Eliza

The First Pioneers of the West

Tom Jiroudek

A Historical and Biographical Novel

Bluebird Feather

Weyekin is a Nez Perce word for a spiritual being.

Children approximately twelve to thirteen years of age undertake a vision quest to find a channel into the invisible world of spiritual power.

The Weyekin, a spirit helper, can take on almost any form, such as a bear, tree, mountain lion, or wolf. Often an object such as a bluebird feather or bear claw found during a vision quest is saved and protected as a symbol of a personal weyekin.

https://www.whozoo.org/ZooPax/ZPFeather.htm

North America, 1836

https://www.kolbefoundation.org

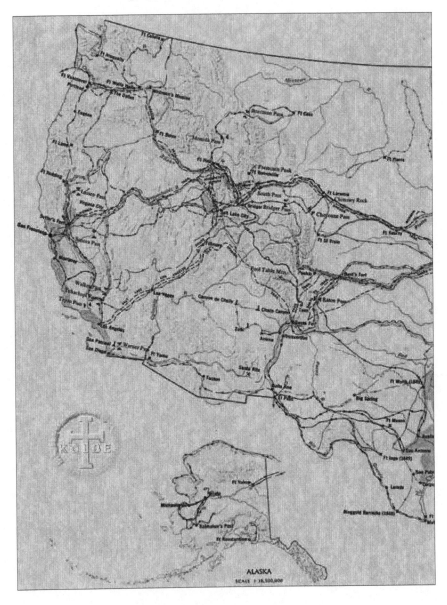

North America, 1836

5,215 miles, seven grueling months, one foot in front of the other.

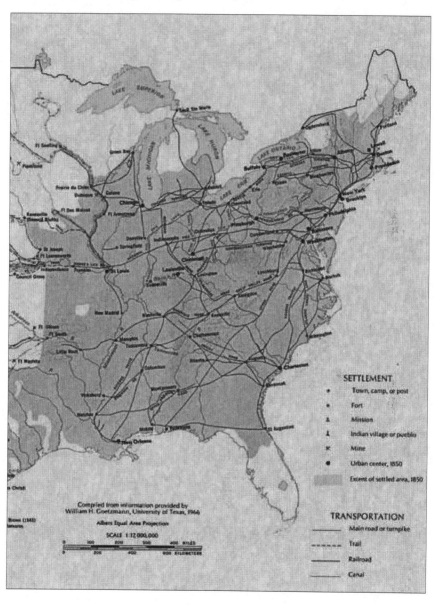

Dedication

Eliza is dedicated to my wife, Laurie, the love of my life and the
inspiration for this book.

It is also dedicated to my children, Harmony, Flynn, Evan, and
Lake, all descendants of the Spaldings.

A special thank you ...

Joanne Spalding-Stacy, Spalding family historian
for her letters and insight.

Barbara Wilson, my dear friend,
for her guidance and encouragement.

Lawrence Hussman

Betsy Ayres

Larry Dean

Rance Babb

Steve and Linda Mayer

Vera Haddan, for her brilliant editing, research, design, and
inspiration. Without her help, *Eliza* would not have been possible.

Prologue

As I walked through the ashes and ruins of the Whitman Mission for the first time in many years, memories of the massacre came flooding back. I often wonder what my life would have been like had my parents stayed in New York, and never ventured westward beyond the daunting Rocky Mountains.

Before 1835 no white woman had ever journeyed over the Oregon Trail. Seven grueling months, one foot in front of the other, 5,215 miles. For a young woman like my mother, from a comfortable home and loving family, the journey was no less epic than that of Christopher Columbus, crossing the Atlantic Ocean. Forever gone were the gently rolling hills and farmlands, flower gardens, Sunday picnics, and loving family and friends who adored her. For mother, the most difficult and terrifying part of going was leaving behind her family and everything she cherished forever.

That was not how she chose to live her life. She and my father were of a different ilk, fully committed to the ideal of sharing their beliefs no matter what the cost, no matter what kind of hardships or fates lay ahead.

They rose every day before the sun and worked until long after it had set. I can still remember seeing their candlelit figures casting shadows across the crude log cabin walls of our first home, night after sleepless night. Yet no one was ever left wanting no matter how weary Mother and Father may have been in body or soul.

They struck out fearlessly toward an unknown world of unimaginable beauty and danger, inhabited by a people of fierce passion for life and devotion to Mother Earth, the Nimiipuu, known to us as the Nez Perce.

Mother and Narcissa Whitman were the first white women to challenge the Oregon Trail, and I was the first white child born and raised in the Northwest. The pioneer women rarely received credit for the sacrifices and contributions they made; in almost every instance, accolades were given to the husband, whether he wanted them or not.

On November 29, 1847, one of the most brutal massacres in Northwest history took place. I know, because I was there and witnessed it: I was ten years old at the time.

Doctor and Mrs. Whitman, along with nine other boys and men, were killed that day by a band of Cayuse Indians. Two other men were killed several days later in a way that defies description; I was there also. Having escaped, another man was hunted down, scalped, mutilated and then killed while seeking help for his family. During the second week of captivity, several young children sick with the measles died for lack of Doctor Whitman's gentle care.

The day of the massacre, 54 terrified women and children were forced into the living room and brutally shoved against the walls while the warriors decided whether or not to burn the mission down with us in it. I was the only one who understood what they were saying. The room was a horror beyond imagination, and we saw things that no one, especially children, should ever see.

We were all in a deep state of shock; there was no crying, and not a sound to be made. Our fates hung like an invisible thread. When I approached the chief to suggest that we were more valuable alive than dead, I knew it might be my last moment on earth.

Because I was the only one who spoke the Sahaptin language of the Nez Perce, Cayuse, and Umatilla Indian tribes, the chief used me as an interpreter. As the interpreter, I saw and heard more than anyone else, more than I ever wanted to see or hear. I was also the designated food taster so that if the foods were poisoned, I would be the first to die.

Other than the nightmares, I have no idea how many ways that this must have affected my life, or what I was thinking or feeling at the time. I do know for certain that I never expected to see another day. That night was a living hell, and for the next 30 days, we never knew from one moment to the next if we were going to be tortured or killed in the same way as the other victims. For several of the women, the next 30 days held a fate worse than death.

Let me get one thing straight: only a few of the men involved in the massacre were truly evil. Most of the Cayuse men did what they thought they needed to do to save their people and rid themselves of the Americans, our diseases, and greed for land.

To our culture, the abomination was in the way in which they were killed, but their customs are often incomprehensible to us, as ours are to them. There are instances in which the U.S. Army has done much worse, things that make you sick, and ashamed to be part of the human race.

I grew up in the Nez Perce village of Lapwai and had very little interaction with other white people until I was eight years old. The Nez Perce were my family, and my heart breaks whenever I think of what has happened to them and the other tribes of the Northwest. They believe they are one with the earth, the Great Spirit, the very nature of existence. They have a deep and abiding respect for all living things, respect we cannot begin to understand since it is not part of our culture. If there is food, no one goes hungry. If there is warmth and shelter, no one goes cold. Elders are revered, and children are given freedom unknown to white children, along with the responsibility that comes with it.

Fate is often mysterious, and I will always be grateful that the day before the massacre my father fell from his horse and was unable to return to the mission that night. For six days and nights father was on foot, soaking wet in the middle of winter with no shoes or food, pursued by a band of Cayuse warriors. My father's story will forever be a testament to his indomitable strength, spirit, and will to survive, a symbol of his love and devotion for our family.

Because of the sensational nature of the massacre, it is what most people remember from that time in our history. For various reasons, the Whitmans have been glorified because of it, and often given undue credit, The Spaldings have been all but forgotten.

The missions were responsible for bringing the "Book of Heaven" to the Nez Perce, Cayuse, and Spokane tribes as well as helping them adapt to the inevitable changes on the horizon. It was a direct result of my mother's deep love and respect for the Nez Perce People and their adoration for her courage and "quiet heart," that my parents' mission at Lapwai was acknowledged as a great success. The other three missions at Waiilatpu, Tshimakain, and Kamiah were utter failures.

The Cayuse people distrusted the Whitmans, and one of the contributing factors to the massacre may have been Narcissa Whitman's obvious disdain for the Indian people. She and Doctor Whitman were good people, and I loved them both, but they were not well-suited for the task before them. Still, their lives and those of my parents, Eliza and Henry Spalding, were woven together, a tapestry of human experience unlike any other. Torn between east and west, they put their souls before their hearts, and it all began with the Oregon Trail.

Eliza

Part One

The Trail

"The pioneer did not wait for the government to mark the way—he marked the way for the government. His path was not blazed, his course was the setting sun. Plains were neither too broad nor mountains too high to deter him. His own right arm was his defense and his heart supplied the never-ending inspiration."

—Eliza Spalding Warren

Chapter 1

Leaving Home

Most of what I recall about the lives of my parents before I was born was told to me while sitting around the fireplace after supper. Along with stories of Mother's family, the trail was one of my favorite subjects, one I never grew tired of hearing. When I was eight years old, I spent my first school year with Doctor Whitman and his wife, Narcissa.

They were also remarkable storytellers who shared many of the details that my parents had intentionally left out. Like the time Mother was nearly dragged to death by her horse, or when Father almost drowned under a wagon while crossing a storm swollen river.

They treated me as if I were their daughter, a gift of kindness that rests gratefully in my heart to this very day.

Mother's family had first emigrated from England to America in 1652, and though I never met my Grandparents, I felt as though I had known them all of my life through the stories Mother told. Her parents had settled in an area called Holland Patent, New York, which at the time was still a wilderness. Mother told me that on the farm, she learned the skills that would become essential to the success of their Mission at Lapwai. It was a home rich with love and open to freethinking and creativity.

Father was born in a rustic log cabin in Steuben County, New York. You could say that he had been a pioneer all of his life. He was unfortunate to have been born out of wedlock, a cross he would bear his entire lifetime. His childhood, often harsh and cruel, was the exact opposite of the warmth and affection Mother had experienced.

Their relationship began as pen pals in 1830. They met in the fall of 1831 and were married on October 13, 1833, in Hudson, New York. Father was studying to become a minister at Lane Theological Seminary while working as a printer. Mother was auditing classes in Greek and Hebrew, tutoring for extra money. Together they applied to the American Board of Commissioners for Foreign Missions and were assigned to work among the Osage Indians in Missouri.

In December of 1835, as they were making preparations for their mission, the board informed them that a Doctor Whitman had just returned from the Oregon Territories.

He was planning to return west, and looking for associates to accompany him over the Oregon Trail to establish a mission among the Indian people. Still single, the doctor was told by the commission that they were only interested in sending married men and women. Within two weeks, he and Narcissa Prentiss were married and assigned the task of establishing relations among the Nez Perce. Since Father was an experienced minister with a myriad of other skills, someone at the missionary board suggested that he and Mother might be a good match to join the Whitmans.

This was fraught with complications since Father and Narcissa were previously involved. There were still hard feelings between them, and at one point, Father questioned Narcissa's suitability for such a journey, creating an even wider rift between the two couples. He told the board that she had been brought up in a privileged environment, that she was extremely social and outgoing, and he felt her nature better suited to that style of life rather than the rugged and unknown challenges of the Oregon Territory. There was also a question in his mind as to whether she had the necessary skills, or would be able to endure the hardships and difficulties associated with life in the wilderness among a potentially hostile people.

This eventually got back to the Whitmans, and they decided to look for another couple while my parents continued to prepare for their mission among the Osage Tribes.

The Whitmans were unable to find anyone else, and time was running out. If they didn't prepare to leave soon, their plans would have to wait another year. At that point, Doctor and Mrs. Whitman put aside their personal feelings and asked if my parents would meet with him to discuss joining the expedition. With a good deal of trepidation, Mother and Father agreed to meet, putting aside their differences. The missionary board then gave them their approval to either join the Whitman party or continue to Missouri to serve the Osage Indians.

Mother told me that saying goodbye to her family was the hardest thing she had ever done, that she never expected to see them again, and never would.

The morning before they were to leave was bathed in soft, late winter sunshine and everyone was trying their best to stay lighthearted. Mother's parents, Levi and Martha, called everyone together and told them they had a going-away present. Her three younger brothers ran playfully pushing and shoving around the back of the house where the barn was located and came out several minutes later, leading two beautiful horses pulling a fresh oak and pine prairie schooner. It would be the first covered wagon to cross the Rocky Mountains over the Oregon Trail.

Mother ran to her parents' waiting arms, and the three of them huddled together in a profoundly sweet sadness. Her two sisters and brothers joined in as Father longingly looked on at the kind of intimacy and love he had missed growing up, but hoped to have one day with his own family.

Martha was inconsolable. Levi put $100 in Father's hand and told him not to let any harm come to his daughter; Father promised to protect her with his life.

It was the most heartbreaking moment of Mother's life as her father lifted her onto the wagon, and she waved goodbye to her family for the last time. She was never to see any of them again except her younger brother, Horace, but a foundation had been formed that would carry her bravely and steadfastly into a new life, into a new world.

By the time they reached Prattsburgh, New York, Mother was wavering between a mild case of homesickness, and the excitement of the unknown.

On February 20, 1836, they finally met up with Doctor Whitman. He was a tall, strong, good-looking man with light brown hair and a very fashionable goatee. He was intense, and yet casual at the same time. He seemed comfortable with himself and had an air of confidence that my parents found reassuring. They felt his first-hand knowledge and experience in the Northwest would come in handy if they decided to join them on the trail.

Mother's first impression was a good one; she found Whitman honest and sincere. He gave them a compelling account of the Nez Perce and their desire to learn about the "Book of Heaven" as they called the Bible. He introduced them to the two Nez Perce young men named Tackitonitis and Ais, who had accompanied him back east. They were in their late teens, both medium builds, strong and athletic with long shiny black hair tied into ponytails. They were curious and bright with a distinctively noble bearing.

Doctor Whitman had given them the Christian names of Richard, and John. Richard Tackitonitis already spoke English, and John Ais was quickly learning.

Before they took their leave, Richard asked if he could say a prayer for their safe journey together if the Spaldings decided to join them. It was a surprising and powerful moment to hear this young man from another world express himself so eloquently in a manner that spoke to their own beliefs. In some ways, it was a subtle epiphany validating Mother's feelings toward the mission they were now committed to. It was at that moment that they decided to accompany the Whitmans to the Oregon Territory. The next day they left Howard, New York, for Pittsburgh, Pennsylvania, with a sense of joy and purpose, at peace with their decision.

After two weeks of getting used to the wagon and their new way of life on the trail, they arrived in Pittsburgh, where they planned to travel by steamboat to Cincinnati. While there, Father also had the opportunity to meet and talk with a well-known artist named George Catlin, who had gone to the West in 1832 to paint the Indian people.

It caused Father a good deal of concern when Mr. Catlin told him, "I wouldn't take a white woman into that wilderness for any reason whatsoever. It's unpredictable and dangerous even for the most trail hardened man."

Father explained that once his wife's mind was made up, there was no turning back. Mr. Catlin wished him good luck and Godspeed.

When he told Mother about his discussion with Mr. Catlin, she said, "I would prefer to put my faith in our Lord rather than Mr. Catlin," exactly what he expected to hear.

They left Pittsburgh on the morning of February 29 aboard the steamboat *Arabian*, bound for Cincinnati. It was another sad time for them since they were unable to take the horses they had become so attached to. Thankfully they were allowed to bring the wagon and provisions.

They arrived in Cincinnati on March 4, and had to wait until March 17 for the Whitmans to join them. It was the first time Mother had met Mrs. Whitman, and she thought her a lovely woman, very friendly and outgoing. She seemed a perfect match for Doctor Whitman, who also had a strong and charismatic personality.

My parents and the Whitmans were like night and day. Mother was of a calm and solemn nature, not inclined to socialize without a reason. She seemed to have a sixth sense about people and preferred to hear their stories one at a time. To the contrary, Mrs. Whitman seemed to gather people about her and took great pleasure in being the center of attention.

Mother was surprised and somewhat dismayed when Mrs. Whitman told her, "I adore being in the shelter of my husband's protection, and appreciate him telling me of my failings and love to act under his judgment."

Though Mother understood that this was the way most women of the time had been taught to think and act, it was far from how she felt or had been raised.

In her relationship with Father there was no master. They were a team and made important decisions together as equals. She was the calm and quiet one who took her time to think things over; Father was more passionate and impulsive. At times he had shown a bit of temper and impatience with people, especially those who were lazy or idle. However, he had never been that way with her, and she felt they were a good match.

By March 25, 1836, they had traveled to the mouth of the Ohio River aboard the steamboat Janius. As Mother stood along the railing of the steamboat staring out at the golden sunset, she marveled at the Ohio River and the life that flowed with it.

At the same time, there was also a persistent sadness for the life she was leaving behind.

The land was so graciously rich and went on as far as the eyes could see without a person or building to interrupt its graceful lines. The soil was chocolate brown and looked as though anything that touched it would grow like a healthy newborn babe. She envisioned that one day it would be blanketed with people, farms, and towns.

On the 29, they boarded the steamboat *Majestic* for the trip to St Louis. The name was certainly appropriate since it was one of the largest and most elegantly appointed boats on the river. The accommodations were by far the finest they had ever known, with excellent foods and someone to attend to their every need. Mother told me that it made her feel like royalty.

There had been a steady flow of steamboats coming and going up and down the river, and two of the boats they had recently passed were now far behind. The captain of a smaller steamship called the *Adeline* was obviously angry when he noticed the *Majestic* beginning to pass and swerved toward their bow to try and cut them off. Mother was worried that there might be a collision. At the last moment, the river opened up, and their captain sped by to the cheers and jeers of the passengers and crew. It was not much longer before they merged with the Mighty Mississippi, running swiftly south toward the Gulf of Mexico. Mother was sitting on deck and began to drift off, feeling as though she were flowing with the river, gliding lazily toward the unknown. In the afternoon, they were enveloped in a dense fog bank, and by 5:00 PM, they were high and dry, stranded on a sand bar.

The next day both the fog and the *Majestic* lifted and gently they resumed their journey peacefully along the immense waterway. It was cold and damp as they hung to the slippery rails, but they couldn't pass up the opportunity to see the dramatic landscape of ragged bluffs and low plains rising and lowering above the sparkling waters.

After St. Louis came Liberty, Missouri, where they hoped to catch a ride aboard the steamboat *Diana*. The *Diana* belonged to the American Fur Company, which Doctor Whitman had arranged to travel with until they reached Council Bluffs. This was the last stop before they would make the rest of their journey by land. From there, they hoped the Fur Company would allow them to continue with them, providing protection against the possibility of hostilities.

Mother told me that in St. Louis she saw a side of Father that she had never seen before or wanted to see again. When he was in Seminary College, he and a group of his friends organized an informal boxing club. He told her that it was just a way for them to blow off steam, that they used padded gloves, and always pulled their punches so that no one ever got hurt. He told her it was a great way to stay sharp and get some exercise.

Having grown up with three brothers, Mother figured that it sounded harmless enough and never gave it another thought. That was until they ran into one of his friends from college on the *Majestic* named John Holt. After Father's abysmal childhood, college had come as a liberating relief. It was a place where he was able to grow spiritually and intellectually, making friends of like mind. Mother was happy to see her husband relaxed and reliving some of the better moments from his past.

Somehow, they got onto the subject of the boxing club and exchanged what information they knew of the friends who had belonged. John smiled and asked Mother if Henry had ever mentioned the boxing club? She told him that they had only discussed it once before. Father tried to change the subject, but John was not to be denied a good story and went on to say, "Henry never lost a single match, and no one even wanted to spar with him."

John then paused until Mother said, "Alright, you have my attention?"

John continued, "He was fast, real fast." Mother burst out laughing, which then got the men laughing.

John went on, "You wouldn't think it was so funny if you were on the other side of him and could see his head rise with that wild look in his eyes. He beat men a good head taller and 100 pounds heavier like he was swatting flies."

Father laughed it off and told Mother that it was only a game.

John said, "It may have only been a game to you, Henry, but not us. No one had ever seen anyone move that fast. The best we could do was put our hands up in front of our faces until he got bored. I was one of the better boxers, but every time I took a swing, he would smack me before I knew what happened, then smile at me with an unsettling grin on his face."

Father tried to laugh it off and change the subject by telling John, "You haven't seen tough until you try to change Eliza's mind once it's made up."

They had disembarked in St. Louis, then separated, as each couple undertook a different responsibility for gathering the goods and supplies they would need for the trail. Father and Mother were asked to locate and purchase flour, beans, and other food staples. On the way back to the boat, they were passing what looked like the rear entrance of a ratty old tavern. Three men who had obviously been drinking were loafing around outside. As my parents passed by, one of the men made a rude comment toward Mother. Father was very calm and courteous, showing no anger or fear when he went over to the man and asked him to please apologize. When the man got up to confront Father, he was easily six feet five inches tall and 200 plus pounds to Father's five foot ten, 160 pounds soaking wet.

Mother called out to Father, asking him, "Please let it go, Henry, we need to be on our way."

Smelling of alcohol, the man stepped right up to Father's face and mimicked Mother in a high voice saying, "Please Henry, we need to be on our way," then turned to his friends and curtsied. The other two men thought this the funniest thing they had ever seen and started laughing hysterically. They didn't bother to get up since they figured he surely wouldn't need any help with the smaller meek-looking man. The big man was obviously a bully, and when he turned back, he knocked Father's hat off his head. Father calmly picked it up, dusted it off, and put it back on without moving. The man did it again, and the other two broke out, laughing even louder. Father calmly picked his hat up, dusted it off, and put it back on.

At this point, Mother didn't want to say or do anything for fear that the man would mimic her again, making things even worse. Father looked straight in the man's eyes and repeated, "I am waiting for an apology to my wife, sir." They broke out laughing again until they could hardly breathe.

The big man put on his most serious face and slapped Father hard on his cheek then said, "You two look kinda churchy, are you gonna show me that other cheek," then slapped Father hard on the other cheek? Father was unfazed.

The man stepped back, removed his coat, and took a couple practice swings at the air. He then stared at Father with a fierce and intimidating look saying, "This should be fun."

He then told Father, "When I get done with you, SIR, we're gonna have some fun with the little lady over there."

Mother said that at that instant, the change in Father's eyes was much more frightening than the big man's threat. The man turned to his friends and said something, then quickly spun around and threw a punch at Father. Mother said she was looking right at them, but didn't even see what had happened. She saw Father duck, and the next thing she knew, the big man hit the ground like a sack of potatoes. The other men started to get up, but Father charged menacingly toward them with a look that made them back off. The bully was lying in the dirt holding his face and started to rise when Father put his foot on the man's chest and told him to stay put.

Blood was starting to run over the man's cheeks as he said, "You broke my damn nose."

Father very calmly told the man, "My wife and I are still waiting for an apology, mister."

Mother begged, "Henry, could we please just leave?"

Father told her, "As soon as these men remember their manners."

He looked at the big man in the dirt, holding his bloody nose and asked, "Do you have a mother?"

The man didn't seem to understand, "What?"

Father repeated, "Do you have a mother?"

"Yes."

"How would you like it if someone talked to your mother like you did to my wife?"

The bully paused a long time while holding his bloody nose and then replied, "I wouldn't like it."

"Then what do you think you should do?"

Father took his foot off the big man's chest and backed up as the man got to his feet, dusted himself off, and wiped the blood from his face. Mother was terrified when he started walking toward her, but Father stayed just in front of him.

When the man was about six feet from her, he stopped. Looking stone sober, he lowered his head and said, "I'm very sorry, ma'am, I hope you'll accept my apology."

The whole event sobered the other men up who took off their hats, ambled up beside the big man, and offered an apology. Mother told me she wasn't sure what to think or feel at that moment since she was still in a state of shock at how everything had happened so fast.

When she finally regained herself, she looked at them intensely and said, "I forgive you because I can see that you are sincere. I want you all to promise me that you will never do anything like that again."

They shuffled their feet like children, and each took turns, saying, "I promise."

Father shook hands with each man in turn and said, "Good day, gentlemen."

When they were once again alone, Mother asked, "What about turning the other cheek, Mr. S.?"

He took a while to think before he replied, "I used them both up ... but that's not the point, Eliza. I don't know if what I did was right or wrong in the eyes of God, so I will get on my knees tonight and ask for forgiveness. I wasn't afraid for myself, but I couldn't bear to think of what they might do to you if they put me down. I didn't feel like I had a choice. I gave your father my promise to protect you with my life, and right or wrong, that's what I am going to do."

"All right, Henry, I can accept that, but the look in your eyes before you struck the man was so cold that it frightened me. What were you thinking?"

"I wasn't thinking at all, and I wasn't angry. I knew he was coming at me, and it was as if time slowed down, and I was caught in the moment with nowhere else to go."

"Well, I hope I never see that side of you again."

"Me neither."

There would be times in the future when Mother would see Father angry, impatient, or frustrated, but not that cold empty look again. She never told anyone else but me what took place that day, and it was the last time that they ever discussed it. By the time they returned to the boat, it was as if it had been a bad dream and had never happened at all.

On April 1, they left St. Louis aboard the steamboat *Chariton* for Liberty, once again merging with the Missouri River. Mother was afraid that she had isolated herself to the point of being unsociable but felt there was so little time to prepare and so much to learn before reaching the Oregon Territory. She spent most of her time with Richard and John learning the Nez Perce language and culture. She told me that she had never known any other young men to be so calm and patient with such a great love for sharing and learning.

They reached Liberty, Missouri on April 8, 1836. They were joined by Mr. William Gray, Doctor and Mrs. Satterlee, and a young Nez Perce man named Samuel Temoni, who had met with Mr. Gray and told him he was going west, asking if he could join them. It so happened that he was friends with both Richard Tackitonitis and John Ais's families. He was in his middle twenties and spoke English, French, and several Indian dialects.

He was a large and powerful young man with broad shoulders and long black hair that he wore loose and untied. He dressed in traditional Nez Perce clothing and had a quiet and humble nature that everyone found admirable—a welcome addition. He told them that he had spent years traveling and exploring the West and would be glad to guide them if needed.

Mr. Gray was an outspoken man in his mid-thirties with brown hair, brown eyes, and medium build. He had been hired as a carpenter by the missionary board to accompany the party to the Northwest and construct their homes and buildings, also a welcome addition. The Satterlees were a very pleasant couple who had been assigned as missionaries to the Pawnee nation, happy to temporarily share the company of other missionaries.

The last addition was a young man of 19 who had simply attached himself to the group. His name was Miles Goodyear from New Haven, Connecticut. He was a tall, athletic 19-year-old with light reddish-blonde hair and deep blue eyes. He was gregarious and full of youth, telling everyone that he was going west, "with or without them." Mother said she couldn't help but like him, though she could see the rascal in his eyes. He was brought up on a horse ranch and seemed to know as much, if not more, about horses than anyone other than Samuel.

They were uncertain how long they would be waylaid in Liberty, so they set up their tents and arranged a comfortable campsite. With all of the anticipation concerning the future, it was an exciting time of shared memories, mostly of home and family. Everyone questioned Samuel mercilessly since he was a fountain of knowledge concerning the land as well as the Indian people. The only concern was for Mrs. Satterlee, who was very weak and had been sick for some time with a disturbing cough. Doctor Whitman feared that she might have developed pneumonia, and they were all praying for her recovery.

Mrs. Satterlees health continued to decline, and they feared that she might not survive. Their hearts went out to Doctor Satterlee, who was doing everything within his power to keep her spirits up and help her to recover.

Expecting the steamboat Diana at any time, Father, Mr. Gray, Richard, John, Samuel, and Miles Goodyear all left on the morning of April 23 with the wagons, supplies, horses, mules, and cattle since they needed to take the overland route. The rest of the party, including Mother, were expecting the Fur Company boat any day so that they would be able to meet up with the caravan at Council Bluffs.

The time had come for Doctor Whitman to tell Mrs. Satterlee that he didn't expect her to live much longer. Mother was there, holding one hand, while Doctor Satterlee took the other.

17

Mrs. Satterlee looked at her husband and asked, "Who is going to take care of you? I truly thought that I was going to recover, that we would spend our days together ministering to the needs of the Pawnee people."

Mother said that along with leaving home, it was one of the most heartbreaking moments of her life. They left them alone, and when Mother returned sometime later to comfort her, Mrs. Satterlee seemed resigned to her fate and was talking about putting her affairs in order. They prayed together and, Mrs. Satterlee quietly fell asleep. Mother had only known her for a short time but could tell that she was a brave soul with a true heart. The next day she was struggling to breathe, and it was obvious that she was slipping away. Doctor Satterlee held her in his arms and told her how much she meant to him.

Just before she took her last breath, she opened her eyes, and he told her, "I love you, dear, we will be together once again on the other side."

She smiled and held up her hand to bid them all farewell, then closed her eyes, and without a sound or complaint, she took her last breath and gently left this earth. There was not a dry eye among them as she departed this world within the full embrace of love.

Mother told me that on May 1, 1836 they said their final goodbyes to Mrs. Satterlee and laid her to rest, Doctor Satterlee seemed so lost. They were still young and excited to start their new life together. Mother wondered how anyone could prepare for such a tragic circumstance, and what she would do if something were to happen to Father. They had no sooner left Doctor Satterlee at the gravesite and were returning to camp when they saw the American

Fur Company steamboat *Diana* in the distance. They all ran to the riverside as the horn sounded, announcing its arrival. As the boat approached, it became obvious that it was not getting any closer to shore or slowing. They all began whistling and calling out at the top of their voices, waving and trying to get the captain's attention. He intentionally ignored them, refusing to take on passengers or cargo. It was like the air going out of a balloon mixed with a sense of disbelief that they had been abandoned at the edge of the known world. They confronted the man who attended the dock and way station, asking him why the boat didn't stop?

He told them, "Some of the trappers and traders aren't inclined to encourage the missionaries to come into the Northwest. They kinda like things the way they are and don't care to have any interference."

He also explained, "There's a new captain on the Diana who may not know anything about your previous arrangement."

This was discouraging not only because they were left behind without the passage and protection, they had hoped to have with the Fur Company, but also the idea that they were unwanted by their fellow Americans.

With no time to waste, Doctor Whitman immediately started making arrangements for them to leave as soon as possible. He sent a message ahead with a man who planned to join the Fur Company. It told Father and the other men what had happened, and to wait for them at their next stop. The Doctor was then able to hire a wagon and purchase enough supplies to get them to Fort Leavenworth, where they hoped to meet up with the rest of their party.

Chapter 2

The Oregon Trail

It was May 3, 1836 as they anxiously departed with nothing more than their blankets and the stars above for shelter. It was a rude awakening, especially for Mother and Mrs. Whitman, but they hadn't expected it to be a Sunday picnic and made the best of their circumstances. Fortunately, the weather was accommodating, and they didn't find themselves scorched by the sun or drenched in a rainstorm. Doctor Satterlee decided it best to accompany them until they were all safely reunited.

They reached Fort Leavenworth on May 6, only to find that Father's party was nowhere to be found, that he was wasting no time or effort getting to Council Bluffs. They spent that night at Fort Leavenworth and left early the next morning for the Methodist mission among the Kickapoo Indians, hoping the messenger had reached their party by now. When they arrived at the Kickapoo mission, there was still no word from Father, who was obviously unaware that they had missed the Fur Company steamboat. They left bright and early the next morning for Council Bluffs, once again in the hope that the messenger had reached Father's party.

On May 14, within 20 miles of the Otoe Agency near Council Bluffs, after 11 strenuous days of trudging, they finally caught up with the rest of the party. Mother said she had never been so happy to see her husband, and they spent the remainder of that day catching up on their experiences. Father informed them that he had recently gotten a message that the American Fur Company caravan had left Council Bluffs two days ago led by a Captain Fitzpatrick on their way to the Rendezvous. That meant they would have to travel day and night to catch up. Doctor Satterlee said his goodbyes, and my parents told him how truly grateful they were to have such a good and considerate friend stay by their side when he was most needed. Oddly enough, the rough conditions seemed to have improved Mother's health, and she felt better than she had in a long time, but they were now out of fresh foods and running low on staples like flour, cornmeal, and beans.

They planned to make it to Council Bluffs that day before the Fur Company could reach the mountains, hoping they could continue under their protection. They would soon be approaching Sioux and Blackfoot country, which was unsafe for travel without a large and well-armed party. Many of the men were experienced hunters and trappers who knew the Indian people well and knew how to avoid a confrontation. They were still uncertain why the Fur Company had not stopped for them at Liberty, nor did they know how they would be received if and when they did catch up.

When they reached Council Bluffs, they were informed that the Fur Company was moving fast, that they were still several days behind. With that information, they decided to travel as long and hard as possible to try and catch up before the Fur Company reached the Rocky Mountains.

There were endless dangers along the trail, and unfortunately, Father experienced two within the same day. As he was checking the packs, one of the mules kicked him square in the chest. Mother saw it happen out of the corner of her eye and said he was lifted off the ground and thrown several yards through the air, landing in a heap of dust. She hurried to help and immediately called out for

Doctor Whitman, who came running. Father was lying motionless, trying to get his breath and had just started to move around when the doctor arrived. Doctor Whitman told him to be still until he could examine him.

The doctor asked, "Where did he get you, Henry?"

Hardly able to breathe, Father pointed to his chest. Doctor Whitman unfastened Father's vest and shirt, finding two large red welts shaped like horseshoes beginning to rise on his upper chest. The doctor took his time examining, trying to make sure that there were no broken bones or internal damage.

He then asked, "Is there any place that feels damaged or broken?"

Father asked, "Well, my pride has surely been damaged, but let me ask you, Doc, have you ever been kicked by a mule?"

Doctor Whitman smiled and shook his head no.

Father smiled back weakly, "Well, let me tell you, Marcus, it feels as though every place on my body has been broken or damaged."

It was a moment of relief since Father was well known to use his levity sparingly.

Mother started to help him up, but he kindly waved her off, saying, "I better see if I can do this myself."

He was slow to rise, and the bruises were starting to turn a dark purple. By this time, Mrs. Whitman and the rest of the party had arrived and were wondering what had happened.

Miles Goodyear looked at Father and said, "Mr. Spalding, that's a darn fine head of hair you have on your chest, sir."

Mother was afraid that Father was going to be mad, but he just smiled and shook his head as he buttoned up his shirt and vest.

Father replied, "I think I might loaf around for a while and ride up on the wagon. Miles, why don't you take a look at the rest of those packs, and be sure to stand right behind that big brown mule."

Father took his time getting up on the wagon, but Mother felt reasonably confident that he was going to be all right.

They had been traveling for several hours when they came to a section of the Platte River they would need to cross. The current was running fast, but it looked shallow enough to cross safely. My parents' wagon was the last to go, and Mother was on Father's left side holding the reins. They had just dipped down into a small hole when they were hit on Mother's side by a log that no one had seen coming. The wagon tipped as far as it could without going over, and Father went headfirst into the water. Miles was riding behind them, and when he saw Father go in, he sprung forward and dove in to help.

Father had just come up coughing water as Miles pulled him to his feet and said, "Mr. Spalding, you sure know how to have a good time, sir."

This time Father didn't think it was so funny. That night he came down with a cold and fever. Doctor Whitman came by to bleed him and give him some calomel, both of which we have learned do more damage than good. The next day he was even sicker with a terrible headache and riding with a wet dishtowel over his head to keep the dust out of his face and light out of his eyes.

At midday, they stopped to eat and rest. When they were once again ready to go, Father told Mother, "Maybe you should leave me here for a while with a horse and some food and water, I'll catch up later."

Mother told him to "Get up on that wagon, Mr. S. You're not going to lay around soaking up the sun all day while there is still plenty of trail in front of us."

Father gave the doctor a pitiful smile, climbed on board, and put the wet towel back over his head. They did cover a lot of ground that day, and I am certain Father must have felt every inch of it.

On May 24 they crossed the Elk Horn River. Thankfully for Father, it was routine and uneventful. Later that day, their intended guide, Mr. Dunbar, finally caught up with them. He planned to stay on until they were able to join the Fur Company caravan. He then needed to return to his Mission and join the Otoe Indians with their summer hunting party. At this point, they were starting to run low on dry goods and wood for cooking. Mother received instruction on how to collect and use buffalo dung as a cooking fire, not the most pleasant chore she had had to perform so far. The next day Samuel took down an elk, giving Mother and Father their first taste of fresh game since they had left home. Doctor Whitman told of having to live off elk on his last journey and professed to be an artist in the preparation and cooking of the gangly beast. After a diet of biscuits and dry foods, Mother admitted that it was delicious, that the doctor was indeed a fine cook and was welcome to do so anytime.

Fear is a powerful motivator. May 27, was a hot, grueling, long haul of a day. They had traveled almost 60 miles in 18 hours, the most ground they would cover in one day during the entire journey.

This came after a four-day forced march in the hope of catching up before it was too late. Everyone, including the animals, had been driven past the point of exhaustion, and by midnight they reached the south side of the Loup Fork of the Platte River. When they spotted the campfires of the American Fur Company in the distance, it was as if they collectively exhaled after holding their breath for days. At first light, Father and Doctor Whitman crossed over the river to talk with the leader, Captain Fitzpatrick, and ask if he would allow them to continue with their party.

The captain apologized profusely for the misunderstanding and said that they were welcome to join his group, that it would be an honor and privilege. He told them that the new captain of the steamship *Diana* had not been instructed to stop and pick anyone up along the way and didn't want to risk losing his position by disobeying orders.

Once the men heard there were two ladies with the group, almost every able-bodied man volunteered to swim their horses back over the river and help them cross. Some of the men hadn't seen what they considered to be a real lady in years and fell over each other vying for Mother and Mrs. Whitman's attention, even helping set up the campsite and get a fire going. Later that evening, they came to swap stories about their experiences in the wilderness and tell of their longing to see their homes and families again.

Recollecting, one of the men told how his mother used to sing to him when he was a boy. It was quite a sight to see those rugged mountain men wiping the tears from their eyes and faces as Mrs. Whitman began singing a hymn in her beautiful soprano voice. When she finished, another man told Mrs. Whitman and Mother how they reminded him of his mother and sisters; that he hadn't realized how much he had missed them until that very moment. For a time, the experience made everyone feel like a big family, and for Mother and Mrs. Whitman, there was a comfort in knowing that these men were there to protect them the rest of the way in case anything dangerous or unexpected should happen.

The next day, as the sun rose over the prairie and began warming the mountains, there was a call for everyone to rise. Within minutes the camp was deluged with activity and noise, a seemingly chaotic mass of people moving in every direction, though in reality, everyone had a purpose and knew exactly what to do and when to do it. After the animals were fed, they prepared and ate their breakfast, by 6:00 AM wheels were rolling, dust was rising, and they were on their way.

It was like a small moving village with hundreds of animals, men, and wagons spread out over half a mile. In front, Captain Fitzpatrick rode side by side with the company guide. Next were the men with the pack animals and mules. Then came the seven company wagons fully loaded, followed by Mother and Father's party in the rear. Miles led the horses, Richard and John led the cattle and mules. Mr. Gray was in one wagon with Doctor Whitman. Mother, Father, and Mrs. Whitman were in the very last wagon where the dust was so thick that you could almost eat it. Several men rode along beside them, including a Captain Stewart, and Mr. Chelam. Both were intrepid adventurers and romantics who planned to cross the mountains and see the Oregon Territory and Rendezvous for the thrill of it.

The cattle Father had purchased at Liberty would be the first driven over the Rocky Mountains, and if it had not been for the milk they gave, Mother was not sure she would have survived. Even before they met up with the Fur Company, she was feeling ill again and growing weaker by the day. The only thing they had to eat at this point was dried buffalo jerky, and she was continuing to grow less tolerant of eating it each day.

By June 4, 1836, they had reached the wide-open, seemingly endless plains along the Platte River. Captain Fitzpatrick told them that not long ago, these plains had been covered with vast herds of buffalo and the Indian people who hunted them. Both were beginning to disappear as the white hunters continued to kill thousands of the animals for their hides. It was no wonder that many of the Indian people in this part of the country felt such animosity toward the white people who had invaded their land and were quickly destroying their way of life.

Chapter 3

A Dangerous Crossing

By June 13, 1836, they had reached another crossing point of the Platte River, not far from Fort William. It was the Sabbath, so they decided to honor it and let the Fur Company go ahead, meeting up with them at Fort William. The Fur Company moved at a slower pace than they did, so they were not worried about being left behind again. The next day as they stood on the bank of the Platte River, it seemed to be flowing much faster and more powerfully than the day before, possibly from a flash flood in the mountains or heavy spring runoff. They faced the dilemma of trying to cross or attempting to find a safer crossing further upstream.

Father looked to Samuel and asked, "Are you familiar with this part of the river Samuel?"

"I have crossed it several times, but never when it was this fast or strong."

"Is there another place we can cross nearby?"

Samuel thought about it for a few moments before replying, "There is another place we can cross that is about 30 miles upstream, but with this much water, I am not sure it is any better."

Father turned to Doctor Whitman, "What do you think, Doc?"

"It looks pretty fast."

At that point, Miles blurted out, "I can do it, my horse is the best swimmer, I can take the rope across."

Mother got down off her horse, took off her boots, and stepped into the water up to her ankles. She looked up at the men and said,

"The bottom might be too soft and sandy for the wagons. We should look for a better place to cross or wait to see if it eases up."

Samuel was squatting by the river and gazing at the current. Doctor Whitman saw him watching and asked, "What do you think Samuel, can we get across?"

"We can get across, but it might be wiser to wait."

Father looked to Doctor Whitman and asked, "What do you think, Marcus?"

"If we move upstream, it will cost us another day or two with no guarantee that the crossing will be any better. If we get too far behind, we'll have to go the rest of the way without the protection of the Fur Company. Crossing Blackfoot country without their help could be a lot worse than getting across this river. I say we take two guide ropes over instead of one, let Samuel and Miles each take a rope to be on the safe side. I think I already know Mr. Goodyear's answer, how about you, Samuel?"

Samuel thought another moment and replied, "Two ropes should be enough, is there anyone who can't swim?"

No one replied, so Miles blurted out, "I guess that does it, I could use a bath anyway, let's get some rope, Samuel."

No one objected, so Samuel and Miles took their coats off and found the ropes. They started a good 100 feet upstream, and when they hit the water, they were immediately swept along with the current. Fortunately, the ropes were long enough, or they would have had to let go and do it again from further upriver.

Mother said she had never seen two horses that could swim any better, or men to handle them. It was serious and dangerous work, but they made it over without any trouble, staked the ropes down, and pulled them tight. Richard Tackitonitis, John Ais, and Mr. Gray rounded up the spare mules, horses and cattle, all reasonably good swimmers and herded them in. One of the cows got away, so Miles went in after it, bringing it in almost a quarter-mile downstream. The ropes continued to hold, and the rest of the animals made it over safely. Now it was time for the wagons. Miles, Samuel, and Mr. Gray went upstream and waded back into the water to help the wagons cross.

When they had worked their way back, Miles looked at Mother and Mrs. Whitman and asked, "Would you two dear ladies care to be escorted over this gentle little stream by two handsome and debonair young men?"

Mrs. Whitman and Mother looked at each other and burst out laughing. Both were excellent horsewomen, so they took off their boots and bonnets and plunged into the water before Miles and Samuel could position themselves to help. Mother told me it was one of the most exhilarating experiences she had ever had. She felt safe knowing that Samuel and Miles were close behind. For her, it was over far too fast, and she would have gladly done it again if she could have. I have never even tried riding sidesaddle, so it's hard to imagine that they rode that way almost the entire trip. River crossings and perilous mountain trails were the few exceptions to riding sidesaddle.

When they reached the other side, there was no place to change, so they had to wring their clothes out as best they could while still wearing them. They could hear Father, Doctor Whitman, and Mr. Gray cheering as Mother and Mrs. Whitman waved back to them from the other side. Samuel and Miles once again crossed so that they could help in case there was a problem with the wagons. Mr. Gray took the first wagon over with Richard and John beside him having little trouble crossing. This inspired Father and the doctor to cast off into the current without hesitation, Doctor Whitman at the reins, and Father by his side. Miles and Samuel seemed to be having the time of their lives racing their powerful horses across the river, now bringing up the rear in case they were needed.

No one knows for sure exactly what happened, but just a little over halfway across, they must have gone into a hole, and the doctor lost control, the wagon tipped over going on its side. The ropes were holding it in place, and the mules somehow managed to set their feet, keeping their heads above water, but both men went under and out of sight.

Mother saw Doctor Whitman come up gasping for air, but there was no sign of Father. She was just about to jump into the water herself when she saw Samuel come flying up beside the overturned wagon on Father's side and dive in. The doctor was holding on to the overturned wagon trying to get his breath, until he realized that Father must be stuck underneath. He then went back under to see if he could help Samuel.

Somehow Father had gotten his foot stuck underneath the wagon and was trying desperately to get loose before he lost consciousness. Mother said it seemed like forever, but was more likely less than a minute or so before Samuel finally emerged with Father in his arms gasping for air like a newborn. Miles had worked his way around to help, and together he, Samuel, and the doctor put Father over Samuel's horse and swam him to shore. The ropes were straining to the point of breaking. As soon as they could see that Father was breathing, everyone but Mother and Doctor Whitman ran to the ropes and started pulling as hard as they could to keep the wagon from getting away. Miles found another rope, swam out and attached it to the wagon then swam back and helped everyone drag it in. Father had swallowed so much water that he was doubled over and vomiting a small river of his own.

By the time the wagon had been dragged in and set back upright, Father was telling everyone to go about their business of drying out. Other than a sprained ankle and one overwrought cow, everything, including the animals and wagons, had made it across safely.

Miles broke out with, "I thought you were a goner for sure, Mr. Spalding, but I told you we could do it."

Everyone including Father, who was still sputtering, burst out laughing. It was one of those moments branded into their memory forever. They laughed until they were sick; when they recovered their senses, they started getting fires lit to help them dry out. Some of the supplies and bedding were wet, but it was a miracle that all of the goods and personal items on the wagon were still intact. Clothes and personal belongings were strung out on every available bush and box for 100 feet in the hope that they would dry out, and they could be on their way as soon as possible. They were still damp when they took off later that day, but it had warmed up nicely, and thankfully, no life was lost or anyone badly injured. Father told me that it was the last time he would cross a river in the wagon for the rest of the trip.

Mother told me that at times like that, she honestly wondered whatever possessed her to undertake the journey, that it would be a miracle if everyone survived. She said she missed her family and the simple feel of a warm blanket. She was tired of being dirty, wet, and homesick. It didn't make her feel any better when Doctor Whitman told them that from now on the journey was only going to get more difficult. If that was true, she couldn't imagine what the future had in store. As if that were not enough excitement for the day, they could see five riders in the distance coming their way fast.

Father handed his telescope to Samuel and asked, "Can you tell who they are?"

Samuel told them, "They are Blackfoot in war paint. I suggest everyone get their rifles out but don't aim at anyone or make any sudden moves, just be ready."

The warriors were well-armed and intimidating in their manner and appearance. Samuel held his hand up, palm out to show goodwill. The gesture was not returned, alarming the three Nez Perce who clearly understood its meaning.

Speaking the Blackfoot language, Samuel said, "I am No Heart of the Nez Perce; what is it that you want?

The Blackfoot replied, "I am Bloody Hand of the Blackfoot; I want the whites to turn around and leave our land."

Doctor Whitman asked Samuel to tell Bloody Hand, "We have been traveling for many days and come in peace with many things to trade. The Nez Perce have asked us to tell them of our God and share the "Book of Heaven" with their people."

Mother was inside the wagon, listening and watching through a slit in the canvas. She said that you could almost cut through the tension in the air, and it made her extremely anxious to see that everyone had a finger on his trigger. She was especially alarmed at the Blackfoot man who had his rifle pointed in the general direction of Father. She looked over at the spare rifle they kept inside the wagon and was now faced with a moral dilemma. Could she just watch as her husband was killed, or should she act to protect him if it became necessary? She picked up the rifle and from cover aimed it through the opening toward the chest of the man who was pointing his rifle in Father's direction. The last thing she ever wanted to do in this world was to hurt or kill another human being, but if he raised his gun to fire on Father, she planned to fire first and beg forgiveness later.

Samuel continued to translate as Bloody Hand spoke. "Tell the white man that we have no need of his God, we have our own, that he has nothing we want, that this is no place for the white people.

Doctor Whitman was trying to keep things calm when he replied, "We have come to live in peace with you as brothers and sisters, but we have come too far to turn back now."

"You have been warned ... If you do not leave, you will pay with your lives."

Bloody Hand gave my parents and the Whitmans a fierce and terrible look of hatred before he raised his gun and shook it, signaling the others to leave. They then turned as one and rode off toward the distant hills, firing their guns in the air as a final warning.

Samuel told them, "That was not an empty threat."

Father asked, "Are we in danger?"

"Yes. They think of anyone who encroaches on their land as an enemy. When I was 14, the Blackfoot killed my father for crossing over their land to hunt the buffalo; they will not hesitate to attack anyone who they feel is an intruder."

It was a day they would not soon forget, and hoped never to repeat.

They pushed on until that evening traveling by moonlight until they were once again relieved to see the campfires of the Fur Company in the distance outside of Fort Laramie. They could smell meat cooking over an open fire and couldn't wait to eat something fresh. The Company men were anxious to hear Mrs. Whitman sing again and retell their own tall tales about wild animals and Indians. When the doctor told Captain Fitzpatrick and several trappers about the near-tragic river crossing and their encounter with the Blackfoot Indians, he assigned four men as a rear guard to watch over them.

The captain told them that they planned to rest up for several days and would be leaving their wagons at the Fort, packing everything on mules and horses the rest of the trip. The Whitmans decided to leave their large wagon behind since it was becoming more of a burden than a blessing. Captain Fitzpatrick told Mother and Father that at some point, they may need to leave their smaller wagon behind, that there were mountain passes too narrow and steep to get it through. It had become a home away from home, an important part of my parent's lives, and Mother was hoping they could take it all the way to the Oregon Territory.

The captain also let them know that he didn't plan to stop again until they reached the Rendezvous. He explained that it was an annual gathering held by the American Fur Company and Hudson Bay Trading Company. Trappers, traders, and the Indian people came from all over the Northwest to sell their furs and hides, replenish provisions, and let themselves go. He told them that everyone was invited, including women and children, that different tribes from all over the territory came to trade and join in the festivities. He warned that it was a boisterous and rowdy group, that there would be dancing and singing, contests for running, jumping, knife and tomahawk throwing, and target shooting. They even had an event to see who can tell the best yarns, that travelers from as far away as Europe had come to be part of it. He warned them that there were very few pious men or women, that whiskey ran like water, and everyone ate and drank to their heart's content. This year it would be held at the lush Green River Valley near the foot of the Wind River Mountains, still 400 miles from where they were now standing.

June 21, 1836, they were packed and ready to leave Fort William for the Rocky Mountains, which they would start to ascend in the next week. They were now 2,800 trail miles from home, and Mother felt they could have just as well been on the moon, it seemed so far away. The buffalo they had been eating was starting to get rancid, and Mother was doing all she could to keep it down. Samuel was planning to look for fresh game that afternoon, anything, even a rabbit stew was starting to sound good to her.

Thankfully the next two weeks were uneventful. There were several rough river crossings and an occasional sighting of

Blackfoot Indians stalking them from a distance, but nothing overly dangerous or unexpected. They continued to follow the Sweetwater River until they were finally able to make out the outline of the Rocky Mountains rising into the sky, an omnipotent wave of jagged earth and snow. They planned to take the South Pass since it was wider, less steep, and less dangerous. They reached the foot of the mountains early the next day and decided to rest, starting again at the crack of dawn the following morning. Mother said that the ascent up the east side of the mountains seemed a never-ending climb into the clouds that went on forever.

When they finally reached the summit, it was July 4, 1836, Independence Day.

For Mother and Mrs. Whitman, it was a highly emotional moment since they were the first white women to bridge the Rocky Mountains. This was where the headwaters flow south toward the Gulf of Mexico, and west to the Pacific Ocean. They raised the American Flag, and everyone bowed their heads as Father said a prayer.

They were still on the plateau of the summit and had been riding less than an hour when they saw dust rising and riders coming hard and fast from the west. Everyone grabbed his gun in the event that it was an attack. My parent's party was especially alarmed when they began to hear the eerie sound of riders yelling like banshees and bullets whizzing above their heads. Captain Fitzpatrick told everyone to hold their fire, that this was a traditional greeting of trappers and mountain men. In the distance, they could make out 15 to 20 men who looked like Indians.

The captain said, "Nothing to worry about folks; it's just some crazy trappers and a friendly group of Indians. I think that's Kentuc waving his gun around like a madman."

As the riders drew closer, they could see that there were five or six trappers and about a dozen Indians. You can imagine my parents' relief when they learned that it was a greeting party sent from the Rendezvous and not a party of bloodthirsty hostiles.

The leader of the group was a big grizzled mountain man named Kentuc, who was half French and half Indian. He and Captain Fitzpatrick gave each other a hardy handshake and then began the introductions. After the captain introduced Mrs. Whitman and Mother, Kentuc took his hat off and started shuffling his feet around as if he were embarrassed.

He then said, "Mrs. Whitman and Mrs. Spalding, I mean no offense, but you two are the purdiest things I have seen in my whole dang life." Everyone broke out laughing.

Captain Fitzpatrick said, "Kentuc, you are a charmer, but the next time you greet strangers like that, you might send a rider out ahead so you don't look like you're on the warpath. You darn near got your heads shot off."

Kentuc gave a big smile, "Then it wouldn't be no fun."

He told Father and Doctor Whitman that he had a message from Mr. Parker saying that he wouldn't be able to meet them at the Rendezvous, that he was on his way to Hawaii, and then back east for family-business. Doctor Whitman had previously arranged for Mr. Parker to guide them the rest of the way from the Rendezvous to the Oregon Territory and show them the best possible sites for a mission. This created several problems they hadn't anticipated. They wouldn't have Samuel as a guide since he planned to go south from the Rendezvous, and they had no idea where to look for a mission site.

Mother was continuing to grow weaker by the day and couldn't hold down the buffalo jerky any longer. The next day when Doctor Whitman came to check in on her, she was unable to rise or even speak. She was aware that everyone was alarmed but felt helpless to do anything about it. Mrs. Whitman took her hand and spoke gently to her as Doctor Whitman felt her forehead and began rubbing her face and arms with a cool, wet towel. When she was finally able to speak, the doctor gave her some water and told her to rest and lie still. Mother felt as though her spirit was slipping away—uncertain that she could go on any longer.

She told them that they needed to keep moving and leave her there and tell her parents she was not sorry that she had come.

Father told her, "Eliza, I know how bad you must be feeling, but you're not thinking straight. You can't give up; we have too much work to do that would be impossible without you, think how far we've come, and why we came in the first place."

Deliriously she told Father, "Henry, please don't make me get back up on that horse, I can tell he doesn't like me."

Father smiled, assuring her, "You don't have anything to worry about, especially that horse. I'll make you a comfortable place in the wagon, and we can rest here as long as it takes. I'm going to stay right here until you feel better and are ready to go on. We're only two days from the Rendezvous, Eliza, and there'll be plenty of fresh food to eat when we get there."

Mrs. Whitman took over rubbing Eliza's forehead with a cool towel and told her that they weren't going anywhere until she was feeling better, that they started this together, and would continue together. The entire party made camp early that day so that Mother could rest. It was a great kindness considering how badly everyone was looking forward to the Rendezvous. Later that afternoon, she started feeling a little better and was able to drink some milk and eat a biscuit that one of the men had brought for her. She slept that whole night and woke the next day feeling better. She told Father and Doctor Whitman that she was sorry for what she had said; that she wasn't herself, and they needed to be on their way. The doctor told Captain Fitzpatrick that he thought she looked well enough to continue. They broke camp quickly and were once again headed west.

Chapter 4

The Rendezvous

On July 7, 1836, the missionaries arrived at the Rendezvous. Mother didn't think she had ever seen so many people in one place before. There were over 400 trappers and traders, and as many as 5,000 Indian men, women, and children. What a joy to see the children running around playing games, she felt her spirit lift just watching them. The Green River Valley was immense and easily capable of accommodating the 10,000 or more horses and mules out to pasture. She was told that there were over 125,000 acres of grazing land and the clearest, sweetest drinking water anyone had ever seen or tasted. The Indian people were inquisitive and friendly; many of the women came right up to Mother and Mrs. Whitman and kissed them on their cheeks, another very emotional experience for both of them.

The Indian women also wanted to touch their dresses and feel the fabric. The men were curious about the cattle and wagon, which they called a land canoe. They were led to a small crude building of about 20 feet square made of rough timber and covered with a roof made of brush. They called it the trading post, but it looked like nothing more than a shack to store hides and supplies. They were then introduced to the man in charge of the trading post, Captain Bonneville of the American Fur Company. He was a big, strong, rugged-looking man of about 35 years with broad shoulders, a full beard, and full head of hair. Doctor Whitman introduced everyone and then asked the captain if he knew Mr. Parker, or had been given a message from him.

Captain Bonneville told them, "It's a real pleasure to meet you, folks. A messenger told me you were coming, so I've made accommodations for you to camp with another group of missionaries. I know Mr. Parker, but all I heard was that he couldn't make it and had left for Hawaii. I know you need a guide to Fort Walla Walla, and this puts you in a bind, but I'm sure that we can work something out. There are several groups headed your way after the Rendezvous, so there's no need to worry."

Captain Bonneville told Mother and Mrs. Whitman that they had caused quite a stir. Most of the Indian people had never seen a white lady before, and many of the trappers hadn't seen one in years. He said that for the most part, it was safe, but they needed to understand that many of these folks lived isolated for a good portion of the year under the harshest conditions imaginable, that this was their chance to let loose. He let them know that there was a lot of drinking, dancing, gunfire, and Indian women for the men. He told them that he realized that this was not acceptable behavior in their world, but they needed to understand that they were not in their world, that it would be bad manners to say or do anything that made these people feel as though they were being judged. The one thing he recommended was that they post a guard on their camp. With so many people, there was bound to be someone with sticky fingers. He had arranged for a Sergeant Wilcox to show them to their campsite and a good place to graze the animals. He told them to let him know if there was anything more that he could do and to enjoy the festivities.

This was unlike any festival they had ever attended before, but they were grateful for Captain Bonneville's courtesy and the first sight of anything that resembled civilization.

Sergeant Wilcox was a big, gregarious man with a jolly laugh and gift for making people around him feel comfortable. He showed them to their campsite and told everyone to let him know if they needed anything, then bid good day.

At the campsite, a Reverend Warren and his small party greeted them heartily. He was a Presbyterian missionary who had traveled all over the world, spreading the gospel. After introductions, he asked if there was anything they needed. Father explained that Mother had been feeling poorly, and asked if there was some place she could rest while they set up camp. She was taken to a comfortable cot and given one of her favorite things in this world, a hot cup of tea with milk. Doctor Whitman told Mr. Warren that they were without a guide or anyone to advise them concerning the Indian people or possible sites for their missions. Mr. Warren expressed his apologies and told them that, unfortunately, Mr. Parker hadn't given him anything to pass on either. The tea and milk, along with a short nap, had worked wonders for Mother, the fever almost gone.

Later that afternoon, Doctor and Mrs. Whitman, Father and Mother all decided to visit the Nez Perce camp so that they could meet the families of Richard and John and give them their thanks. When they arrived at the camp, there was a great stir of excitement.

When Doctor Whitman had been to the Oregon Territories the previous year, he had arranged with the boys' fathers for them to return with him to the East. Richard's father was the head chief of his tribe, and John's father was also an important chief, both very happy to see the doctor again. They embraced and shook hands heartily. Richard translated for them as they were all introduced.

Doctor Whitman told the fathers and their families, "You have raised two fine boys and should be very proud. They will be a bridge between our people that we can cross at any time in peace and friendship."

Richard's father said, "They have brought much honor and pride to our people; they left as boys and have returned as men. Now it is time for them to hunt buffalo and share the stories of their travels at the campfire. You and your people are always welcome at our lodge to smoke the pipe of peace and share the meat."

When they returned to the camp, several of the trappers who had accompanied them with the Fur Company were already waiting for them with their friends. They wanted to hear Mrs. Whitman's beautiful voice again and continue sharing their tall tales. The visit with the Nez Perce had worn Mother out, so she excused herself to get some rest. Father soon joined her, and they fell asleep that night entwined together listening to the angelic voice of Mrs. Whitman singing their favorite hymns.

Soon after breakfast the following morning, Sergeant Wilcox came rushing into the camp with a big smile on his face.

"Mornin folks, you are in for a real treat. Everyone's heard of your arrival, and all of the different tribes would like to honor you by putting on a parade. I saw it once about five years ago; let me tell you, it's something to see. They dress up in war paint, buckskins, feathers, and moccasins, then parade past the camp, everyone trying to outdo the other."

Miles exclaimed, "This I've got to see."

Mother asked, "What about the women?"

Sergeant Wilcox said, "They dress up real pretty in white buckskins decorated with beads and shells. Some of them can ride as good as the men; they're a feast for the eyes on those high wooden saddles. Even the horses are all painted and braided up."

Father asked, "How soon, Sergeant?"

"They're gettin' ready now, sir, I'd say about an hour. This is a real honor, something you might only see once in a lifetime. You don't need to go anywhere to see it; they're plannin' to come ridin' right by your campsite."

Everyone hurried to get into his or her best clothes and tidy up the camp. They were all standing around anxiously waiting when they heard the thunder of horses approaching at a blazing speed. Several of the fastest riders and horses came charging past doing the most amazing tricks they had ever seen. After several minutes of the most incredible horseback acrobatics imaginable, the rest of the tribes began appearing to the sounds of drums and rattles. The horses were powerful and dazzling, artistically painted with tassels and beads intricately woven into their manes and tails.

Each tribe had their own traditional dress, war costume, and hairstyle. Some of the men, especially the younger ones, made every effort to look as ferocious as possible between smiles. The Chiefs were easily recognized because of their elaborate feather headdresses, and the tribes were spread out for almost a mile.

Since it was well known that Richard, John, and Samuel had traveled with their party, they and their families were honored by

45

being last in the parade, the grand finale. Mother thought the Nez Perce women were the most strikingly beautiful women she had ever seen. They were wearing white deerskin dresses with intricately beaded patterns on them. Their hair was worn down or in braids, shiny and black, flowing over their shoulders and down their backs with ornate beadwork and feathers. They sat in their beautifully decorated wooden saddles like princesses of a foreign nobility. The very last to parade by were Samuel, Richard, John, and their families; they had never seen a more impressive sight. They were like royalty, mounted on the most magnificent horses, dressed in their traditional ceremonial costumes. They wore no war paint, and when they smiled, it was as if the sun had broken through the clouds and filled the valley with a pure and divine light. Sergeant Wilcox was right; it was "a once in a lifetime experience."

That afternoon a rider came into the camp and introduced himself. "You folks must be the Whitmans and Spaldings. I'm Thomas McKay of the Hudson Bay Trading Company. I was asked by Mr. McLeod to look in on you."

There were introductions all around, then Doctor Whitman told Mr. McKay, "I met Mr. McLeod when I was here last year."

Mr. McKay replied, "He mentioned that you two had met. The Hudson Bay Company has the two of us out looking for new trade routes that haven't been trapped out. I've got a letter here for you from Mr. Parker. It seems he needed to go back east to take care of family matters, and won't be able to help you folks get to Fort Walla Walla. We can take you as far as Fort Hall. You're welcome to join us if you like, there's a good chance we'll have orders to go on to Fort Walla Walla after we reach Fort Hall."

Mr. McKay dismounted and handed the letter to Doctor Whitman, smiled, and tipped his hat to Mother and Mrs. Whitman. He was about 40, very fit, and rugged looking.

There was a brawny look to his face and a twinkle in his eyes. He seemed to have a sense of calmness and humility that inspired confidence and trust. About that time, Samuel came strolling in for a visit. When Mr. McKay and Samuel saw each other, they greeted with powerful bear hugs and patted each other on the backs, creating a minor dust cloud. It was a joyful reunion that drew everyone in with its sincere and good feeling.

When they were finished talking, Mother turned to Mr. McKay and said, "Mr. McKay, you have no idea what a relief this is. We were in a quandary as to how we were going to proceed without a guide or interpreter. Providence seems to be watching over us."

Mr. McKay replied, "It will be an honor, ma'am. We plan to be here for five or six more days to do some trading and see if we can find out anything about new routes or explorations. We're just on the other side of those trees if you folks need anything just let me know. It gets a little wild around here at night; it might be best if you ladies stayed in camp after dark.

"Thank you, Mr. McKay; we are very grateful for your help."

"It's no trouble whatsoever, ma'am. I'll check in on you tomorrow."

Mr. McKay and Samuel gave each other another bear hug; he then tipped his hat and rode off.

Mrs. Whitman asked Samuel, "How do you know Mr. McKay."

Samuel said, "It's a long story, Mrs. Whitman."

"If there is one thing, we have plenty of, it's time."

Samuel smiled and then became thoughtful before he began his story. "Three years ago, Thomas hired me as a guide to help him explore the Blue Mountains and Snake River area. Since then, we have shared many campfires and become good friends. He is the greatest rifleman I have ever known, a legend among the mountain men and Indian people. Here at the Rendezvous, I once saw him hit the head of a nail from over 50 paces five times in a row. His father, Alexander McKay, was hired by Mr. Astor to establish the Pacific Fur Company at Fort Astoria and brought Thomas here from Canada when he was only 14 years old. His father was killed that same year when a tribe from southern Canada blew up his ship the Tonquin; only one man survived. Thomas started trapping the Northwest when he was 15 and has explored more of the Northwest Territory and California than anyone I know, white or Indian. I can't think of anyone who does not like and respect him; he is always fair in his trading and fearless in the face of danger."

Samuel stopped for a while as if he were recalling a memory, then continued. "Thomas seems to have a sixth sense about danger and once saved my life ... After his father's death, he was stranded alone at Fort Astoria. His half-Indian mother decided to come to the West and married Mr. John McLoughlin, manager of the Hudson Bay Trading Company in Vancouver. Mr. McLoughlin is a good man and has always treated Thomas like a son. The thing about Thomas is that he has no greed or need to be recognized. He is a simple man who cares more for the Indian people than any white man I have ever known. He is a shrewd trader, but never takes advantage and never trades for whiskey.

He was once married to an Indian Princess of the Chinook Tribe near Fort Astoria and was very close to her father, Chief Comcomly. He had gone for several months looking for new lands to trap, and when he returned, his wife and her father had died of a mysterious disease. People who knew him say he changed, became thoughtful and quiet, that his wife was very beautiful, and they shared a deep bond."

Mother said, "You can see it in his eyes."

"I told you it was a long story," said Samuel.

"Please go on, Samuel."

Thoughtful, he said, "He was the first white man to scout the Willamette Valley all the way to Alta, California. He has explored the Snake River Basin, Deschutes River, Blue Mountains, Klamath Lake, Great Salt Lake, and as far as the San Joaquin River over the Siskiyou Trail. In 1833, the Hudson Bay Company gave him a farm near Astoria at a place called Scappoose so he could be close to his friends of the Chinook. He also has a small farm in the Willamette Valley. He was asked by Nathaniel Wyeth of the American Fur Company to establish Fort Hall as a trading post, which he did. The next year he was asked by the Hudson Bay Company to establish a trading post called Fort Boise to compete with Mr. Wythe, which he also did. He guided the Methodist Missionary Jason Lee from Fort Hall to Fort Vancouver and helped him find and pick out the sight for his mission in the Willamette Valley. I have never known him to be anything but kind and generous, but when trouble comes his way, he becomes a different man and will do whatever it takes to protect his men, I would trust him with my life."

Doctor Whitman said, "Eliza, I think you're right; providence has smiled on us."

Samuel replied, "Three days from here, you will travel through Blackfoot country. As you can see, there are many tribes at the Rendezvous; some come from hundreds of miles away. The one tribe you will not find here is the Blackfoot, though you can be sure they are watching and waiting to take horses and lives. Thomas knows them well."

The following day, July 9, Samuel came to their camp with Chief Tackensautis, Chief Ishholholhoatshoats, and Chief Rotten Belly. Samuel introduced everyone and then told them that the chiefs had come to ask that they settle among their Nez Perce villages so that they could learn of the "Book of Heaven." Doctor Whitman told them that they were honored and had just recently decided to establish two missions, one with the Nez Perce, and one among the Cayuse. The chiefs thought there was wisdom in this decision and told them that this would bring great honor to their villages, offering to guide them after the buffalo hunt, which would take up to two moons. The doctor thanked them but told the chiefs that they needed to get settled before winter set in, that Mr. McKay had offered to guide them as far as Fort Hall.

Chief Rotten Belly had gotten his name from a wound he had received in the abdomen during battle and told them that he would like to accompany them and guide them the rest of the way from Fort Hall. He suggested that they bring young Tackitonitis and Ais along to interpret and help with the cattle, that he would arrange it with their fathers. The doctor told him that they would be honored, that John Ais and Richard Tackitonitis were like sons to them.

It was a great relief to know they now had someone to guide them all the way to the Nez Perce and Cayuse villages, as well as John and Richard to translate for them. There were good feelings all around as everyone shook hands and said goodbye.

Samuel said it was time for him to say farewell, that they had been good friends to him and that he would carry their spirit with him always. He told them that since his people had no word for goodbye, he would surely see them again one day in this world or the next.

For Mother, it was a tearful parting since she had spent a great deal of time with Samuel learning the Nez Perce language and exchanging ideas. She would always remember him as one of the most honorable and brave men she had ever known.

She was overjoyed that Richard Tackitonitis and John Ais would be continuing with them and that she would be able to carry on with her Sahaptin lessons. She also looked forward to continuing the sessions in which she had begun teaching them the Greek and Hebrew languages.

During the rest of their stay at the Rendezvous Mother spent as much time as possible with the Nez Perce women learning their language and skills. She always kept paper and pencil at hand to write down words and sentences. The women would take turns pointing at different objects and then say the Nez Perce words. Mother would write them down phonetically and try to repeat them verbally. She would say them in English, and they would try to repeat them. It was great fun, and there were always peals of laughter as they did their best to repeat the words correctly. Sometimes Richard or John would stop by to visit and interpret for them, honestly seeming to enjoy the banter and teasing from the older women.

It was hard for Mother not to feel concern for these women who were continually on the move, knowing very little in the way of home and comfort in the way that she had. She could see that they had to do all of the dull and uninspiring work, preparing the food, gathering firewood and water, packing and tending to the horses, caring for the children, skinning the animals, and making clothes. They also put the camps up by lashing wood poles together to make their lodges, then tore them down when it was time to move on. They worked from dawn until dusk and often well into the night without complaint while the men often spent much of their time hunting, playing the stick game, riding or breaking horses, and gambling, all things they enjoyed. Mother understood that everyone has a role and responsibilities, that it was the only way to ensure survival. Still, she hoped that one day she could find a way to make the women's lives less demanding.

By July 18, 1836, the camps were beginning to break up and everyone was preparing to leave. All of the packing was finished, and they were saying their farewells to new and old friends. In the distance, they could see the jagged mountains they would soon need to traverse, ominously looming. Mr. McKay told them that the next three mountain ranges were unlike anything they had encountered up to this point, to expect a challenge. The next several days were through steep and treacherous mountain trails, trees and brush often had to be cut and cleared to make room for the wagon.

On July 20, they barely averted disaster. They were passing through a switchback of narrow trails less than eight feet wide with a drop off of several hundred feet into deep ravines. As they rounded a particularly dangerous and narrow part of the trail, one of the horses reared up and lost its footing. Miles was leading it and tried to steady the animal from going over the cliff. The horse lost its footing and went over the side with Miles holding on until the last split second. As Miles let go of the falling horse's reins, his horse regained its footing, both barely escaping certain death. When he reached a wider area on the trail, he found the rest of the party taking a break. Mother and Mrs. Whitman were off looking for a private place to relieve themselves; Father and Doctor Whitman were resting.

Richard had been just behind Miles and saw the whole thing as it happened. When he caught up to Miles, he said, "You came very close to joining your ancestors."

Miles smiled, "Tell me about it, brother."

Father said, "It looks like we have one less packhorse, Mr. Goodyear."

Miles replied, "I'm awful sorry, Mr. Spalding, that horse has always been skittish and darn near took me with him. By the time I knew what was going on, he was going over the side."

Father asked, "Besides the horse and the pack, what else did we lose?"

"I think it was mostly Mrs. Spalding's personal belongings in the pack."

Father shook his head seriously and told Miles, "Well, I'm glad to see that you are still here with us, I'm not too sure if Mrs. Spalding will feel the same way when she finds out about her pack.

I'm going to let you tell her what happened to her things; I hope you have a thick skin. She doesn't get mad very often, but when she does, it's best to lower your head and stay quiet until she gets it out of her system."

Smiling, Mr. Whitman added, "If she doesn't say a word, you might want to get down on your knees and say your prayers."

Miles looked stricken and unsure of what to think until they burst out laughing, then Doctor Whitman said, "Well, Henry, the clothes can be replaced, but I doubt that we could ever find ourselves another Mr. Goodyear. I think I'll mosey along before Mrs. Spalding returns and hears the bad news."

Father added, "I think I'll join you, Marcus."

The following day they started descending the mountains in a southwesterly direction and reached the valley floor a little after noon. It was hot, dry, and dusty. Everyone was uncomfortable, especially the animals. The bright spot, if you could call it that, was a big range of dark clouds off in the distance and the sound of thunder announcing the arrival of a coming storm. Silver sprinkles began to fall, followed by huge drops. Things had cooled off, and the dust had settled, but they got a lot more rain than they had wished for.

The earth was drinking it up as fast as it could, but it wasn't fast enough. A flash flood sent rivers of water cascading in every direction, making it hard traveling on the animals and wagons. Mud was up to their ankles and axles, but at least it had cooled things down and revived their spirits.

Father and Doctor Whitman had been riding with Mr. McLeod. trying to gather as much helpful information as possible about the land and its people. Miles had attached himself to Mr. McKay, bombarding him with a non-stop rapid-fire series of endless questions. Mother thought that Mr. McKay must have seen a little of himself in young Miles since he was so patient and accommodating.

On July 23, they once again began ascending into the mountains. By the next day, the traveling had become punishing and dangerous. When they reached a clearing, Mother and Mrs. Whitman told Mr. McKay that it was the Sabbath and asked to spend the rest of the day worshipping.

Mr. McKay politely told them, "This is Blackfoot country, a very dangerous place to be caught in a confrontation. When I sent hunters out to look for game this morning, they spotted a small band watching from a distance. There are only 30 of us, and who knows how many are out there. They have nearly extinguished the Flathead Tribe, and would dearly love to have our horses, weapons, supplies, and scalps. I think God will forgive us under the circumstances, ladies."

Mr. McKay looked closely at Mother and asked, "Mrs. Spalding, you don't look so well, is there anything I can do?"

She told him, "Buffalo jerky doesn't seem to agree with me. I should be fine once we reach Fort Hall."

"I'm sorry you aren't feeling well, ma'am, I was planning to send a party out to look for fresh game this afternoon."

Mother thanked him, and later that day, he left with a party of ten men, including young Miles. Several hours later, they heard the sound of gunfire off in the distance. Not the kind you hear while hunting, it was the rapid-fire of a skirmish. The men all formed a close circle around Mother and Mrs. Whitman for protection. The gunfire went on for ten or more minutes then stopped, everyone was starting to worry that something may have happened to Mr. McKay and the hunting party. About ten minutes later, they came riding into camp fast and hard. One of the young men was wounded in the shoulder, so Doctor Whitman immediately went to see how badly he was bleeding. Mr. McKay told the men to close ranks and be ready for an attack as the doctor removed the injured man's coat and shirt to examine the wound.

He told him, "I'm going to have to go in and dig that ball out, son. It isn't going to be pleasant, but I don't feel any broken bones. You're going to be pretty sore for a while, but you'll live to use that arm again.

Mr. McLeod asked Mr. McKay, "What happened out there, Thomas?"

"It was a party of Blackfoot looking to ambush us. We were on the trail of an elk when Chloe's head turned sharply to the right, and her ears shot up. It was the wrong direction for the elk, so I figured we were being trailed. I saw some movement through the trees and told the men to dismount and find cover. Just as we were dismounting, bullets and arrows started whizzing all around us, and Charlie got hit. We got to cover, but the bullets were still flying. I figured there couldn't be too many of them, maybe ten at most, or they would have rushed us. I was able to get a bead on one and brought him down. When his friend went to help him, I did the same. It gave us time to get organized and form a skirmish line. This went on until one of the warriors got too close, then I put a hole in his leg, and they let out."

Miles broke out, "It was the darndest shooting I've ever seen. Those first two must have been over 300 yards away through the trees and didn't even know what hit em."

Mr. McKay looked at Miles and told him kindly, "This isn't something to rejoice over Miles, I only tried to wing those men. I shot high on the first one and may have killed him. Remember that we're the intruders; they don't want us here and are doing what they feel they need to do to keep us out. I would have gladly given them a couple of horses to avoid having to fire on them, but it didn't look like they were going to give me the chance to parley. Doctor, as soon as you get Charlie patched up, we need to be on our way. They may be going for help right now and decide to try again later. We better double the guards and be ready to move."

Doctor Whitman told Mr. McKay, "I'll be done in another five or ten minutes."

Mother told me that the rest of that day, there was an eerie feeling that they were being watched and that a bullet or arrow could come flying in at them any second.

By July 25 they were deep into the mountains where it was extremely rugged and narrow. It had become far too dangerous for anyone to ride on the wagon, and twice it had overturned. Each time it took a group of men to pull it free and set it back upright. Miles was in charge of keeping it moving, and they could tell he was becoming flustered with the responsibility since he wanted to be part of the scouting and hunting parties.

On the 28, they were descending an extremely steep section of the mountain trail when the front axle broke. They were faced with the decision of whether to leave it there or try and fix it. Mother couldn't bear the thought of leaving it behind. It was the only home they had known through all of the difficult months of traveling and an important link between herself and her family. She had to stay out of the decision since she wouldn't be the one to fix it or keep it moving. They decided that it could not be repaired since there was no replacement axle. However, Father came up with an idea to replace the front axle with the back, cut it in half, and use it as a cart instead of a wagon.

They spent the next several hours working on it, and by that afternoon, they were ready to go with half of their home away from home.

When they cleared the trees at the crest of a mountain, it took their breath away as they looked down onto the valley floor. There were large pine and spruce trees and a giant oval-shaped meadow surrounded by mountains. The river water was sparkling clear and clean, the valley and hills covered with wildflowers. The soil was dark and rich, reminding them of the fertile farmland they had left behind in New York. Doctor Whitman told them that there was a plant that grew in the valley called camas root. It had a large purple flower, much like a lily, and bloomed in the spring. It also had a large onion-shaped root and was one of the primary sources of food for the Indian people of this region. The tribes came from all over each summer to harvest and prepare it. They baked it by digging a hole and throwing in red-hot rocks. They then covered the rocks with grass and put the roots over that; they add more grass and then covered everything with a layer of dirt. Even though it has the appearance of an onion, it's sweet, almost like a fig when cooked. By late winter, when game is scarce, it can be the difference between life and death.

Mr. McLeod and a party of six men were able to catch a dozen fish resembling rainbow trout. One of the men brought in an antelope, and they had their first fresh meal in over a week. It didn't take long before Mother was almost herself again, but unfortunately, Mr. Gray had taken ill and felt too weak to continue on horseback. Chief Rotten Belly and Miles helped him up on his horse, and the chief got behind to keep him from falling off. He held on to him like that for over ten miles until they were able to make camp. Once there, Mr. Gray fell into a sound sleep and was able to get the rest he badly needed to revive himself and continue. Through Richard, the chief explained that because the Nez Perce People spend much of their lives on horseback, this was not unusual for them.

The following day my parents and the Whitmans decided to go off their route to see a place called Soda Springs. Mr. McLeod and several of his men accompanied them as the rest of the party continued moving forward. He reminded them that they were still in an area where Blackfoot hunting parties had recently been spotted and that they would need to stay on guard in case of attack. Mr. McKay told them that he hadn't seen any signs of the Blackfoot this last week and felt it should be safe to explore.

It was an amazing place with crusty white mounds of soda coming out of the ground above the mineral charged streams. They found a small crater that was full of dead insects and small birds that had choked on the noxious gas it was emitting. When they got close enough, they could hear a rumbling sound coming from far below the steaming crater. They found several other streams with water as clear and clean as crystal. The water was bubbly, almost like champagne, and tasted almost as good. Mr. Mcleod told them to drink only a small amount, that too much could make them sick.

It was a pleasant diversion that no one could have anticipated, more like a day trip instead of the hard labor they were used to. They easily caught up with the rest of the party shortly before dark and enjoyed another fresh supper. Mr. Gray was feeling better, and everyone was content with a full stomach, reveling in the warm, gentle breeze and pristine skyscape, a perfect nightcap.

On August 3, 1836, they arrived at Fort Hall and were looking forward to resting and relaxing for the first time since they had left the Rendezvous. At the Rendezvous, they had briefly met with Captain Wyeth, who was on his way back East to settle some of his business arrangements. He was an adventurer and inventor who designed the first insulated icehouses and tools for harvesting ice, and shipping. At that time, it completely revolutionized the fishing industry and opened the door for shipping fresh foods all over the world.

They were greeted by Captain Thyng, who was put in charge of the fort while Captain Wyeth was away. He was a kind and generous southern gentleman, well-educated, and a gifted storyteller. He had come west as an assistant to Captain Wyeth, arriving on Christmas

Eve of 1834. He invited them to dine with him that night with none other than dried buffalo. However, to Mother's delight, they were also treated to fresh turnips and mountain bread, which is dough fried in buffalo fat. For dessert, they had tea and stewed serviceberries, a much-appreciated departure from their earlier diet.

Captain Thyng, Mr. McLeod, and Mr. McKay shared stories of their explorations and adventures that were hard to imagine. However, Mother had learned that these kinds of men were more likely to understate rather than exaggerate. Captain Thyng told them to be careful when walking around the fort; since it was situated on the south side of the Snake River, they were exposed to the Blackfoot who had killed several men during surprise sniper attacks.

Sadly, Miles Goodyear decided to leave them at this juncture of their journey. He wanted to explore the lands to the south where the Ute Indian tribes resided. He was a wild one with a good heart and had become a trustworthy friend, brave, honest, and hard-working with an infectious enthusiasm for life. They were all sad to see him go.

There was now a serious discussion as to whether to keep the cart or leave it at Fort Hall. Miles had been the one responsible for digging it out of the mud or swimming it across the rivers, and no one else, including Father, wanted to take on the extra burden. After talking it over, Mother and Father decided to take it as far as they could, hoping it would make it all the way to their new home.

Chapter 5

A Wild Ride

On August 6, 1836, Mother came close to losing her life. They had recently left Fort Hall and were on their way to Fort Walla Walla. Her horse had bruised its foot, so she was giving it time to heal while riding one of the extra horses that Chief Rotten Belly had brought along. For some reason, she was having trouble controlling him. When the horse stepped into a hornet's nest, it reared up on its hind legs, throwing Mother off with one foot firmly stuck in the stirrup. The horse bolted and took off dragging Mother's bouncing body beside it for almost 100 yards before one of the trappers caught and stopped it.

Miraculously she was not seriously injured. Doctor Whitman was there right away to examine her for contusions and broken bones. Fortunately, he found nothing but bumps, bruises, and several shallow cuts on the side of her head and elbows. Father was visibly shaken and couldn't stop asking her if she was all right.

Mr. McKay approached saying, "I saw what happened, Mrs. Spalding; you are a lucky lady, that could have gone badly ... that was quite a ride, how are you feeling?"

"The doctor says that nothing is broken. I should be ready to go again after I catch my breath and get a cool drink of water."

He looked at her, shook his head, and said, "They must make women different where you come from, Mrs. Spalding. I see you keep a journal; you should write a book about your experiences on the trail one day."

"If I were to write a book about all the things that we've seen and done so far, Mr. McKay, no one would ever believe it."

He smiled, tipped his hat, and said, "I better find you a different horse, Mrs. Spalding."

Mother said she got to thinking after he left about how much they had been through and wondered if she had changed in any way besides losing weight. She certainly felt stronger not only on the outside, but also on the inside. She figured that whatever she took from this experience, it would help her survive whatever lay ahead.

On August 20, 1836 they reached Fort Boise. It was a rough and rugged trip from Fort Hall, and they were all weary from the drive. Most of the terrain had been high desert, hot and dry. The next morning, they woke to a searing wind that cut through the desert, sending shards of blinding sand through the air. Mother said that she had seen little that would make her want to settle in this part of the country and that water was extremely scarce once you left the Snake River. It was a hard land, and she didn't envy the Indian tribes that inhabited it. Sadly, and finally, Mother and Father abandoned their cart at Fort Boise. Mr. McKay told them that the Blue Mountains were the most treacherous in the entire Northwest, and there would be no hope of getting it through on the route they planned to take. It had been such an important part of my parents' lives, and they hoped they might be able to retrieve it at a later time.

They rested for two days, and with a strong sense of excitement, they departed for Fort Walla Walla, knowing they were getting close to their final destination, grateful to still be in the company of Mr. McKay. Mother and Mrs. Whitman had an unexpected and exhilarating experience crossing the Snake River. The water was not moving quickly, but it was going to be another deep and wet crossing. Several men from the Snake River Tribe who were accompanying them had devised a way to take goods and provisions across the river without getting them wet.

Small rafts were quickly made out of twigs and cattails, then tied together with rope. They put everything on the raft, then got into the water and swam it across, pulling the rope in their teeth. Father told Mother he would swim beside her if she chose to give it a try. The Indian men were confident that the women would make it to the other side completely dry. Since Mother was quite a bit lighter and a good swimmer, she told Mrs. Whitman that she would go first. Father helped her on, and she lay completely flat, splayed across the raft. Lo and behold, she made it to the other side exactly as promised. When Mrs. Whitman joined her on the other side, they laughed like schoolgirls at the thought of crossing in such an undignified manner.

In the distance, they could see the intimidating Blue Mountains rising upwards over 9,000 feet into the deep blue sky. Mother was having a conversation with Mr. McKay when he told her about the crossing. He said that even though the mountain range would only take several days to cross, it would be the steepest and most treacherous they had yet to encounter during the entire journey. He was not exaggerating. It was also the narrowest trail they had ever crossed, winding and zigzagging in a way that almost made them dizzy. Just when they thought they were through the most difficult part they would find themselves facing an even more demanding challenge. In some places, the ground was strewn with broken black rock that was extremely slippery and hard on the animals' feet. At times it was so narrow and steep that even the horses seemed unsure where to step next.

They finally made camp at the widest part of the divide as the sun was setting.

In the distance, they could see Mt. Hood and Mt. St. Helens, and below was the Columbia River and valley. Far off in the hazy distance, Mr. McKay told us the Coast Range was the final gauntlet before reaching the Pacific Ocean. Mother said that it was one of the most spectacular sunsets she had ever seen. It started with golds and yellows, turning to red, pink, and purple, finally to shades of gray and black. She felt that words could never accurately describe or capture the beauty of a scene like that; it needed to be experienced.

The next day they slowly descended the Blue Mountains. Fortunately, it was not as steep or rocky as the east side had been, and they were able to make camp early enjoying a much-needed rest that evening. Mother considered it a small miracle that they were able to cross over safely with all of their belongings intact and no injuries.

The land had changed drastically from the high desert and mountains to rich and fertile lowland. The valley was nothing less than euphoric for the senses. Flowers were in bloom, rich with their divine perfumes; birds were calling out to one another in their most musical voices. The area, a circular shaped valley with the mountains enclosing it like the tender arms of a mother's love, was called Grand Ronde. There were giant spruces and pine trees, shimmering clear blue river water. The soil was so dark and rich that anything that fell to earth would begin to grow, a welcome sight after the hot, dusty, barren high desert. The next morning as the wildflowers opened to the morning sun, they rose to the dawn, rested, but restless, hungry for the salty taste of a new day.

September 3, 1836, Mr. Pierre Pambrun, chief trader for the Hudson Bay Company, met them at the gates of Fort Walla Walla. It was a tremendous relief to be so close to the end of their journey. Since they were now so poorly provisioned from having to leave the wagons behind, it was necessary to continue to Fort Vancouver to try and replace what they would need to get the missions underway. Mr. Pambrun was a very kind and generous man, and since he was also planning a trip to Fort Vancouver, he offered to let them join him. They said goodbye and thanked Mr. McKay and his party who departed in search of new trade routes and explorations. After a week of rest, they were once again on the trail heading toward what would be their farthest destination west.

September 7, they had been waiting for several days for the winds to die down so they could be on their way to Fort Vancouver by boat. Mother reminisced that they had now been on the trail for six and a half months, though it felt more like six and a half years. She was musing over what her family and friends might be doing at home, and if they were thinking about her. When they met with Captain Wyeth at the Rendezvous, he offered to take their letters home with him since he planned to be in New York, so she was hoping to hear from home in the next year or so.

The Columbia River was and is one of the most magnificent bodies of water in the world. It has everything from narrow, swiftly moving rapids and waterfalls to glassy river crossings almost five miles wide. The scenery was constantly changing from high rocky cliffs on one side, to wide-open plains of grass and sand on the other. It was another memorable sunset as they made camp that night as the rising stars began to appear and silently circle the earth.

The river sound was like a deep baritone voice rising from the earth. The food they were eating was considerably better than the dried buffalo jerky they had eaten during much of their journey. That evening they feasted on ham and potatoes with bread and butter. Mr. Pambran also made a delicious tea that he told them had come all the way from India. The next day they encountered a 20-foot waterfall making it impossible to continue downriver by boat. They needed to unpack everything and haul it along with the other boat for almost a mile downstream. Fortunately, there was a large group of Paiute Indians nearby who were willing to carry the provisions and boats to the next landing for a large bag of tobacco. Mr. Pambran had come prepared to barter. Other natives continued to join in, knowing that they would be needed again several miles further downriver.

On September 11 they came to a place called The Dalles. Once again, they had reached a gauntlet of rapids and waterfalls and were unable to continue by boat. The Hudson Bay Company had a small trading outpost set up since this was the most prodigious fishing area on the entire river, maybe the world. Different tribes had been coming to fish and trade for hundreds, if not thousands of years. One of the Indian men had caught a sea lion just below a place called The Chutes. He was selling and trading its blubber, meat, and valuable waterproof skin, used for coats and boots.

Their possessions and supplies would be portaged between two and three miles downriver this time. Afterward, it would be smooth sailing all the way to Fort Vancouver as long as the winds were not overly strong from the west. At The Dalles, they feasted on the most delicious smoked salmon and roasted hazelnuts that they had ever tasted, then camped overnight. In the morning, they came to the Chutes and were dazzled by one of the most astonishing spectacles they had ever witnessed. The Indian people had built wooden platforms out over the falls and were catching giant salmon with large nets and spears. The salmon were jumping into their nets as if begging to be caught. That afternoon they were buffeted by high westerly winds that stopped them dead in their tracks.

The next day they again made little progress and were assailed by strong winds at a place called the Gorge. This was a canyon well known for dramatic landscapes, a geology that created a natural wind tunnel causing waterspouts, whirlpools, and even high waves when there were opposing currents and tides.

That day they were visited by a group of Indians called The Flathead Tribe. The tribe had taken their name from flattening the heads of young children less than one-year old by taking two boards and tightening them together with cords. They kept them bound for up to four months. There seemed to be no practical purpose whatsoever, and Mother felt deeply sorry for the little ones who had to suffer this form of torture regardless of the reasoning.

Along the river, they had seen some of the Indian people living in miserable conditions, and their hearts went out to them in the hope that they could one day help. Their social structure was no different than American society; there were rich and poor tribes and people. The Nez Perce and Cayuse were among the richest, but even they had times of hunger from the bitter cold winter conditions.

Some of the poor looked so drawn and hungry without adequate homes or shelters, especially the women and children. Mother said she could see the depth of suffering reflected in their eyes. This struck home, prompting her to reaffirm her commitment. She hoped that they could make a difference by helping the Indian people plant crops and build homes so that they would never be hungry or cold again.

On September 13, they docked at a riverside landing with a sawmill only five miles east of Fort Vancouver. It was customary for the men to prepare themselves by cleaning, shaving, and dressing for their arrival. Mr. Pambran sent a messenger ahead to let them know that they were coming and to expect the first two women who had crossed the Oregon Trail.

Chapter 6

Fort Vancouver

On September 14, 1836, Fort Vancouver was a sight to behold. There were two ships anchored offshore, fully dressed, and flying flags of all sizes and colors.

Hundreds of people were gathered along the shore and on the dock, waiting to greet them. Mother found it hard to believe that there was so much excitement and fanfare in their honor. It was a simple pleasure to see buildings that reminded her of home. A very distinguished man with long silver hair named Doctor John McLaughlin and his associate James Douglas were there to formally greet them. Doctor McLaughlin was a very imposing man in stature and appearance. He was tall with long white hair and beard like a lion's mane. Everyone was extremely courteous and friendly as they were introduced. Doctor McLaughlin took Mrs. Whitman's arm, and Mr. Douglas took Mother's and gently guided them to the Fort.

It was at that point that Mother first became truly aware of the significance associated with being the first white women to journey over the Rocky Mountains and Oregon Trail. As they made their way to Doctor McLaughlin's home, he remarked that this would undoubtedly be chronicled as a historic moment in the settling of the Oregon Territories, that he was proud to be a small part of it. He pointed out the two ships in the harbor and told them that they were the *Neraide* from London commanded by Captain Royal, and the *Columbia*, which had just returned from exploring the Sandwich Islands for trading routes. It was under the command of

Captain Dandy, who had taken Mr. Parker to the Hawaiian Islands in April.

They were informed that both captains had invited them aboard the ships and were looking forward to meeting their party. They were again introduced to Mr. Townsend who they had met briefly at Fort Walla Walla. He told them that he was an ornithologist from Philadelphia sent to collect various bird and animal species for the Audubon Society. He had spent two years in the mountains collecting and was planning to return home sometime soon. He was extremely grateful that they had brought along letters and journals for him from home and offered to do the same for them when he returned east.

When they arrived at Doctor Mclaughlin's home, they were greeted by Mrs. McLaughlin, Mrs. Douglas, and Doctor McLaughlin's daughter, Mariah, a very lovely and bright young woman. Mrs. McLaughlin and Mrs. Douglas were both half-white, and half-Indian, Mrs. McLaughlin, the mother of Thomas McKay, was a fascinating woman. She was considered the matriarch of one of the most prominent families in the Oregon Territories, a strong woman who made them feel at home. Mother liked her very much.

Their quarters were beautifully arranged with soft beds, fresh flowers, and bowls of fresh fruit, a vast improvement from the hard ground and hardtack they had grown used to. It was unfortunate that they were unable to meet with Mr. Parker before he left since they understood that he had spent a great deal of time researching the best locations for possible mission sites. He appeared to have done a good job ministering and was well-liked; they understood his need to return home and the difficulty in obtaining timely passage, and they wished him Godspeed.

Doctor McLaughlin was the chief factor and superintendent of the Columbia District of the Hudson Bay Trading Company. He had done an admirable job of developing what had been a crude village into a civilized colony. He took them on a tour of the grounds showing them orchards ripe with fruit and gardens overflowing with vegetables of every shape and color. Every quarter of the Fort was well-groomed and arranged. One of the smaller guesthouses was covered with grapevines they used to make their own wine.

Mother would always have the greatest respect for Doctor McLaughlin's ingenuity, kindness, and manners. In various ways, he had helped to make that part of the country what it was, and he was considered by many to be the Father of the Oregon Territories.

If it were not for him, she was uncertain how they would have initially fared, or if they would have made it through the hardships of the first years without his help. It certainly would have been a much more arduous and questionable beginning. They had lost almost all of their possessions along the trail and had come to him nearly empty-handed. Doctor McLaughlin gave them food and shelter, providing them with everything they would need to get started.

The ship *Nariade* had recently filled Fort Vancouver's stock rooms, and they were able to find almost everything they needed. He supplied them with household goods, tools, seeds, and other supplies, even the horses to carry their heavy packs. He gave them wheat, oats, barley, cattle, hogs, turkeys, and sheep. All this he did on loan, asking nothing more than that they do the same thing for other immigrants and settlers who came to their missions in need.

At this time, the Oregon Territory was dominated by British and Scottish trappers and traders working for the Hudson Bay Company. The political climate in England did not approve of Americans settling in the Northwest and hoped to establish it as a British colony, keeping the land and resources to themselves. A Scotsman, Doctor McLaughlin was not a politician; he was a generous and compassionate human being who took a risk with his career by helping them. There was also a large group of French-Canadians who worked as laborers at the fort. Many of them had Indian families, and the post provided an excellent school for the children who were generally very bright and well educated. One of the teachers had taught them to sing together and had started a choir that filled the church with angelic and heavenly voices every Sunday morning.

By September 17 Father and Doctor Whitman were getting provisions ready to explore the territory where they planned to establish the two missions. They needed to decide as to whether Mother and Mrs. Whitman should accompany them, or stay comfortably at Fort Vancouver. Neither Mother nor Mrs. Whitman wanted to be separated from their husbands, but Doctor McLaughlin felt strongly that they would be safer under the protection of the soldiers. He was also persuasive in convincing them that the men would be able to move faster and more freely while living off the land. Several days later, they all met and decided that Mother and Mrs. Whitman would stay at Fort Vancouver until the men returned for them. Mother continued to work hard at learning the Nez Perce language as quickly as possible from Richard Tackitonitis, who had stayed with her for that purpose. Both Richard and John planned to help the missions as interpreters until they were established, then they would rejoin their own people.

September 21 was a bittersweet parting as the men left with a small party going upstream against the powerful Columbia River. They hoped to make good time, but going against the current and possible headwinds had always been dangerous and unpredictable. Fortunately, everything went extremely well, and on October 29, the men returned with the good news concerning the mission sites.

Doctor Whitman had decided on a section of land among the Cayuse Tribe, near the Walla Walla River called Waiilatpu, which means, "Place of the Rye Grass." It was approximately 30 miles from Fort Walla Walla, the land rich and fertile. He felt that it would take well to agriculture and produce crops by the next spring and summer. There was no timber close by, but the Indian people had offered to help cut and transport whatever was needed.

Father had decided on an area approximately 120 miles northeast of Waiilatpu on the Clearwater River. It was among the Nez Perce People near a village called Lapwai, which means "Valley of the Butterflies." The land was also fertile, the timber close by and plentiful. Father had spent a good deal of time with Chief Rotten Belly, who was returning to his village near Lapwai. Before parting, John Ais translated as the chief told him that the Cayuse are good people, but not as friendly toward having the white people among them. It was the Nez Perce, not the Cayuse, who asked to know about the "Book of Heaven," and he hoped the Whitmans would not regret their decision to live among the Cayuse.

On November 1, Mother was helping to prepare and load their boat for the last leg of the journey when she became aware of a young Indian woman paddling a canoe with one arm. The woman had a young man lying in her lap who showed no sign of life. It was her dead husband who had been shot by their chief because of a disagreement over a horse.

The ball had gone all the way through him and entered her chest. They quickly helped her to shore and took her to Doctor McLaughlin, who said she was lucky to be alive and likely to recover. He told them that this kind of thing was not uncommon, that there is no recourse; the chief is the last word in these situations.

When Father heard about it, he told them that they had witnessed something even more harsh and heartbreaking while at Fort Walla Walla. A young mother with a small child had gotten sick and died at the camp outside of the fort. After the burial, her husband left the little girl with a friend and then went to find someone to care for her. Shortly after leaving, the young mother's father arrived and took the little girl of about two years old to the gravesite and dug it up. He then placed the child into the grave and buried her alive with her dead mother. Father said he wanted to intervene, but was told in strong language not to interfere, that it is extremely dangerous for white people to do so. When the woman's husband returned, he was understandably angry and wanted to have his wife's father shot and killed, but no action was taken. This was a graphic and violent reminder that they were the foreigners, and would be the ones who needed to adapt to the laws and customs of the Indian people, far different than anything they had experienced in their pasts.

November 3, 1836, they were ready to take their leave of Fort Vancouver.

Mother told me that she had never met a more kind-hearted and loving person than Mrs. McLaughlin, that she made her and Mrs. Whitman feel as if they were part of her family. She would also miss Doctor McLaughlin; his kindness, wisdom, and generosities were a beacon that would guide them forward into the unknown. Mrs. Whitman had grown fond of the school children that she sang with each evening. Their departure was a mixture of tears and smiles as they bid farewell to their new friends.

As they parted, Doctor McLaughlin took Mother and Mrs. Whitman by the hand and said, "Thank you both for your courage in coming to this new world. I know that you have had a difficult journey and had to leave your families and friends behind. You have done what no other white women have ever done before. Your determination to cross the Rocky Mountains and Oregon Trail from one coast to the other will open a door that will change this land forever. I know we will meet again, and if there is anything I can do, please do not hesitate to ask."

As they said goodbye, Mother felt as though they might be leaving behind the last safe and familiar place she would ever know. Unsure of the future they had chosen, she prayed that the sacrifices they had made would be meaningful.

When she looked back at the journey, there were times when she didn't think she would survive. On several instances, she felt as though her soul was preparing to depart from her body, that there must be some purpose why they had made it this far. She was now in the best health she had experienced in years, possibly the strongest she had ever felt in her life.

The excellent fresh foods, horseback rides, and long walks with Mrs. McLaughlin seemed to have revived her body and spirit, giving her strength she needed to go on.

She and Father were now ready to start living the reality of the hopes and dreams they had so long envisioned. The trip back up the Columbia was formidable. The currents and headwinds were relentless, causing them much longer delays than they had anticipated. They encountered strong winds and heavy rainstorms, creating rapids and whirlpools, unlike anything they had ever experienced.

Once again, Mother came close to losing her life and felt that someone must have been watching over her. They were at a difficult branch of the river where all of the men had to get out and pull the boat upstream by rope to make any progress. Mrs. Whitman had decided to get out and stretch her legs. Mother was quite comfortable and decided to stay with the boat. When they reached an especially rough section of the river, one of the men slipped and let go of the rope. Several men next to him lost their footing and fell to the ground letting the rope go slack. When the men below them caught the slack, it pulled them over the bluff and into the water. Thankfully they didn't hit any rocks and were able to swim to safety. The boat then quickly caught the current and flew away for several hundred feet before it crashed into a large rock. Somehow both the boat and Mother were undamaged for the time being, though the boat was trapped and tightly wedged in between the rocks. Father and several of the Indian men took two of the canoes and paddled as fast as they could before the boat could become submerged or pulled loose and crushed upon the rocks below by the deadly current.

When they reached her, they made sure that she was unhurt, then took her safely to shore before they started pulling the boat loose. They had to reattach the ropes and struggled for several hours before freeing it from the rocks. Mr. Pambran told them that numerous boats had wrecked upon the rocks, and many lives had been lost in the past. He went on to say that it was nothing short of miraculous that neither she nor the boat was lost. Mother told him that it would have been nice to have known that earlier, that she would have gladly hiked that part of the trip with Mrs. Whitman.

They reached Fort Walla Walla on November 22, 1836, now nearing the final leg of their journey. They were met and greeted by over 120 Nez Perce men, women, and children, who now considered it their responsibility to get the Spaldings, their packhorses, and possessions safely to the village at Lapwai. It was an exciting time, and everyone was anxious to be on his or her way.

The Whitmans decided that it would be best for Narcissa to stay at Fort Walla Walla until Marcus was able to build a structure for the coming winter. The one thing they found disconcerting was that none of the Cayuse people had shown up to greet the Whitmans, perhaps there was a misunderstanding concerning their arrival. Mother and Father stayed at the fort that night, but by first light, they were ready to leave.

It was not easy saying goodbye to the people they had been so close to for so long, whom they had relied on in almost every way.

Doctor and Mrs. Whitman had been a lifeline when Mother felt tossed upon an ocean of unknown forces. The doctor treated her with his skill and thoughtful care; Narcissa had taken her hand and brought her back to this world when she thought herself slipping away. They were good people, committed to a higher calling; Mother would always think of them as Brother and Sister Whitman.

Mr. Gray and John Ais were coming along with Mother and Father to Lapwai. Mr. Gray was planning to help Father build a house. John was planning to return to his village, then help them with the stock, and planting of the crops. Richard Tackitonitis would be joining the Whitmans after he had visited his tribe and family for a time.

Late that afternoon, they crossed a shallow but powerful stream. They had hoped that there were no more challenges of the trail, but that was not to be the case. Two of the packhorses were swept away and cast over a waterfall of about 15 feet. One hit the rocks and died instantly the other pulled to safety. One of the packs was lost along with its precious supplies.

As they approached the last hill, Mother said she could hardly contain the deep feelings she was having about finally reaching their destination. As they cleared the last grove of pine trees, they feasted their eyes for the first time upon the "Valley of the Butterflies."

Everything appeared perfectly placed by the eons of time and elements, like shells upon the shore, Lapwai. They had left everything behind and survived innumerable hazards. Father and Mother had traveled a total of 5,215 miles on horseback, riverboat, canoe, wagon, cart and foot, and were now finally home.

Eliza

Part Two

The Mission

"Those were years pregnant with heroic self-sacrifice. They were to make their homes where the first tree had not been felled to build it. They must wrest a living from the soil when the axe had not yet been laid to the first tree toward clearing the soil. They must live among a people whose language they did not know one syllable and not one word of which had been reduced to writing. All of this must be endured in such isolation as is scarcely possible on the face of the earth today."

—A.M. McClain, 1912

Chapter 1

Lapwai

Poised thousands of feet below the Bitterroot Mountains, Lapwai is known as the Valley of the Butterflies. Mother told me that even in her dreams, she had never imagined such a magnificent place. Lapwai Creek is a lifeline that runs through lowlands of lavish dark earth. The grass sways to the rhythm of the wind, and the creek moves side to side as it dances over the mossy rocks, slowing and surging.

The valley is some four miles wide and eight miles long, surrounded and sheltered by mountains to the north, east, south, and west. The canyon walls climb like an enormous stairway into the heavens. When the winds blow down over the mountains, the entire valley fills with the scents of sweet pine and fir. To the east is an immense prairie of tall grass and forest extending to the Bitterroot Mountains. In springtime, the valley is covered in wildflowers of every color. Thousands of birds mate before soaring off to their summer nests.

When my mother and father first arrived, it was fall, and the land was covered with a carpet of orange and yellow leaves spread out like a warm cotton quilt, comforting the earth beneath.

A new world lay wide open before them, inviting, inspiring, terrifying. This was the place where my parents planned to spend the rest of their days, where they hoped to raise a family and live in peace among their new brothers and sisters of the Nez Perce People.

Nez Perce villages of almost every size, ranging from several dozen to over 600 people, populated the Oregon Territory during the 1830s and 1840s. The largest was perched along the winding Clearwater River some ten miles to the north of Lapwai.

My parents had made an extraordinary friend named Chief Tamootsin, whose village was three miles north. Though he was not an old man, the elements had carved an ancient face lined with creases of wisdom and patience. He was broad-shouldered with a noble bearing and the eyes of an eagle. He had termed the Bible, "The Book of Heaven," and because of his spiritual nature and agile mind, he was curious to understand its meaning.

He made my parents feel welcome as if they were returning home to family and friends instead of having just arrived in a strange and unknown land. Mother found the Nez Perce People to be among the most elegant she had ever known, and her deepest wish was that they would find harmony together.

My parents were surprised, even awed by the amount of time and energy that had been spent preparing the camp for their arrival. There were dozens of ornate teepees set up to accommodate them and those who planned to stay and help with the building and planting. Many were beautifully crafted with intricate designs of animals, stars, and personal symbols. The biggest ones could take up to 20 buffalo hides, tediously sewn together with buffalo ligaments.

Mother was amazed that the women were able to assemble and furnish them so quickly. They could complete a comfortable lodge with a fire burning in under an hour, then tear it down and pack up in less than half that time.

There was so much to do, they had no idea where to start or how they would fit in. They were led wide-eyed to the largest and most beautifully decorated teepee, their new home sweet home. They began by locating and moving in their personal belongings, trying their best to make it feel comfortable and familiar. The supplies that needed to be put under cover were placed next to their lodge underneath the well-worn tent that had sheltered them on the trail.

Father had no lack of helpers, and I can't help but smile at the thought of all of those people running around like happy children with absolutely no idea what they were trying to accomplish.

Head Chief Tackensautis of a nearby tribe was doing a fine job of acting in charge; the women and children were gathered around Mother watching her every move. They were so curious, wanting to touch everything, her hair, her clothes. For no reason other than simple joy, a member of the group would spontaneously reach over and give Mother a big hug or kiss, creating even more cause for celebration. They were loving and devoted people with great reverence for family and friends.

For the Nez Perce, it was a sign of respect that Mother had come to them with a basic understanding of their language. Initially, John Ais helped explain that he and Richard Tackitonitis had been teaching her their language while journeying the trail together over the past seven months. She also told them about the word game she had played with the Nez Perce women at the Rendezvous. Of course, that was all the invitation they needed to start the game up again. Before long, there was a large group of women and children laughing and playing.

Of the Indian people, the Nez Perce were among the most affluent, some owning vast herds of horses. During the warmer months, fish and game were plentiful. In the summer, they collected a plant called camas root, which, when prepared, resembled a biscuit. This, along with dried salmon, buffalo, and elk jerky, was used to help them through the harsh winter months. They had extensive knowledge of the trees and edible plants used for nourishment as well as medicine.

They made their clothes out of the most exquisite deer hides with beautiful quill and beadwork, as good if not better than anything Mother had ever seen. Doctor Whitman told my parents that their territory was so large that it covered over 17,000,000 acres of land with as many as 100 permanent villages. They were a proud and powerful tribe with a remarkable history.

Many of the women were stunning, with beautiful shiny black hair, like the feathers of a raven. The men had strong, intelligent faces, some very fierce. They were curious, inquisitive, and quick to learn and share their skills and concepts.

Other than an occasional trapper, the Nez Perce first came into contact with the white man in April 1806 when Lewis and Clark ventured into their territory. Their party had just crossed the snow-covered Bitterroot Mountains and was near starvation. William Clark was leading a hunting party of six looking for game when the Nez Perce first observed them. The braves were initially uncertain of what to do; some were in favor of ambushing and killing them.

They decided to return to the village and discuss it with the elders. As they were deciding, one of the elder women overheard and told them about her experience with the white people. When she was a young girl, she had gotten lost in the forest and become very weak, hungry, and cold. She was found by a small party of white trappers who kindly nursed her back to health and returned her to her people. She told them that the ones she had known had good hearts, that these people might also have good hearts, that they should find out why they were here, and listen to what they wanted.

I can't help but wonder how far back it would have set the expansion into the west if the Lewis and Clark party had been killed that day. The Nez Perce generously fed and lodged them, freely sharing their knowledge of the land. They stayed for several days before moving on toward the setting sun. Before they left, the Nez Perce helped them cut the dugout canoes they would need to continue downstream.

On the return trip, the Lewis and Clark party stayed at the same village from April 29 through June 9, 1806. During those days, Meriwether Lewis spent most of his time and energy collecting plant and animal specimens. William Clark spent much of his time treating sick members of the tribe, mostly minor ailments. Fortunately, he was successful since Indian custom gives the family of a deceased person the right to put a medicine man to death if the patient dies while they are being treated.

Several days after my parents' arrival at Lapwai, the new village was bustling with activity. Under Mr. Gray's supervision, the Nez Perce were cutting down pine and hemlock trees of the right length and diameter for log cabins. Further upriver they floated logs downstream under the direction of Chief Tackensautis. Men with whipsaws were shown how to cut larger trees into boards. Father was busy measuring and notching the cut logs before they were put into place. Amazingly enough, the building moved along very quickly, and my parents were able to live in a section of their new home by December 3, 1836. The floor was partially finished with a chimney, stove, and several completed windows. It was still drafty since they needed to complete two doors and two windows in the schoolroom area, but already comfortable with a warm fire burning.

The Nez Perce did most of the roof work and filled in the chinks between the logs with pine pitch, giving the rooms a wonderful smell. They also did the hard labor of bringing in all of the timber and rock. Father and Mr. Gray spent most of their time doing the windows, doors, and rockwork for the fireplace. They held all of the services outside until a room was finished for worship. The Indian people had so many questions about the "Book of Heaven" that outdoor services would sometimes go on for hours until they were covered with snow.

One of the things that surprised my parents since coming to Lapwai was how many of the different tribes already had a fundamental knowledge of Christianity. When my parents questioned Doctor McLaughlin, he told them that there was an extraordinary Indian man named Spokane Garry, bright and well educated. He traveled the Oregon Territory teaching a basic form of Christianity to the Indians. His sermons were often attended by hundreds of native people curious to know about the "Book of Heaven."

With the help of John Ais, my parents were both working hard at learning the language as quickly as possible so that they could communicate directly without the need for an interpreter. After supper, Mother and Father would talk about their day, drilling each other on new words they had learned and how to pronounce them correctly. As they lay together, face to face, in the dark, they would often carry on until well after midnight, exhausted but unable to sleep because of the excitement and anticipation of the coming day.

Chapter 2

White Eagle

Mother said she couldn't put into words the joy she felt when they opened up the school on January 27,1837. The first day there were over 200 men, women, and children; grandmothers and grandfathers, women nursing babies, old and young. She had no books or even a clear idea of what or how she was going to teach, only a burning desire to do so. Thankfully John was there to help interpret for her until she was able to speak directly with her classes. He had been diligently studying the Bible since meeting Doctor Whitman over two and a half years ago, and his wisdom was far beyond his years.

From the time he was a young boy, he had apprenticed with a powerful shaman and headman of the Nez Perce named Hinmahtutekekailt, also known as Thunder Eyes. Mother felt she had learned as much or more from John, as he had from her. John was also translating Father's sermons, but unlike Mother, who had a gift for languages, Father was slower to learn and found it harder to master.

Mother's first attempts at teaching were to try to describe scriptures and proverbs from the Bible.

Some of them, such as "Greater love has no one than this, that he lay down his life for his friends," seemed easy for her students to understand, but concepts such as the parting of the Red Sea were much more difficult.

At times she had become extremely frustrated with her inability to communicate concepts, and out of desperation, she thought to use her pencil and watercolors. As she began to draw and paint the scenes, there was a collective ahhh of understanding that words could not express. It was like a revelation to her that they were instantly able to visualize what she was trying to communicate.

Mother was busy illustrating the moment when you find God, and how it changes your heart when everyone started nodding approval and understanding. One of the women raised her hand and said the word Weyekin. Several others then encouraged a young woman named White Eagle to come forward. Mother could see that she was timid about being pressured, so she gently took her by the hand and led her to the front of the class.

John explained to Mother that the young woman was being asked by the others to share a similar belief. White Eagle asked if she could use the pencil and paints to illustrate a concept that they called Weyekin. For Mother, the prospect of having a student she could share her artistic skills with was as exciting as the breakthrough in communicating concepts and learning about the Nez Perce beliefs.

White Eagle took a long time staring at the paper before she picked up a pencil, turning it in her hand to feel its weight and texture. She started by making nonsensical marks on a piece of scrap paper. She then did the same with a brush and watercolors. At first, Mother was unsure what White Eagle was trying to do until she took a full sheet of paper and started to outline an image.

At the beginning, it didn't seem to make sense because she would move from one part of the paper to another, seemingly without any discernment for organization. As she continued sketching, it slowly started to come into focus, and Mother could feel the fine hairs on the back of her neck rise.

This young woman had a perfect grasp of perspective. My Father, Mother's parents, and friends had always told her how gifted she was as an artist. She was grateful for their encouragement but well aware that she was in no way extraordinary. This experience clearly illustrated the difference between someone who does as their teachers have taught them and a person who can extemporize what they see in their mind's eye—good art, versus great art. Mother had a good hand and eye, and could accurately translate what she saw, but what she was watching now was far beyond anything she had ever conceived or executed. White Eagle was lightly outlining the image of a young girl of maybe 12 or 13 sitting on the edge of a mountain overlooking a valley.

The girl was looking into the sky at an eagle gliding by barely above her head. She then picked up a brush and made a few strokes, experimenting with colors on the scrap paper. As she began to fill in the tones, Mother became aware that she was watching something extraordinary, a scene that had never been witnessed before. White Eagle's lines and colors were as perfect and natural as the rain falling from the clouds. Once she understood the pencil and brush, there was no longer any hesitation until she had finished. Mother said that her eyes and mouth must have been wide open as she stood before nothing less than a masterpiece. For Mother, it was an awakening, a perfect example of how some people are born blessed with a special gift. Mother told me that they looked into each other's eyes for a long time, and she could feel the instant bond of understanding and sisterhood.

John then went on to explain the concept of Weyekin to Mother. "It is the belief that everything in the world, including animals, trees, even rocks possess a living spirit. Every child between the ages of ten to 15 is required to go on a pilgrimage called a vision quest. It is always at a location of great power, usually on a mountaintop that has been used by others since the beginning of our history. It is a time to be purified, find spiritual guidance, and a deeper understanding of one's purpose in life.

It is considered a rite of passage from childhood into the full acceptance and the responsibility of adulthood. One or more of the village elders or shamans tutor each child for a number of years until they are were considered ready. The child then fasts for several days until highly attuned to the spirit world. Then they are sent out into the wilderness with no food or shelter. In this high state of consciousness, they remain exposed to the elements for up to a week, focused on receiving his or her weyekin when it presents itself.

The weyekin is a spiritual symbol and guide that comes in the form of an animal, bird, or force of nature. The eagle is considered sacred, signifying courage, wisdom, and strength. Because it is the highest flying of all birds, it is believed to be capable of carrying prayers to the Great Spirit. Those who have it as their weyekin are highly revered and respected. White is considered the color of purity, and White Eagle was among the most highly revered young women of the Nez Perce People.

Until that moment, Mother had not fully realized the significance of their beliefs or how beautiful White Eagle was. She was slim and petite with raven black hair down to the middle of her back. She was dressed more simply than any of the other young women with nothing more than the single white feather in her hair as adornment. Her eyes were large and black, dreamy, bright, and intelligent. Her humility and grace made her all the more alluring. It began to dawn on Mother how much she had to learn before she could ever gain or deserve the trust or respect of the Nez Perce.

John continued by telling Mother that White Eagle was much sought after to design clothing and jewelry; that she had painted many of the most beautiful teepees. Her father was well respected, but not a chief among the tribe. Many of the most powerful and wealthy chiefs of the Nez Perce and other tribes had offered many horses and other gifts for her marriage.

It was well known that there was a deep bond of love between White Eagle and her family. Knowing that this kind of arrangement would make her parents rich and powerful among the tribe, they still insisted that the choice would be hers, that her happiness was their happiness.

That night Mother explained to Father what she had experienced during the day and showed him the painting that White Eagle had given to her. These ideas were hard enough for her to comprehend, even more so for Father, who was much more rigid than she in his beliefs.

He asked, "Do they pray to these weyekins as Gods?"

"I asked John the same question. He explained to me that they were not like Gods, but more like saints that you might ask to help or protect you during a time of conflict, confusion, or important decisions."

They lay there in silence for a very long time looking at the picture White Eagle had painted.

Father finally smiled and asked, "Do you think this is what is meant by the saying, "The Lord works in mysterious ways?"

They had not spoken of it since that night, but the painting became one of our family's most treasured possessions, and Mother would often find Father looking at it while drifting off to sleep.

With so much to do, there never seemed to be enough time in the day. They worked from sunup until sundown, after supper, they prepared lessons for the coming day. Several days before Sabbath, Father would often be awake long after midnight working on his sermons, which now drew as many as 500 Nez Perce. At this time, Mr. Gray was a great help, and when the mission house was almost completed, he left for Waiilatpu to help the Whitmans with their buildings.

Mother once told me that there are all kinds of men, but few were like Father. When he put his mind to something, there was nothing he couldn't do. Even as they lay entwined together at night, she could sense that he was working on whatever project he faced the coming day. He never seemed to tire, and never complained or stopped working even when he was sick or injured.

She told me that there was little glory in being a hardworking, responsible family man, that they were seldom ever thought of as heroes, but that was exactly what Father was to her.

His accomplishments were those of a humble man. He had his faults, a quick temper for laziness and impropriety; and though he had studied the many religions of the world, he was so passionate in his own beliefs that he had a hard time accepting others. Mother felt it her calling to calmly help him with these things rather than criticize.

They had barely placed the glass in the windows and doors to the house when Father was already at work on a blacksmith shop, woodworking shop, gristmill, lumber mill, and dormitories. He was still putting on the finishing touches to the schoolhouse, but it was far better than having to teach outside in the snow. With the help of the Nez Perce women, he had started clearing some of the fields close to the house for winter wheat, hoping that it was not too late.

It was hard to get the men to help since they felt that any kind of digging in the dirt was women's work and below them. Mother had been collecting and saving vegetable and fruit seeds for almost two years. With the flower seeds that Mrs. McLaughlin had given her, she had started growing a garden in the yard. Father had set aside a field that looked perfect for a fruit orchard of apples, pears, plums, and cherries. Before they left New York, Mother was able to purchase the plans for a spinning wheel and loom. Father promised to get started on it as soon as the woodworking shop was completed, and he had a place to build them. If there were ever two more productive people in this world, I would never see or know of them in my lifetime.

The coming spring was an endless quilt of colors, sounds, and smells. Before the forge was operational, Father was having trouble making the tools he needed and finding the right wood for his plows. He decided to undertake the journey to Fort Colville, which was owned by the Hudson Bay Trading Company some 200 miles northwest.

On March 27, 1837, he left with 20 packhorses and five Nez Perce men to guide and help with supplies. Mother remained on her own at Lapwai with 1,500 Nez Perce.

She hadn't thought about how vulnerable she was until the day Father departed. By the next day, she was far too busy to give it any more consideration. If Father had known what the conditions were going to be like, he would have certainly delayed two or three weeks.

Long before he reached Spokane, he had to travel through deep and treacherous snowdrifts, at times covering less than one mile per hour on horseback. It took him four days to reach Spokane, but to his delight, his friend William Gray was there to greet him. From Spokane, it was another 60 miles to Fort Colville, but the Nez Perce refused to go any farther north since it was too hard on the horses. They offered to walk to Fort Colville and carry the goods on their backs, but Father would never ask that of them, so they waited for the trail to clear.

While in Spokane, Father finally became acquainted with the man named Slough-Keetcha, also known as Spokane Garry of the Middle Spokane Nation, who he had heard so much about.

When only 14 years old, he had been chosen by the Hudson Bay Company to attend an Anglican mission school called the Red River School, run by the Church of England. The trip to the school was an arduous journey of over 1,000 miles through snowdrifts and frozen rivers, taking 75 days to complete. He became fluent in English and French with an amusing Scottish accent he had picked up from his teachers.

In 1827, he was the first Indian baptized by the Protestant Church west of the Rocky Mountains. In early 1829, Spokane Garry returned as chief of the Middle Spokane Tribe and began preaching his simplified form of the Protestant faith to his people. He became a circuit preacher and started traveling and preaching all over the Northwest. He also began training his people in the new methods of agriculture he had learned while at the mission school. He built a large schoolhouse that measured 20 feet by 50 feet, where he taught and held religious services. He eventually quit teaching after the first missionaries came to the Spokane territory and instead concentrated on agriculture. He became a rich man and was well known for the remarkable crops of potatoes he cultivated.

It turned out that Father was able to find all of the tools and goods he needed in Spokane, as well as 15 bushels of seed potatoes Spokane Garry agreed to sell him. They started back for Lapwai on April 3. Because of the melting snows, almost all of the river crossings were treacherous; thus, he didn't arrive home until April 7.

To Father's amazement, the Indian population at Lapwai had grown to over two thousand while he was gone. In his absence, Mother had taken over his duty of prescribing medicine for minor ailments, mostly stomach problems from bad food or gluttony. Little did she realize how much time it took until she had taken over the responsibility. Each morning there would be anywhere from six to ten Nez Perce waiting for her before she had even dressed. It seemed they now preferred her tender hands and gentle nature to Father's, which were considerably less sensitive.

During the spring salmon run, the Nez Perce men took Father with them to their favorite fishing spot. They caught over 200 salmon weighing between ten and 25 pounds each, giving him 40.

It took them an entire day to salt the salmon in four large barrels that Father had brought along. He told Mother that it was hard to believe his eyes; they were pulling them in almost as fast as they dropped their nets. There were dozens of other groups at the same place, pulling in as many as they could pack. Several days later, a hunting party went out and came back with ten deer, three of which were used for a feast, the rest salted and dried for summer. Mother could hardly believe the bounty and asked Chief Tamootsin if there was always such an abundance of fish and game.

He told her, "It has been a good year, but it is not always so. When the winter is harsh, many of the animals and plants die, and we must do what we need to survive, even if it means eating our horses and dogs. This abundance of fish and game is only a small portion of what we will need to last the summer; then we will need to rely on our brother the buffalo and camas roots to survive the winter."

Father knew that drastic changes were on the way that would be hard for the Indian people to accept, which is why he was so insistent they learn to farm. The white hunters were mindlessly depleting the once vast buffalo herds to the point where they would become nearly extinct within the next two decades.

The Pawnees had once lived so close by the herds that at times the buffalo surrounded their entire village as they passed. They were now forced to trek hundreds of miles in search of the herd. The Sioux had to roam the prairie for as long as 20 days or more to find a buffalo herd, at times yielding to starvation before they could do so. John Ais told Father that many of the Indian people nearly died of starvation two winters ago for lack of enough buffalo and game.

Father proposed to the chiefs that for every acre of land they helped him plow and seed, he would provide two for them, that they would never need to suffer hunger again. Chief Tamootsin could see that the future would change their way of life and understood the dilemma, convincing several of the braves to help him with the planting. Father was hoping to get 100 acres under cultivation that spring. Because there was so much other work to do and reluctance by the Nez Perce men to dig in the dirt, he was only able to get 30 acres planted, certainly not enough to feed everyone.

With the help of the Nez Perce women, Mother was able to plant a large assortment of vegetables in her garden. Father set out what would become the first nursery of fruit trees in the northwest. Roots had taken, and by late summer, the winter wheat was ripe, and Mother's Garden was providing a bounty of fresh vegetables.

My parents held prayer meetings each morning and evening and full services every Sunday. They were astonished to see how fast the Nez Perce had learned the lessons by sharing them with each other verbally.

Both Mother and Father had a deep love of music, though Father had a much better voice and understanding of the fundamentals. He started out teaching simple gospel hymns, and within five or six weeks, he had organized a choir. The intonation and pronunciations were rough at times, but the voices were sincere and exhilarating, especially the angelic sounds of the children's voices. About this same time, Father first began the daunting challenge of translating Nez Perce into English, and English into Nez Perce. Before long, he was able to teach the choir to sing simple hymns by translating them into their language phonetically, which he had taught them to read. On Sunday mornings, their voices echoed throughout the valley in the Sehaptin language.

When their good friend Chief Tackensautis returned from a month-long visit to his sister's village, he was so deeply moved by one of the hymns sung in Nez Perce that he could not hold back the tears.

The chief was concerned for my parents' safety and wanted to make clear to them the danger involved in treating an Indian for illness or injury. He told them that while he was at his sister's camp, one of the medicine men, known as a Tewat, was treating a powerful war chief who later died in his arms. To be avenged, a younger brother of the chief came to the village and shot the Tewat dead. Chief Tackensautis explained that this was an acceptable custom in which no action was taken toward the chief's brother. My parents talked it over and decided to confine their practice to minor ailments for the time being.

On one of Father's trips to Waiilatpu, Doctor Whitman had told Father that his life had already been threatened several times because he was unsuccessful in saving a life. He, too, was having a moral dilemma but had decided to treat all problems regardless of the risk; that he had taken the Hippocratic oath to do so.

Chapter 3

William Gray's Fiasco

During Father's previous trip to Spokane for supplies, Mr. Gray had expressed an idea to raise money for the missions. He had proposed taking a herd of horses back east in trade for cattle and sheep. He also planned to try to recruit more settlers to come west to help with the planting and mission work. Horses were only eight to $14 each in the Oregon Territory and would sell for much more back east. Father thought it a good idea, and since the Nez Perce were eager to acquire cattle, he convinced them to contribute 20 of their best horses to trade.

Doctor Whitman didn't think it a good idea and refused to encourage the Cayuse from participating. He was in favor of recruiting reinforcements to help with the overwhelming amount of work to be done at the missions but worried about the repercussions of something going wrong. They would have to travel through hostile territory belonging to the Blackfoot and Sioux, who would love nothing more than to get their hands on a herd of fine horses. He was outvoted, and Mr. Gray began preparing for the journey.

Four of the Nez Perce braves volunteered to accompany Mr. Gray during the trip. They were curious to learn about the white man's world and eager to acquire the prestige of returning with cattle and a worldly knowledge to share with the others.

Mr. Gray left Spokane in the middle of April, accompanied by the Hudson Bay Company brigade, picking up the horses and men Father had arranged along the way. The Hudson Bay party was headed for the Rendezvous to do their annual trading and celebrating. When they arrived at the base of the Bitterroot Mountains, they were joined by a group of Flathead and Iroquois Indians also on their way to the Rendezvous.

Since the party was so large, Mr. Gray decided to go ahead of the slow-moving brigade and join up with another Hudson Bay party that had left several days earlier under the command of Mr. McLeod. Before joining the McLeod party, they were involved in a brief but intense skirmish with the Blackfoot Indians in which one of the men was wounded. On May 31, they caught up with Mr. Mcleod, and several days later, combined with a group of American trappers led by Mr. Andrew Drips, also on their way to the Rendezvous.

To Mr. Gray's consternation, he was once again part of a large and slow-moving party. They arrived at the 1837 Rendezvous, held at the Green River between Horse Creek and New Fork two weeks later. Other than the Blackfoot, tribes from almost every nation in the Oregon Territory and some beyond were in attendance. Only a handful of Nez Perce had come since so many had decided to stay at Lapwai with my parents. The conditions were so hazardous, and the Rendezvous so important, that if a trapper were missing, he was considered dead.

Mr. Gray had his good and bad sides but was not well-liked among the trappers or Flathead Indians. He was making a pest out of himself, constantly demanding that Mr. Fitzpatrick's party immediately depart and accompany him going east. He was anxious to be on his way and had no interest in taking part in the trading or revelry, threatening to leave without them. Mr. Fitzpatrick told him that they would be staying until the end of the Rendezvous. He warned that it would be foolish and dangerous to travel with such a small party and so many horses through Blackfoot and Sioux country.

Mr. Gray finally became so restless that on July 25, he left with his party of three French-Canadians, four Flatheads, three Iroquois, The Hat, and Big Ignace of the Nez Perce.

The other two Nez Perce were fed up and tired of the bickering, deciding to stay at the Rendezvous with their horses. When Mr. Gray's party reached Fort Laramie, the officer in charge also warned him that it was not safe to continue with such a small party that the Sioux had recently attacked a small party of settlers. At that point, one of the French-Canadians decided to leave, heading back to the Rendezvous.

Mr. Gray and his group pushed forward, and on August 7 near Ash Hollow, on the Platt River, a small party of Sioux was lying in ambush and attacked. Mr. Gray's party was able to flee a short distance before finding a good defensive position before anyone was hurt.

A French-Canadian trader who was with the Sioux called out to Mr. Gray that they were only interested in killing their enemies the Flatheads, that he and the rest of his party could go about their way if they put their weapons down and surrendered. Mr. Gray convinced the French-Canadian trappers to submit, so they stepped out into the open and laid their weapons down. The Sioux rushed by them, and within minutes killed The Hat, Big Ignace, three Flatheads, and the three Iroquois. In the melee, three of the Sioux were killed.

The leader of the Flathead group was wounded but still alive. The white men were about to witness something that would haunt them to their graves. Mr. Gray and the two Canadians were taken prisoners and tied to a tree as the Sioux were deciding whether to kill the Flathead warrior or humiliate him. The Flathead warrior expected to be killed and wanted it over quickly, so he taunted the Sioux warriors, calling them cowardly dogs. This infuriated the Sioux, so they began torturing him by cutting off his toes. Screaming with pain, he spit at them and continued to assault them verbally. When they cut off his fingers, the Flathead warrior went mad with rage and hoping to find a swift death as he insulted their families and ancestors. This only inspired the Sioux braves to test his manhood even farther. They slowly continued torturing him by cutting off other parts of his anatomy until he finally went unconscious and bled to death. The leader of the Sioux was impressed with the Flathead leader's show of courage and opened the dead man's chest and cut out his heart. He then held it up to the others as an act of respect and let out with a blood-curdling yell. Expecting to be next, Mr. Gray and the two French-Canadian's had turned a sickly shade of color.

Feeling he had nothing to lose, Mr. Gray threatened that if they were killed, the American Army, as well as the British Hudson Bay Company and Nez Perce would take revenge upon them. After a heated council, the Sioux party decided that they didn't want any trouble with either the Americans or Hudson Bay Company, and turned the prisoners loose. They gave them each a horse and told them to return to the settlements. The rest of the horses, weapons, and supplies were confiscated. Word spread like wildfire of Mr.

Gray's part in allowing the Indians to be slaughtered. Had he returned to the Rendezvous instead of continuing east, he would have surely found an irate group of Flathead Indians, Iroquois Indians, and trappers waiting to spill his blood. The Nez Perce were angry because of the loss of The Hat and Big Ignace, as well as the prized horses. They hoped to take revenge on Mr. Gray one day for not having the courage to protect the men under his leadership.

This was the first serious rift between the missionaries and the Nez Perce People. By the time the first two Nez Perce had returned from the Rendezvous with their horses, word had already spread throughout the village about Mr. Gray's disgrace and the death of The Hat and Big Ignace. Father was angry because the two young men had abandoned the group. Chief Tackensauris was angry because his brother, The Hat, had been killed.

When father scolded the two young braves for not continuing with Mr. Gray, Chief Tackensauris admonished him for getting them involved in the first place. He told Father that the two warring parties were said to be of equal size. If Gray had fought instead of surrendering, it would have been a standoff, and his brother, along with the other men, might still be alive.

He told Father that, as leader, it was Gray's responsibility to protect his men, even if it meant his own death. There was a bitter quarrel between the two of them, and when it was over, Tackensauris struck his teepee next to the mission house and returned to his own village along with several dozen men and women of his tribe.

From the beginning, there had always been a group of Nez Perce and Cayuse who felt it was a betrayal of their traditional beliefs to adopt those of the missionaries. The fallout with Chief Tackensauris helped validate these feelings and was a serious blow to the missionary movement. The loss of Chief Tackensauris as a friend and strong advocate was a significant setback. Still, many of the Nez Perce continued supporting my parents, but a chink in their trust had opened up.

Mother and Father continued to prepare the land for planting, but Father felt it was necessary to have a pair of oxen to supply the labor to provide for so many people. They were already running low on supplies and would need considerably more to get through the winter.

On August 28, Father left for Fort Colville with 20 men and 75 pack horses. Once again, Mother was left alone. This time she was six months pregnant. Two days after Father had gone, a cry was raised proclaiming a large war party of Snake Indians were quickly approaching from the east and would soon be upon them. Mother took out the telescope and could see that it was nothing more than a herd of wild horses. She told everyone to calm down that there was nothing to worry about.

The next night a woman with her two children came scurrying into camp crying that the Snakes had come upon her and shot her horse, that she and her children had barely escaped certain death. Mother told her to please be calm, that the Snakes might steal her horse, but they would not shoot innocent women and children. That night a large group of women and children decided to spend the night in the mission house with her. For the next two nights, many of the women and children slept in the house, and extra guards were put on the horses. Shortly after, the woman's horse was found nearby unharmed. Mother could tell that it was going to be an eventful time without her husband and that she certainly would not be lonely for companionship.

The conditions were good on this trip north, so Father was able to cover between 40 and 50 miles per day, reaching Fort Colville on September 1. The Indian people in the Colville area had heard that a white holy man was coming and were curious to meet with him and hear him speak. John Ais was one of the men with his party and was nearly fluent in the Salish language, so Father asked him to translate.

From that point on, he was asked to preach at every camp they made, and on the return trip, Father said as many as two thousand native people followed for several days to hear the words from the "Book of Heaven." At Colville, Mr. Archibald McDonald, the new factor in charge of the fort, warmly greeted Father, showing him every courtesy. Though it was not policy to provide oxen to the missionaries, Mr. McDonald broke with protocol and sold him a yoke of oxen as well as 1,200 pounds of flour and other supplies. Many of the Indians who were attending the sermons were from the Pend d'Oreille tribe. Two of the chiefs were so impressed that they decided to follow Father to Lapwai and stayed for several weeks to hear his prayer services and sermons.

Chapter 4

First Born

My parents have told me many times that November 15, 1837, the day I was born, was the most blessed day of their lives. Father insisted they name me Eliza after Mother. The Whitmans, along with their eight-month-old daughter Alice Clarissa, were with us for the occasion, Narcissa helping with the birth.

They had made the difficult journey on horseback, much of it in the freezing rain and snow. We had not seen another white person since the previous December when Mr. Gray left. It was a joyful reunion. Emotions ran high, especially when Father baptized both Clarissa and me. Clarissa and I seemed to bind them even closer together, and the women agreed that each morning between 5:00 and 9:00 AM, they would unite together in prayer. On December 2, The Whitmans began their journey back to Waiilatpu, much of it by log canoe.

Mother told me that I was such a favorite among the Indian women and children that she often had to subtly wrestle me away in order to breastfeed me. When she was busy working, she would occasionally return to the cradle to find me gone and in the arms of one of the Nez Perce women. It was impossible for her to be upset since it was their way, and their only intention was to show me love. There were times when she would have to pick fleas or lice off of me, but these were small things to her, ones that she could find no place in her heart to complain about.

By early spring, Mother and Father hadn't seen or heard anything from Chief Tackensauris and were feeling badly about the loss of his friendship. They talked it over at length, and Father acknowledged that he had handled the situation poorly, that he should have talked with the chief first and let him decide what should have been done. Bringing me as an olive branch, he decided to visit the chief, hoping it would break the ice that had formed between them. He also brought along one of the pigs that the chief had learned to relish, just in case I didn't do the trick.

As he slowly entered the village, he sensed a feeling of apprehension bordering on hostility until they saw that he was carrying a little child in his lap. As he dismounted, several of the women came up to look at me and feel the blanket that Mother had woven. Father recognized one of the women as the chief's wife and held me out for her to hold. She proudly took me into her arms and started showing me around to the other women. Father told me that I had spent so many days and hours in the arms of the Nez Perce women that this seemed completely natural to me, that I was all smiles.

I was passed around for a good 15 or 20 minutes, Father then asked if he could see the chief. The chief must have already heard of our arrival and was waiting for him with a big smile and open arms for me. As Chief Tackensauris took me in his arms, I laid my head tenderly in the crook of his neck and touched his smooth face. Father didn't think that he was ever going to get me back, and it was obvious to all that there were no hard feelings to be found anywhere.

Father told him that I was still nursing, and they could only stay for the night, that we would have to leave first thing in the morning. He told the chief that he was sorry for what he had said and done, that he could be stubborn and sometimes had a bad temper that he was ashamed of.

He also told the chief how much he valued his friendship and wanted them to live as brothers again in the future.

The chief told him that all was forgiven, that he also wanted them to live in peace together. He explained that unlike the white man, the Indian men do not tell each other what to do, they only make suggestions that are either accepted or rejected. That in the future, he should always speak to him first and let him decide what to do concerning his tribe. Father was surprised when Chief Tackensautis called a large group together for evening prayers, asking Father to perform the service. It was a powerful moment of absolution.

As Chief Tackensautis was holding me, he told Father, "Eliza is a good name for this little one, one day she will be like her mother, strong but gentle. Women must be strong to face so many hardships; yes, Eliza is a good name."

The chief went on to tell Father the story of a legendary Nez Perce woman he had once known. "Twenty-five winters ago, a French-Canadian man named Dorio was working for a small trading post on an island of the Snake River. One day in the middle of winter, the post was attacked by a band of Snake Indians, and everyone except Dorio, his Nez Perce wife, and their two children were killed. They had hidden in an underground supply cellar away from the main building and had been overlooked.

When the warriors had taken all they wanted, they fled, leaving the bodies of the dead strewn hideously about the post. Before Dorio had joined his wife and children in the supply cellar, he had been badly wounded with a gunshot to the stomach. His wife did her best to stop the bleeding and bandage him. She then rounded up two stray horses and a small cache of food to take with them as they fled, fearing the Snake warriors might return at any moment. Because of Dorio's injury, they were forced to travel slowly. The next day he fell to the ground unconscious from the loss of blood and could go no further. That night he died in her arms. It took her until dawn of the next day to dig a grave in the hard, frozen ground with nothing more than a knife.

She left that day, headed west with one child in front, and one in back while leading the spare horse. She knew the direction she needed to take and that she must keep off the main trails that led to Fort Astoria on the Oregon Coast, where she hoped to find sanctuary. When they reached the Grande Ronde, she realized that the snows were far too deep to attempt to cross the mountains with her tired and hungry children. They were out of food, and the only place to take shelter was under the trees and bushes.

She led one of the horses off several hundred feet and tied it securely to a tree. When she returned it was with a large rock, that she used to club the horse with. The horse was staggered, so she cut its throat as quickly as possible, killing it. She then led the other horse close to where the first lie dead and did the same. She then skinned the horses, dried the meat, and made a tent over the bushes with the horses-skins, preparing to wait out the winter until spring. As if her cup of sorrow was not already full, her youngest child died later that winter.

Somehow, she and the surviving child managed to stay alive and elude the Snake Indians.

In the early spring, as the snow began to melt, she put her child on her back, and with nothing more than a blanket and small portion of moldy horsemeat, she left, managing to cross the snow-covered mountains on foot. Her family had gone to Fort Astoria each spring to trade and fish, so she continued, covering over 600 miles on foot until she reached the Fort. Because of her strength and determination, they both survived, her son, Baptiste Dorio, becoming a well-known fur trader and interpreter in the Oregon Territories."

Before Father left, he felt he needed to discuss Mr. Gray with Chief Tackensauris. He heard from a trapper who had recently returned from the East that Mr. Gray was also returning with a group of Americans to help at the missions. Father asked the chief to forgive Mr. Gray for what he had done, that hate was unchristian, and no good would come of killing him. The chief agreed, and told Father that what had been done would be forgiven, but not forgotten, that he could only speak for his village. Father thanked him, and the next morning had to wait until the chief was finished playing with me before he could leave. When Father returned to Lapwai later that day, he told Mother that peace had been restored with Chief Tackensauris and that their little olive branch was very hungry, fussy, and stinky.

My parents had been considering the possibility of moving the mission three miles upstream to the mouth of the Lapwai Creek on the south bank of the Clearwater River closer to chief Tamootsin's village. The new site had large shade trees to keep the house cooler in the summer, and they would be away from the mosquitoes, which had become almost intolerable.

It was difficult to leave a place where they had put so much time and energy, but they were looking at what would be best for the mission in the long run. They would continue to use the fields until the new ones were providing for their needs and then turn the old ones over to the Nez Perce.

They were continuing to have problems with chief Thunder Eyes, whose land the mission was on. They told him that he could have the buildings they had constructed if he would let them build on the new site. He agreed, and they immediately went to work on the new mission. Doctor Whitman came for a week to help cut and float logs from further upriver. The new house was going to be two stories, approximately 32 feet by 22 with fireplaces at each end. Downstairs there would be two bedrooms, a buttery, and a kitchen. Upstairs were three small bedrooms and a storeroom. The house would be without floors or ceiling until October and finished sometime in December.

It was a good summer, busy and productive. When Father told the Nez Perce that he was going to build a new schoolhouse, which would also serve as a house of worship, it inspired them to work even harder on the mission. At the same time, he started on a dormitory for students and visiting families, as well as a blacksmith shop. With help from the Nez Perce, he was able to collect enough logs for a flour mill, sawmill, and workshop that he planned to build that winter.

Crops from the summer and fall of 1837 had been insufficient, and in some cases, a complete failure. The harvest of 1838 was considerably better, providing the first surplus my parents had known. There were 75 Nez Perce families who had grown over 100 bushels of potatoes, a considerable crop of vegetables, grains, corn, and peas. Their efforts had produced an abundance of vegetables and grains, as well as four new hogs, three calves, and 30 hens.

At the beginning of summer, a Hawaiian couple named Mr. and Mrs. Joseph Maki came to Fort Walla Walla from the mission in Hawaii with a small herd of sheep. My parents were given five females and three males in the hopes of creating a new source of wool for clothes and food when the herd had grown large enough.

Initially, Mrs. Maki stayed with the Whitmans to help Narcissa around the house, and Mr. Maki came to help my parents with the building and farm work. He was a big, strong man who worked extremely hard to help us establish the new mission site.

In August, Doctor Whitman asked if we would come for a visit and if Father could help him with religious services. We left on August 8, and arrived at Waiilatpu on August 12, I had just turned eight months old. It was during this time that the idea for a church was discussed between Father and Doctor Whitman. By August 18, 1838 they had organized the first Protestant Church west of the Rocky Mountains.

Chapter 5

The New Missionaries

In September of 1838, Mr. Gray returned with his new wife and a small party of reinforcements to help with the missions and establish new ones. The other three couples with him were the Eellses, Walkers, and Smiths, as well as a single man named Cornelius Rogers. Everyone, especially Mr. Gray, was nervous that one of the Indians or tribes would take revenge on him. Fortunately, Father and Doctor Whitman had convinced the Nez Perce and Cayuse to forgive him, that his death would only bring them trouble.

The four new couples were like a tempest that had been building across the Oregon Trail. They had been quarreling the entire way and were not speaking to each other by the time they reached Waiilatpu. Over two years had passed since my parents and the Whitmans had first broken the land for their missions. They had had their differences before and during the journey over the Oregon Trail, but since Alice Clarissa and I had been born, there had been unity and cooperation without any instances of discord.

My parents and the Whitmans had experienced almost every kind of hardship and emotions together. There had been birth and death, sickness and health, hunger and cold, danger and fear, and the satisfaction that they had blazed the trail together, laying the foundation for their church.

The new reinforcements were coming into a world where the houses had already been built, church and schools had been established, the land had been plowed and harvested, storehouses were full, and most importantly, friendly relations had been established with the Indian people.

My parents and the Whitmans were the pioneers; everyone who followed after was an immigrant or settler.

Originally, Mr. Gray had been hired exclusively as a mechanic and carpenter. He was employed to do the work that neither Father nor Doctor Whitman had the time nor experience to do. He spent six weeks at Waiilatpu helping Doctor Whitman and four weeks at Lapwai with us, then decided he wanted his own mission. When he first returned East and informed the missionary board of his intention of starting his own mission, he was severely reprimanded. With quick thinking, he was able to turn the focus from his irresponsible actions to the need for more help at Lapwai and Waiilatpu. Since it was true that help was needed, they forgave his misconduct and turned toward the idea of having him recruit more missionaries. However, like Doctor Whitman, he was told that they were only interested in married couples.

On February 19, while visiting his home in Ithaca, New York, he met a young woman named Mary Augusta Dix, and they were married on February 25. He let the board know that he was enrolled in medical school and that since he was now married, he planned to lead a group of reinforcements back to the Oregon Territories.

He quit medical school after several weeks, but still attached "doctor" to his name.

Knowing how badly the Spaldings and Whitmans needed help with their missions, the missionary board appointed Doctor Gray and his new wife to lead three newlywed couples into the Oregon Territories. The three couples, not including the Grays, were then permitted to start their own missions once they had made plans with Father and Doctor Whitman for future sites. Two couples were married quickly on the same day, March 5, but in different places. Mr. and Mrs. Smith were married on March 15 and joined the party on March 18.

These are not Mother's words, but those of Mrs. Gray concerning the journey.

She said, "Mr. Smith was the most highly educated and had studied medicine as well as theology. He was also prejudiced beyond all reason with an arrogant and superior attitude, practically resistant to friendship. His wife appeared to be the perfect match. Small and prudish, she seemed a little dear after our first encounter. Once we were on our way, she proved to be a vicious gossip and agitator. She complained the entire trip, and whenever she was admonished, she would break into a pathetic medley of tears. The Walkers and Eellses were little better. Mr. Eells had constructed an abundance of self-esteem and pretentiousness, but void of the character and qualities necessary for a successful missionary in the New World among the Indian people. Mr. Walker was studious and kind as well as awkward, timid, and indecisive, making him unsuited to do the work that he had come to do. They were all strict Calvinists, intolerant and without sympathy for the Indian people."

Mr. Rogers was the last to join the group as a helper, not a missionary. He was younger and less bigoted but was said to have a prissy nature, not a particularly advantageous quality for the ruggedness of the West.

According to Mr. Smith, Mr. Gray was next to impossible. He wrote a letter back to Mr. Greene with the missionary board stating, "We have not found Mr. Gray such a man as we hoped to find. I presume you are already aware, and I should judge so from the letter he read from you at Independence, that he is not judicious in all his movements. He is rash and inconsiderate and not at all calculated properly to fill the station he now does. He has assumed a great deal of authority over us and talked to us in a very harsh and unbecoming way, and I may say an abusive manner, without regard for the feelings of others, even of the ladies. These things have been a severe trial for us."

It must have been quite a challenge for all concerned, especially poor Mr. Rogers. Mother was told the Rendezvous was a soul-shattering experience for the four newlywed couples. Mr. Smith was said to have set up a separate tent for his wife and himself away from everyone else. I am almost certain that the others were more than glad for a reprieve from his complaining and fault-finding.

One night a group of four intoxicated mountain men, staggering and swearing up a storm, barged in on the missionaries looking to take revenge on Mr. Gray for the death of their Flathead friends. When Mr. Eells opened the tent flap, they told him that they only meant to kill Gray, that no one else was to be harmed. Mr. Gray and his wife were hiding under covers in the back of the tent, badly frightened and hoping not to be discovered. The mountain men were extremely inebriated, and for no apparent reason, one of them began to sing. Soon they all joined in trying to encourage Mr. Eells to have a drink and sing along.

When they had mellowed, Mr. Eells told them that they had woken, disturbed, and frightened his wife and Mrs. Walker; that if they were good Christian men, they would leave them in peace. The men apologized and, arm in arm, staggered away, singing a profane and bawdy tune, forgetful of the vengeance they had come for in the first place. Word spread throughout the camp about Mr. Gray, and though several threats were made, no other action was taken against him at the Rendezvous.

One of the men had collected a scalp from a Blackfoot warrior and wore it tied to his rifle. One night the mountain men, along with some of the Flathead Indians, got good and drunk and started dancing Indian style, half-naked around a large bonfire. Dancing about wildly, the man fired his gun as he displayed the scalp as a sign of a past victory.

Mrs. Eells and Mrs. Walker happened by and later told Mother that it was like a satanic ritual, nearly terrifying them to death. They tried to convince Mr. Drips to leave early with the caravan, but he had grown weary of their fighting and complaining and told them that if they wanted to leave, to be his guest. They understood the slight, and dangers involved, and decided not to bother him again.

As they were leaving, the Nez Perce wife of a well-known trapper, Joe Meeks, decided to join them, saying, "Me and my drunken husband had a terrible argument, I am going home to my village and people."

They had been traveling for several days before Joe came out of his drunken stupor and realized that his wife was missing. Still intoxicated, he saddled up and took out to try and win her back. Along the way, he came across a distraught woman standing next to two horses and a man lying on the ground next to her. When he got close enough, he realized that it was Mrs. Smith standing over her prostrate husband.

She told Mr. Meeks, "My husband says he is dying of thirst, do you have any water that you could spare?"

He threw a canteen on the ground next to Mr. Smith before he remembered that it was full of whiskey. Lethargically, Mr. Smith took a huge gulp and immediately spit it out, choking so hard that he could hardly catch his breath. Mr. Meeks almost fell off his horse, thinking it to be the funniest thing he had ever seen and using the opportunity to berate Mr. Smith into getting up.

He told him, "I have seen little Indian girls who are more of a man than you are, and you are keeping your lovely wife out in the sun. I'll bet she is more of a man than you are."

Laughing hysterically, he then lifted the frightened Mrs. Smith into her saddle and led her away in tears.

As he did, he called to Smith, "You can lie there and die like a suckling mouse, or get on your horse. There are plenty of better men than you who would be glad to take care of your widow."

Later, when they had joined the rest of the group who had already made camp, Mr. Meeks made light of the situation, telling them that Mr. Smith was resting and would be along shortly. Oddly enough, no one seemed to care or offered to go back and look for him. That evening while everyone was gathered around the campfire, Mr. Smith came ambling into camp to Mrs. Smith's great relief and Mr. Meeks' dismay. It seems Mr. Meeks had had enough of his current wife and was already making designs on Mrs. Smith, in case her husband expired. When they reached Fort Hall, Mr. Meeks and his wife had another passionate argument, and he decided the marriage was off, riding back to join his trapper friends at the Rendezvous.

From what I was told, it had not only been a miserable trip emotionally; it was an unusually wet year and had rained on and off the entire time.

In one of Mrs. Walker's letters home, she wrote, "It was raining, and the water came pouring into the tent. To make matters worse, I was sick. I cried to think how comfortable father's hogs were compared to myself."

Mr. and Mrs. Gray had ridden ahead of the main party, arriving at Fort Walla Walla on August 21, 1838. He told the other three couples and Mr. Rogers that he needed to go on to Fort Walla Walla to acquire supplies. I believe he and his new wife were also in need of a reprieve from the bickering honeymooners. The main party arrived at the Whitman Mission August 29. The first order of business was to decide who was to go where after the initial work to be done at the Whitman mission was completed.

It was made abundantly clear by all of the new couples that they refused to be at the same mission with Mr. Gray, and Doctor Whitman made it known that he did not want him at Waiilatpu. The Eellses and Walkers were to be assigned to the Spokane Nation, the Smiths would stay with the Whitmans for the time being, then join us at Lapwai, Mr. Rogers was to go to Lapwai, and reluctantly Father agreed to have the Grays at Lapwai. Since it was initially Mr. Gray's idea to have a mission among the Spokanes, he was not happy with this decision.

Mr. Gray had brought along a letter from Mr. Greene of the missionary board stating that Father should spend more time on spiritual matters, and less on secular activities such as farming and animal husbandry. It infuriated Father that Mr. Gray had spoken poorly of him with the missionary board behind his back. He sent the letter to Doctor Whitman, who was also upset with the content as well as the backstabbing. Father wrote back right away to the board, explaining that with so little money and support, they could not survive without attending to their farming and animals. He also explained that the progress they had made with agriculture had helped to unite them with the Indian tribes, making them much more open to the teachings of the Bible; that Mr. Gray had become a troublemaker and done little since his return.

He went on to ask," Why have you sent three more preachers when what we need are men willing to work with their hands, farmers, carpenters, blacksmiths, mechanics, and mill workers? When we have eaten all of our reserves, do we then butcher our horses and dogs? Do we then walk the hundreds of miles it takes to spread the word of God on an empty stomach? Am I to continue to preach in open rain and snow? Should Mrs. Spalding continue to teach her lessons to the women and children, huddled together shivering in blankets, in the freezing cold? I do not think Mr. Gray begins to understand the situation here. We will accomplish much more by teaching those who are fed and sheltered, but it will take time, money, and manpower."

The reaction of the missionary board was to reduce the amount of money they sent in the way of expenses and salary, which was already far below subsistence.

Doctor Whitman had noticed that Mr. Gray had signed correspondence to the missionary board as "Doctor Gray." He questioned him thoroughly and found that he had only listened to lectures for several weeks and had no practical experience whatsoever. He demanded that Mr. Gray immediately remove the title doctor from all documents, and told him that impersonating a doctor in Indian country could get him and others associated with him killed.

By the first part of January 1839, Father had as many as two thousand or more Nez Perce attending his sermons and pledging to live their lives according to God's commandments. He sent a message asking for Doctor Whitman to spend a week helping him with prayer services and lessons. It was a busy time, and Mother could tell that the doctor was happy to be away from his demanding practice, bickering, and cramped quarters. When he left, the Smiths who had been with us for over two months, returned to Waiilatpu with him hoping that they would soon be assigned a mission of their own. They complained nonstop, and it was a great relief for my parents to have the Smiths gone, but my parents felt sorry for the Whitmans who would now be forced to share a house built for three with six other agitated individuals, constantly at each other's throats. It was not long before the Whitmans and Smiths grew to dislike each other intensely. Mr. Smith was trying to undermine the missions by sending back critical and derogatory messages to the missionary board behind the Doctor's and Father's backs.

Doctor Whitman had hired Chief Lawyer to teach the missionaries the Nez Perce language. The chief had been asking to have one of the missionary couples come to his village at Kamiah to live and teach among his people. Doctor Whitman was quick to recommend the Smiths to be rid of them, and the Smiths were anxious to be far away from the Whitman mission. In February, after they had visited Chief Lawyer's village, they stopped at our mission on the way back to the Whitman's home. They constantly complained about the conditions at Kamiah but said that it was preferable to living at Waiilatpu with the Whitmans.

On March 5, 1839, the Eellses and Walkers left to establish their new mission among the Spokane people. Although there was much more room in the Whitman's home, there were still hard feelings and frustration between the Smiths and Whitmans. By the end of April, the Smiths decided to go to Kamiah to work with the Nez Perce at Chief Lawyer's village. Doctor Whitman didn't feel that Mr. Smith's personality was suited to the work, but he was willing to go along to keep the peace and see them gone. Before the Smiths left, they had been constantly arguing, and even Narcissa was at her wits' end.

We will never be certain why, but for some reason, Mr. Smith decided to go after Father's standing and reputation with the missionary board. It was about the same issue Mr. Gray had brought before the board, that too much time was spent on secular rather than spiritual duties. Standing up for Father, Doctor Whitman tried to explain that a productive man, with food in his stomach, is much more likely to listen to what you have to say than one who is hungry and cold. Mr. Smith was no longer listening and had become a bitter critic of everyone except himself.

This is part of a letter he sent to the board criticizing Father: "I take issue with Mr. Spalding regarding his providing them with seeds, hoes, and cattle to get them settled so they can be taught. It is wrong to cater to the Indians' avarice for material goods. They would do or say anything to get hoes and cattle, and the more we do to encourage their selfish desires, the more difficult it will be to bring them the true gospel. My only hope is in giving them the pure unadulterated word of God and enabling them to understand it."

He went on to say this about the Nez Perce: "They are like the Pharisees of old, they often tell of their own goodness in the extreme. They have no fondness for the plain truths of the gospel."

Mr. Smith also made an issue out of Mother's method of teaching with drawings and paintings. He had this to say: "Natives filled up the pictures from their own imaginations and in this way have acquired a vast amount of error, which I find no easy matter to eradicate."

It was not his place to eradicate anything. He and his wife came into a ready-made mission with no effort on their part and had no idea what those first years were like. There was no set way to approach a situation or environment that had never been approached before. It was only through the grace of God that Mother came upon the drawings as a way to communicate. Had she not, it would have taken her far longer to accomplish what she had. My parents were happy to have people with a strong sense of imagination and were not looking to convert them into mindless mimics, walking around in a daze, mumbling words that had no meaning to them.

The real problem for Mr. Smith establishing a mission was that he never liked or respected the Nez Perce or any Indian people for that matter. He thought of them as sub-human savages to be manipulated. Father is human and has his faults, but right or wrong, he has never wavered in his devotion to the Nez Perce People. He had a deep respect for their ethics and morals and loved them as individual souls, not as people to be conquered or converted.

Right or wrong, he truly believed in what he was doing. He knew that if he labored hard every day of his life, for their benefit, whether it was writing sermons, or laboring in the fields until long after sundown, he could help to improve their lives. He felt a sense of urgency to help them become self-sufficient since the buffalo were disappearing, and the immigrants were depleting the fish and game at an alarming rate.

It never occurred to Father to criticize Mr. Smith even though he and his wife had done nothing but cause problems from the day they joined the missionary party on the Oregon Trail.

The Nez Perce could sense Mr. Smith's disdain for them and distrusted him. They could not understand what in the world he was trying to teach them with his heavy-handed and pontifical manner. In frustration, he turned his poison on Father and Doctor Whitman. Instead of using his intelligence and gift for languages for the good of the Indian people, he used it to undermine the people who had toiled for years developing relationships with the Indian people. What he never understood is that you must win a person's trust and friendship before you could ever hope to win their hearts and souls. Like a faithful dog, Mr. Smith's cynical and temperamental nature would follow him wherever he went throughout his entire lifetime.

On April 17, 1839, Mr. and Mrs. Hall, who had been doing missionary work in Hawaii, brought the first printing press to the

Northwest Territories. Since Father was the only experienced printer, it was decided to bring the press to Lapwai. With it, he would produce the first Nez Perce translations of the Bible, educational books, and a Nez Perce dictionary.

On May 24, Father finished 400 copies of an eight-page booklet designed to teach children and beginners the alphabet and instructions on how to pronounce words in English. It was an early attempt, but a beginning.

Chapter 6

The Wallowa Valley

Father and Doctor Whitman decided to formally bring Chief Tamootsin and Chief Tuekakas into the church, giving them a ceremonial baptism. Chief Tamootsin was given the name Timothy, and Chief Tuekakas given the name Joseph.

When Chief Joseph was getting ready to return home, he asked Father if he would like to visit his village. Father had never been before, but had heard stories of the Imnaha and Wallowa Valleys as being the most beautiful places in all of the Oregon Territories, and was happy to go along. After crossing the Snake River, they reached the Grand Ronde Canyon and were joined by a group of Indian men from Joseph's tribe. They traveled for three days through pine meadows and mountains, a land abundant with elk, deer, and bear.

When they arrived at the Wallowa Valley surrounded by the Wallowa Mountains, Father could only describe it as "paradise." It was the home of the Wellamotkin tribe, of which Joseph was head chief. Most of the men were leaving to do seasonal fishing, but Joseph told Father that he had a special place he wanted to show him, a place no white man had ever been before. It was not far, but the terrain was rugged, and they had to cross over a steep mountain pass.

When they cleared the last summit, Father felt as though he was looking down upon a great masterpiece that could only have been created by God. The air winding through the trees was thick and spicy with the heady scent of cedar. In the center of the mountain range was the most perfectly, crystal-clear lake he had ever seen, reflecting a transparent azure blue sky. The outside of the lake was a light blue turquoise that transposed into darker shades of blue as it deepened toward the center. The center was a violet blue, deep and mysterious. The entire lake was about four miles long and two miles wide. There was no wind, so the lake was like a sheet of glass reflecting every detail of the sky, billowing clouds that drifted by like thoughts in a daydream. He told Father that because his heart was pure and his intentions good, he had brought him to this sacred place as a brother.

As they descended to the lake, they watched dozens of white-headed eagles soaring through the sky, and others perched upon their nests in the trees. Chief Joseph showed him a burial ground where many of his ancestors had been brought to rest. He told Father that this was sacred ground only for burials and visits, never to be traveled or walked upon. He also told Father that this is where he planned to be buried with his medicine bundle. It would help him on his journey to the spirit world to meet with his ancestors, Jesus, and the Great Spirit in the Sky.

When they reached the water's edge, Chief Joseph dismounted and began undressing until he was naked, as uninhibited as a child. He looked to Father, who had dismounted and was also undressing. Father was reluctant to remove his underwear, but Joseph told him that God must surely love him with or without them. Father took the last of his clothes off and dove into the lake. The water was cold, but the sensation was exhilarating, freedom like nothing he had ever experienced before. It was as if he were a child once again, liberated like the eagles above with no sense of restriction or gravity. They swam for over an hour until their skin turned blue, it was another form of baptism, holy and purifying. After they dried off and dressed, Joseph built a fire and took out some smoked salmon and camas cakes that his wife had prepared for them. They spent the night in their blankets around the campfire talking and listening, watching the shooting stars race across the sky. It was a day and night that Father would never forget, the first time in his life that he had truly understood what brotherhood meant.

When they returned, there was a feast in Father's honor. The braves had caught over 600 salmon and were smoking many, and drying the others on racks made of long branches. For the next couple of days, the Nez Perce continued to show Father the mountains and valleys. He said it was the richest landscape he had ever seen, constantly changing like a living work of art with each stroke of nature's brush. It rained that night and when Father awoke the next day it was as if the entire world had been washed sparkling clean. The grass was as young and fresh as a newborn baby. Chief Joseph and several of his men showed Father a site where they had fought and defeated a band of Snake Indians who had come to steal their horses and women. They re-enacted it for him, falling from their horses and reveling in the more dramatic scenes.

On July 29, 1839, Father left the beautiful valley, taking with him an even stronger conviction to serve the Nez Perce and help preserve as much of their way of life as possible. These were the same mountains and valleys where the American army would one day hunt, persecute, and evict the Nez Perce People. Among them would emerge the greatest Nez Perce leader of all, Hinmatóowyalahtqɨt, also known as Young Chief Joseph.

When Father returned home, he was immediately thrust back into the reality of Mr. Smith's world of malice and contempt. Smith was growing more frustrated with the Nez Perce, and at one point, had written that they were "hopeless, and a waste of his time."

He was also angry because he felt that Father and Doctor Whitman had gone behind his back in baptizing Chief Timothy and Chief Joseph. This was another wild presumption on his part since it was never his decision to be a part of in the first place. He and his wife had both become quite ill, and when his cow ate a poisonous plant and died, he begged Father to give him another. Father explained that he only had one extra milk-producing cow at the moment and had given it away for labor done at the mission.

Smith's frustration and failures with his mission unleashed a bitterness in the form of continuous letters to the board, attacking both of my parents. He was an excellent writer and manipulator who used these skills to cloak his vindictive spirit with the dishonest guise of objectivity.

Father was also continuing to have problems with Mr. Gray, who wanted to start his own mission without the permission of the board, the Whitmans, or my parents. Father told him that it would have to come later, that he had been hired as a worker, not a missionary, that there was still a great deal of work to do at both missions. Mr. Gray and his wife left without permission to look at prospective sites, finding an area among the Yakima Indians where he wanted to establish a mission. When he returned, he started packing their things to leave, but Father reminded him that it had not been authorized, that there were no extra funds or supplies. This led to an angry argument in front of the Nez Perce People, creating confusion and a fissure in their respect for the missionaries. Mr. Gray left for Waiilatpu, and in a meeting with the other missionaries, he was told to return to Lapwai and resume the duties that had been assigned to him.

He returned frustrated and humiliated at the rebuke, using it as an opportunity to join with Mr. Smith in attacking Father and our mission.

That winter, he hardly lifted a finger, spending most of his time sulking or complaining, resulting in more open arguments. Mr. Rogers was staying at the mission at Kamiah with Mr. Smith, and together with Mr. Gray, they fired off one letter after another criticizing Father.

Father was unable to attend the next missionary meeting held at Waiilatpu where it was decided Mr. Smith would compose an objective letter describing the meeting and issues discussed. It was then to be looked over and edited by Doctor Whitman before being sent on.

Mr. Smith sent it off under the guise of having been officially authorized, without it having been read or edited by any of the other members, including Doctor Whitman. It was a 52-page report with 40 pages of vindictive character assaults on Father and my parents' missionary practices.

He said, "Mr. Spalding's actions had been a deliberate conspiracy against the wishes of the missionary board, that he was an enemy of the board and only interested in personal enrichment. Neither the Whitman nor Spalding missions had made even the least bit of progress with the Indians."

He went on to say: "It would be best to return Mr. Spalding to his native land and dismiss him from service without bringing him to trial or making public charges that might embarrass the board."

He finished by charging that, "Henry Spalding has gone insane and was no longer fit to serve."

These charges were an extraordinary defamation of Father's character, a total fabrication. They were based on the neurotic fears of a miserable and insecure man filled to the brim with jealousy, hatred, and self-righteousness. It had all been perpetrated behind Father's back.

My parents and the Whitmans had had their differences, and Father could be stubborn, but they had always resolved their problems, face-to-face, like responsible adults. It seems that no matter how much you help people like the Smiths, it is never enough to curb their insecurities and vexations.

When the report was read, the board was horrified and felt that something drastic needed to be done. They decided to recall our family as well as the Smiths and Grays. They instructed Doctor Whitman to close down both missions at Waiilatpu and Lapwai and join Mr. Walker and Eells since no complaints had been made against them. Because of Mr. Smith's letter, the board was ready to write both missions off as failures. The Walkers and Eellses somehow managed to find peaceful resolutions to their problems as they immersed themselves in the work of their new mission. They also managed to stay out of the conflict brewing at Lapwai and Waiilatpu.

Ironically, while Mr. Smith was making these accusations, Father and Mother were experiencing a massive spiritual awakening by the Nez Perce, with thousands attending Sunday services and hundreds attending classes each day. Thankfully, the mail was extremely slow, and they would not receive a return message from the board for well over a year.

In the meantime, another problem was raising its head to strike at the Protestant missionaries. Catholic priests had recently come into the territory. They were disregarding all rules of decency by remarrying and re-baptizing the Indian people, bribing and giving them gifts and money to convert. They were attempting to proselyte as many, as fast as possible, without any consideration for a proper understanding of the religion. They were also intruding into areas previously established by the Presbyterian missions, trying to turn the Indian people against the Spaldings and Whitmans.

The Catholics not only openly expressed hostility toward the Presbyterian missionaries, they proclaimed they worshiped a false God and depicted them as devils sent from hell to destroy the Indians' souls. This type of practice was not uncommon to the Catholic religion; it had been practiced for hundreds of years. At the time, Father was far too busy with work at the mission to do anything about it, hoping the Nez Perce and Cayuse would see through the deceptive tactics.

On June 24, we received heartbreaking news; the Whitman's two-year-old daughter Alice Clarissa had drowned. An Indian messenger had ridden all day and night, bringing a letter asking for our family and the Halls to come to Waiilatpu. Father had taken a bad fall from his horse the previous week and broken several ribs. There was nothing to do for broken ribs but wrap them tightly.

Since he was still unable to ride, we traveled by canoe down the Snake River, arriving at Fort Walla Walla several days later.

We reached Waiilatpu the next day to hear the sad details of the accident. They found two small cups near the river where she must have gone to fill them. As soon as she was found missing, several of the Indian men immediately dove into the stream and discovered her body lodged against branches by the waterside. She had only been missing for several minutes, but by the time she was found, it was too late to resuscitate her.

The funeral was the day after we arrived, and Mrs. Whitman used her wedding dress as a shroud. It was a sad and solemn time of sorrow for us all. Though Father and Doctor Whitman had not always seen eye-to-eye, Mother and Mrs. Whitman had gotten along well with a sincere affection for each other. The tragedy had softened everyone's feelings.

As the Whitmans laid little Alice Clarissa to rest on the hill to the north of their home, they also laid to rest their hopes and dreams of having children. The loss had taken something intrinsic out of Narcissa. She would always be kind and loving to me, but Mother said she was no longer the same outgoing and joyful person she had once been.

My parents decided to return to Lapwai on July 4, arriving on July 6. The Whitmans left the day after to join us at Lapwai. On July 8 we all left together for Kamiah to see how the Smiths were doing, and to settle on an alphabet to use for the Nez Perce books my Father was working on. Because of the drought and lack of physical labor to provide water, the Smith's garden was barren. They were living off of pudding and milk from the cow my parents had recently provided. Their health had rapidly deteriorated, especially poor Mrs. Smith, who needed help to move.

Mr. Smith had done nothing to help the Nez Perce and a dreadful job of providing for his wife. The floors were still of dirt with no windows and a very poor roof that constantly leaked water and mud. Mr. and Mrs. Smith were outwardly grateful for the bounty of food and supplies my parents had brought along, but there was an undertone that bothered Mother.

It seemed especially ironic how Mr. Smith had admonished my parents about their wasted time spent in the fields and building up our mission instead of spending their time instructing the Nez Perce in the gospels.

When Father offered to help him devise an irrigation system for his garden, he declined, saying that he had more important spiritual matters to attend to. Mother could see that Father was losing his patience and placed her hand on his shoulder before he spoke again. He calmly told the Smiths that the Bible was food for the soul, not the stomach. If they wanted to continue their work with the Nez Perce, they would need to find a way to feed themselves and become self-sufficient instead of dependent on others. Mr. Smith replied that the Lord would provide. Father and Mother looked at each other with the same thought in mind, how could an intelligent man be so ignorant and arrogant?

It seems ironic to me that many of the simplest people I have ever known have the most common sense, and some of the most learned, like Mr. Smith, are crackpots.

It had been a very hot, dry summer with temperatures soaring to 115 degrees. Father had devised a way to irrigate our crops and was still able to produce a substantial amount of food to feed our village, as well as provide for the Smiths, Eellses, and Walkers. It was the first irrigation system of its kind to have been designed and used in that part of the Oregon Territories.

Father had made another trip to visit Chief Joseph and treat several sick members of his tribe. When he returned on July 30, he found that Mr. Gray had not finished the adobe workshop as he had promised, also neglecting to harvest the barley crop. Father did it himself, and when he finished, he immediately began a 20-page book to be used for the Nez Perce schools with the new alphabet. On August 6, he printed 500 copies.

I had become very sick and was having trouble breathing, so on August 25, Doctor Whitman rushed to Lapwai to attend to me. By the time he arrived, I was feeling better, but the good doctor hardly left my side for the next two days. The annual missionary meeting was scheduled to take place at Lapwai the first part of September, so Doctor Whitman had decided to stay on and help around the mission until then. Mrs. Whitman was to join us on August 30.

Doctor Whitman had decided to ride out on the south side of the river and meet her. He asked if it would be all right to take me with him, that the fresh air would be good for us, and we wouldn't be long. My parents were glad to see the two of us ride off together with me sitting in front of the doctor on his old mule. I was two, almost the same age Alice Clarissa was when she drowned, and I can't imagine the emotions he must have been feeling as we rode off with me pulling on his whiskers.

It was to be one of many rides we would take together, me chatting away, and dear Doctor Whitman patiently listening to every word. Mother said that the sound of his laughter as we rode off together was like music. Somehow the Whitmans missed each other. Narcissa had taken the trail on the north side of the river instead of the south and had arrived hours before us. Mother was sitting on the porch, becoming concerned when she heard Doctor Whitman and me approaching just after sunset—me sound asleep in his lap.

Fortunately, the meeting was relatively uneventful except for Mr. Smith's charge that it was wrong for the women to pray aloud at the prayer meetings in front of the men. Narcissa was especially upset, and it was never implemented. After everyone had left, Father started work on the first of his translations of the Bible, as well as elementary English and math books.

Two new missionary couples, the Griffins and the Mungers, arrived at Waiilatpu, independent of any organization. They had set out in May of 1839 and arrived at Waiilatpu in September. The question now before Father and Doctor Whitman was what to do with independent missionaries who showed up unexpectedly without the support or endorsement of the church, without resources of any kind to start their own missions. Mr. and Mrs. Munger were to stay at Waiilatpu and help the Whitmans with their building projects, and the Griffins unexpectedly showed up on our doorstep on September 9, 1839. There was nothing else to do but take them in since there was nowhere else for them to go, and they were destitute.

The missionary board had a policy toward independent missionaries stating that we "Provide every Christian kindness and courtesy, but to be certain not to entangle the two missions, that they did not want to be held responsible for any actions or behavior taken by the visiting missionaries."

We had another unexpected visitor on October 4, 1839. Mr. A.M. Blair had left the Oregon Territory late that summer to return east, but his party decided not to risk the mountains so late in the year. Doctor Whitman told him that we could use his help at our mission and sent him to us. He borrowed a horse from the doctor and arrived in dreadful condition, without any supplies, and nearly starved. He was quite elderly, and Father doubted that we could get much use from his labor, but Mother said she had a good feeling about him.

It turned out that he was a highly skilled carpenter and cabinet-maker. Father had all but given up the idea of building another mill since Mr. Walker, Mr. Gray, and Mr. Rogers had failed to find any suitable stones. Mr. Blair was able to locate what Father needed, and with the help of Chief Timothy and several Indian men, we were able to get the mill operating. Mother said that if there was a kinder hearted soul than Mr. Blair, she had never met him. He would do anything asked of him without question or complaint. He was a truly honorable man with a peaceful benevolence that brought a sense of comfort and contentment to the mission.

I seemed to be especially drawn to his gentleness and would follow him wherever he went until he would pick me up and tickle me. He stayed with us for over two years and then moved on to California, where my parents heard that he had passed away. He was a simple, good, and humble man whose kindness and generosity of spirit would remain permanently lodged in our hearts.

On October 6, a Mr. Conner joined us with his Nez Perce wife and their baby. They were both hard workers, and with the additional help, we were once again making good progress on the mission buildings. Mr. and Mrs. Gray returned on October 18, informing Father that they had found a suitable location for their new mission and were making preparations to move. Father reminded him that he had been given permission to explore the area for a site and that no authorization had been given for him to establish a new mission. Father also reminded him that he had never completed the farming or building that he was contracted to do.

This resulted in another heated argument between Father and Mr. Gray, so on October 21, Mr. Gray decided to leave the mission to look for employment for himself and his wife, who had been a teacher with the Hudson Bay Trading Company. His previous conduct, which brought about the death of the Flathead, Nez Perce, and Iroquois Indians attached to his party, was spread far and wide, resulting in no offers of employment. He returned to Lapwai frustrated and disappointed at his failure to find work.

On November 11, Mrs. Gray and their seven-month-old baby left for Fort Walla Walla with two Nez Perce to look for work. Father thought it a bad idea for Mr. Gray to let her go, but Mr. Gray was planning to stay and plead his case at the next missionary meeting to be held at Lapwai.

On November 14, Doctor Whitman arrived. He and Father discussed the situation concerning Mr. Gray and were agreed that he was negligent in fulfilling his obligations. They refused his request, telling him that before they would consider it, he would need to complete his commitments. The Eellses, Walkers, and Smiths were unable to attend, so it was left to Father and Doctor Whitman to decide Mr. Gray's fate. He was furious, but there was no other course for him to take, so he returned with Doctor Whitman to Waiilatpu to complete one of the buildings. Because of their previous experience with Mr. Gray, the Walkers an Eellses would later confirm that they, too, were against his starting a new mission.

Chapter 7

Little Henry

On November 24, 1839, our family was blessed with a baby boy. Mother insisted we name him Henry, after Father. I was just a little over two years old and immediately assumed the position of little mother to my new plaything. There are so many precious memories of countless hours we spent together growing up among the Nez Perce, a childhood like no one else I would ever meet in my lifetime.

It would be hard to imagine a child receiving more love and attention than I did. Every worker or person who visited wanted to hold me or take me with them. I had found a new best friend named Timps-te-te-lew, who was about my age.

When Alice Clarissa drowned, there was a terrible sadness not only with us but also among the Nez Perce. Chief Timothy had spent a good deal of time with the Whitmans and had grown to love little Alice. Since we also lived right next to the river, the chief wanted to make sure this would never happen to me, so he assigned old Mustups as my guardian. Nearly blind, old Mustups, who was once a proud warrior, found himself with little to do, feeling as though he had become a burden to the tribe. He was told that caring for me was a very important responsibility and would bring great honor and peace of mind to everyone at the mission.

Mother told me that the change in Mustups was immediate; his life force seemed reborn overnight as he assumed his responsibility with great care. Mother said that having someone around at all times was a bit disconcerting at first. However, with a new baby, her life was so busy that it soon became a great relief knowing that I was safe and being watched over. He would rock my cradle and bring me to Mother when I cried, fix my small hurts, and never rest when I was sick.

When little Henry was born, Chief Timothy told Mustups that he wished for him to do the same for the new boy child, and gave him a beautiful new blanket and buffalo robe as a gift for a job well done. Mother was amazed at how he responded to having a sense of purpose; it was as if Mustups was growing younger by the day instead of older.

Unfortunately, our peace and harmony were short-lived. Mr. Gray returned to Lapwai several weeks later and immediately started making trouble. Rather than helping with the innumerable projects of the mission, he either stayed in his room sulking or idly walked around the mission criticizing the work being done. He and Mr. Smith sent off another letter of condemnation to the missionary board. It stated that Mr. Rogers was attending a class taught by Chief Timothy in which he told his people to start building houses, farming the land, and raising cattle. These were things he had been taught by Mr. Spalding in which they felt undermined the missionary board. They also claimed that Mr. Spalding had been too lenient and liberal in helping the new missionaries and workers who had arrived.

When Doctor Whitman told Father about the charges they had made to the board, Father responded by saying he was absolutely guilty, but to any sane mind, he would be found innocent of any wrongdoing. He explained that he was not conspiring against the mission, but was told by the mission that the goal was to improve the lives of the Indian people so that they would be open to the teachings of the Bible. He also asked if it were wrong to give food and shelter to our Christian brothers and sisters who had unexpectedly arrived? He said he was well aware of the missionary board's policy. That he had in no way involved or mixed his mission with the objectives the Griffins and Mungers may have brought to the Oregon Territory.

On April 2, 1840, my parents were presented with a shocking development. Mr. Gray came to Father and demanded, "You are neglecting your spiritual duties, I am going to take over all secular duties and take possession of the property. I forbid you to cultivate any part of the property."

Father reminded Mr. Gray that he had not done a bit of work in months, and asked on what authority he based this decision? Mr. Gray told him that he, Mr. Smith, and Mr. Rogers had reached this decision. Since none of the three had any authority whatsoever, my parents were dumbfounded at their arrogance and presumptuousness.

With strong reservations, Father and Mother decided that it might be good for Mr. Gray to have some responsibility, giving Father more time to devote to his religious duties. It would still be some time before the board's decision would reach them. In the meantime, Father received an earlier letter from the board praising the work he had done.

Several missionaries returning to the East, including Jason Lee, had told the board that the Spalding mission was by far the most productive, not only materially, but also spiritually. The board told him to keep up the good work and let them know of his needs. Father finally lost his patience with Mr. Gray and presented the letter of praise from the missionary board to him, informing him that his trial was over. He let Mr. Gray know that he had failed miserably and to get out of his way so they could do their spring planting.

The Griffins turned out to be great helpers and good friends. They were the first couple my parents had living with us with a stable and healthy attitude toward hard work and life in general. An enduring friendship developed between the four of them. Later that spring, the Griffins left to try and start their own mission at Fort Boise on the Snake River. My parents were sad to see them go but knew how much it meant to them, doing all they could, and wishing them well. Through messengers, Father learned that things were not going well for them. Without the support of the church or committed individuals, it was almost impossible to acquire the resources necessary to establish, build, and maintain a mission. They returned that summer and eventually moved to Fort Vancouver, where Mr. Griffin became the post chaplain and tutor for the school children. They then moved to the Willamette Valley, where they were able to establish their own church successfully. Our families remained loyal friends and communicated through messengers whenever possible.

Mother had received a letter from a dear friend of hers, Mrs. Lydia Sigourney. Mrs. Sigourney had been one of her teachers when she attended the female seminary in Clinton, New York. She wanted to know how Mother was doing, what life was like in the Northwest, and had sent along a collection of new poems. Mother considered her one of the best poets of their generation; she had opened her mind to so many new ideas. There are many different kinds of teachers and styles of teaching, but most of Mother's teachers had been very strict to the point of being cruel. She said they often used fear as a method of motivating their students to work harder, that it does work, but leaves scars in places that don't show.

Mrs. Sigourney's way of doing things was to teach with love, love for her students, love for the written word, and love for life in general. She was one of those rare human beings who knew how to open doors for her students that they didn't know existed. Each week they were assigned to write a poem of any length and read it to the class.

Creative writing did not come easily for Mother, and the first week she was embarrassed that she had been unable to come up with a concept or write a single line. Everything she tried to write sounded shallow and trivial to her. She was the only one in class who had nothing to show. Mrs. Sigourney made nothing of it and kindly continued to another student. However, when class was over, she casually asked Mother to see her after school.

Mother was terrified. It was the first time in her life that she had failed to turn in an assignment, and she feared that her teacher would be upset and disappointed with her. When Mrs. Sigourney entered the empty classroom, she walked over to Mother, took her by the hand, and led her to a table where they sat down. Mother started to blurt out some kind of excuse but was stopped right away and asked what she loved to do for herself. She thought about how much she loved to ride, take turns around the fireplace with her family reading books to each other, and a hundred other things. By the look on Mrs. Sigourney's face, Mother realized that this was not what she was asking for, and began to tell her how much she loved to draw and paint.

Mrs. Sigourney asked if Mother would make a drawing while she read aloud. It took a while to get started, but slowly she began to lose track of time until she realized that she had completed a drawing of her family sitting around the fireplace together. She had no idea how long it had taken, but Mrs. Sigourney never stopped reading until she was done. Mrs. Sigourney told her that art was just a different kind of poetry and that Mother was a poet with the pen and brush.

She went on to say that she had seen thousands of drawings and paintings that she was unable to feel, but this drawing invited her in, to feel a part of the family.

She then asked Mother to write a poem the next week based on the drawing she had done. With that in mind, it made perfect sense, and the task became effortless. Mrs. Sigourney asked Mother if she would bring some of her artwork, that she would like to see how the class would interpret her work as a writing assignment.

Like Mother, Mrs. Sigourney was a very spiritual person whose faith was her guiding light. She was also an advocate for women creating their own social organizations so that they would have more influence over their voices and identities. She was an outspoken advocate for the abolition of slavery and resolving the injustices done to the Indian people. Mother felt that Mrs. Sigourney helped her define what she wanted to do with her life, to teach, and to give to those in need. It had also given Mother the strength to make her voice heard among even the most powerful men, including her father and husband. Along with Mother's parents, Mrs. Sigourney's guidance and friendship became the foundation of her life's work, and Mrs. Sigourney's poetry had become an inspiration that she would continually draw upon.

***

Sadly, the gentle soul of Joseph Maki passed during August 1840 and he was buried at Waiilatpu. His lonely wife returned to the Hawaiian Islands with little more than a broken heart.

Mr. Maki was such a big strong man that it seemed almost impossible that he could die so young. They had brought with them such happiness and joy of living. His hard work had been a great addition to both missions, and it was difficult to imagine them no longer a part of our lives.

Fall 1840 marked the beginning of the end of the large fur companies, and that same year was the last of the great Rendezvous. It would take several decades for the fur trade to come to a complete end, but for the most part, the colorful life of the mountain man was like a forgotten language. It was a life that had been overly romanticized, leading many young men toward a harsh and deadly lifestyle that they were neither suited nor prepared. For every successful trapper, there were at least two others who either froze to death, died of hunger, infection, or were killed by Indians or wild animals. I think it was something that young men felt they needed to do to prove themselves, like going into the military. The idea of being free to do as you please in a beautiful and pristine land, where the mountains and valleys promised a vast bounty of adventure, was intoxicating.

From my experience, it took a certain kind of man to survive. They were hardy men with an abundance of endurance and strength, a high threshold for pain, hardship, and privation. There were those looking for a solitary existence, who wanted to be left alone, and those who loved the company of other mountain men. It was not unusual for a group to share a winter camp where they could relax together or with their wives and children. They would play games, wrestle, have various kinds of contests, clean and skin animals, and hunt whatever game exposed itself during that time of year.

When the early trappers came during the late 1700s, they were mostly French-Canadians, and some from America, England, and Scotland. There was plenty for everyone; for the most part, they got along well with the Indian people by trading together. The trappers rarely settled in one place, so the natives didn't see them as invaders bent on taking their land. The beaver hat was the rage in England, so it was the primary animal they would hunt. They would also trap muskrat, fox, ermine, otter, rabbit, raccoon, deer, wolf, and bear. As the beaver population started to dwindle, they shifted to hunting buffalo. This was when problems started to arise between the trappers and the Indian people who considered the buffalo sacred.

As the trading companies began to establish themselves throughout the Oregon Territory, the Indian people also got involved in the fur trade. They would take their furs and hides to the stations where they would trade for guns, whiskey, iron goods, and trade beads. Beaver pelts were worth about $3 each, and a beaver pack of 60 was worth approximately $183. The value of a doeskin was 50 cents, and one buckskin was worth $1. That is where the nickname for a dollar came from, a buck. A common riding horse would be worth approximately eight buffalo robes, or one gun and one hundred loads of ammunition, as much as three pounds of tobacco, or 15 eagle feathers. A good racing horse would trade for about ten guns—four buffalo robes for a Hudson Bay Blanket, and 30 beaver pelts for a keg of rum. One buffalo robe might trade for three knives, or a large kettle, or half-yard of calico fabric.

The Indian people loved to ornament their clothes with beads and placed a high value on them. They would trade a beaver pelt for six Hudson Bay beads, or three light blue padre beads, or two large transparent blue beads. In England, the Hudson Bay Company had been stockpiling beaver pelts for years, eventually auctioning off over five hundred thousand when the market started to dwindle. As the larger companies first began to grow, it wasn't long before almost half of the trappers were working for trading companies, and the other half working independently. Spring and fall were beaver season. By fall 1840, the beaver was almost hunted out of existence, and many trappers headed back to the states. Some moved on to even more remote or extreme regions. Others banded together and began stealing horses and supplies from the trading posts, Indians, and even each other. A few went into politics or government.

The last Rendezvous was held in 1840 at Green River, the same location that it had been held when my parents passed through four years earlier. It was a sad affair with few trappers, traders, and Indians since the fur trade was winding down. By the middle of the 1840s, the focus had shifted to buffalo hides for robes and rugs. The American Fur Company alone was shipping as many as one hundred thousand hides per year back East. It would only get worse until the buffalo were almost exterminated.

In April 1841, Andrew Dripps and Jim Bridger were leading a caravan from the United States to the Northwest for a second time. Joe Meek had also joined them along the way with his two-year-old daughter Helen. When they reached Waiilatpu he asked if he could leave her with the Whitmans since he was unable to care for her on his own. After the loss of little Alice Clarissa, they were happy to have a little girl in their home.

Another priest, Father Pierre De Smit, had joined the Dripps party, continuing to add to the problems of the Protestant missions. Three more independent missionary couples, the Clarks, Smiths, and Littlejohns, had also made the journey. Mr. Clark and his wife would spend the winter at Kamiah with the Asa Smiths, the Littlejohns would stay with the Whitmans over the winter, and the Smiths were to join us at Lapwai. Mr. Smith and his wife Abigail were a welcome addition. They were from Connecticut, and though they planned to have a mission of their own, they ended up staying with us for almost a year before moving on to Tualatin Plains. He was a skilled carpenter, and along with helping Father build two sawmills, a gristmill, and other buildings, he and Father would build the first loom and spinning wheel in the Oregon Territory.

It was a disappointment, yet a relief when Asahel Smith and his wife Sarah decided to give up and abandoned their mission at Kamiah. Mr. Cornelius Rogers, who had been living with them for some time, also decided to leave. My parents had gotten along quite well with Mr. Rogers until he moved to Kamiah with the Smiths. He must have taken a dose of Asa Smith's poison, becoming critical and antagonistic toward Mother and Father, who had helped him so much in the past. It had become obvious to the Nez Perce that the

Smiths disliked them and felt vastly superior, leading to a dangerous lack of trust and respect.

In one letter to the board, Mr. Smith had written about the Nez Perce, "They are evil and sinful and possessed stupid degenerated minds."

Unfortunately for the Smiths, their mission with the Nez Perce at Kamiah was a complete disaster. In just over a year, they gave up, blaming ill health and leaving behind nothing but bad relations. They departed on April 19, 1841, stopping briefly at Lapwai.

Asa Smith and his wife probably expected a tearful goodbye, instead, Father looked him in the eyes and told him, "I have read and heard reports of all the terrible things you have written to the board about myself, my wife, and Doctor Whitman. You, sir, are a troublemaker and backbiter who has done everything in your power to turn us all against each other intentionally. Your ignorance and arrogance have undone much of the backbreaking and treacherous work we have spent years accomplishing. Because of your high-handed attitude and treatment of the Nez Perce, you are leaving the territory a much more dangerous place than when you came.

We will pray for you in the hope that you will learn from your mistakes and not take your sinful ways with you wherever you decide to go next. In the future, I would recommend that you act like a real man and resolve your differences face to face before going behind a person's back like a lowly coward. Your time here has been a complete failure, and you have done far more damage than good, good riddance."

It was not exactly what Mr. and Mrs. Smith had expected to hear. Unfortunately, his troubles would follow him throughout the rest of his career and lifetime.

Another problem arose when two mountain men named William Craig and John Larison moved to the Lapwai area. Craig was a rough, hard, plainspoken man who disliked all missionaries, considering them narrow-minded intruders who took advantage of the Indian people. He was trying to incite his new father-in-law, Thunder Eyes, against my parents and our mission. Father had paid Thunder Eyes for the land, but Craig was telling him he should demand more money or goods. Thunder Eyes had become more and more antagonistic over time since Father had unintentionally usurped his standing within the tribe as medicine man.

Craig told the chief that Father treated the Nez Perce like "dogs and hogs," using them as slaves. He told him that they should send us away, that he should take possession of our mills and property. When my parents heard from one of our loyal Nez Perce friends what Mr. Craig was trying to do, they were discouraged and unsettled.

Father went to Thunder Eyes camp to ask Mr. Craig for some kind of explanation, but Craig refused to talk with him. The next day Craig sent several Indians to destroy our milldam. Father rebuilt it, but the seeds of turmoil had been sown. Mr. Craig usurped much of the goodwill my parents had worked so hard to establish. He and Thunder Eyes were now telling the people not to cut or stock lumber for our mill unless we paid them more, though my parents were already paying as much as they could afford.

Thankfully our good and loyal friends Chief Timothy and Chief Joseph continued to help us. They each told their people that Mr. Craig had come to make trouble for the Spaldings and was trying to steal our land and possessions for himself. In March, not long after that incident and to our great relief, Craig and Larison departed for the Willamette Valley. Slowly Father's relationship with Thunder Eyes and his people began to improve, and my parents felt a renewed sense of peace that they had not known since Mr. Craig had first come.

In May, we learned of two sad events. Mr. Pambrun and Mr. Cornelius Rogers were on a riding trip when Mr. Pambrun was dozing and fell from his horse. He was badly injured and died several days later from internal injuries. Mr. Rogers then decided to go on to Fort Astoria to look for work. There he met and fell desperately in love with the daughter of a well-known magistrate named Reverend David Leslie. Mr. Leslie's wife had recently passed away, and he didn't feel properly prepared or equipped to raise five daughters on his own in the Oregon Territory. He decided to sail for the Hawaiian Islands, where there was a well-established Methodist mission and school for girls and young women. Mr. Rogers met one of Reverend Leslie's daughters named Satira as the Leslie's were awaiting favorable winds. She secretly slipped off the ship and eloped with Mr. Rogers without her father's permission. It was a great shock to Reverend Leslie, and after an impassioned meeting with the young couple, he decided to give his consent to the marriage, finding Mr. Rogers, "an outstanding young man."

With favorable winds, Leslie and his remaining four daughters left for the Hawaiian Islands. Cornelius and Satira decided to take a honeymoon trip by canoe down the Columbia River to the Willamette River in search of possible sites where they could settle and start their own mission. Tragically their canoe was swept over the falls along with two Clatsop Indians at Oregon City, and all were drowned. It was almost a year later before Reverend Leslie and his daughters received the sad news. Reverend Leslie would remarry and have two more daughters. Sadly, he would outlive all but one of them.

At the annual missionary meeting held in June 1840 at Waiilatpu, a bitter argument erupted between Father and the Whitmans over a statement he had made questioning Narcissa's ability to effectively handle the responsibility of a life dedicated to the Indians' welfare. Father was well aware of her dislike for Indians in general, and it was well documented that she was high handed and rude with them. She would not allow them in her house or to play with the white children, often referring to them as filthy savages. He felt this attitude was obvious to the Indians, making it more difficult and dangerous for all of the missions.

During the quarrel, Father learned of all the charges and letters that had been sent to the missionary board. He was shocked and told them they should have come to him directly instead of going behind his back if they had a problem with him or the way that he was running his mission. He was also heartsick to find that Asa Smith had sent a letter to the board insinuating that he was insane and calling for his removal back to the states. Ironically Narcissa would later confide with Mary Walker, "I am entirely unfit for the work. Henry has correctly assessed my character flaws." In her own words, she told Mary that she "regarded herself as the most unfit and unworthy of all the missionaries."

Her pride rarely ever allowed her to be wrong, and even when she was, there was rarely, if ever, an apology. It would eventually be Father who apologized in order to keep the peace.

When Father returned to Lapwai, he was disillusioned and confused by his colleague's behavior and betrayal, causing him to question his own conduct and the value of the work they had done to that point.

Shortly after returning to Lapwai, five members of the United States Navy commanded by Charles Wilkes joined us. They were three years into a four year-long expedition of the Pacific Northwest looking for new trade routes and had been sent to examine the forts and missions of the Oregon Territories. They asked to be shown around the mission and to meet with the Nez Perce that Father had been working with. When they had finished and were preparing to leave, Father briefly explained that there was a possibility he would be recalled, and the mission shut down because of allegations regarding his lack of attention to the religious aspects of his mission. He explained that one of the other missionaries had charged that he had spent far too much time and energy in cultivating the land and building up the mission instead of tending to the Nez Perce spiritual needs. Commander Wilkes told my parents that those charges were absolute nonsense, that our mission had accomplished more than all of the others in the entire Northwest Territory combined.

He was especially impressed with Chief Timothy's and Chief Joseph's remarkable knowledge of the Bible. He went on to tell my parents that they should not be discouraged and that he would not only write to the missionary board on their behalf but to the heads of our government as well. It was what Father and Mother needed to hear at that moment in time, encouraging them to work even harder for the good of the Nez Perce and our country. This is an excerpt from the letter Commander Wilkes sent to the board, Navy, and government officials:

"His, Spalding's, efforts in agriculture are not less exemplary, for he has 20 acres of fine wheat, and a large field in which were potatoes, corn, melons, pumpkins, peas, beans, etc. the whole of which were in fine order. The great endeavor of Mr. Spalding is to induce the Indians to give up their roving mode of life and to settle down and cultivate the soil; and in this, he is succeeding admirably. He shows admirable tact and skill, together with untiring industry and perseverance in the prosecution of his labors as a missionary, and he appears to be determined to leave nothing undone that one person alone can perform."

There seemed to be no end to the challenges my parents had to face. On October 7, 1841, Mr. Craig and Mr. Larison returned.

Chief Tiloukaikt was the leader of a Cayuse tribe within one day's ride of the Whitman mission. Mr. Gray was still living at Waiilatpu when he and the Chief got into a heated argument over the horse-trading incident. The Chief ordered Mr. Gray to leave his territory, or he would kill him. Doctor Whitman tried to intercede, also telling the chief that he should not be practicing the papist's ceremonies. The chief then struck the doctor in the face. As the quarrel became more heated, Chief Tiloukaikt grabbed Doctor Whitman by the ears and pulled on them, then threw his hat in the mud. When Mr. McKinley at Fort Walla Walla heard about what had taken place, he scolded the Cayuse, telling them that their behavior was worse than dogs. This just made the chief even more angry.

On October 2, a small party broke down the Whitman's door with an axe, tore the doctor's clothes off, and assaulted him, putting a gun to his head. Showing no fear and standing his ground, the war party finally left. However, the next day they returned waving their guns and tomahawks in a threatening manner and breaking out several of the mission windows.

Ironically it was Mr. Craig and Mr. Larison who intervened and managed to calm the Cayuse down. The same party who had done the damage at the Whitman mission decided to go to Fort Walla Walla and punish Mr. McKinley for what he had said to them by setting fire to a section of the fort. Mr. McKinley extinguished the fire and managed to make peace by giving them several pounds of tobacco.

When Craig and Larison arrived back at Lapwai, they told my parents what had happened. Father immediately set off for Waiilatpu with a group of Nez Perce in case his help was needed. By the time he arrived, peace had been restored.

When Father returned to Lapwai he went to see Mr. Craig to thank him for helping the Whitmans. They would never see eye to eye, but Mr. Craig told Father that he would try to help him restore the peace with his father-in-law Chief Thunder Eyes. In their discussion, Father offered to cut and mill the logs necessary for Mr. Craig to build a house. Several weeks later, Mr. Craig came to work for him at the mission. That fall, the Nez Perce produced the best crops they had ever grown, and school and Sabbath attendance were at an all-time high. Our own crops and cattle were flourishing, and most of the mission buildings were near completion.

In late Fall 1841, my parents received sad news concerning Asahel Munger. He had been struggling for some time with a deeply seated mental illness that he was unwilling to talk about. He and his wife Eliza had spent the better part of two years with the Whitmans. They were hard workers who kept mostly to themselves and had become disillusioned by the hardships of life in the west. On June 25, 1840, they had a daughter, who they named Mary Jane, and appeared overjoyed with the new addition to their family.

Sometime in early spring 1841, Mr. Munger started acting strangely, complaining about visions and voices. With the help of Doctor Whitman, they decided to return to Oberlin, Ohio, in the hope that he could recover his health with proper care. They were to join the American Fur Company caravan at the Rendezvous. Unfortunately, the Rendezvous was almost non-existent, and the American Fur Company decided not to send a caravan back East that year. The Mungers were forced to return to Waiilatpu, and it soon became apparent that Mr. Munger was becoming mentally unstable. The Mungers then decided to move to Salem, Oregon, to see if he could find suitable work.

As well as being a fine carpenter, Mr. Munger was an able blacksmith. He found a job working in a blacksmith shop, but continued to get worse, constantly erupting out loud with Biblical quotations and scripture.

On December 1, 1841, we were told that he was having some kind of fanatical religious experience. Believing he was able to perform miracles, he put a nail through his hand and threw himself onto his forge, severely burning himself. His coworkers were able to pull him out of the fire, but he died a most excruciating death over the following two days. Delusional, he had consumed himself in glorious misery, the mountains and valleys of emotions had become an unbearable crown of thorns. It was a shock to those who knew him. Although suicide is an unforgivable sin, everyone prayed that God would forgive and understand that he was not himself when he took his life, that he was possessed by something far beyond his control.

On June 2, 1842, all were in attendance for another missionary meeting at Waiilatpu. The letters sent by Smith, Gray, and Whitman to the missionary board criticizing Father had come up once again, causing Father and Doctor Whitman to become engaged in another heated argument.

Doctor Whitman was still upset about the comment Father had made concerning Narcissa being unsuited to do missionary work. The Eellses and Walkers were surprised and shocked by the hostility. Mr. Walker told everyone that if they were to save the mission effort at Lapwai and Waiilatpu, they would need to restore the peace and find a way to get along together.

He told Doctor Whitman, "Even though most of the criticism has been pointed at Henry, you are equally to blame by showing unreasonable pettiness and resentment toward Mr. Spalding. Your disregard for the consequences by threatening to leave the mission without a doctor could be ruinous to all of the missions. Henry is right that Mrs. Whitman has low regard for the Indian people; we have all witnessed it."

The lecture from Mr. Walker must have sobered Doctor Whitman and Father since they decided to spend the next day together privately trying to work out their differences. By the end of the day, they had managed to find common ground and peaceful resolution to the situation and toward each other. This helped bring about a new sense of hope between the missionaries for an enduring commitment to their work and each other.

Anticipating that the board may have already taken drastic action, it was decided that Mr. Walker should write a letter to the missionary board to that effect, and they would disregard any letters received from the board until his letter was delivered and replied to.

Chapter 8

The Sham Battle

The wind of heaven is that which blows between a horse's ears.
—Arabian Proverb

One of my earliest memories is from when I was five years old. I remember that Mother and Father had visitors to the mission, including the new Indian agent named Doctor White and several of his intimidating looking friends all dressed in black suits and hats. They had heard stories about the legendary horsemanship skills of the Nez Perce and asked if Father could arrange a demonstration. The Nez Perce told them that they would do more than that; they would reenact one of their most famous battle scenes, but it would take a day to prepare.

I can still recall a long line of beautifully painted ponies dressed with beads and feathers parading by us the following day. The younger Nez Perce warriors wore loincloths with war paint on their faces and bodies, holding their guns and tomahawks high in the air shouting and making coyote and wolf calls. Many of the men were covered in red paint with pennants of the same color streaming from the horses since this is said to be the color of courage during battle. Most of the older chiefs were dressed in their finest buckskin robes with large feather headdresses.

All of a sudden, they charged past us like lightning bolts. There was a thunderous sound of horses' hoof beats as they flew past at dazzling speeds. The air was filled with an exhilarating intensity as the warriors put on their fiercest expressions, performing tricks that defied the imagination. After they had all ridden by and finished doing their most dangerous stunts, they automatically broke into a fast gallop with a larger group circling a smaller group. The smaller group in the center began preparing to do battle.

With a signal, they started yelling and whistling as loudly as they possibly could with bone whistles. In the center of the circle, they had placed a large pile of brush and wood to take cover and return fire upon the warriors that were madly circling them. When they started shooting at each other, I became so frightened that I hid behind Mother's dress but could not take my eyes off the scene that was taking place before me. Mother tried to reassure me that it was just pretend, that there were no bullets in the guns, but it looked and felt real enough to give me the shivers.

It's so odd what you remember at different times in your life. I can still remember looking down at my small hands and fingers that had turned white from squeezing them so hard. As one gunshot after another erupted, I had to place my hands over my ears to keep the sound from penetrating. After each series of shots, several of the Indians from the center would drop to the ground, and ones from the party circling would fall from their horses into the dirt as if they had been shot. Someone had turned the brush pile into a burning inferno, which seemed to send the warriors and their horses into a kind of madness. I finally became so frightened that I pulled my apron over my head so I wouldn't have to watch my friends being hurt and killed.

Again, Mother reassured me that this was not real; that the Indians were just pretending, and I should not be afraid. It calmed me for a few minutes until the warriors all started jumping off their horses with their knives and tomahawks drawn. They then went into hand-to-hand combat with each other. One of the Indians grabbed the head of a fallen warrior and took his scalp off, screaming AIEEEE as loud as he could. I screamed and bolted for the house as fast as my little legs could carry me. Father came up behind me and lifted me into his arms and told me it was a fake scalp; that no one was hurt, but he would take me home if I wanted. I asked him why they wanted to kill each other?

He told me that it was all make-believe, a show for Doctor White and his friends. He held me in his arms for a long time, and before he could take me to the house, the sham battle started breaking up as the warriors got up and started dusting themselves off. It seemed so strange that they were now all laughing and slapping each other on the backs as if nothing had happened. Mr. White told them that it was the most amazing show he had ever witnessed; that they were indeed the greatest horsemen and actors he had ever seen.

By this time my heart had started beating again, and I calmed down, watching the Nez Perce as they lined up so that they could parade by us. All of the women, children, and elders from several villages, including ours, applauded wildly as the warriors rode past. Some of the men were actually injured and bleeding from the falls, though no one seemed to be badly hurt. The sham battle is one of the most vivid memories that I have, one I will carry with me for the rest of my life.

As frightened as I was, I couldn't help but wonder what it would feel like to be up on the back of one of the horses, blazing over the ground at full speed. The chiefs were the last ones to parade by. At the very end was Chief Timothy dressed in pure white buckskins with colored beads and the largest feather headdress in the parade.

He was waving at me and riding the most beautiful horse I had ever seen in my life, Tashe. She was painted in beautiful designs with red and blue streamers flowing behind her. Tashe was not a large horse, but one that had been bred over many generations for speed and endurance. Though still young, she had become one of the most sought-after horses in the entire Nez Perce nation, almost legendary. Her shiny coat was a sandy white color with spots that went from pale gold to a rich chocolate brown.

One of the favorite pastimes of the Nez Perce men was racing their ponies against each other. It was something that bothered Father since there was usually gambling involved, which he considered a sin. Tashe had never lost a race, and one chief had even offered one hundred horses and his youngest daughter for her. Chief Timothy had become father's closest friend and had begun to accept the ways of Christianity. He had given up racing, gambling, and the practice of having more than one wife, so there was no chance for any of the other chiefs or warriors to win Tashe in a bet or race. When the sham battle was over, Chief Timothy came straight to me and took me in his arms, saying, "I could see that you are frightened little one, the battle was not real, nor were the scalps."

He took out a clump of hair that was tied to a piece of animal hide and said, "See, it is not real." I knew he was telling me the truth but still didn't want to touch it or even look at it.

With his war paint on, he still looked frightening, but he looked me in the eyes and said, "You know that I would never let anyone do anything to hurt you ... I have someone who wants to meet you."

He then led me over to where Tashe was standing and let me rub her nose and feed her a carrot that he had grown in his garden. When she had finished the carrot, she nibbled at my shoulder and placed her head against mine. Chief Timothy swooped me up onto her back and led me back to the house. I still remember almost every detail of that day and how riding Tashe was one of the finest moments I had experienced in my childhood. From that point on, my love of riding was like an unquenchable thirst I could never satisfy.

When it was all over, Father told everyone that a feast had been arranged and everyone was invited. He had slaughtered and dressed a cow and pig for the occasion. Mother and the other Nez Perce women had been preparing the meal since before first light and had brought dishes of every kind for the feast. Mother called for old Mustups to take me to the house so that I could help set up the plates and dishes while she continued to get everything else ready. Matilda had become an excellent baker and cook and was busy taking a hot yeasty pan of bread out of the oven. She pinched my cheeks and then cut me a big piece off the end and put a swatch of butter on it and stuck it in my mouth. It was the most delicious thing I had ever tasted, and still is to this day.

It's hard to put into words the kind of feelings I had when Mother and I were in the kitchen together preparing meals, but there was a deep sense of peace that I have never known at any other time or place in my life. She brought with her a kind of grace and comfort that filled the kitchen with soft light, like a benevolent sun rising behind a gathering of transparent clouds. Everything was in the moment, like shifting sands, no future, and no past. She once told me that here at Lapwai she had found the rhythm of a simple life, like gentle waves breaking on the shore. I had never seen the ocean, but I understood what she was trying to say. There was no question that the Indian people loved and respected Mother for her courage and what they called her "Quiet Heart." She reciprocated with genuine love and respect she felt for the Nez Perce People.

My little two-year-old brother Henry had wandered into the kitchen, so Matilda picked him up, squeezed him, and stuck a giant piece of bread and butter in his mouth. He heard father and the other men approaching the house and ran outside into the gated yard to see what they were up to. Father scooped him up like a feather pillow as he led everyone to supper. At the table Doctor White, Reverend Hines, Reverend Perkins, Mr. Littlejohn, Chief Timothy, Chief Joseph, and Eagle joined us for supper. There was a lively conversation in which both Doctor White and Reverend Perkins commented on how astounding Chief Timothy and Chief Joseph's knowledge of the Bible was.

Afterward, we joined everyone else outside for fun and games. Later that evening, Father asked the Nez Perce if they would sing the Lord's Prayer for our guests. Mr. White and the others told my parents that they could hardly believe their ears, that it was an astonishing achievement, the perfect end to a perfect day.

September 1842, Doctor Elijah White returned to the Oregon Territories with the letter they had all feared. The two missions that were now operating at Lapwai and Waiilatpu were to be closed down and abandoned. Though the mission at Tshimakain run by the Eellses and Walkers had had no success with the Spokane People, it was to remain open. The Spaldings, Grays, and Smiths were to be recalled, and the Whitmans were to join the Eellses and Walkers at Tshimakain.

Everyone was stunned by this decision that was based on Mr. Smith's vindictive letter. They all felt it was terribly unfair that they were unable to respond to or defend themselves from the false accusations. Father and Doctor Whitman felt that something drastic needed to be done right away to save their missions. The Eellses and Walkers were undecided as to what should be done since they had nothing to lose. Mr. Gray was indifferent since he had decided to take a position with the Methodist mission in the Willamette Valley, using the opportunity to resign officially from the mission. With Mr. Gray out of the picture, they voted to send someone back to Boston to let the missionary board know the truth of the situation and try to save both missions and Father from the disgrace of being recalled. Doctor Whitman volunteered to go, and all were in agreement.

It was late September, a very dangerous time to begin crossing the mountains. If the snows were to come early, the doctor and whomever he decided to travel with could be trapped in the mountains and never heard from again. He started making plans to leave as soon as possible. The party that had come over with Mr. Elijah White was the largest to cross the Oregon Trail so far, with over one hundred members. There were a number of people in that party who had already returned to the east, with plans to return to the Northwest the following year with friends and family. Doctor Whitman saw this as an opportunity to lead the largest group of immigrants ever to come west. He felt that with a substantial group of skilled workers and missionary families, he could enlarge the

Whitman community to the size of a village, making it easier to "assimilate and civilize" the Indian people.

Mother and Father wanted to see the missions expand gradually and were uncomfortable with the idea of bringing so many new people into the Oregon Territory so quickly. The Nez Perce had established their own civilization thousands of years earlier, and though my parents wanted to share their faith with them, they also wanted to make sure that their culture was respected and their way of life preserved.

Doctor Whitman left for the East October 3, 1842, with Mr. Asa Lovejoy. Mr. Lovejoy was 34 years old at the time and had come to establish his law practice in the Oregon Territory. He was from Massachusetts and had attended Cambridge and Amherst Colleges. He was a very bright and kind man who would play a major role in establishing the state of Oregon.

He would one day become the mayor of Oregon City, which was the established center for the provisional government. He also helped to establish the town of Portland, where he would be elected mayor and where he and his wife Elizabeth would raise their five children.

On Mr. Lovejoy's first trip over the Oregon Trail, he was captured and held captive by the Sioux with one of the other immigrants. Fortunately, they were able to trade their way out but decided not to continue along the Oregon Trail route through Blackfoot territory without the protection of a large party. Instead, they took the southern route cutting through the Rockies and on to Taos. With just the two of them, they were able to make good time, eventually arriving safely in the Northwest.

Several mountain men joined Doctor Whitman and Mr. Lovejoy until they reached St. Louis in early March. He made several stops at both Washington D.C. and New York before arriving in Boston after five months of hard and fast traveling. The missionary board was far from happy to see Doctor Whitman, giving him a very cold reception. They were angry that he had disobeyed their orders and returned without permission.

He made an impassioned appeal, explaining that the conditions had changed drastically and that Mr. Smith had used the opportunity to slander Mr. Spalding. He showed them the letters from Commander Charles Wilkes, Mr. Walker, and Mr. Eells in favor of keeping the missions intact. It helped him confirm that they had resolved their problems, that Mr. Smith and Mr. Gray had made every attempt to disrupt and divide the missions and were now gone.

He went on to explain that they must also protect their interest from a Catholic domination in the territory; that the territory was on the verge of expanding drastically and that the missions were needed more than ever. He also warned that there was still the possibility the Northwest could be lost to Great Britain and that his bringing another party of immigrants west would help establish American control and preeminence.

On April 4, 1843, the committee agreed to reverse its decision, allowing the missions to continue. Doctor Whitman would be permitted to lead a wagon train, but it would need to be a separate endeavor from the Protestant mission. They only granted that he take a small party of Protestant missionaries back with him since they did not want to be responsible for the added expenses. To

Doctor Whitman's dismay and disappointment, he was only able to enlist one person to come with him, his 13-year-old nephew Perrin Whitman.

In the meantime, Mrs. Whitman was the only white person at Waiilatpu and unable to find someone to help her run the mission and provide protection if needed. One night as she lay sound asleep, she was startled awake by the sound of breaking glass coming from the kitchen door. She grabbed her gun and started screaming as loud as she could, which frightened away whoever was trying to break in.

The next day she fled alone on horseback to Fort Walla Walla. Once there, she was given an escort to The Dalles, where she was welcomed to stay with the Methodist mission. Soon after, a party of Cayuse set fire to their gristmill and several hundred bushels of wheat and corn.

When word arrived through one of the visiting Cayuse about what had happened at Waiilatpu, Father immediately packed and left to help, not knowing that Mrs. Whitman had already fled. When he arrived at Waiilatpu, he was told that Mrs. Whitman was safe at The Dalles. He immediately went to work trying to repair the fire damage, separating the ruined and burned grains from the good.

Father had only been there several days when he received a message from Mother that she had suffered a severe hemorrhage and was in dire condition. All he could think about was that she was alone with the children, without any kind of medical attention other than what the Nez Perce could provide. He asked the messenger who had come if he would be willing to turn around and make the ride again without rest. He consented, so Father picked out the four fastest horses, two for spares, and set out for home. It was 9:00 PM when they departed in the rain with no moon or starlight.

In a later letter to Mr. Greene at the missionary board, he wrote, "Oh those hours, only death can blot them from my memory. Must my dear wife die alone—her last moments embittered—hastened on with the indescribable thought of having no civilized being with whom to leave her two little children untill the return of their father—this seemingly for want of someone to administer timely relief."

They had covered 65 miles by the time the sun was coming up and only stopped once to change horses and have a quick drink of water. As the sun was fading into the west, they arrived at Lapwai. Mother had stopped bleeding but was very weak and pale from loss of blood. Father burst into the room muddy and soaked from head to toe, then dropped to his knees and thanked God that she was still alive. Though there must have been a hundred things to attend to, he didn't leave her side for almost three days until she had improved.

In less than 17 hours, they had ridden over 120 miles, much of it in the dark, and all of it in the rain. It was rough country through mountains and rivers and very little in the way of a trail. To this day, I still find it hard to believe that any human being or horse could do it. My Father may not be the biggest man I have known, but he has a will of iron, and I have never known anyone with more strength or tenacity. He later sent a fine horse and supplies to the Nez Perce man who bravely made the arduous and dangerous trip with him.

Doctor White had been put in charge of Indian Affairs at Oregon City. After hearing about the damage at Waiilatpu, he felt it his duty to send a party to protect the missionaries. It included six armed guards as well as Tom McKay with Baptiste Dorion as interpreter. They left Oregon City on November 15, 1842, to investigate what had happened and rescue Mrs. Whitman if necessary, reaching The Dalles on November, 24, Mr. McKay commented, "Mrs. Whitman looked worn and lonely, her noble and intellectual spirit was much depressed and her health suffering."

Mr. Geiger and Mr. Littlejohn had also arrived at The Dalles and volunteered to take charge of the mission until Doctor Whitman returned, leaving right away. Mr. McKinley joined the group, and the next day, November 20, they reached Waiilatpu. Though Father had done a great deal of work at the Whitman Mission before returning to help Mother, there was still much to do, and the Geiger party was shocked to see the destruction that had been done during the Whitmans' absence.

Doctor White had heard rumors that my parents were experiencing some opposition from the Nez Perce and decided to ride to Lapwai in case help was needed. He also sent word to the Nez Perce that he wanted to meet with the chiefs while he was there. They arrived at Lapwai on December 3, finding hundreds of Indians gathered around the mission. My parents were especially glad to see their good friend Tom McKay.

Though we hadn't experienced any hostilities, Doctor White spent the next two days visiting the Nez Perce lodges, observing our classes, and inspecting the farms, barns, and stables. He told my parents that they had done an excellent job with our mission, that it was by far the best he had seen, and was gratified to see how well the Nez Perce were coming along with their own fields and cattle.

On December 5 he met with 22 chiefs as well as many other family and tribal members. They were curious but uncertain of who he was, or what his purpose was in coming to meet with them. He told them that he had been sent on behalf of the United States Government to establish a code of laws that would protect the native people as well as the Americans. Doctor White was a powerful force, known to have very high regard for himself.

He had run into troubles with Jason Lee and the Methodist mission, accused of spending unauthorized funds and compromising himself with his behavior toward various Indian women. As captain of a large party, he led over the Oregon Trail, he became so unpopular because of his heavy hand that he had to be replaced.

At the meeting, one of the elder chiefs, well into his nineties, talked of having met with and befriended Lewis and Clark and held up a small flag that they had given him. He talked of how Clark had told him that one day a big chief would come to better the way of peace between them, that he was glad to have lived to see that day. Doctor White was highly inflated by the comparison between himself and Captains Lewis and Clark. Though no government yet had the authority to administer or take command of the Indian people, Doctor White presumed that this was his decision to make and treated them as if they were now under his control and supervision.

He was wrong; their sovereignty was still their own. The primary difference between Doctor White and Lewis and Clark was that they saw the Indians as free men, beholding to no man. Doctor

White was indifferent to this fact and took it upon himself to place and enforce his own set of rules and regulations. They were:

1. "Whoever willfully takes a life will be hung.
2. Whoever burns a dwelling house will be hung.
3. Whoever burns an outbuilding shall be imprisoned for six months, receive 50 lashes and pay all damages.
4. Whoever carelessly burns a house will pay all damages.
5. If anyone enter a dwelling without the permission of the occupants, the chief shall punish him as they see proper. Public rooms excepted.
6. If anyone steal, he shall pay back two-fold; and receive 50 lashes.
7. If anyone take a horse and ride it without permission or take any article and use it without liberty, he shall pay for the use of it and receive 20 to 50 lashes as the chief shall direct.
8. If anyone enter a field and damage the crops or throw down the fence so that the cattle or horses go in and do damage, he shall pay all damages and receive 20 to 50 lashes.
9. Those only may keep dogs who travel or live among the game; if a dog kill a lamb, calf, or any domestic animal, the owner will pay the damages and kill the dog.
10. If an Indian raise a gun or other weapon against a white man, it shall be reported to the chiefs, and they shall punish him. If a White person do the same to an Indian it shall be reported to Doctor White, and he shall redress it.
11. If an Indian breaks the laws, he shall be punished by his chiefs, if a white man break the laws he shall be reported to an agent, and be punished at his insistence."

While Doctor White may have thought that these provisions were well-considered, in reality, they would create more problems than they would solve. Now that the Indian people understood that the Americans were to administer punishment, and not God, it took away the most powerful means the missionaries had to control behavior. For the Indians, it had brought their customs and ways of dealing with behavior into question, taking away their option to discipline in the old ways that they had used effectively for hundreds, if not thousands, of years.

Beginning their journey West, Doctor and Perrin Whitman arrived at Independence, Missouri, in May. They were overjoyed to find over one thousand immigrants prepared to take the Oregon Trail to the Northwest and California. There were over one hundred fully loaded covered wagons with as many as five thousand heads of cattle, horses, oxen, and mules.

Doctor Whitman offered to help guide them through the mountains and over the trail. He was also able to administer medical assistance and advise on river and mountain crossings. The British trader who was in charge of the wagon train told them that they would have to leave their wagons behind at Fort Hall. Doctor Whitman explained that the mountain man Joe Meek had safely guided wagons to the Willamette Valley, proving it was possible. The immigrants decided to take his advice, and he was able to personally guide them to the Grande Ronde Valley.

By 1842, with the influx of so many immigrants, the Americans would soon take control and force the English out of the Oregon Territory. At the time, the Indian people were unsure of what to think of so many white people coming into their territory. Some thought it an opportunity to gain wealth by trading; others thought it a threat to their long-term survival. For the time being, most immigrants were continuing to the Willamette Valley and coastal areas; however, the Nez Perce and Cayuse were becoming concerned that the Americans would soon attempt to settle on their lands. They had heard of how the whites had taken lands from the Sahaptin people in the Willamette Valley, reducing them to vagabonds and forcing them to steal and beg to survive. By this time, measles and smallpox were beginning to spread, creating even more tension between the Indian people and the Americans.

After Doctor White left, our mission experienced a period of relative harmony. Doctor White, Mr. McKinley, and Mr. McKay had taken it upon themselves to write to Mr. Greene at the missionary board after hearing of our problems with Mr. Smith and Mr. Gray.

Mr. White wrote, "I found nearer approaches [at Lapwai] to civilization and more manifest desire for improvement than I have elsewhere met with, in this or any other Indian country. Mr. Spalding is an ardent man and certainly a zealous individual and most efficient missionary and with his incomparable Lady doing much good in this dark portion of the earth. Too much praise cannot be given to that courageous woman who shares her husband's love for the Nez Perce. Their prospects are much more flattering than at any mission station in Oregon of this side of the mountains."

Mr. McKinley wrote, "I was most agreeably surprised at the great progress of the school. I had formed no adequate idea of the labors of himself and Mrs. Spalding."

Mr. McKay wrote, "I am happy to inform you that the mission under the care of Reverend H.H. Spalding is above all missions in this country, that it surpasses them all. Notwithstanding all that had been said against him, he stands like a pillar; unshaken by his opponents."

My parents decided that if the missionary board recalled them, they would resign and stay on independently to fulfill their commitment to the Nez Perce since they were now self-sustaining. The schoolhouse had become far too small to hold the 230 Nez Perce, who regularly attended, so Father decided to build a larger one, 30 by 50 feet with the help of Mr. Philo Littlejohn. Mr. Littlejohn and his wife Adeline had joined us in January of 1843 with their 20-month-old baby boy named Everette, who had stolen everyone's hearts with his joyful spirit and limitless smiles. When Mother first met them, little Everette came to her and put his hands out to be picked up. When she did, he leaned his head of golden curls next to her cheek and gently took a handful of her hair, twirling it in his pudgy little fingers. How sad that as we grow older, we lose the ability to trust and love without conditions.

I had found a new baby to mother, and little Henry had found a new playmate. I remember once dressing them up like little girls and having them model for the parents. Everyone laughed until out of breath, and the two little boys lapped it up like warm milk and honey.

Adeline and Mother would become the best of friends, lifelong. Adeline stepped right in and started helping with household duties as well as sewing and spinning classes, allowing Mother to devote more time to the school.

Mother told me she sometimes wondered if we are born with a gift for doing a certain thing, or had to learn it from our parents and teachers. How is it that two people can attend the same classes, and one will become a natural teacher, another may become a natural healer?

She said that with that in mind, she couldn't help but think that I was born to teach.

Every morning she would find me with a small group of Nez Perce girls and boys and an open book, reviewing what she had recently taught them. I had just turned six years old, and had never been around any other white children. I spoke the Sehaptin language of the Nez Perce, Cayuse, and Umatilla as well, if not better than English. I had also vicariously picked up the Chinookan language, which was made up of Indian, French, and English words. Most of the girls in my class were rapidly learning to speak English, especially Timps-te-te-lew, who was now almost fluent. Mother told me that I probably would have gone on all day if I were allowed to do so.

After what had happened to Alice Clarissa, Father had fenced in our yard so that we wouldn't have to worry about little Henry or Leverette. The little boys spent nearly every day in the yard playing in the dirt, or with baby farm animals Father would bring in for them to terrorize. About the only time I ever heard Leverette cry was when he couldn't play with little Henry, who was now learning how to do basic chores around the house.

On March 29, 1843, I came into the house asking where Leverette was. Adeline and Mother were immediately alarmed and went into the yard where they found little Henry building something with sticks and rocks. When they asked him where Leverette was, he responded that he had last seen him playing in the corner of the yard. He was nowhere to be found, and while searching, they discovered a hole large enough for him to have crawled through and quickly called out for help.

Mr. Littlejohn arrived first and immediately sent several of the Nez Perce off to look for Everette. Mr. Littlejohn then went to the millrace that powered the gristmill less than a hundred yards away and pulled the fence down to stop the water. When the water was low enough, Leverette's little body came into view, still and lifeless. Mr. Littlejohn rushed to pull him out and started trying to get the water out of his lungs and revive his heartbeat; it was too late. It was every parent's worst fear come true, losing the life of one of their children. For the Littlejohns, it was their only child, and Mr. Littlejohn had to pick his wife from the ground and carry her away weeping from the deepest part of her broken heart.

Since our family has been here at Lapwai, my parents had seen and experienced much heartache, but this was the worst we had known so far. The next day we buried little Leverette, and Mother couldn't help wondering why God had taken this tender little soul and what kind of wonderful man he would have become had he lived. How terribly sad that Alice Clarissa and Leverette should die in the same way at almost the same age. I can't begin to imagine how my parents would have felt if it had happened to little Henry or me. However, that was the life they had chosen, and it exposed us to these kinds of dangers almost daily. We would never know how the hole got in the fence, but suspect it must have been one of the animals digging in the yard.

After another meeting with the Cayuse, Doctor White chose Ellis to be the head chief of all Nez Perce tribes. He was the grandson of a great and powerful chief named HohatsIlppilp.

He had also gone to a Christian school at Red River, where he learned to speak, read, and write English.

Several problems would arise because of this decision. The first was that the Nez Perce had never had a head chief. Each village was autonomous and chose their headman for his bravery and wisdom. No leader could tell another what to do or how to run their village. The other was that Ellis was only 32 and had never been proven in battle. Because of this, many of the elder chiefs would refuse to obey Ellis or allow him to punish members of their tribes. This break with tradition didn't make sense to the Nez Perce and was doomed from the start, planting seeds of misunderstanding that would eventually lead to conflict.

Shortly after Chief Ellis' selection, his manner changed and he became high-handed and arrogant. This angered and provoked not only the chiefs from other villages but those of his own tribesmen who refused to recognize his authority. Doctor White received no cooperation from the Cayuse leaders when he returned to Waiilatpu. Most of the chiefs were still out hunting buffalo. Those that attended the meeting greeted him suspiciously, without warmth or friendship.

When Doctor White lectured the Cayuse on the damage that had been done to the Whitman mission, one of the chiefs became agitated and told him, "The white people are much worse. The whites preach one thing and do another; their treaties are nothing but lies so that they can steal the Indians' land and kill our buffalo.

At the Rendezvous and buffalo camps, the white men break with almost all Christian doctrine with women and drink. Worst of all, the Protestant and Catholic missionaries fight over whose God is right or wrong. How are we to trust such people when it is obvious you do not trust each other?"

Doctor White had no reasonable answer and was unable to make any progress with the Cayuse chiefs. He then asked that they have another meeting when the rest of the chiefs returned from the buffalo hunt in April.

Father had a pretty good voice and loved to sing. Inspired by the progress he was making with the Nez Perce choir; he printed a 32-page hymnbook in the Nez Perce language. He then helped Mr. Walker print a 16-page book in the Spokane language for their services. Some of the Nez Perce People were making amazing progress in agriculture and animal husbandry. Last season over 140 members had cultivated almost 400 acres. One of our orchards was covered with peach blossoms, and our apples, though still small and tart would be good enough for pies that fall. We had over five hundred bushels of corn, then planted the same ground with winter wheat. We were sharing with the village, so they were doing much of the labor and spending much less time roving for food. We were not only self-supporting at this point, but we were selling to the immigrants and helping provide for the other villages and missions in need.

Even before Doctor Whitman returned from the east, the tribes were becoming restless and concerned about the growing number of immigrants coming to the Oregon Territory. The Cayuse were especially unsettled since the Oregon Trail passed directly through their hunting grounds. One of the Cayuse chiefs was spreading false rumors that Doctor Whitman was returning with American soldiers to take their land and start a war. Some of the young warriors suggested that they take a war party and strike the Willamette Valley before he returned. There had been threats made at The Dalles where Mrs. Whitman was staying, but she remained calm and confident that they would not be attacked.

She sent a message to her husband, stating that Doctor White was meddling in something he did not understand and making matters worse. She was hoping that Doctor White would not return before her husband since it was obvious that he was "quite ignorant of Indian character, especially that of the Cayuse."

She went on to explain that the Cayuse were not looking to start trouble; they simply "did not wish to be forced to adopt the white man's laws." While at The Dalles, she had been visited by Doctor McLaughlin. He explained that with so many different religious groups coming into the territory, the Indian people were becoming distrustful and confused by all of the antipathy and division between the missionaries. He told her, "They are a fiercely independent and proud people who are not likely to accept the idea of being forced to adopt these new laws."

His last warning was that if the American immigrants continued pouring into the territory, there could be a serious uprising that may lead to war.

Doctor White arrived at Lapwai on May 13, 1843, with a small party, including two Methodist missionaries. He planned to use the Nez Perce to convince the Cayuse to accept his laws. He felt that Ellis could be bought and manipulated, that he could count on him to help deliver the message. The Nez Perce had had no need to use the laws, so they were open to meeting with him and listening to what he had to say.

Over five hundred men, women, and children rode with Doctor White to Walla Walla to meet with the Cayuse. They were curious more than anything else and decided to make a big party out of the meeting. After Doctor White had read the laws, Peopeo Moxmox stood to ask a question. He wanted to know if these were the laws of the white man or the laws of God? Doctor White would become one of the first Americans to begin the chain of lies and dishonesty used to deceive the Indians when negotiating treaties.

He told them, "The laws were recognized by God and imposed on men in all civilized countries." Peopeo Moxmox told Doctor White, "I am glad to learn that it is so. Many of my people have been angry with me when I whipped them for a crime and told me that God would send me to hell for it. I am glad to know that it is pleasing to God."

Father had recently baptized Chief Five Crows, known as Hezekiah, into the church. Chief Ellis was beginning to lose respect and credibility, so Doctor White felt that Hezekiah would be best suited to the position as new head chief. Mother had been feeling lonely because of the long separation from Father, who had returned to help at Waiilatpu, so she accepted Doctor White's invitation to join him and his family at their home in the Willamette Valley. She stayed through the summer, and when word arrived that Doctor Whitman was through the Rocky Mountains, she started back up the river to join Father, who was tending to Waiilatpu until the doctor returned.

Later that same summer in August, Mother became very ill with a high fever, headaches, patchy sore throat, nausea and vomiting, swollen tonsils and glands, and red dots on her tongue.

It was obvious to Father that she had all the symptoms of scarlet fever, with which he had no experience.

He put her to bed and made sure she drank plenty of fresh water, but Mother continued to get worse. After a time, she was unable to even drink water and felt as if she were sinking into an abyss and dying. She could see the worry in Father's face and told him that it was important he prepare himself for her death, giving him farewell instructions. They had lost all track of time, but later, Father told me that she was teetering on the brink of death for over two weeks. He felt that no one could survive being that sick for so long and decided to send a message to Mr. Geiger, the Eellses, and Walkers. In it he explained how close she was to death, and that she may not survive. Then Father started coming down with all of the same symptoms and was severely stricken; then little Henry and I.

The Littlejohns had taken on the responsibility of caring for us since we were incapable of caring for ourselves. Had it not been for their gentle and continuous care, one or more of us may have perished. They were like angels of mercy, committed to our recovery even if it meant exposing themselves to the dreaded disease.

Mr. Geiger arrived on September 14, 1843, the Eellses and Walkers, on September 15. Having heard by messenger that Doctor Whitman was already through the mountains, Mr. Geiger sent a messenger to let him know how serious our condition was. The messenger found the Doctor at Grande Ronde, east of the Blue

Mountains, and gave him the message. Doctor Whitman turned over the responsibility of the caravan to Chief Stickus, who had joined them at Grande Ronde and rushed to our aid. He reached Lapwai on September 25, finding all four of us sick, but Father and Mother on their way to recovering. Little Henry and I were still seriously ill, so the doctor did all he could, but had to leave for Waiilatpu the next day to meet the wagon train. There were over one thousand hungry immigrants, some sick and desperately needing care and supplies. He told the Littlejohns that they had done an excellent job and gave them further instruction on caring for us.

Once at Waiilatpu, he was able to arrange for the immigrants to be cared for and spend some time with Narcissa, who had returned from The Dalles. Two days later, he mounted his mule and rode 160 miles to Tshimakain to attend the birth of Mrs. Eells' second child.

They were blessed with a healthy baby boy, naming him Myron. Two days later, the Doctor was on his way back to Waiilatpu. If there was ever a man more committed to helping heal and care for his fellow man, I have not met or heard of him. From that time forth, there was never another unkind word spoken between our families. My parents and the Whitmans had been through and endured things that most people could hardly believe or understand. When the Whitmans were needed, they were there; when we were needed, we were there, and the words brother and sister had replaced the word friend.

In time everyone recovered and got right back to work. Doctor Whitman had brought back the good news that we were going to be allowed to stay at our missions, even given the role of vanguard for the new church and the Oregon Territories' eventual statehood.

Other than the illness, this past year had been the happiest and most productive my parents had experienced thus far. The school and sermons were at capacity, and Father had brought many new members into the church. The fields and orchards were productive, and even the more dissonant voices had quieted. Little could we have guessed the troubles and heartache that lay ahead.

There was a sense of peace on the surface, but an undercurrent of fear and foreboding beneath due to all of the immigrants who had come with Doctor Whitman.

As the Indian people watched the long caravans of settlers pass through their lands on their way to the Willamette Valley, they suspected it wouldn't be long before the invaders would turn to the Nez Perce and Cayuse lands. Unfortunately, the Whitman mission was located directly in the middle of these two powerful forces and would eventually become the target of a growing conflict between the two races.

With the good news from the missionary board, Father set about with a new sense of purpose. Mother said it didn't seem possible for a human being to work any harder. She said that a strong sense of urgency seemed to be driving him forward. Most of our helpers, including the Littlejohns, had moved on, so it was with grateful hearts that my parents welcomed Mr. Henry Lee from Nashville, Tennessee to our mission that fall. He was a very bright and easygoing young man of 25 who had come to help teach at the school.

He was also willing and able to do whatever was needed or asked of him. One of his goals was to learn the Nez Perce language as quickly as possible. There is very little that a six-year-old girl loves more than bossing someone around, and I had willingly become his teacher. Mother thought that it was quite amusing for a pig-tailed girl to be quizzing a grown man and correcting him like an old schoolmarm every time he made a mistake.

For the six months that he was with us, we were almost inseparable. Before he left, he confirmed Mother's suspicion that I was born to teach. He told her that he could hardly believe how quickly he had picked up not only the language but the customs and habits of almost every individual in the village. He told Mother that I was like a whirlwind of energy that drew people to me. He recalled the first time he came into the classroom and saw me over in the corner of the room with my books open, teaching a group of children. I was trying to explain something or other and gesticulating wildly with my hands.

Mr. Lee had watched for a time before he turned to mother and said, "I hope I don't have to compete with the other teacher."

Mother smiled, telling him, "Oh, don't worry, Mr. Lee, that's the advanced class; you will be teaching the beginners."

He shook his head as they laughed together.

Most of that year and the beginning of 1844 were relatively peaceful and productive times. The laws Doctor White had instituted were rarely followed, especially since there was no one to enforce them. The only undertone of unrest was from the settlers continuing to pour in and the uncertainty of those projected to arrive in the future. None had settled on Nez Perce or Cayuse lands so far, so raids and attacks were still rare.

Chapter 9

Little Owl

By the time 1844 started to roll in, the mission was in full bloom, a beehive of activity.

A young girl of my age, about seven or eight, was brought to the school by one of the children's mothers. She had been found wandering through the forest to the north and east by a small band of Nez Perce who were hunting game. The hunting party hadn't planned to go so far from home, but they needed fresh game and had had little luck. The girl was skin and bones and had nothing but a blanket, dress, moccasins, and a small pouch of herbs and plants, none of which gave any clue as to where or what tribe she was from.

When they returned to Lapwai she was put into the care of a kind woman named Blossom who felt so sorry for her that she took her in with her own family. It had been almost two months, and the little girl had not uttered a single word. Everyone was beginning to fear that hunger and exposure might have damaged her mind, so Blossom did everything she could to make her feel loved.

Because of her silence and big eyes, she was given the name Little Owl. It was thought that she may have been traveling with a parent or other adult and had gotten separated and lost. It was also possible that she had been abandoned, or perhaps the person with her had died or been killed. One thing that mystified them was a small pouch of carefully chosen herbs and plants that she had tied to her dress. Blossom had run out of ideas to help her communicate and brought her to the school.

I could see Mother listening carefully to Blossom as she explained how they had found Little Owl, and that she was unable to get any response from her. I was curious, so I placed myself close enough to overhear their conversation. The little girl was so shy with those big brown eyes, and I could feel Mother's heart going out to her.

Blossom told Mother that she didn't know what else to do with Little Owl and asked if she could bring her to the school with the other children to see if it would help. Mother told her that they were both welcome any time, that she would do all she could to bring Little Owl back to the world. I could see that the little girl was frightened by all of the people and was probably seeing and hearing a white person for the first time in her short life. Mother took her small hand and led her to the table where she was working with the younger children, including little Henry, who was her helper that day.

When all of the children were asked to greet her, Little Owl's only response was confusion and fear. She sat there for a long time with her head down until Mother got up to attend to one of the other groups that needed help. When Mother returned, she found that Little Owl was gone. She looked at little Henry, who pointed to the corner where she was balled up with her head tucked into her knees.

Timpstetelew and I had seen the little girl come into the room and could tell that something wasn't right since she didn't respond to anything going on around her.

When I took over Mother's group, she got up and went to Little Owl and started speaking to her gently in Nez Perce, trying to comfort her. At some point, Little Owl raised her head and looked at Mother with tears in her eyes. Mother gently lifted her into her lap and rocked her for a long time. Everyone was watching, but trying not to be obvious.

When she began to calm down, Mother brought her to our group and told us briefly what had happened, asking us to be kind and help in any way we could. She told us that she had been given the name Little Owl, but that was not her true name. Mother also told us that she was frightened, and to be gentle and see if we could get her interested in what we were doing. She went back to her class, leaving us with Little Owl.

Since she was sitting next to me, I put a pencil and piece of paper in front of her hoping she might become curious and try to write or draw something, but there was no response. Several times I had turned to her and asked a question, but it was as though she didn't hear me. For a time, it was awkward for the group trying to include her, and eventually, everyone but me went back to our studies, and for the most part, forgot that she was there.

I was still trying to think of some way to make contact, so I picked up her hand to hold it. I must have frightened her, and she instantly withdrew in alarm. I told her that I was very sorry, she didn't understand. I probably should have let Timpstetelew or one of the other girls try and make contact first, but in those days, I rarely thought of myself as being white. We took a short recess to run around to let out some of our energy; when we returned, Little Owl was back in the corner with her head buried in her knees. When Blossom came to pick her up, Mother told her what the day had been like and to bring Little Owl back the next day; with time, she might be able to reach her.

At supper, Mother told Father about the little girl and asked me how it had gone when she put her with our group. I told her that Little Owl didn't seem interested in anything, but I felt as though there was something I was missing. Mother told me that she must have been through something terrible that had caused her to shut down, but she could see understanding in her eyes and thought that with a gentle hand, she could be reached.

I asked that if Little Owl left the group again to sit alone if Timpstetelew and I could sit with her and try to interest her in our studies. I told her that everyone had been kind, but boys will be boys, and they could be loud and intimidating. She gave me her beautiful smile, and wrapped me in her arms and held me in her soft embrace. It felt as if I had been enveloped in a warm cocoon smelling of sweet lavender.

When Mother and Father had first come to the Oregon Territory, they had purchased supplies, and vegetable seeds from Doctor McLaughlin since most of theirs had been ruined or lost on the trip over the Oregon Trail. Mother and Mrs. Whitman had stayed with Doctor McLaughlin and his wife Margarite for almost a month when Father and Doctor Whitman had gone searching for their mission sites. They had all grown very fond of each other, and as they were preparing to leave, Mrs. McLaughlin handed each of them a full leather pouch. Mother asked what it was, and Mrs. McLaughlin said it was a surprise, but to be sure to plant them as soon as possible.

Once planted, it was as if the seeds immediately began seeking the shelter and comfort of the good earth, then slowly began popping their heads out to feel the warmth of the sun. It turned out they were a mixture of flower seeds, lavender among them. From the labor of her gifted hands, Mother now had a beautiful garden of flowers thanks to Mrs. McLaughlin. She would always keep a pouch of lavender in with her clothes to give them that wonderful scent. Even now, if I smell lavender and close my eyes, it's as if I have been transported back into my mother's sweet embrace.

It took the better part of a week for Little Owl to get comfortable with Timpstetelew and me joining her in the corner. I could see that she was becoming more and more curious, so I talked to her as if we were good friends and she understood every word I said. I wrote down letters and tried to get her to repeat them. She seemed interested but still wouldn't try to speak. This went on for over a week, and though I could see she was curious, it seemed as if I wasn't making any real progress.

One morning Chief Timothy announced that he had arranged something special for us that day. He had recently met and befriended a powerful chief among the Shoshones named Washakie. Washakie had come to visit his favorite nephew Bear Hunter who had recently married a Nez Perce woman and moved to her village. Bear Hunter was a well-known and respected warrior even amongst the Nez Perce and Cayuse. When he was still a young man of 15, he had gone out to hunt the giant silvertip bear, also known as the grizzly, with nothing more than a thin spear and knife. He had been badly wounded on the shoulder, leaving long dark scars but managed to drive the spear into the heart of the bear and now wore a necklace made of its giant claws and teeth.

When Washakie was very young, he had learned the Nez Perce language from a boy he had befriended who had come to live with a relative among the Shoshones for the summer.

Washakie was now very old but with a young and joyful spirit. He was a wonderful storyteller who had come to tell us of his land on the plains, what it was like to live where there were almost no trees, but many buffalo.

He had also come to show us what he called the hand language, something that his people learned as children. In this way, they were able to communicate with other tribes of the plains, including the Cheyenne, Sioux, Kiowa, Arapaho, Crow, and Blackfoot. There was a hiss when he said the word Blackfoot because they had been enemies of the Nez Perce for so long.

He raised his arms in a gesture to quiet us down and said, "We will talk of this later."

Before he showed us anything, he explained that each gesture had a different meaning; that the meaning can change with a touch to a different part of the body such as the nose, ear, or eye.

He also told us that the meaning could change with a different facial expression or body movement. Since Timpstetelew and I were fascinated by his stories, we had moved up to the front so we could see and hear better. Little Owl was still sitting in the corner but watching.

Washakie told us that he would first show us some simple gestures, such as a greeting or name. When he made the hand gesture of greeting, Little Owl jumped up and started gesticulating wildly. We were all completely confused as to what was taking place since she had shown so little interest in anything up to this point. When she stopped, the chief started making hand signs to Little Owl. Mother immediately asked what was happening. Chief Washakie told us that this little one could not hear or speak but understood the sign talk. He went on to tell us that she had been separated from her mother and lost during a terrible rainstorm in the mountains. She says her father is a powerful Chief, and her mother is a highly respected medicine woman. She and her mother had wandered far into the mountains looking for plants when the storm hit; that she is worried about her mother. It was completely quiet and felt as if a bolt of lightning had passed through the room and stunned everyone silent.

It now seemed so obvious that I could hardly believe we had missed it. So many times, I had talked right in her ear, and she had not reacted at all. Everyone but Mother, Timpstetelew, and I had all but given up on her, thinking that her mind had been damaged. Washakie asked her if she knew where she had come from. She signed that she did not know, but was of the Blackfoot tribe, that her name was Fawn. The word Blackfoot brought about restlessness among the group. The Blackfoot tribe was often hostile and extremely protective over their territory and ordinarily attacked tribes from the west trying to cross over their land to reach the buffalo hunting grounds.

The chief raised his hands once again to quiet everyone down then went on to say, "The Blackfoot people can be a fierce and deadly enemy, but you must understand that there are many people among them with good hearts. They live in a land that is very harsh, and unforgiving and it has made some of their people the same as the land. Some of you may know my nephew Bear Hunter who now lives among you in his wife's village." There was a loud ahhh of approval.

"He can speak the sign language and may be willing to return this little one to her people. Remember she is a child that has done you no harm ... one who has endured hardships that few of you can imagine. Then you may think of her as Blackfoot." We all watched in complete silence as he talked with the girl using the sign language.

When they were done, the chief told us, "She had never seen a white person before and at first thought that you were ghosts. When the white mother talked with her for a long time and took her into her arms, she knew that she was not a ghost but a human being."

Washakie asked one of the older boys to get his nephew Bear Hunter who was at a nearby village. He stood to take a break and told us that he wanted to talk more with Fawn. Mother told us that it was time for us to have a break and get something to eat, that she would stay with the chief and Fawn as he interpreted for her. Afterward we bounded back into the classroom and found Mother with Fawn once again in her lap. It was the first time I had seen Fawn's beautiful smile, now completely at ease.

Several minutes later, we all watched in awe as this big strong, strikingly handsome man with long black hair to his waist entered the room. His face was fierce but kind, and he seemed to fill the room with a presence of strength and dignity that only comes from a lifetime of danger and adventure.

It was a mild day for winter, so he wore no shirt and had terrible scars across his right shoulder that he wore like a badge of honor.

The scars, necklace of claws and teeth, and story of his courage had brought him great respect among all Indian people. Chief Washakie stood to greet him, and you could feel the bond of love between them as they locked hands and forearms and looked into each other's eyes.

The chief introduced him to Fawn, then went on to tell him her story with words and sign language.

When he had finished, Bear Hunter smiled at Fawn and said in the hand language, "You have endured many hardships, little sister, I am greatly honored to meet you."

Fawn smiled shyly at the imposing man, but never lost eye contact.

Bear Hunter then told her, "You no longer need to be frightened little one, I promise to protect you. I have come to help you and will not rest until I have returned you to your family and people."

She leapt out of Mother's lap into the open arms of Bear Hunter and wept tears of happiness down his massive chest. He held her tight and ran his fingers gently through her silky hair until she was once again calmed. There was not a sound in the room or heart that had not been touched. He gently took her head in his giant hands and wiped the tears from her face. He told her that it would take him two days to prepare for the journey, that he wanted her to stay with his wife and him until they left. Fawn went to Mother and settled back into her lap as they embraced. She then embraced Chief Washakie and thanked him. She came to Timpstetelew and put out her hands to us. We each took one, and then the three of us held each other. Bear Hunter then gently took her hand and led her to the door.

Two days later, Fawn, Bear Hunter, and his wife's brother, Standing Buffalo, stopped by the mission so that she could say goodbye. Standing Buffalo was a giant of a man, and I could see why Bear Hunter would want him to accompany them. All three of them, including Fawn, were riding beautiful ponies with colorful blankets. She was wearing a pretty doeskin dress with colorful beads and new moccasins that someone had given her.

She dismounted and ran straight for Mother, who took her into her arms. Timpstetelew and I showed her how we had learned to say hello and our names in sign language. She was a different person, and my heart was full of happiness for her. Through Bear Hunter, she told us that she would never forget our kindness and always have a place for us in her heart. We were never to see her again, though I often wonder what became of her life. Washakie returned almost every day for several weeks to teach the basic hand and body gestures.

Each day Timpstetelew and I quizzed him mercilessly until he would finally say, "I am an old man, you two magpies are going to wear me out and send me to my ancestors early if I am not allowed to rest."

I have forgotten most of the sign talk but will never forget the tenderness and humanity that the Nez Perce showed to a helpless little girl named Fawn.

When Bear Hunter and Standing Buffalo returned, they were leading three of the most beautiful ponies I had ever seen; one was almost pure white. Buffalo Standing took two of them, said goodbye, and left for his village.

Bear Hunter came into the classroom and talked for a long time about what had happened on the journey and the reunion of little Fawn with her family. He told us that it was cold through the mountains, but for the most part, it had been uneventful and pleasant until they reached the Blackfoot territory. Once there, he said they could feel eyes watching their every movement. When they came into an open meadow with no protection, a small band of nine Blackfoot warriors came charging at them, waving their weapons and screaming war cries. He said that he and Standing Buffalo raised their hands, palms out, to show that they had come in peace.

The Blackfoot circled them, looking as though they were threatening to strike until one of the men stopped and said in broken Nez Perce, "You are not welcome here, what do you want?" Fawn was wrapped in a buffalo robe withdrawn and frightened by all of the hostility.

Bear Hunter drew her robe back from her head and said, "We have come to return this young girl named Fawn to her family. She was lost in the mountains and found by Nez Perce men who were hunting for game. She cannot hear or speak, but talks the sign language."

The one who spoke Nez Perce said, "I know this little one, she has been missing for over two moons, we thought her dead. I know her father and mother, and I will take her to them."

"I am Bear Hunter of the Shoshone, and this is Standing Buffalo of the Nez Perce, we have given our word to Fawn that we would not leave her until she is returned to her family."

The leader of the Blackfoot party said, "Your name is known to me. Her father is a powerful chief, and her mother is a medicine woman much respected. I will take you to their village."

Bear Hunter turned to Fawn and told her in sign talk that they were taking her to her family, and that she was safe. By the time they arrived at the village, word had spread that they were coming, and her mother and father were waiting for her.

It was a heartwarming moment when the three of them reunited, and the entire village started cheering. With sign language Fawn's father told Bear Hunter that she was their only child, that they had searched the mountains and plains for one full moon, finally giving her up for dead. He also told them that, like her mother, Fawn had a great gift for finding plants and was expected to be a medicine woman for her people.

Bear Hunter told us that there was a celebration feast in which they were the guests of honor, that they ate so much food they were afraid their stomachs would burst. They rested the next day and night and then started making preparations for their return home. Before they left, Fawn's father told Bear Hunter that he and his wife had gifts for them, that they had done a brave and good thing, and he would always be grateful. The chief's wife came out with a bundle of assorted items beautifully decorated and told Bear Hunter that this was for the family that had taken her in and cared for her. One of the warriors came from behind the chief's lodge leading three beautiful horses.

The chief told Bear Hunter and Standing Buffalo, "You and Standing Buffalo are to each have one of these ponies for returning our daughter. The white stallion is for the white woman of the Nez

Perce. Fawn has told me that the white mother brought her out from the darkness with her kindness."

Bear Hunter told the chief, "We are deeply honored and will give great care to these fine animals. The white mother is highly respected among the Nez Perce People, and it will be a privilege to present her with this gift."

As they mounted and prepared to leave, Fawn ran to Bear Hunter and wrapped her arms around his waist. He picked her up and held her for a long time until he could feel that her heart slowed. When he put her down, they looked into each other's eyes until he told her with his hands, "You were very brave and will one day be a legend among your people. I will proudly tell your story at my lodge."

Fawn's father said, "You are always welcome at our village. I have told my people that the Nez Perce are not to be harmed while traveling through our lands. Go in peace."

When Mother and I first heard that Bear Hunter and Buffalo Standing were on their way to Lapwai we were all waiting outside to greet them.

Mother was shocked when Bear Hunter presented the horse to her, she put her hands to her mouth and then said, "Dear me, what a beautiful animal."

She told him, "I am truly grateful, but did nothing more than any mother would do for a lost child."

She went to the white stallion and gently rubbed his neck and long velvet nose.

Then looking up at Bear Hunter, she said, "I rarely have time to ride anymore; it would be selfish and unfair for me to have such a magnificent animal. You did not hesitate to put your life in danger; I want your wife to have this pony." There was a long and loud ahhh from all of the children and adults.

I knew it was selfish thinking, but couldn't help picture myself on such a beautiful horse, though I knew that it was the right thing for Mother to do. Anyway, my heart already belonged to Tashe though I knew that the most I could ever hope for was an occasional visit or ride.

Bear Hunter thanked Mother and told her that his wife would be deeply honored.

It was almost two weeks later when Standing Buffalo arrived with a packhorse and message from Bear Hunter asking to see, "The Quiet Heart." It was a Saturday afternoon, and there was no school, so Mother and I came out of the house with flour on our hands to greet him in the front yard. After greetings, he dismounted and went to the packhorse and grabbed two large bearskin robes. He then went back and took down two of the most beautiful baskets that I had ever seen. He told Mother that he had been sent by Bear Hunter to deliver a message and these gifts.

"Bear Hunter would have brought these himself, but he was called to help a friend in need. He asked me to tell you that the white horse has brought great happiness to his wife; that they have spent many hours riding together and have named the pony "Quiet Heart" in your honor."

He handed her one of the robes and said, "Bear Hunter's wife is named Espowyes, it means "Light on the Mountain." She has made these robes to keep you and your husband warm. It would be this same buffalo robe that would one day save Father's life. They took them over to the porch so that she could lay them out. As she opened the first one, she uncovered a beautiful white doeskin dress with blue beads and a buckskin vest like Doctor Whitman's. Both Mother and I must have gasped at the incredible handwork. The strange thing was that the dress was far too small for Mother, and the vest was too small for Father. Standing Buffalo said, "These are for your daughter and son."

It felt as if my heart had stopped beating as Mother handed me the dress. It was exactly the right size with a little room to grow. Timpstetelew told me later that they had used her to get the right size. Just about that time, little Henry came barging out of the house, wondering what was going on. Mother picked up the vest and told him it was a gift from the wife of Bear Hunter. He put it on and started dancing all over the yard, making even the stoic Buffalo Standing start laughing. When Mother unwrapped the other robe, there was a matching set of moccasins for the dress and a small bow with arrows for little Henry. It was more than I could have ever wished for, and Little Henry almost went wild when he saw them. Buffalo Standing told him, "Bear Hunter has made the bow and arrows, and Chief Timothy has offered to show you how to use them wisely." Little Henry and I ran to Buffalo Standing and wrapped our arms around him. He picked us up in his powerful arms, and little Henry let out with the best wolf call I have ever heard. When Mother picked up the baskets, she held them out at arm's length and said, "These are the finest I have ever seen; they could surely hold water." Buffalo Standing gently let us down and told her, "That is what they were made to do." Mother told Standing Buffalo, "Please thank Bear Hunter and his wife and tell them that we are in awe of the beauty of these fine gifts and will always treasure them." He smiled as he mounted the powerful horse that had been given to him by Fawn's Father and Mother.

As soon as he left, I ran into the house and showed them to Matilda, who took me in her arms and said, "Now you are truly of the Nez Perce." Then I ran to my room, and as I pulled the dress over my shoulders, I couldn't believe how soft and warm it was, and the moccasins fit perfectly. I closed my eyes and pictured myself dashing through the hills with Tashe. When Father came back from the mill, I was showing the dress to Mother. He smiled and said, "It looks as though my little papoose has become a beautiful Nez Perce princess," I ran to his open arms and was immediately enveloped in his strong but gentle embrace and one of my favorite smells, fresh-cut cedar. When he let me go, he made a gesture for me to turn around so he could see the whole dress, I know it was showing off, but I did it three or four times until I was almost dizzy. I thought it was the happiest moment of my life.

The peace lasted until spring 1844 when a Delaware Indian scout and trapper named Tom Hill came to Waiilatpu. He was extremely intelligent with a near-photographic memory and gift for languages. Aside from his own Algonquian language, he spoke English, French, and the Sehaptin language fluently as well as several other Indian dialects. He was a powerful, handsome, and fierce-looking man with shiny black hair down past his waist with eyes that penetrated and challenged. The Nez Perce had asked him to come and speak with them, and though my parents were not invited to listen, he also came to our mission along with Chief Joseph and his son, young Joseph, who was four years old at the time.

Tom Hill was thought by the Indian people to have special powers, able to find water in dry places and game where there was none to be found. Some said he was a shaman who had the power to see the unseen and know the unknown. He had been trapping for a number of years with Kit Carson, Joe Meeks, and other trappers throughout the Oregon Territories and California until the beaver started to disappear. He married a Nez Perce woman and rapidly began gaining power and respect among the Nez Perce People because of his reputation for courage. It was said that he had a large collection of scalps and had made a name for himself as a warrior fighting the Comanches at Cimarron, the Shoshonis at the Great Basin, and the Blackfoot at Yellowstone. He had been a guide this past year for John Fremont, who had been assigned by the President to map the Northwest and look for new passes over the mountains.

What Tom Hill told my parents changed the way they looked at what the American immigrants and government were doing to the Indian people. He was not an angry man, but he was direct and extraordinarily intense. Mother said his eyes seemed to search your soul to determine if you were honest and sincere. He asked what my parents hoped to achieve with their mission.

Father told him, "I believe the American immigrants and settlers will one day predominantly populate the Oregon Territories; that there is no way to stop white civilization from expanding into the Northwest. I fear that the buffalo and much of the game the Indian people need to survive will soon disappear. Our desire is to help prepare the Nez Perce for that time by teaching them how to grow crops and raise farm animals. We are also Disciples of Christ and live by the lessons and laws set forth in the Bible, and hope to share these beliefs with the Nez Perce People."

Tom Hill thought about what they had said for a long time and then told them, "I can see that you have good hearts, and I will never intentionally bring harm to you or your family. The best thing you could do for the Indian people is to go back where you came from and let us live our lives our way, though I know this will not happen. I too can see that the whites will be coming in great numbers and strip the land like locusts. Our laws are just and cannot be bought like the white man's justice. Your people call us sinners because Jesus said it was so thousands of years ago. I have read the Bible, and have spent many hours over the campfire discussing God and the Great Spirit. Your people have spent millions of hours attempting to justify contradictions in the Bible until you find one that suits your needs. A contradiction is something no one can understand because it makes no sense, how are we to understand these things? You expect the Indian people to follow you like sheep stampeding over a cliff. Be warned, one day you will find that we are not sheep. When we fight, it is for survival; food, horses, and to protect our families and villages. Your people fight over things you do not understand or truly believe in, for leaders who betray you with their greed. For people who profess God's love, I have never known such hatred. I have seen first-hand how your people have enslaved the people of Africa and fear you will do the same to us. In our villages if there is food, everyone eats, everyone has a place, a lodge to sleep in and stay warm. I have seen your people starving and freezing to death in your streets, your religions all think they are right and will kill each other to prove it; none of this makes sense to us."

Father and Mother were struck speechless; they had never heard anyone talk like that about their religion or government. When Father came out of his thoughts, he told Tom Hill that he spoke the truth, that there were many things the white people should be ashamed of.

He said that he also had seen the "greatness and nobility of the Indian people and witnessed the meanness and wickedness of the white man."

He told Tom Hill that they now considered the Nez Perce to be brothers and sisters, and would not abandon them. When Tom Hill left that day, it was with good feelings between them, but uncertainty toward the future.

Over time Tom Hill became a powerful chief and managed to acquire the support and attention of other powerful chiefs among the Nez Perce and Cayuse people. He had seen first-hand what the Americans had done to his people in the east, how they had been forced off their land, and reduced to beggars. At one of his speeches, he told the Cayuse that it might be necessary to kill all white people before they themselves are destroyed. He told the people to go back to the old ways of living, hunting buffalo, and listening to their own ancestors, not those of the white man.

Chapter 10

The Angry Bull

Today Father, little Henry, and I barely skirted death. One of the old chiefs came to us with a wound to his arm that had happened two days earlier. He was lucky that an angry bull had only injured him instead of taking his life. After Father had cleaned and dressed his arm, he asked where the bull was now. The chief explained where it had happened and told Father that the bull had gone mad; that he would show him where he had last seen it. Mother was deeply involved in her classes, so Father grabbed a rifle and took little Henry and me with him to investigate. It wasn't long before we reached the bank of a river where the chief pointed to the bull on the other side. Father first thought it might have been one of his bulls, that there would be no danger as long as he had his rifle in hand. They located the canoe the old chief had used to cross, and we paddled to the other side.

When we reached the other side, Father could see by the bull's markings that it was not his and was reluctant to destroy it without permission. With no reason or warning, the bull charged at us like lightning, and Father didn't even have time to get a shot off. As the bull came charging, I spotted a tree and scampered toward it as fast as my legs would carry me. Just as Father picked up little Henry, the bull hit him in the rump at full speed, lifting them off the ground and throwing them high into the air; thank goodness neither was gored. Father had protected little Henry from the fall with his body, but when they started to get up, the bull was already turning to come at them again.

By this time, I was up the tree yelling and waving my dress at the bull. It worked, and the bull turned and tore after me. When it realized that I was out of reach, it turned to go after the old chief— Father had grabbed little Henry and ran for the tree. Before the old chief could reach the water, the bull hit him from behind and sent the poor old man flying through the air and crashing to the ground. Father thought for sure that the chief must have been mortally wounded. He then got down out of the tree and started throwing stones and yelling at the bull since his rifle was far out of reach lying on the ground where he had dropped it. This attracted the bull's attention but only seemed to make him angrier as he came charging at us again. When he started to get close, Father climbed safely back into the tree.

In the meantime, the old chief miraculously picked himself up off the ground, reached the canoe, and barely escaped as the bull came charging at him again. He paddled out beyond reach and waited. When the bull had gone after the old chief the second time, Father had gotten down out of the tree and found several good-sized rocks as big as his fist. The bull was still angry as it slowly snorted and pawed its way back to the tree. When it was directly below us, Father hit the bull hard right between the eyes with the biggest rock. At first, it was stunned, then charged the tree head-on as if it had thrown the rock. With a terrible thump, Father hit it in the head again just above the eye. That was enough for the bull; it circled several times from a distance and then wandered out of sight.

When we got back to the mission, Mother could see that both Father and the chief were limping badly and ran to help. Little

Henry and I were wild with excitement, both jabbering as loud and fast as our mouths would work. Father told Mother that he didn't think he had broken anything and could wait for her to take a look at the old chief. Mother asked little Henry and me to please calm down, that she couldn't hear herself think. The poor old chief looked pretty bad and had wounded his other arm as well as his leg. Father took over since the arm needed to be reset and bandaged. He told Mother that his pride had been badly damaged, and he should have never taken us with him across the river. The old chief stayed with us for several days, and Mother had to feed the poor old man since both of his arms were bandaged, and he was too sore to walk.

Several days later, one of his sons came to pick him up, but he didn't want to go. He said that he liked it here, that Mother was the best squaw he had ever known, and was taking good care of him. Father was finally able to bribe the chief to go with a bag of tobacco and assortment of apples and potatoes. Little Henry and I never grew tired of listening to the old chief tell the story over and over again and were sad to see him go.

Each night after supper, we would spend time together doing different activities; some nights were game nights, some were study nights, and some were story nights. It was something Mother had learned from her parents. We all sat around the fireplace and would take turns telling a story, each saying one sentence or paragraph. Then someone else would continue with the same theme. For the next couple of weeks, the theme always turned to the bull story when it was little Henry's or my turn. Little Henry's sentences became long paragraphs as he went on and on about how they had flown through the air, landing in the dirt and making a big cloud of dust. When it was my turn, I talked about how mad and mean the bull looked until Father bonked it in the head with the rock. Father went along and said that if I hadn't thought to use my dress like a matador's cape, little Henry and he might have gone to meet their maker. Mother stayed quiet most of the time, but I could tell that she was thinking about how badly things could have gone.

Though I deeply love Matilda, Mustups, and Chief Timothy, my dearest friend in the world was Timpstetelew, also known as Cherry Eyes. Her hair was a shiny raven black with the biggest, deepest dark eyes I have ever seen.

The sweet breath of June had tenderly guided me safely into my seventh year, and we were hosting the annual missionary meeting at Lapwai, so I was dressed in my most uncomfortable clothes. One of my favorite games to play with Timpstetelew was tag, chasing each other through the apple orchard. Sometimes, I was allowed to wear comfortable clothes and moccasins around the mission and house. The Sabbath was a different story, and I had to wear an itchy wool dress, wool socks, and shoes that were too tight, trying to remember to be quiet and respectful at all times.

I remember Timpstetelew tagging me and taking off. The next thing I knew, we were running through the orchard as fast as we could, and even with my tight shoes, I was almost ready to tag her when she tripped trying to avoid Mrs. Whitman. We went flying through the air and landed in a pile of arms, legs, dresses, and pigtails surrounded by a cloud of dust and our laughter. Mother rarely got mad, but when she did, I wanted to get as far away as soon as possible.

She put her hands on her hips and said, "Eliza, this is the Lord's Sabbath; you should know better than that." The other two women who were with mother and Mrs. Whitman looked very serious and stern, and I knew I was in big trouble. I looked up and told her, "I'm really sorry that I forgot, Mother. I promise it will never happen again."

Mrs. Whitman reached down and gently lifted me off of Timpstetelew and started dusting me off. Timpstetelew got up and took off like a rabbit, leaving me there to take my medicine alone. Mrs. Whitman took a handkerchief and started wiping my pathetic, dirty face off, then put her hand over her mouth and started snickering. Before long, the other ladies joined in, and soon after, they were all laughing out loud; all but mother, who was still doing her best to look angry, which is not easy for her.

When they calmed down, Mrs. Whitman said to Mother, "I'm sorry, I don't know what came over me or who is more at fault here, myself or little Eliza. I really should know better, but for a moment, I remembered what it felt like to be a little girl again."

Mrs. Whitman patted me on the bottom and told me to be on my way, that she would do her best to make sure my father didn't find out what had happened.

The Whitmans had brought what is called a missionary barrel with them to Lapwai, mostly clothes, but sometimes there are things like paper and pens or small tools. It takes over a year from the time they send it from New York, so I had usually outgrown the clothes and shoes before they ever reached us. After lunch, I overheard one of the missionary wives complain that because the barrels went to Waiilatpu first, Mrs. Whitman always took the pretty dresses and nice clothes before anyone else had a chance to choose. Mother reminded her that Mrs. Whitman had the important responsibility of greeting dignitaries and the new immigrants coming into the territory; that it was important she made a good impression for all of us. Father rarely showed much concern over the clothes that came in the barrel, but when he pulled out a new tool that he had asked for, his eyes lit up like two lanterns.

That afternoon, Father gave a sermon to almost one thousand Nez Perce and Cayuse as well as our guests. Some of the Indians had traveled over 50 miles to attend. Father had a voice that could cut through rock, and it was easy for anyone to see that he believed every word he spoke without equivocation. When he said something that the Nez Perce liked, they would all nod their heads and make a sound something like ahhh. However, no one likes to be scolded, so he had to be careful about when and how he admonished what he considered sinful deeds like gambling and alcohol. When he said something they didn't like, it was like a symphony of silence, and you could feel the tension crawl up the back of your neck and leak into your forehead.

By this time of year, the Nez Perce were usually at the camas fields digging the bulbs or at the rivers and lakes fishing for salmon. Some of the men were preparing to go over the mountains for the annual buffalo hunt. They had decided to postpone for several days so that they could talk about the new laws Doctor White had brought with him. Father's sermon was especially long, and my clothes were especially itchy, and all I could think about was Tashe. I knew that Timothy would be coming that morning, so I had several carrots in my pocket to give Tashe. When they arrived, she came straight to me and nuzzled up against my shoulder; I felt the hairs on the back of my neck stand up as I rubbed her beautiful long neck and gave her one of the carrots.

Chief Timothy looked down and smiled, "She is happy to see you with or without the treat. I would let you ride her, but it is the Sabbath, so we will have to wait for another day."

Another day was going to be at least a million years away as far as I was concerned. He asked me to take off her bridle and blanket and let her out to graze, so I took the long way around to the grassy hill where the other horses were grazing and gave her the two carrots I was saving before turning her loose. I was watching Tashe and had lost all track of time until I saw little Henry running up the hill to find me. He told me that Mother had been looking for me and needed me to give her a hand with the dishes. Later as I sat there listening to Father's sermon, again, all I could think about was Tashe, beautiful Tashe, and the feel of her velvet coat. For me, she was the essence of a young girl's dream of happiness.

Since there were so many people, Father had to hold the service outdoors, making it even harder since I could see Tashe running and playing with the other horses. There is something almost telepathic about the way a group of horses move together as one. Like the way the wind moves the trees or the way the water turns through a fast-moving stream, they seem to know instinctively how to move together without colliding.

Mother could see that I had drifted off and had to gently squeeze my leg to bring me back to Father's sermon. I know it must be a sin of some kind, but I couldn't remember a single word he said later on, and yet it didn't feel like I had done anything wrong. I also knew that deep down, no matter how hard I tried, I could never be as good as Mother; I don't think anyone could, for that matter. She never loses her patience and always has time for everyone, even when she has a hundred things to do. Father says that without her, the mission would have never succeeded, that it was her calm and gentle ways that won the hearts of the Nez Perce People. They respected how she had learned to speak their language well enough to communicate before she ever reached the Oregon Territories, now speaking it almost like her native language. They also knew that when her mind was made up, that her stubbornness was monumental. Father once told me that sometimes she scared him because she so rarely got angry. She would store her anger like a squirrel stores nuts for the winter. When she blew up, it was like a volcano, something not to get in the way of.

The one thing I do remember from that sermon was when the Nez Perce choir sang Amazing Grace. It was as if the Holy Spirit had risen through my feet into my heart. They did it first in English and then in Nez Perce. Father had tirelessly translated and printed a whole book of hymns phonetically so that they could sing them in their language. At the time, I was too young to understand the significance of the work he was doing, especially the Bible translations. My memories of the printing room are mostly of the smell of ink and sound of the press.

After the hymns, my gaze quickly turned back to the hill where the horses were grazing. Tashe stood out as if dressed for the sham battle painted with streamers flowing red and blue behind her. I couldn't stop myself from wondering what it would be like to have a horse like her, how far could we go together? Could we take the

Oregon Trail to New York like Mother and Father had; could I meet my real Grandmother, Grandfather, aunts, uncles, and cousins?

Growing up so isolated at Lapwai and hardly knowing any other white children, I often wondered if I would fit in or if they would even like me. Mother knew how much I loved to hear about her growing up on a big farm in New York, in a beautiful home with a loving family and friends, and never refused to tell me about it. I could almost hear the sounds of her family and picture what it must have been like. She told me that leaving was the hardest thing she ever had to do, but she felt compelled to do something meaningful with her life; that she had grown to love the Nez Perce like her own family and never planned to leave.

Chapter 11

The Camas Harvest

It was time for the annual trip to the camas fields, and everyone was excited as we prepared to go. It was hard, hot, dirty work digging up the plants, but it was a festive and social time that everyone looked forward to, and we were allowed to play almost as much as we worked. That summer, looking back, was one of the best of my life. Timpstetelew and I were old enough now that we were free to roam, exploring every nook and cranny.

The morning we left for our trip; I could hardly wake up. I had lain in bed tossing and turning most of the night in anticipation and couldn't sleep. Father came in, picked me up, and carried me to the window so that I could see Timpstetelew in the yard already packed with her blanket on her horse. That was all it took to get me going; I had packed the night before, and in minutes, I was dressed in my favorite blue calico dress, wool socks and shoes, and ready to go.

Timpstetelew was dressed in a beautiful white doeskin dress with beads and a matching pair of moccasins that her mother had just made for her. It made my worn dress and shoes look pretty drab, but Father told me I could wear the one that Bear Hunter's wife had made for me when we reached the camas fields. Mother felt it was best only to wear it for special occasions; that we should be careful not to take pride in material things. She had always told me that when I see someone with something beautiful that I should be happy for them, that a person's real beauty is in their heart. I was truly happy to see my best friend looking so pretty and couldn't wait to get outside and share in her joy. I knew it was probably a sin, but

I couldn't help but picture myself on Tashe's back with my beautiful doeskin dress and moccasins flying through the hills beside Timpstetelew with the wind in my hair.

By the time I got to the breakfast table, the whole household was bustling with activity, and Father was looking for his watch. Little Henry was running all over the house, and Mother was trying to make breakfast and get us all packed at the same time. As I sat there at the table, my wool socks started itching, but I knew that Father would let me put on my old moccasins as soon as we were on our way. He had asked me to collect all of my things, including the gathering baskets that Matilda had made for me, that we were running low on medicinal plants.

Matilda had always taken me with her looking for herbs and plants since I was a toddler, and over time, I had developed a keen eye. It made me feel good inside when Father told me that I had the best eye for plants that he had ever seen in a white person.

After breakfast, I grabbed all of my things and ran outside to join Timpstetelew and saddle up old Ricketts. Ricketts was Father's old horse, and I had been riding him for what seemed like forever. He was a big gray stallion that must have been about 100 years old. He was sweet and gentle, and I loved him, but he was not very exciting to ride, and it took a lot to get him going fast. Timpstetelew's father had just given her a beautiful new spotted pony and taught her to ride with just a blanket. I still had to use the hard, old squaw saddle with the long pommel in front and the high curved back. It was made out of wood with leather stretched over it, but I was so happy to be going that I didn't mind the hard saddle.

When I got outside, Timpstetelew threw her arm over my shoulder, turned me to the east, and said, "Look." I had been so caught up in getting my things together that I hadn't noticed the sunrise. We stood there with our arms around each other and watched as the sun slowly rose over the Bitterroot Mountains. Since we rise before the sun every day except on the Sabbath, I have seen hundreds of sunrises, but this was like nothing I had ever seen before, almost like a dream world. It felt as if God wanted to show us His majesty, just how beautiful the world that he had made for us could be.

There was a layer of clouds hovering above the mountains, and as the sun cleared, they turned a luminescent cream and gold color. I heard Father and Mother coming out of the door talking, but they must have seen us there with our arms around each other, looking at the sky, and stopped. I felt Father put his hands on my shoulders, and saw Mother do the same with Timpstetelew. I half expected one of them to tell us to quit dawdling, but they didn't. I could hear the footsteps of others coming up behind us, but no one said a word.

The clouds were starting to turn orange with red streamers stretching across the horizon, and it seemed as if time was stretching with the clouds. The sky then turned pink and violet with white and cream patches peeking out through the swirling patterns. It made me think of a piece of maple that Father had just milled. He told me that it had the most unusual grain he had ever seen in a piece of wood. It didn't look like much to me until he took a cup of water and poured it over the board, like magic, it changed colors and came to life with dark and light patterns. That was what the sky and clouds reminded me of that morning, except for the pale blue backdrop of a limitless sky.

No one said a word; we instinctively seemed to know that we were witnessing something immensely beautiful together. In minutes the colors began turning a thousand shades of gray and white, and it was time to go. Father was talking with little Henry, who was making his first real trip.

Mother came and wrapped me in her arms and asked me, "Eliza, do you remember a while ago asking why I loved to paint so much?" I told her that I did. She told me, "I never felt like I gave you a good answer. I remember talking about themes and light and color, but nothing about how it made me feel. That sunrise made me feel like I was as close to heaven as I could get here on earth, that's why I love to paint." Looking back, I can't imagine anything more beautiful than that moment, the feel of her arms around me, the sweet smell of her body, her precious gift of unconditional love. The sunrise had put everyone in a good mood, especially Father, who, for no reason at all, picked me up in his strong arms and swung me around in the air as if I was weightless.

We spent that night out under the stars listening to stories and the sound of the wolves and coyotes in the distance. I know how dangerous they can be, but they sounded so lonely that my heart went out to them. Chief Timothy had a dog that was part wolf, with the most beautiful blue eyes that I had ever seen. He could be fierce with strangers, but was always gentle and loving with me, especially since I made a point of bringing him a piece of jerky whenever I visited.

We traveled single file much of the time since the trail was very narrow in places, especially through the hills. The Nez Perce were singing a song that had no words, just rhythmic sounds and feelings. Somehow, I felt it might have been a song that celebrated and gave thanks for the beauty and bounty of the land. Father let me ride next to Timpstetelew when there was enough room, and we could see the men ahead sitting up so straight and proud on their beautiful war ponies. They had brought along a group of wild horses and colts to be broken before they went on to the next buffalo hunt. For me, it was about the most exciting thing I could imagine and couldn't wait to watch the horses twisting and turning, running and jumping, wild with fear and excitement. Chief Timothy once told me that there are people who are gifted with horses, that they have the ability to feel their hearts and understand their fears.

We reached the camas fields about mid-morning and there was a layer of fog covering it like a soft down comforter over a bed full of sleeping children. When it started to clear, small purple flowers began poking their heads through the fog, and as the sun warmed the earth, the entire valley began to smell like sweet perfume. When we visited the Whitmans last year, Mrs. Whitman let me smell a small bottle of perfume that her sister had sent her in one of the mission barrels. She put a dash on her finger and rubbed it on my neck, and the smell was so wonderful that I refused to wash my neck for days until the scent was completely gone.

This was almost everyone's favorite time of year, especially the children who were allowed to explore the forests as long as we didn't wander off too far. The women were busy putting up the teepees and preparing to dig the camas roots. The men had built a corral and then gone out to find fresh game. Timpstetelew and I were completely absorbed in our own world of make-believe. We had constructed teepees with blankets and had made dolls out of cloth and sticks. We pretended that they were our babies, and even designed packs that we could put on our backs to carry them so we wouldn't get too tired holding them.

Every morning the women and girls would ride to a nearby stream so that we could bathe together. The water was freezing to me but didn't seem to bother the others at all. Everyone else had taken off all of their clothes, not seeming to notice, let alone feel embarrassed that they were completely naked. Mother had told Matilda that I was to wear my old dress with the holes in it if I went swimming. All of the other girls were laughing and swimming back and forth from one side of the creek to the other. Every time I tried to swim across, the dress would pull me down, and I would sink like a stone and come up gasping with a mouth full of water. Matilda was trying to quiet the other children who were laughing at me as I struggled. I know that they didn't mean any harm, but it hurt my feelings.

The Indian people don't have swear words, or even words to hurt each other like we do. They tell you directly or by their body language what they are thinking or feeling. I finally gave up and got out of the water, shivering in my old dress that was stuck to me as if it had been glued on with ice water. I sat down on a warm rock, trembling as I watched the others swimming, splashing, and having fun.

Timpstetelew got out of the water and sat next to me and asked why I had to wear the dress, that it made no sense at all. I told her that Mother didn't think it proper for me to be undressed in front of other people. She thought about that for a while and then told me that white people had a strange way of looking at things, that it was just not smart to swim with clothes on, that I should take them off, so I didn't drown myself. I told her that Matilda was supposed to be watching over me and would tell Mother if I did. Timpstetelew jumped in the water and swam over to Matilda and was back in less than a minute.

She said that Matilda was going to turn her back to us, and wouldn't see anything I did. Timpstetelew helped me take off the clothes that were stuck to me until I was as naked as everyone else was. I thought that an alarm would sound throughout the entire valley, and my Mother and Father would come running out of the bushes, but no one even seemed to notice or care. This time I jumped in the water, not noticing how cold it was, it was the most wonderful feeling I had ever known, and I skimmed through the water like a slippery fish. Timpstetelew dove in next to me, and we joined the other girls splashing and racing back and forth across the crystal stream. Several times I looked over at Matilda, who was heating rocks for a steam bath, but never saw her look at me.

When we finally decided to get out, I went to where my dress had been, but it was gone. At first, I was alarmed, but then noticed a blanket in its place that had been warmed by the hot rocks. As we approached the camp Matilda had arranged, I could see that my dress and underclothes had been placed over a bush next to the fire to dry. The warm old blanket felt like a divine shroud draped over my shoulders. Every day after that one, I bathed with the others, completely unselfconscious of my nakedness. I have no idea if

Matilda ever told Mother or Father what had happened, but if she had, nothing was ever said to me.

Not long after we had returned, the young men came thundering back into camp with two deer and an assortment of birds. Father and Chief Timothy had gone for the day to a nearby village to visit with old friends. Chief Timothy had left Tashe at our camp to rest from the long ride, and Matilda gave me one of the camas bulbs that she had cut into several pieces to give Tashe as a treat.

When I got to where the horses were grazing, young men were gathered around preparing for their favorite activity, racing. There was a disagreement going on between two of them. One of the younger men was saying that since Chief Timothy had become a Christian, he had not allowed Tashe to race and that he would race her to see if she was still the fastest. Timpstetelew's father, Golden Eagle, was telling him that Chief Timothy had not given him permission, that it would be wrong to race her without it.

When it was finally decided that Tashe should not be raced without permission, the young man said that Tashe had become an old nag, that his horse could beat her easily in a race. I was so mad that I walked up to him and told him that Tashe was not an old nag and that I could beat his horse, riding backward on old Rickets. They all started laughing out loud and slapping each other on their backs, even the young warrior.

Timpstetelew's father said, "Like her mother, she has the heart of a warrior."

He looked at the others and asked, "Are you not frightened by that look in her eyes and the way she puts her hands on her hips, like Mrs. Spalding."

They erupted in laughter again and try as I may to be serious, I couldn't help myself and finally joined in with them until I could hardly breathe. It was good that Father was gone since he didn't like to see them gambling. I didn't care one bit about the gambling, but couldn't wait to see them race. I had to admit to myself that I was disappointed that Tashe wouldn't be able to show them her tremendous speed.

It was one of the most exciting things I had ever seen. The men had arranged several different kinds of races. The first was the longest and started where a pole had been placed with banners hanging from it. They had put streamers from certain trees that they would race out to and around several times. If I had to guess, I would say that the race was about two miles or so.

For the next one, they put another pole in the ground about three hundred yards away and raced around it and back twice. The last race, they arranged six thin poles between the one that was out three hundred yards. They had to swerve between them and only went around and back once. They could bump into one, but if they knocked it down, they were disqualified.

Once they got started, all you could hear was the sound of horse's hoofs beating the ground like the drums of a Nez Perce war dance. The rhythm seemed to be beating precisely the way my heart was pounding in my chest. The most exciting part was when they set me down at the finish line and told me I was the guest of honor, that if it were close, I would decide the winner.

I think it had something to do with the earlier scene I had made.

One of the older men was sitting right behind me in case I got excited and made a wrong decision. When they were done racing, there was a feast of roasted venison and camas cakes. The cakes reminded me of the sweet potatoes that we grew and were delicious. That afternoon was almost as exciting as the races when the men began breaking the colts and wild horses. Several of the young men were thrown, but thank goodness no one was badly injured.

Timpstetelew's father was said to have a gift with horses and was often asked to help the others with the wild ones. He would always approach each horse very slowly, talking softly and calmly until he was close enough to touch them by rubbing their neck or nose.

With one of the horses, he just squatted down for the longest time, never saying a word or even moving. The horse pawed at the dirt for a while and then slowly took a step at a time until they were almost face-to-face. Timpstetelew's father then gently rubbed the horse's face and began talking as if they were old friends. I could watch him for hours as he demonstrated and explained his method to the younger men. He had a gentle but firm touch, telling the young men that the most important thing was to gain the horse's trust; that the young ones were like children and needed to be given love and respect mixed with discipline.

He told them that horses have a language of their own, and you could tell by the way they moved their body, ears, or tail what they were thinking. He explained that an angry man would usually have an angry horse, that a quiet heart was the way to calm a horse and gain trust, just like a child. He told the young men that twice his horse had saved his life by alerting him that enemies were nearby by shaking its head and turning its ears in a certain direction. Within less than an hour, he could have a horse moving in any direction he wanted, left, right, slow forward, fast forward, stop, backward. He said that a well-trained horse could feel where you wanted to go by the way that you put pressure on its back, that this was life or death when hunting buffalo with a bow and arrow.

With three other girls, we had our own teepee, but slept most nights out under the stars listening to little Henry's endless questions and the sound of the wind murmuring through the trees. I could almost see myself up in the heavens, racing to keep up with the shooting stars, wondering if we were made out of the same stuff. Since that summer, I have never felt closer to the earth and sky, or more loved as a human being.

Chapter 12

A Mad Dash for Home

We had been home for a little over a week when Father received word that the Whitmans were running low on supplies and wanted to know if we could bring them flour and grains for the coming winter. The Whitmans now had so many immigrants to provide supplies for, that it was hard for them even to provision themselves. It had been a bumper year for Father's crops and cattle, so he was glad to do all he could to help.

It took him the better part of a week to get the flour milled and everything prepared and packed. Since we had just returned from the camas harvest, Father was concerned that it might be too much traveling for me but knew my feelings would be hurt if I wasn't asked to go. My answer was to run to my room and start packing. He and Mother had decided to keep little Henry home since he had developed a mild cough and fever. Father told him that he had an important job for him, and that he was to take care of Mother while we were gone and protect her if she needed help. I think little Henry knew he was being tricked, but he still loved the comfort of being with Mother, so he told Father that he understood and would make sure that nothing bad happened to her.

Chief Timothy decided to go with us and bring two young men to help with the packhorses. He had friends and a favorite young nephew that he wanted to visit with the Cayuse tribe. His nephew had just gotten married, and he was bringing him two horses, a stallion, and a mare as a wedding present.

The 120-mile trip was going to take us at least four days and three nights since Father planned to take three cows and four sheep. When Chief Timothy showed up on Tashe, I could feel my heart speed up. As we prepared to leave, he handed me her reins and told me that I could ride her. Father finally had to tell me to stop spinning and jumping up and down, that it was beginning to make him dizzy. It was the first time I had ever ridden without a saddle, and I was so comfortable that I could have ridden all day and night without getting the least bit tired. Chief Timothy told me that Tashe would respond to any small movement that I made. If I leaned left, she would go left, if I leaned right, she would go right, and if I leaned back, she would stop. The harder I leaned, the more she would respond. I asked him how he made her take off so quickly, and he told me that he leaned forward with a small hop and gentle kick to the ribs.

I asked, "Would it be alright if I try it?"

He looked at Father, who must have taken what seemed like half an hour to nod his head. It's a good thing that I was leaning way forward, or I would have been thrown off her back. In a matter of seconds, I was going so fast that everything was a blur. I had never gone that fast in my life, I had never even seen anything go that fast, and I could tell that she was enjoying it as much as I was. When I gently leaned back, she immediately started to slow down, and by the time we turned around, I could hardly see Father and Chief Timothy. When I got back, Father shook his head, and the chief was smiling.

Father told me that I better not try that again, that he didn't want to have to explain to Mother how her daughter had gotten injured or killed on a lightning-fast horse without a saddle.

Later on, when Father was talking with one of the other men, Chief Timothy leaned over and tapped me on the leg, "She goes fast, huh!"

My face automatically broke into a smile so big that it almost cracked my lips as I said, "She goes fast."

We had planned to stay for three or four days so Father could have a meeting with Mr. Gray, Mr. Walker, and Mr. Eells about the direction of the missions. They also planned to discuss Doctor Whitman's return trip to New York to address the problems with the missionary board that they had finally resolved among themselves.

We had just arrived at Waiilatpu as a Nez Perce messenger came riding up in a cloud of dust. He told Father that Mother was very sick and might be dying, and that we needed to return immediately. I have seen Father get pretty emotional over small things, but when something big happens, he gets very calm. He asked one of the men to get the horses and told me to get my things together and be ready to go in five minutes.

I hadn't heard the part about Mother dying, but I instinctively knew that something was very wrong. Mrs. Whitman told Father that it would be best to leave me with her, and that he could travel faster on his own. Father thanked her but said that it was important I come with him, that I had never slowed him down in the past. I think he was making sure that if Mother was dying, that I would get to see her again and be able to say goodbye. Chief Timothy said that

I might not slow him down, but old Rickets would, and that I should take Tashe. I was so worried about Mother that it was hard for me to think about riding Tashe, but I still knew that this was a great honor.

Within minutes, we had gathered all of our things. Father dropped to his knees in the wet grass and asked that we pray together. We all did the same as he asked God to please grant his mercy and spare Mother's life and give us a safe journey. Now I knew that something was seriously wrong and started to worry. As soon as he finished the prayer, we were ready to go, Father on his big black stallion Thunder, and me on Tashe.

It was a mad dash for home, unlike anything I would ever experience again in my lifetime.

In some places, the trail was too narrow to ride side by side, so Father led the way throwing up a cloud of dust and flying dirt from Thunder's giant hoofs. Tashe instinctively knew how far to stay back to keep the dust and dirt out of our eyes and not fall behind. Maybe it was just my nerves standing on edge, but I felt as though Tashe could sense our urgency and was willing to do anything I asked of her.

At first, Father stopped every couple of miles to make sure that I was all right and keeping up. After several hours of hard riding, he stopped to rest the horses and have some water and food that Mrs. Whitman had prepared for us. We said another prayer before leaving and were on our way like two shooting stars racing across the sky.

On Tashe, even the squaw saddle they had given me to use on the trip back felt smooth and comfortable. Neither horse ever faltered or stumbled even at high speed over the uneven and rocky elk trails. I had never done anything like that before and had no idea how long the horses could keep up the pace. I had heard of horses being ridden to death or ruined, but I couldn't imagine that happening to Tashe. The next time we stopped to rest and get a drink of water, Father told me that if we rode through the night, we could be there by morning. He looked concerned and asked me if I was too tired to go on. I told him that if I had a horse like Tashe, I could ride to New York without getting tired.

We said another prayer for Mother and were on our way. We rode like a windstorm over the plains' knee-high grasses barely slowing through the heavily wooded forests, spraying water droplets in every direction as we charged through the shallow creeks. It usually takes three days to ride from Lapwai to Waiilatpu, and we were going to try and make it in less than one full day. That morning had been cool and comfortable, but by midday it was hot and dusty, and the horses were starting to lather up.

It was afternoon when we stopped at a small creek to rest and eat before starting into the mountains. The horses drank deeply, and we poured water over them to try and cool them down. I was getting tired, but I knew that resting might be the difference between life and death, so I told Father that I could keep going as long as he could.

Lifting his eyebrows, he gave me a sideways smile and said, "Just like your mother ... alright, papoose, let's go."

The red sun was sinking into the west as we arrived at the summit and started our descent down the narrow and dangerous trail. I started to nod off at the worst time and had to slap my cheeks and pinch my hands to stay awake. Father alerted me before we reached a dangerous section where it dropped off over a cliff five hundred feet below. I could feel my stomach tighten up as we passed by, but I was so tired that there was little fear left in me.

Thunder was having much more trouble with the narrow rocky trail because of his big hooves and powerful body. With her small hooves and strong legs, Tashe moved along the trail with the sureness of a mountain goat. Try as I may, I couldn't stay awake, and as I drifted off, I started to slip out of my saddle. Tashe came to a sudden stop, jolting me wide-awake before I fell off.

I was so grateful that I leaned over her neck and hugged her to thank her for saving me. Father must have sensed something and turned around to ask if I was still able to ride, that there was a wide spot coming up where we could rest. I told him that I was thanking Tashe for being so brave, and that we should keep going. I then asked God to forgive me for the white lie.

That night the temperature dropped close to freezing, and my fingers and toes had gone numb; my teeth were chattering like a room full of four-year-olds all talking at once. When we finally came out of the mountains, it was still pitch dark. We could hear the river, sounding much louder than it had when we crossed just days earlier. We had crossed this part of the river several times before, during the same time of year, with no problems at all, but there had been a flash flood several days earlier farther north, and it sounded fast.

Father asked, "There's a safer crossing about ten miles south, what do you think?"

I told him that I wanted to go since we were getting close to home, and both horses were good swimmers.

I could just see his silhouette ahead as he said, "Let's go."

When we hit the water, it was like liquid ice, and the swift current was instantly dragging us downstream with no bottom for the horses to take hold of. I had no idea what to expect, yet it still took me by surprise as the freezing water surged up to my chest. Father yelled for me not to hold the bridle too tight—to grab the saddle and hold on for dear life. The river felt mean, and I could tell it was trying with all of its might to tear me off of Tashe's back and drag me to a cold, watery death.

Just a hint of light was beginning to come up over the mountains, and I could see that Father was about ten feet in front of me. Thunder became frightened and panicked, trying to throw Father off of his back so he could swim easier. I urged Tashe forward, and to the right, in case I had to help. I'm not sure what Father did, but he finally managed to get Thunder under control and swimming toward the shore. When we reached the other side, the horses came out blowing steam from their nostrils, even more frightened and exhausted than we were.

We had to rest for about 15 minutes for the horses to catch their breath. My clothes were so cold that it felt as if they were on fire, and I couldn't feel my hands or feet any longer. I was shaking like a leaf in a strong wind and having trouble breathing. Father started rubbing my shoulders and arms as hard as he could until I was breathing evenly again.

It was starting to get light as Father said, "It's about 20 more miles, papoose, we better get going before we freeze to death."

He turned Thunder toward home, and when I was pointing the same way, I leaned forward, hopped, and yelled he-yah. Within seconds Tashe and I were streaking toward home. I would guess that Thunder didn't want to be outrun by two young girls, so he gave it his best effort to keep up, so I decided to hold Tashe back a little.

By the time we reached home, I couldn't feel anything, which was almost a blessing. I didn't intend it, but Tashe had beaten Thunder by over five minutes. As I dismounted, I fell to the ground, and my legs collapsed like a broken chair. I wasn't hurt, so I started crawling toward the house as Mustups came running out to help. When Father arrived, he dismounted and started running toward me, but I waved him off and told him that my legs had just gone to sleep, to take care of Mother first.

Father jumped the gate and was in the house before Mustups could pick me up off the ground. Mustups took me into the living room where a warm fire was burning and put a blanket over my shoulders. He told me I should get out of my wet clothes before I got sick; I told him I would as soon as I knew how Mother was doing. The door to the bedroom was closed, but I could hear Mother and Matilda talking with Father. The five or so minutes I had to wait, felt like five years being dragged over hot coals. When Father finally came out, he was smiling. I broke into tears as he pulled me into his arms to comfort me. He said that Mother was very weak and sick, but Matilda told him that she was getting better instead of worse and that the fever was coming down.

"She wants to see you, but remember she's weak and shouldn't get excited. You better save the story about our trip for when she gets better."

As he carried me to the bedroom, my face was snuggled down into the crook of his neck, but when I entered the bedroom, I looked down onto the most beautiful smile God had ever placed on a human being's face. Father set me down on the bed next to her, and I put my frozen hands into her warm ones, and she squeezed them tightly. Hope surged through my soul as I realized the world my mother had made for me with her warm and loving heart was still alive. As I dropped to my knees to thank God, I saw Father do the same, and I knew everything was going to be all right.

Whatever Mother had contracted, it was not going away, and we were all becoming alarmed. The Nez Perce were also concerned, lingering around the house, wanting to know what was wrong with "Mrs. Spalding." Several of the women wanted to come into the house to see if they could be of any help, but Father told them that it might be contagious, and that they would have to wait until she was well. Once again, it was Doctor Whitman who came to her rescue, and within hours Mother was feeling better. He thought it might be acute anemia. I don't know if it was the medicine or the comfort of having Doctor Whitman there to help, but Mother was feeling much better by the next morning. I could smell Matilda's wonderful cooking and knew that she had made the doctor breakfast with fresh hot bread and butter.

When Doctor Whitman came into the room to check on her, he smiled and said, "It looks like the medicine must be working."

We each took turns thanking him before Father said, "Marcus, just having you here is the elixir Eliza needed."

Father paused for a while, thinking about what he needed to say, "Eliza and I are concerned about so many people coming into the territory; if it causes trouble, the Indian people may turn against us."

"I have the same concerns Henry, but like it or not, they're coming, and the only thing we can do is try and help prepare for it. The government wants this territory to join the rest of the United States."

"Is there anything we can do to slow it down?"

"I don't think so. People back East are hungry for land. The government has started offering parcels of 320 acres to anyone willing to come west to settle. I think all we can do for now is try to keep the ones coming into the territory moving on to the Willamette Valley and coastal areas."

He then said, "There is one other thing I wanted to discuss with you. Narcissa and I have talked about starting a school for the white children and families staying over for the winter to help us at the mission. We plan to hire a teacher and wanted to ask if Eliza would like to join us, little Henry could come the next year when he's a little older."

Mother was the first to speak. "Henry and I had been hoping for something like this. I think it's a good idea."

I didn't realize that I had been shaking my head no the whole time they were talking until Mother said, "Eliza, I know how much you love it here, but it's time for you to know about your people. Everything you learn, you can bring back and share with the Nez Perce."

Father nodded his agreement, but I was still shaking my head no. No matter how much I liked the Whitmans, I couldn't imagine leaving my family and friends to go off to school with a bunch of strangers who might not even like me.

Doctor Whitman looked at me and said, "What do you think, Eliza?"

I shook my head and said, "No, thank you, Doctor Whitman."

He smiled and said, "Well, you have almost a year."

I was still shaking my head no as he said, "You think it over and talk about it with your parents; you have plenty of time."

He stood up, shook hands with Mother, Father, and little Henry and tousled my hair again and said goodbye as he readied his old mule for another 120-mile trip.

By the next week, Mother was once again her old self. Father was working harder than ever cutting the trees needed for the school and floating them down the Kooskoosky River to our mission, where it took at least a dozen men to carry each of them to the mill next to the mission.

He had the mill going almost every day, and I loved the smell of the fresh-cut pine and cedar boards. The building was going to be 50 by 30 feet, hopefully, large enough to accommodate everyone for all of the classes and meetings.

Little Henry and I used the stacks of lumber to play on until Mother told us that she was tired of trying to clean the pitch out of our clothes, that if we didn't find some other place to play, we would be doing the laundry from now on.

The weather was still mild outside, and all I could think about was riding through the hills with Tashe and Timpstetelew on her new horse. When school got going, I was asked to help a group of the other children, including Timpstetelew and Charging Elk, with their reading and writing. Most of the assignments were taken from the Bible, and I was trying to teach the parable about the Good Samaritan as best I could. When I reached the part that says, "Thou shalt love thy neighbor as thyself," one of the boys asked me, "What is a neighbor." I told him that it meant that we are supposed to love everyone. Charging Elk asked loudly, "Are we to even love those who would steal our horses, or try to keep us from the buffalo hunting grounds?"

Mother had been listening and asked Mr. Lee to watch her group of younger children as she gathered her pencils, paint, and brushes. She took a piece of paper and started sketching a scene in which a man was lying in a ditch on the side of the road. He had been badly beaten and robbed. When the sketch was finished, she filled it in with watercolors as she explained that the man had gone to town to purchase supplies and was robbed, beaten, and left for dead by a group of thieves.

She then started another drawing of the man lying in the ditch with a priest looking at the injured man from the other side of the road, refusing to help. When she finished painting that one, she started drawing another scene in which a wealthy man with a trail of donkeys loaded with riches went past the injured man without offering to help in any way. When that was finished, she started one showing a man from a place called Samaria covering the injured man with his blanket and helping him onto his horse.

She explained that the Samarian man treated the injured man's wounds and was taking him to a lodge where he could rest and recover. The last drawing was of the injured man lying on a bed with the Samarian man and innkeeper looking down on him. Mother explained that it was the custom among the Samarians to help all in need. He told the innkeeper that he would be back in several days and gave the innkeeper money to care for the injured man; that he would give him more when he returned if necessary.

Eventually, this attracted everyone in the schoolroom, and we were all squeezed in together watching.

When she finished, she said, "That is what a neighbor is," there was a long and loud ahhh sound of approval.

Chief Timothy stood and said, "It is good when Mrs. Spalding teaches us from the Book of Heaven, I have seen many things in my life that tell me this is a true story; that the Nez Perce are like the Samarians, of good hearts." Once again, everyone let out a long ahhh.

By early winter, the new school and meeting house were finished, and we were ready to start moving everything over from the old one. Father was going to move Mother's spinning wheel and loom as well as his printing press out of the storeroom and into the old schoolhouse. The new school was big and bright, with neat rows of windows on all sides and fireplaces at each end. The aromatic smell of the freshly cut cedar and pine was almost intoxicating. Everyone wanted to come inside and see it. The children automatically started dancing around the room as if that was its sole purpose.

When classes resumed, there were so many people that we still couldn't fit everyone in and had to hold some in the old schoolhouse. Mother and Father were so busy preparing lessons that they were often up all night and had to designate others to help with the things they couldn't find time to do. There was a small group of students who were so advanced that Father and Mother would work with them in the house after supper.

It was their hope that these students would one day become teachers and learn to run their own missions, helping their people build homes and cultivate the land. This was the pot of gold that Mother and Father had dreamed of, the reason they had endured so many hardships to come to this land, and I had never seen them so happy and fulfilled.

Later that year, a regrettable event took place that would eventually lead to further tension and conflict between the whites and Indians.

During the summer of 1844, a party of over 50 Indians from various tribes, including the Nez Perce, Spokanes, Cayuse, Umatilla, and Walla Walla, departed for California in the hope of trading horses and furs for cattle. Among the tribes, only a few owned cattle that they had traded with the immigrants who were passing through their lands. They were highly prized and desired not only for their value as food but as a sign of status. Since the Hudson Bay Trading Company refused to sell cattle to the Indian people, they decided to take the perilous journey over the treacherous Klamath Mountains with peaks reaching over nine thousand feet, hostile tribes, and rivers like the Klamath, John Day, and Rogue that ran hard and fast. The leader was Peopeomoxmox, also known as Yellow Bird of the Walla Walla tribe.

His eldest son Toayahnu had attended Jason Lee's Methodist school in the Willamette Valley and been christened and named Elijah Hedding after a well-known American bishop of the

Methodist Episcopal Church. He had seen firsthand the value of the cattle that had been brought in from the Northern California settlements. Their party included Tauitau, Spokane Gary, Kipkip Pahlekin, and several other headmen from different tribes. Because of the highly prized horses they had brought to trade, they traveled as a war party to deter any of the other Indian tribes they might encounter from attacking them.

The Klamath and Shasta tribes were tight-knit groups who disliked trespassers and poachers, threatening war with anyone who lingered on their lands. They were a rugged people who lived under extremely harsh mountain conditions, but it was a land rich with fish and game that they had no intention of sharing with any of the other tribes. Along the way, the men encountered mountain lions, grizzly bears, black bears, bobcats, gray wolves, lynx, raccoons, martens, fishers, beavers, gray fox, red fox, flying squirrel, elk and deer. Bird species included golden eagles, bald eagles, woodpeckers, band-tailed pigeon, several species of hawks, and various owl species, including the spotted owl.

In spring, the tribes would fish along the rivers, which were abundant with salmon. Peter Skeen Ogden of the Hudson Bay Company was the first white trapper to cross and hunt these mountains in 1826. His success was due in part to the fact that he offered valuable trade goods with the possibility of repeat business.

As the Indian party descended the Klamath Mountains, they eventually came upon the Sacramento River Valley before arriving at Fort Sutter. The Swiss immigrant John Sutter, who had first arrived in New York in 1834, had constructed it. He was a brilliant man who spoke Swiss, Spanish, English, French, and passable

Miwok he had learned from a local tribe he had befriended. He discovered one of the largest gold concentrations ever found in California but was unable to keep it secret. His fortune was made and then lost as thousands of gold seekers flooded into the valley.

Mr. Sutter had previously met and traded with several of the Indian tribes of the Oregon Territory, so things went smoothly at first. Five Crows had made a good trade of their horses and furs for cattle with the ranchers in the area and were making plans for their return trip.

They decided to go on a hunt before they left and found themselves in a skirmish with one of the local Indian tribes. They captured over 20 horses and mules, then returned to Sutter's Fort to gather their cattle and supplies. Before leaving, several of the ranchers identified the horses as ones that had been stolen from them earlier and demanded their return.

Elijah Hedding and the other Indian leaders refused. One of the Americans named Grove Cook was a notorious Indian hater who had killed in the past with no provocation whatsoever. During an argument with Elijah over the horses, Cook pulled his pistol, shot, and killed Hedding, leading to an intense fight between the Indians and the ranchers and settlers. Greatly outnumbered, Five Crows and his men fled without their cattle, extra horses, or supplies.

They arrived at Fort Walla Walla in the fall, enraged at the Americans, reaching out to all of the tribes to unite and seek revenge for the murder of Elijah. There was a great council that included the Walla Walla, Nez Perce, Cayuse, Pend d' Oreilles, and Shoshones, in which Peopeomoxmox called for the extermination of all Americans in the Oregon Territories.

It was suggested that they take several thousand warriors to the Sacramento Valley and annihilate the Americans there as well. The fever of war ran high, but there was nothing that could be done until the extreme winter conditions melted into spring. In the interim, cooler heads prevailed, and eventually, Peopeomoxmox met with Doctor McLaughlin, who explained that a war with the Americans would lead to certain disaster for his people. He told him that the Americans would send armies with weapons that the Indian people could not even imagine; that the British would not get in the middle of a war between the two to protect them. He reminded the chief that the new laws instituted by Doctor White could be used to punish the man who had killed his son. He then suggested that the chief petition Doctor White to take action against the offender Grove Cook.

Chief Ellis was sent as representative to request that Doctor White bring the killer to justice. Fearing that Elijah's murder might lead to an attack on all whites in the territory, my parents and the Whitmans also wrote letters that reached Doctor White at the same time as Chief Ellis's.

Under his own laws, Doctor White was obligated to find the killer and hang him. He had no idea how he would enforce the law on a man so far away under a completely different government jurisdiction. Instead, he wined and dined Chief Ellis to keep him from pressing the issue.

He promised, "I will write to the Governor of California as well as Captain Sutter, and to our great chiefs, respecting this matter. I will use every measure to get this unhappy affair adjusted and bring the murderer to justice."

245

He even promised cattle and money from his pocket to appease the chief. Eventually, he did send a letter to the Governor who never bothered to reply. At the same time, Doctor White found himself politically criticized by the settlers. On August 15, 1844, he left for the East without providing any of the cattle or funds he had promised to the Indian people. When he arrived in Washington D.C., he asked Congress to give him jurisdictional autonomy and a salary increase. Messages from the settlements had already reached Congress concerning the displeasure and disappointment with the job he had done. He was dismissed from government service, returning to New York without a thought given to the promises he had made to the Indian people. He would continue to find himself embroiled in troubles of one kind or another throughout the rest of his career.

Chapter 13

The Whitman School

In the fall of 1844, Father had to take a pack train of supplies to the Whitman mission for the immigrants who had just come over the Oregon Trail. I had been sick and had to stay home, but when he returned, he said he had some exciting news to share with us.

"The Whitmans just adopted seven children all from the same family. These poor children have had a rough time; their parents both died along the trail. Mrs. Whitman told me that when they pulled up to the mission house in a broken-down old wagon being pulled by a team of half-dead oxen, they looked so sad and pathetic that her heart immediately went out to them."

Mother said that with the seven Sagers, Helen Mar Meeks, Mary Ann Bridger, David Malin, and Perrin Whitman, Narcissa was going to have her hands full.

Father replied, "That's 11."

Father also told us that the Whitmans had decided that they were committed to starting a school for the white children this year and wanted me to stay with them and go to their school this fall.

I told Father, "I don't want to live with the Whitmans or go to their school. I don't even know who those other people are."

Mother said, "You know Helen Mar and Mary Ann, you played with them the last time we visited Waiilatpu.

"I remember that they couldn't even speak or understand their own language. Mrs. Whitman insisted everyone speak English."

I could tell Father was unhappy when he said, "This is the way it's going to be Eliza. Your Mother and I have already decided that it's what's best for you."

When Father was serious like that, I knew there was no sense in arguing with him, that it would only make him more upset with me; I was going to have to make the best of it.

In so many ways, Mother was the strongest person I had ever known, but she was prone to spells of bad health. She would never say anything to Father when she was feeling poorly, so he would have to pay close attention to how she looked so that she wouldn't overdo. Just days before we were ready to leave, Mother came down sick and looked weak and unwell.

Father told me that he couldn't leave her in that condition, and there were still hundreds of things to do around the mission before winter set in. They had arranged for Matilda to take me since we were so close and she had made the trip many times. I was disappointed at first since Father and I had developed such a close companionship during our trips together, but I dearly loved Matilda and knew that she would take good care of me.

Since I had never been away from home for any length of time, the morning we left was one of the most difficult I can remember. Mother asked me to be strong and not cry; that it would make her cry, and then everyone would be crying like a bunch of hungry babies. She told me that this was a good thing and would make me stronger, and that I would make new friends and learn about the world beyond Lapwai. So many of the Nez Perce People showed up to say goodbye that I couldn't count them all. Timpstetelew's father, Golden Eagle told her that she could ride with me to the river crossing, almost 20 miles. I couldn't stop the tears from running down my face, but I didn't cry aloud and get Mother upset. Matilda was riding old Rickets, and without hesitation, she took the reins of the packhorse, quietly turned and started for Waiilatpu.

The warm fall sun was beginning to dry my tears as I sped past Matilda, who was smiling as I raced by on Father's horse Thunder. The trip would take us four days and three nights, and when I had to say goodbye to Timpstetelew at the river crossing, it felt like my world was coming to an end; that I might never see her again. This must have been something like Mother felt when she left home for the Oregon Trail, though I knew it was not forever, that I would see my family again in the spring. The wind was still, and the Snake River was shallow and almost glassy as we crossed over. I could feel Thunder quivering below me and could tell that he wanted to run. We hit the river hard, sending a shower of sparkling water cascading on both sides, yet we were moving so fast that I barely got wet.

When I turned around to wave goodbye to Timpstetelew, she let out a high-pitched call that could be heard from miles away, one I had never mastered. I was worried that Matilda might be upset that I had sped across the river so fast, but she gave me one of those "girls will be girls" smiles, and I was having a hard time pretending to be sad even to myself.

That night we camped next to a singing creek and listened to the musical water tell its story as we gazed into the infinite stars. Before we settled down for the night, I thanked Thunder for taking my mind off of leaving home by rubbing his neck and shoulders and giving him two of the turnips Mother had put in my bag. I could tell that he was happy.

Matilda built a cozy fire and made a comfortable bed for us to share. It would be hard to put into words how much she meant to me at that moment. Like Mother, she had a quiet heart and listened to every word I said even when I babbled. Whenever I had been sick or had bad dreams, she would get into bed with me and quietly sing to me or tell me stories of her ancestors.

We ate our dinner of brown bread and dried salmon that Mother had prepared and then said our prayers and went to sleep. The creek sounds began to wash over me as I dozed and dreamed of places far away that I had only read or heard about.

The next morning, we left the flatlands and started into the hills. Before long, we were in a forest so thick that the sun hardly ever touched the ground, covered with a thick bed of pine needles. As we came out of the trees, I had to shade my eyes from the dazzling meadow flooded with sunlight. I felt something akin to a deer as it leads its fawn out into an open and unprotected field for the first time with hungry eyes watching every move. Of course, it was nothing more than my overactive imagination.

The second night we were lying under the blankets watching the heavens again when we heard a wolf's lonely cry far off in the distance. I could feel Matilda tense up for a long time as we waited to hear if it would howl again or get an answer from another wolf.

She had told me last year when we were camping out that the single howl of a wolf meant that something bad would happen in the future. Mother told me that every culture has its superstitions, and if we worried about all of them, we would never get any sleep at all. It still took me a long time to get to sleep, and I couldn't help wonder if there was some special meaning in the solo warning.

The next day and night were uneventful, but on the last day, we came to the Cayuse village closest to the Whitman mission. Something felt wrong since there were no friendly greetings; even the dogs were trying to nip at Thunder's legs. There was a group of young men nearby led by Chief Tiloukaikt's son, Edward, racing horses at the edge of the village. When he saw us, he called to the other men nearby and slowly approached us with a menacing sneer on his face.

He rode around us without saying a word, and I knew something bad must have been going on at Waiilatpu for them to be so rude to us. It was a great relief when we finally cleared a nearby hill and no longer had to listen to the men racing and dogs barking.

As we descended the hill to the mission, we could see the Walla Walla River lazily stretching out before us. Smoke was coming from the mission fireplaces as I asked Matilda why they called this place Waiilatpu.

She told me, "If you look across the open plains, you will see that the grass stands as high as a man's head, Waiilatpu means place of the ryegrass."

I told her, "That's a perfect name."

The first image I recall seeing on this trip as we approached the mission was of the millpond and a large building where the immigrant families were housed. Next was the blacksmith shop and a building called the mansion house where more of the families and individuals lived who were long term or permanent. It was the first time I had ever seen a covered wagon. Some of them were whole; others were in pieces with shabby and ripped covers. The ones without covers reminded me of a picture Mother had once shown me of a whale's skeleton.

Men were working on the wagons, wearing what Mother had described as "Boston clothes." The women and children were all wearing clean and pressed white dresses and aprons. They looked too fancy and uncomfortable to work in as far as I was concerned. It was an eerie feeling since everyone stopped working or playing and silently stared at us as we rode by. There were just too many of them, and I felt deep down that I would never be able to belong in a place like this with so many strangers.

I reached over and tugged on Matilda's dress and begged, "Please take me home, Matilda, I don't belong here."

She told me, "There is nothing to be afraid of. These are your people, and you will soon make new friends."

The mission house was so big, and painted a brilliant white that almost glowed in the sunlight. A large group of children playing in the front yard stopped to stare. I was getting more anxious with every step Thunder took. Doctor Whitman must have seen us coming since he was out of the door and walking straight toward us. When he reached us, he lifted me out of my saddle and gave me one of his bear hugs. He held me at arm's length and said, "How is it that every time I see you, you get more beautiful?" I hugged him back, taking in that wonderful smell of pipe tobacco and buckskin.

He looked at Thunder and said, "I'm surprised that old Thunder could ride this far without collapsing on the trail."

I slapped him on the shoulder and said, "I know you're just jealous because you have to ride that ugly old mule that Captain Fremont gave you."

He broke out in his terrific laugh and said, "You're right Eliza, I am jealous, but that old mule has taken me more miles than I could ever count, and I have grown to think of him more as an old friend than an old mule."

As Doctor Whitman greeted Matilda and asked about her family, I could see all of the children staring at us. It made me nervous. The doctor turned to me and said, "Eliza, I want you to meet our new family."

He tied Thunder up to the fence and took my hand, leading me to the house where everyone was starting to gather. Just then, Mrs. Whitman came out of the door and hurried to give me one of her heavenly scented hugs. After she had kissed me several times on the cheeks, I peeked around her to find a whole clan of children staring at us. The girls were all nicely dressed in matching calico dresses, and the boys had matching blue and white striped shirts. They all looked as if they had just taken baths and put on freshly laundered clothes.

Matilda had parted my dark brown hair in the middle and braided it on both sides. I was covered in dust and deeply tanned from the trail and still wearing my doeskin dress and moccasins.

One of the younger girls asked, "Are you an Indian?"

I certainly felt more like an Indian than I did one of them, but before I could say anything, Mrs. Whitman said, "Of course she's not an Indian, she is just like the rest of you. Eliza, the doctor and I hit upon a treasure trove of children. You already know Mary Ann, Helen, and David, these other boys and girls are the Sagers, all from the same family."

When she introduced them, the girls curtsied, and the boys bowed, something I had never seen before.

Mrs. Whitman told everyone to go about what they were doing, and that I needed to settle in. She asked Matilda to help put my things in the room I would be sharing with Matilda Jane, Louise, and Henrietta. The doctor asked John and Frances if they would mind taking Thunder over to the corral, so everyone scattered as Matilda and I took my packs to my new room. Mrs. Whitman asked us to be careful not to wake the baby; she was still weak and needed her rest.

I couldn't help but worry about how I would fit in with all of these strangers. As we were putting things in the room, Matilda told me not to be sad, time would go quickly, and we would all be together again soon. She planned to return to the Cayuse village of her cousin and spend the night before returning to Lapwai. As she started for the yard, I asked her one more time to please let me go with her. She gently shrugged me off, climbed up on Rickets, and left without saying goodbye or even turning around to wave. She had never treated me like that before, and I started to cry.

Mrs. Whitman put her arm around me and said, "Matilda knows that it would only hurt worse by prolonging your parting."

She led me toward the house and said that supper would be ready soon, that I wouldn't want the other children to see me crying. When everyone was seated at the big new table Doctor Whitman had built, she said grace, thanking God for bringing me safely to Waiilatpu to be part of their family.

Doctor Whitman smiled at me and said, "I don't think you are going to be lonely this winter Eliza."

There was a bouquet in the center of the table, and when Helen Mar peaked around to see me, she gave me a mischievous smile and stuck her tongue out, reminding me of Timpstetelew and making me smile for the first time. Then little Matilda Jane leaned her head against my shoulder and snuggled like little Henry had done so often. I could feel the emptiness slowly starting to fade away.

I did have times of loneliness and a longing to be with my family, but I was making friends, and it was getting easier, except at bedtime when I would lay there wondering what my family was doing, and if they missed me.

The teacher, Mr. Hinman, was strict, but seemed to know the answer to almost every question.

I could read and write as well as any of the other students, including Perrin, but was having trouble with math. Mr. Hinman would have me come a little early or stay late so I could catch up. He wanted to know all about the Nez Perce and asked me if I would help him learn the language. I hadn't spoken any Nez Perce since arriving and was happy to hear the words again, but told him not to tell Mrs. Whitman.

He told me that he had recently come with the immigrant wagon train over the Oregon Trail the previous fall of 1844. Like Mother and Father, he was from New York, a place called Chinago County, not too far from Holland Patent where Mother was from.

He knew so much that it was hard to believe he was only 23 years old.

Mrs. Whitman told me that he had gone to a very good private school and was at the top of his class. I must have asked him a thousand questions about life back East and what it was like to live in New York compared to Waiilatpu. He told me that they were two entirely different worlds, that there were towns back East with thousands of people and farmland that stretched for hundreds of miles. He had come west in search of adventure and fell in love with the rugged lifestyle and planned to settle here. He was just as curious as I was and wanted to know what my life had been like growing up in an Indian village with no other white people beyond my family.

Talking with him made me feel closer to my family. The only problem was that he seemed to be nicer to the girls than the boys, and was especially hard on Frank.

Playing with Mary Ann and Helen was easy since we were all girls close to the same age. Poor David had been terribly mistreated and abandoned when he was very young. He was withdrawn and harder to reach at times. The only other children who seemed interested in the Nez Perce language were the Sager girls, but for the wrong reason. They thought the words were silly and sounded funny, yet to me, they were much more natural sounding than English. I had taught them simple words like ilp-ilp, which means red, mox-mox, which means yellow, and pits-pits, which means kitty.

One evening we were sitting at the supper table when Catherine said, "What beautiful ilp-ilp and mox-mox flowers are on the table." The other children all laughed, but Mrs. Whitman looked confused.

Then Elizabeth said, "Look at pits-pits over by the fire," and the children started laughing again. John said it sounded like Elizabeth was trying to spit.

Doctor Whitman said, "It sounds like we have a small group of Nez Perce with us tonight."

Mrs. Whitman asked if I had been teaching the children the Nez Perce and Cayuse words. I told her that I had.

She was very quiet for a while, and then in a serious tone, she said, "Eliza, this is to be an English only school and no Nez Perce, or any other Indian languages including sign language are to be spoken or used here. You have come here to learn about your own people and culture, not those of the Indians."

I didn't say anything, but deep down, it made no sense to me. How were these other children, especially the half-Indian ones going to learn to live among their own people without knowing anything of their language? I could tell that Doctor Whitman didn't feel the same, but he kept silent since the school was Mrs. Whitman's domain.

She went on to say, "I know this will be hard for you at first, but you will quickly get used to our ways since you are a very bright young girl.

The next morning after breakfast, I was doing dishes and looking out of the kitchen window when I saw a Cayuse man named Tomahas ride into the yard, dismount and knock on the door. He was one of the warriors I had seen earlier at the Cayuse village, and when he turned his gaze to me, I could feel my blood run cold. Father had once told me that within each tribe, different people take on different roles. Some are peacemakers, some are healers, and some are warriors, Tomahas was a warrior. It was more than that; his eyes appeared dead, as if there was no human warmth in them. He was someone I would never feel comfortable turning my back on.

Doctor Whitman went outside to see what Tomahas wanted and was back inside within several minutes. He came to me and said, "There is a sick man at the Cayuse village that I need to attend to, would you like to go with me?"

I was afraid of Tomahas, but I would take any opportunity to ride. I was saddled up and ready to go before the doctor had gotten his medicine bag together.

Once we were on our way, he said, "Eliza, when I am traveling, which seems to be most of the time any more, I get to make up my own rules. What do you say that we speak nothing but Nez Perce the entire trip, that no English can be spoken until we return to the mission?"

I was so happy that the Nez Perce words started flowing out of me like a waterfall.

For the first time since I had come to Waiilatpu I felt like my old self, and I could sense that Doctor Whitman was almost as happy as I was. When we reached the chief's lodge, the doctor asked me to stay outside while he checked to see what was wrong; he didn't want to risk my getting sick if it was contagious. I had been so engrossed in our conversation that I didn't notice the same group of Indians gathered nearby glaring at me.

Another warrior named Tamsucky had joined them, and I remembered Father telling me that he was a very violent man, and always to stay clear. It was suspected that he was one of the Indians who had been attacking the immigrant wagon trains. He had the most fierce face I had ever seen, and I felt my heart skip when he turned it in my direction with his half-open lizard eyes. By now, most of the village had gathered around me and were staring silently. Thankfully the doctor came out breaking the spell with his gregarious manner and authority.

Since the sick man was Tomahas's uncle, the doctor told him, "Here is the medicine, make sure that he takes it twice a day, and that he does not take a sweat bath or cold swim, it would kill him. Keep him warm and under his blankets and give him plenty of water to drink. If he isn't better within two days, I will come back and see if there is more I can do."

After we started back, I told him what father had said about the Indian people putting a medicine man to death if he fails to heal a sick person, and they die. "Could they do that to you?"

He told me that since he had been in the Oregon Territory, it had happened only twice that he knew of, that he had been threatened several times but ignored it any more. Two days later, as I was brushing and combing Thunder's coat, four Cayuse riders came storming into the mission, looking very angry. Edward was not with them, but Tomahas and Tamsucky were among the four. Doctor Whitman must have heard them ride up since he came out of the house as they were dismounting.

Tomahas walked right up to the doctor's face and said, "Your medicine is bad and has killed my uncle."

"The medicine is good and can have no harm. I just received word yesterday that he was much improved, did he take a sweat bath or go swimming?"

The other men were now closing around the doctor, and I became afraid that they were going to hurt or kill him, so I walked over and took his hand in mine. The doctor asked Tomahas again if the chief had taken a steam bath or swim, which he had warned could kill him if he did.

"That is our way; it was your medicine that killed him."

He then slapped Doctor Whitman hard on the face knocking his fur cap off. The doctor didn't flinch. Tomahas then backhanded him on the other side of the face, and once again, the doctor didn't react. The doctor quietly asked me if I would mind picking up his hat for him. When I did, he calmly dusted it off and put it back on his head. This incensed Tomahas who grabbed the hat and threw it in the mud and then used his foot to repeatedly step on it. The doctor asked me again if I would mind picking his hat up for him, that it had somehow fallen off again.

When I did, he casually took out his handkerchief and wiped the mud off and then put the hat back on. This unexpected reaction from the doctor seemed to confuse Tomahas, and he didn't know what to do. He must have thought the doctor was crazy, and since it was bad luck to bring harm to anyone who was, they mounted up and rode off, leaving a trail of dust.

When we reached the porch, the doctor squatted down so that we could be eye to eye and said, "Jesus told us that if someone strikes us on the cheek, that we should turn and offer the other, I guess we showed them. It isn't always easy, Eliza, but it was the right thing to do since the last thing I wanted was to put you in danger. You are the bravest child I have ever known, and you can't imagine what it meant to me when you walked into that mess and took my hand."

I told him, "I sure didn't feel brave; I was so scared I don't even remember doing it."

He laughed out loud and then wrapped me up in one of his glorious hugs, saying, "If there is one thing the Cayuse respect above all else, it's courage. You may have felt afraid, but you didn't look it and may have saved my life. Your parents must be the luckiest people in the world."

One morning before returning home, I awoke early and was sitting on the porch by myself watching the sunrise. The early spring sun had begun painting a thousand shades of color on the landscape, and like a mother's breast, the spring showers had nurtured the land. My parents were right; I was no longer afraid, and had made a whole new family of friends.

Doctor and Mrs. Whitman were in the kitchen, and I remember overhearing Mrs. Whitman telling the doctor that there was never enough time in the day to do everything. I looked inside the door just in time to see him kiss her on the forehead and tell her, "You're right about that, and I have never seen you happier or more beautiful."

Chapter 14

Martha Jane

A messenger arrived with news that Father would soon be on his way to pick me up. When I heard he was coming, it made me realize how much I had missed my family and needed to see them. Yet I had learned so many new things and had also grown to love the wide-open spaces of Waiilatpu. Something else had happened to me that I didn't anticipate; I had grown to love the Whitmans and my new friends. Mr. Hinman had good and bad moments, but he taught me so much about the world and my own culture. I enjoyed every minute spent teaching him the Nez Perce language and what I knew of their ways. I didn't see it coming, but some part of me now wanted to stay and continue to learn and grow with my new friends; it was bewildering.

I was out in the Whitmans' garden planting beet and carrot seeds when I heard this high-pitched voice yelling in the distance. I looked up to see little Henry pushing old Rickets as fast as he could go, which was not very fast. He was wildly waving one arm and yelling something about a secret. When he reached the yard, he leaped down and ran into my arms and held me around the neck in the same way he always had, making me feel like I was already home.

When he pulled away, he said, "Boy oh boy, have we ever got a secret for you. Papa told me I could ride ahead, but not to say anything until he and Doctor Whitman get here with the pack horses."

I was wondering if it had anything to do with Doctor Whitman leaving last week to visit Lapwai. I couldn't believe how much little Henry had changed, the way he had jumped off Rickets like an old cowhand. His round face was starting to get longer, and his soft little body had grown longer and leaner. It looked as though there might be some muscle underneath the buckskin vest that Bear Hunter and his wife had given him. Once he started talking a mile a minute, I knew it was the same little Henry with ants in his pants that could never sit still for more than ten seconds. I stopped him in his tracks by planting a big kiss on his nose and telling him how much I loved and missed him.

Barely pausing to breathe, he said, "I love you too, Eliza, but you are not going to believe the surprise we have for you."

When Father and the doctor reached the house, Father picked me up and swung me around. He gave me one of his big hugs and told me, "I love you more than all the stars in the sky."

As I held him around the neck, I told him, "I never thought I could feel so happy, Papa, I love you more than all the stars in the sky, too."

It was our way of saying that our love for each other was infinite and unconditional; something we had both learned from Mother, which she had learned from her father.

Little Henry was pulling on my dress and asking, "Can you guess what the surprise is?"

Jumping up and down, he finally blurted out, "Mama had a new baby girl!"

I could feel goosebumps coming up all over my body and could hardly believe that I now had a little sister like the Sagers.

Father said, "It's true, Eliza, and Mother wants you to give her a name."

I told Father that I would have to wait until I could see who she looked like. He and Doctor Whitman looked at each other and shook their heads.

"Can we leave right now, Papa?"

They started laughing, then Father said, "Hold your horses, you still have one more day of school, and the Whitmans have a celebration planned. Besides that, we have 22 horses to unpack. I suggest you start giving some thought as to what we are going to call your little sister."

The next day, after an hour in the classroom, until Mr. Hinman said it wasn't possible to teach a mind that wasn't even in the room. I showed Father all of the lessons I had learned and told him that he had been right; I had grown to like school and my new friends.

I could tell that he was proud of the work I had done, and he told me that I could return next year, that little Henry would be joining me.

My mind was racing as I thought about Mother, the new baby, Timpstetelew, and all of my friends at home. Still there was a part of me that was already beginning to think of the next school year and being with my new friends again.

The next thing I knew, Father was lifting me onto Thunder's back and we were on our way home. That night I was so sore that I could hardly sit down and had to sleep on my side. The next morning was even worse until the soreness started to ease up. To add to my misery, it started pouring rain, lasting all that day and the next. By the fourth morning, we were completely soaked, along with all of our bedding and supplies. A gauntlet presented itself, the same river we had crossed last spring, and once again, it was raging from the heavy spring rains. The storm had filled the river to the top of the banks and was moving faster than I had ever seen it. The only good thing was that it was light out, and we could at least see what we were getting ourselves into.

Father said, "It couldn't be any worse than crossing it the last time in the dark, but I want Henry with me, and we can tie Rickets to Thunder since he isn't as strong as he used to be.

I told Father, "We couldn't possibly get any wetter than we are now, and I can't wait to see Mother and my new sister." When Father said, "Let's go," I went right in, and we were instantly swept downstream in the cold water that was nothing but recently melted snow.

Father called out, "Remember to hold on tight to the saddle with one hand and loose on the reins with the other like the last time." Thunder never faltered or hesitated even with old Rickets in tow. The water was up to my chest and trying to rip me from his back, but I was more worried about Father and little Henry and kept turning around to check on them. Father yelled out, "Don't worry about us, and don't look back; you could lose your balance." I could hear Father trying to calm his horse and encourage Rickets to keep going. When we emerged from the river, we looked like drowned rats and had been swept well over a half-mile downstream. The horses were blowing water out of their nostrils, and little Henry was so excited that he asked, "Can we do it again, Papa ... pleeeease?"

As children, we see our parents as strong indomitable figures that we rarely think about what is going on inside of them. Father was at a point where he just needed to let it go, and he did. Little Henry must have hit Pa's funny bone, and we laughed until our stomachs hurt, a sweet relief from our wretched condition.

I was the first one home and ran as fast as I could into the kitchen, where Mother was rocking the baby. Matilda began heating warm milk and honey for little Henry and me. As I started for Mother, Matilda handed me a warm, dry blanket that felt like heaven. I hugged and kissed her and then went to Mother and did the same. Mother pulled the blanket back and showed me the most beautiful and precious sight I had ever seen. She was wiggling around, and when I touched her hand, she took my finger in her little hand and squeezed it along with my heart. Some feelings are beyond words, and this was one of them. After another hundred or so kisses and hugs, Father and little Henry arrived.

After they had finished their greetings, little Henry asked, "What do you think, not bad. huh?"

"Not bad," I said as I pulled his nose.

I'm not sure what I expected, but my room looked the same with warm clothes already lying on the bed for me to change into. When mother handed me my new little sister, I could hardly believe how small and fragile she was. There was a sweet scent that I would know once again when I had my own children. It was like nothing I had ever experienced before. I fell in love with her instantly as she touched my face with her tiny fingers and then drifted off into her own dream world. As I lay there under my warm blankets that night surrounded by everything in this world I loved, I thanked God for his Blessings.

I must have tried on at least a thousand names, but couldn't decide who my little sister looked like or what her name should be. I think Mother, Father, and especially little Henry were growing impatient since they didn't know what to call her, and it had been over a week. They made suggestions, but nothing seemed to fit. I was holding her and finally decided to ask what she wanted to be named. Bang, just like that, the name Martha Jane popped into my head. Everyone was in the living room. Mother was sewing, Father was reading, and little Henry was playing with the little wooden men that Father had carved for him.

I blurted out, "Grandmother's name; her name is Martha Jane."

Mother asked, "What was that, dear?"

"I said her name is going to be Martha Jane, and I have spoken."

They all broke out laughing, and Father said, "You've spent far too much time listening to Chief Joseph."

Father nodded toward Mother, and she said, "It's a good name ... Martha Jane Spalding."

There was a storm brewing among the Indian people. A Delaware Indian named Tom Hill had come to the territory and married a Nez Perce woman. Among the chiefs who joined him in his dissent against the missionaries was Golden Eagle, Timpstetelew's father. This would lead to one of my greatest heartbreaks.

When we returned home, I couldn't understand why I hadn't seen Timpstetelew for almost two weeks. In the past, her father or one of her relatives would bring her to see me almost right away. When I saw her riding up to our house, my heart leapt out of my chest as I dropped what I was doing and ran to greet her. When she got down, I threw my arms around her and told her how much I had missed her.

She just looked at me sadly for a moment and then tore my arms away and said, "Once I thought of you as my Nez Perce sister, but now I realize that you are one of the white intruders here to take our land."

Her usually smiling eyes were smoldering with anger as she turned her back to me, mounted her horse, and rode off without looking back. It felt as if my heart had been ripped from my chest and torn in two as I ran to the house crying hysterically. Father was gone delivering wheat to one of the villages, but when Mother saw me come running into the house, she asked what was wrong, if I was hurt. For a long time, I couldn't say anything, I just buried my head in her bosom and cried. When I was able to speak, I told her what had happened as she brushed the tears from my face.

After a time, she said, "I am so sorry, Eliza, I know how much you love Timpstetelew, as do I."

She let me cry myself out and then told me, "Her father joined with Tom Hill and turned against us, he must have told her that she could no longer be friends with you. Eliza, I know this is hard to understand, but I am sure Timpstetelew still loves you; we can only hope that things will change."

I understood what she was saying, but it would be a long time before my heartache would subside. When father returned, he took one look at my long face and asked what was wrong. When I told him I started crying again, so he held me until I had calmed back down.

He told Mother, "Tom Hill has been out spreading his hatred for the missionaries like wildfire, I heard he left for Chief Joseph's village and suspect he'll try and turn him against us."

This worried my parents deeply since Joseph had been a good friend and was a powerful ally among the Nez Perce People.

Father was planning to make another trip to the Willamette Valley for winter supplies and told us that he wanted us to come with him. I was so happy to be starting a new adventure together, but it didn't start quite as I had hoped. It was bright and clear for the first couple of days, but by the third day, it had started pouring rain. By the time we reached the mountains, it was slippery and treacherous. It was a miracle that all 17 packhorses, little Henry, Father, and I made it without injury or losing any of the horses or packs.

As we came out of the mountains and cleared the trees, we found the valley painted with wildflowers of every shape and color emerging from a background of lush green grass.

Nearing Oregon City, we could see the flags of a ship tossing in the wind. It turned out to be the British man-of-war called the Peacock. The captain invited us to his cabin for dinner that night, and the cook prepared a wonderful leg of lamb and plum pudding for dessert.

Little Henry told everyone, "One day, I am going to be a sea captain and sail my ship all over the world."

The captain said, "Captain Henry Spalding, I like the ring of it," making us laugh.

He went to the sideboard, picked up his hat, and set it on little Henry's head. It went all the way over his nose, and we started laughing again.

As we started back, I was looking at my little brother thinking what a sweet and gentle boy he was and how much I loved him. I remember musing about what it would have been like to have grown up with a big family in New York. I wondered what my grandparents were like and how I would have looked in a fancy dress and shoes. Even today, I find it hard to imagine anyone having a better childhood than we had.

As a child, I didn't understand the significance of what I was doing or the people that surrounded me; it was just a way of life. There were hardships, times when I thought I would freeze to death, or my blood would boil from the heat. There was a never-ending supply of hard work, but I had two parents who I worshipped and the sweetest brother and sister in the world. With the Nez Perce as my second family, every day was an adventure.

There are favorite memories we all carry. Mine are of Mother and home, the companionship I experienced on the trail with Father and little Henry. Riding all day through mountains, forests, and valleys, sleeping beneath the stars and asking a million questions about everything we could dream up. Holding my little sister and helping her learn to walk and talk.

That night as we were going to sleep, little Henry crawled into bed with me and laid his head on my shoulder as he had done so many times before.

He said, "You're the best big sister in the world," and I knew that there could never be a better feeling in this world than being loved.

At this point, my parents were busy almost every minute of the day. Father had become a preacher, teacher, doctor, farmer, horticulturist, mechanic, printer, lumberman, weaver, miller, carpenter, music director, translator, and author. He took weather readings at least twice or more per day, which were so accurate that the Wilkes expedition included them in their own reports. A German botanist named Karl Andreas Geyer had come to stay with us for several weeks and had inspired Father with a new passion. Together they collected hundreds of specimens of plants and animals that Mr. Geyer was paid to send to London. Father sent the same specimens to Mr. Greene at the missionary board as well as the National Institute in Washington, D.C. Mr. Greene then sold them to a well-known botanist named Mr. Asa Gray at Harvard University. Mr. Gray asked Father to send more and named three species in his honor. Mr. Geyer was so impressed by the Mission at Lapwai that he asked permission to write a letter of recognition to the missionary board. In it, he states that the Spalding mission, "Is by far the most successful and productive Indian missionary deputed by the American Board of Foreign Missions." He berated the Board for not giving Father more support and declared, "The credit and praise belong solely to them." At the end of the footnote, Geyer wrote, "The scientific reader will pardon this digression from my subject, for I have longed to do justice to Mr. Spalding and took advantage of this occasion." Botany would become one of Father's great pleasures and lifelong pursuits.

Peopeomoxmox was still extremely angry about the murder of his son and continued to try to raise a war party against the settlers in the Willamette Valley and upper territories. Doctor McLaughlin asked to have a friendly council with him and other headmen to avert an attack that might lead to a possible war.

Wanting justice for his son's death and still interested in acquiring cattle, Peopeomoxmox decided to try again and took a party of 40 Indians from different tribes to Fort Sutter. The ranchers in the California settlements were misinformed that 1,000 warriors were on their way to take vengeance, and put on high alert.

Peopeomoxmox had assembled a highly experienced group of veteran warriors including, Tom Hill and Kentuck, also known as Bulls Head. The Californians were relieved but still concerned when they heard that only 40 warriors were approaching; they knew they had a far superior number of soldiers and militia in case there was any trouble.

Once Peopeomoxmox and his men arrived at Fort Sutter, he realized everything had changed because of the conflict brewing within the Mexican province. He then took his complaint to John Fremont, who was now in charge of the fort.

Peopeomoxmox told Mr. Fremont, "I have come from the forests of Oregon with no hostile intentions ... We have come to hunt the beasts of the field, and trade our horses for cattle, for my people require cattle, which are not so abundant in Oregon as in California. I have come, too, according to our tribe's customs, to visit the grave of my poor son, Elijah, who was murdered by a white man. But I have not traveled thus far only to mourn. I demand justice!"

Captain Fremont explained that Grove Cook was long gone, but promised to review the incident and take proper action once the current situation with the Mexican government settled down. Tom Hill and Kentuck had run into several of their trapper friends, including Kit Carson, who had joined Fremont's forces as scouts. They were offered land and a fair salary if they would join up as scouts, which they did.

Peopeomoxmox's mission was put at the bottom of Mr. Fremont's priority list. The conflict brewing between the Mexican and American people would become known as the Bear Flag Revolt. Up to this point, many of the immigrants coming into California were required to become Mexican citizens. The Mexican government was worried that the Americans would push for annexation of California into the United States. The Americans were worried that the Mexican Army would make a preemptive attack.

Tom Hill was made a personal bodyguard to John Fremont; Peopeomoxmox and the rest of his party headed home with few cattle and no justice. To make matters worse, they came down with measles they had contacted at Fort Sutter, and over half of the party died on the return trip.

By the time they finally arrived home, they had been gone for over a year. The survivors were again angry and bitter at the white people who had given them the dreaded disease, and they wanted to take revenge. Relationships between the Indians and the missions were starting to deteriorate rapidly. After serving in the

California conflict, Tom Hill was given a large land grant and settled on a Delaware Indian reservation in Kansas.

In 1843, Doctor Whitman led over one thousand immigrants into the Northwest. In 1844, double that number had come, and in 1845 over three thousand immigrants poured into the Oregon Territory. It was not uncommon for the Nez Perce and Cayuse to meet up with the wagon trains at the Grande Ronde Valley to trade fresh horses for cattle and other goods. Many of the new settlers knew little or nothing of the Nez Perce or Cayuse and had come with a fearful and prejudiced attitude toward them. Some thought of all Indians as scalp takers and thieves, treating them with hostility and suspicion.

The Indians were growing tired of the Americans' arrogance and decided to turn one of the wagon trains around at Grande Ronde Valley. Doctor Whitman got wind of what was about to happen from a Cayuse friend and decided to intercept them, knowing it could be disastrous for the wagon train to attempt to return east at that time of year. He made haste for Powder River, and by the time he reached Grand Ronde, the settlers were already in a defensive position. There was a heated argument between Doctor Whitman and the Cayuse chiefs in which his life was threatened. He eventually diffused the situation, offering a payment of cattle and supplies to let the caravan pass.

Many Indian people were beginning to believe that Doctor Whitman was the person most responsible for bringing whites and their diseases into their territory. This led to an even wider gap between the loyal Indians who had converted to Christianity, and the ones who still held to traditional beliefs. Several of the chiefs, including Timothy, had been cultivating the land now for some time with very good results. The more militant, traditional Indians began threatening them, demanding they break with the missionaries, vandalizing their villages and destroying their crops when they refused. Out of fear, many began to return to their traditional nomadic ways, rejecting the white ways and Christian teachings.

Everything had been going so well at the mission that we were all taken by surprise when the attendance of the classes and Father's sermons started to drop off. It was just before the salmon run, camas harvest, and buffalo hunt, so the classes and sermons should have been at capacity. At first, my parents just thought it was a cycle of some kind, but as the numbers continued to decline, Father decided to call a meeting with Chief Timothy, Chief Lawyer, and Chief Joseph to ask if they knew what was happening.

When they entered the house, I could sense that something was wrong. Chief Timothy had always greeted me with a warm smile, but he was now very somber and sad looking.

It was hard to tell what Chief Joseph was thinking since he almost always wore a serious but kind face. Chief Lawyer's judicious and intelligent expression was also more serious than usual.

Since Chief Timothy had arrived on Tashe, I had been daydreaming about riding her while trying to churn the butter at the same time, not paying much attention to what they were saying. I accidentally slopped some on the floor, so Mother looked over at me and told me to be more careful with what I was doing. She also told me to slow down, or I was going to wear myself out before we had any butter.

Lawyer was the first to speak. He said, "The Delaware Indian named Tom Hill has been telling the Cayuse and Nez Perce that the white people will keep coming until they take all of our land and possessions. He tells us that where he came from in the East, the missionaries came first, then the settlers, and then the army; that this is what will happen here. He says that if the whites do not kill us, they will take us from our ancestors' homes and move us to a barren land of no buffalo or salmon. He tells us that the army men will make us like dogs with nothing to eat but the scraps they throw to us, that is all."

Joseph spoke next, telling Father and Mother, "Tom Hill says not to listen to the missionaries any longer and to stop going to the white man's school; that they will destroy us and our ways as they did to his people of the Delaware. Many of my own people want the old ways back, to move with the game, and take as many wives as we can care for. They also feel that Doctor White's laws are no good, that it was a mistake to make Chief Ellis the head chief of all Nez Perce. It is not our way for one man to tell another man what to do or how to live. Chief Ellis has become arrogant, not even capable of leading his own village any longer, that is all."

Chief Timothy told Father and Mother, "My heart is heavy. Chief Thunder Eyes has demanded that I leave his land and return to my own village. I will not do so. Without my protection, there is no telling what would happen to you and your family. He tells me that because I live in a wooden house and have many cattle and planted fields that I am nothing more than a dark white man. He also says that because of my pride for Tashe, I have become vain and selfish. I do not believe I am selfish; I give more than I take."

I could tell that Father had been anxious to speak, but would not interrupt until they were finished.

When they had finished, he told them, "Many of the things Tom Hill says are true, the settlers are coming, and nothing will change that. That is why it is important that the Indian people of the Oregon Territory use the land to grow crops and raise cattle. If a white settler looks out upon a piece of open land and sees nothing, he will feel that it serves no purpose and try to claim it. If he looks out upon five hundred acres of wheat, corn, and cattle grazing, he will know that it has an owner who has worked hard to grow it, that only a thief would try and take it.

They do not understand the Nez Perce ways. It is not that they have bad hearts; they are ignorant of your way and life. If you kill them, more will come, if you kill them also, then an army will be sent to kill the Indian people. The only hope is to show them that this is your land by what you have done with it and to try to live in peace together. I know that what they do is wrong, but nothing will stop them from coming, and they are like grains of sand, so many that you could not count them in a lifetime. You are my people now, your family is my family, and I will stand with you to do everything I can to protect your people, even if it means my life. I know that you three understand what I am saying, but we must make the rest of the people understand before it is too late."

Father was getting very emotional, so Mother put her knitting down and walked over to the table, put her hands on his shoulders, and asked, "Would you men like a cup of tea and piece of cake?"

It was as if everyone had been holding their breath, and her calmness made them relax.

Chief Joseph said, "There are many things that we must discuss with our people, but I warn you that there are those among the Nez Perce and Cayuse who would rather die in battle than to be driven from their land or told how to live."

Father said, "I understand this, but we must try to make them understand that change is coming, whether they like it or not."

When I went to the window to clean up, I looked out into the yard and saw Tashe looking right at me, and that was the last thing I can recall of their conversation.

Chapter 15

The Trip to the Oregon Coast

Father was planning to visit Oregon City for supplies, and then do some trading with Mr. Ogden at Fort Vancouver. He told Mother that there was a possibility we may continue to the Oregon Coast to see the Pacific Ocean and visit Mr. Gray's family at Clatsop Plains, ten miles south of Astoria. Little Henry and I had read about and seen drawings of the ocean, but we had no idea what it was going to be like. When Father told us that we might be able to go, we grabbed hands and started dancing wildly around the living room.

We had grown to love and respect Chief Timothy as if he were a part of our family. His face was like an emblem that reflected the wisdom and understanding of his people. He had an infinite amount of patience, and never tired of telling little Henry and me stories of his life and ancestors. We were so happy that he would be joining us.

Chief Timothy once told me that his body was earth-born, but his spirit was heaven-sent; he was part of all that had come before him and all that would come after he left this earth.

It made me wonder what my ancestors were like a thousand years ago, and what they would be like a thousand years from now.

He and his nephew Chipowits, meaning "Many Coyotes," planned to accompany us for most of the trip. The chief had a brother in the Willamette Valley that he planned to visit while Father was busy at Fort Vancouver. They planned to take a shortcut through the Cascade Mountains to save a week of travel going to

Oregon City. The only problem was that no one with our party had ever taken that route before.

As we began preparing for the trip to Oregon City, Mother again became apprehensive about the idea of little Henry and me going to the coast. The fact that no one of our party had ever taken the shortcut over the Cascade Mountains along the little-used trail on the north side of the imposing Mount Hood did not ease her mind.

Mount Hood stood monumental, like a grand cathedral whose body contained the earth's history and all living things within it. Chief Joseph had taken that route once to Oregon City and said that it had not been overly difficult, but his trip was with a swift-moving party, no packhorses, or young children. He told us that it was covered in fir trees, which are among the largest in the world, so tall and thick that they blotted out the sun. At the summit, he told me they stood as a proud and venerable family, impervious to mankind.

I have always found it amusing how people will act like they understand directions even when they don't, not to appear stupid. My Nez Perce language skills were quite good at that point, but I couldn't understand Chief Joseph's directions. A tree here, a big rock there, a trickling stream by the side of the big rock next to the tall tree all meant nothing to me. Father and Chief Timothy shook their heads as if they understood every word, so I stayed quiet, hoping the setting sun would get us to where we needed to go, anticipating the adventure of a lifetime.

Once we were underway, we made a quick stop overnight at Fort Walla Walla to rest, catch up on local news and visit with Mr. McKinley. We then spent two days at The Dalles resting and visiting with the Brewer and Walker families who were working hard to establish their mission.

We then departed for the Cascade Mountains, hoping to cross in two days and make camp the first night somewhere near the summit. However, it was slow going through dense forest with 63 fully loaded pack animals. During the entire trip over the Cascades, we rarely saw each other's faces, but I got to know the rear end of little Henry's horse in front of me quite well. Father said that it was as though we had been swallowed into the belly of a whale, like Jonah.

By the time we reached the summit, it was obvious that we were lost. Chief Timothy blamed Chief Joseph for the bad directions, saying that he must have envisioned them during a spirit dance. Father knew that we needed to stay west and follow the setting sun, but when we reached a fork that split left and right, we had no idea which way to go. Father and Chief Timothy chose northwest, and after five or so miles, we came to a dense brush that made going forward impossible. We backtracked to the fork and took the southwest trail. We were near the summit when we reached another fork in the trail and were once again uncertain which way to go. It was starting to get dark, the trees and brush so thick that we could barely see. Father decided to camp for the night and figure it out in the morning. The chief lit a fire so that we could warm up and make something to eat.

Shortly after dark, we heard horses slowly approaching, and the men reached for their rifles. The horses stopped before they approached our camp, and a man called out in the Sahaptin language that it was just himself and his family. We were still on guard until the man; his wife and children appeared before the firelight. Father explained how we had gotten lost and were planning to take the south trail in the morning. The Cayuse man told them that he had been this way many times before and that the south trail would be good if we planned on visiting California. Only little Henry and I thought that this was funny. The man offered to lead us the rest of the way to the Willamette Valley where he was planning to do some trading and visit family members.

It was rough going, and several times packs were stripped off of the horses. There were occasional streams of crystal-clear water coming up from below the earth, also bound for the Pacific Ocean. When we reached the bottom of the mountain, we had to cross a river that was running fast and deep, almost losing one of the packhorses.

When we reached Oregon City, I could hardly believe my eyes; there were over a dozen houses and a general store. It was the first time little Henry and I had ever been to a store. Father gave us enough money to buy peppermint candy and licorice, a treat we had only heard about, but never tasted before.

Other than the Whitman house, these were the first painted houses we had ever seen, and the first time we had seen men and women dressed up in fancy clothes. We stayed for several days, and then Father, little Henry, and I took rowboats down the Willamette River until we reached the Columbia River. Chief Timothy and his nephew Chipowits were planning to lead the horses to Fort Vancouver, where we would meet up some time later after they visited his brother.

We passed by Portland, which consisted of one log building at the time. When we reached Fort Vancouver, Mr. Ogden, who was now in charge of trading at the post, greeted us. He was very kind to little Henry and me, showing us all around the Fort. We stayed two nights, and on the third day when Father and Mr. Ogden had concluded their business, we climbed aboard a very crude rowboat and continued down the mighty Columbia River to Fort Astoria. In places where the river was narrow, it ran extremely fast, where it was wide, it slowed to a crawl, almost like a lake, but always moving with the tides and mountain runoff.

At Fort Astoria, the Columbia River was over four miles wide with tides that could drag a small boat out into the ocean in a heartbeat. An experienced seaman told us that this was the most dangerous river channel in the world. Astoria was little more than a crude fort and ratty shack on the side of the hill. A British man of war aptly named the Peacock was docked on the south bank with its proud banners flapping in the wind. It was the same one we had seen on our earlier trip to Oregon City. It was the same captain, and he made a big to do about how much we had grown up.

When Father told the captain of our plans, he offered to take us to Mr. Gray's mission at Clatsop Plains since they were planning a short excursion south. The Clatsop Plains, named after the Clatsop Indian Tribe, had a village on the south side of the Columbia River. Their territory ran south about 75 miles from the Columbia River to the land of the Tillamook Indians. A few of their people had intermarried, and they sometimes traded together.

As we left the Columbia River channel and entered the Pacific Ocean aboard the Peacock, swells started to rock the ship like a toy boat, and nothing could restrain the excitement that little Henry and I were feeling. When we reached Clatsop Plains, it was a wild ride to shore on one of the rowboats. We caught and rode a wave to the beach, another experience we would remember as long as we lived.

Though Father and Mr. Gray had not always seen eye to eye and had had their problems in the past, they put it behind them like water under a bridge and greeted each other with a warm and joyful spirit. Mr. Gray now had five children, and we all spent the first day outside playing in the ocean.

He told Father that he had to make a trip of about 15 miles south to trade with the Clatsop Indians for salt. He then planned to continue south another 15 miles to trade for dried salmon with the Tillamook Tribe. He asked Father if he would like to go along with him, but warned that it was an extremely rugged trip from the salt works to the Tillamook village. He told Father that it was one of the most beautiful places he had ever seen, worthy of the hardship. He suggested that little Henry and I stay with his family since it could be treacherous in places. Father told Mr. Gray that he would be glad to go, but he would need to let us decide for ourselves if we wanted to go or stay. He assured Mr. Gray that both of us were experienced riders and had never been a problem for him. Father explained everything Mr. Gray had told him, and it took us all of one second to decide to go. Mr. Gray told Father that the Clatsop Indians were friendly, but the Tillamook Tribe was suspicious of whites and could be hostile.

When Lewis and Clark undertook their expedition to the west, William Clark had made the same trek to the same village in

January of 1806. When he arrived at the Tillamook village, there were over two thousand Indians and 50 wooden houses they used as a spring and summer fishing village.

Mr. Clark had been told that a whale of over one hundred feet long had washed ashore, and the Tillamooks were boiling the fat and selling whale oil to the British and Canadian traders. He decided to make the trip to trade for the salt they needed to preserve meat and fish, and whale oil that they needed for cooking and lighting their lamps. At the time, the Tillamook tribe was open to trading, hospitable, and friendly with Mr. Clark's party.

In 1843 the Tillamook Indians contracted smallpox, and it decimated the tribe. There were now less than four hundred people left and only ten houses at the summer camp. They had become extremely leery of white people whom they now considered dangerous intruders. Mr. Gray told Father that we would be accompanied by a man from the Tillamook tribe who now lived in Astoria to make introductions and assure the Tillamook that we carried no sickness and had come only to trade.

When we reached the salt works, little Henry and I were in the water almost immediately helping the native children carry saltwater to the kettles. We spent most of the day filling the big pots and gathering driftwood to burn. Later that afternoon, we took a long walk south along the beach until we came to a half-moon cove jutting out about a half-mile to a rocky point.

The walk was over small to medium-sized boulders, smooth from the eons of rolling and crashing along the shore. When we reached the point, the waves were breaking close in over the rocks with pelicans flying just above the perfectly shaped breakers.

Behind us rose a cliff of about two hundred feet in the air with giant spruce trees shrouded in a mystical layer of clouds or fog, it was hard to tell which.

The pelicans were in a frenzy, diving for fish less than a hundred yards away from where we stood. We had never seen a bird like that before, and could hardly believe the giant beak, and wingspan. We watched them for over an hour and threw smooth flat rocks out into the ocean, trying to make them skip across the water before they dove into the waves.

We slept like rocks that night and camped out on the beach. Both Mr. Gray and Father arranged to stop and pick up the salt they had bartered for on the return trip.

The next morning, we were up at daybreak, and after a hearty breakfast, we were soon underway. Mr. Gray had not exaggerated one bit about the ruggedness of the terrain. The path was nothing more than an elk trail with thick, thorny brush all the way. The small range of hills was not overly high or long but became intimidating as it rose sharply into the air with no sense of secure footing.

We were still a mile from the summit, and about a mile inland when Mr. Gray asked if we would like to see something extraordinary. He told us that it would add at least two or more hours to the trip, but it was one of the most magnificent places he had ever seen. He told us that travelers who had journeyed this far felt they had never seen a more beautiful sight. As far as little Henry and I were concerned, this was an adventure, and we didn't hesitate for a second to vote "yea."

As we cleared the tree line, we dismounted and walked the horses out onto a flat triangular piece of land that protruded about a thousand yards into the ocean. When Lewis and Clark had made their journey west, Captain Clark was guided along with a young Indian woman named Sacagawea, her new baby, and 12 other men to this very spot.

Father described the experience as coming out of an intensely dense forest and walking out to the edge of a spear-shaped point that took our breath away as it unfolded before our eyes. We stood on a cliff that rose several hundred feet above the ocean, watching waves crashing onto the rocky cliffs below to the north. There was a steep faced bay with jagged rocks over a half-mile out into the ocean where many ships had been lost. To the south, rolling waves washed up onto the beach for as far as the eyes could see.

Beyond the long stretch of beach also to the south was a creek, running to the sea. The Indian people below looked like ants from this far away. Beyond the whale was another long stretch of beach with a huge monolithic rock shaped like a haystack in the distance.

When Mr. Clark stood at this same viewpoint, he decided to honor the moment by naming it "Clark's Point of View." The creek where the whale skeleton was beached would be the farthest point that the Lewis and Clark expedition would travel south.

Father said he wished he could have spent a week camped there watching sunrises and sunsets over the most spectacular view he had ever seen. The Indian guide told us that this was a sacred place where many Indian people had come to seek their spirit guides.

He showed us a rock where sitting for any length of time aroused a sense of peace and energy not known before. This rock had been used for thousands of years by the Indian people while seeking their weyekin or spiritual force and was said to possess supernatural energy. He explained it as lines of energy running through the earth; that this spot was one of those rare places where two lines intersected, creating a powerful life force coming from the center of the Earth Mother. As we left, I felt sadness that I might never see anything as spectacular as this again in my lifetime. Within minutes we were once again in the dense brush trekking down a treacherous hillside.

When we finally emerged from the trees, we crossed a small creek and were right in the center of the village. Our Tillamook guide gave a greeting to the approaching Indians and told them that none of us had any sickness; that we had come to trade. There were ten long wooden houses surrounded by racks used to dry the salmon. It was then ground into a powder that they would use during the long dark winter months for food. Most of the Indians had never seen a white child before and were curious, wanting to touch little Henry and me on the head.

Once introductions were made and the ice was broken, we were treated to a delicious lunch of smoked salmon. Several of the native people spoke a little English from having traded at Fort Astoria. Two Nez Perce brothers had decided to take an adventurous trip to the "big saltwater," years before, and had to stay when they reached the village. They were gladly accepted into the tribe and had found wives and had children who all spoke some of the Sahaptin language. When little Henry and I started speaking Sahaptin, the natives were surprised and talked all at once, though we couldn't understand a word of their language. This not only softened the hearts of the Tillamook people toward us, it endeared us to them as human beings because of our desire to know the Nez Perce language.

For the next two days, all of the children and even some of the adults argued over who would get to show little Henry and me around. When we returned home, Father told Mother that they took us to the giant rock shaped like a haystack and showed us how the tides went way out, and then came back

We explored the tide pools finding all kinds of little sea creatures and fish shaped like stars. The big rock was covered with hundreds of birds of all different varieties, and every time an eagle would swoop by, they would all roll off the rock like a solid wave of feathers. We saw several kinds of eagles and an osprey, which the native people call a "fish eagle." We watched as one of the fish eagles dove into the water and snatched a large fish with its powerful talons. At the creek there was also a stork with wings even longer than the pelicans.

The Indian people made their camps in two areas; one was closer to the ocean on a flat but slightly raised area. The other was further back up the creek on a flat piece of land that flooded during high tides and rainstorms. The higher camp was where they smoked the salmon; the lower was where hundreds of horses grazed, both places immensely beautiful.

The elk were plentiful, so graceful and powerful. The bulls with their giant antlers have been known to charge and kill a person who accidentally stumbles upon them during rutting season. The Tillamook chief told us that it rarely snows or gets extremely cold, but it is not uncommon for it to rain for weeks and stay overcast for months during the winter.

Little Henry and I begged to stay longer, but it was time to turn north and start making our way home. Father traded goods, then packed as much dry salmon as he could carry, while leaving room for the salt he had purchased. It was another rough trip back with several packs being torn off.

When we reached Mr. Gray's house, we stayed overnight and then headed back toward the Columbia River the next day with the horses that Mr. Gray had loaned us. Since the Peacock was long gone, Father traded with the Clatsop Indians on the south side to take us across the river in their rough log canoes and return Mr. Gray's horses.

From Fort Astoria, we were able to get a ride with one of the Hudson Bay vessels to Fort Vancouver, where Chief Timothy and Chipowits were waiting for us. Not long after we left Fort Vancouver, I became very ill with the flux and had to be carried a good part of the way home in Father's arms. By the time we reached Waiilatpu, I was better, though still weak. It was the adventure of a lifetime I had envisioned, but sadly I would never see the ocean again.

Chapter 16

Tashe

There are those mornings when you wake up, and everything feels wrong. You can't get your eyes to focus, and it feels as if gravity is crushing you into your bed, making it almost impossible to get up. You start to put on your socks, and one of them tears a big new hole; your shoes are too tight, and your dress is too snug and binding. Everything, including your underclothes is binding or itchy like ants have moved in and are making cross-country trips over every part of your body. It's pouring rain outside so hard that you can't go out and play with your friends.

This was not one of those days. As soon as I became conscious, I could feel that something good was going to happen; my body felt light as a feather and seemed to almost lift itself out of bed on its own. Even though my clothes were old and getting ragged, they seemed to feel just about right. The sun was already coming up over the mountains, warm and friendly with big fluffy white clouds passing by like true believers on their way to the Promised Land.

I had just gotten dressed and looked out the window when a radiant bluebird settled down in the front yard. In no time at all, it had snagged a big fat worm and flown off to join its family in the trees. We had gotten word that a mission barrel had arrived at Waiilatpu and that our things would soon be on their way to us. My clothes were comfortable but old and getting too small for me. Mother had mended them so many times that it was hard to tell what was original and what was patched. A mission barrel was like Christmas for us and would only arrive once every year or so.

Except for Sunday services and when we had guests, I was allowed to wear an old comfortable pair of moccasins that Matilda had given me since my shoes were too small. Even though the clothes were hand-me-downs from the church families back east, they were new to us and much nicer than the ones we had. It was springtime, and Mother's flower garden was beginning to burst out of the ground, spewing every color under the sun.

Little Henry and I were excited because Father told us that we could go to the camas harvest. I don't know if it is possible for any six-year-old boy to sit still for more than ten seconds, but little Henry was so wound up that he was starting to get on everyone's nerves. I am almost certain that when I was that age, I was never like that.

Mother is the most patient person I have ever known and is so highly revered among the Nez Perce that when they say their prayers, they end with "In the name of Jesus Christ and Mrs. Spalding."

Even she was getting tired of telling little Henry to stop running in and out of the house and slamming the door. He kept asking me questions until I felt like my head was going to explode. When I would tell him that I needed a break and to ask someone else, he would beg for just one more question, and then one more, and on and on. I was hoping that little Henry would have to ride old Ricketts, and I would have a different horse to ride to the harvest.

Though Mother and Father were concerned about the declining students and sermons, they were never happier than when there was work to do, and the mission was buzzing like a swarm of bees.

Father was in the fields from sunup until sundown, and Mother was taking this time to show a group of Nez Perce women how to spin yarn and use the loom. They sounded like a flock of geese each time they learned or made something new.

I felt so wonderful that morning because of a dream that I had. I dreamt that I was on a mountaintop lying down, watching the clouds drift by on the wind. A bluebird came gliding by and perched on a limb right next to me almost within touch. It started singing and making chattering sounds that I couldn't understand, but somehow felt they had a meaning related to me.

In my dream, I remember looking down at my feet and thinking that they were so far away that they must belong to someone else. As I began to listen closely to the bluebird, I could have sworn that it told me to spread my wings. At first, I was too dreamy to understand what it was trying to say until it opened its wings to show me what it meant. As I stood up and put my arms out, I couldn't believe that I was lifting off the ground. The bluebird hovered next to me as if to help me understand that there was nothing to fear. I opened my arms like wings, and the next thing I knew, we were gliding through the air above the trees.

At first, I was afraid I was going to fall, but then realized that I was capable of anything I could think of as long as the bluebird was next to me. This must be what an eagle feels like when they catch a current of wind and glide effortlessly through the sky and clouds. For just a split second, I must have wondered if it was real or if I was dreaming and started to fall out of the sky. When the bluebird landed on my shoulder, I forgot what I was thinking of and started to glide again. I could see Father out in the fields and Mother with little Henry in the garden as we flew by the mission. We were soon over Chief Timothy's village, and in the distance, I could see Tashe running through the meadow with a golden glow surrounding her.

I couldn't help wondering if that was her soul, what she loves, and what makes her happy. The last thing I remember was going into a bright white cloud with the bluebird still on my shoulder. As everything began to turn white, I found myself waking up in my room with the best feeling I have ever known. I tried to go back to sleep and will myself to return to the dream, but it was no use, I could only get little glimpses before I was fully awake.

I was busy helping Mother hang clothes out to dry when Chief Timothy arrived. He and Tashe usually came galloping up with big warm smiles on their faces. He climbed down from Tashe's back and walked slowly toward us with a sad look. I began to fear that something was wrong. He looked older than I could ever remember, and instead of greeting me as he always had with a smile and hug, he asked if I would get Father.

I wasn't sure where Father was, so I started running around the mission looking everywhere until I found him in the old schoolhouse working on the printing press. I told him to come quickly, that something was wrong with Chief Timothy. He looked worried, and we both took off for the house as quickly as we could. When we reached the house, Father asked if something was wrong, if someone was sick or hurt. Chief Timothy told Father that there was something he needed to discuss with him. Mother gently touched my arm signaling that we should leave them alone.

The chief told us, "This concerns all of you; I would like you to stay and hear what is in my heart." He looked so miserable that I started to worry, and tears began to fill my eyes. He said, "I am not sick or injured, nor is anyone of my family, but my spirit is deeply troubled. For the past two nights, I have sat by the fireside looking into my soul and have seen that my pride for Tashe has made me into a vain man, a bad man. I know that I can never be humble like Jesus Christ or Mrs. Spalding. I also know that as long as I have Tashe, I will continue to be filled with pride and have decided I must give her up." I could feel my heart breaking for him, and the tears started to fall.

He went on, "I have decided not to give her to my people since they would want to use her for racing and gambling."

He looked at Mother and Father and said, "I thought to give her to one of you so that she would not be used for gambling, but I realize that she should belong to little Eliza."

As he said this, he walked toward me, and put the reins in my hand and said, "You have a kind and gentle spirit like your mother, and I know you will love and care for Tashe as I have."

My heart felt as though it were going to leap out of my chest and split in two, one side was sad and broken for Chief Timothy, the other was flooded with the joy that my dream of dreams had come true. I started toward him as his arms opened to me, but was surprised as he lifted me onto Tashe's back instead of taking me in his embrace.

He looked at me and said, "Do not be sad for me little one, I am already feeling happiness at seeing the two of you together, and I have many fine horses."

I knew that he had a large herd of horses, but I also knew there was none like Tashe. Mother and Father were talking quietly, and it suddenly dawned on me that they may not allow me to have her, and I felt a shiver go up my spine. What if they wouldn't let me keep her!

Mother went to Chief Timothy and took his hands in hers and said, "You must never doubt that you are a good man, you are one of the finest human beings I have ever known, and your friendship means more to us than you will ever know. Without your help and protection, I don't think we could have succeeded with our mission. God bless you for your kindness and generosity. We promise always to be kind and gentle with Tashe."

For the next several days, I found myself constantly looking out the window every few minutes to make sure that she was really there, that this was not just another wonderful dream like the bluebird.

Mother told me that I would need to be humble about Tashe, that there were more important things, and I should not let her become the center of my world. She explained that it was going to be difficult because of all the attention that she would draw to me.

Word soon spread like wildfire among the Nez Perce People about Chief Timothy's decision. I know that most were genuinely happy for me, but there were also many, especially among the young men, who resented my having such a fine horse. They felt that it was wrong for any young girl to have a proven war pony and buffalo hunter like Tashe.

Father needed to make a trip to a village called Kamiah, about 60 miles southeast of Lapwai to deliver badly needed flour and grains. It was a fairly uneventful trip, but when we returned, I was in for a joyful surprise. Timpstetelew was waiting for me with a big smile and open arms. As we walked back to the house hand in hand, she told me that she was sorry for how she had treated me the last time we had seen each other. She told me that her father and others were saying bad things about our family and that she would be beaten if she tried to see me.

I took her in my arms and told her that I was sorry for what she had been through, that I understood, and we should forget that it had ever happened.

She told me that she had come to live with us for a while, and we started jumping up and down and dancing around in circles. When we stopped, she put her head down and started to cry. When I asked what was wrong, she told me that her father had been killed in a buffalo hunt.

Her mother had been sick for a long time and when she heard the news about her husband, her heart stopped working. When Chief Timothy heard what had happened, he offered to bring Timpstetelew to Lapwai.

I told her how sorry I was for what had happened to her, that we would always be sisters, and she could stay with us as long as she wanted.

Chief Timothy had told her about giving Tashe to me, but she could hardly believe it when we went out the next day to give Tashe a bunch of carrots.

Father must have known what we were feeling and told me, "You two magpies look like you could use a day off, just don't get carried away and get yourself hurt."

I gave him a big hug, we mounted and were off like a flash. We spent the entire day sprinting through the hills and valleys, throwing splashes of water as we ran full speed through the creeks. It was one of the most wonderful days of my life, and by the time we returned to the mission, my face and throat were sore from smiling and laughing so much.

This trip to the camas fields was much like the first time, pure joy, a time to be free as only children can be. Watching little Henry on old Rickets trying to keep up with us was hysterical, and Timpstetelew and I almost fell off our ponies laughing.

Little Henry was happy helping the women since playing in the dirt was one of his favorite activities. I wanted to watch the men as they worked on breaking the new horses. This was my idea of paradise, and I would often spend the entire day cheering them on, bringing water and food. One of the men had spent the previous day breaking a beautiful palomino mustang until it was calm and gentle. He called me over and immediately boosted me up on the mustang's back. Several other men were there with ropes as they led me around the corral.

Father came over to watch and later told me he was concerned but felt it best to stay out of it. At one point, I kicked the horse to try and spur it on, and it worked. The horse bucked several times and bolted before the men could get control. We made several fast circles before they regained the rope, and the mustang calmed back down. By then, the men were all laughing at the look of wild excitement on my face, Father was standing with white knuckles at the fence post. I have taken several pretty bad falls, but that's the price you pay to do something you love.

The head chief was an elderly Cayuse man who told us that they were going to hold a war dance for the young braves, that the young men needed to learn about the proper way to behave during the dance. The entire village gathered around in a large circle with the chief in the middle. It would have been uncomfortable for most white people since the warriors wore only a loincloth, war paint, and feathers, but we had been raised with the Nez Perce, so it came as no shock to us.

The chief talked for some time about the tactics they used during a battle and the proper behavior. When he was done speaking, he invited the young men into the circle, and the drums started pounding. In their faces, you could see that their young lives were directly connected to the ancient song of the earth and sky, a fierce, virgin force of nature beating and dancing its rhythm in time with that of the Great Spirit.

At first, it was so loud and powerful that I had to put my hands over my ears. The young warriors were doing their best to look and act fierce, making threatening gestures and howling like hungry wolves. Every once in a while, the chief would stop them and explain or demonstrate certain steps or actions of the dance. At first, I was frightened by the loud yells, swirling knives, and tomahawks, but little Henry loved it. Only the men were allowed to dance the war dance inside the circle, but outside the women and children would dance and sing chants. It was not long until little Henry and I had joined in and were whooping it up. One of the women put war paint on little Henry's face, making it official in his mind that he had become a Nez Perce warrior. They danced all day, and that night there was a giant bonfire in the middle of the circle.

For the young warriors, this was a test of endurance, and the dancing went on until the next morning. With one of the men's help, Father carried us back to the tent late that night and said he had never seen us sleep so soundly. The next day little Henry refused to let anyone remove the war paint, and throughout the day, different men would hoist him up on their shoulders, and start dancing and chanting—a memory burned deeply into my consciousness.

The only problem that summer at the camas fields was the resentment from some of the young men toward me because of Tashe. The second day I went to watch the men breaking the horses and colts, I made the mistake of taking her with me. One of the men was giving me a hard time, telling me that it was wrong for a little girl to own such a horse, that it should belong to a Nez Perce warrior.

I was starting to feel guilty when I saw Bear Hunter walking toward us and was hoping he wouldn't feel the same way about Tashe. I was wearing the doeskin dress his wife had made me and just about to thank him when he put his hands over his eyes and rubbed them. I was not sure what to think, but when he took them off, there was a great big man smile that made me feel a little funny inside.

He walked up and put his arm around me, saying, "Is that little Eliza, I thought you were a princess."

I tried not to feel proud but couldn't do it. I started giggling and then thanked him again for the beautiful dress and other gifts that he and his wife had given us. He told me that his wife wanted to thank us for the pony Mother had given her, she thought it the most beautiful she had ever seen. He told me, "It is a good horse, powerful and fast." He winked and said, "Like me, she has trained it well."

The young men standing nearby were in awe of his reputation as a warrior and hunter, vying for his attention. I think he either overheard what the one young man was saying to me or sensed it, ignoring them and giving Tashe and me his full attention as they listened to every word he said.

He was rubbing Tashe's neck and shoulder when he said, "I have heard that Chief Timothy has given Tashe to you; he is a very wise man, and there is no one I know of who is more deserving. The ride you and your father made over the mountain to save your mother is a dangerous ride during the daytime; at night, it would take the heart of a warrior."

He looked over at the braves without smiling and said, "When I was young, I did not understand these things. I wanted the fastest horse and the best weapons. I did not know that these things are not what make a good hunter or warrior, that a good warrior makes the most of what he has, and does not desire what belongs to another.

I have learned that the quiet man who watches and listens is to be most respected and feared. He is the one who is calm when the enemy or buffalo is charging and sees and hears only what he needs to see and hear at the moment of life and death. Chief Timothy is such a man. I have also heard that you crossed the Kooskoosky after a spring flood and almost drowned; that you made the trip from

Waiilatpu in one day without stopping to sleep. When I was young, I did not understand that a child could also have the heart and courage of a warrior, that they too are to be respected. Yes … Chief Timothy is wise to choose one so brave."

The young men heard every word he said, and in his own humble way he had shown them that they had been wrong without offending them or being condescending.

He smiled and picked me up like a feather, putting me on Tashe's back and said, "Show me how fast she is." I think Tashe understood him because as soon as I leaned forward and hopped, we were off like a gunshot. We didn't go far, but when I returned, he rubbed her neck and said, "I have never seen a faster horse, she holds nothing back and runs with no fear."

He tapped my knee and tousled my hair to say goodbye, then walked to the young men and slapped one of them on the back. He told them how well they were doing with the wild ones.

I could see why he was so well respected and why he would become a great leader one day.

I never heard another word of criticism from the Nez Perce men that trip and was allowed to fully share in the joy of watching them work the horses.

After a long day riding, Timpstetelew and I were currying and combing our ponies when we saw a new group approaching the camp. Even though it had been several years since I had seen White Eagle, I recognized her instantly. I don't know how else to say it; she is a radiant human being. The very air around her seems to shimmer, and she has the gift of drawing people to her like a lodestone. There is something pure and honest about her that is irresistible. Timpstetelew told me that she had married a young chief who was very brave and handsome. As her party got closer, I could see that she had a cradleboard with a baby on her back. When she saw us, she gave a big smile that reminded me of Mother, so warm and full of love. She stopped to greet us, ask about our families, and if we would come by her camp later, that there was someone she wanted us to meet.

Later that day, we went to visit. White Eagle's husband could have been the brother of Bear Hunter. He was so handsome and big and strong that Timpstetelew and I both felt flushed as he walked by and gave us a smile that turned us into giggling little girls. When White Eagle handed her baby to me, I felt as if I were hovering two feet off the ground. I turned to Timpstetelew and said, "Look, she has your cherry eyes." It was such a wondrous moment to be in the presence of such beauty. When White Eagle began breastfeeding her baby, I could almost feel a tingle and wondered if I, too, would one day have children of my own.

Chapter 17

The Bluebird Feather

At the camas harvest, one of our favorite games was cloud gazing. Timpstetelew, and our friend Charging Elk and I would lie on our backs looking up at the clouds and take turns describing the images we imagined in the shapes of the clouds. Most of them were of animals or birds, but once in a while, we were able to find the shape of a person's face or body who we knew. If it were a really big nose or belly, we would laugh ourselves sick.

As time went by, I rarely thought of myself as a white person any longer; I had come to feel that I was simply a person. Chief Timothy and Mustups were like Grandfathers; Matilda was like my Grandmother, Timpstetelew like a sister, and I hoped that it would always be that way, that we would always be together.

One day as we were cloud gazing, Timpstetelew told me that if I wanted to be Nez Perce, I would need to have a weyekin. When I asked what that was, she looked at Charging Elk, who explained that a weyekin is a spirit helper sent by the Great Spirit to help guide and protect them.

I told them that it sounded like our God, who Mother and Father said always watched over us. He thought about it a while, then said that they must be of the same spirit family. I asked how to get one? Timpstetelew said, "You must not eat anything for several days before you go on a quest, and only drink a little water to prepare yourself. Once your spirit is ready, you must go to a sacred place and wait until your weyekin presents itself. You need to let your mind rest, and when you are somewhere between the dream world and the real one, you and your spirit will enter an invisible world."

She then said that if my heart was a good one, I would be given the gift of a weyekin. They told me that there was a sacred place not far up in the mountains, that if I wanted to try, she would show me where to go, what to wear, and how to prepare. Timpstetelew told me that this way, the Great Spirit would know my heart was of The People.

I would later learn that the one thing they forgot to mention was that most children spend years with one of the elders preparing.

I wasn't sure what my parents would think, so I decided to keep it between the three of us. Since we always ate in a large group together, it was easy to hide the fact that I wasn't eating anything. By the next morning, all I could think about was food, but I was determined to find my weyekin.

We were free to go after breakfast, so Timpstetelew and Charging Elk accompanied me to a place where I could change into her clothes. I couldn't believe how wonderful they felt as I started hiking up into the mountain, so smooth and warm. They told me which direction to go and the trail I should follow, and that the first time it would take most of the morning to get there. When I was at the right place near the top, I would find a large rock next to the edge of a cliff where I could see the entire valley.

It took me all morning to find it, and by the time I did, I could have eaten it, I was so hungry.

I lie there all day but couldn't seem to turn my mind off and get into that dream world between being awake and asleep that they had told me about. When I finally got back down from the mountain, I was cold and hungry, disappointed that nothing had happened. The Indian children are told to stay as long as it takes, but there was no way I could stay overnight with Father and Matilda watching over me.

The next morning, I was able to get to the rock much faster since I now knew the way. I wasn't as hungry as I had been the day before and drifted in and out of sleep, feeling as though something was going to happen, nothing did. That night Matilda came to me and asked what I was doing, that she knew I hadn't eaten in two days and was gone from morning until late afternoon. She told me that if Father were not so busy, he would have noticed as well.

Reluctantly I told her that I had been going into the mountains to find my weyekin. Like Chief Timothy, she had also become a Christian but continued to practice the old ways as well. She was quiet for a long time, and I was afraid she would be angry or tell Father before I had a chance to continue my quest.

Instead, she asked, "Do you understand the importance of what you are doing?"

"I do, and even though I am white, my heart is of the Nez Perce."

"Have you had visions?"

I told her, "I felt as though I was in a dream world, but nothing had come to me yet."

"Tomorrow morning, I will make you a special tea that will help, but we will be leaving the day after tomorrow." I threw my arms around her and told her that I loved her. She held me at arm's length, looked me in the eyes and told me that she had learned to love me like I was her child.

The next morning Matilda made me a special tea and filled a canteen to take with me. I felt something different right away, as if colors were brighter, sounds more distinct, even the smell of the air was more intense. Time slowed like a caterpillar crawling over a leaf, and the rush to find my weyekin no longer felt that important. There seemed to be no worries about yesterday or tomorrow, only the beauty of here and now.

Timpstetelew kept looking at me funny and finally said, "You look different today, do you feel alright?"

I told her that I had never felt better in my life and was no longer hungry, afraid, or in a hurry to do anything. She smiled as she watched me make my way into the mountains once again.

I was having a strange but pleasant experience as if the trees and earth understood what I was experiencing. It felt like I was walking slightly off the ground as if gravity hardly existed.

When I reached the rock, I sat for a long time watching the clouds move over the valley. After a while, it was as if they were moving over and through me. I wondered how far they would travel before they disappeared, moving in a perfect circle around the earth. It made me wonder if life was like a circle, no beginning and no end, just a constant state of consciousness. I began to imagine that we were somehow connected like a giant spider web, an extension of the creator like the hand is an extension of the arm. I was lost in these thoughts until it seemed as if they started drifting away like tiny clouds, the last thing I remember thinking was ... I am ... I am.

I had lost all track of time until I became aware of a bluebird nearby chattering with the other birds of the forest. I had never realized how beautiful their voices were, or how their conversations made such perfect sense. The sound was something like tu-aw-wee, tu-aw-wee, which was repeated by another bird from somewhere in the distance. When I sat up to watch, it spread its wings and flew above my head over and over until I felt as if I was floating. I have no idea how long this went on until a small blue feather fell from the sky and landed on my dress. I knew that I had found my weyekin without having to think about it.

When I reached the bottom of the mountain where Tashe was tied up, even she seemed to know that I was different than I had been earlier. Looking into her kind and gentle eyes, I could sense that I was truly seeing her for the first time, that her eyes were so much more expressive than I had ever known before, and I suddenly realized that like me, she had a soul.

When I reached camp, it was almost dark, and Timpstetelew and Charging Elk were waiting for me looking worried. When I told them what had happened, they hugged me and told me I was now of The People. I started to take the feather out to show them, but Charging Elk stopped me. He told me that it was a personal object, sacred, and should only be taken out and contemplated in private. He said that I should make a small doeskin pouch, put it inside, and always keep it with me. He showed me the medicine bag he wore around his neck and told me that it is where he keeps the elk's tooth that he found during his vision quest. He told me that he had seen a pack of wolves trying to bring down a large elk during his seeking. The elk was fearless and charged the pack with its powerful antlers.

One of the wolves came at it from behind to grab its leg and was kicked high into the air and badly hurt.

Like mist, the wolves disappeared into the forest. The charging elk went to where it had happened and found the tooth, and that is how he got his name. He and Timpstetelew talked quietly for a moment, and then she said, "Your new name is Bluebird." Nothing had ever sounded so right.

Later that day, Timpstetelew brought me a beautiful little pouch that she had made of white doeskin with a blue bead on the outside. I put the blue feather inside and then in my pocket. As we began riding back to the mission the next day, I constantly put my hand in my pocket to feel the medicine bag and make sure that the little blue feather was still with me.

There was a sweet sadness to leaving that summer—like watching a beautiful sunset fade into the night or the last note of a beautiful song—longing for more, but knowing it could never be any better and letting it go.

It was the best and most important time I was to ever have among the Nez Perce People. I am certain that my weyekin still guides and protects me to this very day.

When we returned home, I was in for a momentous surprise. My Uncle Horace had arrived with the most recent wagon train. It would be impossible to put into words the joy that I felt when I saw his face for the first time. He hoisted me up into the air, kissed me on the forehead and nose, and told me that my grandparents, uncles, and aunts loved me dearly and couldn't wait to meet me one day.

Mother said it was hard to believe how he had grown into a powerful man in the ten years that they had been separated, that having him here was like having a piece of home. I spent the next couple of days drilling for gold. I wanted to know everything about our family and places that I loved but had never known.

Chapter 18

Matilda

It was a beautiful fall day when little Henry and I left home for the Whitman mission to start school. Both Father and Mother were too busy to go, so again they asked Matilda if she would do it. Matilda had been like a grandmother to us and was glad to accept. It was at least 120 miles over rough terrain and very little in the way of a path or trail.

Matilda had made the trip many times, so my parents were confident that she would get us there safely, though neither Father nor Mother would sleep soundly until she returned to let them know that all was well. They waved goodbye and watched us disappear over the first hill. It would take us three days to get there, camping each night under the stars, cooking supper, and telling stories by the campfire.

Little Henry and I loved to hear Matilda's stories about her life, especially those as a young girl. It is often difficult to tell the age of Indian men and women since they have such beautiful hair and skin, but live much of their life outdoors among harsh elements. Matilda guessed that she was about 45 years old, but she had lived a hard life and looked older.

She was a cousin to Chief Timothy and had been abducted when she was little older than I was and held captive for over a year. To our culture, this is one of the most horrific fates that could ever happen to a child or their family. Among the Indian people, it was not all that uncommon. Younger children are usually adopted and treated as family by tribal families that have lost loved ones. Matilda was at an awkward age where she was not yet a woman and not quite a child. Because of her beauty, several of the wives were jealous and resented her, treating her harshly.

She was not taken in with any of the families and was kept as a slave, though given a place to sleep and food to eat. There was one other girl who had also been abducted, but because she was younger, one of the families had taken her in. She was the only one Matilda could talk freely with, who understood what she was going through. The girl would often bring her food and small gifts to ease her suffering and loneliness. She also gave her one of her old blankets, since Matilda had told her that she was often very cold at night. Matilda was lonely, miserable, and missed her family terribly.

She had decided that next spring, she was going to escape or die trying. She knew that she had been taken east toward the sunrise and that she would have to go west toward the sunset to find her home. Beyond that, she had no idea where she was going. She decided to wait until there was a rainstorm so that her tracks would be covered. She had little more than the clothes she was wearing, a blanket, and enough dried food to last her several days.

She left the lodge at night during a rainstorm pretending to relieve herself, though no one seemed to care or even notice. She had taken her bearings over the last couple of days, and her only plan was to head directly west. The rain had done as she had hoped and covered her tracks, but a flash flood nearly drowned her when she tried to cross a small creek that was moving quickly. She attempted to use her blanket as a tent, but it had become so saturated that the rain easily soaked through.

She was wet from head to toe and as wretched as a person could be. She had grown strong from the hard work, but after two days of wandering aimlessly, she was out of food and growing weak. Fortunately, the sky cleared, and she managed to dry off, but it was still freezing at night with only the damp blanket to comfort her.

On the third night as she lay on a bed of old leaves, under her blanket she heard the call of a wolf nearby. Soon there were several of them howling, getting closer. She found a tree and was able to climb into it just as they discovered her scent and started leaping wildly for her legs. One found a limb and was almost able to get to her before it fell back to the ground. They stayed there stalking back and forth, and growling for the meal that was just out of reach.

By morning they had gone looking for easier prey. She was exhausted from going without sleep, having sprawled over a limb all-night, cold and frightened senseless. She had dozed several times and almost fallen to the ground right in the middle of the pack. When she felt it was safe to continue, she climbed down out of the tree and started walking away from the sunrise.

Right away, she was faced with her biggest challenge. In her path an unknown mountain range climbed sharply into the sky. She headed toward the lowest point and continued west. By sunset, she had almost reached the first summit before it was dark, and she was too tired to continue. It was freezing, but she was so exhausted that she slept through the night wrapped in her blanket covered with pine needles.

The next morning, she reached the summit only to find another even higher mountain directly in her path. For the first time she began to question her choice of leaving a life in which she was lonely and mistreated for the possibility of death by starvation, freezing, or even devoured by wild animals. She realized that even if she wanted to return, she couldn't since she had no idea whatsoever which direction to go.

Imagining herself with her family in the comfort of her village drove her on, and by sunset, she had reached the summit of the second peak. From there, she could see a beautiful valley below with a wide river running next to it. Excited, she wanted to go on, but her legs had given out, and she could go no farther. She had learned to cover herself with branches and pine needles to keep from freezing and hide her scent from whatever predator might be looking for an easy kill.

By midday she had descended the mountain and was facing a powerful river. The current from the spring runoff was so strong that she knew she could never swim against it. She eventually found a log small enough to drag, but big enough to help her float across the deep and fast-moving river. She wrapped her blanket around her shoulders and pushed off into the ice-cold water. She kicked as hard as she could for as long as she could but was unable to reach the other side. She was ready to give up and just let herself drift off when her feet finally touched the sandy bottom, and she pulled herself up onto the opposite side. Completely exhausted, she could not feel her arms or legs as she crawled to a flat spot in the sun and collapsed after drifting miles downstream.

Feeling disoriented, she laid on her back, watching the clouds gently drift by as if in a dream. She thought of how easy it would be to let her spirit go, like one of the clouds and join her ancestors. She was beyond the point of worrying or even caring where she was going or if she would ever make it home. She had lost all sense of time, but as she warmed in the sun, she began to hear the sound of horses approaching. She quickly scurried into a bush, crawling inside as far as she could go. Her deepest fear at this point was that the tribe who had kidnapped her had found her and after all she had been through, she would be punished and returned east.

One of the horses rode up next to the bush where she was hiding and stopped. Her thoughts went dark, as she realized that she had been discovered. Brought on by hunger and exhaustion, it seemed to her as if a voice was coming from the spirit world; but somehow it was speaking a language that she understood, asking what she was doing in this place. She was uncertain if she was dreaming or awake, but the voice was concerned and speaking Nez Perce.

They dismounted, and one of the men asked her again, "Why are you here, little sister?"

She wrapped her arms around his neck and cried for a long time. His smell was earthy like perfume, and his words were gentle and reassuring. When she finally looked at his face, she asked him where they were? He recognized the tattered and emaciated girl as the daughter of a friend from a neighboring Nez Perce village. He told her that he knew her family well; that she was safe. He pointed in a southwesterly direction and told her that they were less than two days ride from her home.

He asked how long she had been on foot. She had to recount how many sunsets she had seen and then answered that she thought it had been ten sunsets and pointed in the direction she thought she had come from. He told her that the Great Spirit must have guided her; that few people would have survived the mountains and wilderness with no food or shelter for so long. He went on to say that her people would be proud to tell her story of courage. The men built a fire to warm her and slowly let her eat some of the camas cakes they had brought along, patiently waiting for her to recover her strength.

When they reached her village, there was a joyful and tearful reunion with her family and loved ones. The men told everyone of her journey and the condition she was in when they found her. They told how they had never seen such courage and tenacity in one so young, that she had brought great honor to her family by escaping and making the perilous journey alone on foot.

She once told me that by the second night, she never expected to survive, but had decided that life had no meaning any longer if she was to be mistreated, unloved, and without her family.

Several years later, she was married to a brave young warrior named Running Deer. He and his father had paid 20 horses for the honor of marriage. She told me that on her wedding night, she was frightened speechless, but he was gentle and patient with her, and in time, a genuine love grew between them. They had two beautiful boys before he was killed on a buffalo hunt.

Brokenhearted, she vowed never to marry again, and devote the rest of her life to her sons and their families. Her sons were now powerful young men who adored their mother. They had married and moved to the villages of their wives. They had asked her many times to live with them, but she still felt her duty was to Chief Timothy for the kindness and generosity that he had shown her after her husband's death. She would continue to do as he had asked and look after our family. Her sons came to visit often, and she would sometimes stay with them for several weeks when Father and Mother were not so busy.

Matilda had her own lodge next to our house, but usually spent most of her time helping around the house and sleeping on a buffalo rug in little Henry's or my room. Mother said she couldn't imagine us having grown up with more love and attention than Matilda and old Mustups had given us.

As the three of us continued toward the Whitman mission, we made camp along the barren and rocky plains with the sound of coyotes and big gray wolves howling in the night. I have always loved sleeping under the stars, but this night was different, and I was frightened. The moon was full and hung low with the yellow color of a mad dog's eyes. There was an ominous wind that moaned as it slithered through the brush and trees. We were bathed in moonlight and surrounded by shadows that seemed to be silently seeking a life of their own with each puff of wind.

I tried to get Matilda to talk about it, but she told me it was best if we were quiet and went to sleep. We all shared a bed for warmth and comfort and held hands as Matilda chanted until little Henry and I drifted off to sleep. Matilda later told me that it was an evil spirit searching for a human body to possess, that her weyekin and spirit chant had protected us.

There was never to be a more faithful friend to our family, and I would always carry warm and loving memories of the woman I thought of as Grandmother throughout my life.

Chapter 19

Whitman School of 1846

I don't think it was nearly as hard for little Henry going away for the first time as it was for me since he had already met many of the other children, and had me to talk to and look out for him.

We had a new teacher named Mr. Rogers, who I instantly took a liking to. Like Mr. Hinman, he was young, only 24 and well educated, having gone to some of the best schools back east. I told him about the arrangement Mr. Hinman and I had made the previous year, and he was happy to do the same since he needed to learn the Nez Perce language, and I wanted to study music from him.

Like Mrs. Whitman, he had a beautiful singing voice but also played the violin exceptionally well. He and Mrs. Whitman often sang and played together after supper, and in my mind, I can still hear the intricate harmonies they wove together. He also taught the class to sing so that we would have a choir for Sunday services. It was the perfect arrangement since he gave me private music lessons, and I taught him the Nez Perce language and customs. He was very encouraging and told me that I had a lovely voice, and the lessons soon became one of the highlights of my year. He had a gift for language, and by the end of the winter term, he was almost fluent in the Sahaptin language.

I would never have a voice like Mrs. Whitman, but I had found a new passion through music. The biggest surprise was how close I had become to Mrs. Whitman. She had always been kind and loving with me but was often so busy that it was hard to find time to talk for more than a few minutes. It started with my curiosity about everything that had to do with New York, her family, and friends. I think talking about the people and places she loved made her feel closer to home, and like Mother, she had come from a large and close-knit family. She had arranged to give me cooking lessons, which gave us a good deal of time to talk.

She had such a beautifully sweet and clear soprano voice that the Indian people would travel from all over the territory to hear her sing at the services. She said that she learned from her father, who had a powerful baritone voice and was the choir director at their church. I have come to believe we are all born with a gift, but mine was not music. Even if I had worked hard all my life, I would never be able to sing like Mrs. Whitman. I also believe it is what we do with what we are given that defines who we are.

This year the Whitmans had a full house of children they were either caring for or had adopted, both whites and mixed. Including little Henry and myself, there were 15 children as well as several children of immigrant families who might stay for a time while preparing to make their way to the Willamette Valley.

There was Helen Mar Meek, who was now nine years old, Mary Ann Bridger was 11 and David Malin, who Little Henry would spend most of his time playing with, was eight.

Narcissa had named him after a close school friend. He was half-Indian and half-Spanish. His father had been an employee of the Hudson Bay Company and had abandoned his baby son David and his wife at a village near the mission. David was a quiet and sensitive boy who had been through so much in his short life and was very happy to see me again since I spoke his native Sahaptin language.

Perrin Whitman was 16-years-old and was more of a teacher's assistant to Mr. Rogers than student. He was continuing much of his education privately with Mr. Rogers and Doctor Whitman, as well as learning many of the skills necessary to operate his own mission one day.

There were also the seven Sager children who had already experienced too many unimaginable hardships and tragedies in their young lives. They were now embraced in the loving arms and hearts of Marcus and Narcissa Whitman. The oldest were the two boys, John, 15, then Francis, who was 13. The five girls were Catherine, 12, Elizabeth, nine, Matilda Jane, six, Hannah, four, and the little baby Henrietta who was now two.

Lastly was Cyrus Walker, who was nine years old. He was the first son of missionaries, Elkanah and Mary Walker and had grown up on the mission site at a place called Tshimakain among the Spokane Indians. His father Elkanah was prone to moods of depression and bad temper, sometimes embarrassing his wife Mary with outbursts in front of friends and strangers. Mary had also mentioned to Mother that he was often critical of her, and she felt that it was almost impossible to please him. She had barely known him before they were married and left for the journey over the Oregon Trail. She soon became pregnant, suffering from morning sickness as well as the mood swings of her new husband. To add to her suffering, there were three other bickering couples and the hardships of the trail.

Cyrus Walker had been born at the Whitman mission on August 29, 1838, the first white male child born in the Oregon Territory. He was one of six children who spent nine years living in a 14 square foot log cabin with a roof made of poles, grass, and mud. It leaked dirty water on the dirt floor whenever it rained and must have been miserable. They lived in that cabin for nine years until the fireplace wall caved in, almost crushing Elkanah.

In January of 1841, the Eells' cabin burned down during a winter night when it was eight degrees below zero outside, and they were forced to move in with the Walkers. Myra Eells had been sick for some time, so Mary was, now responsible for caring for Myra as well as her own family. A typical day for Mary was 16 hours long if everything went right. During the nine years at Tshimakain, she never had a stove, having to cook and bake in the fireplace. She was also responsible for the garden, helping with the fieldwork, milking their six cows, washing, ironing, cleaning, soap making, candle making, sewing clothes, making shoes, making repairs on the cabin, and on and on. Her deepest regret was that she didn't have more time for the Spokane natives. The mission experience had been a heartbreaking failure, in large part because they had never mastered the language. When they were forced to leave Tshimakain, Mary wrote this poem for her children to remember it by:

Tshimakain! Oh, how fine, fruits and flowers abounding,
And the breeze, through the trees, life and health conferring.
And the rill, near the hill, with its sparkling water
Lowing herds and prancing steed round it used to gather.
And the Sabbath was so quiet and the log house chapel

Where the Indians used to gather in their robes and blankets.
Now it stands, alas forsaken: no one with the Bible.
Comes to teach the tawny Skailu (people) of Kai-ko-len-so-tin
(God)
Other spots on earth may be to other hearts as dear;
But not to me; the reason why, it was the place that bore me.

When we had first reached the Whitman mission, it was a beehive of activity with men working on the buildings and children playing in the yard. All of the activity came to a halt as they quietly watched us approach the mission house. Little Henry and I both felt awkward and shy with all of the attention until Doctor Whitman bolted out of the front door, lifted us off our horses, and gave us each one of his bear hugs. He greeted Matilda warmly and thanked her for bringing us. Just about that time, Mrs. Whitman came rushing outside, taking both of us in her arms at once.

Everyone was excited to see each other again or meet for the first time. Mr. Rogers came out to greet little Henry and me, making us feel at home with his warmth and kindness. Mrs. Whitman told us that she wanted everyone to get to know each other, and there was a celebration dinner and dessert in our honor; that she and Mr. Rogers had something special planned. John and Frances Sager had to return to the stockyard, and Perrin Whitman needed to help Mr. Whitman, but otherwise, we were all free to play for the rest of the day.

Matilda ate lunch, unpacked the horses, and helped us get settled in our dormitory before she told us that she was going back. I wasn't ready for her to leave and tried to talk her into staying a couple more days to rest. She told us that the sooner she returned, the sooner our parents could stop worrying about us. It was a tearful goodbye as Matilda whispered in each of our ears that we were always in her heart. Before long, we were all playing games in the yard and had forgotten our sadness for the time being.

The dinner and dessert were delicious, and the treat was hearing Mrs. Whitman and the new teacher Mr. Rogers perform together. They both had wonderful voices, and Mr. Rogers played the violin beautifully that night. They played mostly hymns that we were able to sing along with as well as several popular songs I had never heard before. It was a magical night, and I could hardly contain my excitement when Mr. Rogers told me he would give me music lessons as soon as school started.

In contrast to all of the joy and light that we were feeling about school starting, there was a dark cloud hanging over the mission. The measles had become an epidemic among the Cayuse, and the immigrants continued to flood into the Oregon Territory. The Whitman's home was the epicenter of the two opposing peoples pulling in completely different directions. Their mission was littered with covered wagons and Indian teepees. Fear and superstition mixed with anger and resentment is a bad combination, and as if a tornado hovered above us, almost everyone was getting sucked into the contention. Many of the Cayuse felt that the Whitmans had something to do with their misfortunes and started vandalizing the mission by breaking windows, tearing down fences, and dismantling machinery.

The winter of 1846 was the harshest that anyone could remember. The rivers were frozen solid, and the plains were covered in a deep layer of snow. Many of the horses and other animals had come into the valley to try to find food and shelter, but there was none to be found.

I worried about our mission at Lapwai but knew that we had a barn full of hay and grains and were better prepared than anyone else. The Indian people had never found it necessary to store food for their animals before this winter, now half of their horses and cattle had died from exposure and starvation. Doctor Whitman was afraid that the buffalo skin lodges were not going to be enough to keep the Indian people warm this winter, that many might get sick or die from cold and hunger. The measles had spread to epidemic proportions, and the Cayuse were angry, blaming the doctor for bringing the white people to their territory.

The Whitmans had a lean-to on the side of the blacksmith shop with hay and grains piled up, but the doctor was worried it wouldn't be enough to get through a winter like this and started rationing it out.

It broke my heart to see Tashe under the shelter, cold and hungry with her head down to her knees. I was able to save most of my fruit and vegetables to give her when I went out to comb her each day. One day the doctor caught me giving her my vegetables but never said a word, instead he gave me an old blanket that I used to cover her with at night.

Like Father, he seemed to know when I needed a boost and asked me if I wanted to take a ride. When I went back into the house to change my shoes, Mrs. Whitman asked what I was doing. I told her that the doctor and I were going to take the horses out for some exercise. As we were leaving, she put her wool scarf around my neck that covered me from my eyes to my shoulders.

I felt like I had been stuffed into a warm and cozy perfume scented cocoon. Unfortunately, my red wool mittens were old and worn, so before long, both my hands and feet were completely numb. I tried to rub and pound them against my legs, but it didn't help; still, Tashe and I were moving like one being, oblivious to the biting wind.

By the time we got back to the mission, my feet were numb up to my ankles, and as I dismounted Tashe, I started to fall forward. I think the doctor must have anticipated it and caught me as I fell. He lifted me up and said, "I bet you wouldn't mind some hot milk and mush about now." Was he ever right.

Another blessed event was the birth of my new little sister Amelia on December 12, 1846. Doctor Whitman once again traveled from Waiilatpu to assist in the birth and make sure that Mother and the baby were well cared for afterward.

He and Father spent a good deal of time talking about the troubles that had flared up recently because of the many deaths from the measles epidemic. The Indian people couldn't understand why so many of their people had died, and so few of the whites died even when they had the sickness. Father told me that even the best doctors still had no idea why some people had a resistance to a disease, and some didn't. For a short time, it was like the calm before the storm, we could feel something ominous in the air.

As 1846 came to an end, the position and outlook of the missions was growing bleak. My parents had closed the school since no one was willing to attend. Faithful followers had been threatened and intimidated into staying away by a hostile group of young warriors. The same went for Father's sermons, only our family and a small group including Chief Timothy, Matilda and Mustups attended. A militant group of Nez Perce started vandalizing the mission by breaking windows, tearing out our fences, and destroying the crops. They had even managed to tear away a section of our roof. At first, Father tried to repair the windows, but he soon had to settle on boarding them up since he had run out of glass.

The most serious incident occurred one night when Uncle Horace was away, taking supplies to the Whitmans. A group of about 15 Nez Perce had gathered in the front yard and started tearing our fence out and using it for a giant bonfire. They also began burning a large stock of recently milled wood that Father planned to use for construction. They then showed their contempt by gambling and drinking whiskey and had become loud and belligerent, shouting threats and making it impossible to sleep.

Mother tried to stop Father as he got out of bed and started dressing, telling him that they sounded as if they were out for blood. He told her that he could not sit by and let them destroy our home and openly insult our family.

The last thing he did before he left the house was to put on his heavy buffalo robe to keep warm. When he reached the fire, he began pulling out pieces of the fence; four of the Nez Perce grabbed Father and threw him to the ground. This happened several more times before they picked him up and threw him on his back into the fire. When Mother saw this, she ran out the door and helped him up and out of the fire. He received several minor burns, but his thick buffalo robe had saved his life. Father told her he was fine and began pulling boards out of the fire again. As the leader started toward Father, Mother stepped in front of him and told the brave that she knew his mother and father well, that he was bringing dishonor on his family this night. She also told him that we had never done anything but help the Nez Perce and his family.

I am not sure what changed their minds, but they slowly gathered their possessions and left. When my parents entered the house, I saw tears in Father's eyes and have never seen him more despondent. He didn't stop to talk; he went directly to his room and I could hear him weeping for the first time in my life. Mother told us to leave him alone, that it would embarrass him to have us see him like that. The next morning at breakfast, he was very solemn and told Mother that this was the fault of the white man who had taught them the sins of alcohol and gambling.

The following day another group rode by throwing rocks at the few remaining windows and telling my parents to get out of the territory, or they would tie them up, throw them in the river, and take our belongings.

The freezing winter conditions just added to our problems and everyone's misery. Father estimated that the temperature had dropped as low as 30 degrees below zero. The people were not only cold, they were hungry because so much of the game and plants had died. Teepees were not adequate to handle the extreme cold and caused many people to become sick, in some cases freeze to death. Resistance was low, and measles began spreading like wildfire, killing many of the Nez Perce, and almost half of the Cayuse population.

When spring came, the Indian people brought the little wheat and grains they had to be ground, but Father was unable to do so since the mill had been vandalized and damaged. He tried to explain that we couldn't even grind our own wheat, but they would not listen and became agitated, once again threatening to take his life.

Through all of this, there was never one word between my parents about giving up or moving on. I don't think that either of them were sure that we would survive such hostility, but they felt things would change, and it was a risk they were committed to taking.

Adding to our problems, the Catholic priests were inciting the Nez Perce and Cayuse to take action against "The Protestant devils," as they called us. Over one-fourth of the Cayuse and Nez Perce had converted to Catholicism, in good part due to the money and gifts they were given as an incentive. To try and counteract this, Father went to one of the villages to talk about the evils of the Papist priests, how the Pope and Cardinals lived like kings while their people starved to death. The response was unfriendly, and the next day Father found one of our oxen in agony with its ears and tail cut off.

Making the situation worse, a man named William McBean had replaced Mr. McKinley as prefect in charge of Fort Walla Walla. He was arrogant and cold toward our missions. He was also a devout Catholic, making every effort to bring a Catholic mission to the Walla Walla area and force the Protestants out. He immediately invited and welcomed Bishop Brouillet and his four associates to the fort to discuss sites. Within weeks they had set up a new mission at the village of a Cayuse man named Young Chief. It was less than 25 miles from Waiilatpu, and relations went from bad to worse.

Little Henry and I were anxious for school to be over for several reasons. Of course, we missed Mother and Father, but we were anxious to see Martha Jane and our new little sister Amelia. It was hard to believe how our family had grown, how different we were, and yet somehow the same.

By the time we returned home in early spring of 1847, Martha Jane was at that shy stage, hiding behind Mother's dress. I held out the doll that I had made for her at Waiilatpu and waved it at her. She had the biggest, softest brown eyes that I had ever seen, and as she waddled her way toward me, she fell back on her bottom. She looked around the room to make sure that everyone was watching, put her hands on the ground, rolled around and lifted herself up to her knees, grabbed the table, and got back up on her feet.

I clapped my hands, which got me a big smile, and with a look of total concentration on her sweet face, she started toward me again. Just as she reached me, I caught her in my arms. She immediately grabbed the doll and stuck it in her mouth. She held it out to me several times so I could give it kisses, then leaned her head against my shoulder like little Henry use to do. It was a timeless moment of pure innocence, and my heart melted as I held her in my arms.

Amelia was a three-month-old bundle of joy, constantly smiling and wanting to be carried around so that she could see everything going on in the house. Other than a few more gray hairs, Father seemed the same, but Mother looked frailer than I had ever seen her, so I vowed to myself to help her in every way I could.

Chief Timothy was also there to greet us. He told me that he had lost over half of his horses, but was happy to see Tashe looking so well. He asked if she had suffered over the winter?

I told him how the Whitmans let her stay in the shelter next to the blacksmith shop and gave her extra oats and hay; that the doctor gave me an old blanket to cover her with at night and let me ride her almost every day.

"It was right for you to have Tashe," he said.

It didn't take long for me to realize that something was very wrong at our mission. I went to the schoolroom to look for a book and found the room dusty and lifeless. In the past, it would have been overflowing with children and adults, now it was empty. The same went for Father's Sunday services. There were often as many as two thousand Nez Perce in attendance; that Sunday, there were only about a dozen loyal friends. The meetinghouse had part of the roof missing, and most of the windows had been broken out. In Father's printing room, there was paper and type spilled all over the floor. My heart ached for my parents, who had given so much and worked so hard these past years.

One night I found Father sitting at his desk staring at a blank piece of paper.

I asked what he was doing, and he said, "I can't seem to find words for a sermon that no one will hear, but I refuse to give up hope. My faith tells me that things will get better, that the Nez Perce will return one day."

When Father had come to pick us up earlier at the Whitman mission, I overheard him talking with the doctor about the printing press.

Doctor Whitman told Father, "Henry, if you don't think you're going to use it anymore, Mr. Hinman wants to purchase it and start a newspaper in the Willamette Valley."

Father replied, "I can't say for sure if I will or not, but a newspaper is a good idea, so I'll consider it."

That summer seemed like the end of an era as we watched the printing press being loaded and taken off in pieces to its new home with Mr. Hinman. I could almost picture it making the same trip we had once made on Hudson Bay Canoes westward along the mighty Columbia River and then south down the Willamette River. I had heard that new buildings were starting to spring up in what was now the town of Portland.

Word had come by messenger that there would be thousands of immigrants coming over the Oregon Trail stopping at the Whitman mission to rest and take on badly needed supplies. Doctor Whitman had asked Father to bring all the flour and grains that we could spare when we returned for the next school year. He also warned us that the measles had reached epidemic proportions.

Since little Henry had never been exposed to or had the measles, it was decided that he shouldn't go, but could attend the following year. He took it hard and was upset that he would miss out on all of the fun and excitement of a new school year with his new friends.

He moped around for several days, trying to make us all feel guilty until he finally couldn't help himself and got back to being his rambunctious and noisy self.

There was other news of an ominous tone coming from Waiilatpu. One of the more hostile Cayuse warriors was known to have killed at least one of the immigrants who had recently come over the trail. He had come to the mission looking to get medicine for a sick relative. Doctor Whitman gave him the medicine but refused to shake his hand. The man rode off angry and deeply offended. That night he choked to death on a piece of meat.

The Cayuse were superstitious and believed that the doctor used some kind of supernatural power to put a spell on the man causing his death. The man's village was up in arms and threatening to kill the Doctor. Chief Lawyer was with us when we received the message and told us that it would be best if Doctor Whitman and his family left Waiilatpu until the hearts of the people were better toward them.

During the summer of 1847, a well-known Canadian artist named Paul Kane had come to visit the Whitman mission. He had spent a good deal of time among the Indians and was interested in drawing some of the Cayuse chiefs. Doctor Whitman let Frank Sager take him to the lodge of Chief Tiloukaikt, where the chief and Tomahas both consented to an interview. When he realized he was being drawn, Tomahas demanded to see it. Fearing that Mr. Kane would give it to Doctor Whitman for an evil purpose, Tomahas tried to take it from him and throw it in the fire. There was a struggle between the two of them, and when Mr. Kane was finally able to retrieve it, he and Frank immediately mounted their horses and took off for Fort Walla Walla.

Mr. Kane had considerable experience with the Indians, had lived among them, and dressed like them at times. He later told Mr. McBean that from his experience, he felt that the Whitmans were in grave danger and should come to the fort. He would later tell friends that Mr. McBean seemed disinterested and unconcerned.

Several days later, Mr. Kane took that message to Waiilatpu and tried to convince the doctor that their lives were in danger. He told the doctor that he had never seen such anger and open hostility from the Indian people. Doctor Whitman told him that they had far too much invested in the mission to give up now, that there was no real danger from the Cayuse, that they had often made empty threats in the past.

Doctor Whitman decided to take a trip to The Dalles to look at the recently deserted Methodist mission for sale. When he returned to Fort Walla Walla, he was dismayed to find Bishop Blanchet and his assistants there. He felt that the Catholic priest's negative depictions could one-day lead to the deaths of both Protestant and Methodist missionaries. When he found out the Bishop's brother, Archbishop Francois Blanchet was on his way with 21 assistants and that Bishop Blanchet had arranged to use Young Chief's house as a mission, he confronted him. They had a terrible argument before Doctor Whitman raged out of the fort, headed for Waiilatpu.

He had only been home for two days when he agreed to take a group of immigrants to The Dalles over a new route that he had recently discovered. On his way back, he ran into another group of immigrants from Iowa that included Judge L.W. Saunders. He was so impressed with his experience that he asked if he would take over the teaching position since the current teacher Mr. Rogers wanted to pursue his career as a minister. Mr. Saunders consented to take over for the school year and was joined by a tailor named Issac Gilliland.

Shortly after the doctor's return, there was another incident with the Cayuse.

Narcissa would not allow the Indians in their mission house, which was considered deeply offensive to the Indian people. A group of Cayuse became angry when they were told not to enter the house. One of the men hit the doctor in the face with his fist and threatened to kill him with a club as another man pushed past them and broke down the door with an axe. Had it not been for the intervention of Chief Tiloukaikt, who was visiting the mission, he may have been killed that day. The situation continued to decline as tensions continued to escalate.

Chapter 20

Last Days at Waiilatpu

In the winter of 1847, I had just turned ten years old, and my parents decided that I would be returning to the Whitman mission school alone since little Henry had never had the measles. Father was taking supplies to Waiilatpu and planned to help Doctor Whitman care for many sick people, both Indian and white. My Uncle Horace and Mr. Jackson were going to go with us to the Whitman Mission, then continue to Fort Walla Walla to deliver flour and grains, then purchase the supplies we needed. They planned to hurry back to help Mother and would take a shortcut bypassing the Whitman mission.

The only other white person at our mission was Mary Johnson, who had been with us for several months helping Mother with the children and around the house. Things had settled down for the time being. Chief Timothy, and several of the other chiefs, had recently come to the mission to tell my parents they were sorry for what had happened. He went on to tell them that it was a small group making trouble, that there were still many like him who valued our friendship. When Father told Chief Timothy that he would be gone for a week or more, he and Eagle offered to stay nearby to watch over Mother and the children.

By the time Father and I were ready to leave for Waiilatpu, our mill still hadn't been repaired, so we took 20 pack horses loaded with wheat and other grains to be ground at the Whitman mission.

This would be the last trip that Father and I would take together from our mission at Lapwai.

I was now old enough to understand how hard he had worked for everyone but himself, and my love and respect for him was infinite. Our trips over the open ranges, mountains, and rivers are now like a dream, almost too inconceivably rich to be true. Lying next to the campfires beneath a million stars, asking a million questions, he never once lost his patience or interest in my curiosity. I now see these times as more than trips along a trail, something spiritual, a gift from God.

Tashe was part of that gift. She had become so much more than a horse to me; she was like family. She had learned to anticipate what I was going to do before I did it. My slightest movement told her what I wanted or where I wanted to go. She was like a living, breathing work of art, more beautiful than any other I would ever see in my lifetime, and this would be our last trip together.

Just as we approached the Whitmans' mission house, the door burst open and out ran Helen Mar, Mary Ann, Elizabeth, and Catherine Sager, followed by Mrs. Whitman. We did what girls our age normally do; we jumped up and down and squealed with joy. After we calmed down, I found myself once again enveloped in the soft sweet-scented embrace of Mrs. Whitman. The doctor had come out and was shaking hands and talking with Father before he picked me up and swung me around and gave me one of his special hugs spiced with the smell of pipe tobacco and buckskin.

The Sager girls helped me unpack, Father and the doctor went off to talk privately. Frank came around from the back of the house to say hello and asked if I wanted him to take Tashe over to the corral.

I magnanimously told him, "It would be all right if you want to take her for a short ride."

His eyes lit up, and I knew this was the kind of glue that held a good friendship together. He and John had grown tall and lanky with dusty blonde hair from the sun and deep blue eyes. They were strong from hard work, and I had never seen them once pass by someone who needed help without offering it.

After Matilda Jane and I had finished the supper dishes, we decided to go outside and see what Frank was doing over at the stable. We found him cleaning a rifle and asked why he was doing it. He told us that Doctor Whitman planned to slaughter one of the beef tomorrow and asked if he would shoot it for him. He told us that it was his father's gun and meant a lot to him. We watched as he took an old piece of rag, oiled it, and then pushed it up and down the barrel until he was satisfied with the job.

Matilda Jane asked, "Are you any good with it?"

Frances said, "I think so, I've been practicing all summer. I'd show you, but it's too crowded around here, and I would probably scare people to death the way things have been lately."

He must have felt like one of the famous trappers, like Joe Meek or Jim Bridger, as he sighted down the glistening barrel of his father's rifle.

The next day I was outside talking with Catherine when I looked up and saw Tashe over by the mill with an Indian man jumping her back and forth over the millstream. I ran as fast as I could, calling out to Tashe. The man made a quick turn and charged at me full speed. I could see that Tashe was holding back, but by the time they stopped, Tashe and I were nearly nose to nose. As he slowly dismounted with a menacing look of hatred on his face, I suddenly realized that it was Tomahas.

He was a big muscular man with long black hair and gray eyes. I had seen him before but had never spoken to him; Father had told me to stay clear. He tried to intimidate me by staring at me for a long time, but I just stared right back.

I grabbed Tashe by the reins, and with hot tears of anger in my eyes, I asked him, "What in the world do you think you are doing on my horse?"

Tomahas said, "If it is not little Miss Spalding. I like your horse very much. I think Tashe will suit me well when you are all gone."

I could feel my hands ball up, and I was just about to fly at him when Frank grabbed me from behind and held on to my shoulders tightly.

Tomahas let out an insane laugh and said, "Ahhh, we have a little mountain lion … I like that."

Frank turned away as the man glared at us with his evil eyes, but I glared back at him until he started laughing again. He then slapped Tashe hard on the rump and slowly walked to his horse, leapt up, and rode away laughing. I could tell that Tashe was mad, too, and would have gladly kicked him if he had been behind her.

Frank looked scared and told me, "You need to be more careful around Tomahas. They say he's a killer and hates white people. He and his bunch are looking for trouble, so stay out of his way, or you might get someone hurt trying to protect you."

That night after prayer meeting, I saw Tomahas talking with Chief Tiloukaikt, so I got as close as I could without being noticed.

I overheard him telling the chief, "Why do you pray to the white man's God, they are making a fool of you and planning to poison your people and take your land and horses, why else would they be here? Two of your sons are dead, and one is dying, we must kill the white people before they kill us, before they are too many."

I couldn't hear what the chief said, or even guess what he was thinking, but he looked upset when he left. I ran as fast as I could to where Father was getting ready to give his sermon and told him what I had just heard and what had happened that morning. I don't think I have ever seen Father look so shaken.

He told me, "Frank is right, Eliza, you need to stay away from that man. I'm sorry you've become part of this, but these are dangerous times, and it's best you know who to stay clear of."

Through October and November, all of the rooms at the Whitman mission were filling up. Mrs. Rebecca Hays was recently widowed with a four-year-old son named Henry Clay. Overwhelmed and overworked, Narcissa had asked her to stay on as a cook and help around the house. She and her son were put up in the mansion house with the Hall family.

Miss Lorinda Bewley had come to the mission with her parents, who were planning to settle in the Willamette Valley. She was what Narcissa was looking for in a female to help with teaching. After a great deal of persuasion, she was able to get Lorinda to agree to stay through the winter, and she was given a room upstairs in the mission house. Her brother Crocket and his friend reached the mission several days after Lorinda, both seriously ill with measles.

They were put to bed immediately in a room next to the kitchen, while the rest of the Bewley family continued to the Willamette Valley with the promise that Lorinda and Crocket would follow in the spring.

When the Canfield family arrived, there was little room left. They had become close friends with the Saunders during the trip over the trail, so the Saunders made room for them in the blacksmith shop.

Both Joseph Smith and Elam Young were experienced lumbermen, so when they arrived, they were sent along with their families to the sawmill in the nearby Blue Mountains.

Marguerite Osborne had recently given birth to a baby boy who had died within hours. Ten days later, she became deathly ill with measles. She lay in bed, prostrate for almost two weeks before she began to recover. Her little girl Salvijane then came down with the disease, continuing to get worse each day. Doctor Whitman tried everything he could to save her, but on November 24, 1847, she died in her mother's arms.

There had been much talk among the Indians about how few whites had died of this disease, and how so many Indians had perished. The Cayuse were beginning to think that it was a plan to exterminate their people so that the whites could take their land and horses. For this reason, Narcissa invited one of the elderly Indian Chiefs to see the body of little Salvijane lying dead to show him that the disease killed whites as well as Indians. When the chief looked down upon the little girl, he was quiet for a time; he then broke out with a blood-curdling laugh, turned, and walked out of the room. This was not the response Narcissa had hoped for, and it frightened her badly.

Our lives were not easy, and it sometimes seemed as if there was no rhyme or reason as to who would survive and who would perish. Since Doctor Whitman was often called upon to visit the Cayuse and Umatilla villages to treat the many sick people, Narcissa would help treat minor ailments when he was gone. She was busy working around the house one day when an Indian woman barged into the kitchen and told Narcissa that her husband was dying. It was cold and pouring down rain, but Narcissa bundled up and trudged through the mud for almost a mile until they reached the woman's lodge. The man was in a comatose state and in a condition she had seen several times before. She returned to the mission and gathered the medicine she had seen the doctor use for this sickness as well as tea, sugar, and several other things that she thought might help him recover. After administering the medicine and helping him drink some warm tea and sugar, he started to come to and eventually fully recovered.

The man was Nicholas Finley, whose father was the well-known trapper Jacques Raphael "Jocko" Finlay from Scotland. His mother was Teskwentichina of the Spokane tribe. His Indian name was Schwnmuimiah, and he had been an apprentice trapper to Tom McKay. Once Mrs. Whitman had helped him revive, they could not stop expressing their gratitude. He even moved their lodge next to the mission house so they could be more helpful to the Whitmans. It was an ironic twist that his lodge would become the meeting place where the demise of the Whitman Mission would be planned.

When we had first arrived at the Whitman mission, Father was shocked to see how many people were sick or dying, both Indian and white. The Whitmans were completely overwhelmed and had hardly had any rest in weeks. Doctor Whitman was rarely able to sit and have his meals without interruption and was growing pale and weak from overworking.

Father and the doctor had decided to call a meeting with the Cayuse chiefs to let them know that they would sell the mission at Waiilatpu to the Catholic priests, that Doctor and Mrs. Whitman would move to the Willamette Valley if they wanted them to leave. Of the 15 chiefs, only one accepted, the other 14 rejected the idea and told them that only a small group of trouble makers were talking about killing; that the others were grateful for all the Whitmans had done and wanted them to stay.

At their new mission, the Catholic priests were running out of food and supplies and asked Father and Doctor Whitman to help them out. Father and the doctor talked it over and felt that if they were going to stay, they would eventually need to make peace with the Catholic priests.

Father agreed to bring them the food and supplies they had asked for and arranged for a meeting to try and resolve their differences. It was a cordial meeting, but Father left with an even deeper sense of distrust.

The next day the doctor told Father that he had to visit one of the villages and could use his help. Early the next morning, I watched as they disappeared into a menacing fog that hung eerily over the mission grounds. I went into the living room to offer Mrs. Whitman tea and found her with red and swollen eyes. She had been crying. She thanked me but said that she was not thirsty. Father had asked me if he could take Tashe to carry his medical bag and supplies.

I can't explain it, but I could feel that something was wrong, and watched them vanish with a sense of dread.

That night Doctor Whitman returned long after I had gone to sleep, without Father. The next morning, he told me not to be alarmed, but Father had taken a fall from Thunder. As I started to stand up in alarm, he put his hands up and told me that nothing was broken, that Father would just need to rest up for a day or two. Then he would return to the mission to say goodbye.

For the rest of the morning, I went out into the yard every few minutes, hoping to see Father and Tashe come riding up. Eventually, the school bell rang, and I had to go inside. I just couldn't concentrate and found myself constantly looking out of the window. The air was still thick with fog when I heard a loud gunshot and almost jumped out of my skin. I got up and looked out of the window to see that it was just Frank shooting the cow that they were getting ready to butcher.

It struck me as odd that there were so many Cayuse men standing around silently watching.

I then saw Chief Tiloukaikt and Tomahas ride by with such serious looks on their faces that an alarm sounded inside my soul. As they rode past the schoolroom window, I remember hoping that it was just someone needing medical assistance, but there was a bad feeling I couldn't shake or understand.

Eliza

Part Three

The Nez Perce

"If the white man wants to live in peace with the Indian, he can live in peace. There need be no trouble. Treat all men alike. Give them all the same law. Give them all an even chance to live and grow. All men were made by the Great Spirit Chief. They are all brothers. The earth is the mother of all people, and all people should have equal rights upon it. You might as well expect the rivers to run backward as that any man who was born free should be contented penned up and denied liberty to go where he pleases. If you tie a horse to a stake, do you expect he will grow fat? If you pen an Indian up on a small spot of earth and compel him to stay there, he will not be contented nor will he grow and prosper. ... Let me be a free man, free to travel, free to stop, free to work, free to trade, free to think and talk and act for myself, and I will obey every law, or submit to the penalty."

—Chief Joseph

Chapter 1

Chief Timothy

Growing up in the Nez Perce village of Lapwai, I knew little about my own culture. My life was completely centered on my family and that of the Nez Perce. The white people who came to our mission were like foreigners to me, and I had no practical knowledge of their world, only impressions from the stories I had heard. Everything at the mission was centered on school and church. Along with my family, there was Timpstetelew, who was like a sister to me. We did almost everything together, and I have come to realize that the amazing freedom we had to roam, to investigate every aspect of nature and the earth was a rare gift for a white child in the 1840s. To the Nez Perce, it was simply a way of life. They are people of the earth and sky, attuned to every vibration, every variation of the elements, an ability most of us have forgotten or never possessed.

One person stood out above all others, guided me along the pathway of Nez Perce spirituality and tradition, and taught me to respect all things.

When my father baptized Chief Tamootsin, he was given the name Timothy, and over time he became like the grandfather I had never known. He was not much older than my parents, yet he possessed an old soul; a profoundly wise human being. With me he was infinitely patient and gentle, yet respected among the Nez Perce as a great hunter and warrior. He was a quiet and thoughtful man you would not want to face on the battlefield. He would occasionally invite Timpstetelew and me to stay the night at the lodge of his family or take us on long rides. He often talked of his ancestors, showing us sacred sites where they were put to rest. From these experiences with him, I learned most of what I know about the Nez Perce.

My father baptized Chief Joseph at the same time as Chief Timothy; what I experienced with him and his family also had a profound effect on me. His village in the Wallowa Valley is among the most dramatic and beautiful places I have ever seen.

The two great chiefs were once close friends who willingly, gladly shared their wisdom and love of the land and everything within it. Though they would never clash physically, it is one of my greatest regrets that they would eventually grow apart because of their beliefs.

They were both remarkable storytellers. To the Nez Perce, a story is much more than something to entertain with; it is a history and life lesson to be learned and passed on to the next generation. Before my father wrote the first books in the Nez Perce language, it was handed down exclusively by word of mouth. I wish I could recall all that Chief Timothy and Chief Joseph had taught me, but much of my memory has become like a dream, some as fresh as yesterday's rain, some like clouds long gone on the wind.

I could never understand why the Indian people fought among themselves and remember asking Chief Timothy if they had always been enemies with the Blackfoot people. He told me a legend that had been passed down to him from his grandfather about a time when they were once at peace.

Chief Timothy said, "Our warriors had gone over the mountains to hunt buffalo when they came upon a large band of Blackfoot looking to do battle. Our head chief was a brave and fierce warrior named Red Wolf. Our men were few, and the Blackfoot were many. After the battle, only a few of the Nez Perce, including Red Wolf, survived to return home. There was great sorrow, and many funeral songs and dances were held for the lost loved ones. Plans were made to avenge the fallen warriors. That winter Red Wolf gathered all of the warriors from his village and many of those from the surrounding villages for a meeting. They agreed to spend the winter and early spring preparing for war by making bows, arrows, lances, and shields. When they were ready, they held a war dance that went on for two days to gather their courage. They then journeyed to the Blackfoot country, taking cover in a wooded cove where they remained hidden, waiting for the Blackfoot to appear.

"When a large party of over six hundred Blackfoot entered the trap, the Nez Perce attacked without mercy, killing all but the few who escaped. When Red Wolf and his men returned, there were so many scalps that they formed a great pile for the women to clean and stretch. They also had taken over two thousand horses. It was a great victory, and the Nez Perce People chanted and danced for three days and nights.

"For several years, the Nez Perce went unharmed by the Blackfoot on their way to and from the buffalo hunting grounds that had once been so fiercely protected. When Red Wolf died, his son Young Red Wolf took his place.

"The Blackfoot had been patiently rebuilding their forces and awaiting their moment of vengeance. Several years later, when the Nez Perce returned for the buffalo hunt, they were trapped in a canyon as the Blackfoot fell upon them like a swarm of hornets. The ones who escaped were relentlessly pursued hundreds of miles until only a few remained alive, including Young Red Wolf. When they reached their village, they slipped in under cover of darkness, more dead than alive. Nearly all of the men had been killed. The Blackfoot camped nearby, planning to attack the village, leaving no survivors except for the ones they would take as slaves. There was great sorrow and wailing among the women who mourned the loss of their men. Red Wolf told them to prepare their death songs; the Blackfoot would be coming soon.

"Among the Nez Perce People, Young Red Wolf's only child, Wahluna, was considered the most beautiful and beloved of the entire nation. That night after Young Red Wolf had told them what to expect, she slipped away through the dark forest toward the Blackfoot camp. She was committed to do whatever she could to help her people, even if it meant sacrificing herself to a terrible death by torture. Long before she reached the camp, she could hear the sound of their victory drums and singing. The entire forest was lit up from giant bonfires, and the Blackfoot were all singing and dancing as if in a trance.

"Knowing that weakness would mean certain death, she put her fear aside as she approached the camp. She bravely entered to the sound of war drums pounding in her ears and the sight of painted warriors glistening with sweat, and a horrifying pile of Nez Perce scalps. When they saw her, the drumming and dancing instantly stopped as they glared at her in surprise. With her hands in the air as a sign of supplication, they were unsure what to think of this vision of beauty and courage that had the audacity to invade their sacred rite. Several of the men broke off and began running toward her with their weapons drawn. A voice boomed out above all others, ordering them to stop. It was that of a young warrior who had the respect of his people.

"He slowly and menacingly approached Wahluna, and when he was only inches away, he asked, 'Why have you come here, and what do you want?' Had it been anyone else, had she shown any fear, I believe all would have been lost.

"She told him, 'I am Wahluna, daughter of chief Young Red Wolf, and I have come to talk with the great chief of the Blackfoot people.'

"There were voices raised in anger as he roughly grabbed her by the arm and led her off to the largest and most ornate teepee. Once inside, all conversation came to a halt as the young warrior told the chief, 'This is Wahluna, daughter of Young Red Wolf of the Nez Perce, she wishes to speak with you.'

"It was obvious to her that no one but the chief's son would have been allowed to enter so abruptly and disrupt this powerful group of chiefs and elders. The chief rose towering above her, slowly circling her as if stalking his prey, reluctantly taken in by her beauty and courage. He sat back down and said, 'I will hear you ... why have you come here alone into the camp of your enemy?'

"She didn't expect to survive the night, but still spoke with a soft and steady voice.

"We mourn for our dead warriors, and there are but a few left. Our village is little more than women, children and old ones. You are many and can kill us all or take us as slaves as you wish, but there is no honor in it, no dignity or purpose in taking the scalps of women and children. I ask you to return to your village and families and leave us to mourn our dead."

"She fell to her knees and put her head to the ground, saying, 'Do with me as you please, kill me, torture me, or feed me to the wolves, but please be merciful and let the few who are left live.'

"The young warrior who had brought her to the chief's lodge continued to pace around her until he placed his robe over her shoulders and said, 'I can see your suffering and my heart goes out to yours, I will leave your people in peace.' Wahluna raised her head, confused by what he had said and done, unsure of what this meant and why he had been so bold.

"The chief looked angry as he said, 'These people are no more than dogs and should all die. How is it that my son, a mighty warrior, does not see this?'

"The chief's son turned to his father and said, 'She may be our enemy, but she is not a dog, and her courage deserves respect. Her people have fought bravely, and she is right; there is no honor in killing or taking the scalps of women and children. I say to you all; you see my robe upon her shoulders, I will not remove it.'

"There was a long silence, and no one knew how the chief was going to react. The only thing he loved more than his own pride was his son, and he could see that this beautiful and brave young woman had captured his heart. He said, 'Your words are true words, and I will have no bad feelings between us.' He then rose, went to Wahluna, and put his robe on top of his son's. 'Tell your people that if they willingly give us half of their horses and their word never to make war on us again, we will leave them in peace.' She rose knowing that her people were saved.

"The chief's son took her gently by the arm and led her outside to the edge of the forest in the direction of her village. Before they parted, he told her, 'My Father has tried for many seasons to find a wife for me. For some reason, I felt that I should not marry; now I know why that is. My heart was not with any of them, but waiting for you. I want you to come to my lodge and be my wife.'

"This cannot be; my people are angry and bitter and would kill you if they could."

"You speak to your father, Young Red Wolf, and tell him I will return in six moons to sit and smoke the pipe with him. Tell him that with you as my wife, our people can live together as brothers and sisters instead of enemies; that the Nez Perce will be allowed to pass freely to the hunting grounds in peace to hunt the buffalo. Before you leave, you must tell me if you will have me when I return?"

"Yes."

"With that simple promise, she slipped silently into the woods, making her way back to her village. By the time she had returned, Young Red Wolf was beside himself with worry that she had been captured or kidnapped. When she told him where she had been and what had been said, he took her in his arms and said, 'You have saved our people ... would you have this young man freely as your husband?'

"Again, she said, 'Yes.'"

"During the six months apart, both the chief's son and Wahluna could hardly think of anything but each other. Before the sixth moon, Young Chief Red Wolf held council and told the others that

Wahluna would freely take the chief's son as a husband and that the Blackfoot would soon be returning to make peace. When the Blackfoot returned, they all sat together and smoked the peace pipe.

"The Blackfoot chief told Young Red Wolf, 'The Nez Perce will soon be family when my son and your daughter are married. You are free to pass through our land unmolested to hunt the buffalo.' Young Red Wolf thanked the chief and told him that the Blackfoot were free to fish for salmon on their lake and rivers. The chief pointed to his son and said, 'My son is our greatest hunter and will make a good husband. I am asking Young Chief Red Wolf if you will allow your daughter to become his wife? Wahluna's courage has become legendary among our people; they will be a good match.'

"Young Red Wolf asked for his daughter to be brought to the council and when she arrived, he asked, 'Young Chief Tlaska says that his heart goes out to you and asks that you would be his wife; what do you say?'

"Without hesitation, she looked at Tlaska and said, 'My heart goes out to him as well; I will be proud to be his wife.'

"Preparations were made, and a great celebration soon got underway. The feast was the most lavish either tribe had ever seen with enough to feed everyone three times over. On the day of the wedding, the sun was shining, and the birds were happy, singing their songs of love. The bride and groom were led out separately to be joined together as one.

"No one had ever seen a more stunning couple, Wahluna was dressed in a white doeskin dress and moccasins beautifully beaded and fringed. Tlaska was also dressed in white doeskin adorned with eagle feathers. Their hair hung loose and unadorned, so shiny black from the sun's reflection that it was hard to look upon without shielding the eyes.

"The wedding took place next to the lake, and as it finished the wedding songs began. The lake was like a crystal mirror reflecting an exact copy of the distant mountains and sky upside down. They were led to a ceremonial canoe ornately decorated for the occasion. It was the custom at this time of year for the bride and groom to row out to the center of the lake to pay tribute to the bountiful waters that provided life for the Nez Perce People. As they boarded the canoe and started paddling out, there was great rejoicing as everyone sang and danced.

"When they reached the center, they both stood up and put their hands on each other's shoulders as a sign of having been joined. At that exact moment, a giant serpent rose out of the water and crashed down upon the newlyweds smashing the boat to pieces. The people were in shock, then the wailing began. Several of the most fearless men launched their canoes to see if they could find any sign of the newlyweds. It was as if they had disappeared from the earth, and no bodies were ever found.

"It was believed that the Great Spirit was angry because of all of the fighting and violence they had inflicted on each other over the eons. He had sent the serpent to devour the newlyweds as a lesson to the people. The funeral songs and dances went on for seven suns until everyone was completely exhausted. In the great sorrow that they shared, Young Red Wolf and the Blackfoot chief vowed to live together in peace as brothers.

"The peace lasted for many generations, and the story eventually became legend. However, after many years the legend was all but forgotten by a few. In time, one of our men was thought to have been killed by the Blackfoot while passing through their territory, so revenge was taken and the cycle of violence and war between the two tribes began again. I have sent messengers under a flag of truce to reach out to their chiefs for peace. Because of the diseases brought by the white man, over half of their people have died, and the Blackfoot hold more hatred in their hearts than ever before."

Chief Timothy told me that he had sent several emissaries to various Blackfoot chiefs to ask for peace, but their hearts were cold and harder than ever.

The name Nez Perce was given to their people by white French-Canadian fur trappers. It means pierced nose, which was not a common practice among the Nez Perce. Their true name is Nimiipuu, which means, "The Real People." The Nez Perce territory is immense. The majestic Bitterroot Mountains lie to the north and east, named after a small pink flower. Trapper Peak soars to over 10,000 feet, and the treacherous Blue Mountains to the west were the final gauntlet pioneers faced while crossing the Oregon Trail. The rugged Klamath Mountains were the doorway that opened the Oregon Territory southwest to California. The aptly named Sawtooth Mountains to the southeast have 57 jagged peaks that climb over 10,000 feet into the sky. The Columbia, Snake, Salmon, Clearwater, and Grande Ronde Rivers rush through the Nez Perce territory along with dozens of smaller tributaries, the flowing lifelines, veins, and arteries of a living being.

The Shoshone and Bannock border them to the south and southeast, Flathead to the east, Blackfoot to the Northeast, Coeur

D' Alene to the north, Yakima and Spokane to the northwest, and Walla Walla, Cayuse, Umatilla to the west, Paiute and Klamath Indians to the southwest. Their lands were once the size of a small country covering over 27,000 square miles.

I was still a baby when Chief Timothy married the beautiful Temar on November 17, 1839. On that same day, Father baptized Timothy and Chief Joseph, who was Temar's older brother, the two chiefs were his first converts. In Chief Timothy, there was stillness that ran deep, a serenity everyone who knew him could draw upon, and he would become the bridge between the Nez Perce and my family. He divided his time between his village at Alpowa, ten miles to the west, and his lodge at Lapwai. At Alpowa, he was the first Indian man in the territory to build a house made of lumber that Father had milled for him. He had five children, over a thousand horses, and the largest farm of all the Nez Perce.

When Lewis and Clark first came to the Northwest, their party camped next to Chief Timothy's father's lodge, and his aunt cared for their horses when they journeyed to the Oregon Coast. When Lewis and Clark left, they gave the elder Chief Joseph a rifle, powder, and shot. He eventually passed them on to his son, Young Chief Joseph, who was three years younger than I was and would go on to become the most legendary chief of all Nez Perce.

It was Chief Timothy and Red Bear who selected the four-man delegation of Chief Black Eagle, Man of the Morning, No Horns on his Head, and Rabbit Skin Leggings to go to St. Louis to try and find Lewis and Clark. Their mission was to bring back the "Book of Heaven" and someone to teach it to them. In this way, Chief

Timothy was indirectly responsible for bringing my parents to Lapwai.

I recall a day when Chief Timothy, Timpstetelew, and I had been out riding all morning, and when we returned that afternoon, Temar asked me if we would like to stay the night, that her brother had given her a fine goose to cook. Timpstetelew stayed until after dinner and then had to help her mother. After we had eaten, I couldn't stop thinking about his beautiful pony Tashe and asked the chief where the Nez Perce horses came from, and what was it like before they had them.

He told me that they had had horses for over 100 years. His father told him that they came from the south. They had been brought by the Spanish to trade for furs, and others were stolen or traded. He also told me a story about a legend passed down among his people.

"There is a legend handed down by the Indian people about a man named Hahtalekin, meaning 'Echo,' of the Palus tribe who may have inadvertently been instrumental in bringing horses to the Indian people. Having heard fantastic accounts about the Spanish horses, he had developed an insatiable desire to possess them. Witnesses had told him about the incredible power and speed that these animals possessed, that they could outrun the wind, and had more than ten times the strength of a man.

"He spent years working like a slave to put together a small bag of gold, as well as furs and hides that he and his friend Diego would pack hundreds of miles to a place known as the Yellowstone Rendezvous in the hopes of acquiring a horse. Diego was half-Indian, half-Spanish, unrivaled as a player of the stick toss game, and had agreed to accompany Hahtalekin if he could share in the winnings.

"The game involved tossing sticks, used for betting on almost anything that could be bought or traded, with various symbols and having them land face up or down, and was very popular among both natives and Spanish people. They spent three days looking over all of the goods and precious metals and gems used to bet with during the contests and matches. At the rendezvous, a rich, violent and powerful Spanish merchant with a large beard had a stick game player in his party famous for winning every match he had ever played. The braggart saw the Palus Indians as easy prey, challenging them to a match. The only condition was that he would not bet any of his beautiful horses.

"Once the bet for furs and gold was made, the two men went at each other for hours before Diego won out. The bearded Spaniard was so enraged by the loss that he threatened to kill his player. When he finally calmed down, his man assured him that he could win if given another try, and a rematch was scheduled for the next day. Among the Palus Indian party was a beautiful young woman who the bearded man had tried unsuccessfully to buy. Hahtalekin was a distant cousin of the young woman and convinced her to let him use her as a bet, promising to win and make her rich. The Spaniard became so obsessed with having her that he offered eight horses, including six mares and two stallions along with furs and gold for the woman.

"Word spread throughout the camp that an unheard-of wager had been made, and betting spread like wildfire. Diego had pretended that the first match was difficult, only doing what was necessary to draw it out as long as possible yet still win. Hahtalekin told the other Indians of his tribe to bet all they had; that they had tricked the Spaniard and could easily win in a rematch. The match was over quickly, and Diego won. The bearded Spaniard was so inflamed with rage that he killed his player. Hahtalekin left the next day with eight valuable horses; the young woman, and Palus Indians were now rich with furs and gold.

"Because Diego was of Spanish blood, he had been allowed to own horses. He had worked on a Spanish horse ranch and had become an expert in their care and breeding. With his vast knowledge of horsemanship, they immediately began a plan to breed horses. Within ten years, they had developed a small herd of some of the fastest and most powerful horses on earth.

"After Hahtalekin and Diego had accomplished their goal, Diego decided that he wanted to return home for a time to see his family in Spain. He left with a fat pouch of gold and one of the finest horses, never to be seen or heard from again. Within a generation, the Platus Indian herds had grown vast, and their people had become an equestrian society. As time went by, they began trading horses with other tribes and the horse culture soon became a way of life for the Indian people. However, no one knows exactly when the horse first appeared among the Indian people other than it was some time after the Pueblo revolt with Spain about 1680."

Chief Timothy told me that before they possessed horses, life for the Indian people was very hard, even the teepees were different since buffalo skins were so highly prized as robes and blankets. Their people lived in holes dug in the ground covered over with branches and dirt. It was much harder to hunt on foot, so the men spent most of their time fishing and hunting, and the women spent much of their time gathering plants and berries. The horse changed everything. They could travel hundreds of miles to hunt the buffalo, and with the hides, they were able to make comfortable lodges.

The buffalo gave them almost everything they needed to survive, and with horses, they were able to travel much farther to trade with other tribes and villages. Before horses, they were constantly foraging for food and forced to eat even the sacred animals: coyote, grizzly bear, and wolf. The men would often be gone for many days and weeks only to return home with nothing but empty stomachs.

There were times when they ate inner tree bark and moss. Men hunted in packs, and like the wolves, they would surround the buffalo and stampede them off a cliff. It was very dangerous, and many men were injured or killed. When animals were scarce, and there were no furs, the women wove clothes and blankets from tree bark and grass so that they would not freeze during the winters. He said it was good land, but it can be a hard land; it had made the Nez Perce People strong.

My mind was like a whirlwind of questions as I asked if he knew where the Nez Perce came from?

"There are many legends, some of the ancestors believed we came from the far north where grizzly bears are said to be as white as snow, and fish as big as a small village; I would like to see that one day. They say it is a land covered with snow and ice most of the year, that even their lodges are made of ice. Some ancestors say we come from the far south where it is always hot with so many trees that the earth never sees the sun or moon. They tell of giant water lizards as long as three men with mouths and teeth that can swallow a man whole. There are also small fish that are so ferocious that they can eat a man to the bone in minutes. There are said to be giant cats that are as black as night, and birds of every color. I would like to see these things. Maybe one of the ancestors is right, or maybe they are both wrong, but it is certain that we have been here for many generations.

"My grandfather thought we came from nearby, from a place called Mitseadazi, or the Yellow Rock River. He said that it is a strange place where the water boils and blows out of the earth. The people were said to have eaten giant sheep with long curved horns. They would soak the horns in boiling water until they grew soft, then curve them to make bows. I have seen one that was buried in the earth for many years; they are strong but very heavy. It would take a strong man to use one, but the arrow would fly far."

This made me wonder why the Nez Perce chose this area? He said, "The ancestors chose this place because it is good land with tall grasses for the animals, trees for our fires, and many rivers of fresh water. Fish and game are plentiful, and there are plants for every need. My grandmother has a buffalo robe handed down to her from when the buffalo roamed our lands. That was before we had horses, and the buffalo had to be run down on foot or taken unaware. For some reason they decided to cross over the mountains, maybe it is because they became so many that they needed the endless grasslands of the plains.

"One of our Shamans tells us that in a dream, he saw our land was once covered with ice, and there were few people. As the Mother Earth warmed, the ice turned to rivers, and the people multiplied, I am glad I was not here then. It must have been very cold and hard. The elders speak of a place not far to the south where the people lived in caves along the cliffs for shelter and protection; it may have been about the time that Jesus was alive. There were also many villages along the Nichiwana River, which you call the Columbia. When the people learned where the salmon was, how to catch and preserve it, we multiplied again."

My head was spinning from so much to think about, but Chief Timothy never lost his patience or treated me as a child. He expected me to understand and remember what he had taught me, as that is the Nez Perce way. The more I know, the more I want to know, and I wanted to know how he became a chief.

He told me, "My father was a chief, my grandfather was a chief, and my son will be a chief. It is usually something you are born into, but not always. If a chief does not show wisdom, courage, and generosity toward his people, the council can replace him. Every Nez Perce person has a voice and can be heard, but the headman will make the final decision based on what he hears and what the council advises. If the council decides to go against him, he can-not overrule them."

There was so much to learn, and I got to thinking about the sham battle I had once seen and asked why they painted their horses and wore paint on their bodies and faces?

Chief Timothy made a terrifying face, shouted, and jumped at me, scaring me half to death. He thought it was funny and laughed until he was out of breath. Temar had her hand over her mouth, and before long we were all laughing together. That's another thing I love so much about the Nez Perce; they have a wonderful sense of humor and are always laughing and joking. Our family has its moments, but life with us is much more serious and somber.

He said, "We wear the paint to scare little girls who never stop asking questions," which got us all laughing again.

I told him about the war dance that we had watched the young men learn, and how the drums and war paint were terrifying at first; how our music is so different from the Nez Perce. I told him that though the war dances and death chants frightened me, I love the sound of the wooden flute.

"Like our painted bodies, our songs have many different purposes. Sometimes we sing or play for no reason other than the deep need to do so, and sometimes we wear paint to show others our mood or help us talk to the spirit world, and sometimes to frighten our enemies. Some of our songs are very personal and tell of our joys and sorrows; others are stories of our history and ancestors; we use music to express our gratitude for all things.

"War and death are powerful things; that is why the music is powerful and frightening. The drums and flutes are like the voices of the people, sometimes sad, sometimes happy, and sometimes angry ... Our dances and music cannot be separated from one another, and they bring us closer to our real selves. Many times, I have witnessed the buffalo taking possession of a man during a dance before the buffalo hunt, and when I hear the sound of the war drums, something begins to stir inside of me; it is a powerful thing. You must understand that music and dance are like food to us; they nourish our souls and tell the story of our people."

When Chief Timothy mentioned souls, it made me wonder if the Nez Perce believed in God. He told me that he was certain all people have a god of their own, that our gods are all different, yet alike. Christians believe they are made in God's image; the Nez Perce believe everything is living and endowed with God's life force, which is why they waste nothing. He told me that the Nez Perce God is a benevolent God that they each come to know in their own way and does not judge them or send them to the fires of hell if they do not believe as they are told. Not every person or tribe believes this in the same way, most of his people feel that when they die, their soul passes into the spirit world and rejoins their ancestors. They are still the same soul, but must learn again, and do not suddenly possess all of the knowledge of the stars. In their beliefs, there is no hell, so their people are much less fearful of death and see it as a natural part of life, like being born.

He told me that it was time to sleep and dream; that I had worn him out with all of my questions, and his head was beginning to hurt. I begged for just one more.

He grabbed my nose and gently squeezed it, saying, "This had better be an easy one."

"Why do some of the Nez Perce keep a buffalo skull in their lodge?"

"It is used to bless our burial sites and make confessions, now go to sleep."

I still had a million questions rattling around in my head and, try as I may, I couldn't turn my mind off and fall asleep. It just wasn't fair to me that I was born white instead of Nez Perce, nor did it seem fair that I was born a girl instead of a boy. At that moment, I wanted more than anything in the world to experience the adventure of a buffalo hunt and face a grizzly bear with my bare hands. It seemed to me that being a big powerful Nez Perce man sure was a lot more exciting than being a little white girl.

I had spent two winters with the Whitman family and was going to have to go again soon. I was torn because I wanted to see my new friends but also wanted to stay with my family. Mother and Father still felt that I needed more discipline and to be with people of my own kind. I loved the Whitmans and the friends I had made at the mission school, but having the same color skin did not make them my people. Everything was regimented and controlled, and I felt stifled. I wanted to ride through the hills and valleys of Lapwai together with Timpstetelew after I finished my lessons and chores. I ached at the thought of being away from my family and Nez Perce friends. My head was full of adventure, and I couldn't imagine myself in class six days a week staring out the window and sitting around knitting socks at night.

As I lay drifting between the real world and the dream world, tears came to my eyes, and I knew I would have to do as I was told. My thoughts turned to God, and I became confused. I had been raised to believe that the only path to heaven was through Jesus Christ and could not bear the thought of all my beloved Nez Perce friends burning in hell for eternity because they didn't know about or want to accept the white man's religion.

It didn't seem fair to me, and I needed to believe that my God was fair, and loving. I was also wrestling with the question of whether animals possessed a soul or not. This went against everything I had been taught, but when I looked into Tashe's eyes, I was certain that she was not just a dumb brute animal, but she had come to love me and understood the world in ways that I never could. My dog, Cleo, was also like that. She would give her life to protect me, and I knew that kind of loyalty was of a higher order. When I looked in her eyes, I was certain there was more to her than I would ever understand. What of the land and trees? It felt to me as if the Nez Perce way of understanding the world made so much more sense, and that they were much more in touch with the land and all living things. There had been times when I lay on my back watching the trees sway as if dancing to the rhythm of the wind. I have even felt the urge to put my arms around one to inhale its essence, wondering if it could sense or feel me in some way. These thoughts wouldn't let me sleep, and I began to feel that God is so many things to so many beings, and that I would never understand even a small part of it all.

To add to my sleeplessness, someone in the distance began playing the flute. It was a lonely sound as if that person was sad or thinking of a loved one who they had lost. As I drifted with the sound, I felt as if it were talking to me, and that my listening had made me part of its purpose. There is such a freedom and connection in the way the Nez Perce participate in song and dance. There is no good or bad, no inhibitions; everyone sings, chants, dances, or plays an instrument. I wondered if our culture had music that was of the moment and if some of those orchestral instruments ever interacted spontaneously.

The next morning, I woke barely able to hold on to any of the images or thoughts I had dreamed the night before. I tried to go back to sleep to recapture them but could only catch glimpses of people and places that I had previously seen or heard. They were so real last night as I slept but now were more like impressions, music in the mist.

That morning was a beautiful fall sunrise, warm and clear, the kind of day when every living thing is happy to be alive. I wished that Timpstetelew could have stayed over, but she had to return to her village to help her mother. I had walked over to where Father's apple trees were finally starting to bear fruit, and when I returned to Chief Timothy's lodge, Tashe saw me holding one in each hand, and I could tell that she was smiling. After she finished the two apples I had given her, she kept nudging me for more. I went back to the orchard and gathered several more windfalls.

Temar was up long before I was, but Chief Timothy must have still been sleeping. When he finally emerged from their lodge, he stretched and made a gesture to the sky and earth.

Tashe was already saddled when Chief Timothy looked over at me holding her reins and asked, "Would you mind if I had something to eat before you drag me all over?"

Temar winked at me and said to him, "Have you grown so old that you have forgotten what it is like to be young?"

Chief Timothy smiled, shook his head, and said, "Maybe I should give a lesson on patience and have a sweat bath and swim before we go."

He then went back into the lodge, seeming to take forever getting dressed and eating breakfast. Temar could tell that I was anxious to go, so she came over and started braiding my hair, telling me how impossible men were. When she was done, she went into their lodge and came out with two beautiful strips of white deerskin to tie my hair in braids just like hers. I have always been astonished at how much care is given to the way the Nez Perce dress and groom themselves. Every detail seems to have beauty and purpose. I had never realized how much joy could be had taking baths with the other girls and women until I started taking them with Timpstetelew. Mother made sure that we took a cloth bath each day and washed our clothes often, but still, there was always a musty smell to our clothes that never seemed to go away. Timpstetelew once told me that some of the Indian people called whites the "stinky people."

As we mounted our horses, I looked down at Temar to say goodbye. She smiled and waved as she continued to clean the buffalo robes they used for sleeping. I had never seen a buffalo before and found it hard to imagine by the size of the robes what it must be like to bring one down with a bow and arrow. At the camas harvest, I had tasted fresh buffalo, and it was not that much different to me from elk. Chief Timothy often brought buffalo jerky with him when we went on rides or trips together. I had always found the way Temar prepared it to be delicious, especially when you are tired and hungry. Mother told me she had gotten very sick from it while on the Oregon Trail, and that theirs was poorly prepared and preserved and often smelled bad or even had mold on it. She had to do everything she could to hold it down in order to survive.

To this day, I am still amazed at how many uses the native people find for everything. I was told that buffalo meat is a primary source of food; the hides are used for clothing and covers for their lodges. The bones are used as utensils, weapons such as knives, arrowheads, and shields. Tools like shovels and scrapers, cups and ladles are made from the horns. Robes, rugs, moccasins, ropes, saddles, and drums are also made from the hides. The fat is used for cooking and making soap, the dung for fuel, the tail, hooves, and beards for whips and ornaments. The stomach is used to store and carry water, and the skull is used for religious ceremonies. The sinew and muscle are used for sewing as well as binding arrows and bows. The most prized possession is the tongue, a delicacy that is rich in nutrition and full of fat. As we reached the plains, I closed my eyes and tried to picture an enormous herd of buffalo running at full speed with the Nez Perce beside them, lances, bows, and arrows drawn.

Once we were finally under way I had to ask, "What is it like to hunt buffalo?"

Chief Timothy was quiet and thoughtful for what seemed a very long time, then a smile crossed his face as he started. "It is the most exciting and dangerous thing I have ever done. Many men and horses have been injured or killed during the hunts. Some of the men now use a rifle, but I refuse to do so. With the bow and arrow, it is a fair fight, and because each hunter marks his arrows, they can be identified. A bullet has no such mark and can be fired from a safe distance; there is far less honor hunting with the gun. With the bow and arrow, you must be precise since the hide is very thick. I have seen arrows bounce off as if they hit a rock, and it often takes five or six to bring down a large bull. It takes a great deal of courage and skill since you must get very close. A fall means almost certain death from goring or being trampled by the herd. There are still some brave men who hunt with a lance. You must get close enough to touch the animal, and it takes great courage not only from the man but also from the horse. Tashe is the best I have ever seen during a hunt. She is fearless and will do anything I ask of her. During the last hunt, we found hundreds of buffalo slaughtered and left to rot in the sun. Only the hides and tongues had been taken, and there was a deep sadness among the people as if sickness had come over us. It was not only the white people doing it; Indians were selling or trading with the white traders for money, guns, and whiskey. These people had lost their place in the world and no longer cared about what is right or wrong anymore. It was done for the white man's lust of money, and I fear that before my time here on Earth is done, the buffalo will be no more."

Because of my great respect and love for Chief Timothy and the Nez Perce, the thought of all the buffalo being killed hurt me deeply. I had heard my parents talk about the terrible situation brought about by the American buffalo hunters. Compounded with the diseases the Americans were bringing in over the trail, it had created a great deal of bitterness toward the whites, and they feared that it might, one day, lead to violence. It got me wondering why the Indian people fought among themselves, and I asked if the Nez Perce ever fought with the Cayuse.

"We are closely related by marriage to the Cayuse as well as the Umatilla, and Walla Walla. There have even been arrangements between the Palouse, Coeur D' Alene, and Spokane tribes. In many ways, we are like one people and do not fight with one another."

I told him that I had always wondered why one person would scalp another. It's such a terrible thing to do.

Chief Timothy said," It is done for different reasons. Some believe it is a way of showing courage by displaying the scalps as a trophy. Others do it to frighten their enemies, to keep them out of their territories and villages. Some believe that when you take a scalp, the victim's power becomes your own."

"How is it done?"

"That is something I do not think is right to discuss, no matter how smart or grown-up you think you are. It would give you bad dreams."

Chief Timothy was wise not to have told me back then because I probably would have had nightmares. When I was older, I attended a lecture given by an elder chief of the Shoshone tribe who explained it this way.

"Dead or alive, a warrior would wrestle the man down and turn him over onto his face and pin him to the ground with his face in the dirt. He would then make several deep incisions along the top front of the head and pull back as hard as possible, pulling off a large piece of scalp and hair. It was then stretched over a hoop of wood to keep it from shrinking. Usually, a wife, sister, or mother would scrape the insides out to keep it from rotting. It was then mounted on a long wooden shaft to display as a warning or sign of courage."

As we continued to ride, I couldn't help but feel guilty for what my people had done to the Indian people. Father told me that back east, and in the Willamette Valley, the white settlers had taken the Indians' lands and forced the Indian people to leave or become beggars. Father also told me that the new immigrants were often rude and suspicious of the Indian people. Compounded by the measles epidemic the Americans had brought with them, many native people were dying and very angry.

We were quiet for a long time until I started to wonder when the Nez Perce had first seen the white men.

Chief Timothy told me that, "The first white men came from the far north, from a place the Hurons' call "Kanata," meaning "Village." This was at a time when my father was a young man. The men that came were hunters and trappers who bothered no one and had things to trade that we had never seen before. Several were guided by the Hurons and Iroquois and had wisely taken Indian wives to be more easily accepted.

Not long before I was born, the first Americans came, Captain Lewis and Captain Clark. Chief Lawyer's father, Walammottinin, was the head chief at the time and was related to our family by marriage. A French trapper named Charbonneau, along with his Shoshone wife, Sacagawea, guided the party. Our people were startled to see these strangers with hair the color of dried grass and eyes the color of the sky. It was decided to let them live, so a messenger was sent to Chief Walammottinin, known as Twisted Hair, to come to the village and meet with the strangers. At the same time, one of the white men left to find the rest of their party and bring them to the village. When the rest of the Lewis and Clark party arrived, they communicated with the Shoshone woman as interpreter. As a young girl, she had been captured by the Hidatsa people and had learned the sign language. There were also several Nez Perce among the Hidatsa people from marriages, and she had learned the language from them.

By the time Chief Twisted Hair arrived, gifts had already been exchanged, and food had been given to the guests. A council was called, more gifts were exchanged, and the pipe was passed. Captains Lewis and Clark explained that they were on a journey to the great ocean of salt water they called the Pacific. They had gotten lost and were looking for a river we called the Elabekail, meaning Deep River; they called it the Columbia.

There were good feelings among the people, and after the Lewis and Clark party had rested, our people made maps on white doeskins to show them how to find the Columbia River and make their way to the Pacific Ocean. The Nez Perce felt that they had come in peace and that their hearts were good, so a promise of friendship was made, and to this day, no Nez Perce has ever killed a white man. It was my aunt who cared for their horses while they were gone, and by the time they returned, the animals were fat and healthy again. Our people had traded with one of the tribes from the Pacific Ocean, but none had ever been there or seen it.

When they returned, they told us of the many wonders they had seen. At the farthest point of their journey, they were told there was a tribe called the Tillamooks, meaning "People of the Nehalem," which is a mighty river. They traded for three hundred pounds of whale oil that they would use for cooking and lighting lamps. For the generosity and kindness our people showed, Captains' Lewis and Clark gave us many gifts. This included three of the lamps and several gallons of oil as well as salt, shells, and an assortment of feathers. The most prized gifts were the two rifles, powder, and shot. They gave one to Chief Twisted Hair, and one was given to Chief Joseph's father. The family still has it today. The Lewis and

Clark party stayed on at Kamiah for one moon before returning to the east. During this time, they told our people about the "Book of Heaven."

Mother once told me that the Columbia River was named after a ship that a Mr. Astor sent to the north coast. She also told me that he hoped to build a global trading post that is now Fort Astoria, but there were too many problems, and it was sold to the British and eventually abandoned as impractical and unprofitable.

We had been riding for some time, and I was thinking about how the Nez Perce had so many stories about the world around them and how their origins were so different than the ones I had been taught. Just then, we came to a hill that was all jagged black rock, and I couldn't help wonder where something like that could come from.

Chief Timothy explained: "The ancestors say it came from the center of the earth as liquid rock. This is a sacred place for us and has a legend called 'Ant and the Yellowjacket.'"

"Why do they call it that?"

"I will tell you the story, then show you why it has that name. Legend tells that the Ant and Yellowjacket had lived together in peace since the beginning of time, but for some reason, Chief Ant had grown jealous of Chief Yellowjacket, who was eating his lunch atop this hill. His wife had prepared him a delicious lunch of dried salmon, and he was peacefully enjoying his meal.

"The ant had often used this same place to eat, and when he saw the Yellowjacket sitting there eating his lunch he became angry and yelled out, 'Chief Yellowjacket; why are you eating your meal on my rock, don't you know that you must have my permission to do so.'

"Surprised, Chief Yellowjacket said, 'I have always eaten on this rock, now go away little one,' and started rattling his wings and snapping his legs together to intimidate the ant.

"'How dare you call me little one and try to frighten me with your pathetic wings and skinny legs, no one insults me that way and lives to tell about it.'

"Chief Ant then started climbing the hill as quickly as he could, and when he reached Chief Yellowjacket, he attacked. They locked arms and legs furiously trying to bite and sting each other to death. Coyote just happened to be wandering by looking for something to eat when he heard the terrible racket and looked up the hill to see the two chiefs fighting.

"He called out, 'Hey you, Chief Ant, and Chief Yellowjacket, quit being so foolish and stop that racket, I did not give you permission to do so. There is plenty of food for both of you.'

"They were so intent on their fighting that they did not hear Coyote's warning. Growing angry from their disrespect, he called out much louder for them to stop. They did so only momentarily to look down at him and then went back to their fighting. That was enough for Coyote, so he used his special spirit powers, said one of his incantations, and waved his paws in their direction. They both felt something terrible happening to them and stopped to look down at Coyote once again. As they did, their feet began to turn to rock, and they started begging for forgiveness.

"He told them, 'It is too late, you fools should have listened to me the first time.'

"Chief Ant decided to get in one last blow before he was consumed, so they fought again as they slowly turned to rock."

Chief Timothy pointed to an area at the top of the hill to the south side and said, "If you look closely, you can see their figures still locked in battle."

I told him that I could see it clearly and asked, "Do you have any more stories like that, it was wonderful."

He told me, "There are many, but it would take days to tell them, so I will give you one more, called, "The Coyote's Fishnet."

"As you know, Coyote is the most powerful of all animal spirits because of its cunning and courage. It was a late fall day with leaves gently drifting on the breeze that Coyote was fishing for salmon on the Clearwater River. He was usually on his way to the buffalo hunt by this time of year to fatten up for the winter, but his little son had been sick, and he needed to care for him and make sure that he had plenty to eat before he left.

"When Black Bear came upon him still fishing, he asked, 'Why are you still here? It is my turn; you need to leave.'

"'I have every right to be here, where I am and what I do is none of your concern, so quit being so meddlesome."

"This angered Black Bear, who replied, 'I am not being meddlesome, this is my favorite place to fish, and you need to leave right now. I have heard you brag about your powers, but all I see is a scruffy little pup.'

"Coyote had never been talked to like that before and was inflamed. He threw his fishnet to the top of the hill and then told Black Bear, 'You should know better than to insult me that way when I am trying to provide for my family. I will give you one chance to apologize.'

"Black Bear just laughed and said, 'Apologize to you? You must be crazy. Why don't you come up here and let me teach you a lesson?'

"With speed and cunning that Black Bear could have never imagined, Coyote was on him in a flash with his teeth buried deep in his neck. He started spinning around, and when he let go, Black Bear went flying through the air, landing next to the fishnet where they both turned to stone. This is also a sacred place that I will take you to see one day."

As we rode on, I saw a bluebird land on a tree close by as we passed. It made me think of my trip to the sacred mountain, so I reached into my pocket to touch the pouch that held my weyekin.

I knew that it was supposed to be a private gift that was only shared with close family members, but I couldn't help but ask, "Is it a bad thing to ask what your weyekin is?"

Chief Timothy thought about my question for a long time, making me feel that I may have said something wrong.

Finally, he said, "I have grown to love you like a granddaughter, so I will tell you. My weyekin is the coyote."

I blurted out, "I knew it must be because you are the wisest person I have ever known ... mine is the bluebird."

"The bluebird is also wise, and like you, it is very beautiful and talks a lot. It is a coincidence that you brought this up, because of the place I am taking you."

I waited and waited for him to tell me more, but he said nothing until we reached another hill that was too steep for the horses.

As we dismounted and let them graze, he told me, "I am going to take you to a place shown to me by my father and his before him. It is a very sacred place to me, and the only other people I have shown it to are my wife and son, though many others have been here."

It was a steep climb and took us well over an hour to reach the top. Several times Chief Timothy had to help me when my legs started giving out. The top overlooked the entire valley, and I couldn't believe that I had never noticed it before. Set back about 20 feet from the ledge was a boulder about five feet around and three feet tall. Chief Timothy told me that it had been used by many of the Nez Perce on their vision quest, but he had no idea how the boulder got there, that it would forever remain a mystery.

We were quiet for some time until he told me that this is where many of his ancestors had searched for their weyekins. He was 12 years old when he first came here. His father thought he was too young, but he knew in his heart that he was ready. He had already decided that he would be successful on his first attempt, or die trying. He sat on the same rock that his Fathers before had sat upon, and nothing happened for what seemed like an eternity. He had not had anything to eat or drink for days and was nearly frozen to death from the cold nights. He was beginning to see and hear things that he knew were not there and thought that maybe he was losing his senses. If he had not been half out of his mind, he didn't think he could have endured the hunger or thirst.

By the fourth day, everything had become dreamlike, and several times he thought he might have been given a glimpse of his weyekin. One time a giant buzzard flew by not more than ten feet above his head, and that night an owl landed on a tree close-by and started softly hooting to him. His body and mind were ready to go and wanted to accept one of them, but his heart felt nothing, and he knew it was not yet right. On the fifth day, a large coyote came right up to the rock and circled several times, looking at him hungrily. At first, he was afraid it would attack and eat him while he was still alive, but it just lay down in front of him and watched the sunset until just before dark. Then it rose and started howling so loudly that it hurt his ears, and he knew this was not a dream.

He had closed his eyes and started seeing his ancestors' images dancing around a fire until the coyote stopped howling and started digging in the dirt next to the rock with its paws. Then it looked right into his eyes, a feeling as if it had looked into his soul, and like a puff of smoke, it was gone. He knew for certain that the coyote had come for him and was his weyekin, but still uncertain as to whether the whole thing had been real or a dream.

He had not moved all day, and when he got down to leave, he was so stiff that he couldn't stand up and fell to the ground where the coyote had been clawing at the dirt. He started digging where the coyote had been and soon came to a small flat rock with the marks of the coyote's claws on it.

Chief Timothy opened his vest and showed me a small pouch that hung around his neck from a leather cord. He took it gently in his hand, closed his eyes, and whispered something I could not understand. When he reopened his eyes, I took the small leather pouch from my dress pocket that I kept my bluebird feather in and showed it to him. He smiled and nodded his head in understanding. Without a word, we both climbed up on the rock and watched for well over an hour.

Since then, the years have taught me how to quiet my mind, but I can tell you that staying quiet for an hour back then was one of the hardest things I have ever done. I'm glad I did because I didn't want to spoil the moment with a lot of nonsense. I knew that this would be a special day that I would never forget, and I never have. As we reached the bottom of the hill, the sun was just starting to set, and Tashe was ready to go. The ride home was sublime, dreamlike.

I can't explain why I have never felt conflicted over my strong belief in God and Christianity and my belief in the Great Spirit. To me, they are somehow the same, both quite real and an important part of my life. I think Mother would understand this, but not Father. I am still not sure if it was his complete devotion to Christ or a more rigid and stubborn mindset. Mother was stubborn in her own way but wanted to understand the Nez Perce before everything else.

Chief Timothy had once told me that he sometimes struggled with these things, but believed more in what he felt than what he thought. He felt that there was nothing wrong with believing that both were right, both of the creator, and both good.

He felt that it was man who made these things bad, to suit his own purposes. He told me that Chief Joseph had turned his back on Christianity, feeling it was an arrogant religion with no respect or tolerance for the Nez Perce ways or beliefs. Chief Joseph no longer trusted the white people and had come to believe that the whites now make the Indian people out to be devils so that they could justify taking their lands and possessions. Chief Joseph didn't feel that the white man would ever be satisfied, that they would always want more until there was nothing left for The People; that they would never live in true peace and harmony.

Chief Timothy believed that we are all children of the same family of man, and though we call our gods by different names, they are all of the same spirit. He still had faith in my parents' teachings and was hopeful that we could live together in peace with understanding for one another.

These thoughts would always remain a dilemma for me, so I have tried to live life with an open heart and mind, leaving the judgment of mankind to a higher power.

Chapter 2

Princess Jane

When I was five years old, Chief Timothy and Temar had their first child, a little girl. Chief Timothy brought her to Father to be baptized along with his wife, Temar. Mother suggested the name Jane, so she was christened Jane Timothy, and Temar was christened Fannie. By the time Jane was able to crawl, she would curl up in my lap while her father told us stories. We would remain lifelong friends, even though there were sometimes years between correspondence. She was shy as a child but absolutely fearless, and because of Chief Timothy's prestige as a leader, she was called Princess Jane. Among the Nez Perce, she was also called Princess Like a Turtle Dove.

Petite with delicate features, her beautiful long black hair seemed to shine even in the dark. In school, I was often designated to teach her group, and I helped teach her to read, write, and speak English. She was incredibly fast and bright, and never stopped asking me questions, as I had done with her father. She often helped us around the house, and Mother taught her to knit, sew, spin, weave, make candles, and cook. She would grow up to become one of the most beautiful and sought-after women of the Nez Perce nation. Neighboring Chiefs who wished to have a marriage arranged with her deluged Chief Timothy with gifts and proposals.

He always told them, "Jane has her own mind, and will choose who she wants."

When Jane was only 14, she married a man whose mother was Nez Perce and father was white, and for the life of me, I can't remember his name. They had a son who drowned in the Clearwater River as an infant, and her husband died not long after. Her marriage was one of love, so you can imagine how she must have felt losing both her child and husband.

Although there had been many rumors concerning Sacagawea, Chief Timothy had been told by Bear Hunter that she was living among his people the Shoshones, and he knew her well. Sacagawea's journey with Captains Lewis and Clark and the time she had spent among the Nez Perce had become legendary among the Indian people as well as the whites. Chief Timothy had been hearing stories about her since he was a little boy and wanted to honor her with a collection of gifts if she was still alive. Jane had always been an intrepid adventurer, and at 17, her father asked if she would deliver the gifts, explaining that it would be a dangerous journey. She was not only willing, she spent weeks making a beautifully beaded doeskin dress for Sacagawea with her mother's help. It was a vast territory, so Chief Timothy asked his trusted friend Bear Hunter to guide and protect her.

Bear Hunter had been planning to return to his village and visit his family and friends among the Shoshones, so the timing was right. By the time they left Alpowa, the packhorse was completely loaded down with gifts, so they had to take a second for their supplies. They would be skirting the southern part of the Blackfoot territory, but it was during the buffalo hunt, so they were fortunate not to encounter any hostilities.

It took them several weeks of travel to reach Sacagawea's camp, and when Jane saw Sacagawea for the first time, she was nearly stunned by her beauty. Her skin was still unlined, and though her long black hair had silver streaks, it shimmered like a woman half her age.

Sacagawea put her hands on Bear Hunter's shoulders and said, "I have heard that you married a woman of the Nez Perce, is this her?"

"No, Grandmother, she is the daughter of a friend I have promised to bring to you."

"Have you eaten?"

Bear Hunter smiled and took her beautiful face in his hands and said, "I have missed you."

Among most Indian villages, the children are welcome at any lodge and even breastfed by the other women when they are hungry. For this reason, almost all women are referred to as mother, aunt, or grandmother.

After introductions, Sacagawea took Jane's hand and asked, "Why have you come so far, little sister?" There was an instant connection as if they had known each other all of their lives.

Jane went to the packhorse and brought back a handful of gifts explaining that when Sacagawea was at the Nez Perce village with Captains Lewis and Clark, she camped next to her grandfather's lodge and Jane's great aunt cared for the horses. Jane told how her father has listened to this legend since he was a young boy and wanted to honor her.

Sacagawea was deeply touched, and when she saw the dress, she told Jane, "This is the most beautiful dress I have ever seen. Who did this?"

Shyly Jane told her, "It is a gift my mother helped me with; the others are from my father."

"I will treasure them always."

Sacagawea went through the other gifts, remarking on each one and giving Jane her most heartfelt gratitude. She then went into her lodge and came out sometime later with a bearskin robe, and small satchel. When she opened the robe, there was a simple buckskin dress worn by time, as soft as a baby's skin.

"This is the dress I wore on the journey with Captains Lewis and Clark over 50 years ago. I would like you to have it; it has many stories to tell."

Tears came to Jane's eyes as she held the dress up to look at it. Oddly enough, it was exactly her size. She realized that this was much more than a simple gift, that it was sacred to this woman, a piece of her people's history. Sacagawea then opened the small leather satchel and took out two small items. One was a brass compass, and the other was a necklace made of white glass beads on a thin strip of white doeskin.

Sacagawea told her that the compass was for her father, that it was a parting gift from Captain Meriwether. The necklace was for her mother and was given to her by Captain Lewis, which had been given to him by his President Jefferson to give to the Indian people as a gesture of friendship.

At first, Jane refused to take such precious gifts, but Sacagawea held up her hand and said, "I have often wondered why I have kept these things so long, now I know why."

Jane thanked her and said that she and her parents would always hold them close.

Sacagawea then took out a knife that she kept in her waist belt and cut a lock of her hair and handed it to Jane. Jane took the knife and did the same. Without a word said, this gesture made them forever a part of one another.

The two weeks they spent together seemed to pass like two minutes. Jane felt that she had never met a person so gentle and wise, so attuned to nature with every action she performed. From the respect shown Sacagawea, it was obvious that the people of her village felt the same way.

For Sacagawea, Jane was a glimpse into the future of what the Indian woman would become. She was self-assured and independent, and it was obvious that no one was going to tell her what to do or how to live her life. Hand in hand, they would take long walks together, side-by-side they rode to a sacred place of the Shoshone to watch a final sunset together. Sacagawea told Jane that she often came here to invite her dead friends to sit beside her and watch the sunset, that when the time came, they would help her journey to the homeland of her ancestors. Sacagawea told Jane that she had a son she hadn't seen in many years, and a granddaughter that she had never met, that they lived far to the south and west. During one of their conversations, she sadly told Jane that she also had a daughter named Lizette, who died as a young child.

Her son, Jean Baptiste Charbonneau, had gone to live with Captain Clark, who paid for his education at the St. Louis Academy, where he learned to speak English, French, German, and Spanish. He also spoke his native Shoshone language, and over time, picked up several other Indian dialects. He was an explorer, guide, fur trapper, trader, military scout, prospector, and hotel owner. His last position was as mayor of a small village in Southern California called Mission San Luis Rey de Francia, near the town of San Diego.

When Jane and Sacagawea parted, they both knew it would be the last time that they would ever see each other. It was both joyful and sorrowful, a sad beauty beyond words.

The significance of the gifts overwhelmed her parents. When Jane showed them the dress and explained its history, they were speechless. She felt that it would be more secure for them to preserve and gave it to them for safekeeping. They spent the next two days talking about all of the things Jane had discussed with Sacagawea, everything but the lock of hair. Some Indian people wear a necklace with small, intricately woven baskets around their necks to hold their most important objects. For Jane, it was a place where she kept the lock of hair, something that she would privately treasure for the rest of her life.

A man named Captain Pierce had come to the Oregon Territory after hearing tales of gold. In a discussion with one of the elderly Indian men, he was told that there was so much gold in the mountains along the Clearwater River that he could see it in the rocks. The captain and a group of prospectors decided to try their luck but were met, by a hostile band of Cayuse who threatened to kill them if they continued to trespass on their land.

Having heard that Chief Timothy was a friend to the white man, Captain Pierce asked if he and his men could take refuge at his village of Alpowa, which the chief granted. From there Captain Pierce made several more attempts and was almost killed doing so.

He fled back to Alpowa, and in a meeting with Chief Timothy, he asked if he would help guide him and his men over the Lalo Trail, where he had heard there was gold. Chief Timothy told him that he was already taking a risk by having him as his guest. The Cayuse were well aware of where the captain and his men were, and what they wanted, that it could mean death for Chief Timothy and his men to guide the captain and his men through Cayuse territory after they had been warned to stay out.

Jane was at the meeting and spoke up, saying, "I'll take them, Father. We could go in the spring after the snows have melted. I know a route over the Colville Trail that is seldom used, especially in the spring, when the men are fishing for salmon."

Chief Timothy started to object but caught himself, knowing that she had become her own woman, and would not allow even him to make her decisions for her any longer.

It was the way he had raised her, so he accepted it. He did decide to ferry them across the Snake River at night, nervously leaving Jane and the miners on the other side. She led them along the Clearwater River until they reached a place called Canal Gulch. The men chose to prospect there and struck gold almost immediately.

Little could Jane have ever imagined what she had unleashed by helping these men. Miners started pouring in by the dozens, then hundreds, and finally by the thousands.

A new gold rush was soon in full bloom, inevitably leading to the loss of the lands belonging to the Cayuse and Nez Perce. Jane had been given a new name by the miners, "Gold Rush Jane," which I am certain she took no pride in. She had done it purely for the adventure and received nothing in return. Because of her involvement, a Cayuse man stabbed her brother Edward to death.

Shortly after returning, she became involved with a man 18 years her senior named John Silcott. He had been educated at Harvard as an architect and engineer and hired to help design and construct Fort Lapwai. Father performed the marriage at Lapwai, and they decided to make their home at a place called Tsceminicum. About 25 miles west of Lapwai, it meant, "The meeting of the waters." It was located at a confluence of the Snake and Clearwater Rivers, and would one day become the town of Lewiston, Idaho. It was believed to have been named in honor of Meriwether Lewis.

Together they constructed a ferry and charged to take passengers and wagons across the Clearwater River. By the time Jane was 50, she had developed a terrible case of rheumatism and had started using a medicine that her husband John got for her. She would sit by the fireplace for its warmth and apply the medicine to whatever part of her body was hurting. The medicine had a great deal of alcohol and was highly flammable. One evening she was sitting by the fireplace spreading it over her legs when sparks from the fireplace ignited her dress. She tragically burned to death at the age of 53. She will always be remembered by her people for her courage and audacity, but it is the beautiful and bright little girl who used to crawl up in my lap and ask endless questions that I will always remember.

Chapter 3

Valley of the Winding Waters

The Wallowa Valley is also known as the "Valley of the Winding Waters" and is about a hundred miles south of Lapwai. I have made the trip twice with Father; the second time, little Henry joined us. It is one of the most beautiful and dramatic places I have ever seen. A stunning combination of ancient forests, jagged snow-covered peaks, peaceful meadows of wildflowers, calm and raging waters, deep blue lakes and skies dotted with soaring raptors. In the morning before the wind comes, up the lake is like a piece of glass that perfectly reflects every image. At times it makes it difficult to tell where the earth and sky begin and end.

The lake and rivers hold an endless supply of fish and provide the water necessary for the survival of all living creatures in the valley. The meadows were long ago home to the buffalo, now teaming with deer and elk. The mountains have become a sanctuary for many sacred animals, including the crafty coyote, powerful bear, cunning wolf, and eagles that drift upon the winds with all-seeing eyes. It was the home and village of our dear friends Chief Tuekakas, known as Joseph the Elder, and his people. It is easy to see why they love this land so passionately since it has everything a human being would ever need to survive and flourish.

Chief Joseph was a highly respected head chief of the Wallowa band of Nez Perce called the Willamwatkain people. In 1832, he personally welcomed Captain Bonneville and his party to his village. A few of the Wallowa Nez Perce had come into contact with white trappers, but for the most part, these were the first white men that the villagers had ever seen. Captain Bonneville was a big, baldheaded muscular man with a jovial nature. He was well-liked among the Indian people, and Chief Joseph told us that he thought Captain Bonneville an honorable man. He successfully treated several sick members of the village and was given a feast in return. They were both eager to trade, and quickly formed a friendship and trust for one another.

Captain Bonneville was on a leave of absence from the U.S. Army to explore the Northwest Territories, tasked with making maps and gathering furs. He grew very fond of the Nez Perce and asked Joseph if he could spend the winter of 1833 with them, which was granted. The summer of 1834, he sent the furs that he and his three partners had trapped and traded at the Rendezvous back east.

That fall, he embarked on one of the most perilous journeys ever taken by a white man through rugged and dangerous terrain, unrivaled anywhere in the entire Northwest.

His Indian guide suggested they stay alongside the Snake River where the snow was less deep, but unfortunately, he led them directly into Hells Canyon before deserting them. The snow was over three feet deep, with little to no foothold for the horses. Two packhorses fell in, and only one survived.

The precious food and supplies were swiftly lost downstream. They had to crawl over enormous rocks that had fallen from the cliffs above. They were then forced to cross over precarious bridges of snow and ice, and easily could have ended their lives with one slip or wrong step. They were so desperate to cross the river that they considered killing several of their horses to make boats. They did this by stretching the hides over a wooden frame usually made of buffalo hides called "bull boats." Fortunately for them, they decided against it, unaware that they would have been smashed on the rocks below and thrown over a deadly waterfall not far downstream. By the winter, they were out of food and worn to their cores from the efforts they had already given to the relentless demands of Hells Canyon.

Finally, they discovered an elk trail, and miraculously managed to climb out of the canyon and over a six-thousand-foot barrier called the Wallowa Mountains. They followed the source of the Imnaha River out of the mountains down to a small valley where they were once again faced with another mountain range.

Nearly starved and frozen to death, they again barely managed to clear the mountains and descend into the Grande Ronde Valley, home of one of the lower Nez Perce villages. Word had spread of the white men coming, and the crafty Nez Perce chief of the village was anxious to see what they had to trade. He showed them all possible hospitalities and held a feast in their honor. Through Captain Bonneville's Indian interpreter, the chief presented the Captain with a fine-looking horse as a sign of friendship between them. Knowing that a gift received must be reciprocated, Captain Bonneville took his spare rifle and put it in the chief's hands. The chief was beside himself with pride, giving thanks to the Captain for the gift.

As Captain Bonneville was taking his saddle from his worn-out horse and putting it on the one the chief had given him, an elder woman approached looking sad and forlorn. The chief told Captain Bonneville that his wife had loved that horse very much. The captain reached into his pack and brought out a pouch with beads giving her a small handful. She was thrilled and couldn't wait to show them to her friends. As the captain began to mount and say goodbye, a young man approached, and the chief told the captain that it was his youngest son. It was he who had cared so affectionately for the horse and personally broken it with great tenderness, that they were like brothers. The captain pulled his foot out of the stirrup and once again reached into his pack and pulled out a shiny hatchet and gave it to the chief's son, which greatly pleased him. Captain Bonneville was now trying to get mounted and make his exit before another relative appeared. He was just about to go when the chief gently took the horse's neck in his hands and said, "This rifle is a great and powerful gift, but I fear it will have little value without powder or shot. I could certainly feed my family well with these things. The captain dismounted and rummaged through his pack until he found a bag of powder and shot, and gave it to the chief. He knew he was being taken advantage of, but what else could he do? He quickly said goodbye and made his getaway as fast and courteously as possible before losing his clothes.

The first time I visited Chief Joseph at his home in the Wallowas was in the summer. A messenger had arrived to tell Father that they feared Chief Joseph was dying, and he had asked for Father's help. It was over a hundred miles of the most rugged and dangerous territory in the Northwest. Father explained how hard it would be and let me decide if I wanted to accompany him. I was packed, saddled, and mounted before he was packed. The pace that Father set and the terrain exhausted our horses to the point that we feared they might not survive the trip. About 25 miles before we reached the camp, two young men were waiting for us with fresh mounts.

It was the hardest ride I have ever made, and we were both exhausted for days afterward. When we entered Chief Joseph's lodge, we found him extremely weak with a high fever. Father gave him a big dose of calomel, jalap, and Mother's special tea. I was put in charge of applying a wet towel to his face, chest, and shoulders to cool him down.

He was delirious and shivering with fever, so Father and I stayed with him all that night trying to keep him as comfortable as possible, continuing to give him medicine and tea.

The next morning after a large dose, he leapt up and ran for the bushes where he expelled out of both ends. Later that night, he was still extremely weak, but his fever had broken, and we knew he was coming back to us. We stayed for several more days until he was much better. Our horses were well-rested and fed, so we were just about ready to depart when a young man approached with a spectacular stallion that had been broken and tamed.

Chief Joseph told Father, "This is a gift for saving my life."

Father replied, "I didn't come here for a horse; I came here for the love of my brother."

I could tell that Chief Joseph was deeply touched. He stood up and took the reins from the young man, putting them in Father's hands. Father understood that it would be rude to refuse and thanked the chief for his fine gift. Chief Joseph then went into his lodge and brought out a small bundle wrapped in buckskin and handed it to me. It was a beautiful doll with a beaded doeskin dress and moccasins that his wife had made for me. I jumped into his arms and told him that it was the nicest gift I had ever received and would cherish it always.

The next time we came was in the spring, accompanied by little Henry. As we descended from the mountains, we looked upon a valley covered in wildflowers for as far as the eye could see, the smell was sweet and heavenly. Father had received a message from Chief Joseph that several members of his village were very sick, and he could use his help. We arrived as the sun was setting over the mountains to the west, changing colors every few moments.

I remember waking early the next morning as the first rays of sunshine began bursting with colors as they slowly climbed over the mountains to the east. I could hear the river winding through the rocks, and birds singing their songs of life. When the sunlight touched my face, it was warm and tender, like a mother's love, and I thought that this must be what heaven is like. There were naked brown babies running freely through the camp, including Joseph's two young sons, Hinmahtooyahlatkekt, meaning, "Thunder Rolling Down a Mountain, and his brother, Alocut, who was a year younger. Hinmahtooyahlatkekt was also given the name Joseph and would one day become leader of the Nez Perce.

Father and I had made some perilous trips over the Blue Mountains, but I had never seen anything as wild as the trip we took with Chief Joseph to a place called Hells Canyon. The trail was barely wide enough for a mountain goat, with drop-offs thousands of feet below. He had suggested that Father leave little Henry and me at the village with the other children, Father told him that little Henry was too young to go, but I was big enough to make my own decision, and I was going. It was the most exciting and dangerous ride I have ever taken in my life. Miles before we reached the Snake River, I could hear it rumbling like an earthquake in the distance.

When we cleared the last ridge, I saw the most awe-inspiring and terrifying waters I have ever seen. If the best swimmer, man or beast, jumped in the water, they would drown and be beaten to death on the rocks instantly.

The spring run-off was creating rapids that moved as fast as a mountain lion. Both small and large waterfalls dove like falcons from the sky into deadly swirling whirlpools. Chief Joseph told us that he had seen most of the Northwest Territory; that this was the fastest and deepest river he had ever seen. We had come to fish several miles to the north, where the river widened and gentled. The chief told us that there were fish called matsihnahmack, which we call sturgeon, that were as long as two grown men and weighed even more. He also told us that there were legends of the matsihnahmack dragging men to the bottom of the river where they would devour them. I told him that if he was trying to frighten me, it wasn't working.

Both the Lewis and Clark expedition of 1805 and the Wilson Hunt expedition of 1811 had encountered Hells Canyon. It was so daunting that they never did cross, and were forced to turn back. We rode along the ridge for several miles until we came to a narrow elk trail where we were able to carefully descend. As the river began to widen, the waters became slower, almost calm in some places. The sun started to disappear behind the mountains to the west as we found a place to camp for the night, and I rounded up kindling for a fire. Chief Joseph, Father, and the other two men who had accompanied us found bigger branches for a bonfire. Like Chief Timothy, Chief Joseph was a wonderful storyteller, so I asked if he knew any good fish stories.

He told me that he knew many, so I lay back and watched the stars shoot across the sky, listening to the rhythm of his voice as he told me one called "Coyote and Salmon."

He said, "There was once a cunning and fearless coyote who was traversing back and forth along the steep rocks of the Snake River looking for something good to eat. He spotted a small school of salmon swimming close to the bank and called out to one of them, 'My good friend salmon, I am very hungry. If you would swim close enough for me to gently take you in my teeth, I would promise to honor you by singing your praises to the Great Spirit after I have eaten you.'

"The salmon replied, 'That is very noble of you coyote, but I would much prefer swimming among my brothers and sisters in the cool waters of this sacred river than to be eaten.'

"The salmon kept his distance, so the coyote laid down on a large rock above the water and pretended to be asleep. The salmon became curious and wanted to get a closer look at the coyote, swimming close enough to see the fine hairs of his whiskers. All of a sudden, the coyote lunged into the water, barely missing the salmon with his sharp claws and jagged teeth. Furious, the coyote jumped up and down thrashing the water in frustration. As he lay drying in the sun watching the salmon swimming in the deep waters, he had an idea. He tore his blanket in half and waded out into the water to use it as a net for when the salmon got curious and careless. He stood perfectly still for what seemed like an eternity until the salmon came close enough for him to throw his blanket over him. Unfortunately for the coyote, it was an old blanket with several holes in it, and the salmon slashed back and forth until it found one and wiggled out. Now the coyote was so angry that he started hitting himself on the mouth and was shocked when little creatures began streaming from his lips. He was staring in disbelief as one of them told him that if he wanted to catch the salmon, he would need to take a limb from one of the trees and club the salmon over the head when he approached. This made sense to the coyote, so he found the perfect limb and waded back into the water. He stood as still as a rock until the salmon became careless enough to swim between his legs. With a mighty swing, the coyote hit the salmon on the head and killed him. He built a fire by the waterside and kept his promise by praising the salmon to the Great Spirit. He then feasted on the salmon until he was so full that he fell asleep, planning to eat the rest in the morning.

"Several hungry animals had been watching from a safe distance, and when they finally heard him snoring, they slowly and quietly crept up to his camp and devoured all of the leftover salmon until nothing was left but a pile of bones. They started to worry that the coyote would be angry when he woke up with nothing to eat and come looking for them. They quietly built the fire back up and cut a piece of flesh from the coyote's behind and put it in the fire so he would have something to eat when he woke up. When he awoke, he was once again hungry and could not understand why he had a pain in his behind.

"When he saw the juicy piece of meat by the fire, he forgot about the ache. Just as he started to put it in his mouth, an ant yelled out, 'Stop, you are about to eat your own flesh.'

"The ant then bit him on the behind where they had cut the piece out to show him where it had been taken. At a distance, he could see the animals that had done this to him dancing and laughing at him. This made him furious, and he decided he was going to get revenge. He took the piece of flesh and put it back in place and bandaged it tightly with a strip of his old blanket to hold it together. The animals had found a nest full of eggs, put them in a pot to boil, and lay down to nap while the eggs cooked. The coyote quietly crept up and took all of their eggs but one and ate them. He then took a brush and painted ridiculous-looking faces on the animals. He went a short distance away and started yelling for them to wake up. When they did, the silly faces he had painted bewildered them. Suddenly they realized what had happened and were incensed at having been made fools. They began calling out for their friends to help them catch the coyote. The coyote then held up the last egg so that they could all see him clearly, stuck it in his mouth, and ate it. By now, there were many friends, and they took off after him as fast as they could until they were worn out and could run no farther. Coyote stood atop a boulder and taunted them by shaking his bushy tail at them, then went off laughing and looking for another salmon."

Chapter 4

The Sager Family

When it comes to the Oregon Trail, there has never been a more epic or tragic story than the Sager family. Henry and Naomi met and married in Ohio, but because of his restless nature for greener pastures, they moved to Indiana, then Platte County, Missouri, and then Saint Joseph, Missouri. Henry next made the calamitous decision to take his pregnant wife and six children over the grueling and treacherous Oregon Trail. When and if they reached the lush Willamette Valley, he hoped to find a heaven on earth for his family.

Naomi was tired of moving around and loved everything about the farm they had bought and settled on in Missouri, never wanting to leave. When they met, Henry was working as a blacksmith, and Naomi was teaching school. He was built for the hard work of a blacksmith with a strong stocky body, and big rough hands that knew how to be gentle with children. He had short brown hair and lively brown eyes to go with his kind smile. Naomi was pretty and petite with long brown hair, and gentle blue-gray eyes. She had a kind and generous nature that drew people to her. She was often enlisted to sit patiently and listen to personal problems until friends felt better, and she felt worse.

Henry was one of those men who seemed to know how to fix just about anything and everything. With his friendly and creative nature, he rarely had to look beyond his blacksmith shop for work. When they bought the farm in Missouri, the hard work came easily to him since he was as strong as an ox and had worked on a farm in Ohio. He was also a gifted and highly respected folk healer who was often called upon at all hours of the day and night when there was no doctor to be found. He had been taught by his father, who had been taught by his father, and was thought to have considerably more horse sense than the local doctor.

John and Francis [Frank] were the oldest children; John was 13 with a sweet round face, big blue eyes, and long straight straw-colored hair. Frank also had a round face, but brown eyes and long brown hair that turned golden in the sun. With his rosy face and curly hair, he looked more like eight than 11 years old. They were both lanky boys who could run like the wind on their long skinny bowed legs that looked like those of young fawns.

Catherine was the oldest girl at ten years old, Elizabeth seven, Matilda Jane four, and Louise, who was two. All four girls had clear blue-gray eyes and blonde hair that would eventually turn light brown like their mother's. Rosanna was the youngest, born on the Oregon Trail, with all of the same characteristics as her sisters.

In the Sager family, everyone worked as soon as they were old enough to carry a bucket of water. The two boys were up before the crack of dawn doing the hard labor of cutting and stacking firewood, carrying water from the river, and milking the cows.

The girls helped around the house and in the garden and were taught to sew and knit as soon as they were old enough to learn. Both boys were pranksters, especially Frank, who loved to tease their little sisters by telling them that Indians were in the trees waiting to grab little girls. One time, while the girls were still asleep, Frank took a piece of string and ran it through the window, tying it to their pigtails. He then walked it around the house and tied it to the door handle, knocking on the door. When Naomi opened it to see who was there, it nearly tore the hair out of Catherine's and Elizabeth's heads. His father gave him a harsh whipping, but he was a tough kid and didn't make a sound. They were good boys, hardworking, and respectful rascals.

Being the oldest and most capable girl in a large family isn't always easy. Catherine was responsible for dressing and undressing the two younger girls as well as a myriad of household chores. Elizabeth was either awkward with things like buttons and lacing or pretended to be that way, so the dressing and undressing duty wouldn't fall on her shoulders. Matilda Jane was a sweet and affectionate child who was loved by everyone. Louise was more temperamental and cried or became easily agitated, but was quick to give love and affection. They were a happy and loving family, a home that sang with the music of children's laughter.

When Henry made up his mind that they were going to the Oregon Territories, there was no changing it or turning back. He had met and talked with Doctor Whitman, and when hearing about all of the limitless possibilities of the Northwest, he planned to join his party in the spring of 1843. Unfortunately, Matilda Jane developed a large lump on her right knee that Henry felt needed to be taken care of before leaving. He decided that it would be best if they waited until the next year, and started making preparations.

In early spring 1844, they moved to Saint Joseph, Missouri, to be nearer the starting point of the journey. They had left their comfortable home and farm to live in a tiny one-room cabin with a crude loft for the boys to sleep. It was so small downstairs that the beds and dining table touched the walls with little room for Naomi to use her spinning wheel. She was a good teacher and had spent an hour or more each evening teaching the children math, reading, and writing. However, she felt that she had taken the boys as far as she was able, and hoped to find a good school for them when they reached the Willamette Valley. The change was hard for Naomi to accept, and she never felt good about going. However, it was not her nature to complain, so she made the best of her situation and turned their tiny cabin into a happy home.

She tried to explain to Henry that she had a bad feeling about going west. He wouldn't listen and promised everything would be fine, that when they reached the Oregon Territory, he would build her a big beautiful home and she would never have to move again. The one thing she demanded they take was the cherrywood sideboard her grandmother had given her mother, and *her* mother had given her.

John and Frank were anxious to get started on the adventure of a lifetime and asked why they couldn't leave sooner. Henry explained that it would be far too dangerous to cross the mountains during the winter, and there would be no grass for the animals to graze on. Without the protection of the wagon train, they would be vulnerable to attack almost the entire way. Henry had signed up to make the trip with a group called the Independent Party, consisting of over 1,500 people and 250 wagons.

In March, people started pouring into St. Joseph for the coming immigration west. The past year Doctor Whitman had guided wagons over the Blue Mountains for the first time, proving that it could be done. Most expected to continue to the Willamette Valley with a stop at the Whitman Mission to rest and replenish their supplies. Each year more and more settlers were coming west, and so far, this was going to be the largest wagon train that had ever made the journey over the Oregon Trail.

By late April, the Sagers were preparing for the journey, trying to figure out what they could take, and what would need to be left behind or sold. Henry knew that if the sideboard wasn't coming, neither was Naomi, so he arranged everything else around it. He decided to use it to divide the wagon into two parts, Naomi and the girls would sleep in the front with all of the bedding and clothes. Items they would not need to unpack regularly were stored under the mattresses. The back would have all of their personal belongings, food, supplies, and tools. Henry had made hooks and placed them along the canopy frame for pots and pans, and other tools he would need to get to quickly for repairs and maintenance. On the back were a barrel of water for drinking and cooking, and a toolbox for smaller tools. Henry and the boys would sleep outside in a tent next to the wagon.

The last couple of days before leaving were filled with excitement for Henry and the children, but dread for Naomi. She was heavy-hearted at having to leave behind so many belongings that they had worked so hard to acquire over the years. They sold some of their furniture and tools for a fraction of what they were worth, but most had to be given away or left behind because there were so many others doing the same. The boys could hardly sleep and looked at it as a long camping trip, starlit nights by the fireside, a time to be closer than ever before with parents they dearly loved.

Friends and family of the immigrants began arriving to see their loved ones off, knowing there was a good chance they would never see each other again. It was a time for tears and laughter, a time to remember the past and look forward toward the future, a time to say farewell.

The spring morning, May 10, 1844, was beautiful, clear skies and a light warm breeze that smelled of hope and opportunity. Even though they were up before dawn, other wagons were already passing by, and Henry was anxious to get in line before the dust had risen too high. He had purchased four oxen that he was extremely proud of and was hitching them to the wagon as the children dressed. Oxen were not as fast as horses or mules, but they were much more powerful, easier to feed, and less likely to run away.

As if in a dream, they were suddenly on the trail, but it was not what they expected. Within a short time, they were enveloped in a massive cloud of dust from the wagons in front of them. For Naomi and the girls, it was especially difficult. They were confined inside the wagon, where it was hot and humid, with dust coming in from every opening and crack. Within several hours Naomi and the girls in back were experiencing motion sickness as if out to sea. They were constantly lurching back and forth over an ocean of bone-jarring bumps and ruts.

Two days later, it was Catherine's turn to sit up front, and she asked her father what that strange smell was. He told her that it was the Missouri River, that they were getting close. When they were near enough to see the river, they could see a line of hundreds of wagons waiting to cross on the ferry. As they took their place in line, Henry told them he would walk ahead and ask how long it was going to take to cross. When he reached the spot where the ferry was crossing, he approached a big man standing at the riverbank with a handful of pieces of paper looking bored. When he asked how long it was going to take to get across, the man handed him a ticket with a number on it and said, "Don't lose this or you'll have to take a new number and wait all over again."

He then told Henry that it would take at least a couple of days, so they may as well get comfortable and let the animals out to graze. He explained that generally, it was safe, but to keep an eye on them. By the time Henry returned, everyone was standing by the wagon waiting to hear the news. He told John and Frank to unhitch the oxen, and let them graze with the cattle, that it was going to be a couple of days. He also told the boys that it was their responsibility to make sure the cattle didn't get stolen or mixed up with other cattle. Henry told the girls they could go rinse their faces and hands off, but not to get in the water, that Catherine was in charge and to watch the little ones closely.

As he started pitching a tent, Naomi asked, "That ferry looks pretty dangerous, and none of the girls are good swimmers. Do you think it's safe?"

"Don't worry; it's taken thousands of wagons over. The only tricky part is getting up and down the banks, and getting on and off, but no one is going to drown."

"How about the cattle?"

"Once I get the wagon loaded on the ferry, I'm going to swim them across."

Since they were anxious to be on their way, the two days they had to wait their turn, seemed like forever. When they finally got their turn, everyone but Naomi was excited about the ferry ride. There was a little slip and slide as they went down the bank, but otherwise, it went well. Within minutes the wagon was bobbing up and down like a cork in water, and the boys thought it was about the most fun they had ever had. When they reached the other side, they had to wait for Henry, who had drifted about a hundred yards downriver. He had little trouble crossing with the oxen and cattle and quickly hitched up his two best oxen to pull the wagon out. Coming up the bank, one of the oxen slipped, and they both spooked, sliding back into the water. The younger girls started crying, and Naomi had a hard time trying to calm them down since they were afraid the oxen would drown. With so many people crossing, this wasn't unusual, so several men stationed at the river bank immediately hitched up two more oxen while Henry got his under control. Within minutes they pulled the wagon out and put it in a spot to camp for the night since it was already getting late.

Naomi approached Henry with fire in her eyes; he put his best smile on and said, "I told you it was safe."

She got nose to nose, put her hands on her hips, and said, "That's not funny, Mister Sager; you get to spend the next couple of hours unloading the wagon and drying out our things while we eat supper and watch you work."

Just then, Elizabeth came up and grabbed her hand, saying, "Listen, Mama, someone's playing music. Can we go listen?"

There were hundreds of people camped out that night, so everyone gathered around a giant bonfire and listened or sang along with the musicians and singers as they played favorite songs. It was a beautiful starlit night with a warm and gentle breeze. Naomi started out sitting about an arm's length away from Henry to show him she was still mad, but within a few songs, she was wrapped in his tender embrace humming along.

The next morning Henry went to gather the oxen and cattle and found they had gotten loose and swam back across the river toward home. He was able to borrow a horse from one of the families they had gotten to know and catch the ferry back. After two long days, Naomi was getting worried that something had happened and found herself constantly looking across the river, pacing back and forth. The girls were fully engaged in their own world of play and make-believe as John and Frank stayed by the riverside to help the wagons coming over. Just before dark on the third day, the boys spotted their father and two other men coming across in a rowboat with the oxen, cattle, and horse swimming beside them. Henry looked tired and worn as he approached Naomi and the children. He told them that he had to ride all the way back to their log house at St. Joseph before he found the animals.

Naomi told him sarcastically, "It looks like they were the only ones who had sense enough to turn back."

Henry laughed and held her as she pretended to be mad; finally, she put her arms around his neck and said, "You had me worried sick, don't let that ever happen again."

They had fallen behind the rest of the wagon train and had to drive hard for the next three days to catch up. When they reached the crossroads that joined the St. Joseph trail, they found the entire wagon train had stopped to wait for the stragglers and hold a meeting to decide how they would proceed. With over 1,500 men, women, and children, 250 wagons and thousands of cattle, it was becoming almost impossible to keep a steady pace.

They decided to break up into four companies and chose a leader for each group. That way, it would give the dust time to settle between companies, and they would be able to handle whatever problems arose without constantly slowing the whole wagon train down.

The Sagers were put in the last company commanded by Captain William Shaw. He was a big friendly man with a full beard and a head of brown hair. He and his wife Sarah had six children close in ages to the Sagers and were also headed for the Willamette Valley. With Sarah's sweet and friendly nature, it didn't take long before she became Aunt Sally, and Captain Shaw became Uncle Billy. Uncle Billy had the rare ability to memorize names, and within several days he had learned all three hundred and 75 people in his company. There were some rough characters on the trail, but with his natural air of confidence and authority, there was never a problem with discipline within his company.

The first week on the trail, a party of Indians raided their camp one night, taking a number of cattle. Uncle Billy and a group of men who had lost their cattle went searching for them, but couldn't find any trace of the cattle or the Indians who had taken them. After that, they started drilling military-style for a raid or attack and set up a guard duty each night.

This was Henry's first experience driving oxen, and he was having trouble keeping them under control. He asked Uncle Billy if he had any ideas that might help. The captain looked around, picked up a handful of small rocks, and climbed on board. Each time one of the oxen would slow down or veer off, he would pelt it with a rock. It would immediately straighten up and cooperate. From that point on, Henry kept a small pile of rocks close.

It rained hard and steadily for the next four days. Everything was getting damp, and the air inside the wagon was thick and rancid. Catherine and Naomi were the first to get sick from the dampness and mildewed canvas cover starting to leak and grow mold. Combined with the constant jostling from the rutted and rocky trail, they were a pathetic and miserable crew.

Finally, the skies began to clear, and warm winds dried the soggy lot of people and possessions. The camp was still on edge from the cattle theft, so when a gunshot rang out one night, men grabbed their guns, and the whole camp went on high alert. Henry seized his rifle and leaped off the wagon and ran in the gunshot's direction with John and Frank close behind. Naomi and the girls huddled in the back of the wagon, terrified by the yelling and commotion, fearing it might be an Indian attack. They kept hearing the men scurrying about asking each other if anyone had seen anything, expecting the canvas to be thrown back and scalped at any second.

It turned out to be a young man and his girl out for a stroll in the moonlight. They had startled one of the guards who thought they were under attack and fired in their direction before they could call out. Fortunately, he was a lousy shot, otherwise, it could have been tragic.

The next day Aunt Sally heard that Naomi and Catherine were still sick and not getting any better, so she decided to give them a visit to see if there was anything she could do. When she pulled the wagon cover back, she was shocked to see how pale and weak they all looked. She told them to get dressed and get their shoes on, that what they needed was fresh air, exercise, and sunlight. She finally had to clap her hands loudly to get their attention. When they were dressed, she took two of the girls by the hand and helped them climb down out of the wagon, Naomi and the other girls reluctantly followed. At first, they were so weak and tired that they could hardly walk, and the sunlight felt as if it were burning through their eyelids. Before long, Aunt Sally had them all gabbing about what they were going to do when they got to the Willamette Valley, and no one seemed to realize they had been walking for over an hour. It was exactly what they needed, and would become a regular part of their routine.

With the weather having turned warm and dry, they were able to cover between ten to 20 miles per day, depending on the trail's condition. A strange illness called camp fever circulated throughout the camp, with symptoms similar to typhoid. Pneumonia claimed two lives, but the wagon train stopped only while shallow graves were dug and a short service was held.

The next couple of nights were somber and quiet until two fiddle players started everyone's toes tapping. It lifted the weary travelers out of their doldrums and took their minds off their hardships and sorrows. Before long, a drum and mouth harp were added, and everyone started clapping and singing. Henry and Naomi let the girls stay up much later than usual, all six sitting on the wagon seat together dancing to the music with their feet. The music was like an elixir for the soul, the first time that anyone had heard the sweet sound of laughter for far too long.

May was coming to an end, and Naomi was so ill that she was unable to get out of bed. Catherine took over the cooking while Elizabeth helped with the cleaning. Naomi had always been such a stouthearted woman that everyone began worrying after she was bedridden and unable to eat for several days. On the morning of May 30, she called out for Henry to stop the wagon, alarming the children. He told John and Frank to unhitch the oxen, let the animals out to graze, and then to get Aunt Sally.

When Aunt Sally arrived, she asked Catherine to get some hot water and towels and take the younger children to her wagon and get them something to eat. Catherine didn't say anything, but she was worried that her mother was dying from camp fever.

Captain Shaw compassionately called a halt to the wagon train, causing fear and confusion over Naomi's well-being. After several hours Aunt Sally asked Henry to get the children. When Catherine saw the smile on his face, she couldn't understand how he could look happy when her mother was so sick. As they walked to the wagon, Henry told the children not to worry that he had a big surprise for them. For the first time in days, Catherine noticed how beautiful the day was with the sweet smell of wildflowers wafting through the air.

They let the children into the tent two at a time, and when Catherine and Elizabeth entered, Aunt Sally held up a little bundle and said, "I want you two girls to meet your little sister Rosanna."

Elizabeth immediately went to hold the baby, but Catherine lay down beside her mother, kissing her on the cheeks and combing her hair with her fingers, enveloped in the sweet smell of new life. Both girls were relieved, but right away, Catherine started worrying about how she was going to have one more child to dress and care for.

She was reluctant to even look at the baby; her heart set against loving her. When she finally picked her up, she looked into her little face as Rosanna grabbed her finger and squeezed. Her heart melted like a snowflake in the sun, and she instinctively knew that she would always love this little one most of all.

In Louise's mind, she was still the baby. When she saw little Rosanna in her mother's arms, she started crying so hard that Naomi had to ask Henry to take her outside and calm her down. Henry set up a separate tent for the girls so that Naomi could concentrate on caring for the baby. That night Henry had to bring Louise into the tent with him, John and Frank, since Louise was keeping everyone awake crying.

Once they were underway again, it started raining harder than anything they had ever experienced in their lives. It rained throughout the entire month of June, and almost every wagon had at least one sick person. The closest doctor was with the group ahead. Henry was busy day and night caring for the wagon train even though he was not feeling well himself. Everything was wet, and it was almost impossible to find dry wood or brush. They were forced to eat their food cold and uncooked, adding to the general misery. The wagons were constantly getting stuck in the mud, and almost as much time was spent getting them out as making headway. Men were often covered in mud up to their waists, and the best they could do was a mile or two per day. The lightning and thunder were so intense that they could hardly keep the frightened animals moving.

Out of sheer boredom, Frank made up a new game for himself, Catherine, and Elizabeth. The other girls were too young, and John was almost always with the cattle. They would stand on the tongue of the wagon and jump out as far as they could and try to land on their feet. Catherine and Elizabeth were so light that they seemed to float through the air, often beating Frank. Naomi asked Henry if it might not be too dangerous? He told her that he would keep an eye on them, that it was a good way for them to keep their minds off the monotony of the trail.

On July 4, it finally cleared, and Captain Shaw decided to take a day to rest and dry themselves and their belongings. Many of the people in the company were sick, including Naomi and Henry, often coughing to the point of exhaustion.

When they came to the Platte River, they found a shallow and wide place to cross. The problem was that the bottom was soft sand, and if they didn't keep moving quickly, they would get stuck. The Sagers made it across easily, but as they started to ascend the bank, something frightened the oxen, and they tried to run up as fast as they could. This caused the wagon to overturn, throwing everyone and everything sprawling all over the inside of the wagon. Catherine, Elizabeth, and Louise were frightened but unhurt. Matilda was trapped and calling for help.

When Henry called to see if Naomi was hurt, there was no answer, but he could hear the baby crying. Instantly a group formed and began helping the girls out of the wagon and getting the oxen under control. They found Matilda and carefully extracted her from the wagon, mindful not to cause any further injury. Her arm and legs were badly bruised, but nothing was broken, and outside of a few scrapes, she was not bleeding anywhere.

Naomi had still not responded to Henry's call, and when they found her, she had the baby clutched to her chest to protect it. She had been knocked unconscious by the sideboard that she so passionately demanded bringing with them. The baby was agitated and frightened but unhurt.

When the oxen had started to run up the bank, Henry tried everything he could to stop them, but was thrown over the side and hit by the wagon canopy as it toppled over him. He was bruised with several deep cuts, but not badly injured. However, when he picked Naomi up and carried her to a flat dry spot where someone had put a blanket down, he bled all over her dress. Seeing the blood, the children were frightened that their mother was bleeding, possibly even dead. John instinctively untied the tent from the bottom of the overturned wagon and called Frank to help him set it up.

Aunt Sally arrived to help with the baby, and Captain Shaw was with Matilda, and Louise, checking to see if they had any serious injuries. Henry was holding Naomi in his arms, and the girls were gathered around crying when Naomi started coming to. Her first thoughts were for the children, and as soon as she could talk, she asked if anyone was hurt. Catherine thought it felt as if she had been underwater holding her breath until her lungs were going to burst. When they assured her that only Matilda Jane had superficial cuts and bruises, she asked for Rosanna.

She looked at Henry, who was bleeding with a large knot on his head that seemed to be growing by the minute and said, "Henry, you need to get help for yourself, you may have broken something inside that thick skull of yours."

He smiled and told her not to worry that he could tell he was not seriously hurt, and that everything was being taken care of. Just then, Louise broke loose and lunged for her mother with the other three girls right behind her. Henry tried to hold them back, but Naomi told him she would be fine, and within seconds Naomi was being smothered in little girl hugs, kisses, and tears.

John and Frank had a tent set up, and along with several other men, they were trying to untangle the oxen. When that was accomplished, they set the wagon upright and pulled it to a dry safe place. Word spread quickly, and before long, a group of women from their company had already unloaded everything from the wagon and were setting things out to dry. Naomi and Rosanna were moved into the tent where they could get out of the sun and rest, John and Frank started playing games with Louise to distract her, and Aunt Sally tended to Matilda Jane. Within an hour or so, everyone was calmed down, and the Sager's wagon was being packed and put back together. It was understood that a wagon train was like an extended family and that looking out for each other was key to surviving the dangerous journey.

Later the children were nervously sitting around the tent, waiting to hear how their mother was doing. Henry came out with Rosanna and told them that even though their mother had been knocked unconscious, she was not badly hurt, and would be fine. He handed Rosanna to Catherine and asked her to take care of the baby while their mother rested, and he tended to the wagon and animals. He asked the boys to keep their little sisters occupied until they were ready to go again.

After the boys had taken charge of the younger girls, Captain Shaw left to attend to other duties. Aunt Sally was still in the tent with Naomi when he rode by and asked Henry if they could continue.

Henry told him, "Naomi and Matilda are going to be sore for a while, but if they had to go on, they could do it."

After a short rest, Henry and two other men carried Naomi to the wagon and got her and Rosanna comfortably settled. Then the other girls climbed aboard, and they were once again on the move. As much as Captain Shaw would have liked to let them rest and recover, his responsibility was for everyone in his company. If they were going to get to the Oregon Territory before the snows came, they needed to keep moving.

The rains had stopped, and the summer heat took its place with a vengeance. The dust worked its way into every nook and cranny of the wagon as well as their clothing.

Matilda recovered quickly, and within days, she and her sisters were once again walking beside the wagon for fresh air and exercise. Naomi was now well enough to sit up on the seat with Henry and keep an eye on the younger girls. She commented on how ragged the children were starting to look, that their clothes needed mending, and their shoes were falling apart.

Henry said, "You're right, Naomi, they are a ragged group, but I've never seen them looking healthier."

They were all deeply tanned from the sun, lean and strong from walking. At night they gathered around the campfire, ravenous and supercharged with excitement for the future awaiting them when they reached the Willamette Valley. There were still so many sick people that Henry was constantly being called upon day and night to help. He even had to take over as dentist in several cases, pulling teeth with an old pair of pliers he used around the farm.

The plains stretched out infinitely, and the colors of the sunsets were like ever-changing paintings that no one would believe were real. They would start out gold and yellow, then orange and red turning to pinks and purples, finally a thousand shades of gray. As light turned to darkness, a billion stars appeared as if by magic, twinkling, and shooting, near and far. The children would lay on their backs, staring into the vast and endless sky, taking it all in, lost in the infinite. Like sugar in water, the sound of music and children's laughter helped dissolve the tensions and trials of the trail.

Chapter 5

You Poor Child

It was the first day of August, and Catherine had just come out of the covered part of the wagon to get a drink of water. Henry was walking beside the wagon and told her that they should be at Fort Laramie by evening. She wanted to get down and walk with him, so she got on the tongue of the wagon and prepared to jump. As she leaped into the air, her dress was caught on an axe handle that had not been pushed all the way down, and she fell hard to the ground. Before Henry could stop the wagon, he heard the horrific sound of her leg breaking like a twig as one of the wheels rolled over it. Henry stopped the wagon as quickly as he could, but it was too late. Catherine cried out but was in a state of shock by the time he reached her.

Henry held her in his arms, looked at her leg, and said, "You poor child, your leg is broken to pieces."

Catherine lost consciousness for a few moments and when she came to, Naomi was on her knees, cradling her with tears in her eyes. When Captain Shaw came to see what had happened, he once again brought the wagon train to a halt. He told Henry and Naomi that there was a German doctor named Doctor Dagon in the company ahead of them, that he would send someone to get him right away. They set up another tent for Catherine and told her that they had sent for a doctor who should be there soon.

Catherine begged her father to fix it himself, and he finally agreed to do it, not without reservations. He asked John and Frank to look for some slats that he could use as splints and had Naomi heat water and tear pieces of cloth to hold the splints in place once he had set the leg. Catherine tried as hard as she could not to cry out, but when Henry pulled on her leg, she let out a scream that ran like a shock wave through every heart that heard her cry.

Mercifully, she lost consciousness as he continued to adjust the leg until it looked straight again. When she regained consciousness, she was again in her mother's arms with her leg wrapped and splinted. Naomi tried to calm her as best she could until several hours later when they heard the sound of horses quickly approaching their tent. Captain Shaw pulled the tent flap open, and a small man with glasses, thick curly hair, a bushy beard, and big friendly blue eyes entered. He had a kind and sympathetic face that instantly made people feel more relaxed.

He had come from Germany, and as a surgeon, he had treated many broken bones and limbs. He knelt and introduced himself to Catherine and asked if he could take a look at her leg. She was reluctant at first, but her father told her it was a good idea, so she consented. He gently took off the wrapping and splints and felt down the leg.

When he was done, he said, "This is an excellent job, I could not have done better myself. Who did this?"

Catherine said, "My papa did it." The doctor made a few adjustments to the splints, and rewrapped it carefully trying not to cause Catherine any additional pain, then gave her a mild dose of laudanum. Captain Shaw apologized but told them that there had been too many delays, that they would need to keep moving in order to reach Fort Laramie before sundown. Doctor Dagon said that it would be all right to continue, but he wanted to make a device that would enclose and brace her leg. After he finished, they put her on a stretcher and carried her to the wagon where they placed her as gently as possible, propping her up on blankets and pillows. Even at this young age, she had a strength and courage that would walk beside her throughout her lifetime.

Doctor Dagon felt that Catherine needed to be watched over to make sure there was no infection. He told the Sagers he would continue with them to keep an eye on her. He explained that he was unmarried and traveling with another family, that it would be no trouble to have his things brought from the other company.

Worn but relieved, Naomi said, "Thank you Doctor. Henry has a cough that has me concerned; do you think you could take a look at him?"

"I would be glad to do that, and my name is Theophilus, but please call me Theo."

Henry tried to avoid being examined and told the doctor that he was fine, but Doctor Dagon said, "What could it hurt to take a listen? I have this new instrument called a stethoscope invented by a French physician so that I no longer have to stick my ear on my patients' chests."

He took it out of his bag and listened to Henry's chest, then told him, "You have a good deal of congestion in your lungs, Mr. Sager, I would suggest you lay up for several days to a week so that you do not get pneumonia."

Father told him that he would do his best, but there was a lot of work to be done, and his two boys were also sick. Catherine was resting when they went out of the tent but could hear the doctor when he told Henry that if the leg didn't heal properly, she might not walk on it again. She couldn't stop the silent tears as she thought about the possibility of not being able to run and play. She prayed that God would heal her leg and help her to do the things she loved.

Henry told the doctor that he and the boys had a large tent that he was welcome to share with them. Doctor Dagon thanked him and said that would give him a chance to take a look and listen to the boys' lungs as well.

That evening, just before the sun had set, they reached Fort Laramie. The children had never seen anything like it, there were high log walls, and the entire fort was surrounded by Indians camped in teepees and tents. When Elizabeth asked why the walls were so high, Henry told her that they were there to protect the soldiers in case the Indians attacked. She then asked why there were so many Indians at the fort, and if they would attack them. He explained that they were friendly and were there to trade with the soldiers.

Everyone hoped to stay and rest for a night or two, but Captain Shaw told them they were too far behind schedule and would need to leave first thing in the morning. Two days later, they came to a beautiful grove of trees next to the Platte River where everyone took the opportunity to swim, bathe, and clean their clothes. Naomi told Henry that this would be a beautiful place to settle, that the land was rich, and they could have a farm without being so far from civilization. He explained that there would be no protection from Indian attacks, that the Willamette Valley was considered the richest land in the country with topsoil hundreds of feet deep, and towns where they could buy or trade for all of the things they would need to get started.

The exertion of packing and hitching up the oxen caused Henry to have a coughing fit that left him doubled over and weak headed. Naomi told him that he needed to rest; that if he got any worse, it might kill him. He told her that they were only a couple hours from making midday camp, and he would rest then. The next day he couldn't get out of bed, and the boys had gotten worse. Doctor Dagon had been up all night treating sick people in their wagon train. When he listened to Henry's lungs and felt his temperature, he knew it was serious, and told him that he had better not get out of bed or he would jeopardize not only his life but those of his family as well. He also suggested that the boys stay in bed for a couple more days, that he would ask Captain Shaw to send over two men to help them drive the wagon and cattle. He gave them each medicine and bitter medicinal tea, and by the next day, the boys were feeling better, but Henry was worse.

The camp was growing low on provisions, so when the word spread that there were buffalo nearby, Henry dressed and grabbed his rifle before Naomi could stop him. He returned with buffalo meat and an antelope, but he could hardly stand up, and his body was on fire. Each day he continued to grow weaker, and even Doctor Dagon's medicine no longer helped the fever and chills. Naomi and the older children were growing extremely worried about how badly his condition had deteriorated; even the younger girls knew something was very wrong with their father.

Chapter 6

"What will happen to us now?"

Several nights later, they crossed the Green River, and the wagon train made camp. Uncle Billy went to the Sagers' tent to see how Henry was doing. He could tell by the gray color of his skin and the smell that he was in critical condition.

Henry told him, "I'm dying ... I don't expect to recover. I need to ask a favor of you."

Captain Shaw stopped him and said, "Henry, you have to hold on, man, you can still get better."

"I don't think so, Captain; I need to ask you to look over my family for me until they reach the Whitman Mission."

Then Henry looked at Catherine, who was holding his hand, and with tears in his eyes, he said, "My dear child, what is to become of you?"

Uncle Billy told him to rest and get better, but if anything happened to him, he would care for his family as if they were his own until they were settled.

That night Naomi and Catherine took turns trying to keep Henry's fever down with cool wet rags as he mumbled deliriously about their home in Missouri.

When Catherine awoke the next morning, Naomi was in tears as she pulled the sheet over her dead husband saying, "Oh, Henry, if we had only stayed in Missouri this would have never happened, what will happen to us now?"

There was no turning back, no relatives to ask for help, and Naomi was starting to get the same terrible cough that killed her husband.

The next day Uncle Billy had a coffin made, and there was a short service as Henry was buried in a shallow grave on the bank of the Green River. By the time the next wagon train came through, they would find the coffin broken up and Henry's bones bleaching in the sun. Doctor Dagon tried to take over the duty of driving the oxen but had such a difficult time that Naomi had to hire one of the young men from the wagon train. The young man told her that he would stay on until they reached the Willamette Valley. When they reached Fort Bridger, he asked if he could borrow their rifle, that he planned to go hunting and get some fresh game. That was the last they ever saw of him but later heard by word of mouth that he had gone on to one of the forward companies to be with his girlfriend.

Naomi was now suffering with chills and fever, growing weaker by the hour. She had never fully recovered from childbirth and the traumatic injury to her head. Sick and overwhelmed from the heartbreak of losing her husband, she was now vulnerable and alone to care for her seven children. Initially, she blamed Doctor Whitman for selling Henry on the idea of going west, but now she saw the Whitman Mission as the only hope of surviving the Oregon Trail.

Looming in the near future were the ominous Rocky Mountains, but the days were still hot and dusty, and the nights bitterly cold and lonely. At night the girls huddled together for warmth in the wagon as Doctor Dagon, John, and Frank lay shivering beneath their blankets on the hard ground. Naomi lay wide awake most nights huddled together with her girls, trying to keep them covered and warm. Her cough continued to get worse and the children worried that the same fate might befall their mother that had taken their father.

They reached Fort Hall on September 1, 1844, and found it completely surrounded by Indian teepees. Again, they were friendly and had come to trade. Although the travelers were weary and wanted to stay and rest, Captain Shaw had to firmly remind them that they were at least a week behind the company in front of them, and every hour now counted. The nights were getting bitterly cold, and they still had five hundred miles to go before they reached the treacherous Blue Mountains and then the Whitman Mission.

They shadowed the Snake River to keep the dust down, but it was still so thick that Naomi and the girls were suffocating inside the wagon. Doctor Dagon had taken over when the young man disappeared with their rifle and was barely managing to control the team of oxen. Naomi let Matilda and Louise ride on the wagon seat between the doctor and Elizabeth to make sure they wouldn't fall off.

At times it was like being tossed around in a tiny dinghy on a violent ocean. Catherine was about to go crazy from being propped up and confined in back while Naomi and the baby were mercilessly thrown from side to side. Naomi had grown so weak that her milk had finally given out. Doctor Dagen arranged with Aunt Sally to have little Rosanna passed around from one lactating woman to another to keep her alive. Before long, Rosanna was being cared for most of the time, and the family hardly saw her anymore. Other members of the wagon train brought any food they could spare, but Naomi had grown too weak to eat.

The once joyful company was now reduced to a sad collection of souls intent on simply getting to where they needed to be to survive.

Poor, brave Catherine was not only suffering from her own injury; she had to watch in horror as her mother began to die. Naomi could only imagine how terrible it would be for her children to go on with no parents. She gallantly fought with every ounce of strength she could muster to stay alive as long as possible. She soon became delirious from the fever and constant struggle to survive. They tried to make her as comfortable as possible, with Catherine continually rubbing her face and neck with a cool rag. Aunt Sally told her husband that Naomi's suffering was inhuman, so he decided to halt the wagon train once again.

During her last moment of clarity, Naomi asked to have her children brought to her so she could say goodbye. There were no dry eyes or hearts unbroken. She asked John and Frank to take care of their little sisters and promise to do everything they could to keep them together, to always be kind to each other and never forget her or their father. They promised they would. She then took each of them in her arms and whispered how much she loved them, that she would always be in their hearts.

Her last words were, "Oh, Henry, if you only knew how we have suffered."

She held on to Catherine and Elizabeth's hands as she struggled to take her last breath.

Aunt Sally had Elizabeth look for Naomi's best dress as a shallow grave was dug. There was no time or materials for another coffin, so she was covered with willow branches and buried in an old dress since they could not find her good one. John found a piece of wood and carved, "Naomi Carney Sager, age 37," as a grave marker.

In the 26 days since their father had died, the Sager children had become orphans. Two women, Mrs. Eads and Mrs. Perkins, were still nursing their own babies and took in little Rosanna. There was no measuring the depth of suffering and uncertainty these children must have experienced. Not only were their parents gone, they had no idea where they were going, or what would happen to them, and each child was having his or her own reaction to the tragedy.

Knowing that he was now responsible for what was left of the family, John became quiet, strong, and stoic, understanding that he must set an example for the others. In his blanket at night, the tears flowed freely from the loss of his parents and the uncertainty of his ability to care for his brother and sisters.

Once Frank had shed his own tears, he followed John's example with a quiet determination to make sure that no harm came to his sisters. None of this was made easier by the fact that they were both still weak and recovering from camp fever. Though devastated, Catherine and Elizabeth had developed an inner strength that helped them bravely face the unknown. Matilda and Louise were still too young to truly understand the gravity of what had happened; they just wanted their mama and papa. At times, Louise would become hysterical crying for her mama's comfort, but it was even more heart wrenching to see the soft-hearted Matilda Jane with silent tears in her eyes. The older children did all they could to reassure the younger ones that everything would be all right, though they had a hard time trying to believe it themselves.

At the next stop, there was a camp meeting to decide what to do with the Sager children. Some thought it would be easier to divide them between several families.

Captain Shaw stepped forward and told them, "I made a promise to Henry Sager on his death bed that I would keep his children together ... that's what I am going to do."

It was decided that Doctor Dagen would continue to drive the children, that they would follow behind the Shaws' wagon so that Uncle Billy and Aunt Sally could keep an eye on them in case they needed help. Everyone in the wagon train offered to pitch in with food or whatever else was needed. The children rarely saw Rosanna, who was being cared for by Mrs. Eads and Mrs. Perkins. The two women were trading off breastfeeding so that neither would lose the milk needed for their own child.

In time the children slowly began to reemerge from the darkness of their losses.

Catherine was overjoyed when Doctor Dagon finally removed the splints and told her that her father had done an excellent job. He felt that she should be up and running around with the others again one day soon. In the meantime, he made a crutch and told her no more jumping off the wagon.

It was not only the Sagers that had caused the delays; other families and individuals had also been terribly sick and died. Uncle

Billy thought that by now, most of the other companies must have reached Waiilatpu, yet they still had to cross the Snake River and Blue Mountains. Before they reached the mountains, one of the Sagers' oxen gave out, lay down, and died of exhaustion. Many of the other families were having the same problem, so a meeting was called to decide what to do. One of the men had made the trip before and told them that when the Spaldings and Whitmans came over, they cut the Spalding wagon in half and made a cart out of it to spare the animals and help navigate the mountains.

Within a short time, one could hear the sound of saws as they cut the wagons in half. Sadly, this meant that almost everything had to be left behind except a pathetic assortment of bedding and clothes. Aunt Sally explained to the children that the only matter of any importance at this point was getting them safely to the Whitman Mission.

As they were climbing aboard the cart, Matilda spotted the corner of their family bible under a blanket. It contained records of all family births and deaths, so she handed it to John, who told her he would enter their mother and father's deaths.

Doctor Dagen supervised the loading of the cart and helped the children climb aboard. When he climbed on, it upset the balance of the cart and the girls all leaned back to try and correct the tilt. This caused everything and everyone to go rolling off the back of the cart. John and Frank came running as fast as they could to see if anyone was hurt. When they saw everyone lying in a pile and found that no one was hurt, Frank burst out laughing, and before long, everyone joined in. It was the first time since Henry had died that anyone had heard the sound of laughter, and was exactly what their weary and broken-hearted souls needed to continue.

The three-week trek along the Snake River was grueling, from boiling hot to freezing cold, but always bone-jarring. The trail was so rough that it had become easier for the children to walk the endless miles rather than ride. Oxen and mules were lying down and dying. Provisions were running low and had to be rationed. When the Shaws shared their last two loaves of bread with the Sager children, there was nothing left but rancid buffalo jerky. The children's clothes were torn and tattered; their shoes had worn out long ago, so they walked barefoot. The trail was becoming more dangerous each day with deep ravines and rapid rivers.

John had taken on the role of father, and in some ways, he was stricter and more effective at keeping them in line. Catherine had assumed the role of mother with the younger girls. Nights were the worst, huddled together under filthy and worn blankets trying to keep warm. Poor little Louise cried herself to sleep every night calling out for her mama. Matilda said nothing, but when Catherine stroked her hair to soothe her, she could feel the tears on her cold, wet cheeks. They went to sleep each night, holding hands while praying for their parents. Doctor Dagon refused to eat any more than he needed to survive so that there would be more for the children. When Catherine told him, he needed to eat his share, he told her that he was too fat and needed to lose weight. Their cow Bossy had been like a lifeline, giving the girls enough milk to keep them nourished. She now looked like a sack of moving bones and was starting to run out of the precious liquid.

It was easy to see why Three-Mile Crossing was considered the most dangerous river crossing of the entire journey. It was over one thousand feet wide with a constantly shifting sandy bottom and violent currents. At this time of year, when the water was at its lowest point, three small islands rose above the waterline. There were stories of wagons being swept away with oxen, cattle, and people either pulled under or tangled in the rigging and drowned. Even some of the brave souls who had tried to save them had been drowned. John and Frank tried to make the cart as waterproof as possible, telling the girls to get in the back and lie flat so they wouldn't fall out. As soon as they hit the water, the cart lurched out from under them, and the girls shrieked in terror, holding tightly to one another and expecting the worst. They had been attached to another wagon to give them more stability, but both started to slide dangerously downriver. Finally, the wheels caught the sandy bottom and started to slowly move forward.

It was obvious from the intense tone of voice that Doctor Dagon and the boys were using that all their lives were in jeopardy. As the water began coming in from the bottom of the cart, Louise started screaming for her mother, putting everyone's nerves on edge.

John had tried to caulk the cracks in the cart with tar, but the freezing water was now swirling all around the frightened girls. Catherine was doing her best to calm Louise down even though she was unsure if they would survive the frigid waters of the Snake River.

When they reached the first island, the cart almost jumped out of the water as it hit the bank and water poured out of the back, and began to drain. Just as they started to relax, they were once again thrust forward, slipping precariously down the other side of the bank, sliding sideways. The water came up even higher this time, and the girls were up to their waists in liquid ice as the cart skimmed across the bottom without making solid contact. The next island came at them quickly, and once again, they lurched upward out of the water. Doctor Dagon was yelling at the oxen like a madman, trying to get them back into the water, and Louise was screaming and crying at the top of her lungs.

Finally, the oxen started down the last bank, pulling the most frightened and pathetic looking family of four little girls anyone had ever seen. They were clutching at each other in a desperate attempt to hold on for their dear lives. This time they gained ground quickly, but the oxen were tiring and trying to turn around. The doctor was flailing the whip and yelling, John was beside them on a borrowed horse, whipping and yelling at the top of his lungs. Frank dove off the cart onto the back of the closest oxen and started hitting it as hard as he could.

Maybe it was divine intervention, but as they reached the other side, the girls were thrown to the back of the cart in a tangle of sodden arms and legs, safe. The oxen slipped and slid up the bank, collapsing when they finally reached flat ground. Fires of damp brush were already burning so that wet clothes and bedding could be taken out and dried before they continued.

That night was wet and miserably cold, everyone draped in damp clothes and bedding, smelling of musty camp smoke. Captain Shaw told them that they were now headed for Fort Boise, where they would soon find giant pine trees and forests teeming with wildlife. First, they would have to leave the river and cross the open plains where there would be little water or food. There had been no rain there for months, and before long, they were forced to ration water for drinking and cooking.

The captain was wrong about Fort Boise; there were few trees and no forests. By this time of year, the fort was like a desert with no surplus supplies available for sale. They were unable to find any fresh game, so everyone was reduced to eating buffalo jerky, and once again camp fever was beginning to spread like wildfire. The Sager children were getting as much help as anyone could spare, but they grew weaker by the day.

It got to the point where they had to lay down in the cart and try to sleep to conserve energy.

Doctor Dagon had eaten very little and was also growing weaker by the day. If it hadn't been for Aunt Sally, he and the children would have surely perished. She continued to share every last bit of food they had with the Sager children even as her own children grew weak from hunger. The Sagers' cow Bossy had dried up, and Aunt Sally only had one milk-producing cow that Captain Shaw had traded for with an Indian man. It looked worse than the children and was almost dry, but Aunt Sally managed to squeeze out just enough for the children and Doctor Dagen, who now barely had enough strength to drive the oxen. Aunt Sally told her husband that if it hadn't been for that cow, the doctor and younger Sager girls would have never survived.

The days were growing cooler and more comfortable, but the nights were even colder. As soon as camp was made, everyone would get their fires going as fast as possible and huddle around as close as they could to stay warm.

It was nearing the end of September when they reached the Grande Ronde Valley, where they finally found enough brush and wood to have a substantial fire. The wind had kicked up and was blowing hard from the west. One night, Elizabeth got too close to the fire, and her dress went up in flames. Doctor Dagon jumped up and beat the fire out with his hands. Though seriously shaken, Elizabeth miraculously had only minor burns, but the doctor's hands were badly injured.

Doctor Dagon guided Aunt Sally through the process of cleaning and dressing his hands, but was unable to drive the wagon cart, so Frank took over while John drove what was left of the listless cattle.

Chapter 7

A Cry in the Night

Two nights later, Catherine woke to find Louise gone. There was no moonlight, and she couldn't see a thing in the dark and started calling out, trying to see if she could get a response. There was no reply, so she went to her brothers' tent, calling for help. It was bitterly cold, and the chances for Louise's survival were not good if she wasn't found soon. Louise had somehow managed to crawl over the tailgate of the cart looking for her mother. Her cry was so weak that no one had heard it until she tripped and yelled, waking Aunt Sally. Sally woke her husband and told him that she was certain she heard a child crying out in the darkness somewhere. Weary, weak, and tired, he dressed and went out into the frigid night looking for what he thought his wife might have imagined. His hands and feet were completely numb, and he was just about to give up when he heard a small voice crying, "Mama, Mama."

When he finally found Louise, she was shivering wildly and had turned blue from the cold. He took her in his big arms and ran as fast as he could in the direction of their tent. When he finally found it, he handed Louise to Sally, who immediately started rubbing her limbs vigorously, trying to stop her violent shaking. By this time, Catherine had woken John, Frank, and Doctor Dagon, who were up and searching for Louise. Uncle Billy quickly found them and told the doctor they needed his help right away. The doctor told the boys to warm some blankets by the fire as he took most of Louise's clothes off. He told Sally to undress to her underclothes and hold Louise to her as tight as she could while he turned around. When that was done, he wrapped them in a blanket until John and Frank arrived with warm ones, then rewrapped them together tightly. Louise was shaking so violently that she couldn't even cry out. When she finally did, it was a great relief to everyone. Once Louise stopped shivering, Aunt Sally handed her to Catherine, who rewrapped her in a warm blanket and held her close.

Captain Shaw said, "I know this wasn't your fault Catherine, but we will need to rig something up to make sure it doesn't happen again." Catherine broke down crying, saying that she was sorry over and over again.

Aunt Sally took Catherine and Louise in her arms and said to her husband, "You could have handled that better with all these poor children have been through."

Head down, he apologized profusely, then picked Catherine and Louise up together, putting them back in bed and covering them up tightly. By then, Louise was sound asleep from exhaustion, and Captain Shaw spent the night wide awake staring at his wife's backside, admonishing himself for making Catherine break down crying. Fortunately, he had found Louise before she had done any real harm to herself.

They now often went on ahead of the company because the cart was so light, which was a great relief from breathing in the dust and constantly having to wipe it out of their eyes. One day they had gotten so far ahead that they were able to pull over by a stream to wait for the rest of the company. Doctor Dagon asked Frank to make a fire so they could warm up and have some tea he had saved while they waited. Frank was having trouble starting it since all he could find to burn was damp brush and a few wet sticks.

He decided to use some of his gunpowder on the brush to get it going. He turned his powder horn upside down, and as he started to pour, he saw the flame come up toward him and let go. The horn exploded before he could move, knocking him flat on his back. He jumped up and started running blindly toward the creek, then diving in. Doctor Dagen jumped in the water after Frank and started examining him, hoping that he hadn't damaged his eyes or hands. The doctor found that Frank had, fortunately, let go of the powder horn just before it exploded and must have closed his eyes since the lids and eyebrows were blackened, but the eyes uninjured.

When he returned to the fire, which was now burning brightly, John took one look at Frank's blackened face, singed eyebrows and eyelashes, and started laughing. He tried to hold back, but soon Catherine joined in, and before long, everyone else was laughing hysterically, even Doctor Dagen. It was the first time anyone had laughed since the girls had all tumbled out of the back of the cart, and was another badly needed dose of sweet relief.

It seemed as if there was no end to the dangers they had to endure. As they reached the far point of the Grande Ronde Valley before ascending the mountains, they came upon a beautiful open meadow with plenty of water and grass for the animals to graze on. Once again, almost everyone wanted to rest and get their strength back up for a couple of days, but it was now late October, and if they were caught in a snowstorm, all could be lost.

As Three Island crossing was the most dangerous of the river crossings, the Blue Mountains were the most dangerous of the mountain crossings. They were not that high, but they were extremely steep, and the trail was almost non-existent at times. It was a daunting sight standing at the base of the mountains staring into the sky and wondering if everyone would make it over safely. For three excruciatingly backbreaking days, the men cut trees and brush to make room for the wagons, the first to ever use this trail. Their clothes were torn to shreds, and many of them had deep scratches over their faces and arms from the trees and thorny bushes.

Amazingly enough, no one was killed or badly injured. Descending the west side was by far the most dangerous. They had to tie logs to the back of the wagons and carts and drag them so that they wouldn't run away and go charging over a cliff. Everyone who could walk did so just in case one got away. That way, it would only be the animals and wagons that would be lost.

If it hadn't been for Captain Shaw's persistent discipline keeping the wagon train going, things could have gone far differently. On the third night in the Blue Mountains, it started snowing, and they were able to descend just in time to avoid blizzard conditions. As they made their final descent, they could see the majestic Columbia River in the distance, one of the most beautiful sights they had ever seen.

There were still three hundred miles to go until they reached the Willamette Valley, but the Whitman Mission was only one hundred miles ahead. Here they hoped to find help for the children and supplies for the wagon train. Doctor Whitman had received word from the previous company that they should be coming out of the mountains soon, so he sent a wagon full of provisions to meet them. The sight of a wagon loaded with supplies was almost as beautiful as the Columbia River.

That night Aunt Sally made fresh bread and potatoes, which seemed like a feast fit for a king after what they had eaten and been through. Some complained about having to pay for it since the Whitmans were missionaries. Captain Shaw told them they should pray for the Whitman's consideration and be grateful that they had something to eat that night. He explained that the Whitmans had to pay for seed and labor, just like anyone else. If they gave it away to every wagon train that came out of the mountains, there would soon be nothing left for anyone.

Most of the company went on to the Willamette Valley, but those who were sick or still in need of supplies started for the Whitman Mission. Catherine overheard the captain tell his wife that he would go ahead and ask the Whitmans if they would care for the Sager children until he and Aunt Sally were settled. When he returned, Catherine once again overheard them as he told Aunt Sally that Mrs. Whitman was willing to take the girls, but didn't have the room or resources for the boys. Aunt Sally said to take them with him anyway, that when she saw them, she might have a change of heart. He told her that he would give it a try, but Mrs. Whitman seemed firm about her decision and was already over her head with children and immigrants.

Aunt Sally mended the boys' clothes as best she could and then had them clean up. She then cut their hair, thinking to herself that no matter what she did, they were still going to be a sorry looking lot. Catherine kept the news about the boys to herself so she wouldn't alarm the others. Inside she was nervous and deeply troubled about the possibility of being separated from her brothers.

Uncle Billy was worried about Matilda Jane and Louise, who were now sick. It was a miracle that their cart or oxen hadn't already broken down. He told his wife that as soon as they found land and got a farm going, he wanted to come back and make them all a part of their family. She agreed wholeheartedly. He said that if the Whitmans wouldn't take the boys, they were hard workers, and could help them with a farm. Rosanna was still behind in a wagon with Mrs. Eads since her group had decided to rest up for several days.

Aunt Sally told him that they should get going in case the Whitmans decided to change their minds, that if Rosanna was still alive, she would make sure the baby got to the Whitman Mission if she had to bring her there herself. The last time they had seen Rosanna she was terribly weak and sick, hardly even responding.

As the Shaws gathered the Sager children around them for the last time, Elizabeth ran to Sally and said, "I don't want to go to the Whitmans. I want to stay with you and Uncle Billy," then burst out crying.

This just about broke Aunt Sally's heart, and even Uncle Billy was fighting back tears. She told the children not to worry, as soon as they were settled, they would come back for them. They loaded up their meager belongings and said goodbye to the Shaw family, waving until they disappeared into the hazy distance. Doctor Dagon cracked the whip, and Uncle Billy rode beside them with a spare horse for the return trip as the Sagers rolled on toward another unknown and frightening destination.

There are no words that could accurately characterize the kindness and generosity shown by Uncle Billy and Aunt Sally. They had treated the Sager children as if they were their own and had grown to love them in the same way. This was also true for Doctor Dagen, who nearly starved to death to make sure the children survived. They were good people, the best we have to offer as human beings.

In her heart, Catherine was dreading the moment they would reach the Whitman Mission, and possibly being separated from her two brothers. She said nothing, holding to a thread of hope that they could somehow manage to stay together. They had planned to make it in one day, but the oxen were worn out and barely able to continue. They camped that night for the last time, huddled together for warmth and comfort.

The next morning was bright and clear with a sapphire blue sky and sunshine that warmed their spirits with hope. They feasted on a few pieces of dry crusty bread and cold potatoes before striking camp. For the older children, the thought of being forced upon strangers was not unlike their breakfast that morning, cold and hard to swallow. They had no idea who these people were, or what they would be like. Would they be kind or mean, did they even like children? They also wondered what the mission would be like, expecting it to be something like a fort with high walls to protect them from the Indians.

As they drew near, the road became much smoother, and horses were grazing on the tall grass. There was a small lake with geese swimming about and a rough two-story house made of adobe. As they made the last turn, they finally stopped in front of a big beautiful white house that looked as though it belonged in Missouri.

Captain Shaw asked the children to stay with the wagon as he dismounted and went to see if he could find one of the Whitmans.

Chapter 8

Oh, Dear Lord

When Mrs. Whitman came out of the house with Captain Shaw, she put her hand to her mouth and said, "Oh, dear Lord."

Uncle Billy had told her earlier what the children had been through and the kind of condition they were in, but she wasn't prepared for what she was seeing. Their faces were dark from the sun and dust. Their clothes were ripped and tattered, and not one of the children had a pair of shoes. They looked like skeletons, nothing but skin and bones covered in dirt. On the other hand, the Sager children thought that Mrs. Whitman was the most beautiful woman they had ever seen, perfectly combed and dressed with a kind face. Doctor Whitman came over from the blacksmith shop wiping his hands on a rag with a warm smile that took them off guard.

He went to Narcissa and quietly said, "I have never seen a more pitiful sight in my entire life. These poor children look as if they are less than one step from death's door."

Narcissa whispered, "I told Captain Shaw that we could only take the girls. What are we going to do with the boys?"

"These children have been through too much to be taken from each other now; God would want us to take care of them all together."

She knew that there was no point in arguing with God, so she turned to the children and said, "You children must be tired and hungry. Welcome to your new home."

444

John put his head down and started crying, and Catherine blurted out, "Does that mean John and Frank, too?"

Doctor Whitman walked over to John and said, "If Mother gets the girls, then I get the boys. It's only fair." Catherine broke down and wept like a baby.

Doctor Whitman went to John, who was trying to hide his tears and said, "Son, there is no shame in crying after what you've been through. I suspect you have had to take the place of both your father and mother, and I am sure they would be proud of you. There are a lot of grown men who couldn't have done any better."

To break the somber mood, Doctor Whitman loudly said so everyone could hear, "I hear your father was a blacksmith, and you boys drove these cattle all the way from Missouri. Can either of you use a hammer?"

Frank spoke out right away, saying, "We both know how to use a forge, sir. We can also farm and take care of cattle."

Doctor Whitman turned to Narcissa, smiling, and said, "Did you hear that mother? I just got myself a couple of hired hands, and Lord knows I can use them."

He then turned back to the boys and said, "I can't pay much, but you boys can make a little something if you work hard." John and Frank looked at each other in amazement, then took turns vigorously shaking the doctor's hand and thanking him.

Uncle Billy and Doctor Dagen had been quiet up to that point, but the captain said, "This is what Mrs. Shaw and I have been praying for. Doctor Dagen and I promised their parents that we would do everything in our power to keep these children together."

He then introduced Doctor Dagen to the Whitmans. Mrs. Whitman invited everyone inside and said, "Let's get you children cleaned up and fed. Captain Shaw and Doctor Dagen, you are welcome to join us and stay the night. I was told there was a baby. Where is she?"

Catherine told her that Rosanna needed to be breast-fed and was still with one of the women from another wagon and would be brought later if she were still alive. Narcissa was staggered by the thought of a dead baby, and then she saw Catherine pick up her crutch and start struggling to get down off of the unsteady cart.

Narcissa said, "You poor girl, you've been injured. Marcus, help me get her down. What happened to you, dear?"

Catherine told her how she had fallen off the wagon and was run over by one of the wheels. Narcissa's eyes misted as she put her arm around Catherine and helped her to the house. The other girls were still huddled together in the back of the cart as Doctor Whitman gently lifted each of them out, shocked by how light and fragile they were.

Narcissa came back out and took each of them by the hand one at a time and led them into the house. Even Doctor Dagen was having trouble trying to hold back the emotions that he was feeling for these children. It was the first time he had ever felt like a father, and he had grown to love and respect each child beyond measure. Before supper, Doctor Whitman told the boys that he would take them to Captain Shaw and Doctor Dagen, over at the mansion house to show them where they could clean up and bunk for the night. He told John and Frank that they would make room for them in the main house, but it might take a couple of days.

The feel of a real home and warm, friendly faces was almost too much for the children to comprehend after what they had been through.

When the girls were inside, Narcissa sat down with Louise in her lap and told them, "There is no reason for any of you to be afraid anymore. You are all safe here, and we are going to take good care of you. We can only imagine what you children have been through and how much you miss your parents." She then asked if it was all right to say a prayer for their parents, and everyone bowed their heads.

Inside the kitchen, there was a girl of about eight years old warming milk and bread for the children. Mrs. Whitman introduced her as Mary Ann Bridger. Her father was a famous mountain man named Jim Bridger, and her mother was an Indian woman.

Louise was still in her lap as Narcissa asked the girls their names. Several minutes later, Doctor Whitman came in and introduced the boys to Narcissa. He said that Captain Shaw and Doctor Dagen were still cleaning up and should be over in a little while. The children told them about their parents and what had happened to them; how everyone had helped them out, especially the Shaw family and Doctor Dagen. It was still almost too painful for them to talk about their parents, but when they did, the tears started again. The Whitman's were deeply touched and told them how sorry they were for their loss.

Doctor Whitman asked if he could take a look at Catherine's leg, "Did Doctor Dagen set this?"

She told him, "No, sir, my father fixed it."

After examining her, he said, "This is an excellent job; you should be as good as new before long. Was your father a doctor?"

"He never went to school for it. He learned from his father, who had learned from his father, and they were always treating people for one thing and another."

"I've known some country medicine men that were just as good as any doctors. It's something you either have a knack for or not. Your father must have had a knack for it."

Catherine then asked if the Whitmans had any children. She could tell by the sad look on Mrs. Whitman's face and the way she hung her head that it was the wrong question to ask.

Mrs. Whitman looked up and said, "We had a little girl named Alice Clarissa that would be seven now, but she drowned when she was just two years and three months old. She's buried right outside beside the tree where I can see her; it helps me to feel closer to her."

Elizabeth said, "I wish we could see Mama and Papa's graves; we had to bury them on the trail. Mama didn't even get a coffin; they just covered her with bushes and dirt."

The boys' heads were down, and the girls started getting teary-eyed again. Just then, Uncle Billy and Doctor Dagen came in, breaking the somber mood.

Captain Shaw said, "I can't tell you folks how much this means to my wife and me. We plan to find some land and settle in the Willamette Valley; we should be back next spring to gather up the children. These children are brave beyond anything I have ever seen, and keeping my promise to their parents has been heavy on my mind."

Mrs. Whitman was looking toward the cradle in the corner that had belonged to Alice Clarissa and said, "Doctor, I was looking forward to having a baby in the house, do you think she is still alive?"

He paused and then said, "It's hard to say ... the last time I saw her, she was very sick and weak. When we were running low on food and water, both women were having a hard time nursing their babies, but I know Mrs. Eads is doing everything she can for Rosanna. They're not far behind, so someone should be bringing her here soon if she has survived."

Captain Shaw then asked, "I told the children that you were taking care of several other children, how many are there?"

"You met Mary Ann Bridger; we also have Helen Mar Meeks who is near the same age as Mary Ann; then there is David Malin, who is almost five, and Marcus's nephew Perrin, who is a little older than John."

Doctor Whitman said, "It looks like we are going to have one big happy family around here, once we get a little food in these children."

Just then, Mary Ann came in the room with a large tray of warm bread and butter, then went back to the kitchen, returning with a big pitcher of warm milk. Mrs. Whitman thanked her and then told the children this was a little something to warm them up, that supper would be ready in about an hour. The doctor told them to take it easy and eat slowly, that their stomachs were shrunken up, and they would get sick if they ate too fast.

Narcissa asked the children how old they were; little Louise held up four fingers and said she was three. Catherine told her she was ten, Elizabeth seven; Matilda said she was five, John 13, and Frank 11. Surrounded by these pitiful, frightened, and ragged children, she was touched in a way that she had never felt before and could feel her heart going out to them. She looked at the cradle in the corner and hoped that little Rosanna was still alive so she could once again hold a baby in her arms.

Doctor Whitman went to his wife and tried to pick up little Louise, but she pulled away and tucked back into Narcissa's arms. Narcissa laughed, making her look even lovelier. She told Marcus he was scaring the child, that she was perfectly comfortable where she was. When he sat back down, Matilda came over and sat in his lap, putting her head on his shoulder.

As his heart melted, he wrapped her in his arm, and looking at Narcissa and Louise, he said, "See, I'm not so bad."

Matilda stroked his beard and twirled his hair on her finger like she used to do with her father and mother. Narcissa and Marcus looked at each other as something unsaid passed between them. Narcissa had been guarding her heart for so long that she finally broke down and started weeping. Both Catherine and Elizabeth ran to embrace her. It was a deeply human moment that felt like home and had been missing from all of their lives; even Marcus had to brush back tears.

After supper Mrs. Whitman had Marcus bring the big tub into the kitchen that she used for giving the children baths. She found several old nightgowns that had belonged to Mary Ann and Helen for them to wear to bed. The children hadn't felt so clean and warm since they had left home almost seven months ago. That night they had to sleep on blankets, but Doctor Whitman said he would get busy the next day, building them each a bed. Catherine lay silently listening to her younger sisters breathing as they slept, wondering how they had ever gotten to where they were now. She thought of how badly she missed her parents and wondered what the future would be. She closed her eyes and prayed for her mother and father and thanked God for guiding them to Mr. and Mrs. Whitman.

The next morning as Captain Shaw and Doctor Dagen prepared to leave, Doctor Whitman told them, "Mrs. Whitman and I have decided to take the children in permanently. You won't need to come back next spring unless you want to visit. I think we can give them a good home, and they have already found a place in our hearts."

Captain Shaw said, "Thank you doctor. I know that if their parents, Henry and Naomi, are looking down on us right now, that there is a smile on their faces."

Doctor Dagon added, "These are fine children, the best I have ever known, and those boys are the hardest workers I have ever seen. I was not there when it happened, but I hear that Catherine barely cried when her leg was crushed, I have known battle-hardened men with less courage. I know that you will bring each other great happiness, and I thank you with all of my heart."

They shook hands warmly as Uncle Billy and Doctor Dagon promised to visit as soon as possible. The next day was washing day, and Mrs. Whitman had the big tub outside filled with warm water and soap, another tub to rinse them out. The children's rags nearly dissolved in Narcissa's hands, so she started going through all the clothes she had saved and managed to find enough for them to wear for the time being. She told the children that there were two excellent seamstresses at the mansion house, and they would make new clothes for them. Catherine told her that she and Elizabeth had been taught to sew and knit by their mother, and they would be glad to help.

As the doctor showed John and Frank around the mission, he was amazed at the answers they gave to his questions. They had a thorough knowledge of animals, farming, and the blacksmith shop. Their mother had given them an excellent education. He liked their quiet, bright, and unassuming natures, and it was obvious that John was a born leader.

The next day Catherine watched as an almost steady stream of people came knocking at the kitchen door. Mrs. Whitman told her that the immigrants and Indians came for food, medicine, and treatments from the doctor. An older boy about John's age came into the house with a younger one of about five tagging along behind him. Mrs. Whitman introduced her to Perrin Whitman and little David Malin, whom she had only said hello to the night before. Perrin was tall with wide shoulders like the doctor, wavy brown hair, and blue eyes. It made her think of how John looked so big and strong before they had started the trip, but had lost so much weight that he was much smaller now.

David Malin was dark-skinned with straight black hair and big soft dark eyes. Mrs. Whitman told Elizabeth and Catherine that David had been brought to her when he was four years old. She told them that his first name had been Cortez, but they named him David; he was a shy, sweet and gentle boy.

That night, Catherine and Elizabeth noticed quite a few fires outside the mission and mansion house and asked who they were. Mrs. Whitman told them that, unfortunately, they didn't have enough room for everyone who came to the mission. Those camped outside were mostly immigrants who were still living in their wagons; some of the fires belonged to the Indian people who worked around the mission. Most were from the recent wagon train and were either resting or getting treatment from the doctor before making their way to the Willamette Valley. Some had been asked to stay on and work around the mission, and others were too sick to go on.

After supper, Narcissa told the children that she had exciting news; "We will be starting a school for the white children soon. We found a nice young man named Mr. Hinman who has agreed to stay on until spring."

The children all clapped their hands with joy, and Elizabeth asked, "Do the Indian children get to come to the school?"

The doctor told her, "We already have a school for the Indian children. We need a school for the white children so we can teach subjects like math and science."

That night the doctor and Mrs. Whitman told the children that they had decided to keep them as part of their family if they would like to stay. They all leaped to their feet and enveloped the Whitmans in hugs and kisses.

Matilda Jane looked up at Narcissa and asked, "Does that mean forever and ever?"

The Whitmans both started laughing, and Narcissa said, "Yes dear, that means forever and ever.

Chapter 9

A Ragged Little Bundle

Several days later, as the girls were busy cleaning up, there was a knock on the kitchen door. Narcissa opened the door to find a ragged woman in dirty clothes with a filthy bundle in her hands. The woman held it out, and Narcissa instinctively took it.

The woman was worn and haggard, saying, "It was my turn to feed her, but I can't get milk anymore. Captain Shaw told us you took the other Sager children in and that you wanted this little one."

Catherine and Elizabeth crowded around the baby as Narcissa pulled back the bundle. As they peeled back the blanket, Narcissa gasped when she saw Rosanna's tiny ancient face and body.

Catherine shrieked, "She's still alive. Thank God she's still alive."

Matilda heard her from the other room and came running into the kitchen, asking, "Is that Rosanna?"

Narcissa held her down for Matilda to see, and Matilda kissed her on the forehead. The girls all went to Mrs. Eads and hugged and thanked her for bringing the baby.

Mrs. Eads then said, "That little girl's a fighter. It would have been easy for her to let go, but she didn't. We need to be on our way, we still have a long way to go, and we're anxious to see the land."

Narcissa told her, "You are welcome to stay and rest up as long as you need."

"Thank you, Mrs. Whitman, and thank you for sending the wagon to meet us. We were nearly starved, but we're going to be on our way."

Narcissa asked her to wait a moment and grabbed a sack and started filling it with potatoes, vegetables, and three loaves of fresh bread from the counter.

She then brought over a large bag full of flour and said, "You have gone a long way out of your way. Please take this with you, and thank you for this kindness. These children have been worried sick about their little sister."

They said their good-byes, and then Mrs. Eads climbed aboard their nearly broken-down wagon and waved as the rugged man next to her cracked the whip. Narcissa could see three young children in the back of the wagon who looked every bit as worn as the Sager children had on the day they arrived. She closed her eyes and thanked God for Rosanna, saying a silent prayer for the Eads family.

Narcissa asked, "Elizabeth, would you run over to the mill and get the doctor; please tell him to come right away."

Rosanna was moving, but it looked as if she were in a dream world. Catherine and Matilda huddled up close as Narcissa started to unwrap the filthy blanket from around the baby. The terrible odors of stale urine and feces slapped them in the face. Narcissa immediately asked Catherine to get some towels and warm water off the stove. The baby could barely open her eyes and was trying to cry but was too weak to make more than a tiny whining sound.

John and Frank burst in the door with Doctor Whitman right behind them. Catherine told them, "She's alive, Rosanna's alive."

Frank asked the doctor, "She doesn't look so good. Do you think she'll make it?"

"We're going to do everything we can for her, but this may not be in our hands."

When Narcissa was done cleaning her up, she put a cloth diaper on and wrapped her in a soft, warm blanket. Catherine had prepared a small cup of warm milk mixed with water, and Rosanna started drinking it right away, then threw it back up and started gagging. The doctor told her to give the baby a few drops at a time.

When he was through examining her, he said, "It's a miracle she is still alive. How old is she?"

Catherine told him, "Rosanna is a little over five months."

The doctor shook his head and said, "She doesn't even look a month old. Other than being tiny and undernourished, I can't find anything wrong with her."

Narcissa asked Catherine and Elizabeth to warm some water, that the baby still smelled bad, and a bath might make her feel better.

John asked, "Can I hold her?"

Narcissa handed Rosanna to him, and he kissed her cheeks that were wet from the tears that had fallen from his eyes. After everyone had gently taken turns holding her, Narcissa gave her a few drops of milk and water from her fingertip. This time Rosanna was able to hold it down. Everyone stood around the tub, watching as Narcissa gently lowered Rosanna into the warm water; it was the first bath she had ever had, and she had no idea what to think of it. Suddenly, she let out with a wail that startled everyone in the room.

The doctor told them, "That's a good sign, healthy lungs."

Narcissa gently rubbed warm water over her little body and talked softly to her, reassuring Rosanna that she would soon be running and playing with the other children. Within a few minutes, she stopped crying and started exploring the feeling of being suspended in warm water. She kicked her legs and arms and opened her eyes as wide as she could, returning a noticeable smile to all of the faces smiling above her.

Matilda clapped her hands and said, "Did you see that, did you? She just smiled."

Narcissa asked Marcus to get the baby clothes that had belonged to Alice Clarissa out of the chest, still at the foot of their bed. When Rosanna was dressed and bathed, she began to move like a newborn, grasping at the air. Everyone gathered in the living room where Marcus had a warm fire going.

Narcissa put Rosanna in Catherine's arms and told her to give her a few drops of milk mixed with water every couple of minutes, as long as she could hold it down. When Catherine stuck her finger in Rosanna's mouth, she started sucking as hard as she could, and Catherine let out with a triumphant giggle. Narcissa told the girls if they were careful, they could take turns feeding and holding the baby; that she still had a hundred things to do.

The doctor said, "I think she's going to make it; it's amazing what a little milk and love can do."

He and the boys left to continue working on the mill. Every once in a while, Narcissa peeked into the room to check on the baby. She could hardly contain the feelings she was having looking at these innocent little girls gathered around their precious little sister, with such a deep sense of love and devotion. It was a feeling she had hidden away since losing Alice Clarissa, a feeling far beyond words.

After supper, they gathered around the fireplace and talked about what they hoped to learn at the new school. Narcissa was in her rocking chair with Rosanna asleep in her arms. She then got up and brought the cradle that had belonged to Alice over next to her, laid the baby down inside, and started rocking it with her foot just as she had with Alice Clarissa. This was the life she and Marcus had always hoped to share.

Within days, Rosanna seemed reborn and was becoming much more aware of everything around her. Catherine was happy to see the change but had been given the responsibility of caring for her. She hardly saw John and Frank, who were always busy working. Elizabeth, Matilda, and Louise always seemed to be outside, playing with Mary Ann and Helen. Narcissa noticed that Catherine was beginning to grow moody and despondent. When she found her in the living room holding the baby and crying, she asked what was wrong.

Catherine told her, "I don't know. I miss my parents and being able to run and play outside with my sisters and brothers. It seems all I do is sit inside and take care of Rosanna and mend clothes."

Narcissa said, "I'm sorry, dear. I've been so busy that I didn't notice."

Narcissa sat down and put her arm around Catherine, saying, "I know how it is to lose someone you love ... I felt like a different person when I lost Alice. I was always so happy and cheerful; she had become the center of my life. In a way, I feel that the pride I had

459

in her was the reason she was taken away from me, to teach me humility.

"Any more, it seems one minute I'm happy, the next I'm sad or angry. I find myself weeping for no reason at all, other than a deep sadness I can't resist. As much as I love and respect my husband, nothing has been able to fill the emptiness until now. You children have given me a new sense of purpose that I thought I would never know again."

She took Catherine's face in her gentle hands and said, "As long as I am alive, I promise you will have a home and people who love you."

It was exactly what Catherine had needed, and she put her arms around Narcissa's neck, and they held each other for a long time.

Narcissa said, "I have never told anyone that before ... now, let's get you outside."

It was silently understood that Narcissa's rocking chair was off-limits, so none of the children ever sat in it. She picked it up and carried it out to the porch and set it where Catherine could watch everyone else playing and working. She told Catherine that the chair was now both of theirs and to use it any time she wanted.

Narcissa brought the baby out in the cradle and set her down where Catherine could rock it with her good foot and said, "What a beautiful day. How is that?"

Catherine looked up at her with a big beautiful smile on her face and said, "Wonderful!"

The next day, they were introduced to Mr. Hinman and thought him a nice man, though Louise and Matilda seemed a little frightened. He was short and stout with long brown hair and green eyes. He told them about all of the things they would be learning and let them know that he ran a tight ship, but if they worked hard and minded him, they would all get along fine.

It was not always easy to understand the new rules of the house. The Whitmans were strict disciplinarians with a steady and consistent hand. They were also loving and did everything within their power to make the children happy and comfortable. But the Sager children had had little to no supervision for a long time. Getting used to doing everything at a certain time and in a certain way was a challenge, especially for Frank, the free-spirited prankster. School had started, and Frank was beginning to have problems with Mr. Hinman, who was also a strict disciplinarian, but without the sense of love and kindness that the Whitmans had shown.

After a week or so, the new family had started to fall into the routine of sitting around the fireplace at night with Narcissa and the girls knitting, and the boys reading to the younger children. Louise adored John and would usually sit in his lap. Matilda and Frank had a special closeness, and she would snuggle up with him or the doctor. Rosanna tired easily and spent a good deal of time sleeping, but she was slowly beginning to respond more and more and was putting on weight.

One night the doctor was sitting in the living room with the fireplace crackling, children and books spread out everywhere, observing the scene of domestic bliss when he said, "Mother, I have never seen you more beautiful," making her blush and the girls giggle.

"It seems as if God must have a reason for bringing us all together, and I can rarely remember being so content. Less than two weeks ago, these children showed up on our doorstep barefoot, sunburned, ragged, and starving. Now, look at them. It's like you and I have found the end of the rainbow, angels sent from heaven to bring us happiness. There is just one thing missing ..." He paused for a long time until it was perfectly silent, except for the sound of the cradle rocking and the fire crackling.

The children were all looking around at each other, wondering what could possibly be missing, when he said, "I can't remember the last time I heard you sing." Everyone started clapping and begging her to sing. She held her hands out to quiet them and began to sing "Silent Night, Holy Night." The Sager children had never heard anything like it before. Her voice was flawless, true, and clear, like church bells ringing in perfect harmony. She had a beautiful soprano voice that suspended time, lifting their spirits, giving them an intense feeling of hope and belonging, a spiritual experience.

When she finished, it was completely silent for a few seconds before everyone started to breathe again. Matilda Jane started clapping, then everyone joined in, asking for more. When they quieted down again, Narcissa began singing "Rock of Ages" with such beauty that they were all once again spellbound. She sang several psalms and then told the children it was bedtime, that they had school the next day. They begged for more, but she told them it was too late, and she would sing for them again tomorrow night if they would go to bed. They all surrounded her giving her hugs and kisses.

Elizabeth put her head on Narcissa's shoulder and asked, "Does this mean we are a family?"

Narcissa wrapped her in her arms and said, "It certainly does, dear."

Elizabeth kissed Narcissa on the cheek and said, "Good night, Mother."

Narcissa's eyes filled with tears as she wished them each good night.

The doctor was a wonderful storyteller, and the Sagers loved to hear his tall tales about the Wild West. He knew many of the most famous mountain men, trappers, and hunters and had an endless supply of stories about the Indians. They couldn't get enough of Mrs. Whitman's descriptions about her life in New York and what her sisters and brothers, parents, and home were like. It was an exotic and sophisticated world; unlike anything they had ever known.

The Sager children knew that the Whitmans were missionaries, but didn't understand what that meant besides being very religious. Catherine spent more time helping Narcissa than the other children did, and one day asked Mrs. Whitman what a missionary was.

Narcissa explained, "Everyone has a special gift to share. Back home we belonged to a church that is part of a group of churches that send people out into the world to help the poor, some sent as far away as Africa and China. Our purpose is to serve God and share His message, but we also do whatever we can to help make their lives better by teaching them how to grow food and build homes.

Catherine asked, "Why did you decide to become a missionary?"

"When I was 15, I heard a man speak at our church about the work he had been doing as a missionary. He told us he had been all over the world, talking to anyone who would listen. He spoke of the terrible conditions and hunger they lived with, about the darkness in many of their souls. In some places, they ate each other, and children were slaves. What he said touched me in a way that changed the way I looked at the world, and I knew that I wanted to dedicate my life to something bigger than myself, so I came to help."

Catherine thought about this for a time and then asked, "Would you teach me to be a missionary?"

Narcissa smiled and took Catherine's hands in hers, "When you get older, if that's what you truly want to do with your life, then I would be happy to teach you what I know."

School was Monday through Friday and a half-day on Saturday, but John, Frank, and Perrin only attended half days so they could help with the mission work. Sabbath was strictly observed, and over time the children began to look forward to it. When the weather was good, Mrs. Whitman would take them on outings into the nearby hills or along the river. Doctor Whitman believed in spending as much time as possible outdoors and made sure everyone got plenty of exercise either at play or work. The Whitmans hired extra helpers during the school year so the children could devote themselves to their studies. During the summer, everyone worked, either in the house or on the mission. Narcissa gave each child a small plot of land so that they could learn to grow their food.

During the summer, the girls always took a mid-day break to bathe in the river before lunch. It was a return to childhood, free to frolic in the water without a care in the world. The boys found a spot where they could dive or slide off a big mossy rock. The tricky part was getting up without sliding back down. They were all patient and compassionate with David Malin and taught him to be a playful little boy for the first time in his young life.

By observing Doctor Whitman, they were learning a valuable lesson about life. People came day and night for food and medicine, some of them terribly ill. The doctor was direct, but never lost his patience, and would do all he could to help and answer any question no matter what time of day or night. Sometimes he would eat, get dressed as fast as possible, grab his instruments, and medicine and travel to wherever he was needed, no matter the conditions.

When he was gone, Mrs. Whitman had to take on his responsibilities, often depriving herself of sleep and draining her of precious energy. Unlike the doctor, the constant demands sometimes made her impatient, irritable, or even fearful, especially when he was away. She could be difficult during these times, but other times she was the warmest and most kindhearted person imaginable.

The doctor seemed indefatigable and spent much of his time on his trusty mule, often treating patients hundreds of miles away; no one was ever refused medical help. It was obvious that he loved the children, and they loved him. On many of his trips, he would choose one of them to accompany him if it was not too far, too cold or hot. Visits to the Indian villages were the most exciting since they were often given gifts and shown around the camps.

The doctor always seemed to have a steady demeanor about him, never too high or too low, a consistently calming presence. These times were special for whoever got to accompany him since the doctor was a great listener. With the children he was always smiling and generous with his time and knowledge, never seeming to be in a hurry with them even when he was. He was also fearless and would travel hundreds of miles alone through the freezing nights and boiling days; one wrong step or encounter could mean disaster or death. He understood and accepted the reality that he might be injured and die alone on the trail without help or the comfort of a loved one. As kind and gentle as he was, he was also as hard as a rock, a giant among men.

The immigrants arrived in such large numbers that the Whitmans didn't have enough supplies or resources to take care of their needs. It seemed as if the doctor hardly ever slept because of the illnesses and responsibilities he faced.

Mrs. Whitman taught the children the importance of using all of their resources and never waste anything no matter how small or insignificant it may seem. Every seed, bean, and scrap of food was accounted for, and if someone was caught being wasteful, she would remind them of how cold and hungry they were before they came to Waiilatpu. Their foods were simple and healthy. Coffee and tea were rare, cake and pasties for special occasions, but vegetables, grains, milk, butter, and cheese were plentiful.

They traded with the Indian people for wild fruits and edible plants. During the winter, they ate beef and pork, sometimes venison or dried buffalo when it was available. During the summer, it was fish or mutton, with plenty of fresh vegetables from the gardens. They often had to ration the flour, corn, and grains they produced to feed the Indian people and immigrants, who often arrived near starvation.

On wash days, the whole family was up by 4:00 in the morning so that the children could be to school by nine. Catherine and John were responsible for breakfast on wash days, which often led to a good dose of humor and Frank's notorious pranks.

Like food, clothing was never wasted. If something was torn or ripped, it was mended. If it was too small, it was handed down, and if it could not be worn any longer, the scraps were used to make or stuff into quilts. Shoes were hard to come by, so the doctor paid several Indian women to make moccasins for the children. Mrs. Whitman always had one or more mission barrels that she kept in her room full of clothes and shoes. When someone needed something badly, she could often find or alter what was needed from the missionary barrel. She told them that when the doctor went to Fort Vancouver, he was going to purchase a bolt of cloth for new clothes. At night after supper, Narcissa would show Catherine and Elizabeth the finer points of sewing and knitting and had started teaching Matilda Jane the basics.

John and Frank were settling into their routine with the cattle, farming, and helping the blacksmith. They had to get up early to cut and haul firewood, then get water from the river for cooking and cleaning. Everyone worked hard, and Mrs. Whitman was extremely strict about cleanliness, creating even more need for water and wood to heat it.

Frank was growing tired of all the discipline and responsibilities and had started spending time with the older boys and young men at the mansion house. Mrs. Whitman could tell that his attitude was changing, so she tried to keep him in line by criticizing him, which only made him more defiant. He was also tiring of all the religious assignments and routines and had begun missing morning and evening prayers. Henry and Naomi Sager had gone to church on Sundays, but it was never forced on the children. When Frank misbehaved in class, Mr. Hinman beat him, which terrorized his sisters and made John angry.

Things continued to get worse. Mrs. Whitman was constantly on him, and the beatings were getting more severe each day. Frank was a tough kid and refused to cry out or make any sound at all during the whippings. This only infuriated Mr. Hinman, making him strike Frank even harder. The children were too frightened of Mr. Hinman to tell the Whitmans what was happening. Frank tried to talk to John, but John told him, "If you would just be easier to get along with, Mrs. Whitman would stop picking on you, and Mr. Hinman would stop beating you."

Frank replied, "I've had just about enough of both of them; I'm thinking of leaving for the Willamette Valley."

John said, "After all we've been through, you don't want to do that, Frank. You should be grateful to the Whitmans for taking us in, remember what it was like before we came here? Your sisters need you—I need you. Just stick it out, and things will get better."

They didn't get better, they got worse, the beatings became savage, and Narcissa was constantly on Frank for one thing or another.

When Doctor Whitman left for a short trip to Fort Walla Walla, Frank told Catherine, "I'm going to run away. I can't take it anymore. I'm leaving tomorrow for the Willamette Valley with the Howards."

She started crying, begging him to stay and keep the family together, that it was their parents' dying wish.

He told her, "I don't have any more tolerance for Mr. Hinman or Mrs. Whitman.

"He's beat me for the last time, and I am sick and tired of hearing how I can't do anything right. I'm tired of all the rules and having every minute of my day and night planned out for me. I need to breathe … Don't get me wrong; I'm grateful for all they've done for us.

"I like Doctor Whitman a lot, he's a good man, but I've had enough, and the Willamette Valley is where Mother and Father wanted us to go in the first place."

When Catherine went to her room that night, she got down on her knees and prayed that Frank would change his mind, but when she woke up in the morning, he was gone. She was worried that she would never see him again and went to Mrs. Whitman.

Narcissa said, "I was afraid I was pushing him too hard. Go get John and tell him to come here, I want him to find Frank and bring him back."

When John caught up to Frank, he tried to convince him to come back with him, but it was no use. Frank had made up his mind to go, and that was that. When Doctor Whitman got back, Catherine told him about the beatings but kept the part about Mrs. Whitman to herself.

The doctor told her, "I was afraid this was going to happen, I should have done something when I saw those welts on his back." He told everyone that he had to go to the Willamette Valley in several weeks for supplies and would find Frank and try to work something out.

Frank was always the life of the party, mischievous, but never mean or hurtful in any way, a rascal. When he left, it was as if someone had let the air out of a balloon, deflating everyone's spirits, even Narcissa's. Because of their closeness, it seemed to affect Matilda more than the others. During school, she would often become distracted, staring out of the window. Mr. Hinman had to keep telling her to pay attention and stop daydreaming.

Finally, he asked, "What in the world are you always looking out that window for?"

She burst into tears and said, "I'm looking for Frank. I know he's coming back; he would never leave me here."

He moved her to a different place in the room, so she wouldn't continue to look out of the window, and told her, "If you do not start paying more attention in class, you are going to be punished with a spanking."

John was becoming a big powerful young man from his heavy work in the blacksmith shop and on the farm, and when he stood, he towered over the pudgy, soft teacher.

Without anger or malice, he quietly told him, "Mr. Hinman, if you touch one of my sisters you are going to answer to me, and I promise it will be much worse than anything you did to Frank." Mr. Hinman told him that the Whitmans were going to hear about this, but they never did. John, also, was becoming frustrated with life at the mission, and he missed his brother.

He told Doctor Whitman, "I'm thinking about leaving the mission, Doctor. I don't mind the work at all, but I'm tired of Mr. Hinman, and I'm not going to attend his classes anymore. He threatened to beat Matilda Jane for not paying attention. I told him he would answer to me. I miss Frank ... we were about as close as two brothers could be, and it feels like a part of me left with him."

The doctor was quiet and thoughtful for a time and then said, "I miss Frank, too. I told Mr. Hinman that he was not welcome back next year, so we are going to have a different teacher even if I have to do it myself."

He paused for a moment in thought and then continued, "I'm leaving in a couple of days for the Willamette Valley, and I plan to find Frank. When I do, I'll tell him what I want to tell you now. If you two will stay on for several more years, I'll give you enough cattle and horses to start your own place and help you find and purchase a ranch and farm."

John replied, "I'd be willing to stay on if you can talk Frank into coming back, but there's another problem that I didn't want to bring up ... First, I want you to know that I love and respect you and Mrs. Whitman like you were my parents. You've been kind and generous to us beyond measure. I get along fine with Mrs. Whitman, but she and Frank don't see eye to eye—a big part of the reason he left. I know that she's trying to do what she thinks is best for him, but he's not going to change, and shouldn't have to. He's a free spirit and needs more elbow room than the rest of us. She constantly criticizes or corrects him, and he won't live like that anymore."

The doctor once again looked thoughtful, "I've seen it, but have been reluctant to do or say anything, hoping it would somehow work itself out. If Frank comes back, things need to change, but I need to be careful ... before you children came into our lives, my wife had been so sick and weak that I thought she would die. Her love for you, Frank, and your sisters brought her back to life, and it would kill her if you all left. I know it's hard to understand, but she dearly loves Frank and his high spirits. She's cried herself to sleep almost every night since he left and has begged me to look for him and bring him back. You should understand that she comes from a different kind of world where everything was orderly and proper. I promise to talk with her, but it's going to take some effort on Frank's part. I'll tell Mr. Hinman to make sure he doesn't lay a hand on your sisters, and that you will no longer be attending class."

John thanked him and told the doctor that he understood and would wait to see what Frank had to say before he did anything. He also told him that he would write a letter asking Frank to come back so they could work things out.

When the doctor returned from his trip to the Willamette Valley, he told the family that Frank had agreed to come back in the spring when school was finished. Everyone except Mr. Hinman was elated with the news, especially Matilda Jane.

Chapter 10

Reunion

On a beautiful spring day, just after the school year had finished, Catherine, Elizabeth, Matilda, and Louise were all out working in the garden when they saw a handsome young man come riding up to the mission. It took a moment to register that it was Frank since he had changed so much. As soon as they did, they bolted for the gate as Frank leapt off his horse and started running toward them. They looked like one big animal all huddled together, shedding salty tears. When Mrs. Whitman saw him, she went running with open arms and was warmly embraced by Frank.

Everyone was talking all at once, telling him how much they had missed him and everything that had happened while he was gone. John came running from the blacksmith shop, and when the doctor heard the commotion, he started making his way from the milldam. They all walked to the porch where Rosanna had just woken and was peeking her little head over the side of the cradle to see what was going on. Frank headed straight for her and lifted her out of the cradle and held her up in the air as she smiled down at him.

He then held her to his chest and said, "I can't believe how much she's grown. She looks as healthy as any other one year old."

Mrs. Whitman said, "I can't believe how much you have changed; you left here a boy and came back a man. Frank, I am sorry for how things went wrong before you left; I promise it will be different from now on."

Frank replied, "Thank you Mrs. Whitman. I know a good part of it was my fault. I can't tell you how happy I am to see you all."

He handed the baby to Mrs. Whitman, and within seconds, he had Matilda and Louise in his lap talking nonstop. Several nights later, they were all in the living room after supper, and Frank was playing with Rosanna as he said, "I've been giving this a lot of thought, and think we ought to give Rosanna a new name."

Everyone was quiet and surprised for a moment, then John said, "It's the name Mother and Father gave her."

"I know, and that's what I've been thinking about. I'm having trouble remembering what they look like, and it's started to bother me. I thought we might name her something that would help us remember them better."

Catherine looked around the room thoughtfully and said, "I think it's a good idea."

John added, "I kind of like the idea too."

Both Matilda and Louise said, "Me too."

The Whitmans knew this was something for the children to work out, so they stayed quiet.

John asked, "What did you have in mind?"

"Well, I was thinking Henrietta Naomi for father and mother. What do you think, Mrs. Whitman?"

Narcissa smiled and said, "I think it's a good name, a wonderful way to honor your parents."

"I heartily agree," said Doctor Whitman.

Frank picked Rosanna up in the air and blew air on her belly, making her laugh then asked, "What do you think, Henrietta?"

He blew on her belly some more, and when she laughed, he said, "I think she likes it."

Elizabeth chimed in, "Then it's settled, Henrietta Naomi Sager."

It wasn't always smooth sailing, but with both of them making an effort, things got better between Frank and Mrs. Whitman.

By spring 1845, the Cayuse attitude toward the missionaries was beginning to change for the worse. Frank had started associating with the older Cayuse boys at the mansion house, learning that they had a growing resentment toward the Whitmans. They disliked the doctor telling them to dig in the fields like women and resented Mrs. Whitman for not allowing them in her house or letting her children play with the Cayuse children. This was a great insult, completely opposite from their open way of living.

Though nothing was said at the time, the Whitmans were concerned and worried when Frank began staying overnight with the Cayuse. Frank had a gift for languages and had quickly learned enough to communicate. When he told John and Catherine how the Indians felt toward the Whitmans, it got them both worrying about the future.

That spring the Cayuse became embroiled in a war with the Snake tribe, and many men were killed. It was frightening for the white people at the mission to see them coming back from raids rattling their weapons and shouting war cries. When there was a victory, they would spend days celebrating and repeating their acts of courage. When there was death and defeat, they would sing the funeral songs for days with the women wailing late into the nights. Between the celebrations and funerals, everyone's nerves were on edge.

It was about this time that a group of Delaware Indians came to visit the mission. Their leader was a man named Tom Hill. He was a full-blooded Delaware but had taken the name of a white friend who had died, which was an accepted part of their custom. While at the mission, Tom Hill gave a speech that lasted for over two hours. It was as eloquent as anything the doctor had ever heard, and he was deeply impressed. Doctor Whitman could see that he was a force to be reckoned with, hoping to have him as a friend and ally in the future.

That fall, another large immigrant train arrived with a young man named Andrew Rogers. His traveling companion was very ill with tuberculosis and died shortly after arriving at the mission. Mr. Rogers was tall and pale, kind, and considerate, and everyone immediately took to him. When the Whitmans found out how well he had been educated and his teaching experience, they asked him to stay on as teacher for the next term. He was planning to become a missionary, so he agreed to teach for one year if Doctor Whitman would help him with his ministry.

One night while Doctor Whitman was gone, Narcissa and Catherine were startled awake by the strange sound of wailing and singing that almost seemed inhuman. It was almost like the cry of coyote or wolf. Catherine had never heard it before and asked Mrs. Whitman if she knew what it was. She explained that it was a death chant, that someone in the Cayuse village had died or was close to death. Sitting in the kitchen having a cup of tea, they were once again startled by pounding at the door.

When Mrs. Whitman answered the door, she was face to face with a woman who looked as if she was in a trance.

The woman told her, "My husband is very sick and might be dying; he can hardly breathe and needs the doctor."

"The doctor is not here, but I may be able to help."

She told Catherine to slice and boil two large onions in hot water. When they got to the village, the young man was wheezing loudly, exhausted from breathing so hard that he couldn't talk. The pungent onion poultice, mixed with fresh sliced onions, was so strong that it burned her eyes as she placed it over his throat, neck, and chest.

Within a short time, he was breathing a little easier, and since they had not had a good night's sleep since the doctor had left, they headed back to the mission house. Catherine told Mrs. Whitman that she was frightened because she had heard of how the Indians sometimes kill the medicine man or woman if the person they are treating dies and asked if that was possible.

Narcissa told her that she didn't think so, but it was not in her hands. They were getting ready to go back to sleep, when Narcissa said, "Do you hear that?"

"I don't hear anything," Catherine said.

"That is what I am talking about, the singing and chanting stopped, which means that the young man must be getting better. I've seen that kind of inflammation of the throat and chest many times before. You won't find an onion poultice in the physicians' handbook, but it is about as effective as anything else; the doctor has used it at least a hundred times or more."

That summer of 1845, the annual missionary meeting was to be held at Waiilatpu. Mrs. Whitman was a painstakingly fastidious housekeeper and had everyone scrubbing from dawn to dusk, preparing the house for visitors—every surface and every item was cleaned and polished until it shone, and the house smelled of fresh-cut flowers.

After the meeting, the doctor made his yearly trip to Fort Vancouver for supplies. To everyone's delight, he brought back gifts, delicious candies, and a giant map of the world. The new teacher, Mr. Rogers, was as different as night and day from Mr. Hinman. He was always laughing and had a great sense of humor. Like kindred spirits, he instantly took to Frank and easily won the children's hearts.

He was also a fine violinist with a wonderful voice, and before long, he and Mrs. Whitman began performing duets after supper. Though Mrs. Whitman had enthralled them with her singing, this was like nothing they had ever heard before. The fullness of the harmonies and violin accompaniment was almost like a small orchestra. He told them that he would give private lessons and start a children's choir for Sunday services if they wanted. He brought lightness and a desire for learning that had been sorely missing with Mr. Hinman.

The Sagers' greatest joy was watching their little sister Henrietta grow into a healthy and perfectly normal two-year-old. She was a precocious child who loved to sing and would join in with the choir whenever she could, singing perfectly in tune, totally uninhibited.

Unfortunately, problems with the Cayuse were coming to a head. The Whitmans had tried to keep it from the children, but Frank was spending a good deal of time with the Cayuse boys and

478

keeping Catherine and John informed. There had been several more incidents between Tomahas and Doctor Whitman, one which almost all of us had witnessed. Tomahas had once again shown up at the mill, demanding to have his wheat ground without waiting his turn. When the doctor refused to let him have his way, he started yelling threats and making intimidating gestures.

When he cut in line and tried to take over the milling himself, the miller tried to stop him and was knocked flat on the ground. Tomahas became enraged and threatened to kill the miller and Doctor Whitman. He was coming for the doctor with a knife when Chief Tiloukaikt grabbed him from behind, knocked him to the ground, and pinned him face down in the dirt. The chief was a big powerful man, a highly respected hunter and warrior. He held him there until Tomahas calmed down and agreed to leave. When Tomahas mounted his horse, he spun toward the doctor and once again told him that he had killed before, that he would kill the doctor next. Mrs. Whitman had seen the whole thing and went rushing to the doctor in tears.

He told her, "Don't worry, I have heard it all before, Tomahas is just trying to intimidate me."

"That man scares me, Marcus. I have never seen anyone so cold-blooded with so much hatred in his heart; I think he means what he is saying. What am I supposed to do if he comes looking for you when you're gone?"

Chief Tiloukaikt had been a good friend for many years and told them that Tomahas did have a bad heart and had been making trouble at his village, trying to turn the Indian people against the

Whitmans. He told them he would tell Tomahas to stay away from the mission, but that may not stop him.

It seemed the chief had diffused the problem for the time being, but the threat hung over their heads like a dark cloud and continued to haunt them.

Spring 1845 came early, and before I knew it, Father was there to pick me up and deliver supplies to the mission. For the trip back, Mrs. Whitman had decided to bring the children and accompany us for several miles, camping for the night since it was so nice out. They found a beautiful spot six miles upriver with wildflowers and overhanging trees shading a sandy beach. Catherine told me later that after we had departed, Narcissa made supper over an open fire as she had done so many times on the trail. That night the hills echoed with the sound of children's voices. The sky became a star-filled maze of patterns as they said their prayers and cuddled up in their bedrolls. As Catherine looked into the heavens, she wondered where her parents were, or if they were watching over her as she said a silent prayer for them.

They had come in a cart pulled by two oxen, and when they woke the next morning, the oxen were gone. This wasn't that unusual, so the children saw it as an opportunity to continue the fun. John and Frank left on foot to find the oxen and were gone almost all day.

On the other side of the river was a small group of Indian boys waving hello. Most of the faces were familiar, and sensing no danger, the girls waved back. They hadn't planned to be gone so long, and everyone was getting hungry since they had only brought enough food for one night. Elizabeth spotted a large fish swimming in shallow water that had trapped itself with only one way out. She slowly and carefully positioned herself in front of the opening, and when the salmon tried to escape, she dove on top of it and caught it with her hands, wrestling it to the shore. She was barely holding on when a hand reached over her shoulder and snatched the fish away from her.

Startled, she turned around quickly to find one of the older Indian boys smiling with the fish in his hands. She put her hands on her hips and said, "Give that back to me; I was the one who caught it."

The other Indian boys thought this was funny and started laughing.

The boy who had taken the fish had attended the Whitman Indian school and spoke some English. He put on his most fierce face and said, "This cannot be your fish, because this is not your river. It is my river, a Nez Perce river."

He then smiled and said, "I do thank you for finding our lost friend. We are going to enjoy eating him."

He then held it up like a trophy, and all the boys started whooping and laughing as Elizabeth jumped up and down, trying to grab it, adding to their hilarity. Mrs. Whitman and Catherine had noticed the commotion and were just heading back when a big strong-looking man who was leading the Indian boys on a hunting party took the fish from the boy, pounded its head against a rock, and handed it back to Elizabeth.

It was Tom Hill, and the laughter ceased immediately. He remarked, "There is plenty of fish for all. Did you see the way this courageous little one dove in with all of her clothes on and caught this monster?" That got a few laughs from the boys, but the wind had been taken from their sails.

When Narcissa reached them, she said, "Hello, Mr. Hill. Very nice to see you."

Elizabeth was struggling to hold the fish when Narcissa said, "My goodness, Elizabeth, that fish is almost as big as you are. Would you and the boys like to join us for supper, Mr. Hill?"

"It is good to see you too, Mrs. Whitman. You have quite a brave young one here, but we must be on our way. Boys will be boys."

"I understand. Thank you for your help."

Tom Hill and the Nez Perce boys crossed the river, mounted their horses, and rode off, leaving a trail of dust. That afternoon, as Mrs. Whitman was finishing cooking the fish, John and Frank returned with the oxen.

Frank said, "Man, oh man, am I hungry. We could smell that fish cooking a mile away. How in the world did you ever catch it?"

Narcissa turned to Elizabeth and said, "Why don't you tell them the story, dear, and don't hold anything back."

The boys had found the oxen next to a bush full of early spring berries and were able to add to the feast. When they returned, it was obvious that the doctor had been concerned about their late arrival, but when he heard the story, he had a good laugh and told Elizabeth she would sit at the head of the table that night.

The summer slipped away and soon became a fond memory as we all continued to grow in our own ways. Mr. Rogers had been heaven-sent and had not only captured our imaginations but helped guide us toward our interests. The Sagers had settled into a comfortable routine and were starting to feel like a real family for the first time in a long time. The only wrinkle was that Mr. Rogers had decided to give up teaching so that he could dedicate his life to missionary work. The good news was that he would be staying on at Waiilatpu to study with Doctor Whitman and continue to give the children music lessons.

The new teacher was named William Geiger. He was from Narcissa's hometown, and they had been friends as children, even attending the same church before coming to the Oregon Territories. He had done survey work for Captain Sutter in Sacramento, traveled and taught extensively in California and the Hawaiian Islands. He was of average height, squarely built with short brown hair and beard. He seemed to fit well and was liked by everyone.

In late fall, 1846, I returned with my little brother Henry for the new school year. There were now 18 at the dinner table each night, and had it not been for the help of Mary Johnson, Narcissa would have been completely overwhelmed.

Guests were often included with the family since it was a regular stop for wagon trains, explorers, scientists, military, and government officials. It was the hub of the entire territory, and the supper table was the center of information for the Whitmans as well as visiting travelers.

There hadn't been any recent problems with the Cayuse since the last incident with Tomahas. However, at their next encounter, Tomahas told Doctor Whitman that the Indian people no longer trusted him, and they wanted him to leave or they would kill him. It was the first time Catherine had ever heard the Whitmans discuss leaving Waiilatpu. The doctor told Narcissa that the Methodists wanted to sell their mission at The Dalles, that it might be a good idea to buy it and move there next spring.

The annual missionary meeting was to be held at the Walkers and Eellses' mission at Tshimakain and Catherine was the only child invited. Narcissa felt that Catherine needed a break from Henrietta's constant care and household chores. At the meeting, it was decided to buy the mission at The Dalles, but the Whitmans had decided that they had far too much invested in Waillatpu to leave any time soon.

At this time, a treaty was finally settled between the United States and Great Britain that would forever change the landscape of the Americas. Everything above the Canadian border now belonged to Great Britain, and everything below was the property of the United States.

Winter 1846 was the coldest anyone could remember, and many of the animals and Indian people died. Adding to the misery was that the latest wagon train had brought an outbreak of measles with it. Most of the white people who contracted it had at least some resistance, but the Indian people didn't and were dying by the hundreds. Much of the blame was placed on Doctor Whitman for having helped bring so many new settlers into the territory, and there was a great deal of anger and resentment toward him and the white immigrants. When school concluded that spring, Mr. Geiger left for the Willamette Valley and took up a claim near Salem, later moving on to Forest Grove. Mother was once again feeling poorly, so it was decided that 18-year-old Mary Johnson, who had been working for the Whitmans, would come with us to help. Everyone at the Whitman mission was sad to see her go since she had become like an older sister to the younger children. Father also hired John Sager to do some work for him that winter, the first paying job John had ever had.

Later that year, Mr. Manson showed up at the mission and asked if he could leave his two boys, Steven and John, with them through the next school year. Steven was 12, and John was ten. Mr. Manson worked for the Hudson Bay Trading Company and his wife, Félicité Lucier was half-Indian and half-French-Canadian. They felt their boys needed a more formal education and had heard about the Whitman School while visiting Fort Walla Walla. The doctor was glad to have the extra help, and Mrs. Whitman thought it would be a good idea to have more boys.

About that same time, two artists visited Waiilatpu. One was John Mix Stanley, also an explorer sent by the Smithsonian Institute to paint the west, primarily the Indian people. Thin and wiry, he had long brown hair, a bushy mustache and eyebrows, and big expressive brown eyes. Orphaned at 12, he moved to the frontier town of Detroit when he was 20. As an artist, he was self-taught, and wandered the Midwest painting signs and portraits. When he opened his drawing tablet, everyone gasped. Mrs. Whitman told him that she had never seen such perfect drawings, and they looked like photographs. Catherine told me he was the greatest storyteller she had ever heard and that the doctor let them stay up way past bedtime. He was from Canandaigua, New York, not far from where my parents and the Whitmans had come from and had brought with him all of the latest news.

The other artist was Paul Kane from Canada, who had come to Waiilatpu to paint portraits of the Cayuse and Nez Perce Indians.

Doctor Whitman tried to explain that it was not a good idea, since the Indian people could be very superstitious. He ignored the doctor and talked Frank into taking him to the Cayuse village, where he sketched the image of Chief Tiloukaikt under the guise of writing down his stories. When he did the same with Tomahas, Tomahas became aware of what he was doing and grew enraged, threatening to kill him. Somehow Frank was able to calm him down with a bribe and help Mr. Kane escape. Had it not been for Frank's quick thinking, Paul Kane would likely have lost his life that day. Later, Mr. Kane showed the sketches to the Whitmans and told them the story.

I don't think I have ever seen Doctor Whitman that mad before. He told Mr. Kane that he should have taken his warning and that he could have gotten Frank killed. He told him that Tomahas was an extremely violent and dangerous man who would kill him if he tried that again. He told him that the name Tomahas means murderer, that he should keep that in mind. Mr. Kane asked the doctor why they would get so upset about a simple drawing?

The doctor told him, "The Indian people believe that if someone takes their image, it gives that person the power to control their soul."

Kane said, "That's nonsense, but I'm sorry if I have caused you folks any trouble."

"It may seem like nonsense to you, Mr. Kane, but I promise it won't seem that way if Tomahas ever gets his hands on you."

Unlike John Mix Stanley, Paul Kane was not well-liked, and everyone was relieved when he left. Doctor Whitman told Frank that by taking Mr. Kane to the Indian village, he had put all of their lives in jeopardy and asked him never to do it again.

Among the dusty and well-worn travelers, they hoped to find another teacher to take Mr. Geiger's place, and as the fall of 1847 rolled in, so did the latest wagon train roll down Immigrant Hill toward the Whitman Mission. Fate smiled upon them, and they were able to persuade two people to stay and teach. Since Narcissa's time was so limited, she hoped to find a woman to help. Like Narcissa, Lorinda Bewley was a lovely woman with golden hair and blue eyes, well-educated with impeccable manners. Judge Saunders from Oskaloosa, Iowa, was hoping to find a school for his four children and agreed to take Mr. Geiger's place.

An unwanted guest had also accompanied the wagon train over the trail, the measles. Doctor Whitman had discovered a new route to The Dalles that was considerably shorter and spent a day guiding the wagon train commanded by Captain Bewley toward its destination. When he returned, he was visibly upset, so Narcissa asked him what was wrong?

He explained, "There are a number of people from the group I just led to The Dalles who are infected with measles, and Captain Bewley told me that the group behind is even worse off. If this spreads to the Indians, it could mean real trouble. We'll have to try and keep them moving along without letting them trade with the Cayuse."

It was already too late; a group of Cayuse had ridden back and traded with the wagon train behind them earlier, unaware that they were bringing along the deadly disease.

When John returned from our mission at Lapwai with a pack train of supplies, he found that the measles was taking a heavy toll on the settlers and children at Waiilatpu. He and Frank, with barely enough time to eat or catch a quick nap, were called upon to help the Whitmans treat the sick children. Within two weeks, most of the children and adults were recovering, so Mrs. Whitman decided they could start school by the end of November, and then John and Frank got sick. At the same time, the doctor visited the nearby Cayuse village and found that almost half of the village had been wiped out; the children and adults were dying at a rate of five to six per day. He did what he could, but it was an impossible situation for one man alone.

The happy life the Sagers had known with the Whitmans had come to an end. By this time, the mission was overflowing with people, many of them sick, and threats from the Cayuse were a daily occurrence. The blacksmith shop had been converted into a residence, and the mansion and mission houses were full to capacity.

On November 24, Father and I arrived at Waiilatpu with a train of horses loaded down with supplies. The Whitman mission had been going through supplies at an alarming rate because of all the new people.

The next day a messenger arrived from Five Crows' village asking for the doctor's help with their sick people. Since Father had been very close to Five Crows, having baptized him, Doctor Whitman asked if he would accompany him, that he could use the help. The next day, November 26, they set out together for the village. Mrs. Whitman was left to do what she could for the children and adults who were still sick. Helen Mar Meeks and Louise Sager had gotten worse, and Narcissa was doing everything she could to keep them comfortable while still managing to stay on her feet. She was visibly worn and had lost much of the vitality she normally exuded. John and Frank were quickly recovering, so Mrs. Whitman asked them to help with the little ones so that she could get some rest.

Catherine told me she was startled awake late that night when Doctor Whitman returned home alone. He told the boys to get some rest, that he would take over and check on Helen and Louise. She heard Narcissa come down from her room to join the doctor and get him something to eat, asking where Henry was. He told her that Father had taken a fall from his horse and was going to stay with Chief Stickus for a day or two until he was well enough to ride again, that he was badly bruised, but nothing broken.

After Narcissa went back to bed, the doctor made his rounds and checked on Louise, who shared a room with Catherine and Elizabeth.

Catherine was wide-awake and asked, "Do you think the Cayuse will try to kill us, Doctor Whitman?"

He sat on the edge of her bed and said, "I don't think so. We have good friends among the Cayuse who would never let that happen. Don't worry, dear. You need to get some rest." He then tucked her in and said goodnight.

In the morning, Catherine found the doctor in the kitchen, making breakfast. When I came into the kitchen, I was confused and asked where Father was. The doctor repeated what he had told

Narcissa the night before and told me not to worry, that it was nothing serious and he would be back later today or tomorrow.

When Mr. Rogers joined us, Catherine overheard the doctor tell him that if things didn't start to improve with the Cayuse, they would need to move to The Dalles in the spring, where it would be safer. When Narcissa came down, her eyes were a little puffy, but otherwise, she looked her old self, fresh and neatly dressed. She told the doctor that she was still worried about Helen Mar and Louise, who didn't seem to be getting any better.

The doctor told her he would keep a close eye on them but needed to attend a funeral that morning for one of the Indian boys whose father was an important chief.

When the doctor returned, he said, "I don't understand why there are so many Indian men hanging around the mission this morning with nothing to do."

Narcissa replied, "It's probably because the men are butchering a cow and the Cayuse want to get a share."

There was a knock at the door, and when Narcissa went to answer it, Chief Tiloukaikt and Tomahas were standing there with an intensity that put her nerves on edge. They told her that they needed medicine, so she called the doctor in from the living room. She and the doctor passed each other, almost touching shoulders, and then everything happened so fast that there was no time to react.

Eliza

Part Four

The Massacre

"The bravery shown by ten-year-old Eliza Spalding is an example of the unimaginable courage and heroism that children of any age are capable of under the most horrific conditions."

—The Oregon Lyceum.

Chapter 1

The Morning

On November 29, 1847, dense fog and freezing rain lay like a dark, wet shroud over the mission grounds, obscuring the future and enveloping our collective spirit. An ominous and penetrating presence hung like an eerie curtain over the Whitman mission ... waiting.

I don't think anything could have prepared us for what was about to happen, especially the children kept in the dark about the dangers lurking in shadows and nightmares that would accompany us throughout our lives. The signs were getting clearer and more disturbing. Cayuse greetings had turned to looks of anger, and relationships were becoming more and more distant and tense each day.

My parents and the Whitmans had a deep distrust of the Catholic priests who had arrived in the Oregon Territory several years earlier. They were bribing individuals and tribes with money, goods, and cattle to repudiate the Protestant missionaries. Father had been given a long paper drawing about two feet wide and five feet long called a Catholic Ladder. It depicted him and Doctor Whitman as devils being condemned and cast into hell for their wicked sins against God.

Thomas McKay told Father of having attended a meeting where Bishop Blanchet told the congregation that the Indian people were dying because of Doctor Whitman's bad medicine and immoral teachings. At the same meeting, Tomahas, the Indian man who had clashed with Doctor Whitman in the past, offered to kill the

Whitmans and sell their mission to the priests. If I close my eyes, I can still see him in my mind on the day of the massacre. He was a ferocious and violent-looking man with the intense eyes of a hawk. Covered in his victims' blood, he wore dark leather pants and a wildly striped shirt with a bright red coat and fancy trim that made him look like an eccentric military commander. On his head was a beaver-skin hat with a long white horsehair tail attached to it, flowing down over the back of his head and shoulders. On his face was a look that could turn flesh to stone.

I remember the sounds of the mission coming to life that morning. I could hear the clear, bell sound of Mr. Canfield's hammer in the blacksmith shop as he struck his anvil. The tailor, Mr. Gilliland, was patiently sitting at his worktable, plying his needle with great skill toward making a Sunday suit for Doctor Whitman. Mr. Rogers was tediously tending to the garden as Mr. Marsh was busily grinding flour and corn at the gristmill. Mr. Hall and Mr. Osborne were hammering out a familiar rhythm while putting in a new floor at the mansion house. On the outside were the familiar sights and sounds of another day, but underneath was an uncomfortable feeling that something was wrong.

The doctor was making plans to hold services for the son of an important chief who had died the previous day, then make his rounds of the other buildings. Mrs. Whitman had been feeling poorly that morning and was late coming down. Mr. Saunders was upstairs in the schoolroom, helping us prepare our assignments for the day, and I was busy assisting the younger boys and girls with their reading and writing assignments. When the doctor returned, he treated Miss Lorinda Bewley for a lingering illness that he was having trouble diagnosing.

I recall hearing a racket outside and looking out of the window just in time to see Joe Lewis riding by the kitchen yelling and waving his gun, and I wondered what in the world he was up to. We will never know for sure all of the reasons why the massacre happened, but we do know that while the measles was poisoning the Cayuse bodies, Joe Lewis was poisoning their minds.

Father once told me that Joe Lewis was one of those people who seemed to have been born with a criminal mind, with little or no humanity and completely void of conscience. He was also a habitual liar who told a different story every time someone asked about his past. He once told Father that he was born in Canada and educated in Maine, his father was white, and his mother was from the Chinook tribe. He also had a story about how a group of Americans had stolen him away when he was a child and taken him east. I'm not sure if he even knew the truth himself, but two things were certain; he hated white Protestant and Methodist missionaries and was a devout Catholic.

I remember the day of the massacre, Doctor Whitman was in the living room reading, and Mrs. Whitman was taking a cup of milk to one of the girls when she heard a loud knock at the kitchen door. When she answered it, Chief Tiloukaikt told her that he needed medicine and wanted to see the doctor. Mary Ann Bridger was helping prepare supper at the big table, and John Sager was sitting on a stool winding twine for brooms.

Narcissa called out to the doctor, saying she needed him in the kitchen. As the doctor opened the door to enter the kitchen, Mrs.

Whitman frowned and brushed shoulders with him as she was going into the living room. Chief Tiloukaikt tried to push past him to get into the living room, but Doctor Whitman blocked his way and pushed him back into the kitchen, quickly closing the door and telling Mrs. Whitman to lock it behind him. With a feeling of unease, Mrs. Whitman stood with her ear to the door, listening to see if she could detect any danger. Initially, it seemed to be a routine conversation between the doctor and the chief, and when she thought it was safe, she picked up Henrietta and sat down next to the fireplace in the living room.

Several events had begun to put everything into motion. Six days earlier, Father and I had arrived at the Whitman Mission on November 23. The previous summer, several of the young Nez Perce had gotten angry with Father and destroyed our grist mill, so he was bringing a string of pack horses with wheat and corn to be ground at the Whitmans' mill. I couldn't believe how the mission had grown in less than a year and how many people there were. It had become like a small town, and it was obvious from people who were sick and dying that something was very wrong. The usually warm smiles had turned to glazed looks of hopelessness and in some cases, open glares of hatred.

Doctor Whitman told Father that the Cayuse had been bringing their sick to the mission, and there were as many as four or five deaths per day. Most were elderly and children, but with measles, there seemed to be no rhyme or reason for who lived and who died. They had closed the Indian school since no one came any longer, and only a few loyal followers attended the Sunday services.

495

Father had noticed a change in the Whitmans. Narcissa was still a lovely woman, but she had begun to age quickly from the tension and uncertainty of the future. Father had never felt she was well suited to this kind of lifestyle. She ran a tight ship and had made every effort to create a home like the one she left back east; however, that was not the way things worked in the west among the Indian people.

She had never fully recovered from her daughter Clarissa's death and had deeply offended the Indian people by not allowing them in her home or to play with her adopted children. They thought of her as "haughty and disdainful." The strain was starting to take its toll. Her moods were beginning to swing back and forth, easily upset one moment and bubbly the next. She was an outgoing and social person who loved being the center of attention and interactions with her kind of people, not that of the Indians who she considered savages.

The innumerable hours on horseback under the most severe and hazardous conditions were starting to tell on the doctor as well. He was still the same steady, devoted man, but the deteriorating relationship with the Cayuse had taken its toll on him.

The mission had become dedicated to the needs of the immigrants. The Whitmans had lost the trust and faith of the Cayuse people, and at this point, they were far beyond the point of no return. There had been a drastic shift in priorities, and though Father understood why it had happened, he wasn't happy about it.

The day after we arrived, Doctor Whitman told Father that the Catholic priests needed food and supplies. He told Father that he was too busy tending to the sick and dying to go himself and asked

Father to deliver the supplies. Father had had very little rest since we had arrived at Waiilatpu, and though reluctant, he was first and foremost a man of God who practiced what he preached.

Father hoped to keep things friendly but felt he needed to show the priests one of the paper ladders that depicted him and Doctor Whitman as devils with horns on their way to the fires of hell.

When he arrived at the Catholic mission, he told them that it was inexcusable and could serve no good Christian purpose and lead to bloodshed. Bishop Blanchet did most of the talking, telling Father that it was one of the Vicar's ideas, promised not to distribute any more of the ladders. However, something was condescending and dismissive about his manner that Father felt was untrustworthy. He would always believe that the priests must have known about the plans to kill the missionaries. He felt that their tactics were partly responsible, that they certainly had the most to gain.

Several days after Father had returned to the mission, on November 28, a young Cayuse chief came riding into the station asking for Doctor Whitman. He told him that there were sick people in his village, including Chief Tiloukaikt's sons, who needed his help. The doctor told Father that he could use his assistance and that it would be a good time to talk over their current dilemma. When Father said goodbye, he told me they would be returning late that night. I remember being worried because it was already getting late in the day, and freezing rain was falling. The paths were wet and treacherous, with over 30 miles round trip, mostly in the dark. Watching them disappear into the grave afternoon gave me an eerie feeling, but I would have never guessed that it would be their last ride together.

As they rode, Doctor Whitman told Father that Joe Lewis had been riding by the house waving his gun and about his last run-in with Tomahas.

Father nodded sadly and said, "All of the years of hard work seem to be going up in smoke Marcus."

They stopped briefly at Chief Stickus's village and treated several of the sickest people before continuing.

Sometimes what appears to be bad luck can be a blessing in disguise. Shortly after leaving Chief Stickus's village, Father's horse slipped while he was half-asleep, and he fell hard, badly bruising his hip and leg. It was decided that he should turn back and stay with Chief Stickus at his village for a day or two to recover while Doctor Whitman went on to Chief Tiloukaikt's village to tend to the sick. Had this not happened, Father would have surely been killed.

That night the doctor had the sad duty of helping Chief Tiloukaikt bury three of his sons who had died of measles. Chief Tiloukaikt had always been a loyal friend, but Doctor Whitman could see that anger was beginning to smolder beneath the sadness, and it worried him.

The doctor didn't arrive home until very late that night. He found John and Frank sitting up with three of the sick children. Narcissa was lying in bed asleep, fully dressed, and completely exhausted. The boys were still recovering from the measles, so he told them to get some rest, that he would take care of the sick girls. He examined the first two and gave them some soothing medicine, telling them to try and sleep, that he would look in on them later. When Narcissa got up to help, she looked at her weary husband, thinking she had never seen him look so tired and forlorn. His handsome face had become like leather, and his old frostbite scars had turned white from the long ride in the rain and sleet.

After a hot cup of tea, they went to Helen Mar Meek's bedside to check on her. She had become so frail that he turned to Narcissa, shook his head, and said, "I don't think she will live." Narcissa had loved and nurtured Helen like her own daughter for the past seven years, and the thought of losing her tore into her heart as she held the little girl in her arms.

After the doctor finished his rounds, they went into the kitchen, and he pulled up a chair by the stove as Narcissa sat at the table. He told her that he had heard disturbing news at the Cayuse village concerning Joe Lewis, that he was planning a raid with some of the other Indian men. He told her that Joe Lewis's horse was tied up outside Nicolas Finley's lodge, not more than a hundred feet from the mission house. Nicolas had always seemed a good man until recently when he befriended Joe Lewis.

Most of that night, the Whitmans lie wide awake talking about leaving, wondering what they would do and where they would go. The doctor tried to reassure Narcissa that it was just another attempt to intimidate him; they had been through this many times in the past.

They lay there lost in their thoughts until she finally fell asleep in his arms. It would be the last night they would spend together on earth, the last time they would hold each other close.

The next morning it seemed as if a wet blanket covered the landscape. Mrs. Whitman was still in bed when Doctor Whitman got up to make breakfast. He had continued to check on the children throughout the previous night and had recently finished another round with a heavy heart. Helen had been like a daughter to him as well as his wife, and now she was slipping away, and there was nothing he could do to prevent it from happening.

The measles had also spread to many immigrant families, and it was not unusual for him to bury as many as three to five people each day, mostly Indians, since they had so little resistance. He had seen so much death over the past six months that he had to bury his feelings of loss and desperation deep below the surface to continue.

It was easy to tell when Mrs. Whitman was sad or upset, but the doctor always had such an even temperament that it was hard to tell how he felt. That morning was different, and when I went into the kitchen to say good morning, I could tell that something was wrong. He always looked me right in the eyes and gave me a big smile. His eyes were downcast, and he hardly seemed to notice that I was in the room. He told me what had happened to Father and that he would be fine with a day or two of rest. Still, I couldn't help but worry as I looked out the window, trying to think of something cheerful to say. The weather outside seemed to match his gloomy mood, and for once in my young life, I couldn't think of anything.

I decided to go over and kiss him on the cheek, which seemed to wake him up. He then gave me one of those handsome smiles and a big hug. I asked if there was anything I could do, and he said he would be grateful if I would take Mrs. Whitman some breakfast; he needed to check on several of the sick adults. I knocked lightly and entered the room, and found her softly weeping. When she saw me, she quickly dried her eyes and motioned for me to come and sit next to her. I asked if she was feeling sick, and she said she was fine and held me in her arms for several minutes.

I had always loved the way she smelled when she held me, it was the scent of lavender, and to this day, I always think of her and Mother when I smell it. When I returned, several women staying in the main house had come into the kitchen and started preparing breakfast, which I was to take to the children who were too sick or weak to get out of bed.

I was so tired that the day just seemed to drag on and on. Sometime after lunch, I recall looking out the window and seeing Mr. Stanfield leading a cow into the yard for butchering. I remember the jolt of shock when Frank Sager fired his rifle into the cow's brain, killing it. Mr. Kimball and Mr. Hoffman were also there to help in dressing it.

It seemed odd that there were so many Indian men standing around with long blankets over their shoulders hanging to the ground covering their moccasins ... watching.

It must have been nearing 2:00 PM as the men were finishing up with the cow, and still, the fog hung over the entire mission letting in so little light that it felt as if it were already getting dark. I was looking out of the classroom window when I saw two Indian men coming from somewhere near the millpond at a deliberate pace straight for the kitchen door. One of the men was Chief Tiloukaikt, who Doctor Whitman had just helped bury his three sons. The other was Tomahas, who had always frightened me, and neither of them looked friendly.

Chapter 2

The Massacre

Chief Tiloukaikt told the doctor that he had been feeling poorly and asked if he could have medicine for his cough. Doctor Whitman went to the pantry area where he kept the medicine and chose an elixir. He and the chief were discussing the condition of his other children as Tomahas was slowly sneaking around behind the unsuspecting doctor.

As the doctor was examining the chief, Tomahas took a pipe tomahawk out of his blanket and buried it deep into the back of Doctor Whitman's head. Mary Ann Bridger screamed and immediately ran and hid behind the large stove. When John Sager saw what was happening, he tried to pull a pistol out of his belt. As he was fumbling with the gun Tomahas pulled a pistol from his blanket and shot John in the chest. He then pulled his knife and cut John's throat, though it was not deep enough to kill him.

The doctor tried to crawl toward the back door when Tomahas put his foot on the doctor's back to pull the tomahawk from his skull. Doctor Whitman managed to crawl his way out of the kitchen door when Tomahas hit him with a second blow, then a third. They then turned him over and gave him three more blows to the face and several to his body until he lay still, and they assumed he was dead.

The shot must have been a signal to the rest of the Indians, who numbered between 15 and 20. Chief Tiloukaikt and Tomahas ran out of the kitchen to help the other Indian men who had started shooting, stabbing, and bludgeoning every man in sight. In the chaos, they forgot about Mary Ann Bridger, who slipped through a window and ran around the outside of the house. When she reached the living room door, she pushed it open and breathlessly cried out, "The Indians are killing Father and John."

Mrs. Whitman asked where they were now, and Mary Ann told them that the Indians had run out of the kitchen to the yard where they were butchering the cow. John was on the other side of the door, and the doctor was just outside the kitchen. Mrs. Whitman told the children taking a bath to get dressed quickly and find somewhere to hide. One of the older children took Henrietta out of her hands as Mrs. Whitman, and two of the other women pushed the kitchen door open and found John seemingly lifeless. He was lying on the floor, bleeding badly from where his throat had been deeply cut.

Narcissa then ran to the doctor, and with the help of Mrs. Hall and Mrs. Hayes, they dragged them both back into the living room. Outside they could hear gunshots and the terrifying sounds of men screaming for help.

In the mission yard, Mr. Kimball had been helping dress the beef when he narrowly escaped. He ran to the mission house, where he crashed through the living room door. yelling, "The Indians are killing everyone."

He asked Mrs. Whitman why in the world they would want to kill him; he had never done anything but help them. He was a big man and had run several hundred feet from where they had been working the beef. He had been shot in the arm, which was badly shattered, and asked Mrs. Whitman for a glass of water. He looked down at Doctor Whitman and asked if he were dead, to which the doctor replied, "No," startling everyone in the room.

Mrs. Hayes gave him a glass of water and tended to his arm as Mrs. Whitman locked the door and dragged several pieces of furniture in front of it. They had run out of drinking water, and several of the younger children were getting thirsty and upset. When Mr. Kimball had revived, there was so much confusion that he volunteered to go outside and get water from the well. He haphazardly dressed like an Indian hoping that he could sneak out unnoticed. The Indian men were so occupied at the time that they didn't notice him as he went out the kitchen door. On his way back to the house, one of the men spotted him running and went after him. His daughter Susan was standing at the kitchen door waiting for him to return as a warrior known as Frank shot her father in the back. Another warrior came up behind him and finished him off with a shot to the head. Susan tried to stifle her scream as she ran back into the house to take cover.

While they were gone, Mrs. Whitman went to the doctor who was starting to move and asked him, "Do you know me?" to which he answered, "Yes."

She then asked if there was anything that she could do to stop the bleeding, and he replied, "No."

She then put a wet towel to his face and took ashes from the stove, and packed them into the deep gashes in the back of his head, which were bleeding profusely.

Outside, the Indian men watching the cow being slaughtered had heard the gunshot coming from the kitchen of the mission house and threw off their blankets and started firing and hacking at the white men working there. This included Jacob Hoffman, Nathan Kimball, William Canfield, and Joe Stanfield. Frank Sager had just returned to the schoolroom before the massacre had begun. For some reason, Joe Stanfield was ignored and stood to the side, watching the bloodbath. Mr. Canfield had received a gunshot wound to the hip but played dead and then made a run for his blacksmith shop. He and his family hid in the loft until nighttime, then decided that their only chance was for him to try to get help. That night he made his escape on foot, in the direction of Lapwai.

Mr. Hoffman had also been outside in the mission yard helping with the butchering and was now fighting for his life, the only one that even had a chance to defend himself. Badly outnumbered, he picked up an axe and went for the nearest Indian. Four or five of them circled him, with more on the way. They could have easily shot and killed him, but they respected his bravery and decided to test his courage.

Mr. Hoffman knew that he would die, so he fought like a wild man knowing he had nothing to lose. When one of the warriors attempted to stab him, he anticipated it and countered a blow that almost took the man's arm off. Tomahas decided to get involved and squared off against him with his tomahawk. Once again, Mr. Hoffman countered and struck down with his axe, badly injuring Tomahas' foot. One of the other braves used this opportunity to come from behind and struck him on the back of his head with his war club.

Mrs. Hayes watched through the window in horror as Mr. Hoffman was cut down by several other men. He was lying in the dirt on his back, trying to regain his senses, when one of the men opened up his stomach and pulled out his intestines. Another man then cut open his chest, pulled out his still-beating heart, and held it up as a trophy.

When the fighting broke out, Mr. Marsh had been working at the gristmill. He grabbed an axe and came running as fast as he could toward the fighting. When one of the Indian men saw him coming, he shot him down.

At the east wing of the mission house, Mr. Hall was working on an addition when he heard gunfire and screaming. He went around to the north side of the house and jumped to the ground making his way to the front door. Once inside, he was shocked to find Doctor Whitman so terribly mutilated and John Sager lying unconscious.

His wife Rachel told him that he had to get away immediately and go for help, that the Indians were killing all of the men. He was reluctant to leave since his wife and five daughters' lives were obviously in great danger. Mrs. Whitman told him that he couldn't do anyone any good by getting himself killed, that if he could find help, it may save lives. He was hesitant to go but soon realized that they were right and cautiously went out the door, managing to make his escape.

He headed in the direction of Fort Walla Walla, some 32 miles away, with most of his clothes being ripped or torn from the thorny bushes. The next day, covered in blood from the deep scratches and cuts, he stood at the gate, calling for help until Mr. McBean finally arrived.

Mr. McBean told him that he only had a small detachment of men and didn't want to risk being attacked for helping the missionaries. He refused to let Mr. Hall into the fort and sent him on his way with a small bag of food, a blanket, and vague directions toward The Dalles, a heartless and cowardly act.

Mr. Hall thought his best hope was to get to the Willamette Valley, where he might find help. The next day he was caught and killed in a most horrific manner by a band of Cayuse men hunting for him. His body later washed up on a lonely river shore, and by all accounts, he had been scalped and mutilated before murdered.

The day after the massacre, Mr. Hall's daughter Gertrude saw Tomahas fly off with several of the other warriors in the direction of Fort Walla Walla. When he returned, he was overheard bragging about having captured and scalped Mr. Hall.

Back at the mission, Mrs. Whitman had secured all of the doors and windows. The five Sager girls, Mrs. Hall, Miss Lorinda Bewley, Mrs. Kimball, Mary Ann Bridger, Helen Mars Meek, and Mrs. Hayes joined Mrs. Whitman in the living room.

Upstairs, Mr. Osborne was working on a window frame when he heard the shots and yelling. He climbed downstairs to have a look, and when he saw the other men slaughtered, he reentered through a downstairs window and ran upstairs to where his wife Marguerite and three children were cowering in the corner of their room. Having seen or heard much of the carnage that had taken place, he and his wife pulled up the flooring he had recently installed. They then managed to squeeze everyone underneath, telling the children that their lives depended on being quiet.

At one point, several Cayuse men came into the room searching for survivors, and Mrs. Osborne had to stuff her apron into their youngest child, Alexander's mouth, to keep him quiet. Fortunately, the Osbornes were not discovered. They hid underneath the floor until dark when most of the Indian men had returned to their village or were inside the mansion house. Sometime after midnight, they quietly and carefully crept out of the house, evading the guard who was fast asleep, and then escaped into the darkness with no food or water. It was nearly freezing with snow on the ground, and all they had to keep them warm were two thin sheets.

In the past, Mr. Osborne had worked for Doctor Whitman and had returned with his family from the Willamette Valley to rebuild a new gristmill for the mission. The whole family was recovering from the measles, and Mrs. Osborne had just delivered a baby on November 14, who died after only a few hours. She was still extremely weak as they blindly made their escape into the frigid November night.

They were just barely able to feel their way along in the terrifying darkness, staying closely beside the river that led to Fort Walla Walla some 30 miles away.

Like a death shroud, the bone-chilling fog still hovered above the ground without even a star to guide them. Blindly, they felt the trail as best they could with their feet and what senses they had left. Mrs. Osborne began staggering and became so weak that she almost passed out from exhaustion as they continued.

When they reached a place called Mill Creek, they had to wade through the icy waters, which were almost up to Mr. Osborne's shoulders. As he helped his wife across, she slipped on a mossy rock and would have been washed away had she not managed to grab on to her husband's coat at the last second. He had to cross back and forth four times to get his wife and children across, keeping the children above his shoulders and out of the deathly cold water.

After several hours Mrs. Osborne finally fainted and was too weak to go on. They crawled through the frozen mud until they found a dry spot among the bushes where Mr. Osborne laid a wet sheet on the ground and the other over them. They were shaking so violently from fright and cold that he feared they would never survive the night.

Early the next day, as the sun came up behind the clouds and fog, they heard a party of riders slowly approaching. They were well hidden in the bushes, but the warriors came so close by that Mr. Osborne was afraid the sound of their hearts pounding would give them away. Once again, Marguerite had to stuff her apron into Alexander's mouth.

It was the longest day any of them would ever know in their lifetimes, and Mr. Osborne didn't expect his wife to survive the ordeal. That night they were forced to cross another freezing stream called Dog Creek. They continued for about two more miles until Mrs. Osborne fainted from weakness and exhaustion. Again, they crawled through the frozen mud into the bushes for cover and traveled less than a mile.

That night Mrs. Osborne told her husband that she couldn't go on any longer, that he would have to take their two-year-old Alexander with him and try to find help for her and the two older children. He knew that there was no choice, and because he never expected to see them alive again, he gave them his version of the last rites. His body was so exhausted that he was barely able to cross the fast-moving Touchet creek with Alexander above his shoulders. Several times he had to quickly scramble into the bushes with his hand over his son's mouth when he heard riders advancing in their direction. Each time it turned out to be an Indian party searching for them.

When he finally reached Fort Walla Walla, he and Alexander were both completely exhausted, but all he could think about was his wife and two other children. He explained the situation and begged Mr. McBean to loan him some food, blankets, and horses so that he could find his family and bring them to the fort if they were still alive.

In another incredibly cowardly act, Mr. McBean refused to help, saying that the Cayuse might attack the fort if he did so. Mr. Osborne got down on his knees with his crying son and begged for the life of his family but was refused. He then called to the Catholic priests who were watching and begged them to help. They flatly refused, saying that they did not want to get involved. He asked them to please have some Christian compassion and extend mercy for his wife and children's sake, or they would surely die ... the priests refused.

An artist named John Mix Stanley, who was at the fort, overheard the dilemma Mr. Osborne faced and offered to give him food, horses, extra clothing, blankets, and the help of his Indian guide. He told Mr. Osborne that he would go himself but had just narrowly escaped a hostile party of Cayuse warriors.

Before departing, Mr. Stanley also gave him a bag of tobacco and a beautiful pipe, saying, "This might come in handy."

The Indian guided him through the pitch-black darkness to where Mr. Osborne thought he had left his wife and children. Bitterly cold, they looked for hours but could find nothing in the dark. They were unable to call out for fear that they would attract the attention of the Cayuse men. They searched all night without rest, and the next morning as the fog lifted, they were completely exposed. Mr. Osborne was now beyond exhaustion, almost beyond hope. He had dismounted and told the Indian guide that he and Alexander needed to rest for a couple of hours. The guide told him that his family might be right under their noses, to get back up on his horse and keep looking.

Less than an hour later, the guide found Mr. Osborne's wife and children, all still alive. Mr. Osborne immediately gave them food and water and covered them in the dry blankets Mr. Stanley had given him. Just as they were preparing to cross the Walla Walla River, they came upon a Cayuse warrior who was searching for them. The warrior pulled his rifle and told the guide that he could go, but he had come to kill Osborne and his family.

The Indian guide pulled his rifle and shamed the man by saying, "It takes a mighty warrior to kill a sick and unarmed man, his wife, and three little children. Surely you will want to hang the little ones' scalps upon your lodgepole to show your courage."

Mr. Osborne then remembered the tobacco and pipe, offering it to the Cayuse warrior.

The Cayuse man took the tobacco and pipe and then told the guide, "I will not kill them, but others close by will."

He then spun his horse around and rode off quickly. Once the warrior was far in the distance, they crossed the river. When they reached the other side, the guide told them they must hurry along before the war party caught up with them. The guide had to hold Mrs. Osborne in front of him so that she wouldn't fall off. Mr. Osborne had the two youngest children with him, and his daughter

Nancy was riding alone on one of the horses Mr. Stanley had provided. They were nearing Fort Walla Walla when once again they had to hide in a copse of trees until dark because of a war party passing in the distance.

When they finally reached the fort, they had been in the freezing wilderness for four days without food or shelter. Mr. Osborne lay his wife down at the gate and pounded loudly. When Mr. McBean saw who was there, he told them that he couldn't let them enter, that they had to continue to The Dalles, that he would loan them a small boat.

Mrs. Osborne sat up and told him in her sternest voice, "You, sir, are the lowliest kind of man, a coward. If you do not let us enter, I will lay down and die right here at your front gate."

Hearing his men grumbling behind him in disgust, he finally broke down and let them enter. Once inside, he gave them food and a private room but said he had no extra blankets. Mr. Osborne begged him to find something for his poor wife to lie on, that her bones were almost through the skin, and she was miserable. Mr. McBean told him that he had none to spare but would sell them some from his supply room. Mr. Osborne tried to explain that they had just lost everything they owned, but as soon as he reached the Willamette Valley, he would borrow the money from friends and promised to pay him back. Finally, a heartless Mr. McBean reluctantly agreed and gave them two extra blankets on credit. The next day Chief Stickus came by the fort and gave Mr. Osborne the cap off his head and a scarf for one of the children.

Back at the mission house on the day of the massacre, the killing was at its peak. Mr. Rogers was running wildly through the garden and mission grounds after being struck a glancing blow to the back of the head and on the wrist by a war club. He had managed to escape and was looking back behind to see if anyone was pursuing when he struck the front door and broke out one of the glass panes startling the women and children. After Mrs. Whitman cleared the doorway and let him in, he was in such a nervous state that he could hardly speak. When he looked down at Doctor Whitman, he asked if he was dead. In a loud voice, the doctor shocked everyone once again, saying, "NO."

Upstairs in the mission house classroom, Mr. Saunders had been helping us get our lessons prepared when we heard the commotion. The schoolroom floor sat above the mission kitchen with two windows looking out into the front yard. Two of the bedrooms had been converted into a classroom. When Mr. Sanders heard the first gunshots, he went through the kitchen and found the door locked to the living room. He caught Mrs. Whitman's attention, and she gave him a hand signal to return to the classroom. He was just about to climb the stairs to the classroom when a warrior named Tamsucky burst in through the kitchen door. He was a terrible sight, covered in the blood of the men that he had just helped kill in the mission yard. Like Tomahas, Tamsucky was a fierce and violent man with a deep hatred for Doctor Whitman. Recently, Tamsucky's wife had died shortly after the doctor had treated her and given her medicine for the measles. He believed the doctor had poisoned her, and he had come for vengeance. When Tamsucky saw Mr. Saunders trying to get to the schoolroom, he pulled out a long knife from the sheath on his waist and attempted to bury it in his back. Frank Sager could see and hear what was happening and tried to herd us into the loft, the youngest first.

Two warriors then broke in on Mr. Gilliland and found him still sitting at his table, working on Mr. Whitman's Sunday suit. They shot him in the back and left him there on the floor, though he somehow managed to crawl to his bed, where he later died.

Upstairs in the classroom, my best friend at the mission, Helen Saunders, and I were the last two up the stairs and never made it into the loft. Mr. Saunders was desperately trying to get up the stairs while Tamsucky continued to hack at him. By that time, three other warriors had arrived to help; Mr. Saunders was already badly injured when he fell down the stairs. He tumbled right past them and fell into a heap at the bottom of the stairs. He quickly regained his footing and ran for the kitchen door to try and warn his wife, who was with their youngest child, Mary, at the mansion house.

The four braves gave chase as Mr. Saunders dodged through the garden and into the open yard. Helen and I watched through the window as he tried to mount one of the horses near where they had butchered the cow earlier. As he climbed up onto the horse, two Cayuse men grabbed him and wrestled him to the ground. At that point, they all started hacking and stabbing him with their tomahawks and knives. Helen was screaming, "They are murdering my father; they are murdering my father." It didn't seem real as we watched them cut him to pieces. Her screams haunt my dreams to this very day.

In the kitchen, Mrs. Whitman was desperately trying to block the broken door when she saw Joe Lewis riding by waving his rifle. She yelled at him through the kitchen window, calling him a troublemaker, that this whole thing was his fault and he was a bloodthirsty murderer. He drew his rifle up, sighted it, then shot her in the chest through the shattered window. She collapsed on the floor as several women came running to help drag her back into the living room, where they did their best to stop the bleeding and block off the kitchen door. When she started to recover from the shock, she began praying to God that the children would be spared and that her parents would accept her death.

Outside the mission house[,] the Cayuse warriors had begun breaking in the windows and pounding on the front door. When it finally caved in, they found Mr. Rogers pointing a gun directly at them. They backed out, unaware that the gun was broken and incapable of firing. Joe Lewis carefully peeked in the door and told them that if Mr. Rogers put the gun down, they would spare their lives, and no harm would come to them. They had no choice, so Mrs. Whitman told Mr. Rogers to put the gun down. He was so badly injured that he could hardly hold the rifle level anyway.

Joe Lewis told Mrs. Hayes to go upstairs into the schoolroom and bring all of the children down; they too would be spared if she did as she was told. Tamsucky was covered in blood that he had used to paint his face. He followed her upstairs to make sure that all of us children came down and that none of the adults were hiding in the loft.

When we reached the living room, I went into shock at seeing Doctor and Mrs. Whitman and John lying on the floor covered in blood. At first, I thought that Doctor Whitman and John were both dead until I saw Doctor Whitman's chest still moving.

Mrs. Whitman crawled over to her husband to try and comfort him, but there was no longer any movement from either him or John. About this time, Joe Lewis started strutting around the room looking extremely agitated and angry and trying to intimidate us. I was standing right behind Frank when Joe Lewis came up and grabbed Frank from behind pulling his head back by the hair. He then pulled the trigger, and shot Frank in the throat and through the skull.

It happened so fast that I didn't understand what had taken place. I was all wet and sticky when I suddenly realized that I was covered in blood and a white substance that turned out to be Frank's brains. The other Indians started firing their guns wildly all over the room, and everyone was silently frozen in place. Miraculously no one was injured though several of the children had bullet holes in their clothing. One of the bullets had gone through Lorinda Bewley's dress and burned her fingers.

It must have been the sound of gunfire that made both Mr. Whitman and John try to move. One of the Indians stood menacingly over John and then clubbed him in the head, breaking it open like a melon and killing him. Another pushed Mrs. Whitman aside and hit Mr. Whitman in the face several more times with his tomahawk until he was forever still.

I have used words to try and relate what happened, but no one could possibly understand what it felt like to be in that room unless actually there. It was a grizzly scene of carnage, so brutal that I believe every woman and child there was in a complete state of shock; not a sound or cry was heard. It was as if everyone had stopped breathing, and all of our senses had shut down. At that point, there was not even a shadow of doubt in my mind that we would all be killed.

Chapter 3

Captivity

In the living room, Chief Tiloukaikt began to restore order and told the Cayuse men that there would be no more killing. He ordered the men to move everyone over to the mansion house since the younger warriors were planning to burn the mission house down when they were done looting it.

Since Joe Lewis was rummaging through one of the other rooms, I was the only one who understood the Sehaptin language and had to interpret. Mrs. Whitman asked me to tell the chief that she didn't want to go to the mansion house because she was fearful that they planned to harm the children. Chief Tiloukaikt assured her that no one else would be injured. As Joe Lewis reentered the room, the chief told him and Mr. Rogers to put Mrs. Whitman on the settee and carry her to the mansion house. It took Mr. Rogers several tries before he was able to lift his side of the settee with his injured arm.

Once we were outside, Joe Lewis dumped Mrs. Whitman in the mud and started whipping her across the face with a lash. Mr. Rogers tried to help but was knocked to the ground. Several men tried to run them over with their horses, but the horses refused to trample on human beings and jumped over them.

Joe Lewis continued to lash Mrs. Whitman about the face as I heard her cry out, "Please don't let my parents hear of this."

Then he shot her in the chest, and she lay still, but not dead. Mr. Rogers tried to rise to his feet to go to her, but one of the Indians shot him in the back.

As he fell, I heard him say, "May God have mercy."

I was standing in the yard with several others, having witnessed the entire atrocity. The chief told me to tell the rest of the women and children to get moving, that we were being taken to the mansion house, and no more women or children would be harmed. At this point, his words had no meaning since he had just said the same thing to Mrs. Whitman and Mr. Rogers before they were beaten and shot.

I don't believe it was Chief Tiloukaikt's idea to shoot or even harm Mrs. Whitman and Mr. Rogers, but he did nothing to stop it once it started. We had no choice but to keep moving since the younger warriors planned to torch the mission house.

Back in the mission house, Mr. Sales and Crockett Bewley were very sick with the measles in a room off the kitchen, and for some reason, they had been overlooked. I was worried they would be burned to death but also afraid to say anything for fear they would meet the same fate as the other men. Fortunately, it was decided to wait until the mission house had been thoroughly looted before burning it to the ground.

As we were being marched across the mission yard, Chief Beardy, who had always been a faithful friend to the Whitmans, came riding up protesting loudly about what was taking place. He told the men that what they had done was a very bad thing and that they should let the rest of us go. The younger warriors started taunting him and calling him names, then throwing rocks and dirt at him. One of the Cayuse men started whipping him as another told him that they would kill him if he didn't leave. They were continuing to pelt him with rocks as he slowly rode off, protesting loudly.

As we crossed the yard on our way to the mansion house, we could see Mrs. Whitman and Mr. Rogers lying in the dirt, covered in blood, but still moving. When Miss Bewley saw Tamsucky standing over Mr. Rogers as if to make sure he was dead, she became hysterical, panicked and started running, and screaming for help. Tamsucky quickly caught up with her, grabbing her by the arm to stop her. He then ordered me to translate.

It seemed so out of character when this man who had so savagely killed Doctor Whitman gently took her hand and had me tell her to be quiet if she valued her life. He then carefully led us over to the mansion house as the rest followed. We would later discover his devious intention.

We were herded like cattle to the slaughter and led into the mansion house where they lined us all up on one wall with their tomahawks drawn, and guns pointed at us. I think everyone felt the same way I did, that this was the end, that we were going to be killed, and there was absolutely nothing we could do about it but say our prayers.

I pulled my apron over my head so that I wouldn't see it coming. I understood every word they were saying, and there was a serious disagreement growing between several of the men as to whether they should spare our lives or not. Most of the younger men wanted to kill us and burn the mansion house down with us in it so that there would be no witnesses. Thankfully, Joe Lewis and Tomahas were too busy looting the mission house to give their opinions. Chief Tiloukaikt was quiet, but several of the older men said they wanted no part of killing women and children. There was a brief argument as tensions built, and several of the younger warriors became extremely agitated and started shouting, "Should we shoot, should we shoot?"

I knew that it was now or never, so I took my apron off my head, knowing this might well be my last moment on this earth. Without Joe Lewis or the Whitmans, there was no one else left to interpret. I was the only one left who could speak their language. Like in a dream I remember stepping up to Chief Tiloukaikt, and tugging on his shirt. He had been to our home many times, and I could see that there was still a sense of humanity in his eyes.

Still covered in poor Frank's blood, I asked him, "Chief Tiloukaikt, are you going to kill us?"

At first, he looked at me sternly, then his face softened slightly as he recognized me through the mask of blood. He said, "We will now decide."

I quickly told him, "It would be a bad idea to kill us when you can trade us for guns and supplies."

I knew some of the men in the room from the two missions, but it seemed to startle the others that I was so fluent in their language and had addressed the chief by name. He had turned and started to discuss the idea of a trade when I pulled lightly on his shirt again to get his attention.

This time he looked angry as if he were about to slap me, so I quickly said, "My good friend Chief Timothy once told me that it is not the Nez Perce or Cayuse warrior's way to kill innocent women or children. Is that true?"

He stared at me for the longest time, as if I wasn't there, then turned back to the group. There was a lump in my throat, and my heart was about to explode out of my chest, but my parents had shown me by example that the Indian people respect courage above everything else. I could see by the anger on some of their faces that what I had just done could have easily gotten me killed, but listening to them discuss our fate, I knew that it had to be said. Trading was a way of life for the Indian people and seemed the only possible way we might get out of this alive.

At first, they seemed uncertain, but Chief Tiloukaikt and some other men began advocating for a trade. He told them that we would be more valuable alive than dead and could be used as slaves until they traded us. One of the men asked the chief what they would do if the Americans sent soldiers, and he replied, "Kill them all."

It had been the most terrifying day that any of us would experience in our lifetimes, and the chill of death was like a heavy piece of cold lead in our hearts.

Finally, it was decided to spare our lives and make a trade. That evening we were to be the victims of another wide-awake nightmare, images we carry to our graves. Mrs. Hayes and Mrs. Hall were told to start preparing food, and to be sure that there was plenty of it. In some odd way, this seemed to give us a small hope for survival since both women were excellent cooks, and that might encourage the Cayuse men to keep us alive for the time being.

One thing I was grateful for was that Joe Lewis was no longer among them. His actions had been those of a savage beast, and with him around, none of our lives were safe. How could he be so cruel after the Whitmans had taken him in when he was destitute? It must have been something rancid in his nature or upbringing that had caused him to turn into such a monster. I had always tried to avoid him when I could because of his cold eyes.

It was as if his eyes were dead, the kind of eyes that made me feel afraid. I could understand the Indians' hatred toward Doctor Whitman since they had been lied to about him poisoning them. They believed they were doing what was necessary to save their people. However, I could never understand someone like Joe Lewis.

Poor John and Frank, dearly loved by all for their sweet and gentle natures. What had they done to deserve such a terrible death? That kind of malevolent violence has always been beyond my understanding. I would later find out that Joe Lewis had gone back to the mission house to steal all of the widow and orphans' money and valuables that he could get his hands on. He then fled and was never seen or heard from again.

Beneath the floorboards in the house that night, the Osbornes could hear Mrs. Whitman, Mr. Rogers, and Mr. Marsh lying out on the freezing ground crying for help. Mr. Marsh was begging for someone to be merciful and end his life. The last sound they heard before leaving that night was Mr. Rogers saying his prayers. In the mansion house there was so much noise and confusion that we were unaware of what they were going through.

Once we were inside the mansion house, the women and children were allowed to join together as families or groups. We were a sad and somber collection of helpless women and children, widows and orphans suffering from badly broken hearts, and the horror of the massacre. Three of the sick children had been lying on the settee cradled in Mrs. Whitman's arms and were now covered in her blood.

Several Indian women had shown up and started a fire in the big fireplace, some still taunting the braves to kill us, others sympathetic. Even in the cold, some of the braves were naked or had on a simple loincloth, covered with war paint and the blood of our friends and loved ones.

A group of four or five men started beating a rhythm on the tables and chairs as the others took up their bloody tomahawks, knives, and clubs and started doing the scalp dance. As if we were not already terrified enough, they started darting back and forth, swinging their weapons just above our heads and across our faces. Even though they had told us that our lives would be spared, it was impossible to believe that we were going to survive the night.

It was as if demons had ascended from the depths of hell to frighten and torment us. They were all screaming, dancing, and yelling at the top of their lungs, with men pounding on the tables and some of the women screaming for blood. Once a captive, you are simply property, and several of the white women were dragged off to other parts of the mansion house. There were also rumors of abuse to some of the children, but no one ever talked about what had happened to them that night. Females who had been used in that way were considered damaged goods, dirty and undesirable, so what took place that night went to the graves of the poor women and girls who had been violated.

For the victors, we were the spoils of war, trophies to be taken, and property to be used. They didn't understand our culture, and we didn't understand theirs, and that was probably why this had happened in the first place. The last thing I remember that night was sitting against the wall with my head buried in my hands, asking God how this could happen to us—and to please spare our lives so that we could see our families again.

I was never abused or mistreated. I think they felt that I needed special care since I was constantly in demand as an interpreter and food taster to make sure that the women didn't poison their food.

That night Chief Tiloukaikt told Nicholas Finley to take the two Munson boys and David Malin to his lodge beside the mission house where they would be safe. David was half-Indian and dark-skinned; the Manson boy's father was the chief trader for the Hudson Bay Trading Company. Donald Manson was Scottish, not American, and they didn't want to start a war with the Hudson Bay Trading Company or the British.

When I awoke the next day and went outside for water, I was horrified to see the dead bodies of our dear friends and loved ones so lifeless, twisted, and strewn about the grounds. It was a macabre and ghastly scene of bloody and distorted bodies frozen in death.

Mrs. Saunders seemed to be in a state of shock. She was trying to avoid looking at the remains of her husband's mangled body so close by with the crows busy pecking out his eyes. We were afraid to speak, fearing that anything we said might jeopardize our lives, so we stayed quiet.

The previous night I had heard the wolves and coyotes howling, but I don't think any of them had gotten to the bodies yet since a giant bonfire had been made out in the mission yard. Mrs. Saunders finally asked Chief Tiloukaikt if we could bury the bodies; he told her that he would consider it.

Later that afternoon, Father Brouillet came to the mission with his Indian helper and interpreter, James. I knew not to trust the priest, but still hoped that he might convince the Indians to release us, but that was not to be.

He later wrote a letter to one of his superiors, saying, "Upon riding into the mission compound, I couldn't believe my eyes. Strewn upon the ground and surrounded by burned buildings lay the bodies of Doctor Marcus Whitman, his wife Narcissa, nine other men, and two teenage boys. Huddled together near them were women and children staring at the dead with terror-stricken eyes. They were captives of the Cayuse Indians. Enlisting the aid of Joe Stanfield, a French-Canadian who escaped capture because he was not an American, we loaded the victims on a wagon box nearby the following day. Three of the women captives had been taken as wives of the various Indian chiefs or their sons."

Father Brouillet asked Chief Tiloukaikt if he could bury the dead and pray for their souls. The chief told him that it could be done the next day. That night there was another murder. James Young was the oldest of the three Young brothers, son of Elam and Irene Young.

Elam had been hired to operate the sawmill along with his wife and three sons. It was located almost 20 miles away in the foothills of the Blue Mountains. James was delivering lumber to construct a shelter over the gristmill, and the Cayuse had not yet discovered the Young or Smith families since they were living so far away.

One of the chief's sons named Clark was on his way to his village when he intercepted James. Unaware of what had taken place at the mission, the unsuspecting James was in the process of waving a greeting when Clark leveled his rifle and shot him in cold blood.

Clark tossed him to the ground with no feelings of remorse and left him to die in the dirt beside the wagon, then turned the oxen loose. Clark decided to return to the mission so he could boast about his kill.

Later that night, Mr. Stanfield went up to where James's body lay stiff and dead, burying him where he had fallen. Since Mr. Stanfield was a French-Canadian trapper and not American, he had been spared and used as a laborer. Though it had been very considerate of him to care for James Young's body, something was disturbing about his behavior and how friendly he was with the Indians. Whenever I passed him, he seemed to evade me, and no longer looked me in the eyes.

It was also well known that Mr. Stanfield was strongly attracted to Mrs. Hayes, who had a four-year-old son and had recently lost her husband on the trail. In front of all of us, he had approached her, explaining that if she took him as her husband, he would protect her; that she and her son would be spared since he was a French-Canadian.

She kindly told him that it had been too short of a time since her husband had died, that even if that were not the case, she was uncertain that she would want to be his wife.

He then proposed that they pretend to be married while she and her son were in captivity so that she wouldn't be harmed. Even the other women felt that this would be a good idea. Mrs. Hayes agreed, and he told her that they would need to share a bed and that her son could sleep between them.

Later that evening, he went to bring them to his room in another building when he ran into Chief Tiloukaikt outside the mansion house. The chief asked what he was doing, and he replied that he had come to get his wife and son.

The chief was taken aback, asking, "You have a wife and son?"

Mr. Stanfield assured him that he did, and that they were being held with the other captives. He also reminded him that the French and Canadians were good friends who didn't want war with the Indian people. The chief let him pass and collect Mrs. Hayes and her son Henry. That night one of the braves crept into their room to check on his story and found them together in bed with the boy. This seemed to appease their suspicion, and they were left alone after that. Later Mrs. Hayes told the other women that Mr. Stanfield didn't harm or try to take advantage of her.

Though it had only been days, it seemed forever that we were living under the menacing threat of death, yet no longer being tormented as we had that first day and night. We knew that our lives hung by a thread and could end at any moment, but at least we now had enough food, water, clothing, and bedding to keep from starving or freezing to death. Several of the sick children were getting weaker by the hour, and some were not expected to live without medical care.

I felt myself getting weaker from the constant strain of the fear of death and translating or tasting food at all hours of the day or night. Several of the women had tried to talk with Father Brouillet, but he told them to leave him alone, that they were putting his life in jeopardy by trying to speak with him. My father later told me that between the father and the bishop, the father was the lesser of two evils.

The second day after the massacre was a dreadful and ghastly affair. After we had served the Indians breakfast, we were told that we could wrap the dead bodies in sheets, that Mr. Stanfield would clean and bury them, and Father Brouillet would perform a service. About a dozen women and older girls were chosen to get the sheets and sew the bodies up after they had been cleaned. Helen and I were among them.

I have no idea what I was thinking, or if I was thinking at all while looking upon the frozen and terrified faces of the dead. It was so obvious by the expressions on their faces that they were terrified of dying, and even after so many years have passed, I am still unable to get the images out of my mind. Mr. Hoffman lay there with his heart, lungs, and intestines pulled out of his chest and stomach splayed in the dirt beside him. Doctor Whitman and John and Frank Sager had been dragged out of the house and thrown beside Mrs. Whitman and Mr. Rogers, not far from the kitchen door. Doctor Whitman's brains were leaking out of the side of his head, and part of Frank's face was missing. Mr. Marsh and Mr. Gilliland had been thrown together. Mr. Marsh had been shot in the chest and later shot in the bowels. Mr. Rogers' gentle spirit, beautiful voice, and violin were forever silenced in death. John and Frank were boys who had to become men far too early, and there were no kinder and more thoughtful souls on this earth. All were terribly disfigured and frozen stiff from the cold and rigor mortis.

It grieved me to think that I would never ride beside Doctor Whitman again, or hear his cheerful laugh and see his handsome smile. I couldn't help but think of how beautiful Mrs. Whitman had always kept her hair. It was a lustrous light brown, always perfectly brushed. Now it was bloody and splattered with mud. How incredibly sad that she was murdered in that way with no mother, father, or husband to hold her hand and comfort her as she passed into the next world. Worst of all was helping Helen Saunders as we tried to put her father together and bundle him up in the sheet. Mrs. Hayes had offered to take care of him, but Helen insisted that she do it herself.

He had been cut open in at least a dozen places, and part of his skull was missing with his brains oozing out. Helen seemed as if in a daze. Obviously, in shock, she made no sound, and her face was void of expression. Ironically, Mr. Saunders called her Magpie because there was nothing that she loved more than talking. She saw part of his skull laying several yards from his body and went over and tried to stick it back on his head. It wouldn't stay, so I helped her hold it on while I took my scarf off and wrapped it around his head to hold it in place.

To this day, I wake up drenched in sweat, hearing her cry, "They are killing my father; they are killing my father."

It took us several hours to get the bodies cleaned and sewn into sheets. Then Mr. Stanfield and several of the women dragged them over to a wagon and lifted them aboard. Next, he took them to the mission cemetery and unloaded them next to a shallow common grave about three feet deep, just wide enough and long enough to accommodate them all. Mr. Stanfield had washed all of the bodies before we covered them up and done the digging while we were busy sewing the bodies up in sheets. He placed Doctor and Mrs.

Whitman together, and the Sager brothers side by side. Father Brouillet stood off to a distance rubbing his beads and trying to look solemn and holy without offering to help in any way.

There were so many tears as we said goodbye to the fathers, brothers, sons, husbands, and the woman who had been like a mother to us all. In a strange land so far from home, consigned to a shallow grave in the cold and lonely ground seemed such an inappropriate way to lay them to rest. The only sound was that of our hearts breaking as we said goodbye for the last time.

Father Brouillet faced the head of the grave and started to give a traditional Catholic burial service. Mrs. Saunders seemed to come out of a trance as she stepped up to him and told him to stop, that this may have never happened if he hadn't told the Cayuse that the missionaries were devils. She told him that the last thing her husband and the others would want is a papist ritual spoken over their graves by a Catholic priest. He quietly slipped away as she began a sincere and heart-wrenching eulogy for the dear departed.

These poor families had not only lost their loved ones; they had now lost every possession they had ever owned. Money, jewelry, cattle, horses, property, supplies, even their clothing had been taken from them. We were given just enough to keep from freezing, and some of the poor women and girls were subjected to a fate worse than death.

Chapter 4

Father's Escape

I was afraid that Father would show up at any minute unaware and unsuspecting of what had happened. The Cayuse had made it clear that they intended to kill him on sight.

I waited until the priest was busy talking with one of the Cayuse men and then decided to risk asking his helper, James, if he would try and get a message to Father. I told him that I wasn't sure where Father was or if he was even alive, but if he was, the Cayuse were planning to kill him when they found him and then do the same at Lapwai. I also pleaded with him to tell Father what has happened here, that I was alive and well, and to get home as soon as possible. I wanted Father to know that there was nothing he could do here, that they planned to trade us for guns and supplies. James was reluctant to speak with me since we were out in the open.

Finally, he looked over at the priest talking with Chief Tiloukaikt and said, "What they have done here is wrong, especially to Mrs. Whitman and the two boys; it is not our way. If I see your father, I will do what I can to warn him."

"Thank you, James, God bless you."

James replied, "And you also."

As I passed the priest, he gave me his blessing with his mouth and hands, but his eyes were drawn tight, and said something completely different, something that frightened me. Just as they were leaving, Chief Tiloukaikt's son, Edward, came racing up on his horse and told Father Brouillet he was going with them.

He looked down at me, pointed his pistol at my face, and said, "I expect to find your father, and when I do, I am going to kill him, then we are going to Lapwai for the rest of your family."

I was frozen with fear, and it felt as if the blood in my body had turned to ice. I knew that Father would be completely unaware of Edward's intention and could only pray that someone would warn him and Mother before a war party could reach Lapwai.

They had only ridden several miles when Edward stopped to light his pipe. He had forgotten to get matches, so he was trying to use the flint from the back of his gun. The priest and James continued and came upon Father, slowly making his way toward Waiilatpu with Tashe and another packhorse in tow. When Father spotted them, he waved hello, but there was no response.

He could see something was wrong and asked, "How are things at the mission?"

The priest hesitated and then told him, "All the men and Mrs. Whitman are dead," then rode on.

Father was shocked and started to turn for the priest when James said, "Hold on, Mr. Spalding, the women and children are safe for the time being. The Doctor, Mrs. Whitman, and the men have been killed; we buried them today."

"How did this happen?"

"I was told that Joe Lewis planned it and killed Mrs. Whitman. Chief Tiloukaikt was the leader, and Tomahas bragged about killing the doctor. They plan to trade the women and children for guns and supplies."

"How many are there?"

"I saw about 20; there could be more."

Father had a hundred questions, and James was just about to warn him of Edward's intentions when he came riding up behind them. Father had known Edward since he was a boy and couldn't imagine that he had anything to do with the massacre. Father put his hand up as a greeting, but Edward immediately pulled his pistol and fired. Nothing happened; he had forgotten to reload his pistol after using it to light his pipe. As Father started to draw his rifle from its cover, Edward turned and fled back toward Waiilatpu. James then gave Father the rest of the message that I had asked him to deliver and told him that they were planning to kill him, that he had better hurry.

He gave Father a small bag of food that he had brought along and then said, "Your daughter also asked me to tell you that if they catch you, they plan to go to Lapwai and do the same thing they did at the Whitman mission."

Father asked James if he would take Tashe and the other pack-horse, that they would slow him down.

He then said, "Thank you, friend. I will always be in your debt. God bless you."

"And you, Mr. Spalding."

Father handed the horses to James, spun Thunder around, and went tearing off in the direction of Lapwai. His first instinct was to go to Waiilatpu and try to rescue me, but he realized that it would be suicide and possibly put my life and that of the other survivors in jeopardy.

James hadn't yet caught up with Father Brouillet when a party of five Cayuse, including Edward, came charging toward him.

"Which direction has Spalding gone? If you lie to us, we will kill you," Edward demanded.

James hesitated as if he were thinking to give Father more time and then told them, "He has taken the trail along the Touchet River toward Lapwai."

"Why do you have his horses," demanded Edward?

"He gave them to me; he said he no longer needed them."

Edward snorted a wicked laugh then said, "It is true; he no longer needs them since he will be dead before the end of the day, give them to me."

James handed the horses to Edward, who told one of the warriors to take them back to the mission. He knew that Five Crows wanted Tashe and would pay plenty for her.

Edward added, "You are lucky that I know your mother, or I would kill you for letting him go."

Edward and his men then turned their horses in the direction of the river and hurtled forward as fast as they could in search of Father.

By this time, Father was riding as hard and fast as Thunder could go. He knew that this would be a race against time. The longer he could evade them, the better chance Mother would stand of learning about the massacre and getting our family to safety. If they caught him right away, they would be at Lapwai within two days, before anyone could warn her.

It was getting to be late afternoon, and Father had been riding for several hours when he spotted a low-lying fog on the hill above the river. The trail that runs along the Touchet River was covered in a layer of snow and ice, so he planned to stay as close to the river as possible to hide his tracks. When he reached the fog, it started lifting, and he knew he would not be able to evade experienced hunters and trackers without cover. He decided to cross the river and continue in the shallow water as far as he could instead of just crossing to the opposite bank.

He also knew that getting wet could prove fatal in this cold weather, but it was the only way he could think of throwing them off his trail. He felt that if he could survive until nighttime, he would have a chance. Then he would try and find a place to rest and hide out during the day while traveling at night.

I had been lying down feeling unwell when I looked out of the window and saw one of the young Cayuse men come into camp, leading Tashe behind him. As soon as I recognized her, I jumped up and went running outside, yelling, "Tashe, Tashe."

The young man tried to hold her back, but she immediately came to me and brushed up against my shoulder with her soft nose.

I told him to, "Let go of her; you can see that this is my horse; Chief Timothy gave her to me."

He laughed out loud and said, "You have spirit, I like that; but this horse is going to Chief Five Crows."

"You know it is wrong to take another person's horse; how would you like it if someone took yours?"

"You are in no position to tell anyone what is right or wrong; you are lucky to be alive, now go away."

I knew he was right, and as I stood there with my head down thinking, Tashe continued to nudge me for attention.

I looked up at the young warrior and said, "Could you tell me if there is any news of my father? He was a true friend to Chief Five Crows?"

Reluctantly he told me that they were looking for him, and planned to kill him if they found him ... He then tried to jerk Tashe away from me, but I wouldn't let go, then he looked as though he was about to lash me when Catherine gently grabbed my shoulder and pulled me away in tears.

Father pressed on that night until Thunder was almost spent. It was nearly dark, and he was resting beneath a copse of trees that overhung the river shivering from the cold and looking at his now worthless rifle. Everything was completely soaked, including his bedroll and blanket. Thunder suddenly turned in the direction they had come from, alerting Father. Within seconds he could hear riders coming and went deeper into cover and quietly asked Thunder not to make a sound as he grabbed his nostrils.

The party passed so closely that he could hear them talking about turning back for the night. One of the men thought that Father might have drowned when he entered the water. Father had decided to stay put, and about 15 minutes later, they came riding back toward Waiilatpu. He had hardly noticed the injury from when he had fallen from his horse, but now that he was cold, wet, and tired, the pain was returning with a vengeance. He ate what was left of the soggy bread and dried meat that James had given him, and then continued in the dark.

On the second day, the sky had turned dark gray and was threatening to snow. Father was no stranger to hardship, but the previous night had been the coldest and most miserable he had ever experienced. He figured that he would have an hour or so after sunrise before taking cover. He found a deep ravine next to the river where he and Thunder were well hidden from the trail. Later that morning, as he lay shivering in the mud, he heard riders coming in a hurry and hoped they were looking for him instead of on their way to Lapwai.

The day seemed like a month as he lay shivering in the wet dirt. When the sky darkened again, he decided that it was time to move, though the riders had not yet returned. By now, every fiber of his body ached, and his head was pounding like a sledgehammer breaking rock. Though he was near freezing, he decided it would be safer to stay in the water by the bank so he wouldn't leave a trail they could easily follow.

At times water was up to his chest, and the blanket used as an overcoat to keep the wind off was sticking to him from the cold; he knew it was going to be another long and lonely night.

Sometime near midnight, he heard the sound of horses coming and found a patch of ground covered with high grass and pulled Thunder down on his side. Worried that Thunder might give him away, he put his fingers in Thunder 's nostrils again to keep him from calling out to the other horses. Father was beginning to lose his sense of direction, but it seemed they were coming from Tshimakain where the Walkers and Eells had their mission with the

Spokane Indians. He feared that they, too, might have suffered the same fate as the Whitmans.

Father would later learn that a group had indeed been to Tshimakain and had planned to kill the missionaries. However, the Walkers and Eells were well-liked and had made good friends amongst the Spokane. When the Cayuse came, the Spokane Indians told them to leave, that the Walkers and Eells were under their protection. Threats were made, but no one was hurt. The Cayuse were badly outnumbered and did not want to start a war with the Spokane tribe, especially in Spokane territory.

However, this was the same group that had been hunting Father. When he thought the riders were long gone, he carefully mounted his horse and had just started to continue when he heard them returning. Someone must have suspected that he was near because they doubled back and were riding extremely slow, stalking their prey. The moon was half full, and he was clearly visible. He knew that if he tried to lay Thunder down again, they would hear him, so he gave him a quiet thump on the rear and let him go. One of the Indians saw Thunder and chased him. Within minutes he had a lasso around Thunder's neck and was leading him back to the others.

The night was eerie with moonlight moving through the clouds and stalking sounds of nearby hunters. Father was able to make out Thunders ears and the top of the warrior's head above the high grass. They fanned out and searched in his direction, passing so close that he could hear one of the braves breathing hard. Several times he had to scamper from one bush to another when he heard them closing in. This went on for almost an hour before they made camp not more than 50 yards from where he lay deep inside a bush, in terror of being discovered.

Father lay there for hours without making a sound. They had made a fire, and he was so close that he could hear them debating whether he had drowned or was still on the run. They were cold and tired, so they decided that he had drowned. This way, they could take a short rest and return to the mission to sleep and get something warm to eat.

When they finally left, Father tried to put his shoes on, but they had shrunken so much that he could not get them on and had to throw them in the river. He half expected the group to come back but felt the need to continue for several hours even though the sun was beginning to rise above the mountains to the east. However, he was now barefoot and without a horse, nearly frozen and terrified that the lives of his family were in jeopardy.

The next day I was in the kitchen and overheard Tomahas when he found the young men who had been searching for Father asleep in the living room. He became angry that they had not found him and told them that they were to go back out and continue searching. One of the men told him that Father had probably drowned, that even if he hadn't, he would soon die from the cold. Tomahas told him that if it was so, they were to find the body and bring it back as proof.

This was my first glimmer of hope that Father was still alive. I knew that he hadn't drowned; he was too strong a swimmer, but I was worried about how he would reach home in this weather without a horse. Chief Tiloukaikt was still the group's leader, but because he had softened toward the women and children, Tomahas had all but taken charge. I knew he was planning to send a party to Lapwai once they had found Father, and I couldn't get it out of my mind. My only hope was that Chief Timothy and Eagle would protect my family.

To some extent, Chief Tiloukaikt had become a protector and peacemaker for the women and children. He claimed that he was looking out for his property, but I sensed that he felt guilty about what had happened. When I went to anyone else for help, I was treated roughly, but when I went to Chief Tiloukaikt, he was patient, almost kind. No one knew for sure if a trade was going to happen, but his reassurance gave us hope that it was possible.

On the second day of Father's escape, the sky was again ominous and dark, with a light snow falling. He figured that he would have an hour or so after sunrise before taking cover. He found a deep ravine next to the river where he was well hidden from the trail. Later that morning, as he lay shivering in the mud, he heard riders coming in a hurry and hoped they were looking for him instead of on their way to Lapwai. The day seemed to go on forever as he lay shivering in the wet, cold earth. When the sky darkened again, he decided that it was time to move, though the riders had not yet returned. By now, every fiber of his body ached, and his head felt as though it would split open. Though he was near freezing, he decided it would be safer to continue to stay in the water by the bank so he wouldn't leave a trail. At times, Father was wet up to his chest and used the wet blanket as an overcoat to keep the wind off.

By the third morning of Father's escape, he had discarded his blanket since it was too heavy and wet to drag. His feet were in bad condition, cut and bleeding from the sharp rocks and prickly pears.

He had managed to find a small cluster of bushes next to the river where he was well hidden. He was shivering so hard that he thought his teeth would break from rattling so fiercely.

When he heard horses approaching, he crawled deeper into the bushes. They were moving slowly and looking for traces of his tracks, but he had been careful to leave no prints by walking over the rocks or in the water. They were so close that he could hear one of the men complaining that he was tired of looking for a dead man, that even if he were not dead yet, the cold would kill him soon. One of the other men said that he was not sure; he sensed Father was still alive; they should keep looking. He reminded the other young men that Tomahas had told them not to come back empty-handed, that he was in a rage when they left. Once we find him or his body, we can move on to Lapwai.

Father knew what that meant, and even in his condition, he was able to cover 30 miles that night in the dark over sharp rocks and thorn bushes with no shoes, food, or dry clothing.

Earlier that same day, a most bizarre incident occurred. I was out in the mission yard with Elizabeth Sager getting water when one of the Indian men came bursting out of the mission house wearing a woman's dress. It was some kind of prank that he was involved in with the other men. There was a group by the kitchen door laughing, hooting, and hollering. They were also making lewd gestures as if he were a woman. He then strutted back and forth as they continued to laugh and encourage him.

As deadly serious as everything had been up to this point, even Elizabeth and I had our hands over our mouths to suppress our laughter.

All of a sudden, Elizabeth stopped cold and said, "Oh my goodness!"

I was alarmed at first, not sure what she was talking about. I asked what was wrong, and she told me that the dress the Indian man was wearing belonged to her mother, who had died on the Oregon Trail. She went on to tell me that when her mother died, they had looked everywhere they could think of to find that dress so that she could be buried in it, but never found it. At that point, she didn't seem to know whether to laugh or cry, so we filled up the water buckets, kept quiet, and went back to the mansion house.

Later that same day, the Cayuse had a meeting in which Tamsucky, still seething from his wife's death, gave a passionate speech calling for all women and children to be put to death. I could understand every word he was saying and was becoming extremely anxious, though I kept it to myself to not alarm everyone else. Thankfully, the older chiefs convinced the rest that it would be wiser to keep us alive. They said there had already been enough bloodshed and that they could use the guns and supplies.

On the morning of December 4, 1847, Father found himself huddled in a wet ditch covered in mud and shivering so hard that he thought he could hear his bones rattling. He tried to sleep so that he could get some relief from his misery but could only doze for a minute or two at a time because of the pain that was now beyond description.

If there was one small mercy, it was that his feet had gone numb overnight, and he couldn't feel them any longer. He had found some clay, cleaned them as best he could, and torn a piece of his shirt, and wrapped them, but they were bleeding badly and swollen to twice their normal size. As it warmed, the feeling returned, and Father thought that this must be what it would be like to walk through hell's fire. He was afraid of frostbite, so he rubbed his feet as hard as he could to try and keep the circulation going, then rewrapped them in clay. That day the sky was another shade of dreary dark gray with light hail and snow showers. His only thought was of getting to our family before he died of exposure.

That same morning, Chief Tiloukaikt had all of the girls and young women line up in the main room of the mansion house. There were six Indian men of various ages, also in the room. I translated that Chief Tiloukaikt felt it would be safer for the women to become wives to these more pious men. He explained that they would then be under the protection of their new husbands, and the younger and wilder men would no longer be allowed to harass them. The poor young women stood trembling as he told them to look over the men; they would be given time to make their decisions. He told them that there was no other choice.

Chapter 5

Lapwai

Unaware of what had happened at Waiilatpu, Mother was sitting in the living room that afternoon with the children and Mary Johnson when they heard someone barge into the kitchen. Her brother Horace and Mr. Jackson were working at the mill, but she knew they would never enter the house so carelessly. When she went into the kitchen, she found a man she had never seen before, worn and dirty, barely able to stand. As she went to help, he collapsed in her arms. With Mary's help, they managed to half carry, half drag him to the couch in the living room, giving him time to collect himself. He was extremely weak, and she noticed that blood was oozing from his side.

Without introduction, he said, "You must be Mrs. Spalding. Did Mr. Spalding make it?"

Alarmed, she told him, "No, he hasn't, but we expect him any time. You have been injured, sir. What happened to you, and why do you ask if my husband made it?"

"I'm sorry, Mrs. Spalding, my name is William Canfield, and I have been working at the Whitman Mission. I have terrible news: there was a massacre at the Mission, and I fear everyone may be dead by now. I know the men were killed, but I'm not sure about the women and children. My wife and children were hiding in the loft of the blacksmith's shop when my wife asked me to go for help. I can only pray they are still alive."

Mother had been sitting next to him, and rose to her feet and in her calm and controlled way, she said, "I was not prepared for this, sir, but please go on, let me hear the news."

He told her what had happened and how he played dead until no one was looking and then fled for his family to the blacksmith shop. There, his wife convinced him to try and get help.

"Why did you ask if Mr. Spalding had arrived ... wasn't he killed with the other men?"

"I don't know if he is alive or dead. The day before it happened, he and Doctor Whitman had gone to a Cayuse village to treat the sick. I heard that Mr. Spalding fell from his horse and planned to return when he was able to ride again. That was the last I saw or heard of him."

Mother paused for a time and then looked directly at Mr. Canfield and asked, "Do you have any idea what happened to our daughter, Eliza?"

"I'm sorry, Mrs. Spalding, after the initial gunfire at the mission yard, there were only two or three more shots before I left. It's possible that the women and children were spared."

Mother then pulled back his shirt to inspect the wound and was glad to see that it wasn't badly festered and was reasonably clean where the bullet had gone in and out. She cleaned it with warm water and medicinal alcohol and then told him that she would have to cut away the dead flesh and sew it up.

"There is one more thing I need to tell you, Mrs. Spalding. It's been six days since I left the mission, and I believe the Cayuse are planning to come here; it's not safe to stay."

Just then, Horace and Mr. Johnson entered the house and looked at Mr. Canfield in surprise. Mother introduced them to each other and then explained what had happened. She then told Uncle Horace to get Chief Timothy, that they needed his help. Uncle Horace asked her if it was safe to include the Nez Perce, that they may be involved.

She told him, "You need to trust me on this. Timothy and Eagle are somewhere nearby. I want you to find them and bring them here as fast as you can."

"Yes, ma'am."

When the men returned, Timothy and Eagle were calm as usual but looking concerned.

Mother said, "You have obviously heard the news. Timothy, I need to ask you and Eagle a life favor ... I would like you to go to Waiilatpu and see what has happened to Mr. Spalding and Eliza. If Eliza is still alive, I want you to take our life's savings, and as many horses and cattle as you think it would take to trade for her."

Timothy said, "We will leave now."

Mother took each of their hands in hers and thanked them. She then turned to Horace and said, "I want you to go to Mr. Craig's camp and tell him what has happened. We have had our differences in the past, but I know he will help us."

That night, driven by fear for our family, Father covered another 30 miles. He was hungry, cold, dirty, and limping badly on swollen feet that he could no longer feel.

Since he hadn't heard or seen any other riders that night, he was afraid that they had given up on him and gone on to Lapwai.

By the next morning, December 5, Father was becoming delirious but had managed to find a large enough cavity next to the river to crawl into. His feet were so badly injured that he could barely walk. He found several branches that he was able to break apart to use as crutches. At times he was so weak and tired that he had to crawl on his hands and knees.

Late that morning, after Chief Timothy and Eagle had left, a Nez Perce messenger arrived at Lapwai with news that the men and Mrs. Whitman had been killed, but the women and children had been spared. He told them that the Cayuse planned to hold them hostages until a trade could be arranged and that they were using Eliza as interpreter.

He also let Mother know that Father had been warned before he reached the Whitman Mission and had fled in the direction of Lapwai. As far as he knew, Father had not been captured, but there was no word of where he was or what had happened to him. There was a Cayuse search party out looking for him with orders to kill him on sight. They were then to continue to Lapwai to kill the men and take the women and children as hostages. The messenger recommended that they take only what they needed and leave as soon as possible before a war party arrived.

When Horace returned, he told her that Mr. Craig was sending a party of Nez Perce to escort them to his camp where they would be protected.

She told everyone, "This is the Sabbath, and I don't think the Lord would look kindly on our breaking his commandment. Please send someone back and tell him that we will be ready to leave first thing tomorrow morning."

Mr. Canfield said, "If my family is still alive, I would like to see them again, Mrs. Spalding. These men are butchers. You should think of your children, ma'am. We could all be dead by morning if the Cayuse show up before then."

"I am sorry, Mr. Canfield, we are deeply indebted to you. You are a brave man and have done more than anyone could expect. You are welcome to leave now if you like. I will give you a horse, provisions, and have someone show you the way to Mr. Craig's village, but my family will be staying until Sabbath is over and, God willing, we will all be alive tomorrow. That goes for anyone else who would like to leave now."

Horace, Mary, and Mr. Jackson knew Mother well enough not to argue with her when it came to her faith; it was now carved in stone, and she was immovable. They all agreed that they would go when she and the children went.

Mr. Canfield looked somewhat embarrassed and said, "I would like to stay and be of whatever assistance I can provide to you and your family, Mrs. Spalding."

"Thank you, Mr. Canfield; your help is deeply appreciated."

Tamsucky returned that afternoon and started searching the house as if to find something or someone. When I was brought to him to translate, he told me that he was looking for Lorinda Bewley. I told him that she was ill and in bed. He pushed right by me and started going through the rooms until he found her. I followed him into her room as he told me to tell her that he wanted her to choose him for a husband. He said that Doctor Whitman had killed his wife, that Lorinda was to be his new wife. He then started trying to fondle her, but she pushed him away and managed to hold him off.

549

I was afraid he was going to beat me when I told him that she didn't want to be his wife and asked him to leave. He started threatening her, but she held her ground and continued asking him to leave. He then grabbed her by the hair and dragged her outside.

When he got to the mission yard, he tried to put her up on his horse, but she managed to slide off, causing him to become even more angry and frustrated. She had me tell him that she would scream and tell the chief what he was trying to do to her. He grabbed her again and put his hand over her mouth to stop her from screaming.

By this time, almost everyone was outside wondering what was going on. She then bit his hand, he picked her up and forcefully threw her to the ground knocking her senseless. She lay there, helplessly on her stomach as he tore her clothes off and raped her in front of everyone. I had already witnessed far too much brutality and turned away before he mounted her. When he was done, he told me to tell her she was now his woman, that he would be back soon to take her to his lodge. She was shaking and sobbing, trying to cover herself up with her torn clothes. I could see the blood running down her legs as we half walked, half carried her to her room, and then helped her put on a nightgown. Mrs. Hayes told me to get her some medicine to calm her down.

The beast suddenly came charging back into her room and asked me what I was doing. I told him I was getting medicine for one of the children, so he turned and left. Poor Miss Bewley, her only fault was that she was a beautiful young woman that almost all of the men desired.

When Chief Tiloukaikt heard about what had happened, he came to Miss Bewley and told her that he had found a proper husband for her. She would be taken to the Catholic mission near Fort Walla Walla, then to the lodge of Chief Five Crows. He told her that Chief Five Crows was a kind and rich man. She would now be under his protection so that nothing like this would ever happen to her again. She was told to get her things together, that someone would be there to pick her up shortly. Translating that message was one of the hardest things I have ever had to do. After he left, we all cried until there were no tears left.

That afternoon at the mansion house, there was another sad and mournful affair. Little Louise Sager, only six years old, died of measles and neglect. The women tried to do everything within their power to keep her alive, but what she needed most were the skillful hands of Doctor Whitman, who was now lying in a shallow grave. She had always reminded me of an angel, a sweet and gentle soul, so innocent and fragile. When she surrendered her life—taken so young from the hands of her loving family into those of our Lord— we buried her alone in a shallow grave—not a dry eye to be found, her sisters inconsolable.

As the sun was setting, Daniel Young came into camp accompanied by two young warriors who were guarding the mission. He was looking for his brother and bringing more lumber to cover the gristmill. Mr. Stanfield told him what had happened to his brother and what had taken place at the mission. I could tell that he was in a state of shock, trying to comprehend it all. About that same time Chief Stickus arrived, having heard about the massacre, he wanted to see if he could help the captives.

When Tomahas saw Daniel, he came storming over and started threatening to kill him, restating that it was time to kill the rest of the women and children as well. Several other warriors had wandered over, and a heated discussion started in which Tomahas became extremely agitated. Thankfully, the older chiefs, including Chief Stickus, convinced the rest that it would be easier to bargain with live women and children rather than corpses.

Chief Tiloukaikt finalized it by telling the group that there would be no more killing.

Daniel was told to go back to the mill and bring his family and the Smith family to the mission. He was also told that if they tried to escape, they would all be hunted down and killed. The chief decided that it would be best if his son Clark and Chief Stickus went with him to make sure they didn't try to escape.

December 5, Mother, my brother and sister, Uncle Horace, Mr. Jackson, and Miss Johnson, were all safely taken to the Nez Perce camp of Mr. William Craig.

Mr. Craig was born in West Virginia and had allegedly killed a man in self-defense and was forced to flee. He had become a well-known trapper who had established a crude log cabin in the Green River area called Fort Davy Crockett. On occasion, he shared it with the families of Joe Meek, Jedediah Smith, and Kit Carson until 1840. At that point, the beavers were almost trapped out and many of the trappers, along with their Indian wives and families, decided to try for a new life in the Oregon Territory. At Fort Walla Walla, Mr. Craig met and married a Nez Perce woman to whom he gave the name Isabel, after his mother. She was the daughter of Chief

Thunder Eyes, owner of our mission land and leader of the Nez Perce People at Lapwai.

When Mr. Craig heard about the massacre, he sent a group of men to escort Mother and the rest of the mission party safely to his camp. It was just in time since almost immediately after they left, a group of Cayuse warriors came charging into the compound looking to repeat what they had done at Waiilatpu. Little did Mother know that it would be the last time she would ever see our home at Lapwai.

It had started raining so hard by midday that Father decided it was safe to continue since his trail would be washed away almost instantly. Every step was a test of his willpower, and the crutches had begun cutting deeply into his underarms. Even though he felt he was losing his grip on reality, he thought he knew where he was and that there was a Nez Perce village close by. He was coming over a ridge when he spotted two riders with five horses in tow. His mind was hazy, and his vision was poor at this point, so he quickly ducked out of sight, hoping that he had not been spotted. He found a small ditch and climbed into several inches of freezing water and mud and then waited for well over an hour until he felt safe to go on. Little did he know that it was Chief Timothy and Eagle on their way to Waiilatpu, that he would have been saved had he caught their attention.

He had reached what he thought to be the Nez Perce village of Alpowa, where he needed to cross the Snake River to get to the other side. The river was running hard and fast, and in his condition, it would be impossible to swim. At almost every Nez Perce village, the Indian people kept canoes on both sides to cross. After searching for what seemed an eternity, Father finally found one and crossed. He was hoping it was the village of Chief Timothy, but his mind was playing tricks on him from fatigue and hunger, and he couldn't be sure.

By this time, it was turning dark. He was still worried about being discovered, so he crawled on the ground to have a better chance of going undetected. As he looked for some sign of recognition, he began to question who could still be trusted.

He was certain of Timothy, but in his condition, he couldn't locate his lodge. He crawled up next to one of the teepees and heard someone talking. It sounded as if they were praying, praying for the Whitmans; he thought he might have even heard his name mentioned; since he couldn't recognize the voice or lodge, he continued looking for Chief Timothy. He was suddenly startled when one of the dogs started barking, which set off a whole chorus of barking dogs.

He decided to flee and had to cross the river once again. He drifted for over a mile before he reached the other side. When he did, he found the ground covered with sharp rocks, making it almost impossible to continue with the crutches on his badly torn feet. Still, he continued to trudge over the rocky terrain until he reached the Clearwater River, less than five miles from our mission at Lapwai.

He was completely exhausted and lay immobilized on the bank of the river in the rain; his teeth clenched so hard from the cold and pain that he thought they would shatter. His fatigue finally won out over the pain, and he mercifully fell asleep for a few hours.

On December 6, 1847, Father awoke to the first rays of sun shining down on him since he had left the Whitman Mission eight days ago. The fear that he might need to have his feet amputated was even greater than the actual pain, but that was a bridge he would have to cross later. Right now, his family might be in danger, so it was time to move. The warm rays of the sun slightly revived him as he painfully lifted himself to his feet and continued to stumble over the rocky terrain with the wooden branches cutting deeply into his armpits. The hunger had become more a mental issue than a physical one. He still had the hollow throbbing in his gut, but it was the actual thought of food every few seconds that made it hard for him to concentrate.

The six-day trek since being warned by James would be the most painful and demanding challenge he would face in his lifetime, and there had been many. His feet were so swollen that it caused him to lose his balance even with the crutches. At times he was forced to crawl on hands and knees, even on his stomach.

After what seemed like an eternity, he finally reached the bluff above the mission.

He was quietly resting when he heard a noise and looked over the edge to find a group of Cayuse Indians riding hard into the mission grounds. They were dressed in warm buffalo coats and covered in war paint, so there was no doubt about who they were or their intention. To his relief, there was no sign of life on the grounds, which led him to believe that our family must have gotten away safely.

The war party carefully entered the house and then started whooping and yelling. they were incensed that no one was there, and they started tearing the house apart. He could hear furniture and glass being broken, and then objects were hurled out of the front door. When they were done with the destruction, they took everything of value that they could carry. Everything that he and Mother had spent countless hours making by hand or paying for with their hard labor over the past 11 years was now gone.

Father decided to hide and rest up until darkness came before examining the house. He felt that this was likely to be the end of the mission, but in his heart, he clung to the hope of rebuilding. It was almost dark when he struggled to get up and check on the mission house.

By the time he heard the rider approaching, it was too late; he had been discovered.

The rider stopped next to him, and even in his delirium, he thought he recognized the old woman looking down at him. He was so emaciated and covered in dirt that she didn't recognize him. She asked what he was doing and what he wanted. She was surprised when he answered back in Nez Perce. He didn't want to expose himself and told her that he had been thrown from his horse but had a message for the Spaldings and wanted to know where they were. She told him that they had been taken to Mr. Craig's village that morning because of the killings at the Whitman Mission, that Mr. Craig had promised to protect them until he could deliver them safely to Fort Walla Walla.

Momentarily it felt as if gravity had ceased crushing him, and his pains were temporarily suspended. Then the fear of what had happened to me hit him. Father was so weak that he lost his balance and dropped one of his crutches. When he bent over to pick it up, his cap fell off exposing his bald head. The old woman immediately recognized him and quickly dismounted to help.

"Why did you not tell me it was you, Mr. Spalding?"

"I am sorry, I thought I recognized you, but I am so tired and confused that I was uncertain who to trust."

"You are badly injured; I will go for help. Stay here, and I will send someone back for you and send someone to let Mrs. Spalding know you are alive."

At almost the same time the old woman had found Father, the Cayuse party was charging into Craig's camp looking for our family and the others from our mission.

A lookout had warned the village that they were coming, and by the time they got there, a protective circle of Nez Perce warriors had surrounded everyone.

The leader of the Cayuse demanded, "We have no quarrel with you, Craig; we want the white people you have brought from the Spalding Mission. We will not harm the women and children; they will be held as hostages at Waiilatpu until traded. We have no use for the men; they must die."

William Craig had become a powerful voice amongst the Nez Perce, and his wife was the daughter of a great chief.

He said, "You insult me by coming to my lodge and demanding to take guests of my village who are under my protection. We have no wish to fight, but as you can see, you are far outnumbered. You expect my cooperation, yet you did not consult me before killing the people at Waiilatpu. You are wrong if you think this will rid your people of the Americans, they will come like a mighty herd of buffalo with weapons you cannot imagine. They will want blood for blood and will hang you all like dogs, and we want no part of it. Go now, and if you should try to slip back in the night, you will join your ancestors before the morning light."

The leader held up his spear and said, "You will see me again, white man," then turned his horse and charged back toward Waiilatpu.

Father ignored the old woman's advice to stay put and slowly made his way down the bluff to our home. Bitter tears came to his eyes when he went from room to room in disbelief that everything had been destroyed so quickly. Every piece of furniture was broken, all of the doors as well, and the woodwork that he had taken so much time and care making by hand was destroyed. Everything of value had been taken. Anything left was now worthless. He went on to inspect the rest of the mission and found all of their animals were missing, the gristmill and lumber mill in shambles.

In the distance among a group of Nez Perce teepees, he could hear the sound of mourning and staggered toward it. He knew that if he didn't get help soon, he would die. As he opened the flap door of one of the teepees, he staggered in and fell into the arms of his trusted friend Luke, a loyal follower who he had baptized years ago. Father was more dead than alive as Luke helped him to a buffalo rug and gently laid him down.

He told Father, "We had given you up for dead, dear friend, and were singing the mourning song of your loss."

Luke asked his wife to get some food that would be easy to eat and then looked in shock at his badly swollen and bloody feet. She brought him some cornmeal pudding and fresh milk, which Father choked on at first.

Luke told him, "Slowly, my friend, or you will be sick."

His wife brought warm blankets and covered him and then began examining his feet.

She looked at her husband, trying not to show any emotion, but was also shocked at what she saw. The cuts were deep with puncture holes from the thorns he had stepped on. They were crusted with mud, but the infection was not too bad because of the clay. She washed them as well as she could and then applied an herbal poultice that had been used by her people for 100s of years. Luke told Father that his wife and family were safe at Mr. Craig's camp, that he should rest. Father tried to speak but closed his eyes to rest and fell into the tender mercy of a sound sleep.

The showdown at William Craig's village had shaken everyone but also reassured Mother that she and the others were safe for the time being. After hearing what the Cayuse planned to do to them, Horace, Mr. Canfield, and Mr. Jackson decided to flee over the mountains toward the Missouri River. Mother tried to talk them out of it, telling them that they would never survive the mountains during winter. They wouldn't listen and felt that their only hope for survival was to leave as soon as possible and take their chances.

Mr. Canfield told her, "You wouldn't believe how those men at Waiilatpu died, Mrs. Spalding. I would rather freeze to death than be hacked to pieces."

It was a desperate idea, but they were committed to it, so Mother began helping them prepare as many provisions as they could carry. With her characteristic calm and brave demeanor, she kissed Uncle Horace goodbye and wished them all God's speed, never expecting to see any of them again.

They hadn't been gone more than an hour when two young Nez Perce men came flying into camp with news that Mr. Spalding had been found at Lapwai, that he was in dire condition, but alive. They told Mother how the old woman who had found him on the bluff didn't even recognize him at first; he was so dirty and worn. They had gone to look for him on the bluff, but he was gone, so they looked all over the mission and eventually found him with Luke.

Mother dropped to her knees and thanked God. The entire camp was completely silent, as several others did the same. When she rose again, they told her that Mr. Spalding was resting, and they would bring him to Mr. Craig's camp in the morning. They thought that he must have walked the whole way with no horse or shoes, that he was very weak, and his feet were badly injured.

In her heart, Mother had tried to prepare herself for Father's death; now her heart was racing at the thought that he was still alive.

She told them, "I should go to him; he may need my help."

William Craig said, "It's not safe, Mrs. Spalding. The Cayuse could still be out there waiting, and even some of the Nez Perce have turned against you. He is safe where he is and probably needs rest more than anything else. Luke's wife knows the healing plants as well as anyone and will have already treated him. You should stay here and take care of your children. I'll send a party over at first light to bring him to you."

"You're right. Thank you, Mr. Craig, and God bless you."

The next morning when Father awoke, he wondered if this had all been a terrible nightmare; then, the pain hit, and he knew it was real. Up to that moment, he had been so preoccupied with the thoughts of his family and survival that he hadn't felt the loss of the Whitmans. He silently wept for them as thoughts of all they had been through together flooded his mind. Luke's wife brought him some more warm corn pudding and a healing tea for breakfast and then unwrapped the bandages to check his feet. They were still badly swollen, but the poultice of herbs and clay had already begun clearing up the infection.

Outside Luke's lodge, a group of ten men from William Craig's village waited patiently with our mission wagon to take him to our family. As they approached Mr. Craig's camp, Father could see Mother standing next to little Henry and Martha Jane, with Amelia in her arms. He said it was the most beautiful sight he had ever seen; one he had never expected to see again. When the men helped him down, our family huddled together in each other's arms, giving thanks for God's mercy.

Father had accomplished the unimaginable. Hungry, hunted, weak, and injured, he had covered over 120 miles in the dead of winter over ice, snow, and rock covered terrain. One hundred or more of those miles were on foot with no shoes, food, warmth, or shelter. He was soaking wet most of the time with clothes so cold they were almost frozen to his skin. His feet were so severely injured that every single step was an excruciating test of his courage and tenacity. At times he was forced to crawl on his stomach and knees, dragging his crutches beside him. He was also under the strain of knowing that his family could be captured and killed at any moment. He was well aware that torture and death hung over his head like a dark cloud as a hungry pack of men lusted for his death. Motivated by love and fear, it was a most remarkable feat of endurance, courage, and survival.

Crockett Bewley and Mr. Sales had been taken to the mansion house so that they could be watched more easily. They had been deathly sick from the measles but were starting to recover and would survive the illness. I was in their room, bringing them food and water when Edward Tiloukaikt burst into the room and started lashing them on their faces and chests. This went on for several minutes until three other men came charging into the room. They threw the two men out of bed onto the floor.

They then began tearing the legs off the beds and started beating the two men. I tried to stop them, but someone pushed me into the wall, where I was stunned, helpless. At first, they could only hit them on their backs and sides, but they managed to get both of them turned over and began beating them from the front. Once their arms were useless, they hit them in the face and head. At that point, I ran out of the door looking for Chief Tiloukaikt.

When I found him, I told him what was happening, and he told me that there was nothing he could do, that a decision had been made to kill these men and no one could stop it now. Mrs. Hayes saw me crying and took me in her arms. The beating went on for so long that the men were nothing more than a bloody pulp. When they were done, they dragged what was left of them out into the mansion yard, heaved one on top of the other, and left them there. I had hoped with all my heart that there would be no more killing, but I was finding it hard to believe at this point and beginning to lose hope. With so little rest, I was getting weaker by the day, and at times I needed help to get out of bed.

Chapter 6

Hope

The next day, a ray of sunshine broke through the dismal gray clouds, and my hopelessness exploded into hope as I looked out of the window to see my dearest friend, Chief Timothy, and Eagle coming to my rescue.

As the men approached each other, Tomahas rudely ignored their greeting and without preamble asked, "What do you want here?"

Chief Tiloukaikt looked distant and remained quiet. Chief Timothy and Eagle took their time dismounting and made Tomahas wait for a long time before answering because of his rudeness.

"The Spalding girl is my friend, and I have come here to bring her back to her people."

Tomahas replied, "That cannot happen; the women and children are our hostages and worth a great deal to us in trade."

"I understand that and have brought you fine horses and gold."

"She is not for sale or trade, she is the only one who speaks our language among the white women and children, and we must have her to talk for us." Tomahas added, "If you try to take her, we will hunt you down and leave your bodies lying in the dirt like those two." He then pointed at the two dead men with a war club to intimidate them.

Chief Timothy was legendary for his courage and looked directly into Tomahas's eyes before saying, "We will not try and take her against your wishes. The Nez Perce and Cayuse were family long before you were born, and you should show respect. My people are many, and if anything should happen to us, they would ride here with vengeance in their hearts and turn your bones to ashes ... If anything happens to the Spalding girl, I will crush the life out of you myself."

Tomahas started to advance toward Timothy, who was drawing his knife when Chief Tiloukaikt grabbed Tomahas by the shoulder and stopped him, saying, "What you say is true; we have always lived in peace as brothers. The Spalding child stays here with us, but you can speak with her and leave in peace. This is not between the Cayuse and Nez Perce; it is between the Indian people and the Americans."

The two chiefs had been close for many years and shook hands. I had been watching from the house and could see that it was not a friendly exchange between Chief Timothy and Tomahas. I was too frightened to go near my dear friend Timothy while Tomahas was there. When the chiefs parted, Timothy and Eagle started for the house, and I darted out the door, jumping into Timothy's waiting arms. A look of horror came over his face as he saw that my dress was covered in blood. I immediately told him that the blood was Frank Sager's, not mine, that I was unharmed. He then spotted Mr. Bewley and Mr. Sales, who were completely unrecognizable.

Until that moment, with all of the horror, all of the killing and intimidation, I had not shed a single tear. It was as if a dam had broken loose, and I was drowning, gulping for air. To this day, tears come to my eyes when I recall that moment. Poor Timothy was as broken-hearted as I was as he used my apron to dry my eyes. I could see he was shaken, and his voice trembled as he told me not to worry. He promised that I would be free soon and live to see my family again. He once again held me tight and told me that everything would be all right. It was like being held in the arms of a guardian angel, as a flood of home swept through me. He told me, "Go ahead and cry, little one. I promise you will see your family again. Your Mother has sent us." He looked at the bodies lying outside the kitchen door and asked, "Is that how they killed them?"

When I could talk again, I told him, "It was horrible, they kept beating them after they were already dead. Poor Mrs. Whitman, they shot her twice and then hit her with their clubs and left her to die almost where we are standing. She and Mr. Rogers had laid in the yard that night crying for help in the freezing cold. The next morning, they were dead."

As Timothy pulled back, he could see that my dress was covered in blood and asked, "Have you been hurt or mistreated?"

"No. Some of the other women were, but they haven't hurt me."

When I calmed down, I told him what had happened, how the women had dragged Doctor Whitman and John from the kitchen into the living room. How they had us all line up along the walls. How the doctor was barely alive since Tomahas had repeatedly hit him in the head with his tomahawk, and how he had shot John and cut his throat. They then smashed them with a club and tomahawk until they were dead. I was standing behind Frank when Joe Lewis pulled his head back and shot him in the neck.

Timothy pulled me in tight and let me cry myself out, wondering what would become of my mind and spirit after experiencing something so horrible.

He then asked, "Where is your father?"

I told him, "I don't know. He went with Doctor Whitman to the Cayuse village the day before this happened but fell from his horse and planned to stay with Chief Stickus until he could ride again. They've been searching for him this whole time, but I don't think they have found him. I overheard one of the men say that they thought he might have drowned. He must be on foot if he's alive … have you come to take me home?"

"Your mother sent us to bring you back, but they will not let you leave."

Once again, I started crying until my body began shaking. I felt warm drops falling from Chief Timothy's face, and as our tears mixed together, it was hard to tell whose were whose.

When I calmed again, he told me, "You are not to worry, little one, they have no intention of hurting any of the women or children. They plan to trade you with the people at Fort Walla Walla, and I have told them that if they hurt you, they hurt me."

I continued to tell him all that I had seen, and how Joe Lewis had gone through everyone's possessions and taken off with all of the money and valuables he could carry. Timothy told me about Mr. Canfield and asked me to tell his wife and children that he was alive and recovering from his wound.

I then told him about Tashe. "One of the men from Chief Five Crows has taken Tashe from me and says she now belongs to the chief. Would you please try and get her back for me? She must be scared to death?"

"I will do what I can, but for now, you must be brave like your mother and strong like your father until we can return for you. I feel that your father's spirit is still alive, and I promise I will come back for you, and then we will see about Tashe."

He knew it was time to leave and gently set me down and said goodbye. I wanted to believe him, but with what I had seen, I knew that no one was safe here, that we could all be killed at any time for any reason. However, I needed something to hold on to, and Chief Timothy's words of hope were all I had left at that point.

As I watched them ride off, I felt as if my entire world was collapsing from the outside in. No matter how hard I tried to hold on to his promise, I couldn't shake the feeling that it was the last time I would ever see him or my family again.

On December 8, little Helen Mars Meek died. She was the first child that the Whitmans had taken in and was dearly loved by everyone who knew her precious soul. That afternoon she was buried in the same grave with Mr. Sales and Crockett Bewley. Lorinda hadn't witnessed her brother's murder, but she had heard it and seen what was left of his body lying in the yard. She had been raped in front of everyone, abused and humiliated, and now she had to bury her brother in a shallow unmarked grave before being sent into another nightmare. It was as if she were sleepwalking through the ruins of her life. This time Mrs. Hayes gave a heartfelt and moving eulogy. The next day Mrs. Hayes' baby died of the measles ... she was now inconsolable.

Later that same day, the Young and Smith families were brought down from the mill. Mary Smith was 15 years old and had been at the school when the massacre happened, so she was the one who related all the details to them. Both families were from England with ties to the Hudson Bay Company and were told they would be left unharmed as long as they didn't try to escape.

On December 10, Mrs. Saunders and I went to the lodge of Nicholas Finley to beg for his help. Before we ever reached his lodge, five angry warriors on horseback surrounded us, pulled their weapons, and made threatening gestures. One of the old Indian women came running over, making a sign to cut our throats. Just then, Mrs. Saunders saw Chief Beardy walking across the yard and ran to him for help. I joined her, explaining what the men were threatening to do to us. He told the men to put their weapons away, that the men were all dead, and this woman and child had done them no harm, that their death would do no one honor. I could tell the warriors were still angry, and I expected them to defy him, but they slowly lowered their weapons and rode away. He told us not to go near any of the lodges again, to stay where we had been told, then escorted us back to the mansion house.

At almost the same time, Catherine and Matilda Sager had gone to the mission house to see if they could find any of their possessions. They found that everything had been destroyed or taken, and the cats were wandering through the house looking for something to eat. Later we saw one of the Indian men riding by using the world map as a horse blanket. It was the same one that Mrs. Whitman had taught us to explore the world with.

Catherine Sager was a lovely girl of 13, and unfortunately, she had been attracting the attention of many of the Indian men. That night after going out for water, the two guards who had been ordered to watch the mansion house confronted her. They were grabbing at her clothes and gesturing for her to take them off. She expected to have the same thing done to her that had happened to Lorinda Bewley. She then bolted for the room where I was translating stories to the younger children for old Chief Beardy. Frightened to death, she leaped into his arms and buried her head into his massive chest.

He was very old but still powerful and highly respected. When the young men broke into the room, he asked them what they were doing. They told him that it was none of his business, that they wanted the girl. He gently set Catherine aside and stood up face to face with the young men and told them that she was still too young, that they should be ashamed of themselves. He then told them that he would let Chief Tiloukaikt know that they were neglecting their duty as guards and needed to be severely punished. They quickly turned and walked back to their posts.

To show our gratitude, one of the women made him two peach pies that he completely devoured in minutes. He then rubbed his stomach and belched loudly, making everyone laugh for the first time since the massacre. As he was leaving, he told us to hide Catherine somewhere where the young men couldn't find her, so we prepared a place between the back of the bed and the wall that worked nicely. By the time Chief Beardy arrived back at his village, his stomach was bloated from overeating, and he was nauseous from the bumpy ride. When he reached his lodge, he doubled over and vomited until he almost choked. He assumed that he had been poisoned and planned to return to the mission the next morning and have his revenge. Fortunately, a trader visiting with his Indian wife explained that he had eaten too much too fast and that it was his own fault. When he realized what had happened, he broke out laughing and would never tire of telling the story to anyone who would listen.

About 2:00 that afternoon, we watched as an Indian rider and a spare horse approached the mission. The horse immediately caught my attention and sent my heart soaring. It was my beautiful Tashe. Just as quickly, it plummeted as I began to fear that Father might have been caught and killed. Why else would they have Tashe? When he had dismounted, I asked him what he was doing with Tashe and if he knew what had happened to my father. Reluctantly he told me that he was almost certain my father was dead by now, that they had not found him yet, but suspected that he had drowned.

Another glimmer of hope, since I knew there was no way he would have drowned.

Chief Tiloukaikt greeted the man and told us to get Miss Bewley. We did as we were told and brought her outside. He had me tell her that this man was sent from Chief Five Crows, that the chief was to be her husband. He told her that Tamsucky would be back soon and that she was safer with Five Crows. He also told her that she was to be his property, and he would do with her as he wished. She started crying and got down on her knees and begged not to be taken away, for Chief Tiloukaikt to protect her from Tamsucky.

He told her that it had already been decided, that she would have to go. When they ordered her to get on Tashe, she tried to run for the mission house. The man from Five Crows village easily caught her and tied her wrists. He then put her on the horse and tied her to it so that she couldn't escape. It was another heart-wrenching moment as she was forlornly led away in tears to yet another unknown terror.

When Tamsucky returned, he was furious that Miss Bewley had been taken away. However, he was well aware of how powerful Chief Five Crows was as a leader and knew that it would be more trouble than it was worth to try and get her back.

Later that afternoon, I was getting water when I heard Tamsucky boasting to a group of men that he had caught and killed Mr. Hall. Scalping was not uncommon among some Indian tribes, but this was the first I had heard of anyone from our missions being scalped. It was one of the most horrible tortures imaginable and was almost always done while the victim was still alive. I couldn't bring myself to tell Mrs. Hall what I had heard. I was afraid that she or her children would give up hope and decided to keep it to myself for the time being. There was always the possibility that Tamsucky was lying and had made it up. Shortly before sunset, I had to walk by the lodge where Tamsucky was staying to get wood, and when I saw a lance with a fresh scalp hanging from it, I knew it was true.

When Lorinda arrived at Fort Walla Walla, she was taken directly to the Catholic mission, where she was greeted coldly by Bishop Blanchett and Father Brouillet. After all she had been through, it was hard to imagine that she was at the start of yet another living hell.

She begged the priests not to send her to Five Crows, but they told her that it would be too dangerous for them not to do so, that she had to go. She then begged them to kill her so that she wouldn't have to endure that kind of torture and humiliation again. They told her that it would be a mortal sin for them to take her life and that if she did, she would dwell in the fires of hell forever. She screamed at the top of her voice that she was already in the fires of hell, and asked what kind of men would let this happen, then began weeping uncontrollably. When the two men showed up to take her to Five Crows, she became hysterical and tried to fight her way out of it. They eventually subdued her and once again tied her to Tashe and took her to Five Crows.

Chief Five Crows was about 45, a big swarthy man with a large belly and pocked face. He was dressed in a fancy English officer's uniform and told her that he was very rich and had many horses and cattle.

At first, he made an effort to be kind to her, telling her that she was not going to be harmed, that if she wished to return to the Catholic mission, she could do so, he would call on her tomorrow. She was revolted at the sight of him but greatly relieved that she would not have to endure another brutality. When she arrived back at the Catholic mission that night, she told them that he had been kind and had not forced himself on her.

When they came the next day, she willingly went with them, thinking that it would be a repeat of the previous night. After sharing food, he told her that he had been patient with her and wanted her to disrobe. She became upset and begged him not to make her take her clothes off. He became angry and told her that she was his property, and his women did as they were told. He then grabbed her and started fondling her private parts. When he finally grew tired of her struggling, he slapped her hard in the face and told the men to take her back to the mission. Before she left, he told her that tomorrow night she would be his woman, that if she struggled again, she would be severely beaten until she was willing to do as she was told.

When they came for her the next day, she once again begged for protection and told the priests what Five Crows had said and done to her the night before. They told her there was nothing they could do, and it would be better for all if she cooperated.

She screamed at them, "Cooperate ..."

At that point, she had given up not only the will to fight but the will to live. When they came for her, she offered no resistance, so they didn't bother to tie her up. It was as if Chief Five Crows was taking a dead person, and he became angry at her, slapping her over and over again. She didn't even respond to the hard slaps to the face. When she arrived back at the Catholic Mission later that night, the five priests were gathered together having a late meal.

Father Blanchet sneered at her and asked, "How did you like your new husband?"

She exploded and yelled, "How would you like it if that beast took you into his lodge and ripped you open with that filthy thing? What if that animal puts his bastard inside of me ...? You are even worse than he is, you sniveling coward." At that point, the Bishop stood up and told her to shut up, or he was going to have her gagged and lashed.

She told him, "Go ahead, but if you do, I will show Five Crows what you have done, and he will slit your throats and hang your scalps from his lodge." That shocked them speechless.

With tears of anger and outrage, she continued, "I was a virgin before Tamsucky took me in front of the entire mission. What kind

574

of man is going to want me now? Can you with your cold-blooded hearts even begin to understand what I must feel like or what I have been through … and you have the gall to ask me how I liked my new husband."

She wept alone that night until there were no tears left, then stared at the ceiling in a state of shock and fear until the sun rose on another day of torment.

Each day was the same for almost two weeks. She was abducted, molested, and slapped around for her lack of enthusiasm. The priests tried to stay clear of her so that they wouldn't have to endure her wrath or the threat of retribution from Chief Five Crows.

On the night of December 13, Chief Tiloukaikt called us all to the main room of the mansion house and told us that for the time being, only the two oldest girls, Mary Smith, 15, and Susan Kimball, 16, were to choose husbands. They were frightened, speechless, and unable to make a choice. The chief asked the two young men who they wanted. Clark Tiloukaikt picked Mary Smith, the other man whom Mrs. Whitman had given the name Frank chose Susan Kimball. Since they would not go willingly, they were dragged off like Miss Bewley. We could hear their cries for help as they disappeared into the darkness. To add to the horror, it was Frank who had killed Susan's father, Mr. Kimball, right in front of her.

When he shot Mr. Kimball, he turned to Susan and said, "See how easy I make these Americans fall."

Not long after that, a young brave named Istulest barged into the room where 13–year-old Catherine Sager was sewing shirts for the Indians. He picked her up and threw her over his shoulder, and began walking toward the front yard. Nicholas Finley heard

Catherine yelling for help and stopped Istulest, telling him to put her down. He told him that he must have the chief's permission to take her, or he would be severely punished. Istulest put her down and got right into Nicholas's face. He told him that he would talk with the chief and then be back for his wife, that it was none of his business, and he would settle with him later. Nicholas took Catherine into the house and told the women to hide her well, that Istulest would be back. Nicholas was neither frightened nor intimidated. Three fourths Indian, he was married to the daughter of a Cayuse chief and highly respected as one of the most fearless hunters and warriors in the Territory.

When Istulest found Chief Tiloukaikt, he told him he wanted Catherine for his wife and what he planned to do to Nicholas. The chief told him that she was still a girl, not a woman, and had not had her first moon. He also told him that Nicholas was a legendary warrior who had single-handedly killed a full-grown bear with nothing more than a knife and would surely make quick work of him if he demanded a fight. We had no more trouble with Istulest.

We had seen two different men come to the mission over the last several days. One was a Frenchman I had seen at Fort Walla Walla; the other was an Indian man I had never seen before. When I saw Nicholas, I thanked him for helping Catherine and casually asked if he knew who the men were. At first, he told me that he shouldn't talk with me, that the incident with Catherine had given him several new enemies to contend with. I told him that I was sorry if we had caused him trouble, that we would always be grateful for his kindness.

I had grown so weak from lack of sleep and being in such a nervous condition that I was beginning to have trouble walking. At one point in our conversation, I went blank and started to fall. The next thing I knew, he was at my side holding me up. Mr. Finley said that he shouldn't tell me, but those men brought a message from Mr. Ogden that a ransom was being worked on. He also told me that he knew about the planning of the massacre but had taken no part in the killing. Mrs. Whitman was not supposed to have been harmed; that was the fault of Joe Lewis. He told me that if I would keep it quiet, he would try to let me know how things were progressing. He knew that I wanted to hug him, so he put his hand up to stop me.

Mr. Finley looked me directly in the eyes and said, "I am sorry for what has happened; the women and children were never supposed to be harmed."

I thanked him and started back to the mansion house. I didn't know what to do. I wanted to tell someone, but I didn't want to risk our chance of being set free or Mr. Finley's confidence. This was the first spark of real hope that I had felt since this had begun. I never really expected to survive.

Chapter 7

The Trade

We didn't know it at the time, but on December 15, 1848, Mr. Ogden arrived at the Dalles with three small boats full of goods to trade for our lives. The men who had come to the mission were carrying messages from Mr. Ogden and replies from Chief Tiloukaikt. One thing Mr. Ogden made clear is that if anyone else were killed, there would be no trade. If anyone else were harmed, an army of over a thousand well-trained and heavily armed soldiers and volunteers would be coming to take revenge for the women and children. He also made it clear that all captives were to be returned, that none of the women or children were to be taken as slaves or wives.

Frank Escaloon returned Susan Kimball. Five Crows agreed to release Lorinda Bewley for a price. Clark Tiloukaikt was challenging his father by telling him he would not release Mary Smith now that he had taken her as his wife.

On December 19, Mr. Ogden reached Fort Walla Walla, and on the 20th, he sent a message demanding a meeting at the fort with the leaders. In reply, the Cayuse sent back a list of demands.

Because of his reputation, Mr. Ogden was one of only two men in the Oregon Territory who could have possibly arranged this meeting, Doctor McLaughlin being the other.

Mr. Ogden had been trading with the Indian tribes of the Oregon Territory for almost 30 years, and in all of those years, he had been fair and never had a violent confrontation with either the Cayuse or Nez Perce. He could be a fierce man who was said to have killed several men in physical fights, which gained him great respect as a warrior among the Indian people. He was also respected as one of the greatest explorers of his time and married to a Nez Perce woman named Julia Reava.

A lesser man in the eyes of the Cayuse would have never been acceptable to negotiate. The Cayuse chiefs agreed to the meeting as long as he would agree to their demands. Here is the list they sent to Mr. Ogden.

1st. "That the Americans may not make war with the Cayuses.

2nd. That they may forget the lately committed murders, as the Cayuses will forget the murder of the son of the great Chief of Walla Walla, committed in California.

3rd. That two or three great men may come up to conclude peace.

4th. That as soon as these great men have arrived and concluded peace, they may take with them all the women and children.

5th. We give assurance that we will not harm the Americans before the arrival of these three great men.

6th. We ask that the Americans may not travel any more through our country as our young men might do them harm."

Place of Tawatoe, Youmatilla

December 20, 1847

Names of the Chiefs: Tiloukaikt, Camaspolo, Tawatoe, and Achekaia.

Signed, L.P. Rosseau, D. and G. Leclaire, S.D, witnesses."

They received their reply from Mr. Ogden the next day that their demands would be met. It was agreed by all that there would be a meeting on December 23, to go over the details of the release. The evening of the 22nd, Chief Tiloukaikt called all of us together in the main room and told us that we would be ransomed and set free. He told us that there was a meeting the next day to go over the details and set a specific date.

It was as if we were awakened from a horrific nightmare, and tears of joy flowed freely as everyone embraced. We had been through a terrible ordeal together, and there was finally a sense of relief. We were still apprehensive, but knowing Mr. Ogden was in charge gave us a much stronger sense of optimism.

On the morning of December 23, something happened that once again put us all in fear for our lives. It was the day of the meeting, and instead of a peaceful tribal group preparing for council, all of the Cayuse were decorating themselves and their horses with war paint. They began circling the compound, yelling and gesturing in a threatening manner with their weapons. We thought that something must have gone wrong and that they were preparing for war. I found Nicholas Finley and asked if he knew what was going on. He told me that this is the way Indians prepare for a council. They believe that showing strength will be to their advantage when negotiating. If things go badly, they would be prepared for battle. When I told the others, there was a collective sigh of relief. We then watched as the party left at full speed for the meeting at Fort Walla Walla, each of us saying a silent prayer.

The council consisted of Mr. Ogden, five men from the Hudson Bay Company, Mr. Osborne, 15 Cayuse chiefs and their sons, Bishop Blanchet, Father Brouillet, two Oblate priests, and an interpreter. Mr. Ogden was a no-nonsense man who demanded respect and got it. When he stepped to the center of the room, he looked directly at Chief Tiloukiakt and the other chiefs and gave them this address.

"To the most influential chiefs, on behalf of the American families kept as hostages and prisoners by them. I regret to observe that all the chiefs I asked for are not present, two being absent. I expect the words I am addressing you will be repeated to them, and your young men on your return to your camp. It is now 30 years we have been among you; during this long period, we have never had an instance of blood being spilt until the inhuman massacre, which has so recently taken place. We are traders and a different nation to the Americans, but recollect we supply you with ammunition not to kill the Americans. They are of the same color as ourselves, speak the same language, children of the same God—and humanity makes our hearts bleed when we behold you using them so cruelly! Besides this revolting butchery, have, not the Indians pillaged, ill-treated the Americans and insulted their women when peaceably making their way to the Willamette? As chiefs, ought you to have connived at such conduct on the part of your young men? Was it not rather your duty to use your influence to prevent it? You tell me the young men committed these deeds without your knowledge. Why do we call you Chiefs? If you have no control over your young men, if you allow them to govern you; you are a set of Hermaphrodites, and unworthy of the appellation of men of Chiefs. You young hotheaded men, I know that you pride yourselves upon your bravery and think no one can match you. Do not deceive yourselves. If you get the Americans to commence once, you will repent it, and war will not end until every man of you is cut off from the face of the earth.

I am aware that many of your friends and relations have died through sickness; the Indians of other places have shared the same fate. It is not Doctor Whitman that has poisoned them, but God has commanded they should die. We are weak mortals and must submit, and trust you will avail yourselves of the opportunity, and in so doing it may prove advantageous to you but at the same time, remember you alone will be responsible for the consequences. It is merely advice I give you. I hold forth no promise should war be declared against you. We have nothing to do with it. I have not come here to make you promises or hold out your quarrels. We remain neutral. On my return, if you wish it, I shall do all I can for you, but I do not promise you, to prevent war. If you deliver me up all the prisoners, I shall pay you for them on their being delivered, but let it not be said among you afterward that I deceived you. Mr. Douglas and I represent the Company, but I tell you once more we promise you nothing. We sympathize with these poor people and wish to return them to their friends and relations by paying you for them. My requests on behalf of the families concerns you, so decide for the best. Deliver me the prisoners to return to their friends and families, and I will pay you a ransom. That is all."

"Tiloukaikt replied, "I have listened to your words. Young men do not forget them. As for war, we have seen little of it, but our fathers know something of it. We know the whites to be our best friends who have all along prevented us killing one another; that is the reason why we avoid getting into a war with them and why we do not wish to be separated from them. Besides the tie of blood, the whites have shown us convincing proof of their attachment to us by burying their dead alongside ours. Chief! Your words are weighty—

582

your hairs are gray! We have known you a long time. You have had an unpleasant trip to this place. I cannot, therefore, keep these families back; I make them over to you, which I would not do to another younger than yourself."

It was agreed among the council participants that the Cayuse would start making preparations to deliver the hostages as soon as they returned. Mr. Ogden immediately sent a message to Father telling him that we were to be released from the mission on the 29th and should arrive at Fort Walla Walla on or about the 30th of December. Father and Mother were overjoyed when they received the news. They were still concerned about an attack from a rogue Cayuse or Umatilla party, so they asked Chief Timothy if he would accompany them. The chief was also overjoyed, especially since he had given me his word that I would see my family again. He told Father that he would accompany our family to Fort Vancouver, and he would bring 50 of his bravest men. Father immediately replied to Mr. Ogden that they would be accompanied by Chief Timothy and should arrive on January 1. He warned Mr. Ogden that Chief Timothy had heard that the Cayuse would kill the women and children if they found that any American soldiers were coming to make war on them.

That evening two young women, Mary Smith, and Lorinda Bewley, were returned to the mission. Miss Bewley had fallen off her horse on the way and was badly cut and bruised. When Catherine Sager tried to console her, Lorinda said that she didn't care what happened to her any longer, that she had been disgraced, and no good man would ever want her for a wife and mother of his children. Just then, Tamsucky burst into the room, and when he saw her, he tried to take hold of her, telling everyone that he was taking her to be his wife. She was so despondent that she didn't even react. At the same time, Clark Tiloukaikt stepped forward, demanding to take Mary Smith with him since he considered them to be man and wife, that she was now his property.

Chief Tiloukaikt told them that they could not take the women and that Mr. Ogden had promised guns, ammunition, tobacco, and other goods for them. He told them that if they took the women, many of their people would die, that the Americans would send an army of thousands to wipe their people from the earth. He paused for a long time, then looked at each of them in turn. It is our way to take the women we want after battle, but this was no battle. I will offer you something in exchange for the women. Each of you will receive one of the new guns, 50 rounds of ammunition, one pound of tobacco, one shirt, one blanket, and one flint in exchange.

Both men were in an awkward position, and the chief was giving them a way out. No one would stop them from taking the women, but if the Americans attacked the tribes, they knew they would be killed for their selfishness and their families dishonored.

After several tense moments, Tamsucky looked at the chief and said, "It is a good trade."

Clark knew he must obey his father to have peace, so he agreed.

Chief Tiloukaikt told us that we would be leaving on the morning of December 29. Few of us had anything to pack beyond our dirty and torn clothes, but even putting ribbons and combs into pillowcases made it seem real. We were far too excited to sleep, so we spent the rest of the night talking about what it would be like to have our lives back again.

I would, later in life, find it ironic that we Americans considered the Cayuse savages for having abused us and used us as slaves and hostages; yet, in the south, white Americans had been doing the same if not worse for over 100 years. For us there was at least a glimmer of hope that we would be traded and released. African slaves lived and died without the slightest hope of freedom, and I can't help but wonder if we will ever learn to live together in peace as human beings?

On the morning of December 29, we climbed aboard the two wagons Mr. Stanfield had prepared for us. Four oxen drew each, and Mr. Smith was driving the other wagon. Our last look back was painful. The once beautifully kept grounds thriving with so much activity and life was now void and littered with broken doors and windows, scraps of papers, books, broken lamps, and pottery. The stove had been hauled out of the kitchen door and was lying on its side in the mud. Things that were so precious to us were now just pieces of our broken hearts. As we pulled away, several young warriors approached the main house with torches and set it on fire. We watched it slowly catch and then turn into a raging inferno. It was the last sad image I would have of the once-thriving Whitman home and mission.

We had only gone a short distance when an old Indian woman stepped out of her lodge and warned us to hurry, that she had heard talk of an angry group of Cayuse and Umatilla still set on killing us before we reached the Fort. I was the only one among the captives who understood the warning and told the drivers what she had said, that we needed to hurry.

We slept that night pressed together in the wagons for warmth and awoke the next morning to a beautiful sunrise glimmering behind the Blue Mountain summit.

About noon, we had to cross the Touchet River at the same spot where my parents and the Whitmans had first crossed it 11 years ago to establish the missions.

Knowing that our lives were still in jeopardy, it seemed to me that the oxen were intentionally walking as slowly as they could, as if dragging a house behind them.

We arrived about two hours later on December 30 and were received by Mr. Ogden. He gently lifted me from the wagon like a father would and said, "Thank God I have you safe at last; I had to pay more for you and Miss Bewley than all of the other captives combined. I never thought they would give either of you up."

Mr. Ogden had successfully traded our 49 lives for 62 blankets, 63 cotton shirts, 12 Hudson Bay rifles, 600 loads of ammunition, seven pounds of tobacco, and 12 flints.

He told us to be very careful what we said at the Fort, that it had ears, and the Indians were looking and listening for any indication that there might be American soldiers coming to make war on them. Father and Mother were expected within the next day or two, and we were all told to stay in readiness since we would be departing the morning after they arrived. I felt anxious about my family since I knew there was a band of Cayuse still looking for them. I also knew I wouldn't sleep soundly or breathe easily until I was once again in their arms.

Chapter 8

Dear God, Thank You

Dear God, thank you! Mr. Ogden had brought me a chair, and I had waited almost every minute atop the lookout of the fort for the arrival of my family. It felt as if there was no room left in my soul for another heartbreak. Finally, in the distance, I could see dust rising, then a wagon and large group of Indians approaching the fort. As they got closer, I could see the bonnets of mother and my little sisters.

It was dry, but very cold out, and Martha and Amelia were both wrapped in thick robes. Mother, Father, Henry, Martha, all waved madly as they saw me on the lookout. I could also make out Eagle, faithful Timothy, and 50 or more Nez Perce warriors.

I was still very weak, but I leapt into Father's open arms. There were hundreds of hugs, kisses, and tears. Mother then wrapped me in her arms, and I knew I was home. She held me at arm's length and asked where the girl was that she had sent to the Whitman Mission over a month ago, that I was nothing more than skin and bones.

Tears came to her eyes as she pulled me into her arms and whispered in my ear, "I thought I had lost you."

There was so much to say, but Mr. Ogden came up and greeted my parents, telling them that it was important we ready ourselves to leave first thing tomorrow morning. He had heard rumors that one of the Cayuse bands was still looking for Father and had vowed to kill him. Father told Mr. Ogden that they had been trailed by a party of 20 or more Cayuse men who were unwilling to confront so many Nez Perce warriors. There were mostly tears of joy until I saw Mrs. Canfield looking for her husband and realized that Uncle Horace and Mr. Jackson were also missing.

When Mrs. Canfield finally realized that her husband was not with them, she approached Mother and Father and asked, "Where is my husband? I had heard he made it safely to Lapwai?"

Before they could answer, I asked, "Where are Uncle Horace and Mr. Jackson?"

I could see that Mother was troubled as she told us that Mr. Canfield, Uncle Horace, and Mr. Jackson felt that their lives were in danger even amongst the Nez Perce, and they had decided to return over the mountains. They hoped to find help from the U.S. Army somewhere between Fort Laramie and Independence.

"They will never make it over the mountains in winter," said Mrs. Canfield.

Mr. Ogden told her, "No, I don't think they can. Once they see what they're up against, I believe they'll turn back before they freeze or starve to death."

This was of little consolation for either Mrs. Canfield, or my family, and all we could do was pray that they would return to us safely. Otherwise, there was an overall feeling of joy and celebration at having survived and been set free.

Miss Bewley didn't want to talk about her experience with Chief Five Crows, but she did tell us how cowardly the priests had been and the revolting remarks they had made to her. While she was talking with Mother and Father, she was pointing at Bishop Blanchet and Father Brouillet, who were talking with Mr. Ogden.

You could slice the tension between them with a knife. The priests seemed to be doing everything they could to avoid eye contact with her. When Miss Bewley finally broke down and began to cry, Mother took her in her arms and comforted her.

Father and Mother had brought what they felt was absolutely necessary, but Mr. Ogden told them they would have to leave everything behind. He offered to store their meager belongings at Fort Walla Walla until they could be shipped sometime in the future. They would leave behind 11 years of backbreaking work along with the hope of continuing their mission with the Nez Perce.

Lapwai had been the most successful mission in the Northwest in every way, accomplishing what they had been sent to do by the missionary board. It was by far the most industrious venture among all of the missions on the entire West Coast. The Whitmans had failed. Father had baptized over three hundred Nez Perce while at Lapwai, and the Whitmans had not had a single conversion among the Cayuse. Father would convert over a thousand more souls in the future and lay the groundwork for Protestant churches throughout the entire Northwest.

We left behind 11 buildings, including a blacksmith shop, gristmill, lumber mill, two schoolrooms, student dormitory, spinning and weaving shop, meeting house and church, poultry room, storeroom and granary, two print shops, 44 acres of cultivated land including various fruit orchards with 56 apple trees, 110 head of cattle, 39 horses, 34 hogs, six oxen, chickens, turkeys, geese, two wagons, one carriage, one loom, two spinning wheels, and all household items and goods.

Unlike the Whitman mission that often had as many as 20 or more workers at any given time, almost all of the work over the past ten years had been done by my father and mother with occasional helpers. Unlike the Whitmans, we had also left behind true friends amongst the Nez Perce who would carry on the practices and traditions of Christianity.

This is hard for me to say because I loved Narcissa, but I also loved the Indian people and disliked the way she had treated them. Their dislike for her, combined with the blame they placed on Doctor Whitman for bringing so many white people and their diseases to their land, were certainly contributing factors to the massacre.

I don't believe Narcissa was ever willing to understand the Indian people, and instead, she judged them relative to her own culture. I had often heard her refer to them as dirty, lazy, rude, and unreliable savages.

In 1849, Reverend H.K.W. Perkins, who knew the Whitmans well, was asked by Narcissa's sister Jane how the Indian people could do this to those "who had done so much for them?"

He very politely replied, "The truth is, Miss Prentiss, your lamented sister, was far from happy in the situation she had chosen to occupy ... I should say, unhesitatingly, that both herself and husband were out of their proper sphere. They were not adapted to their work. They could not possibly interest and gain the affections of the natives. I know for a long time before the tragedy that closed their final career that many of the natives around them looked upon them suspiciously. Though they feared the doctor, they did not love him. They did not love your sister. They appreciated neither the one nor the other."

As we made our way to the dock, Mother and Father were not thrilled about traveling on the Sabbath, but it was not a choice they could make. Mr. Ogden hadn't slept in over 48 hours when he gave the order for us to board the waiting boats. We all hurried down the grassy bank and loaded into the boats. The Nez Perce had decided to follow us along the riverbank until they felt that we were safe.

It seemed there was no end to the heartbreaks. Once we were loaded in the boats, a count was made to make sure everyone was accounted for. We cast off and were no more than 50 yards from shore when we heard the cries of little eight-year-old David Malin. He was standing near the dock struggling with one of the priests who was holding him by the collar. Several of us turned to Mr. Ogden and told him that we needed to go back, that we had left little David behind. At first, Mr. Ogden was slow to react, then looking very somber, he put his hands up to quiet us. In the meantime, David was becoming more hysterical, crying, and begging us to come back for him. Mr. Ogden told us that with all we had been through, no one wanted to take him, that the future was too uncertain. He told us that the priests had offered to take him in and care for him.

Lorinda Bewley was sitting close to me when she stood up and told Mr. Ogden to go back, that David was a quiet and sweet boy, that the priests would abuse and destroy him, that she would take him in. He paused for a long time ... then told her that he was sorry, there was no turning back.

David then broke loose and jumped into the water. As he was attempting to swim to us, one of the soldiers jumped in fully dressed and pulled him back to shore. I buried my face in Father's coat and asked why we couldn't take him. He told me that we had lost everything, Mother was ill, and he had no idea where we were going or what we were going to do. We would already be caring for one of the Sager girls and Miss Johnson, and that was as much as we could handle.

The last image I have of David was Bishop Blanchet grabbing him by the neck and pulling him off the bank toward the fort. To my knowledge, no one has ever seen or heard from him again, and as he was dragged away, I couldn't help but fear that he had seen his last happy day in this world.

We had only been on our way for less than an hour when a party of 25 or more Cayuse came upon us at a bend in the river with bows, arrows, and guns drawn.

The Nez Perce were traveling slightly ahead of us, and when they heard the commotion, they quickly doubled back. It was none other than Tamsucky who was leading the Cayuse.

Mr. Ogden told him to lower their weapons, that if they fired on them, they would be declaring war on the British as well as the Americans. Just then, Timothy and his party arrived with weapons drawn. Tamsucky told him that this was none of his affair, if anything, he should join them. Chief Timothy told him that we were all under his protection and to lower his weapons. Tamsucky replied that he did not care about the women and children, that he only wanted Spalding. Timothy told him that Father was his friend, that he would not be taken without bloodshed. He then pointed his rifle at Tamsucky and told him that he would be the first to go. Tamsucky threatened that this would not be the end, turned his horse, and led his war party away, shooting their guns in the air and yelling at the top of their voices.

Chief Timothy and his warriors stayed with us until we reached The Dalles where there was a large group of volunteers and soldiers to protect us. Several family members and friends who had been awaiting our arrival joined us for the rest of the trip to Fort Vancouver. Mr. Ogden let our family go ashore for a short time to say goodbye to Timothy and the other Nez Perce. Timothy had been a wise and loyal friend, and the thought of never seeing him again hurt me deeply. He held me for a long time before whispering, "I promised you would see your family again, and I promise we will see each other again."

Mother and Father then finished saying goodbye to Timothy and thanking him for all he had done, promising to do all they could to return. They then said goodbye to the other Nez Perce and thanked them for their friendship and protection. Mr. Ogden was busy talking with Colonel Lee, who had agreed to escort us to Fort Vancouver with 30 volunteers. Mr. Ogden advised him to be prepared for an attack but not to go on the offensive since they had no idea how many Cayuse were nearby, and he didn't want to start a war.

The rest of the way, we traveled by day and camped at night. It was cold, wet, and windy. We had little in the way of warm clothing or blankets and often had to climb under the canvas boat cover to keep from getting soaked. Father and Mr. John Mix Stanley were asked to care for the Sager girls and try to make them as comfortable as possible. We had to make two difficult portages, one at the Deschutes, and one at the Cascades. At one point, we had to carry the boats and possessions for several miles and then lower them down a dangerous and steep cliff face. Mr. Ogden was taking no chances and had a dozen riflemen watching at all times for any sign of danger.

A party coming from Fort Vancouver met us at the Cascades, and though it seemed unimaginable, there was more bad news for Miss Bewley. One of the men removed his hat and told her that he was very sorry to tell her that her father had died. She dropped to the ground and wept ... Mr. Ogden had to carry her back to the boat where several of the women held her and stayed with her for the remainder of the journey. Now there was only her mother, two brothers, and little sister left, and she must have wondered if she would ever see them again and how they would survive.

We arrived at Fort Vancouver about noon on Saturday, January 8, 1848, and were warmly received by Mr. Douglas. He told us that he couldn't imagine what we had been through, but we were now safe, and there was plenty of food, clothing, and cabins where we would be warm and comfortable. The families were taken to houses along the river that had been prepared with warm fires and food. Families at the fort took in the women and children who had no one to care for them. On Monday, we all departed with Mr. Ogden for Oregon City. For some, it would be the end of their journey; for us, it was a stepping stone to the next phase of our lives.

When we reached Portland, 50 or more volunteers were camped along the river waiting for us to arrive. As we drew close to the shore, they gave us a salute with their guns and three cheers. When we docked, Miss Bewley's family came running to greet her. For the past month, her life had been one horrible event after another, and we all took great comfort in seeing her wrapped in the embrace of her mother's arms. General Gilliam came forward and embraced each of the Sager girls who he had helped care for after their parents had died on the Oregon Trail. Mr. Stanley continued to provide for the Sagers for some time, making sure that they found homes and were properly clothed and fed. They would never forget his kindness. This was Miss Bewley's final stop with us, and I remember asking God to please be kind to her after all she had been through.

We arrived later that day in Oregon City, the final destination for some of the survivors. Governor Abernethy greeted everyone warmly, showing us the greatest sympathy and respect. Mr. Ogden needed to return to Fort Vancouver, so it was time to say goodbye.

It would not be possible to give enough credit to Mr. Ogden. Any lesser man would not have been able to accomplish what he had. He is a man of great courage and integrity, and we owe him a debt of gratitude that can never be repaid. He risked his life for ours and never flinched in the face of danger. He is a force of nature to be reckoned with, and I hope with all my heart that he is repaid tenfold here on earth as well as in heaven.

As we departed, every person that had been held captive, as well as family and friends, embraced or shook his hand and gave Mr. Ogden our most sincere gratitude. As powerful as he was in personality, he was also a very humble man.

As we gathered by the dock, he told us this. "I was acting as an agent for the Hudson Bay Company, and your thanks are due to them. Without their aid and influence, nothing could have been affected, and to them, the praise is due. Please allow me to add, should, unfortunately, which God avert, our services be required under similar circumstances, I trust you will not find us wanting in going to your relief."

Mr. Ogden's memory will always be deeply revered among those of us who owe him our lives. Credit must also be given to the Hudson Bay Company. The expense of men, time, and goods was considerable; it was never charged to the missionaries and was incurred entirely by the Hudson Bay Trading Company.

We were then led to temporary quarters until decisions were made as to where we would go and what we would do.

In Oregon City, I was shown an article that had been printed in the Oregon Lyceum.

"What the Spaldings and other survivors did can never be overstated. The bravery shown by ten-year-old Eliza Spalding is an example of the unimaginable courage and heroism that children of any age are capable under the most horrific conditions. Henry Spalding's will to survive to reach his family exemplifies the breadth of the human spirit; courage, commitment, determination, fortitude, and the power of love."

Not all of those guilty of taking part in the massacre are known, but here is a partial list of those who were:

Chief Tiloukaikt, also known as "Crawfish That Walks Forward."

Tamsucky, also known as "Feather Cap."

Tomahas, also known as "The Murderer."

Clark, son of Chief Tiloukaikt.

Edward, son of Chief Tiloukaikt.

Wai-e-Cat, son of Tamsucky, also known as "One That Flies."

Cupup-Cupup, also known as "Green Cap, and Wet Wolf."

Frank Escaloom, also known as "Ish-al-hal, and Ish-ish-kais-kais."

Kiamasumkin, also known as "Panther's Coat, and Left Hand."

Joe Lewis, the French-Canadian and Indian instigator of the Whitman Massacre.

I believe my spirit was damaged in ways I will probably never fully understand, but I have learned to forgive the men who took part in the massacre. What we find acceptable and what Indian people find acceptable are two very different things, and like seeds that fall from the trees, that is how we grow.

As I have aged, the words of Chief Beardy constantly come back to me, "They believed they were doing what was needed to save their people."

I have also grown to understand how deep the differences are between us and how much we could have learned from the Indian people if we had not been so prejudiced.

To them, the land and The People are one and the same; they are who they are because the land taught them how to live. When I asked Chief Beardy how the massacre could have ever happened, he told me that it was inevitable, and he was surprised that it had taken so long.

The Spalding Mission

Reverend Henry H. Spalding

1803-1874

Eliza Hart Spalding

1807-1851

Eliza Spalding Warren

1837-1919

Henry Hart Spalding

1839-1898

Martha Jane Spalding Wigle

1845-1924

Amelia Lorene Spalding Brown

1846–1889

Marcus Whitman

1802-1847

Narcissa Prentiss Whitman

1808-1847

Eliza

Part Five

Epilogue

"As I am now far advanced in years, I realize that the setting sun of my life is not far distant, and yet once more I have a yearning to see all that is left of those old friends and pioneers. Let me say right here that I do not think the pioneer women have ever had their praise and credit that is due them for their part in making this great northwestern country what it is.

Believing that we will meet with understanding in the new country across the great divide, I bid you greeting and God-speed."

Eliza Spalding Warren

Chapter 1

The Cayuse War

The Cayuse war was in direct response to the Whitman massacre. In January of 1848, after I had been released along with the other captives, a force of over 500 militia was sent to march against the Cayuse and other tribes in that region. A 49-year-old veteran of the Blackhawk and Seminole Wars named Colonel Cornelius Gilliam was chosen to lead them. A minister for the Freewill Baptist Church, he was known to be a belligerent, impulsive, and narrow-minded man.

Colonel Gilliam hated all Indians and was calling for a complete genocide of all nations. He was also dead set on preventing any success in arranging peaceful negotiations. Colonel Gilliam began his violent campaign against the Indian people when his company of one hundred and 30 men came across a small group of Sahaptin Indians who had absolutely nothing to do with the Whitman Massacre. He ordered his second in command, Major Lee, and a small detachment of men to pursue them. They killed one man, took two Indian women and over a dozen horses. On the way back to the main body, Major Lee's party was attacked in a narrow canyon. Though no Americans were injured or killed, Colonel Gilliam decided to send his entire force against the Sahaptin Indians, killing between 20 and 30 men. He then destroyed the Sahaptin village, taking all of their horses and cattle.

On February 24, 1848, a conflict known as the Battle of Sand Hollows took place. The Indian warriors had chosen an area where the depressions in the sand created natural rifle pits. The tribes consisted primarily of Cayuse and Umatilla, but several Palouse and Walla Walla groups were also involved. Chiefs Five Crows and Grey Eagle were in command and hoped that by winning the fight, they could coerce the Nez Perce, Spokane, and Yakima tribes into joining them.

One of the Indian warriors shot a dog of the advancing Americans, giving Colonel Gilliam the opportunity he was looking for to open fire and charge straight ahead.

Tom McKay and a group of veteran trappers had been enlisted primarily to guide the troops through country unknown to Colonel Gilliam. A small band of Indians made the mistake of riding directly at Mr. McKay's sharpshooter unit, made up of some of the finest marksmen on earth. Grey Eagle a powerful shaman and chief, advanced on him as if his medicine was powerful enough to stop bullets. Tom McKay shot him right between the eyes, and Grey Eagle was dead before he hit the ground.

Mr. McKay had known Hezekiah for many years, one of Father's converts, and a loyal member of the Cayuse tribe. When he saw Hezekiah coming, he decided not to kill him, but wounded him in the arm, sparing his life. Five Crows was badly wounded in the stomach but would survive the battle.

The Americans continued to drive forward, firing at will and forcing the Indians to scatter into the hills. After a time, the Cayuse regrouped and began charging at the American soldiers. The fighting went on for several hours, in which five Americans were wounded, including Lieutenant-Colonel Waters. Eight Cayuse were killed that day.

Tom McKay could have taken many more lives had he wanted, but was having doubts about serving for a man like Colonel Gilliam. He knew many of the Cayuse chiefs and warriors personally and decided to become an observer rather than participant as long as his men's lives were not in jeopardy.

The fighting continued the next day, but with far less intensity. Each side was content with harassing each other from a distance. The Cayuse warriors soon felt it was pointless to keep riding close by the American camp and exposing themselves to make their desire to end the battle known. Under a white flag, they got a message to Colonel Gilliam that they wanted peace talks. Gilliam responded by telling them that he would continue moving forward until his troops reached the Umatilla River and that the Indians could either back down or fight. The Cayuse continued to harass the troops until that evening when the Americans reached the Umatilla River. The next day the army crossed the river as the Cayuse watched from a safe distance.

On March 14, a fight took place known as the Battle of Touchet River. The Cayuse had stolen a large herd of cattle belonging to the settlers, and Colonel Gilliam set out after them with a force of approximately three hundred men. At the Tucannon River, they came upon a camp of some four hundred Indians. An old man slowly came across the river under a white flag. He told Colonel Gilliam that he was Chief Peopeomoxmox of the Walla Walla tribe, loyal to the Americans. He also told Colonel Gilliam that the ones they were looking for were further down river and led by Chief Tiloukaikt, the leader most wanted for the Whitman Massacre.

When Colonel Gilliam's force went after Chief Tiloukaikt's party, all four hundred Walla Walla warriors turned on them and attacked the Americans from behind. The battle raged on for two days, and though the American volunteers were outnumbered, they managed to ward off the attacks coming from all sides. That night was nerve-wracking for the Americans; the Indians harassed them by blindly firing into their camp until the sun started to slowly creep over the mountains to the east.

That next morning the fighting continued as the volunteers retreated toward the Touchet River. The warriors had taken hidden positions in the trees and brush close to the only possible river crossing in the area. As the Americans reached the crossing, a fierce skirmish broke out between the two forces, lasting several hours. Finally, the Indians broke off the attack and disappeared into the hills. Of the Americans, there were no casualties, but ten men had been seriously wounded. The Indians suffered four deaths and 14 wounded. Observers from other tribes were disappointed in the battle's outcome and decided not to join in the war.

Unable to stop the Americans from advancing into their territory, the Cayuse withdrew further east into Nez Perce country. They hoped the Nez Perce would join them in their conflict against the Americans, but the Nez Perce were still divided in their decision.

Always on the lookout for another opportunity to decimate the Indian people, Colonel Gilliam moved his forces from Fort Walla Walla to the old Whitman Mission at Waiilatpu. This was so that he would be closer to the Cayuse and Nez Perce if the opportunity to do battle arose. Once there, they encountered one of the most disturbing and horrific scenes that even the most battle-hardened men had ever witnessed: everything destroyed, buildings burned to the ground, the yard littered with broken pieces of pottery, lamps, furniture, and paper from books and journals, and the grounds covered with the remains of the victims murdered at the massacre. The wolves and coyotes had dug up the graves and left body parts everywhere. The troops were sickened and incensed by what they found. Joe Meek was with the party when they found pieces of a young girl's body and hair. He recognized the dress as one he had bought for his daughter Helen. Another man found parts of a woman's head and hair that they suspected must have been the remains of Narcissa Whitman. The men dug a much deeper grave to rebury the mangled and decomposed corpses, and another service was spoken. There was now an even deeper sense of anger running through the hearts of the men. Colonel Gilliam looked at this as an opportunity and was more determined than ever to disrupt any attempts at peace in order to continue the hostilities.

On March 20, Colonel Gilliam started back for Fort Walla Walla with two companies of men to gather needed supplies and ammunition. At this time, it seems fate finally favored the Indian people. While crossing the Umatilla River, Colonel Gilliam pulled on a rope to hitch his horse; the rope caught his rifle and shot him in the head and killed him. They took his body back to Fort Walla Walla, Lieutenant-Colonel Waters was put in charge and immediately found himself embroiled in a great deal of confusion, uncertain who was now friendly and who was not.

On May 21, Major Lee reached our old mission at Lapwai, finding it destroyed and burned to the ground. This was especially disheartening for Major Lee since he had spent part of a year with us helping Father teach classes.

Nearby were several Nez Perce lodges where he asked if they had seen Chief Tiloukaikt or his men. Angered by the military intrusion, they reluctantly told him that he had just missed them by one day, that they had fled to the Blue Mountains where they would be impossible to find.

The failure to capture those responsible for the massacre had created a great deal of frustration and anger among the officers and troops toward the Indian people.

Major Lee was still the Superintendent of Indian Affairs and decided to seize all Cayuse lands in the Walla Walla Valley. He declared that any man who would volunteer to serve in the army would be able to stake a legal claim on Cayuse land. In this way, he was able to attract enough men to keep a presence at the Fort.

Governor Abernathy endorsed the decision and would become the foundation for the devastation of the entire territory. To make matters worse, a notification was announced in the *Oregon Spectator* that Cayuse lands had been seized and any white person over 18 who wished to stake a claim could do so.

This action was illegal and a clear violation of all treaties and arrangements made between the American Government and the Indian people. The justification was that the Cayuse people refused to turn over the fugitives responsible for the Whitman massacre.

The proclamation was stated in such a way that no boundaries were set, that all tribes within the entire Oregon Territory were now in jeopardy of losing their lands. This was a shocking and bewildering act of aggression to the Indian people. They couldn't understand why the entire nation should be punished for the actions of a small group. This would be the end of peaceful coexistence. There was now a real threat that the Indian people of the Oregon Territory would share the same fate as the Kalapuya, Clackamas, and Molalla Indians of the Willamette Valley, who had been deprived and dispossessed of their lands.

The Cayuse involved in the conflict were growing tired of living in exile, tired of being hungry and wandering the plains and mountains. They wanted to return to their homes, to the old way of life, and they were ready to give up the men involved in the Whitman massacre.

A group of both Nez Perce and Cayuse, led by Chief Lawyer, went to Oregon City to meet with Governor Joseph Lane. Governor Lane told them that if they could convince the murderers to surrender, that he would do everything within his power to keep the settlers out of their lands and resume trade negotiations. The Nez Perce and Cayuse held council for two days until they decided to turn over the five fugitives.

The Cayuse fugitives involved in the Whitman Massacre had been on the run for almost two and a half years. The way of life for all tribes in the Oregon Territory had been seriously disrupted, but still, there were those who would rather fight for the freedom of the five accused men, no matter what the cost. The exact details of how the fugitives came to surrender are not known. What is known is that they had left the safety of the Blue Mountains with the understanding that they would be having a council with both Nez Perce and Cayuse chiefs.

When they arrived, they were taken into custody and told that they were to be delivered to Oregon City to stand trial. Chief Lawyer explained that because of their planning and execution of the Whitman Massacre, all of the tribes were being punished. Many of the Cayuse and Umatilla who participated in the skirmishes were still in hiding and unable to return home or hunt the buffalo they needed to survive. Individuals that had had nothing to do with the massacre were being harassed, even killed. Indian people were having their cattle, horses, and land confiscated as a repercussion of the massacre.

After hearing what had been said, the accused indicated that they understood and would do what was best for their people. There was still hope among their supporters that the Americans would understand what caused the massacre and how badly the Indians had been treated; that the American military had done far worse.

Chapter 2

The Trial

Tiloukaikt, Tomahas, Klokamas, Isaiachalkis, and Kimasumpkin were then taken 200 miles to Oregon City to be tried for the murder of Doctor Whitman and his wife, Narcissa, and 12 others. It was an all-white jury, aware of the gruesome details. During the entire trial, the prisoners were kept in chains, and two interpreters had been brought in to assist with translating.

This was to be the first trial of its kind. It was an attempt to have a legitimate and formal trial by the newly formed government designated by President James K. Polk.

The legendary mountain man and trapper Joe Meek was now a United States Marshall for the territory and selected as bailiff. The town of Oregon City had a population of approximately 500 people. It was still a frontier town with a one-room jail located on Abernethy Island, near the foot of Willamette Falls. There was no courthouse at the time, so trials had to be held at a local saloon and could accommodate approximately 200 people. After Judge Pratt had read the indictments, the defense pled not guilty to an over-packed house.

The next day the attorneys for the defense submitted three motions to the court, one asking for dismissal. The first motion stated that since the alleged crime had taken place before the new congress and judicial system were in place, that this court had no jurisdiction over the proceedings. It was denied.

The second motion was for a change of venue. The people of Oregon City were extremely hostile toward the defendants, more likely to seek vengeance rather than justice. That was also denied.

The third motion was for a postponement so that the defense would have time to locate and transport their witnesses the 200 miles from Waiilatpu. That also was denied, and the trial was set to commence the following day.

On Thursday morning, as the trial began, the entire town was buzzing. The first order of business was to select a jury made up exclusively of white men. There were many Indians from all different tribes in the courtroom, but at that time, all women and men of other races were legally barred from serving on any United States jury. The process took up most of the day since the defense challenged all of the original 24 prospective jurors. Out of frustration Joe Meek started selecting random spectators from the make-shift courtroom to serve as jurists. When they were finally able to narrow it down to 12, the prosecutor, Mr. Holbrook, commenced presenting their case.

The prosecution was to have four witnesses, and the defense was to have three.

The witnesses for the prosecution were all female survivors of the massacre who had witnessed the murders firsthand, and I was one of them. The initial questioning was aimed at identifying the five defendants as being the ones who had been present or participated in the massacre. Joe Lewis and several of the other primary perpetrators had fled to parts unknown, so there would be no justice in their cases.

The first witness called was Eliza Hall. She identified Tomahas as the one who had struck Doctor Whitman three times in the back of the head with his tomahawk. Of the other four men accused and present, she was only able to identify Chief Tiloukaikt as one of the possible murderers of Mr. Sanders since he was there when it happened. Her husband had been captured and scalped after the initial murders, and her testimony was extremely emotional, so the defense didn't choose to cross-examine.

Elizabeth Sager was next and also identified Tomahas. She was ten years old at the time of the massacre, and other than Tomahas, she had only witnessed two of the other defendants in attendance. She had seen Isaiachalkis as he pulled Mr. Saunders from his horse, threw him to the ground, and attacked him with his tomahawk. She stated that Klokamas had pointed a rifle at her older sister Catherine's face and laughed when he attempted to frighten her.

Catherine Sager's testimony was basically the same as Elizabeth's, since they had been together through most of the ordeal.

I was ten at the time of the massacre and had done my best to forget it. I was now 13, frightened, and nervous. I had known several of the Cayuse men accused of the murder and couldn't help but feel sorry for them as they sat there stoically with a look of hopelessness on their faces. Chief Tiloukaikt had always been a good friend of the Whitmans, and it was only after his three sons died of the measles that he became involved. After the massacre, I could tell that he was sorry for what had happened and knew he had done his best to protect us afterward.

Tomahas looked intensely angry and had a fierce scowl on his face. I had always been frightened of him and was still having nightmares about his part in the killings. I knew that if he could, he would jump out of his chair and cut my throat right there in the courtroom. Mother had been against my going, feeling that I had already been through enough, that we couldn't afford the expense of traveling or loss of work. Father told her that it was part of our responsibility as citizens, and she finally agreed to let us go.

Thank goodness ... they decided not to have me testify. The prosecution was afraid that I would be sympathetic to the Cayuse because of having been brought up in a Nez Perce village. The defense had a strong enough case and didn't want to see me do more damage than good.

The three witnesses for the defense were Doctor McLaughlin, Chief Stickus, and Father. It came as a great surprise to the spectators that Father was testifying for the Cayuse defense. He told me that he had been allowed to visit with the prisoners under the stipulation that he only provide them with spiritual guidance. Chief Tiloukaikt and Father talked for some time about the chief's beliefs and then briefly about the massacre.

He told Father that he had wanted revenge for his sons but had not participated in the actual killings. He admitted that he had helped plan the massacre, and therefore he was equally guilty. He went on to say that Klokamas was there but had not participated in the killings. Kimasumpkin was never anywhere near the massacre and had only come along as a witness for the defense, and that he should be set free. Father told the chief that he had come as a witness for the defense and would try to keep them from being hanged.

The first defense witness to be called was Doctor McLaughlin. He told the judge and jury that he had been warning Doctor Whitman for the past year or more, that the Indian people were growing increasingly angry with him for bringing the immigrants and settlers into their territory. He explained that the Cayuse were doing what they felt they had to do to save their people and should be shown mercy.

When Chief Stickus took the stand, there was a good deal of uneasiness in the courtroom, and some men began shouting insults. Every time he tried to speak, the prosecution would object that it was immaterial, and people would start yelling at him. Finally, the defense rose and asked the judge if Chief Stickus could be allowed to make his point without being interrupted. The judge told the court that if there were any more interruptions, he would clear the room.

Chief Stickus said, "Only a small group of people had anything to do with the killings, yet we are all being punished. Doctor and Mrs. Whitman were my good friends, and I am sorry they are gone. These men were trying to stop the death of their people and should not be killed. Like me, Kimasumpkin came here as a witness and had nothing to do with the massacre. He should be set free. That is all I have to say."

Father's testimony was brief. He told the court that Doctor McLaughlin had warned them that an attack was planned and to leave while they still had time. He went on to tell the court that Joe Lewis was not only the instigator, he was also the one who brutally murdered Mrs. Whitman and several men, including 13-year-old Frank Sager. He felt that other than Tomahas, mercy should be shown since they believed they were doing what was best for their people and had been misled by Joe Lewis and Tomahas.

Father's final statement was, "These men didn't wake up one morning and say let's go kill all the white people at the mission. You had to have been there to see the terrible deaths these poor people were suffering because of us. Children, mothers, fathers, grandparents, uncles, aunts, everyone was dying ... some of you think these men are savages, but you couldn't be more wrong. I have lived among them for 11 years, and they are the most honorable people I have ever known. I have watched their children suffer and die from the terrible diseases we brought with us. I have seen greedy and dishonest white men steal their land and possessions. I have watched unscrupulous and amoral white men corrupt their souls with whiskey and debase their women. Yes, these men must be punished for what they have done, but we should understand why they were driven to do it and be merciful."

Father's last point was that Kimasumpkin had come as a witness for the defense and had nothing whatsoever to do with the massacre and should be set free. At that point, the defender, Mr. Pritchette, asked if Kimasumpkin could make a statement before the jury retired. The crowd started yelling, and the prosecution objected, so Judge Pratt told everyone to shut up, sit down and let the man talk.

This was Kimasumpkin's statement:

"I was up the river at the time of the massacre and did not arrive until the next day. I was riding on horseback; a white woman came running from the house she held out her hands and told me not to kill her. I put my hand upon her hand and told her not to be afraid. There were plenty of Indians all about. She, with the other women and children, went to Walla Walla to Mr. Ogdens. I was not present at the murder, nor was I concerned in it. I am innocent, and it hurts me to talk about dying for nothing. Our chief told me to come down here and tell all about it. Many of those who committed the murder are dead. If they kill me, I am innocent ... My Young Chief told me I was to come here to tell what I know concerning the murderers. I did not come as one of the murderers, for I am innocent. I never made any declaration that I was guilty. This is the last time that I may speak."

The closing arguments took longer than the testimony, approximately three or more hours. Both Mr. Pritchette and Mr. Holbrook were powerful speakers, and their closing remarks were full of passion for both freedom and death.

On Friday morning, May 24, Judge Pratt spent well over an hour giving the jurors instructions on how to proceed. He told the jury that because the accused men had surrendered that it shouldn't be assumed, they were innocent. He also reminded them that the Indian people knew best who the murderers were, that they brought these men to trial. This was a blatant and obvious attempt to persuade the jury toward a guilty verdict, highly improper and devastating for the accused.

Once deliberations were underway, juror Jacob Hunsaker and one of the other jurymen told the others that they believed Kiamasumpkin was innocent, that not one of the prosecution witnesses had identified him as one of the assailants. Several witnesses testified that he was not present at the Whitman Mission the day of the massacre. The jury explained their dilemma to Judge Pratt, who told them that there was plenty of evidence indicating that all of the accused were armed.

The jury deliberated for another hour before finding all five men guilty. The defense moved for "an arrest of judgement," which was denied, a new trial, denied, and an appeal to the Supreme Court, which was also denied.

That afternoon Judge Pratt announced that all five men were to receive the death penalty and put into the custody of U.S. Marshall Joseph Meeks.

In ten days, they were to be brought to the gallows erected in Oregon City, and hanged by the neck until dead. Chief Tiloukaikt told the court that they were not afraid to die but to be hanged like a dog was considered a terrible disgrace.

He asked the judge if they could be shot instead of hanged. The judge declined his request and reiterated that they were to be hung. I don't think the decision came as a surprise to anyone. The judgment to Kiamasumpkin was unjust, and even those who wanted to see the guilty ones hanged were unsettled by the decision to put an innocent man to death.

The day after the trial, Governor Lane left for California. Territorial law dictated that in the event that the Governor was out of the territory, the Secretary of the Territory would assume his position until the governor returned. Since the defense attorney, Mr. Pritchette, was the secretary, he concluded that he had the power to pardon the prisoners. He gave Marshal Meek the order to let them go and cancel the hanging. Marshall Meek immediately took his predicament to Judge Pratt since he had no idea whether to hang or release them. Judge Pratt concluded that it would take Governor Lane at least ten or more days to make the trip by horseback to California, so technically, he was still governor until he crossed the state line—plenty of time to hang the convicted men.

On June 3, 1850, Marshall Meek led the convicted men through the muddy streets of Oregon City to the gallows constructed specifically for the hanging. They were led up the stairs to where five ropes were dangling and asked if they had any last words. Almost the entire town and even people from surrounding towns had flocked to see the men hang. In my mind, there is something very wrong with the kind of person who likes to watch someone die. Chief Tiloukaikt told Marshall Meek that he would like to say something and asked Mr. Meek to translate for the crowd.

The chief paused for a long time, looking at the faces in the crowd before he said, "Your Christ died to save his people? So, die we to save our people."

Hoods were placed over their heads, then five nooses placed around their necks.

Just before the trapdoor was released, Kimasumpkin yelled out, "Wawko sixto wah! Wawko sixto wah!" In the Cayuse language, this means, "Now we can be friends."

Their remains were buried on the outskirts of Oregon City in unmarked graves.

Chapter 3

Chief Joseph

Sometimes I feel so angry and heartbroken when I think of what has happened to not only the Nez Perce but to all Indian people. I was once asked to lecture at a library function about the Whitman Massacre and my experience growing up amongst the Nez Perce. During my talk, a very rough-looking man interrupted me asking, "How can you defend those ignorant heathen savages after what they did to the Whitmans and a lot of other good white folks?"

I asked him, "Sir, what would you do if invaders came to your home and stole your land, your horses and cattle, almost every possession you owned. How would you feel if they killed your family and friends with a strange disease you had no protection against, force-marched you and what was left of your people to a barren land void of the necessities you needed to survive, and made beggars of you? Are you the kind of man who would sit by and do nothing?"

It was so quiet that it made the hairs on my arms stand up.

When he said nothing in reply, I continued, "Sir, the real problem is that many people don't even see the Nez Perce or any Indian people as human beings. They think of them as you do, ignorant heathen savages, and nothing ... nothing could be further from the truth. Their wisdom and reverence for nature and the land, dedication to their families and friends far exceeds anything I have ever seen from my people. They are highly intelligent and resourceful; they are respectful in ways that elude most white people. Their actions were reactions to what the Americans had done to them. They asked nothing from the white man; they took nothing from the white man until their people were disrespected and desecrated. I ask again, are you the kind of man that would do nothing?"

Once again, there was no answer, but I could hear the sound of several women quietly weeping. I told the audience that I had planned to read this passage at the end of my talk, but now seemed the right time to share it.

"Knowledge was inherent in all things. The world was a library, and its books were the stones, leaves, grass, brooks, and the birds and animals that shared, alike with us, the storms and blessings of the earth. We learn to do what only the student of nature ever learns, which is to feel beauty. We never rail at the storms, the furious winds, biting frosts, and snows. To do so intensifies human futility, so whatever comes, we should adjust ourselves by more effort and energy if necessary, but without complaint. Bright days and dark days are both expressions of the Great Mystery, and the Indian is reveled in being close to the Great Holiness."

I told them that this was written many years ago by a man named Chief Luther Standing Bear of the Lakota People. "I would say he is anything but ignorant, that he writes with an elegance comparable to that of Mark Twain or Charles Dickens. His words remind me very much of my old friend, Chief Joseph."

I explained that the Nez Perce religion is 1,000s of years older than Christianity, and the Indian people have never fought or killed each other over whose God was right or wrong as we have done. I told them how Father had converted and christened and baptized over one thousand Nez Perce and Cayuse, who are among the most devout and pious Christians I had ever known. They have built beautiful churches and have dedicated and knowledgeable teachers.

I then explained, "I hardly think it appropriate to call them heathens or savages. Certainly, there are savage people among the Indians as there are among all races. Several very bad men and others caught up in a blood lust for revenge did what was done at Waiilatpu. All of them had watched their wives, parents, and children die a slow and torturous death from measles or smallpox. If you would like to discuss savage, I doubt that anything could ever match the violence of the Christian Crusades of the Holy Roman Church. It was a war that lasted almost 200 years, with as many as a million Arabs and Jews killed. How about the sadistic and savage torture performed on over 150,000 human beings sanctioned by the Catholic Church during the Spanish Inquisition? These things I would consider to be truly savage.

"A massacre took place at Sand Point, Colorado in 1864 in which Colonel John Shivington of the U.S. Army gunned down an entire village of over 600 human beings, mostly women and children. The whole time the head chief was waving a white flag, trying to surrender. Eyewitnesses reported that some 40 women and children had taken shelter in a hole in the ground. A six-year-old girl was sent out with a white flag, and within several steps, she was shot to death. After that, they shot the rest of the women and children in the hole and left them there to decompose.

"To us, land is a place where we make our homes and raise our crops or cattle. To the Indian people, it is Mother Earth, a living being that they are a part of. The land stolen from them is where their recent and past ancestors are buried, where they had planned to be buried. So, I ask you, sir, to take a good look at what we have done to the Indian people ... then ask yourself how you would feel if it were you, would you do nothing and watch your family and friends be killed?"

Most of my lectures ended on a bright note with a period of questions and answers, but there were no questions that day; people just slowly got up in a quiet and somber mood and left; a few came to thank me for coming.

The man who had made the statement came to me with his hat in his hand and said, "I apologize, ma'am, I never looked at it that way; my answer is that I would have fought to keep my land as they did."

I told him, "Sir, I am not sure exactly why we were put on this earth, but if I were to take a guess, it would be that we are put here to learn." I held out my hand and told him that his apology was accepted.

After the gold rush, there was no turning back. Americans began flooding into the Northwest with a thirst for gold and land that would never be satisfied. By this time, both Old and Young Chief Josephs had made a complete break with Christianity and all of the white man's traditions. They had returned to the old ways and were trying to convince their people to do the same. When it came to treaties, there was no end to the government's treachery and fraudulence.

Buffalo Bill was credited with having once said, "The Indians never broke a treaty, and we never kept one."

Father put it this way. "It is impossible for me to describe in the English language, to convey any of the greatness or nobleness of the Nez Perce Indians, and the unearthly meanness, littleness, and wickedness of the white man, especially as a benefactor."

I never saw Young Chief Joseph again after the massacre but followed everything written about him. From what I could gather, he had grown to be much like his Father, over six feet tall with a deep chest and broad shoulders, a strong man with an iron will. His father had implanted all of his best characteristics into his sons, and Young Joseph enhanced them with his brilliant mind and noble character.

After our departure, most of what I learned was from what I read or was told by mutual friends, that there was never a person more courageous or committed to his people or land. When white people would meet him, they expected a fierce and angry warrior but were surprised to find him gentle and courteous unless aroused by disrespect or condescension.

In the future, there would be many misconceptions, and untruths told about Young Chief Joseph. He was erroneously blamed for the murders that took place under Chief White Bird's clan long before becoming a leader of his people. He tried every resource he could use to bring about peaceful resolutions. Unfortunately, the new settlers and gold prospectors were bent on taking Nez Perce lands with the United States government's cooperation. Even in war, he adhered to a strict code of conduct where women and children were left unharmed, unlike the U.S. Cavalry that murdered innocent women and children indiscriminately. The Nez Perce were then dispossessed of their lands, villages, and horses, and forced to leave the places their ancestors had lived for 1,000s of years. Those who survived became refugees on barren and alien lands where many of their people would eventually wither and die.

By the end of the Cayuse war, the Oregon Provisional Government created the Donations Claims Act. It stated that any white or half-white person over the age of 18 could stake a claim of 640 acres in the Oregon Territory. This was done without any regard for the treaties or rights of the Indian people.

The first treaty council was held in 1855 near Walla Walla, less than six miles from the burned-out Whitman Mission. Six tribes were invited, including the Nez Perce, Walla Walla, Cayuse, Umatilla, and Yakima.

A man named Issac Stevens had been appointed territorial Governor of the Washington Territory. At that time, it consisted of Washington State, much of Idaho, half of Montana and Wyoming. Governor Stevens was a 34-year-old graduate of West Point, veteran of the Mexican War, and a very ambitious politician.

He was in charge of the treaty council and had asked the Supervisor of Indian Affairs, Joel Palmer, of the Oregon Territory to assist him, with William Craig as interpreter.

There were 100 Americans, 40 of whom were soldiers, and over 6,000 Indians. The Nez Perce numbered approximately 2,500, including those who arrived in most dramatic fashion. Six Nez Perce head chiefs, including Chiefs Timothy and Joseph, came ahead to make introductions. The rest blazed wildly through the camp, banging their guns or bows against their shields, yelling and whistling as loudly as possible.

When they dismounted, they circled menacingly around the group of white men, dancing and chanting for almost a half-hour until they were glistening with sweat and worked up into a trance-like state.

They ceremoniously smoked the peace pipe, and then each group returned to their camps to prepare for the planned feast. The Walla Walla, Cayuse, and Umatilla tribes intentionally arrived late to show their disapproval of the council. They refused to accept any of the gifts offered or share in the food provided by Governor Stevens.

Tensions ran high as rumors spread that they had come intent on violence. It is more likely that they were posturing to gain advantage during the negotiations. In essence, Governor Stevens proposed that two reservations be created, one in Nez Perce country that would include the Spokane, Walla Walla, Cayuse, Umatilla, and Nez Perce tribes. The other would be in Yakima Territory, which would include Colville, Okanagan, Klickitat, Palouse, and the Pisquose tribes.

The U.S. Government demanded 24,000 square miles of the 27,000 square miles of Nez Perce land. In return, they would receive $200,000 over 20 years along with supplies, clothing, and equipment to develop the reservation. The Cayuse, Walla Walla, and Umatilla would receive $150,000 over 20 years for their 6,000 square miles of land along with $60,000 to make improvements on their reservation. When full council was in order, everything was formal, but in private, Governor Stevens warned several chiefs that if they did not sign the treaty, the U.S. would unleash a war that would decimate their people.

When it came time to sign, all 58 Nez Perce, even those who could write, signed with an X, and 13 from the Yakima Nation put their Xs on the treaty. Some of the chiefs were happy with the gifts and money, but Chiefs Joseph and Timothy only signed to prevent war, though this treaty allowed them to stay on their lands. Governor Stevens took great pride in praising himself for what he considered a victory for America and believed it would be a final and peaceful resolution. He was wrong.

The treaty of 1855 changed very little in the beginning since few whites wanted to take risks involved in claiming land in an unsettled and potentially hostile territory. When gold was discovered in 1861, everything changed. Prospectors and settlers arrived by the thousands with little or no regard for reservation boundaries or Indian rights. Initially, the Nez Perce chose to keep the peace since the intrusion was in the high country, which had no permanent villages. They didn't want a war and used the opportunity to trade. However, as the settlers and prospectors continued deeper into the Nez Perce reservation, conflicts began to arise, which would eventually lead to the Treaty of 1863.

To the Indians, the treaty of 1863 would become known as the Steal, or Thief Treaty.

It was devastating in several ways. First, it divided the Indian people between treaty and non-treaty Indians. Secondly, it reduced their initial 27,000 square miles to 500 square miles, leaving them less than 2% of their original lands, thus the name Steal, or Thief Treaty.

Superintendent of Indian Affairs, Calvin Henry Hale, acted for the U.S. Government, along with agents Hutchins and Howell.

Father and Perrin Whitman were interpreters. The Nez Perce had always governed individually with a final decision resting on the shoulders of the head chief of their village. Governor Stevens planned to change that and appointed Chief Lawyer, the leading proponent of the treaty Indians, as Head Chief of the entire Nez Perce Nation.

He was happy with the arrangement, which entitled him to a large farm, wooden house, and $500 per year. His village was still within the new reservation boundary, so it affected him very little personally. With this appointment, Governor Stevens made Chief Lawyer a very wealthy and powerful man.

Chief Joseph and his people stood to lose all of their land, including the entire Wallowa Valley, where their people had lived for 1,000s of years. They would be forced to leave the home of their ancestors for a wretched existence on a distant reservation. Chief Joseph the Elder became the main opponent and refused to sign the treaty. The ones who signed were enticed with a small amount of money and supplies. Chief Joseph, Three Feathers, Eagle-from-the-Light, and Thunder Eyes told the commissioner they would never sell their land and that he had no right to take it from them. When all of the opposition leaders left in anger and disgust, the commissioners had little trouble reaching agreement with Chief Lawyer in charge.

Captain George Currey was in charge of security and decided to put his disapproval on record. He wrote, "Although the treaty goes out to the world as the concurrent agreement of the tribes, it is, in reality, nothing more than an agreement of Lawyer and his band, numbering in the aggregate not a third of the Nez Perce Tribe."

Other than Chief Timothy, only the chiefs whose villages were inside the new reservation boundary signed, their only goal was to keep the peace. All of the chiefs outside the new reservation boundary line refused to sign. Chief Thunder Eyes was within the boundary but despised Chief Lawyer so much that he refused to sign.

Before Chief Joseph the Elder left, he made a short statement to the others. "When you go into council with the white man, always remember your country. Do not give it away. The white man will cheat you out of your home. I have taken no pay from the United States. I have never sold our land."

By 1871 Chief Joseph the Elder was dying.

Before he passed, he told his son Young Joseph, "My son, my body is returning to the mother earth, and my spirit is going very soon to see the Great Spirit Chief. When I am gone, think of your country. You are the chief of these people. They look to you to guide them. Always remember that your father never sold his country. You must stop your ears whenever you are asked to sign a treaty selling your home. A few years more, and white men will be all around you. They have their eyes on this land. My son, never forget my dying words. This country holds your father's body. Never sell the bones of your father and your mother."

Young Joseph later wrote, "I took my father's hand and promised to do as he asked. A man who would not defend his father's grave is worse than a wild beast."

Joseph the Elder was now gone, and Young Chief Joseph was the unofficial leader of the Wallowa tribe. There were many treaty violations by the white settlers and prospectors, but Joseph was still willing to make concessions to avoid war, telling his people to refrain from violence.

In 1873 Joseph negotiated with the U.S. Government to ensure that he and his people would be allowed to stay on their land in the Wallowa Valley. In 1877 the U.S. Government reversed its decision, and General Oliver Howard threatened to remove them forcibly if his people did not agree to relocate to the Idaho Reservation.

To buy time, Chief Joseph reluctantly agreed but made this statement to General Howard. "I do not believe the Great Spirit gave one kind of man the right to tell another kind of man what they must do."

General Howard was not used to being challenged or reprimanded, and this angered him. He gave Joseph 30 days to relocate to the reservation, and he would consider a refusal to cooperate an act of war. When Joseph brought this before his people, some felt it was time to make a stand and advocated war, but Joseph was still trying to find the means to a peaceful resolution. White settlers had recently killed the father of a young warrior. The young man warned the council that if they wouldn't do anything about it, he would. He and a small band of men attacked and killed four settlers out of retribution for his father's death.

This signaled the beginning of the Nez Perce War. Until this time, I had only read or heard occasional stories or references concerning what had taken place with the Nez Perce. Most of it was rhetoric from General Howard, who liked having his name and threats against the Nez Perce put in print. The escalating conflict was becoming big news in the newspapers and starting to make waves all over the country; even people back east were taking notice. Father was traveling, and I lived on our ranch in Harney County with my own family. Harney County would later become part of eastern Oregon. The conflict seemed a million miles away, but my heart was still with the Nez Perce People.

At the time, Joseph was the youngest of the five Nez Perce tribal chiefs and in no way considered the leader or spokesman for all of the tribes. Like Joseph, his younger brother Ollokot was a big powerful man. He was six foot two, and over 200 pounds of raw manhood. Many of their tribe considered him a better choice as chief since he had performed more acts of bravery and had more experience as a warrior. The Wallowa band had 60 adult males; White Birds tribe was the next largest with 50. The third-largest tribe was that of Chief Looking Glass with 40 men, then Toohoolhoolzote's tribe with 30. Last was Chief Hahtalekin with only 16 warriors, totaling approximately 196 fighting men.

Chief Looking Glass said that he wanted no part of a war with the Americans and told the other chiefs he would remain neutral, leaving only 156 warriors. General Howard selected Captain Perry to lead two companies of about 200 men, expecting to "make short work of it." He would be very wrong.

The non-treaty Nez Perce had decided to flee deeper into Idaho to try and avoid a confrontation if possible. Joseph urged Ollokot and the other chiefs to determine what the soldiers wanted and only fire if fired upon. The chiefs agreed and sent out six scouts under a white flag of truce. Captain Perry sent out a group of eight scouts that included a hot-headed volunteer named Ad Chapman. He had personally known the four white settlers that had been killed and was looking for vengeance.

When they encountered the Nez Perce, waving a white flag, Chapman fired two shots, and the Nez Perce scattered into the trees. A group of 20 soldiers came charging up behind the scouts with a bugler blowing the signal to charge. When the bugler was shot dead from long range, the soldiers and scouts turned and ran with Ad Chapman in the lead. By now, the main body of Nez Perce had caught up, so Captain Perry retreated as fast as possible, leaving men strung out behind him to be shot or clubbed to death. By the time Perry reached safety, 34 of his men had been killed with many others badly wounded; only three Nez Perce had been wounded.

The news was a stunning blow to the U.S. Army. To save face, General Howard claimed that well over 500 Nez Perce warriors had ambushed Captain Perry and his men.

Up until that point, the U.S. Army and the American people, in general, felt that the U.S. military was invincible. I remember reading about it and knowing that there were no more than 200 men of fighting age among the entire non-treaty Nez Perce. I also remember thinking how foolish the soldiers were to take on the Nez Perce on Nez Perce ground.

Because the Nez Perce were a relatively rich people, it was not necessary for them to be aggressive by raiding other tribes to takes slaves and possessions. However, the men spent a great deal of time practicing the art of war and were among the fiercest and most skilled warriors on earth when threatened.

General Howard began requesting soldiers from as far away as Alaska, San Francisco, even Georgia. He pursued the Nez Perce with a full battalion, hoping to reach them before they came to

White Bird Canyon, but he was too late. They had already crossed an extremely treacherous section of the Snake River, and were well into the rugged mountains. Howard lost a great deal of time looking for a safer passage across the Snake River and by the time he crossed it, the Nez Perce were long gone. Even after Howard had crossed the river, the combination of 600 men, artillery, Gatling guns, and animals progressed slowly. The rear scouts of the Nez Perce were able to leisurely observe the soldiers as the main body rested while deciding what to do next.

Erroneously, General Howard was told that Chief Looking Glass and some of his men had been involved in the hostilities. He then sent Captain Whipple with 66 soldiers to bring him in. Looking Glass had been at Lapwai the entire time, and neither he nor his people had had anything to do with the fighting. When the military arrived at Looking Glass's village one of the soldiers started shooting, causing the other men to open fire.

The only casualties were a woman and child, who drowned while trying to escape, but the village was destroyed, and over 700 horses were taken. It was the end of Chief Looking Glass's peaceful intentions He and his people then joined the main body of non-treaty Nez Perce as they fled northeast. Looking Glass told the other chiefs that he was friends with the Crows whom he had fought the Dakota Sioux with in the past and that they might provide refuge. Looking Glass took over as war chief, and Joseph became the master tactician.

They had come to a place called Cottonwood, where an advance party of 12 soldiers stumbled upon a band of Nez Perce preparing to launch a surprise attack on Captain Whipple's two companies.

Six of the soldiers were cut down almost immediately; the other six fled to a dead end where they had to jump to the rocks below.

It was like a shooting gallery as the Nez Perce took their time picking them off. Only one Indian was killed in the skirmish, a warrior named Weescuatat.

Ironically, his son was a scout for General Howard, and when they reached a place that would become known as the Battle of Clearwater, he discovered that the soldiers had killed his father. During the battle, he charged through the lines drawing fire from both sides until he was able to dive into one of the Nez Perce bunkers. They were ready to kill him until one of his cousins recognized him and stopped them. He told them that he was wrong to have joined with the white soldiers and now wanted to get revenge for his father's killing. Joseph believed he was being truthful and knew they could use every warrior they could get. That afternoon he was shot in the thigh, and after recovering, he fought bravely for the Nez Perce in all of the battles to come.

The Nez Perce had gotten so far ahead of the main body of soldiers that they relaxed their rearguard and were taken by surprise at the Battle of Clearwater. They fought for two days, outnumbered four to one. Because of the extremely accurate Nez Perce sharpshooters, the soldiers were reluctant to send men in, neither side willing to commit totally. The Nez Perce fled again, leaving a small band of sharpshooters to pick off any soldiers who dared to follow too closely.

At the Battle of Clearwater, there were 15 soldiers killed and 27 wounded. The Nez Perce has suffered four killed, and five wounded. As dispatches reached the newspapers, the Nez Perce War continued to be a major headline all over the country, and General Howard was beginning to lose his credibility, not only with his superiors but with the public as well. One thing that neither his superiors nor the public could abide was a loser.

A good deal of sympathy was beginning to take root for the Nez Perce men, women, and children who had lost their lands and were forced to flee for their lives from the only homes they had ever known. Four hundred women and children, 250 men, and many elderly were now homeless fugitives. Courageous and defiant, they were fleeing for their lives to the north along the Lolo Trail.

At one of the tribal campgrounds, Chief Red Heart was returning from the buffalo hunt with 17 warriors and 28 women and children when they met up with the main Nez Perce party. When Chief Joseph asked him to join them, he told them he didn't want war with the Americans and wouldn't join. When he and his people departed for the reservation, they eventually encountered General Howard, who still desperately needed a victory of some sort. Chief Red Heart told General Howard that they had refused to join the non-treaty Nez Perce and wanted nothing to do with the war. Howard immediately seized him and all of his people, their horses and possessions, and put them in chains. He then had them force marched on foot for 60 miles in the blistering heat of mid-July, where they were eventually incarcerated. They were once again marched on foot to Fort Lapwai, where they were imprisoned for nine months. When they were turned loose, it was without any of their animals or possessions. General Howard falsely reported to his superiors and the newspapers that he had captured and taken into custody 45 hostile prisoners.

The Lolo Trail was a narrow, steep, and treacherous trek through mountains and rivers. Its advantage was that it could easily be defended. Five or six warriors were always assigned to the rearguard to alert the main group to how far behind the army was trailing. If the army caught up to them, the plan was to take the women and children into the mountains, and then return and fight to the death.

At the summit called Lolo Pass, they encountered 30 or so soldiers and a number of volunteers from Fort Missoula. A scout had warned the soldiers stationed at Lolo Pass that the Nez Perce were advancing in their direction, and they were told to hold them back until the army arrived. They had cut down several trees and formed a rough barricade in an attempt to delay the Nez Perce until Howard's forces arrived.

The officer in charge, a Captain Rawn, ordered Looking Glass to lay down their arms or they would be fired upon. Looking Glass told Captain Rawn that they had come in peace, that they would not harm anyone or take their property; they simply wanted to pass through. Looking Glass then told Captain Rawn that if he wanted their guns, they would have to take them, but he should look to the hills behind him first.

Captain Rawn turned around and saw that there were at least 50 sharpshooters with rifles aimed at him and his men, ready to cut them down. He knew it would be a massacre and let them pass without incident. When they reached the Bitterroot Valley, another group of Nez Perce, including the Delaware Indian Tom Hill, joined them. Chief Joseph made it clear that no innocent people were to be harmed, that their fight was with the U.S. Army.

Howard's force had fallen so far behind that the Nez Perce believed the war was over and that the Army would not continue to pursue them so far from their lands. They were wrong. Once again, they turned north hoping to Reach the Canadian border's safety and get help from the famous warrior, Chief Sitting Bull.

After Sitting Bull had defeated Colonel George Armstrong Custer at the Battle of Little Bighorn, he and his people fled to Canada, where the Canadian Government reluctantly agreed to grant them amnesty. The Nez Perce hoped that Sitting Bull would join them in their fight if the U.S. Army continued to pursue them. They were only 40 miles south of the Canadian border when they came to a place called Big Hole. They felt that since they were so close to the border, they could relax and rest beside a gentle mountain stream and let the animals graze. Several of the men went out to hunt and came across a small herd of buffalo. Along with fish caught in the stream, they enjoyed their first feast since leaving the Wallowa Valley. There were now 800 people in the group. Only 125 were warriors, the rest women, children, and elderly.

They were unaware that Colonel John Gibbon and his two companies of 190 men had been called up and were covering 25 to 30 miles per day in a forced march. Colonel Gibbon silently reached the wooded hills above the Big Hole Basin before daybreak, catching the Nez Perce completely unaware. No warning was offered; orders were to shoot anything that moved, men, women, or children.

Within 20 minutes, the soldiers had overrun the west part of the camp, and everything was in complete chaos. Women and children were screaming, and the warriors were trying to find any weapons they could to protect their people. It looked to be a short battle, but the Nez Perce rallied and began to inflict casualties among soldiers far less experienced in close combat. Colonel Gibbon called for a retreat so that his men could form a defensive line and make a stand. Ollokot and his 60 sharpshooters were able to keep the soldiers pinned down as Joseph organized another exodus. The Nez Perce then withdrew several warriors at a time until the battle was over.

Thirty-one soldiers had been killed and 38 wounded; 75 Nez Perce had been killed, with many more wounded.

The fact that Chief Looking Glass had assured the people that the war was over and the soldiers had quit the chase cost him his credibility and leadership as war chief.

The volunteers they encountered at Lolo Pass had promised not to take up arms against them in the future, but many were part of the attack at Big Hole. No white men would be trusted or shown mercy from that point on. Lean Elk took over as war chief and directed the Nez Perce to head south in the direction of the Shoshone Nation.

Before the Battle of Big Hole, the Nez Perce had paid or traded for everything they had needed. At this point, they would take what was necessary, especially fresh horses.

One of the most divisive aspects of the war was the U.S. Army's use of Indians as scouts and soldiers, even Nez Perce. The Bannocks were traditional enemies of the Nez Perce, and General Howard had employed 50 of them as scouts and soldiers. They were so brutal that even Howard had reservations about using them.

After battle, they would dig up the Nez Perce dead to take their scalps. When any of the elderly men or women were too sick or tired to continue, they were left behind on the trail. The Bannocks would torture, scalp, and kill them but preferred not to get involved in close combat or hand to hand.

Yellowstone had been made a National Park by President Ulysses S. Grant and was beginning to attract its earliest tourists. When the Nez Perce reached Yellowstone, they were uncertain which direction to continue. Ironically, a white prospector named John Shively agreed to guide them to the Wind River Trail.

They promised not to harm him and gave him a horse and supplies for his help.

While he was with them, two young white women and one man were brought into the camp as hostages. Mr. Shively would later claim that the Nez Perce left them unharmed and treated them with respect, releasing them after two days. One of the two sisters was named Emma Cowan, the other woman was her sister, and the other man with them was her sister's fiancé.

The story of Emma Cowan's husband George has become legendary in the history of human survival and endurance. George was a 35-year-old attorney from Montana on vacation at Yellowstone with his family. They first encountered the Nez Perce when two warriors came charging at them on horseback. George tried to hail them, but one drew his rifle and shot him in the left thigh above the knee, and he fell hard to the ground. His wife Emma leaped off her horse to try and help him. By then, one of the Indians had dismounted, one drawing his revolver. He approached George and tried to put his gun to George's head, but Emma threw herself over George to protect him. The other Indian pulled her off as the man with the pistol shot George in the face. They forced both women and the other man to follow them back to their camp, leaving George unconscious in a pool of blood.

Several hours later, George regained consciousness with what he described as a "buzzing sound" and numbness on one side of his head. When he first tried to rise, he realized that he couldn't feel his legs.

His first thought was for his wife Emma, where had she been taken, and what was happening to her. He was finally able to rise and drag his legs behind him when he spotted another Indian on horseback watching him between the trees. The Indian pulled his rifle, and the next thing George knew, there was a "twinging sensation in my left side." The bullet had entered his stomach and exited his back. He fell to the ground while looking at the man who had shot him expecting to be finished off with a knife or tomahawk. He then put his head in the dirt, pretending to be dead, and the man eventually left. His fear was for his wife, and what she might be going through, so he started crawling.

He crawled through mud and pine needles for the next three days until he finally came to his wagon. His dog Dido ran to him, and when he reached George, he covered his wounds and face with tender licks. George found some hard alcohol hidden under dirty clothes and cleaned and bound his wounds as best he could, but the food had all been taken. The only water available was from the dirty wet holes in the ground. He continued crawling until he came to one of the campgrounds that they had previously used.

He managed to find an old can, matches, water, and used coffee grounds. Other than a few sips of muddy water, it was the first thing he had had to drink in five days. He was so hungry that he considered eating Dido but couldn't bring himself to kill and eat his trusty friend and companion. Several times he had been so close to Nez Perce scouts passing by that he could hear everything they said.

He crawled again for another night and day until he was too weak to continue. He heard riders coming in the distance, and this time he couldn't stop Dido from barking, expecting the end had finally come. It turned out to be two cavalry scouts from General Howard's battalion looking for signs of the Nez Perce. After telling them who he was and what had happened, George's first question was if they had any word of his wife. They told him they had not, but the main force was close behind and might have news. They left him with some food, water, and a blanket. He lay there another night until General Howard arrived the following day.

Unfortunately, no one had heard any news of his wife or any white women, for that matter. The general gave him more food and water and took him to the surgeon's wagon.

The bullets to his stomach and thigh had passed through, but one was still embedded in his skull. The doctor thoroughly cleaned and dressed the stomach and leg wounds. He then executed a very crude surgery with only candlelight to extract the bullet from his head without anesthesia. When George recovered enough to talk again, he asked General Howard to help him find his wife, sister-in-law, and her fiancé. The General told him it would be impossible and put him in the back of one of the supply wagons.

They were traveling over the roughest part of Yellowstone when he was thrown out of the wagon and rolled 30 yards downhill until he came to a stop against a boulder. Badly bruised but not broken, he was hoisted back into the wagon and taken to Bozeman, Montana. The doctor there changed his bandages and deposited him at the Bozeman Hotel to recover. He had been shot three times and had crawled eight days over a dozen miles with only the use of his arms with no food or shelter and little water. He eventually reunited with his wife Emma, three weeks from the time the Army had first discovered him. When they reached home, he had the bullet made into a watch fob that he would carry with him for the rest of his life. He said the only thing that kept him going was the thought of his wife's welfare. To me, this is the greatest love story I have ever heard, more powerful and gritty than Shakespeare's "Romeo and Juliet."

The Nez Perce had narrowly missed General Sherman, who had departed from Yellowstone five days earlier, but three other armies were on their tail. News of the battles, skirmishes, and flights was front page on almost every newspaper in the country, and Western Europe. Every day I hoped to hear news that the search had been called off or the Nez Perce had safely reached Canada. They again turned north until they reached Canyon Creek, ten miles west of Billings, Montana.

An officer named Colonel Sturgis pushed his men past the point of exhaustion and starvation until they were forced to eat their horses to survive. Still, he kept on until he made contact with the Nez Perce rear guard. The Nez Perce marksmen started picking off

Colonel Sturgis's men until they retreated, returning to the main body with General Howard.

Almost 800 weary, homeless, and hungry Nez Perce had been traveling for over three months through the most rugged terrain in North America and were beginning to run extremely low on food and supplies. They had come to Cow Island, which was near a military depot, and decided to send a party to barter.

The sergeant in charge refused to trade and told them to leave. They returned to camp with the news, needing to decide what to do next. The following day and after a short skirmish, the Nez Perce left the fort with as much food and supplies as they could take with them. They were once again headed for the Canadian border, less than 100 miles away. For some reason, it was decided that Lean Elk was to be replaced as war chief by Looking Glass. Everyone was weary, and the rear guard hadn't seen any trace of the army, so they decided to stop for several days while they rested and hunted for game.

Two weeks earlier General Howard, had ordered Colonel Nelson Miles at Fort Keogh to do everything within his power to intercept the Nez Perce before they could reach the Canadian border. Colonel Miles wasted no time, and by the next day, he had assembled 600 troops who were packed and ready to depart. After 16 days of hard riding and a good deal of luck on his part, he caught up with the Nez Perce, who were taken by surprise. Once again, they believed the search had been called off. The Nez Perce were camped in a meadow and had been surrounded from above in what would become known as the "Battle of Bear's Paw Mountain." This would be the last battle of the Nez Perce War.

The women, children, and elderly were evacuated through trenches to an area over 100 yards away from the main camp where they had built several bunkers. At this point, a little over one hundred Nez Perce men fought against six hundred soldiers and a large party of Cheyenne and Sioux scouts and warriors.

That day 20 Nez Perce warriors were shot and killed. It would have been much worse without the extremely accurate sharpshooters giving cover fire. Several chiefs were killed, including Joseph's brother, Ollokot. The next morning was freezing; the ground was blanketed with snow as Colonel Miles sent a messenger under a white flag requesting a parley with Chief Joseph. Joseph agreed, and though he spoke and understood some English, Tom Hill went along as interpreter. Colonel Miles demanded that the Nez Perce give up their rifles and surrender peacefully. Chief Joseph agreed to the surrender but told Colonel Miles that they would need to keep half of their guns to provide enough game to survive. He refused to give up the rest and was taken into custody, put in chains, and held overnight.

The next day he was released to have a council with the other chiefs concerning Colonel Miles demands. The other chiefs refused to give up their guns, and the fighting began again. The fighting continued for the next two days until Colonel Miles could get a cannon into position. He indiscriminately fired into the camp, hitting one of the bunkers containing only women and children; all were killed. Another messenger was sent to tell Chief Joseph that if they surrendered, no one would be arrested and put on trial. They were also promised that they would be given food and returned peacefully to the reservation in Idaho. Chief White Bird refused to surrender, telling Joseph and the other warriors that he would rather die.

He said, "I am older than you. I have my experience with a man of two faces and two tongues. If you surrender, you will be sorry, and in your sorrow, you will feel rather to be dead than suffer that deception."

Joseph replied, "Many of our people are out on the hills naked and freezing. The women are suffering with cold; the children are crying with the chilly dampness of the shelter pits. For myself, I do not care; it is for them that I am going to surrender."

As Looking Glass rose to look at an Indian scout who was advancing upon them in the distance, he was shot in the head and killed. It was decided that when Joseph went back to hear the terms of surrender, White Bird and his people would use the opportunity to flee to Canada.

While Joseph was in council with General Howard, White Bird and two hundred and 33 of his people fled, making it safely to Canada. General Howard was extremely angry for the deception but felt that with Joseph and the other 418 of his people in custody, he finally had his victory.

At the surrender, Joseph had these famous words to say: "I am tired of fighting. Our chiefs are killed. Looking Glass is dead. Toohulhulsote is dead. The old men are all dead. It is the young men who say yes or no. He who led the young men is dead. It is cold, and we have no blankets. The little children are freezing to death. Some of my people have run away to the hills and have no blankets, no food. No one knows where they are, perhaps freezing to death. I want to have time to look for my children and see how many I can find. Maybe I shall find them among the dead. Hear me, my chiefs. I am tired. My heart is sick and sad. From where the sun now stands, I will fight no more forever."

General Howard would later be rebuked instead of praised by General Sherman for spending more time "hunting headlines" than he did the Nez Perce.

The Nez Perce were not taken to the reservations in Idaho as they had been promised; they were taken to Fort Leavenworth, Kansas, as prisoners of war. When I read what had happened in the newspaper, I cried for my friends. To most people, this was just a sad story of strangers who were unknown and foreign to them. I had grown up with many of these people, and over the years, my love and respect for their humanity and courage had only grown.

At that time, Fort Leavenworth was nothing more than a filthy hole, and 21 more died there. They were then marched to a malaria-infested area of northeastern Oklahoma, where another 47 of their people died.

In 1879 Chief Joseph was allowed to travel to Washington D.C. with his friend Yellow Bull. There, he met with many government officials and the President of the United States, Rutherford B. Hayes.

He told newspaper reporters, "At last, I was granted permission to come to Washington and bring my friend Yellow Bull and our interpreter with me. I am glad I came. I have shaken hands with many friends, but there are some things I want to know that no one seems able to explain. I cannot understand how the government sends a man out to fight us, as it did General Miles, and then breaks his word. Such a government has something wrong about it. I cannot understand why so many chiefs are allowed to talk so many different ways and promise so many different things. I have seen the Great Father Chief; and the Next Great Chief; the Commissioner Chief; the Law Chief; and many other law chiefs, and they all say they are my friends, and that I shall have justice, but while all their mouths talk right, I do not understand why nothing is done for my people. I have heard talk and talk, but nothing is done. Good words do not last long unless they amount to something. Words do not pay for my dead people. They do not pay for my country now overrun by white men. They do not protect my father's grave. They do not pay for my horses and cattle. Good words do not give me back my children.

"Good words will not make good the promise of your war chief, General Miles. Good words will not give my people a home where they can live in peace and care for themselves. I am tired of talk that comes to nothing. It makes my heart sick when I remember all the good words and all the broken promises. There has been too much talking by men who had no right to talk. Too many misinterpretations made; too many misunderstandings between the white men and the Indians. If the white man wants to live in peace with the Indian, he can live in peace. There need be no trouble. Treat all men alike. Give them the same laws. Give them all an even chance to live and grow. The same Great Spirit Chief made all men. They are all brothers.

"The earth is the mother of all people, and all people should have equal rights upon it. You might expect all rivers to run backward as that any man who was born a free man should be contented penned up and denied liberty to go where he pleases. If you tie a horse to a stake, do you expect he will grow fat? If you pen an Indian up on a small spot of earth and compel him to stay there, he will not be contented, nor will he grow and prosper. I have asked some of the Great White Chiefs where they get their authority to tell the Indian that he shall stay in one place while he sees white men going where they please. They cannot tell me.

"I only ask of the Government to be treated as all other men. If I cannot go to my own home, let me have a home in a country where my people will not die so fast. I want to go to Bitter Root Valley. There my people would be happy; where they are now, they are dying. Three have died since I left my camp to come to Washington. When I think of our condition, my heart is heavy. I see men of my race treated as outlaws and driven from country to country or shot down like animals.

"I know that my race must change. We cannot hold our own with the white men as we are. We only ask a chance to live as other men live. We ask for recognition as men. We ask that the same law shall work alike on all men. If an Indian breaks the law, punish him by the law. If a white man breaks the law, punish him also.

"Let me be a free man, free to travel, free to stop, free to work, free to trade where I choose, free to choose my teachers, free to follow the religion of my fathers, free to talk, think and act for myself—and I will obey every law or submit to the penalty. Whenever the white man treats the Indian as they treat each other, then we shall have no more wars. We shall be all alike—brothers of one father and mother, one sky above us, and one country around us, and one government for all. Then the Great Spirit Chief who rules above will smile upon this land and send rain to wash out the bloody spots made by brothers' hands upon the face of the earth. For this time, the Indian race is waiting and praying. I hope no more groans of wounded men and women will ever go to the ear of the Great Spirit Chief above and that all people may be one people. "Hinmahtooyahlatkekht has spoken for his people."

In 1885 the Nez Perce were finally returned to the reservations in Idaho, the Christians went to Lapwai, and all others, including Joseph, to the Colville Reservation. There he spent most of his time silently staring into the campfire in contemplation, motionless for hours at a time. He never saw his beloved Wallowa Valley or mountains again, home of "The Winding Waters."

On September 21, 1904, Chief Joseph died at the age of 64 at his lodge in Nespelem, Washington. It was not only the end of his life; it was the end of an era, the echo of a dying way of life sounding over the Wallowa Mountains and valleys.

He was a courageous man, dignified, intelligent, resourceful, and completely devoted to his people and they to him. He was a peaceful warrior unwilling to abdicate the future of his people to a thoughtless government for a handful of beads and grain.

When Chief Joseph's friend Doctor Edwin Latham was asked the cause of death, he stated, "It was due to a broken heart."

Chapter 4

The Survivors

Lorinda Bewley

I have oftentimes wondered what became of the survivors and families of the Whitman Massacre. Some like Timpstetelew seemed to disappear into the mists of time; others I have read or heard about, and a number were scarcely more than rumors. A few like Catherine and Elizabeth Sager became lifelong friends.

These were difficult times for staying in touch. Messages frequently took months or more to deliver and receive. The Whitman experience as a whole taught me that people are very complex. Cruel and divine, craven and brave; it is possible for one person to be all of these things at one time or another. That is why only God should judge our souls at the end of our sojourn here on earth. I have often been asked who among the people stands out from that momentous time.

If a resurrection emerged from the Whitman massacre, it was Lorinda Bewley. The shame and humiliation she experienced were beyond words, beyond imagination. I will never forget one of the last things she said to Mother, "Who is going to want me now ... who is ever going to want someone like me?"

When 21-year-old Lorinda Bewley and her 20-year-old brother Crockett first arrived at the Whitman Mission they were both very ill, suffering from camp fever. Their father John Bewley was captain of the wagon train that had brought them over the trail and had decided it would be best for them to stay for a few weeks until they recovered before moving on to the Willamette Valley. Narcissa wanted Lorinda to help with the children and stay on as a teacher, "Having become very much attached to Lorinda, being much pleased by her refinement and manners." Lorinda reluctantly agreed and John Bewley asked his son Crockett to stay on and watch over her.

Before arriving at the mission, a contingent of Indians, including Five Crows, head chief of the Cayuse, greeted them. He was intelligent, spoke English, and dressed in an immaculate combination of American and traditional clothes.

He was of medium height and build, with a large stomach, strong pocked face, and short cut hair like a European. He understood that change was coming, and it would be to his advantage to know how the white man's world operated. He was also infatuated with Narcissa Whitman and felt a white wife was only fair since many of the trappers and traders had Indian wives. He inspected every wagon train that arrived, looking for "a white girl with golden hair and blue eyes, like Narcissa Whitman," he could take as a wife.

Lorinda and Crockett had barely gotten settled and recovered from camp fever when Crockett came down with the measles. On November 29, 1847, the day of the massacre, Lorinda was lying in bed upstairs ill, wrapped in a blanket, when she heard the commotion downstairs and outside. She was then herded downstairs with the rest of us and lined against the wall where we witnessed the murder of Doctor Whitman and John and Frank Sager.

That night and the following days were a nightmare for all of us, especially Lorinda, whose beauty had attracted the attention of many of the men. For me, witnessing her struggle and rape by Tamsucky was as horrible as seeing the murders. I will never forget how heartbroken and devastated she was afterward.

She had been raised among a highly moral and affluent white society by a close-knit family from Tennessee. She was in love and engaged to a young man named William Chapman. To her, these Indian men were savages, unlike anything she had encountered in the past, unlike anything she had imagined. I remember running to her room after her brother Crockett had been killed and finding her under the bed moaning something that sounded almost inhuman. I can still see her in my mind on her knees, begging Chief Tiloukaikt not to be taken to Five Crows as his wife.

Just before she was abducted, I handed her a small Bible that was lying on one of the tables that she hid in her clothes. When the time came for her to go, she became hysterical and started crying and resisting. The man who had been sent to bring her to Five Crows was a giant man with a stoic face who finally had to tie Lorinda to Tashe. She worked her way loose and fell from the horse badly spraining her wrist. The Cayuse man ignored her injury and was even more brutal in tying her to Tashe the second time.

It was a windy and cold winter afternoon as she departed with nothing more than a small satchel and the little Bible I had given her. She was led away to a terrifying world, completely foreign and beyond her comprehension. Lying over Tashe like a lifeless sack of flour, she looked back at me one last time while holding her injured wrist with a glazed look of utter hopelessness and despair. I will never forget it. We would meet in the future, but it was the last time I would ever see Tashe again.

When Peter Skene Ogden arrived at Fort Walla Walla, he asked for a meeting with the chiefs, including Five Crows, to discuss the details of the ransom and trade. At the second meeting Five Crows expressed how grievous the decision was to massacre the people at the Whitman mission, but was reluctant to give up Lorinda who he now considered his wife. He was a rich man and the ransom meant little to him. Mr. Ogden told him that it was all or nothing, and if it were nothing, the Americans would soon be bringing a well-armed military force intent on war with the Cayuse.

At the final meeting Five Crows didn't show up since he didn't want to be forced to give Lorinda up. Mr. Ogden sent him a message letting him know that there would be no trade without Lorinda Bewley, and there would soon be a price on his head. It was believed that the other chiefs pressured Five Crows into giving her up in order to avoid going to war with the Americans. She had become little more than a corpse to his advances, but still he wanted to keep her; he reluctantly agreed.

On December 28, 1847 an Indian messenger rode to Five Crows lodge with a message that all of the hostages were to be released and that Miss Bewley should immediately be returned to the Whitman mission. When she heard the news, she dropped to her knees to give thanks to God for his mercy, believing the nightmare was over. Five Crows tried everything he could to convince her to stay, even offering to live among the white people if she would agree. She told him that she was promised to another man and wanted no part of the Indian way of life.

In his final plea he said, "There will be no more sunshine in the lodge of Five Crows. I will be alone always and when the wolf howls upon the hill, he will be no lonelier than I. Five Crows will walk alone until he dies, no wife, no children to greet me when I return from the hunt. Only the memory of the golden hair and eyes, the color of the sky, voice like the running brook, and fleet as the wild fawn to run from me."

Mr. Ogden and his men then transported us down the Columbia River headed for Fort Vancouver. The crew started singing, and then the captives joined in. As Lorinda slowly began to come back to life she looked into the sky and remarked that, "No music in this world has ever sounded so beautiful."

Her joy was short lived. Before we reached Fort Vancouver a messenger from Oregon City intercepted us and told her that when her father heard about what had happened to her and her brother Crockett, he had a massive heart attack and died.

At Fort Vancouver she was treated with great sympathy for all she had endured. Along with the other survivors she continued to Portland, Oregon. There she was joined with her mother, two brothers, and sister. She was also met by her fiancé, William Chapman, who she feared would reject her after what had happened. That was not to be the case.

They were married on October 3, 1848 in Oregon City where the happy bride regained her health and beauty, taking her place as a wife and teacher. Her husband William volunteered for the Cayuse war with the Oregon Rifles, possibly to seek justice for what had happened to her.

Their first two children, John and Catherine, were born in a simple home that William built. They then moved to Sheridan, Oregon where William built a comfortable log home and they raised eight more children. Seven would survive into adulthood and they eventually had 15 grandchildren who would become a permanent part of our Northwest history.

On October 3, 1899 they celebrated their golden wedding anniversary with family and friends. A tribute was made to honor the pioneer couple who had endured so much and become an important part of Oregon's history.

Lorinda Bewley Chapman died on November 6, 1899 at the age of 73, her husband William on July 23, 1911.

Like the mythological phoenix, she rose from the ashes of Waiilatpu to live a long and meaningful life of hope and redemption.

Mary Ann Bridger

It would be hard for any of us in this day and age to imagine what the first couple of years of Mary Ann Bridger's life had been like. She was born somewhere in the wilderness of the Rocky Mountains in the middle of a snowstorm. Her mother was an Indian Princess named Cora, daughter of Insula, head chief of the Flathead Nation. Her Father Jim Bridger was one of the most famous mountain men in American history.

Mary Ann's mother Cora died in 1845 from complications after the birth of her third child. Jim Bridger then brought Mary Ann to the Whitman Mission when she was six years old, feeling that life as a trapper's daughter was far too difficult and dangerous for a young child.

She was sick with the measles at the time of the massacre. Without Doctor Whitman's gentle care her health continued to deteriorate until she died on March 23, 1848 at the tender age of 13 years.

The Canfield Family

William Canfield's escape and six-day journey from Waiilatpu to Lapwai on foot in the dead of winter with a bullet in his side is no less epic than Father's.

From Bennington, Vermont, he and his wife Sally Ann were both 37 years old at the time of the massacre. When he, Uncle Horace and Mr. Jackson decided to head back east by crossing the mountains in winter they came very close to death several times. They were attacked by four Indian men they thought to be Blackfoot. Fortunately, the warriors only had bows and arrows, though one nearly took Mr. Jackson's ear off during the skirmish.

Unfamiliar with the terrain they wandered aimlessly toward the rising sun until they ran out of provisions and were forced to eat their packhorse. Deciding to return west because of the cold, they eventually came across a friendly Nez Perce man who pointed them in the direction of the Columbia River. After being reunited at Fort Vancouver, the Canfields traveled to Oregon City where Sally Ann delivered a baby boy who only lived for two days. After two years in Washington State, they and their five children moved on to Sonoma, California where they would peacefully spend the rest of their days. William passed in 1880 at the age of 70, and Sally Ann in 1893 at the age of 83.

David Malin

There can be no more cruel beginning to life as a human being than to come into this world unwanted and unloved; yet that was the harsh and bitter fate of David Malin.

Up until he came to the Whitman Mission as a four-year-old boy, I don't imagine he had experienced any kind of love or happiness. His Spanish father deserted his Indian mother when he was an infant. His mother must have been mentally ill with a heart of stone to leave him in a dirt hole to die.

His grandmother deposited what was little more than a dirty naked skeleton wrapped in a filthy blanket into Narcissa Whitman's open arms. She once told me that when she saw him, "I could not shut my heart against him."

He was so sweet and mild mannered that the other Indian boys at the mission bullied him until Narcissa put an end to it. One time he was pushed into a fire and his foot was badly burned. Another time they shaved his head with a sharp knife leaving him bloody, with strips of hair about an inch wide to humiliate him. This was done because he was friendless and had no one to protect him.

Under the Whitmans' loving care and watchful eyes, he was able to experience four years of relative happiness, quite possibly the only happiness he would ever know.

The last any of us ever saw of him was at Fort Walla Walla. As we were packing to leave it was being decided who would go where, and who would take care of whom, David once again found himself unwanted.

If I close my eyes, I can still feel his anguish and despair as he stood on the dock crying. It was the most heartbreaking sound I have ever heard. When we were about 50 yards away, he jumped into the water and tried to swim out to us. One of the dockhands jumped in the water after him and pulled him back to shore. When they reached the riverbank one of the Catholic priests grabbed him by his spindly neck and roughly led him away crying. It was the last image and impression I have of little David Malin.

The Hall Family

Peter Hall was a 31-year-old architect and builder when Doctor Whitman hired him to work at the mission. He was working on the roof of the mansion house when he saw the men below being attacked. He climbed down through the rafters and jumped out of a window frame seizing a gun from one of the Cayuse men. The man pulled his hatchet and deeply cut Mr. Hall's arm before he managed to escape. His decision was the same as Mr. Canfield's, do I stay and die a meaningless death, or do I go for help in the hope that the Indians would not harm the women and children? He decided to go for help and headed for Fort Walla Walla on foot some 30 miles away. Approximately a week later Peter Hall's body was discovered on the bank of the John Day River where he had been mutilated and scalped.

Peter Hall's wife Rachel was also 31 years old when the massacre took place. Afterward she moved to Yamhill County, Oregon with her five girls, no money, no belongings, or way of contacting other family members. They struggled until she met and married Mr. Robert Beers, a farmer living in Linn County, Oregon.

Gertrude Hall was the only one of their daughters that I had gotten to know well, ten years old at the time of the massacre and smart as a whip. We stayed in contact on and off until I moved to Lake Chelan in my later years. She met and married a riverboat captain by the name of Leonard White, and they were married on July 4, 1853, and had one daughter before divorcing. In December of 1868 she remarried Judge Owen Denny, who had come to Oregon from Ohio when he was 14 years old. He attended college at Willamette University, receiving one of the first law degrees in 1852. They would become a colorful part of the Oregon and United States history. He was appointed as Council General to China, moving to Shanghai where they lived for four years.

They then accompanied General Ulysses S. Grant and his wife Julia around the world starting from Tientsin, China, and ending in Yokohama, Japan. Gertrude lived the good life among high society and was entertained by kings, queens, and emperors. Mr. Denny then became advisor to the King of Korea, and was given a beautiful home furnished in priceless Asian art treasures that they were allowed to take with them when they returned home in 1890. He continued to practice law until he died in June of 1900. Gertrude lived another 33 years and died in Portland Oregon during August of 1933 at the age of 96.

The Hayes Family

Tragically, Rebecca Hayes husband died while they were on the Oregon Trail. She came to the Whitman mission worn and weary with two little boys. Her son Henry was only two, and Napoleon was not yet a year old when he died. A French-Canadian worker named Joe Stanfield was attracted to her and could see that she was alone and vulnerable. He began making advances that she clearly rejected. He was a big burly man who I had always tried to avoid. I remember several instances in which he had her trapped and was talking forcefully at her, her head constantly shaking back and forth.

It was never really known how involved he was in the massacre, but it was certain he knew it was coming and even bragged about it afterward. He had been put in charge of the women and children after the massacre and was a bully, constantly ordering us around. His attraction to Mrs. Hayes turned into an obsession once there were no men to protect her, and he constantly tried to coerce and intimidate her into accepting his proposals of marriage.

She once confided in me that she found him revolting, and still missed and loved her dead husband. She said that she had to be careful and not completely alienate him or he might turn on her and her son Henry. Still, she was a brave woman who risked her life more than once to protect us.

What happened to Mrs. Hayes after the massacre will always remain a mystery since no one that I know of ever heard from her again. Her son Henry became a well-known photographer, but I never did see him again to ask what became of his mother.

The Kimball Family

At 40 years of age Nathan Kimball was a gentle giant of a man. On the trail their youngest girl Clarice came down with camp fever and died and was buried next to the Platte River. Tragedy soon struck again when their oldest boy Omar, who was 14, caught a severe cold and died a week later.

During the onset of the fighting Kimball's arm was deeply cut by a tomahawk and badly broken by a war club. Far outnumbered and knowing he could do no good in the yard, he ran for the mission house and initially hid upstairs with his wife Harriet and their five children. Out of desperation for water to quench the thirst of the sick children he dressed up like an Indian and crept outside. On the way back to the house he was discovered, run down and killed by a Cayuse man named Frank as his daughter Helen watched. Another man later cut his heart out of his chest and burned it in a fire.

Harriet Kimball was 38 and also felt strongly that the massacre was instigated by the Catholic priests. She believed it was done in order to rid themselves of the missionaries and take the territory and missions for themselves. Shortly after the massacre Harriet remarried a man named John Jewett, and moved to Clatsop Plains, just ten miles south of Astoria, Oregon. With her five children and his eight it was a full house. She died in 1892 at the age of 83, leaving behind seven children, seven grandchildren, and 15 great grandchildren.

Their oldest daughter Susan Kimball was 16 at the time of the massacre, one of the three teenage girls present during the massacre. She was forced to become the bride of a young Cayuse man named Frank, the same one who killed her father and then bragged to her about it. No one ever wanted to talk about what happened to her, but it isn't hard to imagine since she was dragged off in the night and was always crying, or on the verge of tears. She eventually met and married a man named Augustus Wirt in 1850 and settled in Seaside, Oregon where they raised five children. Susan died in 1905 at 74 years of age in Seaside.

When the fighting broke out, 12-year-old Nathan Kimball hid under a wagon and watched the carnage, including the men's hearts being cut out of their chests and held up on sticks as trophies and then burned. It may have been because he was small for his age that Nathan was spared and used as a slave to carry wood and water or whatever heavy work was needed.

I was standing next to Nathan on the second day after the massacre when we were all lined up outside. Nathan and one of the other younger boys made a break for it through the cornfields and a bullet passed so close to him that it put a hole in his hat and grazed his head.

They hid in the field until the next day when they were found and returned unharmed. They were then warned that if they tried to escape again, they would be killed. I don't know of anyone who stayed in touch with Nathan, but I did hear that he worked a farm and died at about the age of 68 in Clatsop County, Oregon near Astoria.

Mina Kimball married a man named Issac Boggs when she was only 13 years old and he was 28. Things didn't work out, so they divorced and in 1867, she remarried a man named Alexander Megler.

I ran into her once when we were both in our golden years. She was 75 and told me that she still did all of her own house work saying, "Pooh I'm not an old woman, I'm just trophies." She was spunky and you couldn't help but like her. She told me that she didn't like the way people were changing, that in the past they were less complicated and more concerned about the public welfare. Along with many others she believed that Astoria would one day become a major metropolitan city like San Francisco because of its location on the Columbia River as a seaport. It turned out that Portland would become the heart of Oregon, Astoria all but forgotten by most people.

She and Alexander bought a hotel called the Astoria House, in Astoria, Oregon, and ran it for seven years. They sold it and bought another hotel called the Occident House and ran it until 1900. She once entertained President Rutherford B. Hayes at the Occident and sat next to him during dinner letting him know about all of the benefits that Astoria had to offer. She walked a mile every day until the day before she died in 1938 at the age of 92. She was a colorful character in the history of Astoria, Oregon and the Northwest.

The Marsh Family

Walter Marsh and his family came over the Oregon Trail in 1847 from their home in Springfield, Illinois. His wife Lavisha died on the trail just outside of Soda Springs, Idaho and was buried with no coffin or casket. Like so many others, she was wrapped in a dirty old mattress and left on a lonely plain. At 53 years old Walter Marsh was now responsible for his 11-year-old daughter Mary, and two-year-old grandson Alba.

When the massacre broke out Mary watched in horror from the second story window of the mission house as her father was fatally shot. When we reached Oregon City, Mary found a home with a family named the Lovejoys, who treated her like one of the family. She eventually met and married a man named James Cason when she was 17 and they settled in Wheeler County, Oregon where they raised their ten children. She passed away in 1907 at the age of 71 and was buried at Haystack Cemetery in Wheeler County, Oregon.

The Manson Brothers

Steven and John Manson were smuggled upstairs and hidden behind a trap door when the fighting began. Steven was 13 and John was 11. When they were discovered, the Cayuse threatened to kill them, but John calmly explained that they were not Americans, that their father was Donald Manson, chief trader for the Hudson Bay Company. He clearly explained that if anything happened to them, the Cayuse would soon be at war with the Hudson Bay Company and British Army, that their deaths would be avenged.

I was translating for them and too young to understand whether it was a bluff or not. However, the Cayuse knew their father well, a man with a tough reputation as a fair trader whom they relied upon for guns and supplies. The Cayuse not only reversed their decision toward the brothers; they offered them Cayuse brides. Steven politely thanked them and explained that they were still too young to take wives.

From the time I first arrived at the mission Steven was the one that all of the girls were talking about. It was understandable since he was remarkably handsome and charming with a bright wit and intellect. He never married or had children, settling in Champoeg, Oregon with his other siblings. He passed away in 1880 at the age of 44.

In 1863 John met and married Aurelia Yale while working for the Hudson Bay Company. They had three children together and moved from Vancouver, Washington, to Victoria, British Columbia, where he passed away in 1903.

Helen Mar Meek

Of all my friends at the Whitman Mission Helen Mar Meek was my favorite personality. I think it was the rascal in her that made us all love her so much. She was the life of the party, bright and funny, always being reprimanded by Mrs. Whitman for one thing or another.

She was ten years old at the time of the massacre and very sick with the measles. Like Mary Ann Bridger, her father Joe Meek was a famous mountain man. Her mother was the daughter of a powerful Nez Perce chief and was killed by the Bannock Indians during a raid when Helen was just a baby. Joe Meek then brought Helen to the Whitmans in 1840, when she was just two years old.

I suspect it was for the same reason that Jim Bridger had left Mary Ann, it was nearly impossible to raise a young child constantly on the move in the harsh and dangerous mountains of the Pacific Northwest. It hadn't been long since the Whitmans' little girl Alice Clarissa had drowned, and having this spunky and beautiful little girl in their home helped fill the lonely place left by Alice Clarissa.

Without the tender care of Doctor Whitman Helen died just 11 days after the massacre. Joe Meek had always had close ties with the Indian tribes including the Cayuse. After Helen's death he became bitter toward the Cayuse, blaming them for her death and becoming a strong proponent of the Cayuse War. Legend has it that he was badly injured during a battle with a grizzly bear in which he killed it with nothing more than a hunting knife. He was the first white man to see Yellowstone and described it as, "A country smoking with the vapor of boiling springs and burning gases issuing from small craters, each of which was emitting a sharp whistling sound."

When the beavers were hunted almost to extinction Joe worked as a guide at first, then officer of the law, and later he entered politics. He was one of the few men to witness the transformation of the Wild West into a milder west. He was the first person to bring the news of the massacre and Cayuse War to Washington, D.C.

While in Washington, he met with his cousin Sarah's husband, President James K. Polk to make a case for the Oregon territory becoming part of the United States. As the Federal Territorial Marshall, he personally supervised the trial and execution of the five Cayuse men accused and convicted of the Whitman Massacre. Joe Meeks never resolved his feelings toward the Cayuse for the death of his daughter Helen Mar, nor could he accept the fact that his half-Indian children were ostracized from the Northwest society that he had helped create. He was a legend in his own time, and forever after. Joe Meeks died in Tualatin Plains in 1875 at the age of 65. His wife Virginia lived another 25 years and departed us in 1900.

The Osborne Family

When the fighting broke out Josiah Osborne and his family hid under the flooring in their bedroom for over 12 hours. They then escaped into the pitch-black night with their children in the direction of Fort Walla Walla. They had no food or water and only two sheets to shelter them through the freezing nights.

After two nights and days of traveling it was decided that Josiah would continue to Fort Walla Walla with their two-year-old boy Alexander. Their daughter Nancy and son John would not leave their mother's side. On the third night when he arrived at the fort, Mr. McBean once again refused to help as he had done with Peter Hall earlier.

There are names for people like that, and as much as I would like to, I'm not going to use one because I know Mother in heaven wouldn't like it. If Mr. John Mix Stanley hadn't come to the rescue with horses, food, blankets and a guide, Mrs. Osborne and her children would have surely perished.

After they finally had reached and then departed Fort Walla Walla, they decided to continue to the Hudson Bay Farm near Pendleton Oregon. Once there, they were told that the Cayuse had recently come looking for them with bad intentions. Over a period of weeks, they finally made their way back to The Dalles and then on to their home in Linn County where the small town of Brownsville had recently sprung up.

Nancy was nine at the time of the massacre, and though we had studied and played together, I didn't know her all that well. Several years later that would change when we moved to her hometown of Brownsville, Oregon in the fall of 1848. We had shared the same ordeal of the Whitman Massacre and she became my best friend and confidant.

Though she went on to live a long life, Nancy Osborne was never the same after the massacre and at times she would break out crying for seemingly no reason at all.

She married twice but never had children. At the age of 89 she died committing suicide by jumping out of an upstairs window yelling, "The Indians are coming." For some the nightmare ended only in death.

I never heard another word about Margaret, but Josiah died in Linn County in 1880 at the age of 71.

Joe Stanfield

I don't like to think of myself as vindictive so let's just call it justice when Joe Stanfield was caught, tried and convicted for theft at Waiilatpu. His worst crime was knowing that the massacre was planned and not saying anything to anyone. When Mr. Kimball, his wife and seven children came over the Oregon Trail they had $1,500 in gold sewn into their belts, which was considered a very large sum of money at the time. Joe Stanfield was caught right in the act of burying a watch and the money belt he had stolen from the Kimballs.

Just before we reached Oregon City, he approached Mrs. Hayes and asked her when she wanted to set the wedding date. Knowing she was now safe at that point, she told him that if he ever got close to her again, she was going to have him arrested. She didn't have to wait long, as he was immediately arrested when we reached Oregon City. Two of the widows testified that he had bragged to them about knowing of the massacre beforehand.

He was convicted and sentenced to ten years in prison and then sent away. Unfortunately, he escaped during the trip to prison, then fled to California where he was thought to have died in the gold mines in about 1850.

The Saunders Family

Judge L.W. Saunders was hired as the teacher to replace Mr. Rogers. For me his murder is the most vivid and horrible memory of the massacre. When it started, he bravely ushered us upstairs into the classroom to try and hide us in the loft but was struck from behind with a knife. He was then struck several more times as he tried to fight armed men. Badly injured and bleeding he slipped and fell down the stairs past the men.

As Helen and I were watching out of the window they cut him down and butchered him. It was so heartbreaking to hear Helen calling out, "They are killing my father." I have awakened so many nights in terror hearing her voice.

His wife Mary eventually wrote a book called, "The Whitman Massacre," that was published in 1916. I was able to get a copy, but other than that I have never heard another thing concerning Mary Saunders or her five children.

The Smith Family

Joseph Smith emigrated from England to Canada, Canada to New York, and New York to the Oregon territory in 1847. He had six children from a previous marriage and like so many other immigrants in need of food, supplies, or rest, they stopped at the Whitman Mission to recuperate. Doctor Whitman put him to work at the sawmill to provide lumber for sale and all of the new construction at the mission.

His second wife Anna had also come from England to Canada, but as a child in her mother's arms. She somehow became separated from her mother and was taken in by foster parents who then moved to Illinois. It was there that she met and married Joseph, who was 20 years her senior. After the massacre Joseph temporarily left his family in Oregon City for the California gold rush of 1848. He was able to make enough money to send for his family and buy a hotel in San Francisco where they remained until the gold rush played out. After that they returned to Illinois in 1851. They had six children in Illinois and then returned to San Francisco until they finally settled in Bandon by the Sea in Coos County, Oregon where I never heard anything else about their family.

The Young Family

Like the Smith family, the Youngs were English and miles away working at the sawmill when the massacre happened. Elam and Irene's oldest son James was 24 years old when he was tragically murdered the night after the massacre while on his way to deliver lumber and pick up supplies; simply in the wrong place at the wrong time.

They reached the mission on the night of December 8, to find the bodies of Amos Sales and Crockett Bewley lying in the dirt, mutilated beyond recognition. To add to their horror, the Cayuse put both families in the room that Sales and Bewley had been beaten to death in, with the walls and floor still covered in blood.

After they reached Oregon City Elam Young found a one-room shack to rent. His two surviving boys found work cutting wood per cord and Elam built handmade tools. He then went to work for Doctor McLaughlin who was in the process of building a mill. They moved close to where we were living in Tualatin Plains for a year and eventually settled a donation claim in Green Hills, Washington. In 1855 Elam died at the age of 58, Irene followed ten years later at the age of 67, both buried in Cedar Mills, Oregon.

Nicholas Finley

Nicholas Finley was not involved in the killing, but no one will ever know for sure just how much or how little he was involved in planning the massacre. His father Jacques Raphael Finlay, known as Jaco, was half-Scottish and half-Indian. Nicholas's mother was named Teskwentichina of the Spokane tribe, making Nicholas three-fourths Indian. He had two brothers and one sister and was born in Canada, brought up among his mother's people. He started hunting and trapping the Northwest with his father and two older brothers when he was only ten years old, and his father Jaco died when he was 12.

He began apprenticing with Tom McKay of the Hudson Bay Company when he was 13. I remember some of the older girls saying that he was the most handsome man they had ever seen. He was tall with wide shoulders, jet-black hair down his back, and transparent blue eyes. In some ways he was very traditional and wouldn't eat ducks, eagles, hawks or crows because they were considered spirit birds. Neither would he eat bear, wolves or coyote, all considered spirit animals. My parents and the Whitmans first met him on the Oregon Trail in 1836 when they were at Fort Boise, introduced by his old comrade Tom McKay. In 1846 he set up his lodge at Tshimakain in Spokane country near the Eellses and Walkers' mission. He came to Waiilatpu in 1847 looking for work with a recommendation from Cushing Eells. The doctor hired him as a laborer and he almost immediately fell in with Joe Lewis and his band. It's believed that the planning for the massacre took place in his lodge less than one hundred yards from the Whitmans' house.

The day before the massacre took place Doctor Whitman went to Nicholas's lodge and asked, "I understand the Indians are to kill me and Mrs. Whitman, do you know anything about it?"

Nicholas told the doctor, "I should know, doctor, you have nothing to fear; there is no danger."

No one claims to have seen him during the massacre, so it is certain that he had no part in the actual killing itself. It is also possible that they didn't include him in their exact plans, but I am certain he knew something was coming and could have warned us.

Shortly after the massacre he delivered the two Manson boys and David Malin to Fort Walla Walla and then continued to the Colville Valley near Tshimakain. When the Walkers and Eellses found out about the massacre they became worried that the same thing might happen to them, and that Nicholas was coming to stir up trouble among the Spokane people. He claimed that he was only there to visit his brothers, but for the Eellses and Walkers it was a great relief to have him leave.

One of the ironies of the Cayuse War was that Nicholas and his brothers joined the Cayuse campaign about the same time that his old mentor Thomas McKay was put in command of a company to hunt them down. After the Battle of Sand Hollows, Nicholas and his brothers went to General Gilliam and told him they would quit fighting if he would grant them amnesty. The general didn't fully trust them, but agreed in order to get them out of the conflict. After the war Nicholas returned to Colville Valley with his brothers and wife Suzette where they had the first of eight children together. They lived there from 1849 until 1860, then moved to one of the most beautiful places on earth, Bitterroot Valley, Montana. I was told that the Finleys were still alive in 1891, living a peaceful and quiet life together with their family at the Flathead Reservation in Montana.

William Craig

For many years, William Craig was like a deeply embedded thorn in Father and Mother's lives. He was personally responsible for turning many of the Nez Perce against our family and mission, creating an atmosphere intimidating to even those Nez Perce who wanted to remain loyal. In time his actions, combined with a growing distrust of all white people managed to reduce Father's services from as many as two thousand, to less than a dozen. Our school, which was the center of our mission community, had had as many as three hundred students at any given time, closed since no one was attending.

I don't think this was ever intended as a personal attack on our family; I believe his intention was to help the Nez Perce retain their traditional beliefs and way of life.

My parents' relationship with Mr. Craig had been on and off for many years, but had it not been for his courageous rescue and protection of my parents, brother and sisters, they would have surely been killed or taken as hostages. I say courageous because it would have been easy for him to turn his back on our family and simply let the Cayuse have their way, but he did not. His stand against the Cayuse could have brought his entire village into conflict. For this humanitarian act of valor, I will carry my gratitude for this brave man to my grave.

I was told that Mr. Craig fled his home in Virginia at the age of 17 because of an incident in which he killed a neighbor during an argument. He came west and by the time he was 21 he was a well-established hunter and trapper in the Northwest Territory. He had spent years in the mountains with legendary mountain men such as

Jedediah Smith, much of it in the most dangerous parts of Blackfoot, Snake and Bannock territory. In 1836 at the age of 29 he helped establish Fort Davy Crockett in northwest Colorado, a major supply route at the time. He was the first non-missionary settler in what is now Idaho, and had first came to Lapwai in 1840. This was only possible because he married the daughter of one of the most powerful chiefs and shamans of the Nez Perce People named Hinmahtutekekaikt, also known as Thunder Eyes.

Mr. Craig's wife was a beautiful woman named Pahtissah, who he called Isabel.

He worked on and off for Father, even helping him with the Nez Perce dictionary. Living intimately with the Nez Perce, Mr. Craig had developed a deep respect for their customs and traditions. Because of his dedication and devotion, they not only accepted him as a man, but as a leader.

In 1855 a treaty was made between the Nez Perce and Americans in which Mr. Craig acted as interpreter and liaison. The Nez Perce honored him by giving him 640 acres of land. He was later appointed Superintendent of Indian Affairs by the Oregon Provisional Government and held that position until 1858, when he was appointed postmaster of Walla Walla. At the end of 1859 he returned to his home at Lapwai where he and Isabel opened a hotel and stage stop. They had five children together, one son and four daughters. They continued to live peacefully on their land until he had a stroke in 1869 and died. In his honor there is a mountain just north of the Lapwai Valley named after him. Isabel died in 1886 and was buried next to her husband at Jacques Spur Cemetery, in Lapwai.

Chief Beardy

By the time the massacre took place Chief Beardy was an old man, and though his opinion was sometimes dismissed, he had always been treated with respect for the great hunter and warrior he had once been. Several times after the massacre I would hear him scolding one of the younger warriors in a loud voice, usually trying to stop them from abusing the captives. During captivity, if a Cayuse man would try and take one of the girls or women off, Chief Beardy always came to their rescue and shamed the men for their indiscretion. When he had helped to bury the dead, one of the young Cayuse tried to stop him so he pulled his pistol and said, "If I cannot bury my good friends Mr. and Mrs. Whitman, I will fight."

When Chief Tiloukaikt saw what was taking place he reprimanded the young man and told Joe Stanfield to help Chief Beardy bury the dead. He was a good and loyal friend who will always be remembered by the families for his kindness and protection.

Chief Five Crows

Though it was thought that Chief Five Crows might have known about the planning of the massacre, he had nothing to do with the actual killing. However, after the massacre the Americans used his despicable treatment of Lorinda Bewley as a battle cry.

Among the Indian people he was respected as a powerful and rich chief, with over one thousand horses and head of cattle. He would later become one of the instigators and leading proponents of the Cayuse War, and was considered one of the most savage and vindictive enemies the Americans had ever encountered. In February of 1848, at the battle of Sand Hollow, he was badly wounded and fled to the Wallowa Valley in northeastern Oregon to recover from his wounds. It was at the village of his half-brother Chief Joseph that he was cared for until he healed. No one knows for sure what killed him, but his body was found somewhere near Pendleton, Oregon when he was about 70 years old.

The Gray Family

Maybe it's my odd sense of humor, but I can't help but smile when I recall some of the stories my parents told me about the four newlywed couples that Mr. Gray brought back over the trail including his own wife. From what I was told, the Eellses, Walkers, Smiths, and Grays fought like cats and dogs all the way from New York to Waiilatpu, often unwilling to talk to each other at all. Let's face it, most of these folks didn't get married because they met someone and fell deeply in love.

The simple fact is that they wanted to become missionaries and just did the best they could. With a small twist of fate, they all could have been married to a man or woman from one of the other couples. To think of the four couples trying to get to know their new spouse, let alone the other strangers under such extreme condition must have been a hoot, some kind of honeymoon.

I was too young to remember the William Gray with whom my parents and the Whitmans came over the trail, and had had so many problems with. I only recall the man who showed us such kindness and generosity when we visited him in Clatsop Plains on the Oregon Coast. Whatever their differences, he was to become one of the most respected historians and politicians of all the Northwest pioneers.

I know from Father that their differences centered around the fact that he was hired to build houses and buildings for the missions, but wanted to leave and start his own mission. He must have felt that he wanted to do something more important with his life, and he certainly proved that he was capable. His wife Mary Augusta Dix was a lovely woman, tall and brunette with a stately bearing and beautiful voice. When we were visiting him at Clatsop Plains, he once told us that it was love at first sight, that he proposed the night they met and she accepted. They were married six days later and were soon on the Oregon Trail with the Eellses, Smiths, and Walkers.

The winter that he, his wife and three children left for the Willamette Valley they were caught in a severe snowstorm near The Dalles. Fearing that they were all going to die of exposure, he sent their Indian guide ahead to Fort Vancouver to find help. When the guide reached the fort, he told Doctor McLaughlin what had happened, and the doctor immediately sent out a search party.

With blinding gale force winds and nearly white out conditions the search party had almost given up hope of finding them. They were making little progress going up river and were just about to turn around when one of the men told everyone to be quiet, that he thought he had heard something. As they slowly crept forward in the blinding snow, they began to hear what sounded like a woman's voice. The heavenly, unearthly sound turned out to be the beautiful voice of Mrs. Gray singing a Bible hymn. It was her voice that helped the rescue party locate the Grays and bring them safely to Fort Vancouver.

Once they had safely reached the Willamette Valley, Mr. Gray was offered a position teaching at the new Oregon Institute, soon to become Willamette University.

In the spring of 1843, a pioneer gathering took place at the Grays' home in which the foundation was laid for the provisional government of Oregon. It was to be the first American legislative body of its kind in the Northwest. Mr. Gray was appointed as a member of the legislature and helped write what would become known as its "First Organic Law."

In 1846 the Gray family moved to Clatsop Plains on the Oregon Coast just south of Astoria. It was there that he erected the first Presbyterian Church on the Oregon Coast, which he named "Clatsop Plains Pioneer Church."

In 1853 he and his family moved to Astoria so that his children could attend the new school that had been erected. Mr. Gray felt that Clatsop Plains had some of the best grazing land he had ever seen, and in 1854 he decided to make the journey east once again, this time to Iowa where he purchased four hundred sheep. He successfully drove them over the Rocky Mountains to the Columbia River and all the way to Astoria.

Where the Columbia River empties into the Pacific Ocean is considered to be one of the most treacherous waterways on earth, with storm swells that reach 30 feet or more. The shifting sands are called the Columbia River bar, and only the very best pilots are able to navigate it safely. As Mr. Gray departed Astoria on a river barge with his four hundred sheep, a sudden storm came up near Chinook Point and overturned the scow drowning all of the sheep and nearly drowning Mr. Gray. It was a disaster for him and his family, but he was resilient and fortunately he was offered the position of government inspector for the port of Astoria.

In 1858 he and his family moved to a small village named Hope in what would one day become British Columbia. He started off building riverboats until joining the Fraser Canyon gold rush of 1860. That winter he, his wife, and five children returned to the American side of the river to a place called Osoyoos Lake. He and his sons then hauled logs down the mountain to build their family a log home. Once this was done, they built a boat to haul supplies for miners down the Okanogan River to the Columbia and on to Celilo Falls near The Dalles. Since tools were not available, he constructed the 91-foot-long boat with nothing more than a hatchet and chisel. He then caulked it with wild flax and pine pitch and launched it in May of 1861. Later that year they moved to Portland where he sold the boat and then moved to The Dalles.

He then built his first steamboat called the Cevadilla, and launched it in December of 1862. He was very successful plying the waters and delivering supplies along the Columbia with his new steamboat, but there was only one fly in the ointment. He believed his ship steward Mr. Kimmel, who was in charge of finances, was stealing from him. In a grievous argument he accused Mr. Kimmel of being a thief and put him ashore.

Later that day Mr. Gray was relaxing on deck, lying on his back watching the clouds go by while his 17-year-old son William was loading supplies. Young William looked up in a nick of time to see Mr. Kimmel running across the deck with an axe in his hand. Just as Mr. Kimmel raised the axe to split his father's head open, young William tackled him broadside sending them both flying overboard into the water. When they reached land Kimmel went wild with rage, pulled his pistol and shot young William first in the hand, then in the foot. As he was reloading his gun young William took a rock and struck Kimmel hard in the stomach, knocking the air out of him. William then rushed forward and struck him a mighty blow on the chin knocking him flat on his back and taking Kimmel's pistol. Several of the crewmembers then tied Mr. Kimmel up before he could regain his senses.

Mr. Gray was a man who liked to handle things his own way and decided not to press charges. Several months later Kimmel bought a boat, probably with the money he had stolen from Mr. Gray, and then started a business taking supplies up and down the river. Near The Dalles both he and his boat went over Celilo Falls, and instead of swimming to safety, he decided to go back to his cabin for his money belt. The boat capsized and that was the last bad choice Mr. Kimmel ever made.

In the summer of 1864 Mr. Gray sold the Cevadilla. He then decided to write a book based on the history of Oregon as he saw it. He was a strong proponent for the statehood of Oregon as well as acquiring Canada and Alaska for the United States. In 1867 he started the Oregon Pioneer Society, and in 1870 he published his massive book titled, *A History of Oregon*. The book was no less controversial than his life and actions had been. Many people thought it overly opinionated and lacking in hard facts. Still, it was the most significant book of its kind up to that time.

I think it is quite clear that Mr. Gray was destined to become more than a carpenter and handyman for Doctor Whitman or my Father; that he was industrious, determined and strong willed. He and his family became an indelible part of the past and future of Oregon and the Northwest Territory. His dear wife Mary left this earth on December 8, 1881 at the age of 71. He followed on November 14, 1889 at the age of 79.

The Walker Family

Tshimakain is a Spokane word that means, "The place of the springs." That was where the mission of the Eellses and Walkers was located for nine years, about 200 miles northeast of Walla Walla.

One of the passages that gets to me every time I read it is from a diary that Mary Walker published. In it she says about her husband to be, "I saw nothing particularly interesting or disagreeable in the man. He is a tall and rather awkward gentleman."

I'm not sure if that is the best criteria for a husband, but regardless, he proposed less than 48 hours after they met and she accepted. Life was a pretty rough ride for Mary, but they raised seven children, six boys and one girl and spent the next 40 years together.

Mary once said that she knew she wanted to be a missionary from the time she was nine years old. She had applied to the American Missionary Board to go to Africa, but they were looking for couples and didn't think it wise to send a single young white woman into the middle of the Zulu war. Elkanah Walker had also applied with the board and been turned down because he was single. The missionary board did the next best thing and arranged a meeting between the two; the rest is history.

By the time they reached the Whitman Mission none of the couples were talking to each other. The Smiths were by far the biggest problem, so when they left Waiilatpu to live with us, tensions lifted between the three remaining couples but started straining at Lapwai. The Walkers and Eellses eventually learned to get along together at their mission in Tshimakain, and though they had no success converting the Spokanes to Christianity, they were well liked.

Soon after the massacre the Walkers moved to Oregon City and then on to Tualatin Plains, now known as Forest Grove. They then continued the work my parents had started at the Tualatin Academy. Elkanah died there in 1877 at the age of 71. Mary lived another 20 years and died in 1896.

The Eells

Much of the Eellses' history is woven in with the Walkers' since they traveled the Oregon Trail together and jointly established and ran the mission at Tshimakain. Like Mary Walker, Cushing Eells was redirected to Oregon because of the Zulu war.

He married Myra Fairbanks, daughter of Deacon Joshua and Sally Fairbanks on March 5,1838, leaving the next day for the Oregon Territory. He was scheduled to attend a meeting at the Whitman Mission just before the massacre, but became ill and was unable to go. How fortuitous that he took ill, or he would have surely been killed along with the other men. This is another example of just how precarious our lives are, and the difference a simple twist of fate can make. After the massacre they moved to Salem, Oregon so that Cushing could teach at the Oregon Institute, soon to be Willamette University. They next moved to Forest Grove where he taught at the Tualatin Academy with Elkanah Walker.

He and his family were there for 14 years until the government reopened the upper Oregon and Washington country. They then moved to Walla Walla where Cushing decided to build a school in honor of the Whitmans. He called it the Whitman Seminary, which would one day be known as Whitman College. Myra passed away at Skokomish, Washington in 1878 at the age of 73, Cushing passed in 1893 at the age of 83 in Tacoma, Washington.

The Smiths

Mother used to often say that if you can't say anything good about a person, don't say anything at all. Mr. Asa Bowen Smith, and Sarah Gilbert Smith.

Joe Lewis

There was something missing in the eyes of Joe Lewis that frightened me and made him appear almost reptile like, void of humanity. No one really knew for sure where he came from, what was true, and what was a lie since he constantly contradicted himself.

The best I can make out is that he was probably half French-Canadian, and half Indian. He was both a bitter and violent man, and there is no doubt that he was the primary instigator of the Whitman massacre. One of his stories was that he was kidnapped and taken east and abandoned when he was a child by his white father. If this was true, it might account for his deep hatred for white people. He was smart in the sense that he knew how to manipulate people, especially the Indians who had been mistreated and diseased by the Americans.

It's hard to imagine that he would repay the kindness and generosity the Whitmans had shown him the way that he did. I saw him whipping Mrs. Whitman in the face after he had shot her in the chest, then leaving her in the freezing cold mud to die alone. I will never forget being covered with the blood and brains of Frank Sager after Joe Lewis shot him through the neck into his head, blowing the top off. The truly frightening thing was seeing how much pleasure he took from the killing. I would guess that almost everyone has known someone at some point that seems to take pleasure in other people's pain. I've seen it in people while discussing something painful like the Whitman Massacre; that little twisted smile that throws out a warning.

I think that maybe something terrible must have happened when he was young and it somehow warped him. I would guess that it made him feel better to know that others were hurting. In this case, I believe Joe Lewis was the extreme. After the massacre he pillaged through everyone's belongings taking whatever valuables he could find. He then took off and was never seen again. I did hear tell that he went to Utah to live among the Mormons and was later shot to death while robbing a stagecoach in Idaho.

I have tried to forgive him but it has been hard for me since I can still see the faces of my dead friends. I know that he turned out the way he did for a reason, maybe it was a lack of love, or maybe it was a flaw in his character. Either way I will continue to try and forgive him and pray for his soul.

The Sager Sisters

Henrietta

When the four surviving Sager girls reached Portland, Oregon they were scattered to the winds. Henrietta Naomi Sager was a miracle child that no one expected to live. At six months old she was so small and malnourished that she looked like a newborn baby. She was only three years old at the time of the massacre, so it's hard to say if she remembers any of it, or how it affected her.

After the massacre the Morgan family from Portland, Oregon took her in the for next three years. Her sister Catherine then married and was able to bring her to Salem, Oregon to live with her and her new husband.

When she was 14, they were visited by an uncle named Solomon Sager, who worked with a group of traveling actors and musicians on their way to California. They were like no one Henrietta had ever met before, an incredibly lively group with a lust for life. She was smitten as they played music and put on plays for their hosts. It must have looked to Henrietta like a great life of fun and adventure, so she left with them against Catherine's wishes. Elizabeth and Matilda Jane were also upset and worried for her, thinking it a bad decision for such a young woman to be with such a loose crowd.

Henrietta then traveled extensively and eventually fell out of touch with her sisters and was rarely heard from again. She was said to have gone through several marriages, the last one costing Henrietta her life when she was shot and killed by a bullet that was meant for her husband in 1870 at the age of 26.

Louise

Little Louise Sager would have probably survived if she could have continued to receive care and treatment from Doctor Whitman. For that reason, I would count her among the ones who were killed. She was only six years old when she died, on December 6, a week after the massacre. We were a sad collection of broken hearts when we buried her and then Helen Mar Meek just two days later. I have always wondered what those two beautiful children would have been like as adults had they survived.

Elizabeth

Within seven years after the massacre Elizabeth would end up living with six different families until Catherine was able to bring her into her home. Elizabeth and I were nearly the same age and often worked and played together. When she was 18, she met and married a kind and gentle man named William Fletcher Helm. They had a long and peaceful life together, raising eight children. William passed away in Portland, Oregon at the age of 80.

The last time I saw Elizabeth was in 1914 at a pioneer picnic that had been held every year for the past 26 years. We were both well along in years, but inside of the old woman was the same sweet and wonderful young girl. We talked for hours about everything but the massacre. Mostly it was about our families and how so many things had changed over the years. It was hard for our grandchildren to understand what life had been like for Elizabeth on the Oregon Trail, and myself growing up in a Nez Perce Indian village. Only kids growing up on farms still understand what it's like to raise and then have to kill your dinner. Few youngsters these days know how it feels to spend all day in the saddle or on a buckboard, to be truly hungry or cold.

My hometown of Brownsville, Oregon was more like a village, but Portland had grown into a big city. I told Elizabeth how the first time I saw Portland was in a log canoe with Father and Little Henry.

693

It was in 1845 when there was only one log building on the riverfront. Now there were beautiful houses and buildings everywhere. She told me that near her home there were markets and stores of every kind, in which you could find almost anything you needed on both sides of the Willamette River.

There were now three bridges across the river and they had built a giant train terminal called Union Station on the west side. Trains now ran almost daily between Portland and Seattle, Washington. Streetcars and automobiles were replacing horse drawn trolleys, and a man named Mr. Calbraith Perry Rodgers had flown an airplane all the way across the United States.

We had been talking for hours when I saw her eyes tear up, I asked what was wrong. She told me that she had never stopped missing her parents, the Whitmans, and her life with her brothers and sisters at the mission. I took her hands in mine and we cried quietly for a while as I thought about all the tragedy and beauty our two old bodies, minds, and souls had experienced. When we said goodbye, I knew it was going to be for the last time, that I was coming to the end of my time here on earth and that we would indeed see each other again on the other side.

Matilda Jane

I don't think I had ever known a sweeter and more affectionate child than Matilda Jane Sager. She was eight years old when we left Waiilatpu and I can't tell you how thrilled I was to know that she would be living with us wherever we settled in Oregon.

Mother had been quite ill, and by the time we arrived at Tualatin Plains she was unable to care for Matilda any longer. Father found a home for her with a man named Doctor William Geiger and his new wife Elizabeth Cornwall. When Doctor Geiger came for her the first time Elizabeth and I cried so long and hard that mother decided to keep her with us as long as we could. Unfortunately, it was not much longer until Mother was so weak that she could hardly get out of bed. When Doctor Geiger came for a second time, we knew it was going to happen, and accepted it.

Doctor Geiger was a very strict and stern man often inflicting harsh punishments on Matilda and it was an unhappy time in her life. All of our hearts nearly broke when she came to visit and begged us to take her back, that she was miserable and unhappy with the Geigers. At that point caring for Mother had become a full-time job. She was dying and there was nothing more we could do. Matilda understood.

When she was 15 years old her life changed drastically when she met and married a man named Lewis Mackey Hazlett. She had become a strikingly beautiful young woman with long chestnut hair, wide spaced big brown almond shaped eyes, with full lips that were constantly smiling. She was at the apex of her life with five beautiful children when Lewis became sick. They discovered that he had cancer and so he left for San Francisco to seek treatment from a doctor with a reputation as the best on the West Coast. Matilda was unable to go since she needed to take care of the children.

He died in San Francisco, leaving her a widow with five young children.

She eventually met a man named Mathew Fultz and they were married in the fall of 1865. They had three children together and in 1882 they moved to Farmington, Washington and opened a hotel. It seemed as if tragedy was always waiting around the corner for this dear sweet woman. One year later Mathew died and she was once again left a widow, this time with nine children. It is hard to imagine how her life must have been at that point, raising those children on her own.

Five years later her luck changed for the better when she married a man named David Delaney, who also lived in Farmington. He was a successful businessman and one of the largest landowners in Washington. I never heard of Mr. Delaney's passing, but when I saw Elizabeth at the pioneer picnic in Brownsville, she told me that Matilda Jane was still alive and well and living in Farmington. I have always had a soft spot in my heart for her and wish I could have seen her again, but it was not to be.

Catherine

Whenever I think of Catherine Sager the word courageous comes to mind. Her leg was crushed and badly broken under a wagon wheel at almost the same time that both of her parents died tragically on the Oregon Trail. Still, Catherine became a mother to the younger girls, and her brother John like a Father. When her brothers John and Frank were murdered, she became both mother and father until they were separated, eventually taking both Henrietta and Elizabeth into her home when she married.

When we arrived at Oregon City, the Reverend William Roberts, superintendent of the Methodist mission took her in with his family. She later told me that he was a very stern and strict man, but never abusive. She stayed with them for three years until she met and married Clark Spencer Pringle and they moved to an area about four miles outside of Salem, Oregon. Clark was a Methodist circuit rider and they had eight children together, eventually moving to Spokane, Washington. I went to visit her in the spring of 1862 and she was the same calm and kind person I had known, with a wonderful sense of humor.

It meant a great deal to me to see her so happy and well-adjusted after all she had been through. She told me that she had lost touch with Henrietta, but still stayed in touch with Matilda Jane and Elizabeth, who were both married with children. There was something about Catherine that always brought me comfort, a genuine humanity that is hard to put into words. When I first met her, she was still having trouble getting around on her bad leg, but never complained and took care of those younger girls like they were her own.

During our captivity she was like a rock, someone we could talk to and count on to care for us in our darkest hours.

She and her children were instrumental in settling the Northwest as they branched out into the new world that they had helped create with their own families. As time went by, she began writing down her memories of the Oregon Trail and the Whitman Massacre, eventually putting them into a book called, "Across the Plains."

She had a limited number of copies made and sent one to me, which I thought to be one of the most significant historical documents of its time. She wrote to me that she hoped to publish it and use whatever funds it might accrue to establish an orphanage in the memory of Narcissa Whitman. It was to be a place where orphan children would be loved and cared for as Narcissa had done for her, her brothers and sisters. Unfortunately, it was not published until after her death.

This passage from her book has always touched me deeply, "All of us wept as we drove away from that scene of suffering; wept for joy at our escape and sorrow for those who had been slain and could not go with us."

Before she passed, she wrote to me about a 50th anniversary gathering in 1897 for the Whitman massacre survivors and their families. I had been invited, but I was ill, and was unfortunately unable to attend. She later told me that she was amazed to see over three thousand people there. The reunion with Matilda Jane and Elizabeth turned out to be one of the most joyful times of her life. The three of them were the guests of honor and all spoke at the gathering.

She passed on August 7, 1910 at the age of 75.

The life stories of Catherine, Elizabeth and Matilda Jane Sager are heroic sagas of triumph over tragedy. The hardships and sorrows they endured are almost beyond comprehension, and yet they overcame all of this and lived long and full lives, leaving behind a legacy of courage, dedication, and devotion to their friends and family.

Chief Timothy

If Chief Timothy had not sent a delegation of four men back east to retrieve a copy of the "Book of Heaven," and someone to teach it, my parents may have never married or come west, and I may have never been born. Serendipitous comes to mind.

Chief Timothy was born in 1800, and was five years old when the Lewis and Clark expedition staggered into his village at Alpowa, lost and nearly starved to death. He once told me that he was in awe of, "Their pale skins, eyes the color of the sky, and Captain Clark's red hair."

Chief Timothy and Father were as close as brothers, totally committed to one another, and almost always at each other's side wherever they traveled. Though it is a little-known fact, Chief Timothy said that he was present when Father baptized Chief Joseph's infant son Hinmatóowyalahtqit, giving him the name Ephrain. He would one day become known as Young Chief Joseph, the most famous of all Nez Perce.

One of the few disagreements they had was over me. When I was ten years old, Chief Timothy urged Father and Mother not to send me to the Whitman School, telling them that it was far too dangerous with all of the threats the Cayuse people had been making against the settlers and missionaries. Father told him not to worry, that it was just another attempt to intimidate the Whitmans. He was wrong. Without Chief Timothy's courageous actions after the Whitman Massacre, I doubt we would have survived. At the very least, Father would have been killed and the rest of my family taken as hostages.

In1858 war drums began to beat among the northern tribes of the Yakimas, Palouses, Spokanes, and Coeur d'Alenes who were fed up with the Americans intrusions.

When several miners and settlers were killed in the Colville area, a messenger was sent to Fort Walla Walla for help. On May 6, a military detachment of 152 men led by Colonel Edward Steptoe was dispatched along with Chief Timothy, who agreed to go as interpreter. Chief Timothy also enlisted his son Edward, and nephews Simon and Levi to accompany them as scouts. As they continued to advance north along the Colville Trail, Chief Timothy observed smoke signals, his sixth sense warning him that they were being watched and followed. As they cautiously entered a deep and narrow ravine, the company suddenly found themselves surrounded by over 1,200 hostile warriors, eerily adorned in war paint, shouting and making threatening gestures. Two elderly chiefs slowly approached. As the eldest chief raised his lance, it immediately became deathly quiet. He then asked why they were trespassing on Indian land. Colonel Steptoe assured the chiefs that they had come on a mission of peace, not war. The chief asked, "Why then have you brought the big guns?" Colonel Steptoe and his men were told to turn back, that they would not be allowed to cross the river alive. The elderly chiefs then raised their guns in the air, turned and rode off as the other warriors began whooping and thrusting their weapons up and down wildly.

The company backtracked for the rest of the day until the warriors finally disappeared into the fog lining the canyon ridges. The next day after retreating approximately three miles, they were attacked without warning. In the chaos, Colonel Steptoe was able to deploy a squad of ten men along the ridge and place the howitzers in firing position. However, two of his officers and five enlisted men were killed in the process, and ten men were wounded.

As night fell, there was no doubt in Colonel Steptoe's mind that they would be attacked and overwhelmed in the morning. The pack animals had broken loose during the skirmish, and they were left without food or water. During the fighting, Chief Timothy risked his life locating a narrow gully and trail that had been left unguarded. In single file they hastily made their escape into the terrifying darkness. The next morning, they rested briefly and then rode as hard and fast as they could for almost 75 miles. By the time they stopped to rest, both the men and horses were on the verge of collapsing. Chief Timothy, his son, and nephews stood guard over the soldiers as they rested, then Edward was sent on a dangerous mission to bring reinforcements from Fort Walla Walla. After alerting the Army at the Fort as to what had happened, Edward gathered his mother Tamar, and several other women to bring food, water and supplies to Colonel Steptoe and his men. They packed and traveled fast, reaching the detachment even before help arrived. The women served camas bread and salmon until Edward arrived with two cows that were butchered and served to the ravenous men. Later that day Timothy helped ferry them across the Snake River where they were met by reinforcements who escorted them back to Fort Walla Walla.

In an official report, Chief Timothy was only credited with helping ferry them across the river and not recognized or reimbursed for his service or the food and supplies he provided. Three survivors were interviewed who claimed, "Had it not been for Chief Timothy, we would have all been annihilated to the last man." One of Chief Timothy's sons was later murdered as a direct result of Chief Timothy's involvement with the Americans.

Finally, in 1914, a ceremony was held in Spokane, Washington to honor Chief Timothy for his act of courage during the Battle of Pine Creek, also known as the Steptoe Disaster.

Because of his active participation in the treaties of 1855, 1863, and 1868, Chief Timothy was asked to go as part of a delegation to

Washington, D.C. where he met with President Andrew Johnson. More promises were made, then broken.

On October 26, 1871 Chief Timothy and Father joyfully reunited for the first time in 22 years. I was there, and it was a profoundly moving moment in my life. Chief Timothy later confided in me that along with his weyekin, his two most prized possessions over the years had been the Bible that Father had given him when they first arrived at Lapwai, and the watercolor painting Mother gave him after the massacre on the day we left for Oregon City.

In 1872 the U.S. government built a small church at Kamiah, Idaho on land donated by Chief Lawyer, which was dedicated to Father. Chief Timothy and Chief Lawyer became its elders, and to this day it still stands as a testament to their devotion.

In May of 1874 Chief Timothy and Tamar saw Father for the last time. He had this to say to Father, "Now don't be concerned, I will never turn back. My wife will never turn back. This people will never turn back," a promise that was kept.

Chief Timothy died sometime in 1891 at the age of 91. For almost 25 years no one knew the location of his grave. In 1915, a man named D.M. White was riding near Alpowa when his horse stepped into a shallow grave belonging to Chief Timothy. Around his neck was his precious weyekin, and placed next to him was the Bible and painting Father and Mother had given him wrapped in a doeskin cover. Nearby they discovered his wife Tamar and two of his sons. Several years later a monument was placed over the gravesite to honor him. A plaque now spans Alpowa Creek that reads, "Indian Timothy Memorial Bridge." How appropriate that a man who spent his life attempting to bridge our two people should have one named after him. How sad that Tamar was never acknowledged for her council, courage and commitment, but that was the way things were for women in those days.

There were those among the Indian people who reviled Chief Timothy as a traitor, but he was not. He was a peacemaker who understood that his people needed to change and adapt in order to survive. However, he was also a great warrior, and had he been able to predict how devious and destructive the U.S. government would be toward the Indian people; how negligent they would be as stewards of the land, he would have likely chosen to fight as Chief Joseph had.

There are friendships and loyalties that transcend race, religion, or gender, a bond that goes much deeper than the color of our skin. That is the precious gift my parents and I received from Chief Timothy.

Chapter 5

Life after Waiilatpu

Uncle Horace

My Uncle Horace was the first and only relative I would ever know from either of my parents' families. After the massacre he was taken along with my mother, brother, and sisters to Mr. Craig's village. From there, he, Mr. Jackson and Mr. Canfield all felt that they would eventually be killed by the Cayuse or Nez Perce if they stayed, and decided to cross the Rocky Mountains in December. It was a bad idea even for the most experienced mountain men, and fortunately they turned back before it was too late. Not long after, Uncle Horace joined a group of 50 volunteer soldiers who returned to Waiilatpu in March of 1848. There they found bones and body parts scattered along the grounds including a clump of long golden hair that could have only belonged to Mrs. Whitman.

Uncle Horace was no stranger to adventure, and soon left for the California gold rush. He eventually crossed the continent four times, twice by land, and twice by the Isthmus route around Cape Horn. In 1855 on one of his trips back east he met and married Margaret Mercer of Missouri and settled there until 1860. He then brought his wife and children across the plains and over the Rocky Mountains, settling in the Touchet Valley, 20 miles north and east of Walla Walla. Once there, he took up farming and started raising cattle. It was a good life, a place where he and Margaret would live out the rest of their lives together.

His life was a full one, that of a miner, explorer, adventurer, farmer, stockman, husband and father of ten children. He covered almost every facet of pioneer life in the west. With his wife and children in attendance he passed away peacefully in 1892 at the age of 80. Margaret followed in 1893 at the age of 69.

Amelia

My baby sister Amelia was only one year old at the time of the massacre. She was also taken to the village of Mr. Craig, though I doubt she has any recollections of that time in her life. I'll never forget the feeling I had when I saw her in Mother's arms when we were reunited at Fort Walla Walla. She was just a year old and doing everything she could to squirm out of Mother's arms to get to me. Once we reached Oregon City Father was often asked to preach all over Oregon and Washington. I can still remember Amelia sitting in front of him, Henry, Martha Jane and I behind on our own horses traveling to various churches. Even when she was a little girl, she had a beautiful singing voice and was always asked to sing at Father's services.

We had just celebrated Amelia's fifth birthday when Mother died. Being so young she had a hard time understanding why her Mama was gone and where she went. When I was 17 and Amelia was eight, I married and took her in with me. She was a wonderful companion and we spent countless hours together talking and laughing.

Brownsville was named after Hugh Brown, and when Amelia was 16, she married his son John Brown. With his father's help he bought 400 acres from Father to raise livestock. Mother had left the four of us each a good size piece of land, and added to John and Amelia's 400 acres, they had a substantial parcel of land to start their business.

John was a good businessman who got involved in the woolen and flourmills. Even with their prosperity, sad times were just around the corner. Days after Amelia had her first child she accidentally fell and irrevocably injured her spine. She would be an invalid for the rest of her life, barely able to turn herself over. Despite her terrible condition she was able to give birth to two more children. Only one survived.

In 1885 John built a beautiful and spacious house for Amelia, designed to make life easier for her and those who cared for her. She was only able to enjoy it for four years before she died in 1889 in Brownsville at the young age of 43. John joined her five years later in 1894 at the age of 63. We were very close all of our lives, and it hit me hard. I still think of her almost daily and remember how beautiful she was as a child, and how beautiful she became as a woman, a sweet and gentle soul that I will look forward to seeing again in the kingdom of heaven.

Martha Jane

After we left Lapwai and Oregon City Martha Jane started school at the Tualatin Plains academy with Henry and me. Smart and so beautiful, she was also sweet and generous, almost to a fault. In 1859 when she was 14, she took a trip to Walla Walla and while there she met and married a man named William Wigle. They soon moved to eastern Oregon outside a small town named Prineville where William became involved in the stock business.

Brownsville and Prineville are about 150 miles from each other, and you have to cross the Cascade Mountains so we didn't get to see as much of each other as we would have liked. William and Martha Jane had five beautiful children, John, Minnie, Ida, Albert Lee, and

Eliza, who was named after Mother and me. I can tell you the first time I held that baby I nearly started a flood.

There are people in this life that you don't see all that often, but you still feel as if they are right there with you, that was the way I felt about Martha Jane. When her husband William died in August of 1913 her loss broke my heart, but I knew they had lived a good life together and that brought me comfort. The last time I saw Martha Jane we were old gals, but as I looked into her deep brown eyes for the last time, I could still see the sweet young soul I had always known and loved.

Little Henry

For me the pot of gold at the end of the rainbow has always been the people and times in my life that I treasure most. The times spent with Father and later on little Henry, riding all over the Oregon Territory together was golden. It was such a happy time that it almost seems like a dream at this point in my life.

When Father and I left for the Whitman Mission school little Henry was deeply upset and hurt that he couldn't go because he had never been exposed to the measles. He had been looking forward to it and talking about it all year and I thank God that he was unable to go. I still shudder to think what might have happened to him or how it would have affected his life if he had been there and seen what I saw at his tender age.

In early 1860 Henry left for the Touchet Valley to raise cattle and farm.

It turned out to be bad timing because the winter of 1861-62 was so harsh that he lost almost all of his stock. Some men would have given up, but not Henry, it just made him that much more determined to work harder. He sold his land and what stock he had left and started backbreaking work of packing supplies to miners in the mountains. He saved up enough money to buy more land in the Touchet Valley, but continued to pack during the summers. He met a wonderful young woman named Lucy Knifong from Missouri and they were married on February 4, 1868. Tragedy struck when she died just two years later in February of 1870.

Brokenhearted, he struck out again for the mountains of Idaho and Montana to pack whatever he could and make money supplying miners. With what he saved and the sale of his land in the Touchet Valley he decided to settle on the Snake River about 80 miles northeast of Walla Walla. Once there he established a small town, he named Almota, a Nez Perce word that means, "moonlight fishing." He bought 160 acres of land and started farming and raising stock.

He stayed in touch with his deceased wife's family and in March of 1875 he married Mary Catherine Warren, half-sister to Lucy. Another harsh winter hit and once again he lost a good portion of his stock. Fortunately, he had made and saved enough to build a large warehouse where he charged to let people store crops, seeds and supplies.

He then sold it to the Oregon Railway and Navigation Company in 1878, making a nice profit. He had been experimenting with different plants and trees and came to realize that the soil in Almota was perfect for planting fruit trees. He then started the first commercial apple orchard in the Pacific Northwest. It did so well that he started planting peaches, grapes, cherries, nectarines, apricots, and Italian prunes. He eventually acquired and developed over 1,200 acres of land and became so successful that he was appointed commissioner of the State Board of Horticulture.

He then decided to expand the town by opening a hotel. In March of 1898 a fire broke out on the top floor of his hotel near where his office was located. He ran to the back of the hotel and kicked the door open to try and save his papers and books. The room caved in on him and by the time he was rescued he was badly burned. A doctor was called in from Walla Walla and the next day he performed several surgeries. Henry fought with all he had, but that night his body gave out and he died. This is a clipping taken from one of the local newspapers.

"Buried in flowers, it was an impressive ceremony at the funeral of Henry Hart Spalding. The gathering at the funeral of the late Henry Spalding of Almota was last Thursday afternoon of last week. It was a splendid tribute to the worth of the dead pioneer. Six hundred friends and family followed all that was mortal of this brave and honorable man to his last resting-place. The floral offerings were profuse and elaborate. Among the wreaths and flowers were those from his various lodges, The Knights of Pythias, A.O.U.W, the Red Men, the Rathbones and others."

In those days it was unheard of for 600 people to show up to a funeral unless it was someone special, and that is what my little brother was, special. He was also kind, generous, and beloved among his friends and family; a good man who left his loving wife Mary, and son Henry far too soon.

Father

We all worked hard to build the mission at Lapwai, but no one as hard as Father.

So many backbreaking years of toil and hardship gone in the blink of an eye, like a puff of wind. On January 2, 1848 we had little more than the clothes on our backs when they loaded us on the boat at Fort Walla Walla and we cast off into the unknown.

In Oregon City we stayed in a simple log cabin for four weeks before leaving for the new Tualatin Plains Academy. Mr. A.T. Smith and Mr. John Smith Griffin came to pick us up in an old oxcart. We stayed until that fall, living with the Geigers until Father was asked to open a school and establish a church in Brownsville, Oregon.

Father and Mr. Smith built us a new home and then built a one-room schoolhouse that was also used as a community center and church, where he performed services. Father was also made postmaster and school superintendent, but even with all he accomplished in Brownsville, he was not happy. He told me that his heart was still with the Nez Perce; that he felt as if something was missing among his own people. Mother also missed our life at Lapwai and felt that her life was much fuller and more meaningful among the Nez Perce People.

On August 5, 1850 Mother wrote to her sister Lorena, "I have suffered very much from sickness since we have left the Nez Perce Country. I think the climate is unfavorable for diseased lungs, and I feel I shall not survive."

She died on January 13, 1851 in Brownsville, never to see her beloved Nez Perce again. I think the shock of the massacre, losing

Mr. and Mrs. Whitman, Father's ordeal, and the constant worrying about me being held hostage drained the life out of her.

She told me in early January that she knew she was dying; that her only regret was that she would be leaving us motherless. I remember right before she died that the sun had come out and flooded her room with light and warmth.

Father said, "Soon you will look upon more beautiful skies."

Mother replied, "I have no fears as to that."

Weak and struggling for every breath day after day, her suffering at the end was so intense that I believe death came as a relief.

After the massacre, Father's ordeal took a heavy toll on him, and following Mother's death he was never quite the same man. Mother had been the bow that broke the waves whenever a storm of troubled waters crashed upon our lives. Without her calm and gentle hand to guide him he would easily become upset or angry when provoked, and though he never spoke it, I think he felt completely lost without her. Men like Father don't talk about their grief, so it was hard to know what he was going through or feeling, but these words will always be ingrained in my heart.

He wrote to a friend, "My dear brother in Christ, again I write amid the deep waters of affliction; again, the fountains of grief are broken up. I write from a lonely room! My wife is not there. She lies cold in her grave! No, I do wrong. She is in heaven. At this moment I seem to see her poor white hands, holding in one a golden harp whose angelic notes in harmony with unified millions, floating upon the Zephyrs of heaven, seem to call upon me to not weep for a wife dead, but rejoice on account of a wife glorified."

Near the end of her life, Father had spent a great deal of time and energy caring for Mother, which led to problems financially. It came as a relief when he was appointed as Indian Agent for Oregon. His real hope was that he would be able to return to the upper Columbia area where he could continue his relationship with the Nez Perce.

Priests of the Catholic Church strongly objected to his appointment since they didn't want Protestant missionaries back in the upper Columbia area. The missionary board let him know that since he had accepted the position as Indian Agent, they were terminating their support. Father was extremely upset when several of the more influential priests were able to convince the agency not to send him back to Lapwai. Knowing full well what their intention was, Father was resentful that the Catholic priests were given full reign of the entire upper territory. Because of his criticism, the Indian Affairs Agency fired him. A Catholic named Robert Newell then replaced him.

He wrote to the missionary board, "Our hopes for the recommencement of our mission which were so sudden and so high are completely dashed to the ground." Father's articles in the newspapers circulated all the way back to Washington D.C., even getting the attention of President Millard Fillmore. It caused a storm of criticism toward him, claiming that he had not provided enough specific evidence to make such claims. When Father came into the possession of a document from the Indian Affairs Agency that clearly stated that they were planning to keep all Protestants out of the upper territory he published it, completely vindicating himself. No apologies were ever given from the Indian Affairs Agency or government officials, but the missionary board recommissioned him with a salary and letter of gratitude for uncovering the indiscretion.

It was obvious that Father was lonely and overwhelmed with having to care for us and carry on all of his other responsibilities. He had confided this to his close friend John Griffith, asking his advice. Mrs. Griffith's sister Rachel Smith was planning to come to the west, so the Griffiths became matchmakers. By the time she reached the northwest it had already been agreed through correspondence that they would be married unless either one felt they were not compatible. Miss Smith arrived in the fall of 1852, and Reverend Griffith's married them on July 3rd of 1853, at the old schoolhouse Father had built in Tualatin Plains.

Mother and Mrs. Smith were like night and day. Mother was highly educated, tall and thin with a calm and quiet demeanor. Miss Smith had a very limited education, a large woman with an easily excitable nature. In some ways I was initially glad to have another hand with my many duties such as cooking, soap and candle making, carrying in the water and milking the cows, drying and preserving foods, mending clothes and a myriad of responsibilities Mother used to take care of.

When I asked Rachel if she would like to help me with supper, she said, "I'm sorry dear, I have never had to cook before, I don't even know how." She was odd, and would never be much of a homemaker, but it soon became apparent that she was completely devoted to Father, and would at least make him a good companion.

Father continued to be a thorn in the side of the Indian Affairs agency by publicly criticizing them and continually campaigning for his return to Lapwai, and by 1859 the government finally reopened the upper territories.

My husband Andrew and I decided to move to the Touchet Valley, not far from Walla Walla to start our own cattle ranch. Father soon followed and arrived on August 18th, with Matilda Jane, Amelia, and his new wife Rachel. They set up a tent next to our small home until he was able to build one on his own land. When Chief Timothy showed up after so many years of separation there was a celebration that lasted for days, and tears of joy flowed freely from the eyes of the two old friends. Father was delighted and inspired that his loyal friend Timothy had kept the Sabbath for all of these years. Without wasting any time Father built and established a new church in Touchet Valley as well as one at a post near Waiilatpu.

In 1860 Mr. Eells and his family moved back to the territory and established a new school at the old Whitman site that he called the Whitman Seminary. Father was one of the first trustees and was made Justice of Peace.

Finally, Father's dream came true when he was allowed to return to Lapwai as reverend and teacher. When he arrived, there was a big celebration. The Nez Perce had already started building a school for him to teach in. A new Indian Agent named J.W. Anderson had been appointed to the Upper Columbia County who was fair and impartial to both Protestants and Catholics.

After he had seen what Father had accomplished in such a short time, he wrote in one of his reports, "Mr. Spalding has accomplished more good than all the money expended by the government has been able to effect."

There was a momentous meeting and service held at Lapwai with over one thousand of Father's Nez Perce followers in which many prominent white men, including the Governor of Idaho, Caleb Lyon, were invited. They were astonished to see that the Nez Perce practiced regular family and public worship. Chief Timothy later told me that on that Sunday of January 31, 1864 Father gave a sermon so powerful that all one thousand Nez Perce, the Governor and federal officials were brought to tears.

A new Catholic Indian agent named James O'Neil was then appointed to Lapwai and immediately the skies darkened for Father. Mr. O'Neil had the power to force Father out of the school and then his home. Father once again returned brokenhearted to his land beside us at the Touchet Valley. When Governor Lyon heard what had happened, he immediately came to Father's aid to right the wrong that had been done.

When he saw Father, he threw his arms around him saying, "You are the father of this country and the apostle of these people, and you shall have a place here for your life if you wish."

He not only reinstated Father at Lapwai, he ordered Mr. O'Neil to give him the best house, fence in his orchard, remodel the schoolhouse and build a new church and meeting house. When the Governor left office, Mr. O'Neil dismissed Father and closed the school. Father was now 62 years old, and it gives me pause to contemplate how much a person can take, how many heartbreaks one person can endure before giving up; but that was not my father's way. Before he had even packed up to leave, Mr. O'Neil brought in a contingent of Catholic priests and called a meeting with the Nez Perce.

The priests told them, "As Mr. Spalding has not collected your children and taught them properly and has done them no good, you had better let us come as your missionaries."

The Nez Perce turned their backs on the priests, refusing to listen, then told them to leave Lapwai and never return. At the time Father was the only Protestant missionary working in the entire Oregon territories and I can tell you that he left Lapwai with a bitterness in his heart for the Catholic priests that he would carry to his grave.

This time he returned to his home in Brownsville to reestablish his relations there and lick his wounds. In October of 1870 he took a steamship to San Francisco, then rode the new transcontinental railroad to Chicago, then on to New York, Boston, and Washington D.C. He was asked to testify before the United States Senate and in the process was able to convince them to establish a federally funded Indian school sponsored by President Ulysses S. Grant. In 1871 he returned once again to his beloved Lapwai.

It is hard for me to imagine the myriad of emotions he must have felt going back east for the first time in 35 years, dejected and forlorn; then returning to Lapwai as a hero. I wonder what he must have thought as he sped along the tracks in the comfort of his railway car—if he reminisced about every step that he and Mother had trekked along the Oregon Trail, every mountain, every river crossed all of those years ago. I would think that the struggles, dangers and beauty of the trail must have come flooding back like a winter gale.

Word of his success spread throughout the entire nation and as he made the journey home, he was given a royal welcome at every stop; asked to preach or lecture at churches filled to the rafters with people.

I have read several accounts that say audiences were, "Spellbound as he portrayed life on the mission at Lapwai, the Whitman massacre, and his narrow escape with death."

In Philadelphia he reconnected with his, and Narcissa's old school friend David Malin. He told Mr. Malin how Narcissa had taken little David in and given him their old friend's name in honor of their friendship.

Mr. Malin asked Father if he would give the sermon that Sunday and talk about some of his most profound memories. He told the congregation the story of little David Malin, how the Whitmans had taken him in, wrapped in a wet blanket, filthy with his own excrement. He told them how little David was nearly starved to death and had been thrown in a dirt hole to die by his own Mother. He painted a picture of the Whitmans who had not only taken little David in, but also loved and nurtured him back to health. How they gave him a place in the world, people that he could call family. He then told them that one of his greatest regrets was leaving poor little David on that dock at Walla Walla crying his heart out, to be cuffed instead of loved by a Catholic priest. He told the captivated crowd that even with the future unknown and family responsibilities there was no excuse for what he had done. He told them that he had asked God to forgive him many times for leaving that little boy behind. Before he finished the story it was hard to hear what he was saying over the crying of the congregation.

I had seen him do this many times with the Nez Perce at Lapwai and our other congregations at Tualatin Plains and Brownsville. He was a master composer of words who had spent decades learning how to write his symphonies of emotions that always came to a tremendous crescendo at exactly the right moment, a man completely possessed by the spirit of God.

Father returned to Lapwai in 1871 triumphant and reinvigorated, but his battle was not yet over. During his absence a reverend J.B. Monteith had been appointed and taken over at Lapwai. He had proposed that all missionaries should be men, and not allowed to marry. He also instated a policy in which the Nez Perce language was not allowed to be spoken.

When Father confronted Mr. Monteith he said, "Our missionaries are not to become like Catholic Priests; that women like his dear departed wife were essential to the success of their missions."

He felt that abstaining from marriage was unnatural and unhealthy, that it created abnormal deviations in an individual's personality. He also told the reverend that much of his success had come from using the Nez Perce Bible that he had translated, that the Nez Perce were much more likely to trust someone who was devoted enough to learn and use their language.

When Father returned to preaching at Lapwai it was to large crowds who gathered to hear him speak the word of God from the "Book of Heaven." He baptized over 600 more Nez Perce and laid the foundation for the Nez Perce Presbyterian Church that still exists to this day.

Even with the tremendous success he was having, he was once again exiled from Lapwai, this time by the new Superintendent of Schools Reverend George Ainslie. He was forced to leave Lapwai, but he would not leave the Nez Perce, and moved to nearby Kemiah during the winter of 1872-73.

Once there he immediately erected a new church and started training others to take his place when he was no longer able to carry on. In his customary fashion he continued to make the best out of his situation. Before long, his congregation and sermons began to swell and many of the Nez Perce would ride hundreds of miles to hear his sermons.

In the summer of his seventieth year, he was asked to bring the word of God to the Spokane people. Though his body was ailing terribly, his passion still burned brightly with the light of God and he journeyed over 1,500 grueling miles that summer on horseback, baptizing another 300 souls. He slept on the ground and ate whatever was available in order to bring them the "Book of Heaven."

Few human beings could have sustained their faith through the kind of adversity that my father had experienced. Still, he never lost sight of the mission he had been charged with, though the odds were often stacked sky high against him. I have heard him called cantankerous, stubborn, even crazy, but no other missionary ever accomplished as much as he did in the Northwest. He was the kind of person you were either "all for, or all against," a man who said what he meant, and meant what he said. The men who spoke harshly of him were lesser men, now long gone and completely forgotten. Father could be cantankerous, stubborn, and impatient with loafers, but was also loyal, fearless and faithful with family and friends to his very last breath.

Near the end, his old and dear friend Chief Timothy came to see him for the last time and told him, "You are my great interpreter, you were sent by God to me and this people to teach us life, the word of God. God only is good and great. Jesus alone gives life. Now don't be concerned, I will never turn my back, this people will never turn back."

When Father was near death, he was placed in a farm wagon and taken over 60 miles to Lapwai so that he could receive better care than he was able to get at Kemiah. Once again, his wish had come true and he was allowed to die at Lapwai among the people he loved best, the Nez Perce.

He passed on August 3, 1874. The crowds at his funeral were immense, thousands had come from as far away as Spokane, Washington. With tears in his eyes Chief Timothy spoke of their lives together, of the brotherhood they had found with each other.

Here are just a few of the hats that Father wore: Husband, father, teacher, minister, carpenter, farmer, author, printer, translator, blacksmith, miller, stockman, doctor, post master, U.S. Indian Affairs agent, school superintendent, and missionary.

He is buried in the earth his beloved Lapwai, and in September of 1913 Mother's remains were brought there from Brownsville where they were laid to rest together.

Mother

For me just the word Mother brings back a flood of images and emotions.

I didn't choose to be a pioneer, I was born into it, but Mother consciously chose to leave everything and everyone she had ever known or loved for a fiercely dangerous and unknown world. Eliza Hart Spalding was not a thrill seeker, she was a mild and virtuous young woman from New York who wanted to make the world a better place, to live her conviction by bringing the word of God to the Indian people. She also had an open heart and mind to the Nez Perce People, often telling me that she was learning as much or more from them than she was teaching. Whether or not you share her religious belief, I hope you can respect the magnitude of her commitment to what she believed.

In many ways women have been overlooked, if not ignored, by pioneer history. In Mother's case it may have been her mild manners and gentle spirit, her intention to draw as little attention to herself as possible. Mother went about her way in a serene and quiet way, which made it only natural that she be overshadowed by the fiery and tempestuous nature of Father. Because of its nature, the Whitman Massacre put almost everything else in the background and is what most people remember when they think of that time in our Northwest history.

The mission that the Whitmans and my parents had been given was to help the Indian people become self-sufficient, and bring them the message of God from the "Book of Heaven." In that sense our mission at Lapwai was a complete success, whereas the Whitman Mission was a complete failure for various reasons. It was on a direct route to the Willamette Valley and had become more of a way station for the immigrants than a mission for the Cayuse people. It also failed because Narcissa had a deep dislike and distrust for the Indian people, which they eventually reciprocated. The Indian way of life is very personable and they love to take their time talking about and around a subject. Doctor Whitman was very direct and to the point, busy with his patients, which sometimes created a sense of unease among the Cayuse people. I don't think they were ever well suited to the task primarily because they lacked the desire to truly understand the Indian people or respect their culture and beliefs.

With that said, let me make it perfectly clear that as people, the Whitmans were anything but failures. Mrs. Whitman's commitment to her husband and adopted family was total, as was the doctor's commitment to caring for the sick and injured. They treated me as part of the family and I loved them both dearly. Our mission had the advantage of being remote and completely centered on the Nez Perce People, creating an environment in which my parents could stay focused on their objective. The other advantage was that my parents dearly loved and respected the Nez Perce and the challenge they had been given to teach as well as learn from these noble people.

The women and children used to follow Mother from room to room, school house to meeting house, she was accepted as one of them and respected for her courage and dedication to The People and their needs.

She never lost her patience, never refused to help someone or explain whatever was asked of her. She was capable of staring down an angry mob of violent men with a calm that was legendary among the Nez Perce People, and they loved and respected her deeply for it.

I have heard many mean and degrading things said about Father because of his temper and passionate nature. Because those people had no idea who and what he was, I have learned to let it roll off me like raindrops on the roof. But, when I read something mean or derogatory about Mother, I get mad as an irritated hornet and would dearly love to see those same people say those cowardly things to her face.

Unlike Narcissa, she never cared about trying to impress anyone, she was a woman in charge of her own fate and committed to her own life's work as well as Father's. She understood that trying to be something or someone other than your true self would only interfere, and she quietly accomplished more than the other six missionary women combined.

One of her detractors once said she was, "Of a serious mind," as if that were a fault instead of a virtue.

What they didn't understand was that she was not likely to let a total stranger that she didn't trust see her soft and tender side, let alone her sense of humor.

The unfortunate fact is that this was a time when men got credit for just about everything, including the accomplishments and successes of their wives. This was certainly the case for Mother, though it was certainly not intentional on Father's part.

Without her calm and thoughtful guidance and intervention the mission would have never succeeded.

Father once told me that he would never forget what she said as they stood at the very top of the Rocky Mountains. "Is it reality or a dream that after four months of hard and painful journeying, I am alive and actually standing on the summit of the Rocky Mountains where yet the foot of a white woman has never trod."

In my mind that is how I sometimes picture her, a monumental figure above all other women of that time. Now that I am a mother and grandmother myself, I think that it must have been harder for her to endure the massacre and internment than it was for me.

She not only had to deal with her own danger and that of my brother and sisters, she must have been worried sick about what Father and I were going through or if we were even still alive.

Worry is a powerful thing, and not knowing if we were dead or alive, or possibly even being tortured must have haunted every moment of her consciousness. Mr. Canfield had told her how brutally the men had been butchered before he escaped and that he had no idea what had happened to his family or the rest of the women and children. Yet she went on in her own self-possessed and unfettered way.

She was aware that the same Cayuse who had committed the massacre were on their way to Lapwai to finish what they had started at Waiilatpu, yet she refused to travel on the Sabbath. Some people would have thought her stubborn and foolish, but it only increased the respect she already received from the Nez Perce for her commitment and fearlessness in the face of death.

She had been ill and suffering for several years from either anemia, tuberculosis or both. You would never know it unless she was too weak to stand or get out of bed, which was not often. She was frequently feverish and fatigued with a constant cough, yet she never complained or stopped in her duties. For both Mother and Father having to leave the Nez Perce was tragic. They had worked so hard for so long to see it dashed upon the rocks by one terrible act of violence. Mother constantly prayed that she would one day be able to return to Lapwai so that she could continue to serve the Nez Perce People.

I believe the reason she had such a calm and easygoing nature was that she had a foundation built on love and trust. She knew that she was constantly in the thoughts and prayers of her parents, family and friends, and she was never alone spiritually. There was never a doubt in my mind that her husband and children were the most important part of her earthly existence, that she never let it overshadow the duty she felt for the Nez Perce.

Much has been made of Narcissa taking in the Sagers and several other children, but little or nothing has been said about the eight Nez Perce children who Mother had brought into our home when they had lost their parents. She treated them with the same kindness and devotion that she showed to us.

William Gray once wrote about her, "She was remarkable for her firmness of decision, she never appeared alarmed or excited about any difficulty or dispute around her."

One time an Indian man tried to insult her not knowing that she was perfectly fluent in the Nez Perce language.

A witness said, "Her cool quick perception of the design enabled her to give so complete and thorough a rebuff to the attempted insult, that to hide his disgrace, he fled from the tribe, not venturing to remain among them."

As an example of how highly the Nez Perce thought of her, on another instance a man went about insulting her in front of a large group of Nez Perce. They were so incensed that they took him into custody and were preparing to hang him for the insult. She saved his life by telling the onlookers that he would learn nothing by being killed, that he should be allowed to live so that he could repent his sins and do better in the future.

Out of frustration due to a lack of success some of the other missionary men and women were turning away from the Indian people, and moving more toward their own. The problem was that they were only willing to work with the Indian people on their own terms. Mother was committed to doing whatever it took, including accepting the Nez Perce on their terms.

In all likelihood she was the most respected and venerated white person to ever come to the Oregon Territory up until that time. She was always trying to find a bridge between our people and unite our cultures. Her desire was not simply to convert the Indian people to her religion, it was also to understand their beliefs and culture, and they knew this about her. Many Nez Perce would remain devoted to her throughout their entire lifetimes, often ending their prayers with, "In the name of Jesus Christ and Mrs. Spalding."

When we reached Tualatin Plains she was employed as a full-time teacher while caring for five children and trying to fight her illness. In her own quiet way, she was breaking down the barriers of what the society at that time expected of a wife, mother, and woman while staying true to herself and her family. By the time we reached Brownsville, Mother was dying. Though no one wanted to accept it, we all knew it was inevitable. Even little Amelia must have sensed something since she would hardly leave Mother's side.

In my heart I always carry with me something Chief Timothy once said to Mother as we were leaving Walla Walla as he was saying goodbye to her for the last time.

I will try to recount it as best I can. "Now my beloved teacher you are passing over my country for the last time. You are leaving us forever, and my people, oh, my people will see no more light. We shall meet no more in the schoolroom and my children, oh, my children will live only in a night that will have no morning and I will look upon your face one last time in this world."

He then held out his hands to her with the Bible in one and said, "This book in which your hands have written and caused me to write the words of God I shall carry in my bosom until I lay down in my grave."

Mother died on January 13, 1851 in Brownsville, surrounded by those who loved her most at the age of 44 years old. My wish is that she would be remembered for all she accomplished in her lifetime instead of being referred to as the wife of Henry Spalding, or mother of a Whitman Massacre survivor.

Her journey over the Oregon Trail was heroic in the true sense of the word. She and Narcissa Whitman were the first white women to cross the Rocky Mountains and journey onto the Oregon Territories. She and Father established the first successful mission, church, and school in the Northwest. She collaborated with Father in writing the first books in the Nez Perce language and operated the first loom in the Northwest. However, her greatest achievement was her love and devotion for her family, friends, and the Nez Perce People, and I can't wait until our spirits are together again.

Life after Waiilatpu

The older I get the more dreamlike the Whitman Massacre becomes. I have been asked to speak and write about it so many times that over the years it has become more like a work of fiction I once read, rather than my real life. That is until I wake up in the middle of the night in a cold sweat hearing the screams of those who died so violently. Even the trip from Walla Walla to Vancouver, Oregon City, and the Oregon Coast seem like part of a novel. It wasn't until we reached Tualatin Plains that things started to feel grounded in reality, connected to the present and future. I have also been asked many times what stands out most in my mind about the massacre. That would be the way the Whitmans and Sager brothers were killed, and standing at the window next to Helen Saunders as we watched her father being hacked to pieces through the window. There were also great acts of kindness and courage among the survivors that I will always remember.

The possessions we left behind seem so inconsequential to the people we left behind, especially Chief Timothy, Matilda, Mustups, and Timpstetelew. If there were one possession I could have back, it would be the little pouch containing the bluebird feather I lost during the massacre. I don't include Tashe in that, because she was never a possession of mine, she was a friend, my first love outside of my family and friends.

For years I have wondered where she went and how she was being treated. I know that there were much more important things to think about, but it wasn't something I could control. Worrying about her was like a dark cloud that came over me. The memory has become faded like an old photograph, but how it felt to ride with her at full speed or swim a river together is still fresh, and I know that in her own way she loved me, too.

About the time I began making new friends at Tualatin Plains academy, Father told me that we were moving to a place called Brownsville, about 50 miles south of Salem, Oregon. It wasn't much of a town and there were no houses or towns between Salem and Brownsville, just open land. When we got to Brownsville, even our closest neighbor wasn't very close. My only consolation was that Nancy Osborne lived in Brownsville, so I had at least one friend who understood what I had been through.

Two years passed until five of the Cayuse involved in the massacre were caught and brought to trial in Oregon City. It began in May of 1850, and I was going to have to be a witness for the prosecution since I had seen and heard so much of what had happened as the interpreter. Even with what they had done it was an awful feeling watching them being led in with heavy chains through their hand and legcuffs. Chief Tiloukaikt still looked proud, but sad, Tomahas with so much hatred in his eyes.

When Mother died, we were all expecting it, but it still didn't seem possible when it happened. I expected to see her everywhere I went until the reality struck me, it was like my world had come to an end. She was the first person buried in the new Brownsville cemetery and the service was held at the schoolhouse with people lined all around the building to say goodbye. I had never felt so alone in all my life, even during the massacre I knew that my mother was alive and thinking of me.

At 13 I was the oldest child, and like it or not I was now in charge of my brother and sisters as well as running a household. After what

I had been through, and the changes my body was going through, there was never a time when I needed Mother's love and guidance more. It was as if the weight of the world was resting on my shoulders. I simply did what I thought she would want me to do and ran things to the best of my ability for the next three and a half years without reservations.

When I was 16 years old, I met and fell in love with a young man named Andrew Warren who was 21. He had come from Missouri the previous fall and already established a small cattle business. I was in love and excited about the idea of starting my own life. We were married in 1854 in Brownsville and in 1857 we had our first child, a little girl, America Jane Warren. On January 9, 1859 we had a second little girl, Lizzie.

That spring we packed our things in the wagon along with our two little girls and left for Walla Walla with 300 head of cattle. Andrew couldn't get the cattle over the Columbia River by boat, so he took them over the Cascade Mountains. I drove the wagon with a little one in each arm wishing I had Matilda or old Mustups to help. By the time we reached The Dalles, Andrew was already waiting for us with a big smile on his face.

It was such new territory that from the time we left The Dalles until the time we arrived in Walla Walla I never saw another town, farm, house or white person for that matter. We continued another 30 miles past Walla Walla to a place called the Touchet Valley.

Our life there started in an old canvas tent. Within several months Andrew had built a small log house and we began to settle in. The land was made for cattle with plenty of water and tall grass as far as the eye could see. The only thing I worried about were the big gray wolves that would come right up to the house sniffing and howling. They were fearless and I was afraid to even take my eyes off the girls until Andrew built a high fence so that they could play outside. Some time after, Father and my sisters were to join us and I couldn't wait to see them. Though we hadn't had any trouble with the nearby Indian people, the Whitman Massacre was always in the back of my mind.

One beautiful sunswept morning I was out in the yard with the girls hanging laundry when I noticed a cloud of dust moving our way fast. As soon as I could make out that they were Indians, I grabbed America Jane and picked Lizzie up out of the crib and made for the house as fast as I could. I took the rifle out of the closet and loaded it, then looked for a place to hide the girls just in case it was necessary. It seemed like an hour, but was probably only a few minutes before I recognized them by their dress and markings as Nez Perce.

When they were close enough that I could make out who it was, my heart soared into the clouds. As they reached the house one of the men leaped from his horse like a teenager with long gray hair; it was my dear friend Chief Timothy.

Lizzie was too young to know what was going on, and America Jane was a little frightened not knowing what to think as Chief Timothy gathered the three of us in his arms and said, "Can this be my little Eliza?"

He then stepped back to look at us and I could feel so much love coming from him that I leapt into his arms again and told him how much I had missed him. Then something amazing happened, he bent to his knees and put his arms out and America Jane ran right into them and stuck her face in the crook of his neck. She was at that shy stage where children often hide behind their parents when they meet someone new, but she acted like they had known each other all of their lives. Even though Lizzie was not yet one, she was not to be denied, and let me put her in his arms.

What a sight, both of them taking turns pulling on his nose and the weyekin he wore around his neck. He looked at me with misty eyes as we shared that infinitely precious moment together. He told me that he had heard about Mother and had spent many long nights praying for her, though he was certain she was already in heaven waiting for us.

When I told him that Father would be here any day now, he told me he couldn't wait to see him and ask if he would start teaching again. They camped outside our little home constantly watching for Father to show up on the horizon, which he did three days later. It had been 12 years, but it was as if they picked up a conversation right where they had left off the day before.

We were lucky to have sold our cattle before we moved back to Brownsville in 1861 since the winter of 1861-62 was so severe. Many people including Father lost almost all of their stock. Then in 1873 we packed up our belongings, loaded up the girls and moved to Eastern Oregon. The land was immense open range as far as the eyes could see in any direction, and we almost had it all to ourselves. Andrew gave me a beautiful pony for my birthday and I was able to do something I had been too busy or preoccupied to do for far too long: ride. A flood of memories swept over me as I thought of Tashe and how much I had missed our times together.

On August 3, 1874 Father died. He was like a force of nature, and it hardly seemed possible that a force of nature could ever die. I only wish the people who had criticized him had known him the way that I did, or could at least understand how strongly he believed in what he was doing. Lizzie was very sick and I was unable to attend his funeral but my brother told me that there were thousands of people, mostly Nez Perce in attendance. Henry told me the tributes to Father were emotionally moving and he was often referred to as the Father of Idaho; our family referred to as the earliest pioneer family in the Northwest Territory.

Father and I had had our good and bad times together and he could be a hard man, but he loved me and I knew it, and that was enough. At a given point when I was in my mid-twenties, I seemed to come to the realization that I was now responsible for my own decisions and actions, that I could no longer blame my past or anyone else for who or what I was. It was the most liberating feeling I have ever had and I have learned to love and cherish those parts of me that I inherited from my parents more every day.

By 1875 our stock was flourishing and several other ranchers had joined us at the Harney Valley. This was Modoc Indian territory and we were hearing that they were becoming more hostile all the time because too many new settlers were coming into their territory. Cattle were starting to disappear, so we had to round them up each night. This was still the Wild West and you had to be cautious about where you were and who was around at all times.

Andrew and several of the ranch hands had taken our nine-year old son James, who we called Jimmy to look for cattle that had wandered off and needed to be rounded up.

At camp someone was needed to stay and keep the fire going so they could make beef jerky.

Jimmy had taken a hard fall the day before and was pretty banged up, so he was chosen to stay in camp and keep the fire going. Andrew told him not to worry if they were back late; it might take a while. They didn't make it back until late the next day. When they returned, Jimmy told them that he had been seeing Indians all morning, that they seemed to be interested in the herd. I suspect that the previous night must have been a long one for a nine-year old boy out in the wilderness alone. The stars above were his only company and he was surrounded by the unknown, listening to the big gray wolves howl throughout the night, hungry for meat. I can't imagine what kind of thoughts must have been running through his head.

A group of about 15 Modoc Indians had been trailing Andrew and the other men and they could still see them on a ridge about a mile away. There seemed to be a purpose for the gathering of so many Indians, and Andrew expected that an attack was inevitable.

Prineville was in the opposite direction of the ridge, about 12 miles away straight into the setting sun. It was decided to send Jimmy on the fastest horse to get help in Prineville in case they were attacked. Jimmy tore off like his life depended on it, which it did. Andrew said he saw two riders take off after him, but he had over a mile lead on them. If he had fallen or been thrown from his horse he probably would have been killed. Before he ever reached Prineville the Indians let off the chase since he was making ground instead of losing it. When Jimmy reached Prineville, it was decided that there was no sense in trying to find them at night, so a party

734

planned to leave first thing in the morning. By this time, I was worried sick, having expected them back the previous day.

At first light Andrew and the ranch hands started the cattle moving, reaching home late that morning about the same time Jimmy and the rescue party reached their cold campfire. Neither party saw any more signs of the Indians, but we stayed on high alert for the next couple of days. Eventually the Modoc Indians did raid the valley, and everyone fled with whatever stock they had left, and we headed back to Brownsville.

One of a parent's greatest joys is watching their child become an adult, and one of our greatest sorrows is when they leave home. In 1873 our 16-year-old daughter America Jane married a young man from Illinois named Joseph Crooks. He had come to the Willamette Valley in 1848 when he was five years old and his family had settled in Prineville, Oregon. Joseph opened a butcher shop and grew it into a fine business. They gave me five of the most beautiful grandchildren anyone could ever ask for: Effie, Minnie, Charles, John, and Beulah. Less than two years later our second daughter Lizzie, who was also 16 at the time, married a nice young man named James Calloway and gave me three more beautiful grandchildren.

There is one fear I have had since the day my first child was born, and I suspect it is the same one almost every parent has; to outlive one of your children.

On November 9, 1882 Lizzie died. It was the worst day of my life, worse than the Whitman Massacre, and the only consolation was that she was being laid to rest next to Mother in the Brownsville Pioneer Cemetery and waiting for me in heaven. Andrew and I raised their children until they were adults and loved them like they were our own.

In 1884 our third daughter Martha married F. F. Ellsley and the final chapter in raising our four children was when Jimmy married a sweet young woman named Wauna Wiseman in 1887. A year later they had a little boy they named Carl Byron, who would become the mirror image of Jimmy.

On November 4, 1886 I lost my dear husband. He was buried close to Mother and Lizzie and it seemed as if I was now alone and adrift in an ocean of sorrow and uncertainty.

It was ten years later that I left the Willamette Valley to be with my son Jimmy and his family near Spokane, Washington. Leaving my friends and family behind was one of the hardest things I had ever done, especially after all we had been through together.

It was hard for me to believe that in the sixth decade of my life I was once again living in a tent, a stranger in a strange new land. It wasn't the worst thing that had ever happened to me, nor had it altered my philosophy that "What we could not get, we did without."

While Jimmy was away on a fishing trip both of his boys came down with diphtheria and by the time he returned his youngest son was dead. It seems to me that sorrow and joy are like brothers and sisters, which you just have to learn to live with.

In 1908 my son Jimmy, his family and I took a trip to a tiny mountain village called Lake Chelan in Washington. Besides the view of the Tillamook village on the Pacific Ocean, it was the most beautiful place I had ever seen. The mountains reached endlessly into the sky, and the lake was like a mirror reflecting everything that looked upon it.

Right then and there I decided that this was the place where I wanted to spend the rest of my days here on earth. That's exactly what I did. I built a charming little home right next to the lake with a glorious view that seemed to change every few minutes.

It was a powerful place, almost impossible to describe with words. I could feel that God was in this land, in the wind and sky. It brought me back to what I had learned from Chief Timothy as a child, that we are part of the land, and the land is part of us. Knowing this and realizing that we are all shaped by our struggles, our joys and sorrows gave me a sense that I was not alone any longer, that I was part of something ... holy.

In 1909 I had a strong urge to see my birthplace at Lapwai. I could hardly comprehend the changes. All along the way there were towns and cities, steamboats and railways, big beautiful houses along the rivers.

As I looked out over the "Valley of the Butterflies," I was overwhelmed with images and feelings that I had not experienced in over 60 years. The sacred little cemetery where Father was buried was where my brother Henry and I use to play when we were children. Amongst the Nez Perce there was not a single familiar face, but everyone I met was incredibly gracious and genuinely welcoming.

We held our service in a wonderful little church that stood where Father had built the original one. I watched the most beautiful and angelic children I have ever seen as they attended Sunday school. Afterward with tears in my eyes I watched as they ran and jumped with the same joy I had felt as a young girl. Vicariously I experienced what it was like to be so young and so alive again. I have always tried to keep myself distanced from the word pride, but it is the only one I can find to describe what I felt as the Nez Perce sang a song that Father had taught them, and I cried like a child.

I was kneeling next to Father's grave alone when I saw the shadow of a man come over me. He stood there silently until I turned and asked who he was. The Nez Perce man must have been well in his eighties with a calm and serene nature that felt familiar. He told me that he had been asked to tend to Father's grave, and had been doing it now for the past 35 years.

He told me, "I love to do it, we have spent many hours together and I feel as if Mr. Spalding is like a brother to me."

It was one of the happiest days of my life followed by one of the happiest nights. I was invited for dinner with Chief Timothy's daughter-in-law Maggie, and we spent hours laughing and retelling old stories. As I was leaving, she told me that the community was planning to build a monument in memory of the work my parents had done. Leaving was like turning the last page of a great book, the end of an era for me. In 1914, I attended the Pioneer Picnic in Brownsville and was asked to share my thoughts:

"Without the home builder, exploration would have been in vain. The mere knowledge of the country would have not gained purpose that made the Oregon country a part of the United States. As to the motives we must judge the pioneer as we judge all men, by his actions. In action he was always a patriot, always a loyal citizen, promoting the interest of his government and extending its

738

civilization to the utmost bounds of the continent. He was both a statesman and a soldier, acting from the same motives that prompted them. On this basis he established his fame, and his glory will not fade. In point of endurance these pioneers gave new meaning to the word effort. They made sacrifices to the limit of human possibilities. They all encountered hardships that strengthened; some privations that enfeebled, and others, disease that destroyed. The pioneer did not wait for the government to mark the way, he marked the way for the government. His path was not blazed, his course was the setting sun. Plains were not too broad, nor mountains too high to deter him. His own right arm was his defense and his heart supplied the never-ending inspiration. Toil stained and hungered, men traveled on, hope and care marked the faces of women; children withstood the discomforts and became essential parts of the new states. The days seemed long; months passed; the summer glided into the russet of autumn before the end came. Where now are the fair fields, then became the last resting-place of many a husband, mother, and child; the winds chanted the requiem over the lonely and deserted graves. When the destination was finally reached there was no friend or neighbor to assist or to council. The genial Heavens and generous earth alone could give comfort and hope, but it was sufficient for these courageous, self-reliant people, reckless alike of toil and danger. If your experience has been such to compare the covered wagon with the palace car, the luxurious home with the untended fireside on the plain or mountain; if you can estimate the difference between the protection of our government today and the single barrel rifle then; between the provisions that modern wealth brings and the yield of sod first touched by the rude plow; if you can tell how far the East is from the West, then you can calculate the reward that belongs to these men and women when measured by what they endured. To me, there can be no people like the Oregon Pioneers. To me there can be no other land like the one of my birth, from whose bounty I have always fed. And here let me say that it is with reverence and respect that I bow my head to the old pioneer." —Eliza Spalding Warren.

Author

My Wife's Great, Great, Grandmother, Eliza Spalding, died on Jun. 21, 1919, at the age of 82, in Coeur d'Alene, Kootenai County, Idaho.

Eliza Spalding is buried at the Brownsville Pioneer Cemetery in Linn County, Oregon.

Author

Tom Jiroudek lives on the upper-left edge of the Oregon Coast with his wife, Laurie. Husband, father, musician, singer-songwriter, photographer, business owner, and now author.

Eliza is a labor of love taking over three years to research and write while working full-time and devoting several hours each day to music.

North America, 1836

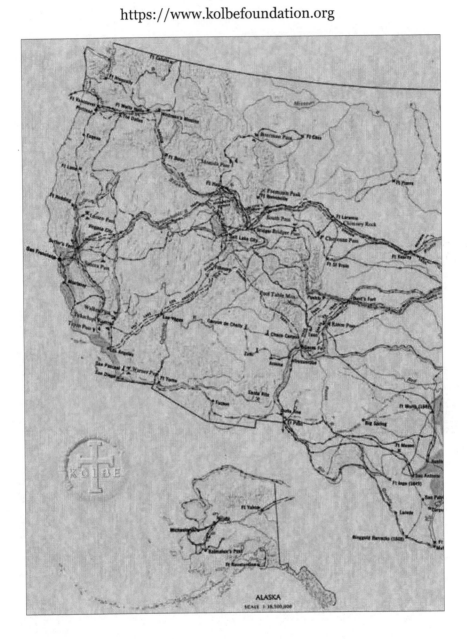

North America, 1836

5,215 miles, seven grueling months, one foot in front of the other.

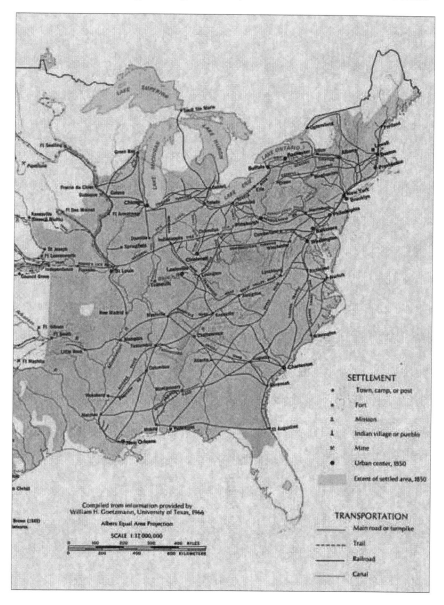